Concurrent Systems

An Integrated Approach to Operating Systems,
Distributed Systems and Databases

Third Edition

SELECTED TITLES IN THE SERIES

Third Edition for the Open University

Concurrent Systems

An Integrated Approach to Operating Systems,
Distributed Systems and Databases

Jean Bacon
University of Cambridge

With contributions by
Robin Laney and Janet van der Linden
Open University

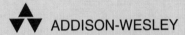 ADDISON-WESLEY

An imprint of Pearson Education

Harlow, England • London • New York • Boston • San Francisco • Toronto • Sydney • Singapore • Hong Kong
Tokyo • Seoul • Taipei • New Delhi • Cape Town • Madrid • Mexico City • Amsterdam • Munich • Paris • Milan

Pearson Education Limited
Edinburgh Gate
Harlow
Essex CM20 2JE
England

and Associated Companies throughout the world

Visit us on the World Wide Web at:
www.pearsoneduc.com

First published 1992
Second edition 1998
Third edition 2003

ISBN 0 321 11788 3

British Library Cataloguing-in-Publication Data
A catalogue record for this book is available from the British Library

Library of Congress Cataloging-in-Publication Data
A catalog record for this book is available from the Library of Congress

10   9   8   7   6   5   4   3   2   1
06   05   04   03   02

Typeset in 10/12pt Sabon by 35
Printed and bound in Great Britain by Biddles Ltd., Guildford and King's Lynn

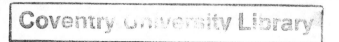

Brief contents

Contents

Preface to the third edition

The Open University (OU) have used *Concurrent Systems* for their course 'Software Systems and their Development' (M301) since 1999. This third edition has been written in collaboration with Robin Laney, Pete Thomas and Janet van der Linden who, with others, developed and taught the OU course. The changes to the second edition are as follows:

- Java is used throughout to illustrate object orientation concepts, concurrent algorithms and distributed programming.
- An operating systems architectural perspective remains, to keep the strong system design focus, but there is less detail on operating system functions and specific operating systems.
- There is a new chapter on security which complements the coverage of distributed systems.
- The case studies in Part IV include a new chapter on web programming and a rewrite of 'Middleware'. The UNIX, NT and Microkernel case studies have been replaced by short case study sections on those systems in earlier chapters.

The philosophy and approach remain unchanged.

The aim of this book is to equip students with an integrated view of modern software systems. Concurrency and modularity are the unifying themes. It takes a systems approach rather than a programming language approach, since concurrent programming is firmly rooted in system design. The language is an implementation tool for the system designer and programming languages are covered throughout the book from this perspective.

The formal theory of concurrency is not included. Rather, the aim is to provide a systems background to which subsequent formal study can relate. Without prior study of real systems a student can have little intuition about the basis of formal models of concurrent systems. For students about to work on the theory of concurrency the book provides a summary of essential system fundamentals.

The structure of the book is:

- **Introduction**, in which some real-world concurrent systems are described and requirements for building computerized concurrent systems established.
- **Part I**, in which the abstraction of a concurrent system as a set of concurrent processes is established and the implementation of processes in operating systems and language systems is studied.
- **Part II**, which shows how a logically single action (an operation invocation) can be guaranteed to run without interference from other concurrent actions.
- **Part III**, which shows how a number of related actions can be guaranteed to run without interference from other concurrent actions.
- **Part IV**, in which some case studies are considered from the perspective developed throughout the book.

Computer systems curriculum

I have taught operating systems, distributed systems, transaction processing and computer architecture for many years. Because distributed systems have come into widespread use comparatively recently, most curricula include them at final-year undergraduate or postgraduate level. Distributed systems are now commonplace and a student is more likely to be using one than a centralized time-sharing system. It is somewhat artificial to cover the functions of a shared, centralized operating system in great detail in a first course, particularly when the rate of development of technology makes it essential constantly to re-evaluate traditional approaches and algorithms.

In general, there is a tendency for closely related specialisms to diverge, even at undergraduate level. An overview of system components and their relationships is desirable from an early stage:

- Operating systems include communications handling.
- Language runtime systems work closely with (and are constrained by) operating systems.
- Real-time systems need specially tailored operating systems.
- Dedicated communications handling computers need specially tailored operating systems.
- Database management systems run on operating systems and need concurrency and file handling with special guarantees.
- Concurrent programs run on operating systems.
- Window systems require concurrent processes.

- Many system components employ databases.
- Distributed systems employ distributed databases.
- Distributed databases need communications.
- Distributed operating systems need transactions.

Concurrent Systems, Third Edition, achieves this integration by setting up a common framework of modular structure (a simple object model is used throughout) and concurrent execution.

I have used this approach in the Computer Science curriculum at Cambridge since 1988, when a new three-year undergraduate degree programme started. A concurrent systems course, in the second year of a three-year degree course, is a prerequisite for further study in distributed operating systems, communications and networks, theory of concurrency, and various case studies and projects. Figure P.1 suggests an order of presentation of systems material. Courses in the general area of real-time, embedded control systems would also follow naturally from this course. At Cambridge, a course which gives an introduction to operating systems functions precedes 'Concurrent Systems' so the students start with some knowledge of file management and memory management. As this may not universally be the case I have included an introduction to these functions, sufficient to set up the concepts that are needed later, in Part I of the book.

In *Curriculum 91 for Computing*, published by the IEEE Computer Society and the ACM (see Denning *et al.*, 1989; Tucker 1991) the general topic 'Operating Systems' includes distributed operating systems and communications. *Curriculum 91* identifies the three major paradigms of

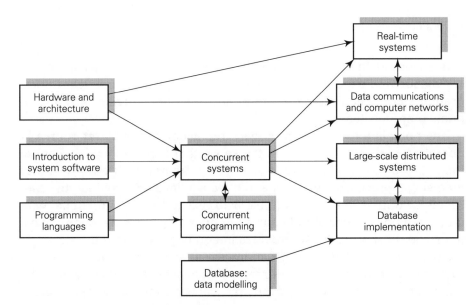

Figure P.1
Concurrent systems in the curriculum.

the discipline as: **theory**, which is rooted in mathematics; **abstraction** (modelling), which is rooted in experimental scientific method; and **design**, which is rooted in engineering. Theory deals with the underlying mathematics of each sub-area of computing. Abstraction allows us to model large, complex systems in order to comprehend their structure and behaviour and carry out experiments on them. Design deals with the process of implementing a system to meet a specification. The approach taken here embodies abstraction and design and establishes the basis for theory.

In December 2001 IEEE-CS/ACM published, in their *Computing Curricula 2001*, a curriculum for Computer Science. Curricula for Computer Engineering, Software Engineering and Information Systems are to follow. They argue that, since the subject has grown extensively and rapidly in the past decade, a minimal core curriculum should be defined, allowing a variety of extensions. The core topics for the 18 minimum core hours in Operating Systems are: overview of operating systems (2), operating systems principles (2), concurrency (6), scheduling and dispatch (3) and memory management (5). The core topics for the 15 minimum core hours of Net-Centric Computing are introduction (2), communication and networking (7), network security (3), the web as an example of client–server computing (3). The ten-hour minimal core in Information Management has transaction processing as an early extension. 'Objects First' is one of three proposed models (with 'Imperative First' and 'Functional First') for introducing programming. The systems view presented in *Concurrent Systems* includes, integrates and extends this core coverage.

Audience

It is assumed that the reader will come to this material with some knowledge and experience of systems and languages. First-year undergraduate courses on programming and systems software are appropriate prerequisites.

The book is intended as a **modern replacement for a first course in operating systems** – modern in the sense that concurrency is a central focus throughout, distributed systems are treated as the norm rather than single-processor systems, and effective links are provided to other systems courses. It is also suitable as a text to be read in parallel with more traditional, specialized courses in operating systems, communications and databases. It also provides integrating and summarizing study for graduate students and practitioners in systems design including systems programming. Graduate students who are researching the theory of concurrency will find the practical basis for their subject here.

An outline of the contents

Chapter 1 describes a number of types of concurrent system and draws out requirements for supporting concurrent activities. Concurrent systems can exploit a wide range of system topologies and architectures. Although this area is not addressed in great detail their characteristics are noted for reference throughout the book.

Chapters 2 through 7 form **Part I**. System design and implementation require software to be engineered. Software engineering, which involves the specification, design, implementation, maintenance and evolution of software systems, has merited many books in its own right. This book focuses on concurrency issues, but a context of modular software structure is needed: first, to give a context for Part II, where intuition on a single logical action is needed; second, in order that the placement of concurrent processes in systems may be understood.

Modular system structure is therefore introduced in **Chapter 2** and the modular structure of operating systems is used as an extended example. The idea that a minimal kernel or 'microkernel' is an appropriate basis for high-performance specialized services is introduced here. The concepts of process and protocol to achieve the dynamic execution of software are also introduced.

In **Chapter 3** device handling and communications handling are covered. These topics are treated together to highlight the similarities (between communications and other devices) and differences (communications software is larger and more complex than device-handling software). The communications-handling subsystem of an operating system is itself a concurrent (sub)system, in that at a given time it may be handling several streams of input coming in from various sources across the network as well as requests for network communication from local clients.

Chapter 4 gives the detailed concrete basis for the process abstraction that is provided by operating systems. Once the process abstraction is created as one operating system function we can show how processes are used to achieve the dynamic execution of the rest of the system. Operating system processes may be used within operating system modules, while application-level processes may be located within application modules. There are several design options which are discussed throughout the book. Later sections are concerned with language systems and a particular concern is the support for concurrency. The relation between operating system and language system processes is discussed in detail.

Chapter 5 outlines the operating system functions of memory management and file management. The address space of a process is an important concept, as also are mechanisms for sharing part of it. File system implementations involve data structures both in main memory and in persistent memory on disk. Both the memory management and file management subsystems of operating systems are concurrent systems in that they may have in progress both requests from clients and demands for service from the hardware.

Chapter 6 introduces distributed software systems. We focus on their fundamental properties then cover time and naming in some detail. Subsequent chapters can then consider distribution of the various functions being studied.

Chapter 7 is concerned with security in centralized and distributed systems.

Part I is mostly concerned with implementation. Knowledge of the material presented here is necessary for a thorough understanding of software systems. Care must be taken, when working at the language or theoretical modelling levels, that the assumptions made can be justified for the operating system and hardware that will be used to implement a concurrent system.

We can now work with the abstraction of a concurrent system as a set of concurrent processes. **Part II** proceeds to explain the mechanisms for ensuring that a given concurrent process can execute without interference from any other, bearing in mind that processes may be cooperating with other processes (and need to synchronize with them) or competing with other processes to acquire some resource.

Chapters 8 to 15 comprise Part II. In Part II we temporarily ignore the issues of composite operations and the need to access multiple resources to carry out some task, and confine the discussion to a single operation invocation that takes place within a concurrent system.

The notion of a single abstract operation is informal and closely related to the modular structuring of systems. A process can, in general, read or write a single word of memory without fear of interference from any other process. Such a read or write is indivisible. In practice, a programming language variable or a useful data abstraction, such as an array, list or record, cannot be read or written atomically. It is the access to such shared abstractions by concurrent processes that is the concern of Part II. Chapters 8 to 13 are mostly concerned with 'load and go' systems that run in a single or distributed main memory. Chapters 14 and 15 start to consider the effect of failures in system components and process interactions which involve persistent memory.

Chapter 8 discusses the major division between processes which share memory, running in a common address space, and those which do not. Examples are given, showing the need for both types of arrangement.

Chapter 9 is concerned with the lowest level of support for process interactions. The architecture of the computer and the system is relevant here. It is important to know whether any kind of composite read–modify–write instruction is available and whether the system architecture contains shared memory multiprocessors or only uniprocessors. Concurrency control without hardware support is discussed. Semaphores are introduced.

Chapter 10 builds on the lowest level to solve classic systems problems. The POSIX pthreads package is described. A discussion of the difficulty of writing correct semaphore programs leads on to high-level language support for concurrency in the next chapter.

Chapter 11 looks at language primitives that have been introduced into high-level concurrent programming languages where the underlying assumption is that processes execute in a shared address space, for example, conditional critical regions and monitors. The support for concurrent programming in Java is described here.

Chapter 12 compares inter-process communication (IPC) mechanisms within systems where shared memory is available and where it is not. In both cases processes need to access common information and synchronize their activities.

Chapter 13 covers IPC for processes which inhabit separate address spaces. Pipes and message passing are discussed. The material here is highly relevant to distributed IPC, but the integration of IPC and communications services is left for Chapter 15.

Chapter 14 introduces the possibility that a system might crash at any time and outlines mechanisms that could be used to provide crash resilience. An initial discussion of operations which involve persistent data is also given.

Chapter 15 focuses on IPC in distributed systems, taking account of their fundamental characteristics, introduced in Chapter 6. We see how an operation at one node of a distributed system can be invoked from another node using a remote procedure call protocol. Node crashes and restarts and network failures are considered. Although distributed IPC is the main emphasis of the chapter, it includes a general discussion of naming, location and the binding of names to locations in distributed systems. Socket programming in Java and Java RMI are given as practical examples.

Chapters 16 through 22 comprise **Part III** where the discussion is broadened to composite abstract operations and the concurrent execution of their component operations.

Chapter 16 introduces the problems and defines the context for this study. Composite operations may span distributed systems and involve persistent memory.

Chapter 17 discusses the desirability of dynamic resource allocation and the consequent possibility of system deadlock. An introduction to resource allocation and management is given, including algorithms for deadlock detection and avoidance.

Chapter 18 discusses composite operation execution in the presence of concurrency and crashes and builds up a definition of the fundamental properties of transactions. A model based on abstract data objects is used.

Chapter 19 discusses concurrency control for transactions. Two-phase locking, time-stamp ordering and optimistic concurrency control are described and compared.

Chapter 20 is mainly concerned with crash recovery, although the ability to abort transactions for concurrency control purposes is a related problem. A specific implementation is given.

Chapter 21 extends the object model for distributed systems and reconsiders the methods of implementing concurrency control in this context. The problem of atomic commitment is discussed and a two-phase commit protocol is given as an example. A validation protocol for optimistic concurrency control is also given.

The concept of transaction, which is fundamental to all distributed systems, has been established.

Chapter 22 covers algorithms which may be used by distributed computations.

Chapters 23 through 25 comprise **Part IV**, in which case studies are presented. Greater depth is possible here than in the examples used earlier. An aim is to show that the approach developed throughout the book helps the reader to comprehend large and complex systems.

Chapter 23 covers web programming – a subject which was invented after the first edition of this book was published and which has grown extensively since the second edition. This style of programming is set to dominate much of distributed systems design and development.

Chapter 24 covers the broad range of middleware, contrasting those based on synchronous object invocation and those based on asynchronous message passing. The former include Java and OMG's OMA and CORBA, and the latter IBM's MQseries and the TIBCO Rendezvous. Microsoft's DCOM and .Net are also outlined.

Chapter 25 first discusses how transaction processing (TP) monitors are implemented in terms of processes, IPC and communications. Some examples of TP systems in the area of electronic funds transfer are then given, for example, an international automatic teller machine (ATM) network.

The **appendix** presents a historical and functional evolution of software systems in a technological and commercial context.

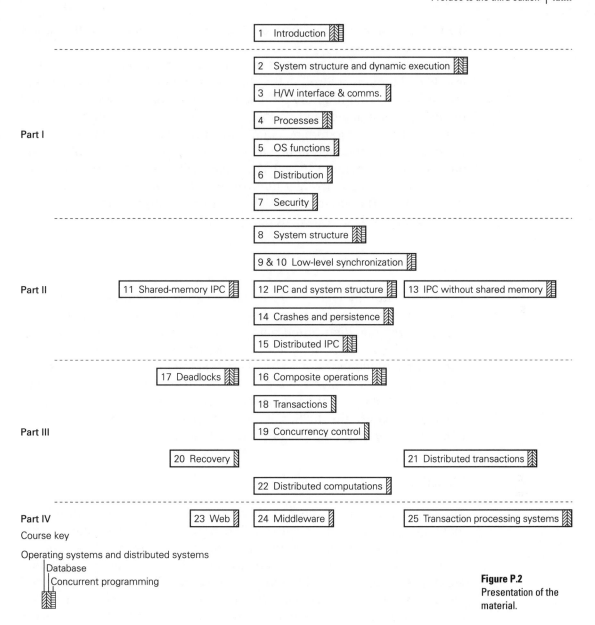

Figure P.2
Presentation of the material.

Order of presentation

Figure P.2 indicates dependencies in the material and shows how the chapters might be selected for courses emphasizing operating systems and distributed systems, concurrent programming or databases. Chapter 17 can be taken earlier if concurrent programming is the emphasis. Sections from this chapter are referenced when they are needed and the topics could be embedded.

The material in Part II could be taken in a different order. Although there is a flow of argument through the chapters as written, there is no inherent reason why shared-memory IPC has to come before that with no shared memory, although distribution follows naturally from the latter.

A concurrent programming course could supplement Parts I and II with full details of a language to be used for project work: Java would be the natural choice. Chapters 16 and 17 from Part III should also be included.

A course on concurrency control in database systems would use Part III, but earlier chapters which cover operating system support for databases provide an excellent background.

Further study

The book naturally leads on to advanced systems courses: specialized operating systems, real-time embedded control systems, large-scale distributed systems, distributed databases. The conceptual framework of concurrency control, naming, location, placement, protection, authentication and encryption are set up, ready for exploitation in systems design.

It is important to have a basis for correct reasoning about the precise behaviour of concurrent systems, and various mathematical models are already in use (Hoare, 1985; Milner, 1989). As mentioned above, theory of concurrency might also be deemed further study.

Objective

The main emphasis of the book is system design: how to comprehend existing systems and how to design new systems. One can't write certain kinds of concurrent system in certain languages above certain operating systems. This book aims to show the reader why. Computers are marketed optimistically. Names such as 'real-time operating system' are used with little real concern for their meaning. In order to survive an encounter with a salesperson one must know exactly what one wants and must know the pitfalls to look out for in the systems one is offered. I hope the book will help systems designers to select the right hardware and software to satisfy their requirements.

Instructor's guide

A web-browsable instructor's guide was developed for the second edition, containing the following:

- Curriculum design. An outline of parts of the IEEE-CS/ACM *Computing Curricula 1991* is given. Uses of *Concurrent Systems* in the curriculum are discussed.
- Points to emphasize and teaching hints. For each chapter, key points, potential difficulties and suggested approaches to teaching the material are given.
- Solutions to exercises and some additional exercises. The solutions include examples of how the various designs that are discussed have been used in practice.
- A description of some environments for project work and how to get them.

The guide is available from www.booksites.net/bacon. Contact your Pearson Education or Addison-Wesley sales representative for a password.

Acknowledgements

Robin Laney, Pete Thomas and Janet van der Linden provided input based on using *Concurrent Systems* for the Open University's M301 course 'Software Systems and their Development'. Their expert knowledge of Java was put to good use in converting all the algorithms and adding new sections on concurrent and distributed programming in Java. In addition, they added study questions and expanded on other areas where they thought it necessary. I gratefully acknowledge the feedback from other OU staff, especially Ray Weedon, and from many OU tutors and students I have not met directly. I am also grateful to Cambridge students who have taken the courses based on *Concurrent Systems* for feedback and to graduate students and colleagues in the systems area for their comments. Thanks are due to those who have used the book in their teaching and were helpful on how it should evolve. Those who advised on the first edition are gratefully acknowledged: George Coulouris and Jean Dollimore, Mark Lomas for the teller machine case study, now Chapter 25, Ken Moody on all aspects but especially the database material. Pearson Education have provided support, motivation and encouragement throughout.

Jean Bacon
April 2002

jmb@cl.cam.ac.uk
http://www.cl.cam.ac.uk/users/jmb/cs.html

Trademark notice

The following designations are trademarks or registered trademarks of the organizations whose names follow in brackets:

ACMS, Alpha, DECintact, DECNET, DECthreads, DEQNA, Firefly, GNS, ULTRIX and VAX (Digital Equipment Corporation); ACTIVEX.COM (used by CNET under license from owner – ACTIVEX.COM is an independent online service); Amoeba (Vrije Universiteit); ANSA (ANSA Internet Inc.); ARM and CHORUS (Acorn Computers); CORBA (Object Management Group); Courier (Xerox Corporation); HP-UX (Hewlett-Packard Company); Java, JavaScript, NFS, SunOS and XDR (Sun Microsystems, Inc.); MC68 000 (Motorola); MIPS (Silicon Graphics, Inc.); Netscape Navigator (Netscape Communications Corporation); occam (INMOS Group of companies); OpenDoc (Apple Computers); OS/2, System 370, MQSeries and SNA (International Business Machines Corporation); Pathway (Tandem); Pentium, 8086, 80 × 86 and 860 (Intel); Rendezvous (TIBCO); REXX (Oracle Corporation); Seagate Elite 23 and BarracudaATA IV (Seagate Technology Products); Tina-C (National Semiconductor Corporation); UNIX (X/Open Company Ltd); Windows NT, Windows 95, Visual Basic, MS-DOS, ActiveX, COM, DCOM and .NET (Microsoft Corporation).

Introduction: Examples and requirements

The aim of this book is to show what concurrent systems are, why they are important and how they may be designed and built. We shall start from an informal, intuitive definition of a concurrent system. System software runs indefinitely, typically supporting other running programs, and users. An operating system running on a single machine is an example of a system. A database management system, which runs above an operating system, is another. Concurrent means 'at the same time'; the system software has to support many users or programs at the same time. The meaning of 'at the same time' is explored more deeply as we progress through the book, but initially we shall assume that the same measure of time holds throughout a system. A concurrent system must therefore handle separate activities which are in progress at the same time. To be a little more precise, we shall consider two activities to be concurrent if, at a given time, each is at some point between its starting point and finishing point.

The broad range of types of concurrent system is introduced in this chapter and their essential characteristics are highlighted. Requirements for implementing these systems are drawn out in each case and the chapter concludes with a discussion of the requirements of concurrent systems in general. The rest of the book is concerned with meeting these requirements.

We hope to build concurrent systems which exploit new technology in emerging application areas. We need to be in a position to bring a good deal of processing power and memory to bear on a given problem and using a multicomputer system of some kind is likely to be the best way to do this. For this reason, this chapter includes a survey of the different kinds of overall system architecture on which a concurrent software system might run.

In some cases, a system is **inherently concurrent** since it is handling activities that can happen simultaneously in the world external to the computer system, such as users who want to run programs or clients who want to do bank transactions. For a system which supports many simultaneous users, the system designers may choose to load a separate copy of some system program, such as a compiler, for every user or may choose to have all users share a single copy. The shared system program is a simple example of a concurrent system.

Application programs are typically initiated by a user and run to completion. For certain applications it might be possible to work on parts of a problem in parallel by devising a concurrent algorithm for its solution. This is a valuable approach when an application involves a massive amount of computation and data and there is a real-time requirement for the result, such as in weather forecasting. These are **potentially concurrent applications**. At present, many problems of this type are solved, if at all, by sequential (rather than concurrent) algorithms on expensive, high-performance computers. A concurrent approach could improve matters in two ways. Either the same quality of result could be achieved at lower cost by using a number of inexpensive off-the-shelf computers, or a better model of the physical system could be built, perhaps giving rise to even more data to be processed but generating a more accurate result. Concurrent algorithms might also bring the solution of a wider range of problems within a reasonable budget. The methods of supporting concurrent activities within systems are equally applicable to supporting concurrent activities within applications.

Application programs are run by systems. We shall study how many applications may be run simultaneously by a system and how systems support concurrent applications.

1.1 Inherently concurrent systems

Systems which must respond to, or manage, simultaneous activities in their external environment are inherently concurrent and may broadly be classified as:

- real-time and embedded systems;
- database management and transaction processing systems;
- operating systems.

In each case the implementation of the system is as likely to be **distributed** across a number of computers (**hosts, nodes** or **sites**) as centralized.

1.1.1 Real-time and embedded systems

The special characteristic of real-time systems is that there are timing requirements which are dictated by the environment of the computer system. It may be essential, for example, for the computer system to respond to an alarm signal in some specific time, although it may be highly unlikely that such a signal will occur and it will never be predictable. The term '**hard real-time system**' is used to indicate that the timing requirements are absolute. '**Soft real-time**' indicates that failing to meet a deadline will not lead to a catastrophe.

Another useful distinction is between **static** and **dynamic** real-time systems. In a static system an analysis of the activities that must be carried out by the system can be done when the system is designed. In a dynamic real-time system requests may occur at irregular and unpredictable times and the system must respond dynamically and with guaranteed performance. Examples are given below.

It is worth emphasizing that 'real-time' does not always imply 'very fast indeed', but rather that timing requirements are known and must be guaranteed.

Examples of real-time systems are process control systems for power stations, chemical plants, etc., military command and control systems, hospital patient monitoring systems, spaceflight, aeroplane and car engine controllers, air traffic control systems, robot controllers, real-time image processing and display systems, videophones and many more.

Process control

A common scenario is that data is gathered from the controlled system and analysed. This may involve simply taking a temperature or pressure reading at an appropriate time interval and checking against a safe level, or more complex data gathering across the process followed by mathematical analysis and feedback to fine-tune the system. The accuracy with which this can be done depends on the amount of data gathered by whatever measuring or sampling devices are employed and the time that can be spent on the analysis. The data gathering and analysis are predictable and periodic. The period depends on the process being controlled. The computer-controlled fuel injection system for a car engine must sample many times per second; the temperature in a furnace is sampled every few seconds; the water level in a reservoir may only need to be sampled every hour.

This periodic activity must be integrated with the ability to respond to unpredictable events. An alarm could occur, indicating that some action must be taken with high priority. Maybe the temperature of a nuclear reactor is too high and must be lowered, or perhaps gas pressure is building up in a coal mine, indicating the danger of an explosion.

Another type of non-periodic event is high-level or coarse-grained parameter tuning. This is initiated by a management system which has a high-level view of the entire system, perhaps gathered from widespread sampling. Management may also wish to make changes, such as to the relative amounts of the various materials being produced by a system. This may be less urgent than an alarm signal, but is the means by which the process is controlled as a whole.

The two types of activity may be classified as **monitoring** and **control**. Monitoring involves gathering data; control involves regular, fine-grained tuning,

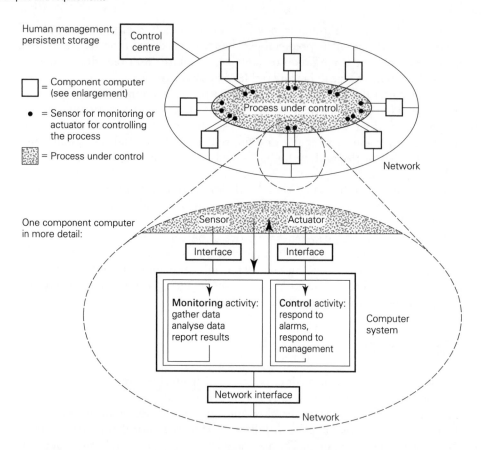

Figure 1.1
Example of a
distributed process
control system.

irregular coarse-grained tuning and response to alarms. Figure 1.1 shows these
two major activities in a computer system which is part of a distributed process
control system. There may be a trade-off between the accuracy of the data
analysis and the system's ability to respond to events: at certain times, accuracy
may be sacrificed to rapid response. But it is critical that if an alarm occurs it
must get immediate attention and that certain events must have response in a
specified time.

There is scope for concurrency in such systems in that many small computer
systems of this kind will work together to control a large industrial or experimental process and each one may have several functions it must perform.

Not all real-time systems are distributed, multicomputer systems. A domestic
appliance, a robot, a car engine, or a missile may have a single **embedded** controlling computer. The software will still have several functions to perform,
associated with monitoring and control. There is, in general, a requirement for
the support of separate activities.

Real-time systems of the kind described here are hard and static. Timing
requirements are absolute and the system's requirements can be analysed
statically at system design time. The approach is usually to design a periodic
schedule for the system, allowing for the possibility of alarms in each period.

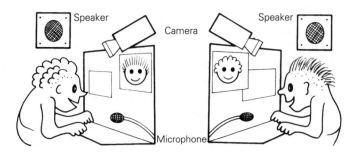

Figure 1.2
Multimedia
workstations.

Multimedia support

An emerging application area for high-performance networked workstations is **multimedia**: the ability to show moving pictures and hear voice in addition to the traditional display of text and graphics. Assuming the workstation has a windowing system, one or more windows could be used for video. Many applications, such as a videophone, videomail or videoconferencing, require a talking person to be displayed (Figure 1.2). In this case the video (picture) and audio (voice) must be synchronized for delivery to the workstation screen; the voice must be synchronized with lip movements.

Videoconferencing and videophones operate in real time. Data can be lost if the system does not keep up. Videomail requires messages which may contain text with video and voice clips to be stored and delivered to the workstation screen when the mail is read. Once the process of reading the mail starts there are real-time requirements on the system to deliver the components at an acceptable rate and in synchrony.

There are many potential applications for stored multimedia documents. For example, a database containing a museum catalogue could include a video clip of an item shown from all angles. A database on ornithology could contain text and drawings for each bird, maps of its territory, audio of the song and video of the bird in flight.

When multimedia data is stored, requests to deliver it to a workstation screen are unpredictable and the system must respond dynamically. Several requests might arrive during the same time period. To achieve acceptable performance the storage system, operating system and communications software must be able to make guarantees of a certain **quality of service**.

Video requires massive amounts of storage space and it must be transferred at a very high rate for a smooth, jitter-free picture to be seen. Taking an example from a local system, a one-minute video clip occupies over 12 megabytes of storage and the required transfer rate is 200 kilobits per second. The voice to be synchronized with the picture has lower storage and bandwidth requirements, typically 64 kbits per second. We assume that adequate amounts of storage are available for video and voice 'across a network' and that the network has enough bandwidth to deliver voice and video 'streams'. The system software design problem is to ensure that both video and voice are delivered to the workstation at a high enough rate for a good picture to be seen and synchronized voice to be heard.

The activities of delivering voice and video are separate and have different requirements for throughput, but both must get sufficient processor time to deliver the image and voice to a standard that the human observer finds acceptable. Although video requires more processing, memory and network resources, we are not too sensitive to temporary hitches in its delivery, whereas we find shortcomings in the delivery of voice infuriating (think of the inaudible announcement that comes over the loudspeaker when your train is due). There are therefore some quite complicated trade-offs to be made.

To what extent should multimedia workstations be considered real-time systems? A videophone requires video and voice to be delivered in real time; if data is corrupted it cannot be recovered except by a human user asking for a repeat. The environment dictates certain requirements for the system to be usable. It could be classified as a soft real-time system.

There is only a quantitative difference between multimedia systems and traditional time-sharing systems; multimedia systems need more processing power, network bandwidth and storage capacity and software that is capable of exploiting them. There is a qualitative difference between such soft real-time systems and power station control systems, where there is an absolute requirement for response, even if some components of the system fail. This is implied by the name 'hard real-time system' for the latter.

Hard real-time applications involving real-time video might be as follows:

- An aeroplane contains a video camera. The pictures it records are compared with an internally stored map of its intended route. This is part of an automatic system for keeping the plane to its planned route and to prevent it crashing into hills or church towers.
- A factory automation system involves many mobile robots, each containing a video camera. The robots must avoid obstacles which may include other mobile robots and humans. There have been fatal accidents in systems of this kind, caused by bugs in real-time software.
- Cars of the future might contain video cameras. The car must stop if a child runs in front of it. The cars behind it must avoid crashing into it. Should the image processing software be able to distinguish between a child and a dog (or a rabbit)?

Requirements

The requirements for building a real-time system that have emerged from the above discussion may be summarized as follows:

- There is a need to support separate activities. Some may be periodic, such as gathering data (taking measurements of temperature, pressure, etc.), and others unpredictable, such as responding to alarm signals.
- There is a need to meet the specific requirements of each activity, which may involve meeting time deadlines.
- There may be a need for the separate activities to work together to achieve a common goal.

1.1.2 Database management and transaction processing systems

Database applications are concerned with large amounts of persistent data, that is, data on permanent storage devices that exists independently of any running program. A typical user of a database system wants to make **queries** about the data, such as 'what is the current level of my bank account' or 'list the owners who live in Cambridge of purple Ford cars manufactured in 1990'. The owners of the database are concerned with keeping it up to date and will want to make **updates**. We assume a **database management system** (**DBMS**) which is responsible for interacting with users and organizing the reading and writing of the database to satisfy their requirements. The DBMS is a concurrent system since it may have to handle several clients simultaneously. The term **transaction** is used for a request from a client to a DBMS.

There are many uses for databases. Commercial systems include banking, airline and other booking systems, stock control for retailing, records of employees, and so on. Engineering systems cover such things as CAD systems, VLSI design and components databases for manufacturing. Statistical databases are held of population census data, for weather forecasting, etc. Public databases are held by police, health and social service institutions. There are also library and other specialized reference systems with expert systems to assist in the formulation of queries to extract the required information from specialized databases.

In applications where it is not critical that at all times the data appears to be up to date to the current instant, updates may be batched and run when convenient, perhaps overnight. This approach simplifies the management of the database enormously and is likely to be used if at all possible. Many of the problems associated with concurrent access are avoided by this means. For example, users may accept that the value given for the balance of a bank account is not up to date; the value at the end of the previous working day may be output with a clear indication of the time at which the value was valid. There is no guarantee in such a system that there is sufficient money in an account to cover a withdrawal. The trend is towards more up-to-date and interactive use of banking databases. Stock control in a supermarket might be managed on a daily basis with consolidation of purchases and reordering of stock carried out overnight.

In some systems the activities of reading and updating data are closely related and updates cannot be deferred. It would be impossible to run an airline or theatre reservation system with an overnight batched update policy. You need to know immediately whether you have booked a seat and not tomorrow morning, and therefore each transaction needs to see the up-to-date system state. Other examples of **transaction processing systems** are the international automatic teller machine (ATM) network service, which provides cash dispensing and other banking services world wide, and point of sale terminals. Both are discussed in Chapter 25.

There is scope for concurrency in database applications because of simultaneous requests from clients. In some kinds of database different clients are unlikely to require access to the same part of the database; it is unlikely that anyone else will be attempting to access my medical record at the same time as my doctor. Concurrent access is desirable for a fast response to queries and there are unlikely to be **conflicting** requests, that is, requests that attempt to update and read the same part of the database at the same time. Any number of transactions which only require to read the database may be run in parallel. If it is possible to update the database as well as read it, the DBMS must ensure that transactions do not interfere with each other.

In order to respond to queries in the timescale required, data will be copied from secondary storage (such as disk) into main memory and reads and updates will use the main memory copy. This introduces the potential problem that the copy of the data held on secondary storage becomes out of date. If the system crashes, the contents of main memory may be lost; for example, a power failure causes loss of main memory. The users of the system may have gone away in the belief that their transactions are complete and their results securely recorded. The management system must ensure that this is the case, even if writing information out to disk slows the system down. A transaction system must therefore support concurrent access and allow for system failure at any time.

Figure 1.3(a) shows the components of a transaction processing system for airline bookings. Many booking clerks can be acting simultaneously on behalf of their clients to book seats on flights recorded in a database. The administration also makes changes to the database. Figure 1.3(b) illustrates the world-wide

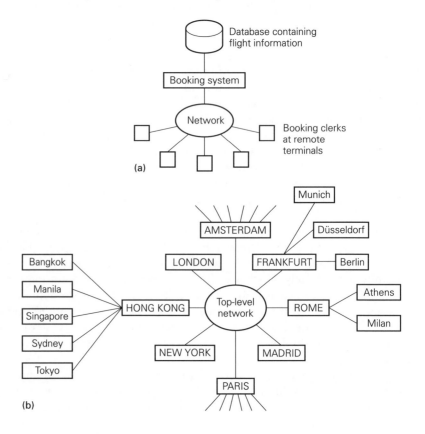

Figure 1.3
Airline booking systems.
(a) Components.
(b) Part of the early SITA private network.

nature of such a system. The diagram shows some of the components of the SITA (Société Internationale de Télécommunications Aéronautiques) private network as it was in the 1970s (Chou, 1977). Even then, over 200 airlines were members of this non-profit cooperative organization.

The kind of problem addressed in Part II of this book is to book a seat on a flight correctly; it is booked but not double booked (assuming that the owners do not have an over-booking policy). The kind of problem addressed in Part III is how to implement a system which can automate the booking of an itinerary consisting of a number of connecting flights or none at all; if one connection can't be booked then none of the others are.

Requirements

The requirements for building transaction processing and database management systems that have emerged from the above discussion may be summarized as follows:

- There is a need to support separate activities.
- There is a need to ensure that the separate activities access and update common data without interference.
- There is a need to ensure that the results of transactions are recorded permanently and securely before the user is told that an operation has been done.

1.1.3 Operating systems and distributed operating systems

We shall first consider self-standing computer systems. It is useful to distinguish between single-user systems and multi-user systems; see Figure 1.4(a) and (b). Single-user systems range from small inexpensive **personal computers** to high-performance **workstations**. Multi-user systems are based on high-performance micro- or minicomputers (with a small number of users) or expensive multi-processor mainframe or supercomputers. We consider the hardware basis for concurrent systems in more detail in Section 1.3.

In a single-user system the user's keyboard and screen are packaged with the processor(s) and memory; a single computer is perceived. The users of a multi-user system access the system via a **terminal**. Terminals are separate from the main memory, central processor(s) and shared devices such as disks and printers. A terminal might provide a graphical user interface and a windowing system and might have internal processors and memory dedicated to these functions. The old 'dumb' terminal has evolved into a special-purpose computer. A system might have large numbers of terminals, remote from the central computer, which are managed in groups by dedicated terminal concentrator computers.

A general-purpose operating system runs in the personal computer, single-user workstation or shared computer. Its purpose is to run the user's programs

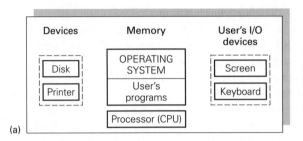

The user's keyboard and screen are likely to be packaged in a single unit together with the memory and processor(s).

(a)

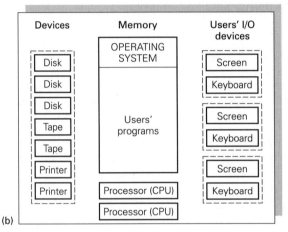

Figure 1.4
Components of
(a) single-user
systems and
(b) multi-user
systems.

(b)

The terminal devices are packaged as separate units. There may be large numbers of them, they may be remote from the computer and they may be handled by an intermediate controlling computer, a terminal concentrator.

and to allocate the hardware resources they need such as memory, disk space, devices and processors.

There is scope for concurrency in both single-user and multi-user systems. We shall see that devices tend to be very slow compared with processors. The operating system will attend to the devices when necessary, but run programs while the devices are busy producing the next input or performing the last output.

In a single-user system the user should be allowed to start off some lengthy computation, such as 'number crunching' or paginating a long document, and carry out other tasks, such as reading mail, in parallel. The operating system should be able to support these separate concurrent activities, running several applications and handling several devices.

There is obvious scope for concurrency in multi-user systems: running many users' programs, handling many devices simultaneously and responding to users' commands. Again, the operating system will attempt to overlap processing and device handling wherever possible. An example is a printer spooler; users' commands to print files are noted and the printing takes place in parallel with general program execution.

In comparison with the statically analysable real-time systems we considered above, the events handled by operating systems tend to be irregular and unpredictable rather than periodic. The load they must handle is dynamic. A user may start using a terminal or workstation at any time and create a heavy computational or input/output (I/O) load. Although timing considerations are important they tend not to be as critical and inflexible as in real-time systems. It is desirable that a user at a terminal should get a response in a short time, but the consequences of not meeting this requirement are not comparable with a nuclear power station blowing up.

A multi-user operating system must manage the **sharing** of system resources between users while ensuring that an acceptable service is given to all of them. It must respond to potentially **conflicting demands** from users for the resources it manages, such as memory, processing time and filing space. Requests will occur dynamically and some will involve a number of **related objects** which are managed by the operating system.

Consider an example involving only one user: the user gives the command to delete a file. The space the file occupies on disk will become free space and the directory entry for the file must be removed. This involves reading the directory from disk into main memory, changing it and writing it back to disk. The details of file management will be explained in Chapter 5, but it is clear that the simple operation of deleting a file involves several different operations by the operating system. The design of a file management system must allow for the fact that a crash could occur at any time, including part-way through a composite operation, and also that different users may make concurrent requests for operations such as creating and deleting files.

Distributed operating systems

Distributed systems consist of computers connected by a communications medium such as a local area network (LAN). LANs are generally owned by a single organization and span relatively small distances, typically a single building or a few adjacent buildings. A university campus network may comprise a number of interconnected LANs. A popular model of a LAN-based distributed system is that of personal workstations augmented by shared server computers available across the network, for filing, printing, etc., as shown in Figure 1.5.

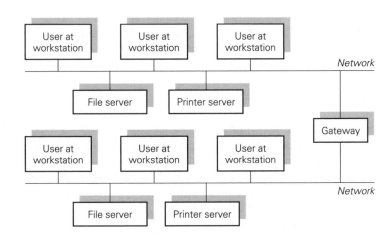

Figure 1.5
A simple distributed operating system.

The workstation operating system is a single-user system with scope for concurrency as described above. The workstations may have local disks, and therefore local filing system software. However, it is likely that the local disks will be relatively small and users will run out of space. Also, users will want to share files with each other. It makes sense to store system files that everyone needs centrally rather than at every workstation. Also, users don't want the trouble of backing up their own files to guard against disk or software failures. For these reasons it is likely that file storage will be provided as a network-based service. It is also likely that a number of file servers will be needed to provide sufficient storage space and processing capacity for all but the smallest systems. These **shared servers** must respond to simultaneous requests from clients and are therefore concurrent systems. The Athena system at the Massachusetts Institute of Technology (MIT) (Treese, 1988) and the ITC system at Carnegie Mellon University (Satyanarayanan *et al.*, 1985) are examples of this kind of distributed system. They provide computing services for all the students of their respective universities.

The operating systems in the computers that are part of a distributed system contain software for **communications handling**. At the lowest level, handling a network connection is similar to handling a high-speed peripheral. However, the data delivered by the network may have come from any one of the other computers in the distributed system rather than just a single device. Computers can send data at very high speed and the network is likely to deliver pieces of data from many sources in an interleaved order. The higher levels of communications software will therefore have a number of incoming communications in progress simultaneously and must deliver complete, reassembled 'messages' to the correct destinations.

The communications software must also take 'messages' from its clients and send them across the network to their intended destinations. Again, a number of requests for this service may be outstanding at a given time. A given message may contain a very large document and may be split into pieces of an acceptable size for the network hardware.

It is clear from the above discussion that a communications handling **subsystem** of an operating system is itself a concurrent system. The term 'subsystem' will be used to indicate a major functional unit within a system.

The above discussion has taken the example of a localized distributed system based on a LAN. There are many distributed systems connected by wide area networks (WANs) and communications software is in general designed to allow world-wide interaction.

Requirements of operating systems

- There is a need for the operating system to support separate activities at the application level (external to the operating system): the independent actions of its users or the multiple activities of a single user. The requirements that applications place on operating systems are dynamic and unpredictable.
- There is a need for separate activities within the operating system: it must handle simultaneous requests from a number of its clients and it must handle simultaneously active devices.

- There is a need for some of the separate activities to cooperate to achieve a common goal; an example is a printer spooler which prints files for users. It must take requests from the various users who want their files printed and liaise with those system components which know how to control the printer and locate files on the disk.
- There is a need to manage competition for resources by separate activities.
- Separate activities must be able to read and write system data structures without interference.
- There is a need for a single task to be carried out as a whole, even when it involves a number of related subtasks. This must take into account potentially interfering concurrent activities and possible failures of the system.

The requirements on operating systems are wide-ranging. Many aspects of concurrency control have traditionally been studied in the context of operating systems, since many problems were first encountered and defined in operating system design. Chapters 3 and 5 expand on operating system functions and Chapter 4 shows how they support separate activities. Part II is concerned with some of the detailed problems of cooperation and competition between related activities.

Part III explores the problems associated with composite tasks. This area has traditionally been studied in the context of database management and transaction processing systems, since these systems have stronger requirements in this area than traditional operating systems. Operating systems may tell a user that the most recent version of a file has been lost after a system crash. If a database system tells a user that a transaction is done it must guarantee that this is the case and the results of the transaction must survive any subsequent system failure. In spite of this difference in emphasis the conceptual basis both for operating systems and for database systems is the same.

1.1.4 Middleware

Distributed systems have become commonplace since first WANs and later LANs (since the late 1970s) allowed network-based distributed software to be developed. Support for distributed programs is now a common requirement and we expect to be able to run widely distributed applications (or services) such as electronic mail, network news or a web browser. They should run irrespective of the hardware or operating system we are using; that is, we expect to be able to work in a **heterogeneous environment**. More generally, industrial and commercial companies need interworking between their distributed components; for example, sales, stock control and invoicing may take place in geographically separate locations.

The idea is to build a layer of software (middleware) above the heterogeneous operating systems to present a uniform **platform** above which distributed applications can run. This simplifies the development of distributed applications by removing the need to port each application to a range of operating systems and hardware.

Chapters 15 and 24

The components of a distributed program may run concurrently and, as we have seen in previous sections, various applications may run concurrently in each component of a distributed system.

1.1.5 Window-based interfaces

Current workstations and terminals typically have **graphical user interfaces (GUIs)** or **window systems**. The advent of such systems has made concurrent activity explicit and natural to all computer users. Even low-end PC-based systems now run window interfaces. You may use the keyboard to type commands in some windows but more often you use the mouse device to move a cursor across the screen to click on a command button or select from a menu within an existing window, to cause a new window to be created or to open an iconified window for use.

For example, consider an email application with a window interface. To run the application you may type a command such as **exmh** in a command window, causing a new window to be created and the mail application to be made available for use via this window. Alternatively, this may be done as part of your login procedure for an application such as email which is part of your working environment. A window may be open or iconified and may be moved between these states by a mouse click.

Suppose you wish to send some mail and click on the appropriate command button. An empty mail template will appear in a new window and you may proceed to type a message. Part-way through you notice that new mail has arrived (by means of a flag and bleep) and click in the original mail window on the 'incorporate new mail' button. One incoming message may need a quick response so you click on 'reply' and get another new window with a reply template. At this stage the mail application has generated three windows and you may move between them at will. That is, the mail application has generated three concurrent activities.

We are familiar with a much higher degree of concurrent activity than this when using window-based interfaces. One may move freely among windows within and between applications. One may also wish to have concurrent activity associated with a single window. For example, one may click on a button to 'purge all mail folders' of messages that have been deleted but not yet removed from the system. This takes some time and in parallel with this background activity one wishes to use other commands, such as reading messages or incorporating new ones that arrive.

1.1.6 The World Wide Web and information servers

In 1990 Tim Berners-Lee developed a prototype hypermedia system called the **World Wide Web (WWW)**. The original application domain had been nuclear physics at CERN, Switzerland. The novel aspect of the system was that cross-network communication formed an integral part of the system, thus creating the potential for transferring hypermedia pages without restriction 'world wide'.

In 1993 the **Mosaic browser** was developed by NCSA (the University of Illinois' National Center for Supercomputing). This provided a convenient window-based interface for the hypermedia transfer system. Since then the growth of the WWW has been explosive. Huge numbers of companies, universities and individuals have built information servers that anyone with a web browser can read.

Each page may contain text, images and links to other pages. A page is created using a hypertext markup language (HTML) which is similar to the standard markup language SGML but also contains instructions on how the page should be displayed. Each page is identified 'world wide' by a name called a **universal resource locator** (**URL**) which forms part of any link to that page. Although the link information appears in the HTML we do not see this in the page we view. Here certain words or images are highlighted (made 'active') so that when we click on them the current page is replaced by the page to which the link refers. To achieve this, the browser contacts the server which holds the page named in the link and transfers it for viewing in the browser. The protocol used between the web browser and web server to achieve this is called the **hypertext transfer protocol** (**http**).

Each client operates sequentially, viewing a page at a time. Any given server may receive any number of concurrent requests for pages; another example where a server may have many simultaneous clients. As use of the web extends we shall increasingly see large databases accessible through web interfaces, thus compounding the need for many clients to have their requests served concurrently.

A recent development in web technology is the addition of animations to web pages, typically written in the Java programming language. Here concurrent processing may be used at the client to speed up the animation and to allow it to occur in parallel with user interaction with the page, for example when the page represents a form to be filled in.

Chapter 23

1.2 Potentially concurrent applications

We now move from systems which are inherently concurrent to applications which might benefit from concurrent implementation. Parallel algorithms are not presented in detail. Rather, the aim is to show the requirements for the support of separate but related concurrent activities that will work together to achieve some result. It is also important to investigate the requirement for some degree of interaction between the parallel computations.

The general motivation for exploiting potential concurrency in an application is that some or all of the following are the case:

- there is a large amount of computing to be done;
- there is a large amount of data to be processed;
- there is a real-time requirement for the result;
- hardware is available for running the potentially concurrent components in parallel.

First, some general approaches to obtaining a concurrent solution to a problem are described.

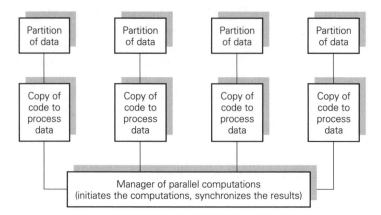

Figure 1.6
Replicated code,
partitioned data.

1.2.1 Replicated code, partitioned data

Perhaps the simplest approach is to use a sequential algorithm but to **partition the data**. Figure 1.6 shows the general idea. If all the components must run to completion the overall time taken is that of the longest component (the other components have run in parallel and have finished before the longest one) plus the overhead of initiating the parallel computations and synchronizing on their completion. The speed-up achieved therefore depends on being able to divide the computation into pieces with approximately equal computation time. This is because we have assumed that the total amount of data processing to be done is the same whether it is done sequentially or in parallel. If we can divide the computation into components which require the same amount of computation time we have maximized the concurrency in the execution of the algorithm.

Examples of problems which are suited to this static partitioning of data are as follows:

- finding all the roots of a given function;
- finding the turning points of a given function;
- searching for specific values in data which has no ordering related to the values required; for example, the data may be records about people which are ordered according to their surnames. You are searching for people with a specific value in some field of their record, for example, those with an Australian grandparent.

A parallel algorithm for searching might be particularly suitable for large amounts of data, some of which is in main memory and some on disk. While one parallel activity waits for more data to be brought in from disk, another can proceed with processing data in main memory.

In some applications, once a solution is found by one component all the others can cease their activity. An example is a search for a single solution to a problem or query. In this case, once the solution is found all the components which are still executing should be stopped. The system mechanisms should make it possible to do this.

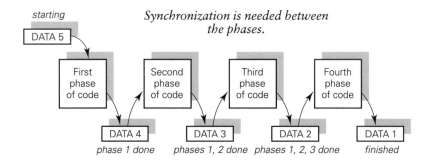

Figure 1.7
A four-stage pipeline.

1.2.2 Pipelined processing

Another simple approach is the **pipeline**. If the total function to be applied to the data can be divided into distinct processing phases, different portions of data can flow along from function to function. Figure 1.7 shows a four-stage pipeline. An example is a compiler with phases for lexical analysis, parsing, type checking, code generation and so on. As soon as the first program or module has passed the lexical analysis phase it may be passed on to the parsing phase while the lexical analyser starts on the second program or module.

The requirements here are for the separate activities executing the various phases to be able to synchronize with each other: to wait for new data to become available or to wait for the next phase to finish processing its current data.

1.2.3 Tree-structured algorithms

Many algorithms can be represented by a tree structure. For example, the evaluation of a function for given arguments may often be split into the evaluation of two (or more) subfunctions, which in turn can be split . . . In this case there is potential for parallel evaluation each time a branch is made as each subfunction must deliver its result to contribute to the higher-level evaluation.

Certain problems require that every branch must be evaluated in full. In other applications the tree structure is a way of dividing a search space where only one solution is required. The whole space should be traversed only if no solution exists. As soon as a solution is found the algorithm should terminate. Again, as discussed in Section 1.2.1, ongoing executions (and the process of creating new ones) should be stopped.

In other cases, such as speech recognition, the parallel branch traversals may represent alternative possibilities for a solution. Each branch has an associated probability of matching the solution and the requirement is to produce the combination of branches with the highest probability of success.

A tree structure introduces more potential parallelism than the simple, static, linear partitioning described above in Section 1.2.1. A new problem here is how to create a reasonable number of parallel computations dynamically, bearing in mind the overhead of each computation and the number of physical processors available to execute them.

1.2.4 Shared data

In Section 1.1.2 we saw that activities in a transaction processing system need to access the same shared data, such as in an airline booking system. The requirements of the application are such that the data cannot be partitioned: you have to book the seat on the flight the client wants, even if someone else is attempting to book a seat on the same flight.

The algorithms outlined above have attempted to avoid the need for concurrent activities to access shared data. We focused on parallel activities carrying out independent work. Even in these cases, their results may need to be merged into a shared data structure. Also, when one activity finishes its work it may be able to request more work from the manager or from one of the other parallel activities. In practice, interaction and cooperation between the activities are likely to be required.

Concurrent algorithms may be designed so that concurrent activities access shared, rather than strictly partitioned, data. For example, the work to be carried out is divided into units and recorded in a shared data structure. Each activity reads a work item from the shared data structure and marks it as taken. A potential problem is that the concurrent activities have to access the shared data one at a time to avoid corrupting it (we shall study this problem later). If the units of work are long relative to the time taken to get the next unit from the data structure then contention for access to the shared data is likely to be tolerable.

1.2.5 Application areas

A full treatment of the different application areas in which concurrent algorithms can be used merits a number of books, for example, Quinn (1987), Almasi and Gottlieb (1989) and Bertsekas and Tsitsiklis (1989). A brief summary is given here and detailed study is left for further reading.

In the area of numerical algorithms, the modelling, or simulation, of physical systems can consume a great deal of computing power and data space. Examples are simulation of nuclear reactions and modelling the atmosphere for weather forecasting. Numerical methods based on the solution of partial differential equations, Fast Fourier and other transforms and optimization in general are candidates for parallel decomposition.

Software engineering tasks, such as the compilation of programs which comprise very large numbers of modules, are an obvious target for parallelization. A library containing the interface specifications of the modules must be available so that intermodule operation invocations can be checked.

Graphics applications, such as those involving raytracing techniques to achieve three-dimensional images, can be parallelized.

The general area of artificial intelligence has a large number of problems which require a large amount of processing power, such as voice and image recognition, natural language processing and expert systems. It is often the case that a number of solutions to a problem must be evaluated and the most likely one selected.

1.2.6 Requirements for supporting concurrent applications

Some simple approaches to designing concurrent algorithms were presented above. They illustrated the approaches of partitioning the data, statically or dynamically, and partitioning the code into a pipeline. For potentially concurrent applications we may have the option of designing an algorithm based on partitioning. For inherently concurrent applications, such as transaction processing systems, we may not have the option of partitioning the data. For some applications it may be more appropriate to use shared data. In general, in a potentially concurrent application, the separate activities are related and cooperate to achieve a common goal.

Some requirements for the support of concurrency at the application level are:

- There is a need to support separate activities.
- There is a need for these activities to be managed appropriately: to be created as required and stopped when no longer needed.
- There is a need for separate activities to synchronize with each other, and possibly to pass data when synchronized.
- There may be a need for separate activities to share the data relating to the application; alternatively, the data may be strictly partitioned.

The application will be written in a programming language and it must be possible to meet the requirements outlined here through the facilities offered by the language and the underlying operating system.

1.3 Architectures for concurrent systems and applications

It is desirable that cheap processing power, large and fast memory and high-bandwidth communications media should be exploited. Conventional architectures and interconnection topologies may be used as a basis for concurrent software. Alternatively, special architectures may be appropriate for certain application areas. Some are well understood and available commercially, while others are novel and still the subject of research and evaluation. This section reviews the options available. Where appropriate, any special language system associated with the architecture is described.

A broad classification that is helpful when considering concurrent systems was given by Flynn (Bayer *et al.*, 1978). It is based on the number of independent instruction streams and data streams being processed by the system.

1.3.1 System classification

SISD: Single instruction stream, single data stream

This is the conventional uniprocessor model, with a single processor fetching and executing a sequence of instructions which operate on the data items specified within them. This is the original von Neumann model of the operation of a computer.

SIMD: Single instruction stream, multiple data stream

In this case there are many processing elements but they are designed to execute the same instruction at the same time. For this reason the processors can be simple: they do not need to fetch instructions from their private memory, but receive their instructions from a central controller. They do, however, operate on separate data items such as the elements of vectors or arrays.

Any machine that has vector or array instructions which execute in parallel can be classified as SIMD. It may be that the array processor component is a special-purpose attached processor such as in the ICL DAP (Distributed Array Processor). This component has thousands of small processors and is loaded to perform matrix calculations. A conventional SISD computer carries out this process. The very high-performance, and expensive, Cray range of computers offers vector operations of this type.

The potential increase in performance through using an SIMD processor depends on the proportion of matrix instructions in the application. It is inevitable that parts of the algorithms concerned will execute sequentially and there is overhead in loading the array processor.

This kind of concurrency is **fine grained**, being at the level of a single instruction on a single data item, and **synchronous**, in that the operations occur together. Many application areas produce problems that require vector and matrix solutions. Some of these areas are well funded and are able to use the expensive SIMD computers, often called 'supercomputers', that have been developed specifically for this purpose. In this book we are concerned with more general-purpose concurrent systems and will not consider SIMD machines further.

MIMD: Multiple instruction stream, multiple data stream

Systems with more than one processor fetching and executing instructions are MIMD. The instructions need not be closely related and they are executed asynchronously. This is a very broad category (the classification scheme has been criticized for this reason) and includes networks of computers and multiprocessors built from separate computers.

Another broad classification that distinguishes conventional systems from experimental ones is into the categories **control-driven, data-driven** and **demand-driven**. The conventional von Neumann model of a computer is control-driven. The processor fetches and executes a sequence of instructions, the program counter acting as sequence controller. It is argued that sequencing is usually overspecified in conventional programming languages and that, very often, instructions that are written down in a sequence could be executed in parallel. The problem is how to detect automatically when instructions are independent of each other and exploit this potential concurrency.

Consider the following program fragment:

$$x = a \times b;$$
$$y = c \times d;$$
$$z = x + y;$$

In this simple example, x and y can be evaluated in parallel, but both must be evaluated before z.

An outline of the range of possible hardware on which a concurrent software system might be implemented is now given. Sections 1.3.2 to 1.3.4 consider control-driven architectures with increasing numbers of constituent computers. The data-driven and demand-driven approaches are discussed briefly in Sections 1.3.5 and 1.3.6. Finally, network-based systems are considered.

1.3.2 Conventional uniprocessors

A single uniprocessor computer may be used to implement some kinds of concurrent system. A time-sharing operating system is an example. Many users are interacting with the system simultaneously and many programs are in the process of being executed (that is, they are at some point between their start and termination) at a given time. We shall see in Chapter 4 that the fact that there is only one processor may be transparent to the programmer. At the application software level it is as though each program is executing on a dedicated processor.

An important point about uniprocessors is that the technique of forbidding interrupts may be used for controlling concurrency. Device handling, including interrupts, will be explained in Chapter 3, but the basic idea is that you can prevent the processor from doing anything other than its current activity until it reaches the end of it, when you 'enable interrupts' again. In the meantime, mayhem may have broken out and alarm signals may be pending but the processor carries on regardless. We shall expand on this technique for simplifying the design of concurrent software in Chapter 8. It obviously has to be used with great care and for short periods of time. The system designer has to decide whether, and to what extent, to make use of the fact that software will run on a uniprocessor. This dependency can impose a major constraint on possible system upgrades and has often prevented the owners of commercial operating systems from improving the performance of their systems by introducing more processors.

Removing such a dependency retrospectively requires a major rewrite of the heart of a system.

Starting from a uniprocessor system it is common to exploit more processing power by adding dedicated machines for specific device-handling functions. The terminal-handling function might be offloaded into a separate 'front-end' computer. Disk controllers have become quite complex in their functionality and contain dedicated processors. When functions have been moved to special-purpose, dedicated computers to the greatest possible extent, the next step is to move on to multiprocessors to obtain more potential concurrency.

The conventions for processor architecture evolve in response to factors such as the increase in processing power and the speed and quantity of memory. The trend for general-purpose processors is towards reduced instruction set computers (RISC) and away from complex instruction set computers (CISC). There are implications for concurrency control in RISC machines, which are discussed in Chapters 3, 9 and 10.

There is a place for conventional uniprocessors in many large-scale concurrent systems. A process control system may consist of a number of relatively small computers placed strategically around the process being controlled. A network connects them and the system is managed automatically by software whenever possible and manually when higher-level, strategic decisions are required. A program development environment may be based on personal uniprocessor workstations and uniprocessor machines may also be used for controlling printers and file servers. This style of concurrent system was introduced above in Section 1.1.

1.3.3 Shared-memory multiprocessors

The conventional multiprocessor model is of a relatively small number of processors (ranging from two to about 30) executing programs from a single shared memory. Note that only one copy of the operating system and any other system software is needed. We now have the situation that software from the same memory is being executed at the same time on a number of processors. A fundamental distinction between different kinds of concurrent software is whether or not the components which run in parallel share memory.

It is more difficult to write operating systems that run on multiprocessors than on uniprocessors. Aspects of this problem are still being researched. Sometimes, to simplify the design, one dedicated processor will execute the operating system and one dedicated processor will handle all I/O. At the end of Part II the reader should understand the trade-offs involved in such decisions.

When more than some fairly small number of processors access a single shared memory, contention for memory access becomes too great. The effect can be alleviated by providing the processors with hardware-controlled caches in which recently accessed memory locations are held. If we wish to get more concurrency into a system we have to look to a different system topology.

1.3.4 Multicomputer multiprocessors

There are very many different computer system designs based on interconnected computers. Let us make the simplifying assumption that each processor accesses only its own local memory directly. The processors may be placed on a shared bus, typically up to 10–15 of them before contention becomes excessive. They communicate with each other through the control and data paths of the bus. A hierarchy of buses may be used to increase the number of processors in the system, as for example in the early Pluribus and Cm* systems (Siewiorek *et al.*, 1982).

To exploit massive concurrency we may wish to use many tens of processors. In this case their connectivity is a major design decision. It is sometimes argued that a tree structure is appropriate for a wide range of problems and that each processor should be connected to three others (its parent and two children). The Inmos transputer has four high-speed serial links for the construction of interconnected systems. A tree-like structure could be built or indeed any topology appropriate for the application.

A crossbar switch arrangement allows any processor to communicate with any other, but only if no other processor is already doing so. It is expensive to connect everything to everything using a switching arrangement and we must not forget that a motivation for using large numbers of computers is to take advantage of inexpensive, off-the-shelf components, so the cost is important.

As network performance has increased, interconnection by this means is an alternative to multicomputer multiprocessors for some concurrent applications; the components may be loaded onto separate machines connected to a network.

A general problem with multicomputers is the complexity of the software systems required to manage them and the time to load software prior to execution. There is little advantage for general applications if loading concurrent software into a multicomputer is a lengthy and complex process, involving transfer through many computers en route, even if execution completes in a fraction of the sequential execution time. At present, such topologies tend to be used for software that will run indefinitely once loaded, such as in embedded control systems.

1.3.5 Dataflow (data-driven) architectures

In a conventional (imperative) programming language you have to write down a sequence of statements even when there are no dependencies between them and they could be executed in any order or concurrently. Dataflow is a response to this overspecification of sequencing.

It is also argued that conventional von Neumann computers have a fundamental design flaw in their bottleneck for memory access. Instructions are fetched in sequence and their data operands are then read or written as specified in the instruction. It is difficult to speed up program execution by fetching instructions or data in advance so you have to rely on getting them quickly when you find out where they are.

In the dataflow model, an instruction may execute as soon as its data operands are ready. Any number of instructions can execute in parallel, depending on the number of processors available. It is possible to arrange for the operations to have at most two arguments. The first argument to be ready for an operation will detect that its pair is not yet available and will wait in memory provided for the purpose. The second will detect that the first is ready, by an associative match on the memory, and they will then go off together to a processor for execution. The result of the operation will become an argument for another operation, and so on.

It is necessary to distinguish between different executions of the same operation, such as in separate calls of a given procedure and the executions of a loop in a program. To address this problem special languages have been developed for dataflow in which there can be at most one assignment to a given variable.

The concurrency made available by the dataflow approach is potentially very great and at a very fine granularity: at the machine instruction level. The challenge is to devise an architecture that can exploit the concurrency.

A problem with a data-driven approach is that unnecessary processing may be carried out for paths in a program that may never be followed; for example, in a simple if-then-else statement, both the 'then' path and the 'else' path may have been computed before the condition is evaluated. This computation may have been done in competition with other computations which were needed. To solve this problem a 'demand-driven' approach is advocated with the aim that only those values that are needed are computed. Function application has seemed attractive as a basis for this approach.

1.3.6 Architectures for functional languages

A pure functional language does not have destructive assignment statements. When a function is applied to its arguments it always produces the same result since there can be no side-effects; that is, in a functional language you can assume that $f(a) + f(a) = 2 \times f(a)$. This is not true in all imperative languages because the first call of f with argument a may have caused an assignment to some variable within the body of f (a side-effect). The second call $f(a)$ may then deliver a different result from the first.

It is argued therefore that functional languages are inherently concurrent. Any number of function applications can be carried out in parallel; as soon as the arguments are available the function can be applied. There is greater potential for controlling the concurrency than in the dataflow approach if we can defer a function application until we are sure that the result is needed: so called 'lazy evaluation'. Again, the challenge is to design a machine to exploit the idea.

Both data-driven and demand-driven architectures, and associated software systems, are still in the research domain. In the meantime, conventional von Neumann machines have exhibited a regular and dramatic increase in performance and decrease in cost with which it is very difficult to compete (Hennessy and Patterson, 1996).

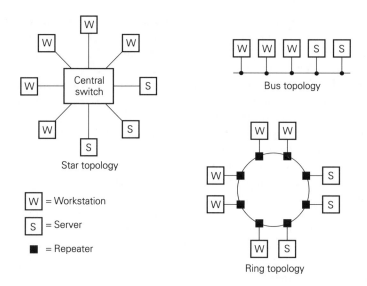

Figure 1.8
Star, bus and ring
LAN topologies.

1.3.7 Network-based systems

Local area networks (LANs)

A local area network (LAN) offers **full connectivity** for some number of computer systems. This contrasts with many multicomputer multiprocessor topologies as discussed above: for example, a transputer can be connected to at most four other transputers. Each transputer in a multitransputer topology may need to handle data which comes from an external source and is destined for an external destination. In contrast, each computer on a network is only concerned with data which is sent specifically to it.

Figure 1.8 shows three basic LAN topologies, namely star, bus and ring, for the popular workstation–server model discussed in Section 1.1. In the star topology every message is first directed to a central switch which forwards it to its intended destination. The central switch is an obvious reliability hazard and should, perhaps, be a reliable multiprocessor. In a bus topology an attached computer that wants to communicate puts its 'message' addressed to its intended recipient computer on the bus. All computers monitor the bus and extract the messages addressed to them. Failure of an attached computer usually does not stop the bus from working. The problem to be solved is how to determine when the bus is free to be used. We shall see one solution in Section 3.7. In the ring topology an attached computer that wants to communicate puts its 'message' on the ring. When the message passes through the intended recipient's station it is extracted. Failure of any repeater causes the whole ring to fail and methods of duplicating the links and stations are used in applications which cannot tolerate failure.

The approach to communications handling in component computers of multi-computer multiprocessor systems and computers attached to networks is very different. This is partly because they have evolved to meet different requirements and partly because of their different emphasis on hardware and software to support data transfer. The former employ **hardware protocols**, such as in a computer's internal bus, to transmit data from source to destination. The higher levels of software, which interpret the data (introduced in Section 1.1.3), tend to be much simpler than in network-based systems. The **software protocols** which the latter employ will be introduced in Section 3.8. These handle more options for sending information to different destinations, allow for loss of data due to network errors or shortage of storage space and in general are more complex.

The basic philosophy of network communications software is to regard the network as a shared resource which must be managed. For example, a user of an attached workstation may have started a background compilation, which requires several files to be read from a file server and, in parallel, may be reading mail from a mail server. Certain attached computers exist solely to support communication, for example, when two LANs are connected by a **gateway computer** or a LAN is connected to a wide area network (WAN).

A simple outline of data communication using a LAN is that a packet of information is composed by a connected computer system, addressed to some other connected computer system, and put on the LAN. The addressing information in the packet ensures that the intended destination computer will take the packet. It is a function of the software in the attached computers to compose and interpret the information.

The LAN design determines the size of the packet of information that it can accept. An Ethernet packet can contain up to 4 kbytes of data and a Cambridge Fast Ring cell contains 32 bytes, for example. This should not have to be a concern of application-level software, so communications software manages the transmission and safe reception of information between networked systems. Communications hardware and software are discussed further in Chapter 3.

LANs are widely used as a basis for program development environments. Each user has a workstation and there are shared server computers such as file servers; that is, the LAN is the interconnection medium for a distributed system, such as is described in Section 1.1.3.

The bandwidth of the LAN medium is shared by the attached computers. In certain types of LAN a proportion of the bandwidth can be guaranteed to each attached computer. This kind of guarantee can be essential for some applications. It is also important to know the overhead imposed by the communications software. The network may be able to guarantee a high, sustained throughput of data but the application software is concerned with the time taken for data to be transferred between application levels on different computers. The design of the communications software and the operating system greatly affect this, but as LAN bandwidth increases it becomes increasingly feasible for a LAN-based system to be used for many kinds of distributed application.

A single LAN, with associated communications software, can handle a certain number of attached computers. If more than this were to be attached, contention for access to the network might become too frequent, and some networks might become congested. For this reason, and also for reasons of geographic separation, a number of interconnected LANs are often used in a company or campus, sometimes called a local internet.

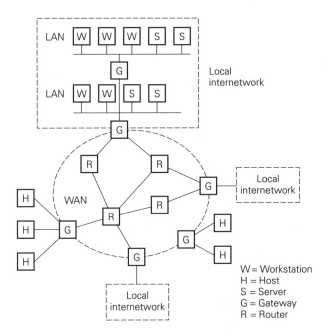

W = Workstation
H = Host
S = Server
G = Gateway
R = Router

Figure 1.9
LANs connected by
WANs.

Wide area networks (WANs)

When computers or LANs need to be connected over long distances, wide area networks (WANs) are used, as shown in Figure 1.9. There are now many world-wide WANs which are used for applications such as electronic mail, information retrieval services, dealings on the international stock exchanges, banking, commerce and science. Figure 1.9 indicates that certain computers are dedicated to the communications-handling function. A gateway computer is shown attaching each LAN and host system to the WAN and a communications subnet comprising computers called 'routers' is shown. These communications computers cooperate to route each 'message' from its source to its destination.

Like the international telephone service, basic WAN infrastructure is provided by the public telephone companies. There are also WANs with private, dedicated connections.

In general, LANs operate at 10s to 100s of megabits per second and are highly reliable. WANs comprise many different links with different characteristics; some may be slow and unreliable. A world-wide network may contain a satellite link through which a large volume of data can be transferred but with a long end-to-end delay; some computers may be attached to a WAN by telephone lines. The trend is towards the provision of high-speed connections which have the characteristics of LANs.

We discuss networks in more detail in Chapter 3 and Chapter 25 includes a case study which involves the use of high-speed WANs.

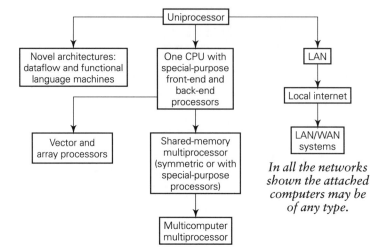

Figure 1.10
Summary of
concurrent system
topologies.

In the figure:
Uniprocessor → Novel architectures: dataflow and functional language machines; One CPU with special-purpose front-end and back-end processors; LAN.

Novel architectures → Vector and array processors.

One CPU with special-purpose front-end and back-end processors → Shared-memory multiprocessor (symmetric or with special-purpose processors) → Multicomputer multiprocessor.

LAN → Local internet → LAN/WAN systems.

In all the networks shown the attached computers may be of any type.

1.3.8 Summary of hardware bases for concurrent systems

Figure 1.10 summarizes the topologies that might be used as the hardware basis for a concurrent system. The arrows indicate the direction of increasing concurrency achieved through different paths of development.

Architectures based on dataflow or function application are an alternative to the conventional von Neumann machine. They attempt to exploit all the potential concurrency of the application rather than that written down in a conventional programming language. Their challenge is to devise an efficient implementation, able to compete with the sophistication of current conventional processor and compiler technology. As they are still in the research domain and are often associated with specific languages they will not be considered further in this book.

The central path takes a single uniprocessor as starting point and attempts to introduce an increasing amount of processing power. Special-purpose processors can handle devices, but a major design change comes when several processors are used to execute programs residing in a single memory. Above a certain number of processors accessing a given memory, a topology comprising interconnected computers is necessary. There is a variety of possible interconnection structures. Vector and array processors may be seen as special-purpose multiprocessor machines.

An alternative to the complexity of the interconnection structures of multicomputer multiprocessor systems is a network. A LAN medium may be used to achieve full connectivity of a certain number of computers, but communication is achieved through software rather than hardware protocols. As LAN performance increases, networked computers can be used for distributed computations as well as the more conventional program development environments, provided that the operating system and communications software impose an acceptable and bounded overhead.

1.4 Defining a concurrent system

The discussion so far has been based on an intuitive notion of what a concurrent system is. We have looked at a number of types of computerized system in which different activities are in the process of being executed (are at some stage between their starting point and finishing point) at the same time, that is, concurrently. System software runs indefinitely and supports a number of applications and/or users. Applications are usually implemented as sequential programs but certain applications may benefit from being implemented as concurrent programs. The concurrency in the application must be supported by the system that runs it.

Figure 1.11 shows some of the concurrent (sub)systems that have been mentioned. In each case a number of activities may be in progress simultaneously within the system, either because components of a concurrent algorithm have been started off in parallel or because a number of clients may simultaneously make demands on the system, as shown in Figure 1.12. The concurrent system may be an operating system, a subsystem within an operating system or an application-level service running above an operating system. In all cases, the concurrent system shown may be distributed across a number of computers rather than centralized in a single computer.

We have made an implicit assumption that it is meaningful to assert that two events happen 'at the same time'. We shall examine this assumption more deeply when we look at systems in which the time at which an event happens is defined by a clock local to the computer in which the event takes place. If many computers, each with their own clock, are cooperating together to achieve some goal the times their local clocks indicate are not guaranteed to be the same.

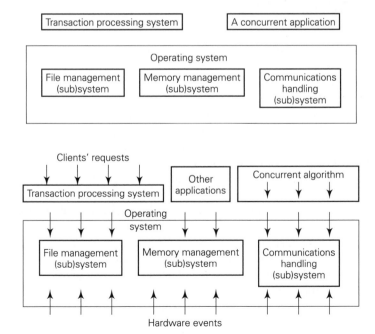

Figure 1.11
Examples of concurrent (sub)systems.

Figure 1.12
Concurrent activity.

We are concerned with **software systems**, implemented on a variety of hardware, in which a number of **separate activities** are in progress at the same time. The separate activities are **related** in some sense; we assume that it is possible to define the **goal** of the concurrent system. The goal may be general, such as 'to run the applications of a number of users of an operating system', or more specific, such as 'to allow users controlled, secure access to their bank accounts'. The goal of a concurrent application may be 'to find the most probable piece of English speech represented by some digitally encoded data'.

In some cases the separate activities may be working together closely, **cooperating**, to solve a given problem. In other cases the relation may be much looser; the concurrent activities may be independent but running above common system software and needing to share common system resources for which they must **compete**.

The activities may need to **interact with the external environment** of the computer system and may need to meet **timing requirements** when doing so.

The activities may need to use the **main memory only** of a single computer (as part of a 'load and go' program execution) or they may use main memory only, but of a number of computers in a distributed system. Finally, the activities may access or record data in persistent memory (for example, a disk-based filing system). In this case they use **both main memory and persistent memory** of a single computer or of computers in a distributed system.

1.5 Requirements for implementing concurrent systems

Some common requirements can be drawn from the discussion on concurrent systems above.

1 *Support for separate activities*. Examples are:
   (a) the monitoring and control activities in a process control system;
   (b) the running of users' programs by an operating system;
   (c) the handling of devices by an operating system;
   (d) the transactions of the customers of a banking system;
   (e) the concurrent computations executing an application.
2 *Support for the management of separate activities*, in particular, the ability to create, run, stop and kill them, and possibly to indicate their relative priorities.
3 *Support for related activities to work together*. Examples are:
   (a) parallel activities each generating part of a solution to a problem;
   (b) device-handling programs which deliver input data to, or take output data from, user programs;
   (c) booking clerks making airline bookings on behalf of clients, when many clerks can run programs concurrently.

4 *The ability to meet timing requirements*. Examples are:
    (a)   that an alarm might require a response in a specified time;
    (b)   the weather forecast must be ready before the time of the forecast arrives;
    (c)   users must hear clear, smooth, recognizable speech and see non-jittering video;
    (d)   users should get response in a 'reasonable' time from systems.

    If a real-time application runs above an operating system the application must know what the operating system can guarantee and with what probability. Note that it might be necessary for the application level to indicate the priorities of its separate activities to the underlying operating system in order that timing requirements can be met. This is not possible in most current operating systems.

5 *Support for composite tasks*. A single task may have several components which are executed concurrently with other tasks. The system may fail after the completion of some of the subtasks but before the whole task is complete.

The rest of this book shows how these requirements are met. Part I is concerned with establishing the abstraction and implementation of **process** to meet the requirement for support of separate activities. Part II shows how related activities may work together to carry out the functions of a concurrent system. In order to keep the complexity of the presentation to a minimum, the discussion in Part II is restricted to the implementation of correct execution of a 'single operation' without interference. Part III addresses the problems of composite tasks which may involve a number of subtasks involving a single main memory, main memory and persistent memory in a single computer system, or the main memory and persistent memory of computers in a distributed system.

1.6 Security, protection and fault tolerance in system design

Emphasis has been given to the dynamic behaviour of systems in which many concurrent activities may be in progress. Support for concurrency is a major aspect of system design, and development of the material presented in this book will be motivated by the support for concurrency in systems. Orthogonal to this development is the fact that all systems have some degree of requirement for security, protection and tolerance of errors and failures. When the details of system design and implementation are given, these aspects will also be covered.

    The topic of security is huge and includes all aspects of controlling access to computers, networks and the information stored, processed and transferred in computer systems. We can express a general requirement that it should be possible for **policies** to be expressed and enforced relating to who (which **principals**) may have access to computers, networks and information.

In Chapter 2 we establish a framework for describing and designing systems in terms of their structure and reasoning about their dynamic behaviour. There, we see how running systems and applications are protected from accidental or malicious corruption. We also establish a general model, a system's **access matrix,** for recording all authorized accesses of all principals known to the system to all objects managed by it. Chapter 5 gives details of how running programs are confined to areas of main memory: **memory protection**; and how access to information stored in files is controlled: **access control** or **authorization.** In Chapter 7 an overview of security in distributed systems is given. In a distributed, networked world it becomes even more crucial to establish securely which principal is attempting to use a system. The secure establishment of identity is called **authentication.** We also outline how secure communication of data is achieved by **encryption** and how cross-network access to services and data is controlled.

Exercises

1.1   (a)   What is a real-time system?
         (b)   Why is it useful to distinguish 'hard' from other real-time systems?
         (c)   In what ways do operating systems which support real-time systems differ from those which support single-user workstations and multi-user, time-sharing systems?

1.2   Classify the following as hard real-time, real-time or non-real-time systems:

An embedded computer system which controls the fuel mixture in a car engine
A robot controller for a car production assembly line
An on-line library catalogue system
A single-user workstation which supports graphics, digitized voice and video
A world-wide electronic mail (email) system
A network of computers for a banking system
A hospital patient monitoring and control system
An on-line medical record system
A weather forecasting system based on a model of the earth's atmosphere
An international stock exchange computer system.

Do any of the above systems have to handle concurrent activities?

1.3   Give examples of monitoring and control activities in real-time and non-real-time systems.

1.4   (a)   Define three general models for concurrent algorithms.
         (b)   On what kinds of hardware could you run a concurrent algorithm and expect to achieve better performance than on a uniprocessor? Are any new overheads introduced for the hardware you mention?

1.5 (a) What is a concurrent system?

(b) Can a concurrent system run on a uniprocessor computer? Give examples to justify your answer.

1.6 What is a shared-memory multiprocessor? Are any of the approaches for devising concurrent algorithms particularly suited to this kind of architecture?

1.7 What is the difference between communications handling for a multicomputer system with hardware-controlled connections between specific computers and a network-based multicomputer system?

Part I

Background and Fundamentals

Computer science is concerned with **exploiting technology**. A prime motivation for the study of concurrent systems is to be able to exploit current and projected processing power, memory size and speed, storage capacity and communications bandwidth. CPU performance is increasing at about 35% per annum (for microprocessors), memory size quadruples every three years, disk performance grows relatively modestly at about 5% per annum. Local and wide area network bandwidths are increasing less uniformly but equally dramatically. The ten megabits per second local area network commonly used since the 1980s is being replaced by hundred megabit networks connected by gigabit backbones.

We are aiming to exploit technology by bringing more processing power to bear on the solutions to problems. In order to do this we must use concurrent software systems. The Introduction started from an informal, intuitive notion of what is meant by a concurrent system and proceeded to a more rigorous definition and some implementation requirements.

A major challenge for computer science is the **management of complexity** since computerized systems which exploit the potential of technology tend to be large and complex. This is achieved by creating abstractions as a means of structuring systems and will be a theme throughout the book. By this means a system can be comprehended as a whole at a high level of abstraction but we can focus on any component part at any level of detail required at lower levels of abstraction.

How to design modular software is the first topic in Chapter 2. Since the **object paradigm** has gained wide acceptance as a basis for designing systems this model is developed in some detail. We then set up the concepts of process, thread and protocol in order to reason about how systems are executed dynamically. Operating systems are themselves large concurrent systems as well as supporting such systems and we spend some time on their design and functionality throughout Part I.

In Chapter 3 we study the hardware–software interface: how hardware is controlled by program and how hardware supports system structure such as the protection boundary between the operating system and the software it supports. A concept that is emphasized is the need for hardware–software **synchronization**. Chapter 4 shows how processes and threads are supported by operating systems and also by language systems and Chapter 5 gives background in operating system functions: memory and file management.

Chapter 6 extends Chapter 2's general discussion of system architecture to distributed systems. We focus on the fundamental properties as background to an integrated approach to concurrent system design. Chapter 7 covers security in centralized and distributed systems.

System structure and dynamic execution

Computer scientists must comprehend, design and build large software systems. A high-level view of how a system is structured and how its components work together dynamically is essential for this purpose. We establish a context of **modular software structure** as a framework for looking at software systems and then progress to considering the **dynamic behaviour** of systems. The classical concept of process is introduced and is refined to accommodate multiple threads of execution within a single application.

Operating systems are themselves large, concurrent software systems as well as supporting such systems. We therefore consider their internal structure, the functions they provide and how these functions are invoked. We sketch how an object model can be applied in the design of operating systems and in the software they support, including distributed software. Issues such as naming, sharing and protection are introduced.

A high-level view of how a software system is structured and how its components work together is essential for understanding the design and implementation of large systems. In all scientific disciplines, the usual approach to making large systems comprehensible is to split them up into more manageable parts, or modules. This process of division is called **modularization**. Software consists of programs written in some programming language but it has long been recognized that attempting to understand a large software system by looking at program code is an extremely difficult task. Therefore, we require a higher-level description of the system that helps us understand its composition and behaviour. The idea that there could be several views of a software system is also helpful when building new software. We can describe the software in terms that we understand then convert this description into program code known as an implementation. Thus, we must always keep in mind the difference between thinking about a problem that involves understanding the problem domain which has nothing to do with programming languages and leads to a conceptual view of the solution, and implementing the solution to a problem in a particular programming language that requires a knowledge of the syntax and semantics of that language, and leads to an implementational view of the solution.

A word of caution is appropriate at this time: the vocabulary that we use to describe these views is often very similar in the two cases so it is important to be clear about which view one is describing. For example, the idea of modularization is common to all views, but a module could refer to a unit of program code in the implementational view (such as a method, procedure or subroutine – depending on the programming language) or an operation in the conceptual view. In what follows, we shall try to ensure that we make it quite clear which view we are discussing.

2.1 System structure: Conceptual views

2.1.1 Types and abstract data types

When analysing a problem it is possible to identify collections of items in the problem domain with similar properties, for example, employees in a firm, for which it is useful to invent a collective name, such as 'employees'. It is then possible to discuss the type 'employee' which is the set of employees in the firm. This implies that certain items have the property of being an employee whereas other items are not employees. Thus, some items are in the set, others are not. We end up with the following definition of type:

Type is a word given to a named set of items having some property in common.

A useful way of defining the property which the elements of the set have in common, is to list the operations that they can carry out and to use the term **behaviour** to stand for this collection of operations. This leads to the idea of an abstract data type:

An **abstract data type** (ADT) is a set of items defined by the collection of operations that they can carry out. The elements of such a set are usually referred to as **values**.

An example of an ADT is a set of bank accounts. Suppose we name such a set **Account**. Being an ADT, all the instances of **Account**, that is, all the individual bank accounts that make up the set, respond by means of the same set of operations. That is, the instances exhibit the same behaviour when invoked. So, for example, there might be an operation that sets the balance of an account named **setBalance**, another operation named **getBalance** that returns the current balance of an account, an operation to withdraw money from an account might be called **debit**, and so on. In other words, all the instances of **Account** are characterized by the same collection of operations – any object that responds to the same collection of operations would be considered a bank account.

If we were interested in building payroll software that would transfer money from a firm's bank account into the accounts of its employees, we could begin by describing the various bank accounts as instances of the ADT **Account**. In addition, we would need to describe the firm's employees in a similar way. That is, we would need an **Employee** ADT having suitable operations related to the amount of pay received by an employee (**getPay** and **setPay**), the frequency of payment (**getFrequency** and **setFrequency**), certain details of the employee's bank account (such as **getAccountNumber**, **setAccountNumber**) and their personal details (**getName** and **setName**). Of course, in this application we would only be interested in those attributes and operations of an employee that relate to the payment of salaries; we would not want to deal with the multitude of other operations that relate to an employee. The process of identifying the operations that are appropriate to the problem being solved is known as **abstraction** because we need to concentrate only on the features of real-world objects that are essential to solve the problem: we ignore all other features. We end up with a definition of an abstract data type, which is a **model** of the real thing at a level of abstraction appropriate to the problem being solved.

Clearly, to define an ADT means defining its operations (its possible behaviours). An operation is defined in terms of syntax and semantics. The syntax of an operation tells you what must be written down to describe an application of the operation, and this includes:

- the name of the operation;
- the arguments of the operation (a definition of the data that the operation works upon);
- the result of carrying out the operation.

Typically, the arguments and the result are values (instances of other abstract data types). For example, the syntax of the **Account** operation **debit** could be defined as follows:

name: **debit**
argument: an instance of the ADT **Money**
result: an instance of the ADT **Boolean**

which says that the operation, **debit**, must operate on an instance of the ADT **Money** (an amount) and returns either true or false depending upon whether the debit was successful or not (an **Account** may not be allowed to become

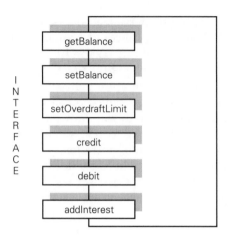

Figure 2.1
The interface of
the ADT Account.

overdrawn and so the operation may not succeed). This information is collectively known as the **signature** of the operation.

The semantics of an operation is a description of what the operation does (often given in terms of what it does to its arguments in order to produce its result). Whilst it is possible to define the semantics of an operation in a formal way, we shall simply use English prose.

2.1.2 Interfaces

It is important to realize that the only way to interact with an instance of an ADT is by invoking one of its operations. That is, the only aspects of an instance of an ADT known externally are its operations. Therefore, we speak of the set of operations that define an ADT as an **interface**. *How* an operation carries out its task is of no concern to any other ADT that uses the operation. These ideas are illustrated in Figure 2.1 where the interface for the **Account** ADT is shown. We have used the same operation names as for the examples in Part III. There, the bank account objects are assumed to be stored in a database, whereas in these introductory examples we are programming objects in main memory. The implementation of the operations is therefore not identical here and in Part III.

2.1.3 State

In our ADT example, **Account,** if we wanted to explain what its interface operations do (you cannot use an operation successfully without knowing what it does), one way would be to describe an instance of **Account** in terms of its state. That is, in terms of a set of values that describe it. For example, an account might have a **balance** (an instance of the ADT **Money**). We could then describe the meaning of the account operations in terms of the effect they have on **balance**. Thus, the operation **credit** would take an amount of money and increase **balance**. The operation **debit** would reduce **balance** by a given amount (but only if the account's overdraft limit were not exceeded) and **addInterest** would increase

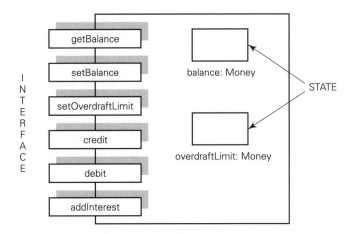

Figure 2.2
The state of the ADT Account.

balance by adding interest to it. Figure 2.2 repeats Figure 2.1 but this time shows the instances of the ADTs which make up the state of an **Account** (**balance** and **overdraftLimit** are both instances of the ADT **Money**).

In a complex system, there will be many instances of a variety of ADTs and the invocation of an operation of one ADT will require further invocations of the operations of others.

In the **Account** example, the operation **credit** must change the value of **balance**, but it can only do this by invoking an operation of the ADT **Money**.

Thus, an ADT normally has two roles:

• a *supplier* of services (another ADT can make use of its operations); and
• a *client* (a user of the services provided by other ADTs).

As a supplier, an ADT makes its interface known to other ADTs; as a client it uses the facilities offered by other ADTs (as described by their interfaces).

If ADTs are designed carefully, they should be general enough to be reused as components in new models.

2.2 System structure: Implementational views

We shall now turn our attention to how the ideas behind ADTs can be incorporated into a programming language. There are a variety of kinds of programming (often referred to as programming paradigms), but in this book we shall concentrate on the object-oriented programming paradigm and will illustrate the concepts in the language Java. Strictly speaking, the correct English term is 'object-orientated' but 'object-oriented' is almost universally used.

2.2.1 Object-oriented programming

An application written in an object-oriented programming language is structured as a community of objects, each of which provides services that are used by other objects of the community when they are activated. That is, an object can perform a number of actions, which can be used by other objects. Objects are defined by their behaviour – the collection of actions that they can carry out. In object-oriented programming it is usual to refer to an action that an object can carry out as a **method** and an **object** as an instance of a class. That is, a class is a set of objects with the same behaviour (the same set of methods). Thus, a **class** is a collection of objects and the objects are defined by a set of methods.

There is a close correspondence between, on the one hand, ADTs and their instances, and on the other hand, classes and objects. Classes can be used to implement ADTs, and an object (of a class) corresponds to an instance of an ADT.

It may appear at first sight that there is little difference between ADTs and classes and indeed they are very similar. However, there is more to classes and objects than straightforward ADTs and their values. Confusingly, problem analysts find that it is useful to describe real-world entities as objects and define classes for them. We then end up with notions such as real-world objects that are similar to, but sufficiently different from, programming objects that we have to be very clear whether we're dealing with conceptual or implementational views of software. In this section we shall confine ourselves to looking at objects in a programming sense and will introduce a notation for manipulating these objects that will be used in the remainder of the book.

Historically, the term **module** has been used to mean a program unit (part of a program) that is used exclusively through an external interface. In the object-oriented paradigm, however, an object is used exclusively through its external interface, and the code that defines that interface (the object's methods) resides in a class. Whilst the two scenarios are different, the same principle applies: code is used only through a well-defined interface.

2.2.2 Interfaces

In our discussion of ADTs we drew an important distinction between an interface and implementation. Because clients of an ADT only need to know about its interface (an interface is the public face of an ADT), there is no need to know about how the operations carry out their task.

In many object-oriented languages this distinction, between the interface of a class and the way in which its methods are implemented, is made explicit. For example, in Java, we can write down an interface for a class that represents the Account ADT as follows.

```
interface AccountInterface {
    float getBalance ();
    void setBalance (float anAmount);
    void setOverdraftLimit (float anAmount);
    void credit (float anAmount);
    boolean debit (float anAmount);
    void addInterest (float interestRate);
}
```

The elements within parentheses are known as arguments and signify what values (objects) are needed by the method in order to give a result (normally another object). Here we have used **float** values (decimals) rather than objects from the class **Money** as the latter is not built into Java (although it would be possible to build a suitable class, but we shall not pursue this here). Thus, the method named **getBalance** requires no arguments and returns a **float** value. The operation **credit** requires a **float** value as an argument but does not return an object (indicated by the use of the keyword **void**). The method named **addInterest** requires one argument (a **float**, that represents a percentage rate of interest to be applied to **balance**) and returns no value. The method **debit** attempts to reduce **balance** and returns a **boolean** value (**true** if the debit was successful, and **false** otherwise).

Hence, each method in an interface is described by a **heading** consisting of three components: the name of the class of the return object (or **void**), the name of the method and any arguments (in parentheses). The heading of a method corresponds to the signature of an operation in an ADT.

2.2.3 Implementation

Having defined the interface of a class (and hence identified the methods that can be invoked on the objects of that class) we must define the processing that is to be carried out when each method is invoked (executed). We describe the process of defining what a method does as **implementing the method.** Once the tasks carried out by the methods in the interface have all been defined, we say that the class has been **implemented** and we have constructed an **implementation** of the class. For example, here is a class named **Account** that implements **AccountInterface** and defines the services provided by bank account objects.

```
class Account implements AccountInterface {
    float balance;           // an attribute
    float overdraftLimit;    // an attribute

    float getBalance () {
        return balance;
    }

    void setBalance (float anAmount) {
        balance = anAmount;
    }

    void setOverdraftLimit (float anAmount) {
        overdraftLimit = anAmount;
    }

    void credit (float anAmount) {
        balance = balance + anAmount;
    }
```

```
boolean debit (float anAmount) {
    boolean success;              // local variable
    if (anAmount <= balance + overdraftLimit) {
        balance = balance – anAmount;
        success = true;
    } else
        success = false;
    return success;
}

void addInterest (float interestRate) {
    balance = balance *(1 + interestRate/100);
}
}
```

The two quantities named **balance** and **overdraftLimit** are conventionally known as **attributes** and together constitute the **state** of an object from this class. In other words, every object from the class **Account** contains two values named **balance** and **overdraftLimit**. Some methods, such as **getBalance** and **debit** not only perform some useful service but in so doing return a value (an object). The value returned is specified in the **return** statement and the class of the returned object is shown preceding the name of the method.

An important principle of object-oriented programming, taken from ADTs, is that the state of an object should be hidden from users of the object. This means that one object should not be able to access directly the values in the state of another object. If there is a need for an object to access the state of another object, then this must be done using a method designed specifically for the purpose. Clearly, such a method must be part of the object's interface. In our example, the methods **getBalance, setBalance** and **setOverdraftLimit** are used to access the state of an object from the class **Account**. This principle is known as **encapsulation**. The principle is important because it provides *controlled* access to the state of an object. If one object were to access the **balance** of an account directly, it could change (either by accident or design) **balance** to a value that exceeded the overdraft limit and leave the account object in an invalid state (in well-regulated circles, such situations should not exist). Ensuring that all attempts at withdrawing money from an account can only occur by invoking the **debit** method enables us to control this process and avoid objects becoming invalid (we also say inconsistent). As we shall see in Part III, even with encapsulation, operations such as **getBalance** and **setBalance** must be used with great caution in concurrent systems.

A major problem in software construction is the continual need to amend the software either to repair it (fix bugs) or to extend its capabilities. Amending software is a major source of error. Separating an object's interface from its implementation means that it becomes possible to change its attributes or alter the implementations of its methods (provided that there is no resultant change to the interface) without affecting any other object that invokes its methods. That is, the effects of any change are localized and errors are more easily rectified. Of course, any change to an interface will affect other parts of a program and great care needs to be taken. However, a compiler will detect whenever one object attempts to invoke a method of another object incorrectly, that is, not according to its interface specification.

2.2.4 Object interactions

An application written in an object-oriented programming language is structured as a community of interacting objects, each of which provides services that are used by other objects of the community. We discuss in Section 2.3 how such interactions are started.

A service is initiated by an object invoking the appropriate method of the object responsible for providing the service. The notation for denoting the invocation of a method varies from one programming language to another, but a common device is to use a full stop between the name of the object that provides the service (sometimes called the receiver) and the name of the method to be invoked. For example, to denote that an amount of £246.50 is to be credited to a bank account object named **myAccount**, we shall write:

    myAccount.credit (246.50)

The construction **credit (246.50)** denotes the method invocation in which the identifier **credit** is the name of a method mentioned in the interface of the **Account myAccount** and **246.50** is an actual argument (a decimal value used by the method to provide the service). A service is defined by some programming code known as a **method**. For example, the **credit** method increases the balance of an account and has been implemented as follows:

```
void credit (float anAmount) {
    balance = balance + anAmount;
}
```

In this example, the **balance** attribute is updated by adding the amount **anAmount** to it. We call **anAmount** a **formal argument**, that is, a place holder for the **actual argument**, the value that is specified in the invocation.

Here is a **sequence** of invocations of the same **Account** object named **myAccount** which make a deposit, add interest to the account (at a rate of 6.5%) and finally print out the balance of **myAccount**:

```
myAccount.credit (250.0);
myAccount.addInterest (6.5);
screen.print (myAccount.getBalance ());
```

The identifier **screen** refers to an object that represents the computer screen and offers a service named **print**. Invoking the method **getBalance ()** on the object **myAccount** returns a float value which is then provided as an argument to the **print** method to be printed on the screen.

The style of programming used here is usually referred to as **procedural**. That is, you write a sequence of instructions which are carried out one at a time in the order they are written down (although the order of execution can be modified

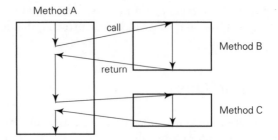

Figure 2.3
A thread of control.

by the use of conditional and loop statements). In the object-oriented paradigm, the predominant type of instruction is a method invocation (also known as a procedure call) in which a method of a specific object is executed. Thus, a program execution consists of a sequence of method calls, and each invocation of a method will often result in further method calls.

A significant point in procedural programming is that, in a sequence of method calls, a call cannot commence until the immediately preceding call has finished. This is known as **synchronous processing**. This may seem an obvious or even trivial point, and you may be wondering why we have invented a new term to describe it. The significance will become clearer once we look at concurrent processing when we allow one call to start before the previous one has finished. Figure 2.3 illustrates what we mean by synchronous processing in which an invocation of method A makes calls to methods B and C. You can view the execution of method A as the execution of a sequence of instructions in which a call to method B is made. Method B is executed and, when it is finished, a return is made to executing A's instructions. Later, a call is made to method C. The main point in synchronous processing is that the instruction in A's code that calls method B does not finish until a return is made from executing method B's instructions. This implies that A's instructions that follow the call to B will not be executed until a return is made from B.

In Figure 2.3, the arrows drawn through the instructions show the order in which instructions are carried out. Such an order is known as a **thread of control**. We return to this concept in Section 2.3.

Terminology

In some programming languages, notably Smalltalk, a synchronous method invocation, such as

   myAccount.credit (250.0);

is called a 'message send'. It is said that the 'message' credit (250.0) is 'sent' to the object myAccount. As such method invocations are synchronous, such a 'message send' generally results in a value being returned. In this book, we are concerned with system design, including distributed systems. In this wider context the term **message** indicates a collection of data that is transferred from one place to another and there is *no* implication that a return value is sent. A message is simply a one-way, point-to-point transfer of data. You can then view a method invocation as (1) the sending of a call message from the caller to the receiver, (2) the execution of the receiver's instructions, and (3) the sending of a return message from the receiver back to the sender. In **synchronous** communication, the caller cannot continue having sent a call message until it receives the return message. We shall discuss **asynchronous** communication later.

2.2.5 The life-cycle of an object

Objects have a life-cycle by which we mean that they are created, enter into collaborations with other objects and eventually die (although some objects will be stored in persistent memory and are, unsurprisingly, known as persistent objects). A non-persistent object has a lifetime that is restricted to the time that the program which created it is being executed. A persistent object exists beyond the execution of the program that created it.

Thus, an object-oriented program must have a notation for creating objects. In this book, we shall use the keyword **new** to indicate the creation of a new object. For example, to create a new bank account object we would write:

```
new Account (350.0, 500.0);
```

where the arguments (the values 350.0 and 500.0 enclosed in parentheses) is used to initialize the object (that is, the new account has an initial balance of 350.0 and an overdraft limit of 500.0). This begs the question of how the process of initialization is effected. In Java, there is the notion of a constructor, a kind of method used to initialize the state of an object when it is created. In the case of an **Account** object, we would wish to create a new account with an initial balance and an agreed overdraft limit. A constructor that does this is:

```
Account (float initBalance, float limit) {
    balance = initBalance;
    overdraftLimit = limit;
}
```

This constructor simply initializes the attributes of a new **Account** object. It would be placed in the **Account** class along with the definitions of the methods that apply to objects of this class.

In order to be able to refer to this new object later in a program we need to associate it with an identifier so that we can keep track of it and distinguish between all the objects that might be created in a program. Typically we would write:

```
myAccount = new Account (350.0, 100.0);
yourAccount = new Account (600.0, 250.0);
```

which creates two separate objects (both from the class **Account**) referred to by different identifiers. In fact, the identifiers **myAccount** and **yourAccount** stand for variables. The main property of a variable is that it can refer to different objects at different times during the execution of a program. Figure 2.4 illustrates how

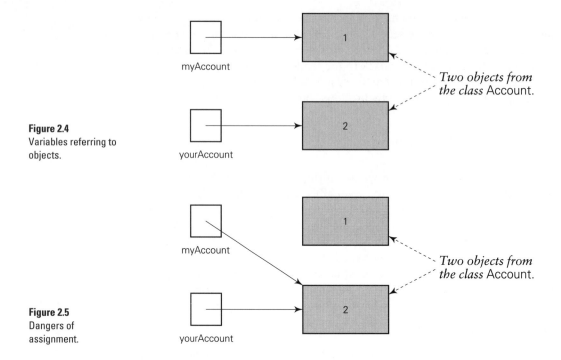

Figure 2.4
Variables referring to objects.

Figure 2.5
Dangers of assignment.

we distinguish between a variable and an object (we've numbered the objects simply to distinguish them).

In our notation, the symbol = stands for the operation known as **assignment**. Assignment means associating a variable with an object and great care must be exercised when using it. For example, having created the two **Account** objects and assigned them to the variables **myAccount** and **yourAccount** as above, if you were then to make the assignment,

    myAccount = yourAccount;

the result would be as shown in Figure 2.5.

In Figure 2.5, both variables refer to the same object (we have created aliases for the same object). However, unless there is another variable that refers to object 1, there is no way to refer to it again, and it is effectively dead (most programming languages would remove the object from main memory, a process commonly known as garbage collection).

Some programming languages are said to be **strongly typed** which, for our purposes, means that each variable has a 'type', which restricts the kind of object to which it can refer. For example, writing (in Java syntax),

    Account myAccount;
    Account yourAccount;

restricts the variables to refer to objects from the class **Account** (and, as you will shortly see, objects from classes that inherit from **Account**). Any attempt to use these variables to refer to objects from different classes will result in an error.

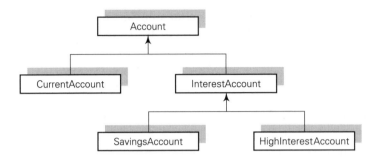

Figure 2.6
The inheritance relationship between different kinds of bank account.

2.2.6 Specialization and generalization

It frequently happens that one kind of object is closely related to another kind of object and we can take advantage of the relationship in a variety of ways. For example, it is common for banks to offer different kinds of account such as current accounts, savings accounts and high interest accounts. Such objects have many things in common – they're all bank accounts, after all – but they also have differences: one may not permit overdrafts, another may not provide interest and so on. We would like to capture both the similarities and the differences, and the mechanism usually used is known as **inheritance**. For example, suppose that a current account is an object from the class **CurrentAccount**, a savings account object is from the class **SavingsAccount** and a high interest account object is from the class **HighInterestAccount**. Because these objects are all bank accounts they should behave like objects from the class **Account**. That is, the methods defined in the class **Account** also apply to these more specialized objects.

Suppose that objects from the classes **SavingsAccount** and **HighInterestAccount** both provide interest, but current accounts do not, and that current accounts are the only kind of bank accounts to permit overdrafts. We can capture these relationships in an inheritance diagram as shown in Figure 2.6.

We say that objects from the classes **CurrentAccount** and **InterestAccount** are specializations of objects from the class **Account**, and objects from **SavingsAccount** and **HighInterestAccount** are specializations of objects from **InterestAccount**. Conversely, an object from the class **Account** is a generalization of objects from the classes **CurrentAccount** and **InterestAccount**, and so on.

The significance of inheritance is that it becomes possible, for example, to define the class **InterestAccount** in terms of the class **Account** as illustrated below:

```
interface InterestAccount extends Account {
    float getInterestRate ();
    setInterestRate (float rate);
}
```

That is, objects from the class **InterestAccount** have the same behaviour as objects from the class **Account** (that is, they have the same methods) but in addition, they also have two further methods named **getInterestRate** and **setInterestRate**. We say that an object of class **InterestAccount** inherits the methods of class **Account**.

In general, depending upon the programming language, inheritance can be used to remove and replace inherited methods as well as to add new methods. In some languages it is possible for a class to inherit methods from several classes and this is known as multiple inheritance.

2.2.7 Composition

An object can encapsulate data in the form of attributes. In general, an attribute is itself an object, illustrating that objects can be composed of other objects. For example, our **Account** objects would be better modelled with a balance that was an amount of money rather than a **float**. In other words, an **Account** object would have an attribute (balance) from the class **Money**, say. The objects of class **Money** would, in all likelihood, contain two attributes, both integer objects, representing pounds and pence (or dollars and cents, or whatever, depending on the currency being modelled).

2.2.8 Object collaboration

An object-oriented program is often described as a collection of collaborating objects in which objects offer services to one another. A service is requested by one object invoking a method of another object. The invocation causes the object to carry out the service. When modelling an object system, a useful design tool is a class diagram which shows the relationships between classes. For example, Figure 2.7 shows the relationships between some of the classes that might be found in a banking system.

The figure shows two kinds of relationships between classes: inheritance, as we have already seen, and association, which is shown by straight lines with symbols attached. The symbols attached to the association lines denote multiplicities. A multiplicity indicates the number of objects from each of the

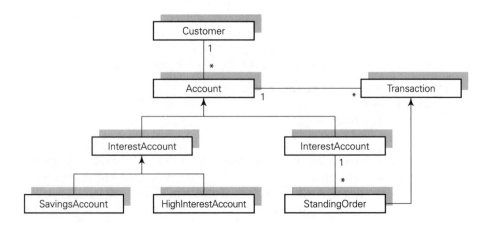

Figure 2.7
A class diagram.

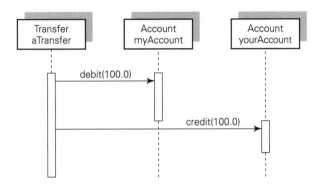

Figure 2.8
A sequence diagram.

two classes in the association. For example, each **InterestAccount** object will, in general, be associated with many (denoted *) **StandingOrder** objects and each **StandingOrder** object will be associated with precisely one (1) **InterestAccount** object. In this model, a **StandingOrder** object is a kind of **Transaction** object (shown with an inheritance association). A **Transaction** object is an object that causes some action to be performed on **Account** objects (crediting or debiting amounts of money, for example). A standing order transaction will result in an amount of money being transferred from one customer's account to another. In general, each **Account** will be associated with many **Transaction** objects.

Another useful diagram is a collaboration diagram, which shows how objects interact by invoking each other's methods. For example, suppose that I want to give you £100: a **Transfer** transaction named **aTransfer** (a type of **Transaction** that transfers amounts between **Account** objects) would ensure that £100 would be debited from **myAccount** and subsequently credited to **yourAccount**. There are three objects involved in this activity and their interactions can be shown on a UML-like sequence diagram (Figure 2.8). The vertical dashed lines represent the passage of time (increasing downwards), with the vertical rectangles indicating an activation of the object. When it is active, the object can invoke methods of other objects. In Figure 2.8, **aTransfer** invokes **debit(100.0)** on **myAccount** and, at a later time, invokes **credit(100.0)** on **yourAccount**.

In a programming language, the same transfer might be represented as:

```
myAccount.debit (100.0);
yourAccount.credit (100.0);
```

which would be a set of instructions in a method belonging to the object **aTransfer**.

2.3 The process concept

The style of modular specification outlined above gives a description of the components of a system and gives the intuition that the components interact as the system executes dynamically. We know that methods are invoked on objects and that the object's set of methods defines its possible behaviour. In Figure 2.3

we saw a thread of control pass from the object containing method A to the object containing method B and back, then to the object containing method C and back, when methods were invoked. We now focus on the dynamic execution of a system: the events that cause method invocations and the order in which invocations take place.

As well as an object model, a **computational model** is therefore required with a notion of **active elements** or **activities** which may call interface procedures or invoke methods on objects in order to carry out a computation. Active elements have been given a variety of names in systems: activities, processes, tasks or threads. We shall use the classical term 'process' for an abstract entity which executes a program on a processor; but see Section 2.3.2 for further discussion of multi-threaded processes.

A process must follow a **protocol** in order to use an object correctly, that is, a set of rules which define the order in which the object's interface operations may meaningfully be invoked. For example, a protocol for an existing file object is likely to be that the file is *opened*, a succession of *reads* and *writes* are then allowed, after which it is *closed*. If the protocol is not followed the invoker of the object may be given an error return, such as 'incorrect argument' if a file's pathname is given where an open file identifier is expected. In the case of a stack object an error might be 'attempt to *pop* from an empty stack' if *pop* is invoked before *push*.

Again, the point should be made that the syntactic specification of the interface of an object is necessary for correct use of the object but is not sufficient, in itself, to convey the meaning (or semantics) of the object's functionality. In the case of the file object, we require that the bytes we read from it are the same bytes that we previously wrote to it. The specification of a protocol is another means by which some of the intended semantics of the object is conveyed.

2.3.1 Process by analogy

To introduce the notion of process let us consider some analogies and see how far each can be taken:

- The text of a book is comparable with the text of a computer program or the specification of a module. The activity of reading a book is comparable with the execution of a program by a process.
- Two musicians sharing a score while playing a piece of music are comparable with two processes executing the same program on two processors simultaneously. Luckily, they need to turn the pages at the same time as they are playing synchronously.
- I start to read a book, make a note of where I have got to and then put it down. My son picks it up, decides it looks interesting and starts to read. Over a period of time the two of us cooperate (or compete) over reading the book. This is again comparable to two processes executing a program. Since only one of us is reading at one time the analogy is with a program that for some reason may only be executed by one process at a time. In the case of the book, we can buy another copy to avoid sharing it.

- I am reading a book; the phone rings; I answer the phone and go back to the book. This is comparable with a processor temporarily leaving the execution of a program to deal with an event such as a disk controller signalling that it needs attention after completing the transfer of some data.

In all cases there are the concepts of the static text and the dynamic process of reading it, which are analogues of the static text (code) of a program and the dynamic process of executing that code.

To put these ideas on a more concrete footing, here are some slightly more formal definitions, taken from Brinch Hansen (1973a):

data	Physical phenomena chosen by convention to represent certain aspects of our conceptual and real world. The meanings we assign to data are called information. Data is used to transmit and store information and to derive new information by manipulating the data according to formal rules.
operation	A rule for deriving a finite set of data (output) from another finite set (input). Once initiated, the operation is completed within a finite time.
computation	A finite set of operations applied to a finite set of data in an attempt to solve a problem. If it solves the problem it is called an algorithm, but a computation may be meaningless.
program	A description of a computation in a formal language.
computer	A physical system capable of carrying out computations by interpreting programs.
virtual machine	A computer simulated partly by program.
process	A computation in which the operations are carried out strictly one at a time: **concurrent processes** overlap in time. They are **disjoint** if each refers to private data only and **interacting** if they refer to common data.

In the case of software, the program text specifies objects' methods and they are executed dynamically by processes on one or more processors. A process may move from object to object by calling interface methods (see Figure 2.9).

A given object may be used by a number of processes simultaneously. In a time-sharing system, for example, users may share a single copy of system utilities, such as editors or compilers. Each user has an associated process fetching and executing the instructions of the shared code. Figure 2.10 shows two processes executing a compiler. Here the processes are shown as cyclic, since they are likely to spend time executing a loop such as 'fetch the next statement and translate it'. There must be different input, output and data areas for the two separate compilations.

In this case the processes are disjoint rather than interacting; there is no connection between the different processes executing the compiler. Although common code is executed, there is workspace private to each process. A main concern of this book is to study the more difficult problem of interacting processes.

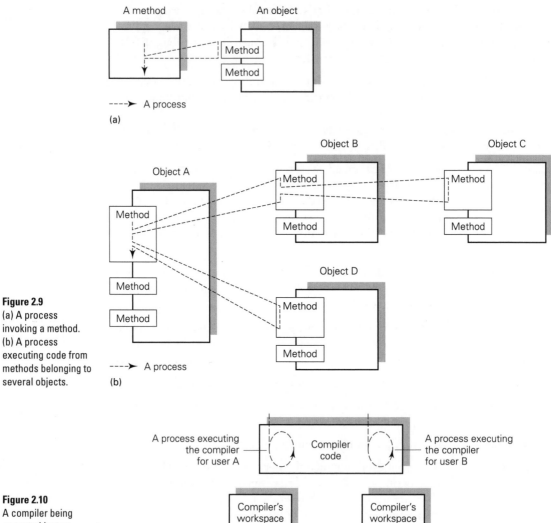

Figure 2.9
(a) A process invoking a method.
(b) A process executing code from methods belonging to several objects.

Figure 2.10
A compiler being executed by two processes.

2.3.2 Multi-threaded processes

Section 4.11

We see from the above discussion that the term 'process' was introduced historic-ally as an abstraction to capture the notion of dynamic execution. In modern systems, particularly since the advent of window-based interfaces there is often a need for a single program (or application) to allow several activities to be in progress at the same time. For example, you may wish to work on the draft of an email message but pause to incorporate and read new email coming in, then reply to an urgent message before resuming your original draft. The mail application, a single 'program' or 'package', then has several activities in pro-gress concurrently, see Figure 2.11.

A mail application

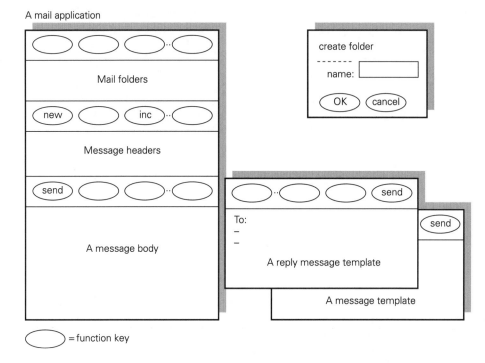

create folder

- - - - - - -

name:

OK   cancel

send

To:
–
–

A reply message template

send

A message template

A message body

send

new   inc ··

Message headers

Mail folders

⬭ = function key

Figure 2.11
Mail: a multi-threaded
application.

In this new situation we shall use the term 'process' for the initial activation of a program; the **resources** needed to activate the program, such as memory, are associated with that process. We shall use the term **thread** or **thread of execution** for each of the separate activities within such a program. The term 'thread' is then used for that entity which runs on a processor: the entity to be scheduled. Systems which support this facility typically create a process with a single thread when the program is first activated. Extra threads are created as required. Note that although the threads execute independently they share the resources allocated to the process.

We shall use the classic term 'process' to subsume the term 'thread' unless it is necessary to draw out the distinction between abstraction and implementation. Process is therefore the general abstraction for a dynamic entity which runs on a processor.

2.4 Operating system functions

Our aim is to comprehend and build concurrent systems. Some, for example transaction processing systems, run on top of (under the control of) operating systems of some kind; others are subsystems which form part of operating systems (see Figure 1.12). It is therefore necessary to understand what an operating system can provide for any system or application which runs under its control and also to understand what the operating system may be hiding or making inaccessible. A study of the concurrent subsystems within operating

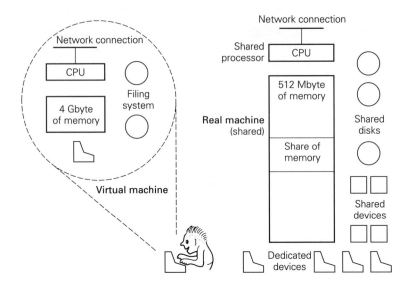

Figure 2.12
A virtual machine and
a real machine.

systems fulfils both of these purposes: it explains the services they provide for the application level and also some of the details of the lower levels which are hidden from the application.

The functions of an operating system are broadly:

Section 2.7

- *To manage resources*
  The resources are typically processors, devices, disk space for files, memory for loaded programs and communications connections to other machines. The operating system is responsible for allocating resources, often dynamically on demand, for resolving any conflicts that might arise over access to resources and for responding to events associated with them. Each resource may be modelled as an object and resources of that type may be managed by a type manager; we expand on this idea in Section 2.7.
- *To provide a service for its clients, which may be utilities, applications or human users*
  Hardware is difficult to program, and the system and its users must be protected from the errors that would be made if uncontrolled access to hardware was allowed. The operating system handles the raw hardware and provides a high-level interface to it. In a single-user system a high-level interface is a convenience; in a multi-user system it is essential to prevent interference between users. This high-level interface can be described as a **virtual machine** (a number of virtual resources) that is easier to use than the real machine (the real hardware resources); see Figure 2.12.

The operating system manages resources and provides high-level interfaces for their use. An implication of this is that clients of the operating system must be prevented from accessing the resources other than through these interfaces. We shall study the **protection mechanisms** that are used to enforce this in Chapter 3. The basic idea is that the operating system is privileged to carry out certain functions (such as device handling) and its clients are prevented from carrying out these functions directly. The part of the operating system which is privileged is often called the kernel, although, as we shall see below, conventional 'kernels' have become larger than is implied by this definition.

If we take a time-sharing system as an example of an operating system there may be many users simultaneously sitting at terminals controlling their program executions, typing input to editors and so on. In Chapters 3 and 4 we show how it is possible for more users to run simultaneously than there are hardware processors to execute their programs or respond to their commands. In Chapter 3, **device handling** is considered in some detail, followed by an introduction to communications handling. In Chapter 4, sharing the available processors between the users is the focus; this is where we see how processes are implemented.

The operating system is also concerned with **memory management**. It must allocate memory to running programs, both on initial loading and when data areas need to exceed their initial storage allocation. It must also interface with memory management hardware, set up the hardware and deal with any errors caused by a running program, as we shall see in Chapter 5. In a system with many users or many processes per user, the memory management subsystem is itself a concurrent system, since it may at any time be in the process of handling more than one request from its clients. Also, throughout the book we shall be concerned with whether memory can be shared between components of a concurrent system.

Most systems require storage that persists independently of the currently executing programs. The provision of such storage through **file management** functions is also described in Chapter 5. Again, the file management subsystem of an operating system is itself a concurrent system and will be used as an example throughout the book. Some aspects of the internal implementation of filing systems are given in Chapter 5 and support this example.

2.5 Operating system invocation and protection

We shall again use the high-level abstraction 'process' to capture the notion of dynamic execution. When we come to implementation examples we shall distinguish between 'process' and 'thread'.

There are two ways of invoking operating system services:

- a process may make system calls;
- a user may give commands to a process running a command interpreter program that causes the process to make system calls.

Once a process is executing a program it may request operating system services by making system calls. The set of system calls is the interface to the operating system module through which the operating system functions are invoked. Section 3.2 explains in detail how this entry into the operating system can be made. Here we shall provide a brief introduction.

First, a process must be created to execute the program. Some main memory must be allocated for the purpose, and the code must be loaded (from a file) into that memory. Some processor time must be allocated to the process to run the program. A process executing the command interpreter program initiates these activities (by making system calls) in response to a command from a user. It must be part of system initialization to ensure that such a process is ready to receive commands. In a multi-user system, we can envisage a process executing the command interpreter program on behalf of every active user.

A **command interpreter** therefore causes system utilities or user programs to be loaded and run. It is concerned with initiating process creation (through system calls to the operating system) and with process management.

As we saw in Chapter 1, current workstations and terminals typically have graphical user interfaces or window systems. You might type commands in certain windows or you might use a mouse to move a cursor across the screen to indicate an object that you wish to use or to select an item from a system menu. Clicking a mouse button is equivalent to giving a command to a command interpreter. The GUI interprets your clicks and invokes the command interpreter on your behalf.

For a detailed example, recall Section 2.3.2 and Figure 2.11 where we saw a running email application with a window interface and several activities in progress. To initiate the application you would have either typed a command such as **exmh** in a command window, clicked on an icon, or this would have been done as part of your login procedure because email is always part of your working environment. The command interpreter, on receiving the command to run the email application, would ask the operating system to allocate memory, load the appropriate files and create a process with a single thread of execution. You then may have clicked to request an empty mail template and started to type a message. Part-way through you might have noticed that new mail had arrived and clicked in the email window on the 'incorporate new mail' button. The GUI would have passed your command to the command interpreter which would have created a new thread within the email application with the correct starting point to execute 'incorporate new mail', and so on.

2.5.1 Protection of the operating system

Operating system code may perform highly privileged operations which are central to the correct, reliable running of the entire system. Application programs should be prevented from executing such operations and from jumping into operating system code by accident or design. The system calls provide the controlled way of invoking an operating system. If this protection and controlled entry cannot be enforced then hardware status may be changed by accident or data structures essential to the correct operation of the system may be corrupted.

In early operating systems, and more recently in those for PCs, the operating system was not protected from application code. Any process could make a simple procedure call into the operating system without restriction. It can be argued that if you are the only user of a system then if you corrupt your operating system it is your own fault, only you are affected, and you will have to reboot it and start again. When multi-user systems came along it became necessary to protect users from each other and to prevent one user from corrupting the operating system, thus affecting other users.

Sections A.2, A.3

When we study the hardware–software interface in Chapter 3 we shall see that typical processors allow us one major protection boundary. Software may run as privileged (or in system mode) or unprivileged (in user mode). Control cannot pass from unprivileged to privileged software except under strict control. In the next section we explore the design choices in allocating operating system services to these two **protection domains**.

2.6 Operating system structure

Early operating systems were monolithic or unstructured, as were those for PCs until very recently. Such systems run without a privilege boundary, and arbitrary procedure calls, reads and writes can take place. The first step in providing structure is to use the hardware protection boundary to make the operating system privileged and applications unprivileged. The system calls can then be the hardware-enforced operating system interface to applications.

An operating system is a very large piece of software; for example, Sun's UNIX kernel (the basic functions described above and shown in Figure 2.13) occupies over a megabyte. Figure 2.13 shows some of the internal modules in a conventional **closed** operating system, such as would be found in a personal workstation or a time-sharing system. The system calls can be partitioned into those which invoke file storage services, those which request terminal I/O, those

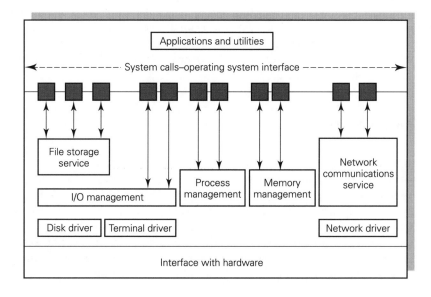

Figure 2.13
A typical closed
operating system
structure.

which request network communication, and so on. The term **subsystem** is often used for the major internal modules of operating systems. We now examine approaches to providing internal modular structure.

2.6.1 Layering

As operating systems grew in size a great deal of research effort was devoted to considering how best they should be structured. One proposal was to impose a strictly layered structure on the functions introduced above. The idea is that each layer in the hierarchy creates a single abstraction. Any layer uses the services provided by lower layers and provides a service for layers above it. An advantage is that a change at a given level does not affect lower levels. The research systems THE (Dijkstra, 1968) and Venus (Liskov, 1972) explored this design idea. In practice, systems have not been designed with their functions in a single strict hierarchy. This is because of the difficulty of choosing one specific layering of functions. In THE, for example, a memory fault could not be reported to the operator's console because the console manager was placed above memory in the hierarchical structure. We consider this example again in Chapter 10.

Section 10.2

Certain modules fall naturally into a hierarchical relationship and this is exploited in system design. For example, a module concerned with driving a disk comes naturally 'below' a module concerned with providing a file service. A layered structure is used for communications software, as we shall see in Chapter 3.

In the Multics system (Corbato and Vyssotsky, 1965) software was allocated to run in one of a number of **rings**. Originally, 64 rings were envisaged but only eight were used in practice. Here we see nine **nested protection domains** instead of the usual two (privileged and unprivileged) provided by modern processors. The most highly sensitive core of the operating system is allocated to the innermost ring, and so on. Services developed to run above the operating system may run in a ring of higher privilege than their clients. Some DEC hardware (PDP-11 and VAX) and operating systems (MVS) have supported three protection domains: kernel, system and user.

Section A.2.2

2.6.2 Microkernels

If a concurrent system is to be built on distributed hardware many of the component computers may have very limited functionality. A component of a process control system may be dedicated to monitoring the process; a component of a distributed system may be dedicated to providing a file storage service or to function as a gateway between networks, concerned only with communications handling. Such components do not need to run a complete operating system, neither would the many programming support utilities provided for human users be needed there. Figures 2.14 and 2.15 illustrate this point.

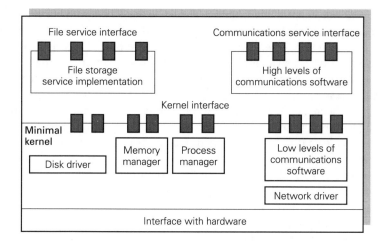

Figure 2.14
A file server.

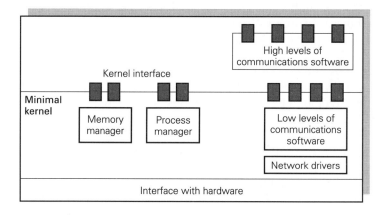

Figure 2.15
A gateway.

For this reason an **open** operating system structure is advocated (Lampson and Sproull, 1979). The idea here is that those functions which are needed universally, by every component of a system, form a **minimal kernel**, sometimes called a **lightweight kernel** or **microkernel**. The phrase '**kernelization** of an operating system' is also coming into use. These names tend to be used now rather than 'open operating system', partly to avoid confusion with the term 'open system' which was also coined in the 1970s for use in communications standards. In the latter case the term means that a system is open to communication in a heterogeneous world.

To give an example, if a computer has no local disks because storage is provided across the network, then modules concerned with storage need not be present in that component of the system. Figure 2.14 shows a dedicated file server with disk handling in the kernel and the file service module running at user level. Figure 2.15 shows a dedicated gateway computer; its function is to receive data from one network and transmit it on another. In the figure, high-level communications handling is shown outside the operating system, but this might not be feasible if very high performance is required. In both cases memory management is shown but this could be very simple for dedicated servers.

A small kernel has the advantage of being easier to engineer and maintain. Also, the services that are implemented above rather than within the kernel can easily be recompiled and loaded and may therefore be changed (or omitted in certain configurations as we have seen). We shall see in Chapter 4 that processes that are executing the privileged kernel functions run at higher priority than user-level processes.

There has been a good deal of experimental work on what should be included in a minimal kernel. Every computer has at least one processor, some memory and at least one device, for example, a terminal or network connection. The aim is to implement efficient mechanisms in the kernel and as much as is reasonable at user level. If you are sure that you *always* want a particular function to run as fast as possible, whatever applications the kernel is to support, you should include it in the kernel. You then give it priority over every function you might ever implement at user level. This is a difficult decision to make. There is a trade-off involved between making a service part of the kernel, and therefore fast but inflexible, and keeping the kernel as small as possible for maintainability and low overhead. Any particular function may provide a **slower service** when it is located at user level than when it is provided as part of the kernel.

The **kernel overhead** is the time spent in the kernel between an event occurring and the user-level process that is interested in it being scheduled. In real-time systems it is essential to be able to **bound** this time; the requirement is to be able to express the maximum possible delay rather than to obtain high speed as such. A minimal kernel makes this feasible. The requirements of the applications that run above a minimal kernel can be expressed by indicating the relative priorities of these user-level processes.

With good design, the minimal functionality of the kernel should lead to low overhead and the potential for high performance, which is essential for many network-based server computers. Any inefficiency in a kernel design affects every application, however high its priority.

To summarize, a microkernel-based system has the following potential advantages:

- The system configuration can be tailored for dedicated servers.
- A small kernel is easier to engineer and maintain.
- The services which now run above the kernel are easier to engineer, tune, update and maintain.
- The time spent executing the kernel can be bounded.
- The kernel provides efficient basic mechanisms; policies are expressed flexibly at user level. Programmers can control the relative priorities of user-level software.

A potential disadvantage is that a given service will respond more slowly to its clients if it is implemented at user level instead of inside the operating system.

A microkernel should be able to form the basis for a traditional operating system which provides a programming support environment. A problem in

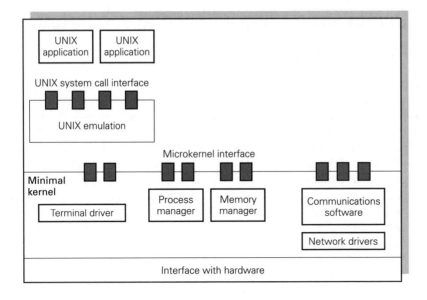

Figure 2.16
Emulation of an existing operating system above a microkernel.

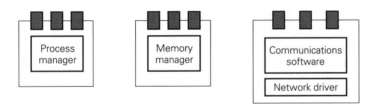

Figure 2.17
A fully modularized kernel.

moving to a new operating system design is that a vast amount of software (so-called legacy software) has been written to run above the old operating system. Ideally, a microkernel should provide a set of abstractions from which higher-level services can be built. It should be possible to build a conventional operating system interface above a microkernel and run existing software above that. This approach has been taken by several microkernel projects, as we shall see in the case studies in Part IV. Figure 2.16 shows the basic idea. The UNIX emulation can take UNIX system calls and translate them into calls on the microkernel's services.

Finally, Figure 2.17 shows the microkernel itself split into separate modules, each with its own interface. Application modules are implemented similarly and the single hardware-enforced protection boundary has been dispensed with. This model is appropriate for a 'single address space operating system' (SASOS) where there is no requirement for protection of the microkernel as a separate entity. This is the case in an embedded computer system, dedicated to run statically defined software or in dedicated servers where efficiency is a primary concern. It is also the model used by personal computers which have run without protection of the operating system until recently.

2.7 Object structuring within and supported by operating systems

Because object modelling is accepted as the standard approach to software engineering, many research projects have explored how objects might be supported by and used within operating systems. **Object support operating systems** are designed to support object structured software; but their internal structure need not be based on objects. **Object-based operating systems** use objects as their internal structuring mechanism. If the latter approach is taken, objects may be used to represent **resources** such as files, memory, processes, devices. A type manager may be used to manage each resource type and an object to represent an instance of a resource of that type. The system calls associated with resources are object invocations.

As well as providing a basis for representing resources uniformly, in terms of attributes and interface operations, there are other benefits. Objects may also be **named, protected** and **shared** using common mechanisms which are provided as part of general object management. That is, once we have learned how to use one resource, such as a file, we know how to use any other resource.

2.7.1 Object naming

It is necessary to **identify objects uniquely** within a system. This is easier to achieve in a single, centralized system, running a single instance of an operating system, than in a distributed system. In Chapter 6 we consider how to design naming schemes that are sufficiently general to work for large numbers of widely distributed objects. In general, naming schemes must scale. Here we will outline the basic approaches.

A potential user of an existing object must have a name for the object in order to invoke it. For example, a type manager for each object type is responsible for creating and deleting objects. Creation is a suitable time for a name to be assigned to an object. Note that such a name may be permanent, i.e. persistent: it lives as long as the named object.

Figure 2.18 outlines a fragment of a possible **naming scheme** which encompasses files and devices and could be extended to include other types of object. Instead of the familiar **file directories** we have **object directories**. The unique object names are **pathnames**, starting from the root of the **namespace**. Note that such names can be used by client software as a basis for sharing objects. A tree or graph structure is therefore one possible approach to **assigning unique names** to objects.

An alternative approach is to say that each object type can be named uniquely in the system and the type manager for that type of object can assign an identifier to each object it creates. A unique object name would then take the form:

type-id, object-id-of-that-type

e.g. type 23, object 456 gives object-id 23456.

This form of name could be more convenient for the type manager to use in its internal data structures and algorithms; it is fixed length and numeric.

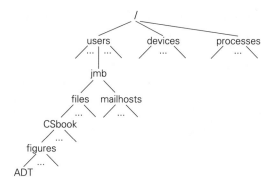

Figure 2.18
An object naming scheme.

We have now seen two forms that unique object names might take. From the client point of view a tree-structured namespace with the ability to store character-string names in object directories is convenient. From the system point of view fixed-length unique identifiers are convenient.

2.7.2 Object protection, invocation and sharing

In this section we are discussing the protection of individual objects by software and not the coarse division into privileged and unprivileged protection domains supported by hardware. Some research projects and commercial systems have attempted to provide fine-grain protection by hardware but the approach was found to be too expensive; the systems ran too slowly to compete in the marketplace.

Section A.2.2

The same access control scheme can be used for all objects: files, devices, processes or memory. The owner of an object may declare that processes acting on behalf of specified users, or executing specific programs, may invoke specified object methods. Such information may be associated with the object and an access check carried out whenever a process attempts to invoke one of the object's methods.

Instead of carrying out such a check on every method invocation, an optimization is usually made as follows. In order to use any object, client software must **open** that object, giving its name and the intended mode of operation as parameters. If the access control check succeeds, the object is 'open for use' and the client is returned an **object handle** which must be used in subsequent invocations. Possession of a handle for an open object is taken as sufficient proof that the access control check was carried out successfully. Note that the handle is a temporary name which is valid only as long as the object is open for use. An example is the integer 13 in the list below.

We have therefore seen three possible kinds of name for objects:

pathname	~jmb/files/CSbook/figures/ADT	persistent, global
object-id	23456	persistent, global
handle (for open object of type figure)	13	transient, private

Any client can attempt to open an object using its name. The protection information held with an object ensures that only authorized processes will pass the access control check and proceed to open it for use. In general, more than one process at a time may have a given object open for use; they will each have a different handle for the open object. It may be, however, that such **concurrent sharing** is dangerous. We shall study this problem in depth, but an example is that where the object is such that processes must take it in turns to make changes to it rather than change it in a free-for-all fashion. In this case, an additional check called **concurrency control** will be needed.

2.7.3 Unified object mechanisms

We have seen that object type managers will support the same mechanisms, whatever the object type, for naming, access control, concurrency control, opening (closing) and invoking via handles. The type managers can **inherit** software to carry out these general object management functions thus avoiding the need to reimplement them for each object type. Alternatively, any specific object type manager may invoke more general objects as appropriate.

Most operating system designs contain elements of the object-oriented approach outlined above. In Chapter 5, for example, we see how files and file directories can be handled in this way. But the object approach is not adopted universally. Some systems support objects but their internal structure is not based on objects; others were designed before object concepts became widely accepted.

2.8 Distributed object systems, platforms and middleware

We have seen above that objects can be used to build an operating system; by implication, a single, centralized system. It is well established that objects may form the basis of general software system design; for example, we can model a transaction processing system in terms of bank account objects or an electronic mail system in terms of mail objects. In general, such systems will be distributed and will be required to run on a heterogeneous collection of computers and operating systems. Since the early 1980s a great deal of research and development effort has explored how such systems can be supported.

Distributed object systems have similar requirements to centralized ones. Objects must be named uniquely throughout the system; access control and concurrency control must be applied before an invocation can go ahead. An additional requirement is that a named object must be located within the system. We cannot expect all operating systems to be rewritten to support exactly the same object model. Instead, a layer of software, called **middleware** or a middleware **platform** runs above the underlying operating systems to provide the

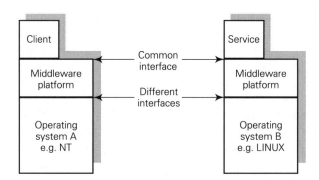

Figure 2.19
A middleware
platform.

unified support. Figure 2.19 gives the general idea. Platforms such as ANSA (1989), Comandos (Horn and Krakowiak, 1987), CORBA (see Chapter 24) and Tina-C have used an object model.

Chapter 24

Although distributed systems are probably the most commonly used style of system, we must study a number of different topics before we can understand them in detail. We lay down the fundamentals of distributed systems in Chapter 6.

2.9 Security and protection

The topic of security is huge and includes all aspects of controlling access to computers, networks and the information stored, processed and transferred in computer systems (Anderson, 2001; Schneier, 1996). In outline, security comprises:

- *External controls – security classifications*
  A general framework for classifying computer systems is given in the above references. A framework may relate only to internal mechanisms or may cover the classification of information into 'top secret', 'secret', etc. The people using the computer system are then tagged according to which categories of information they may read, write and transfer. The system must be able to enforce such specified policies.
- *Encryption*
  The idea of encryption is to transform information so that it cannot be understood by unauthorized parties but can be recovered by decryption. Encryption is often used when data is to be transferred across networks. Data may also be stored in encrypted form. Passwords are usually stored in encrypted form rather than as clear text.
- *Authentication – 'you are who you say you are'*
  The use of a login procedure and a password is part of authentication. The idea is to establish the **identity** of a **principal** involved in any computational procedure. A principal can be thought of as a process running a program on behalf of a logged-on user. Identity is typically based on knowledge of a secret, such as a password, or possession of an object, such as a swipe card. The latter may have an associated secret such as a PIN (personal identity number).

Authentication in distributed systems is more complex than in centralized systems because secret information, such as a password, needs to be transferred across a network. A principal may own **encryption keys** for use in transforming data to and from an encrypted representation. A principal may use a private key, known only to itself, to encrypt the data. The recipient of such data can be sure that the data originated from the expected principal because that principal's publicly available key transforms the data back to an intelligible form. That is, the private and public keys form a pair for use by the algorithms which encrypt and decrypt the data. The login procedure associates the human user with the registered user who owns items such as encryption keys.

- *Authorization, protection or access control*
An authorization policy specifies which principals may access an object and in what way. The system must have mechanisms which can enforce the policies.

    The concept of principal is used because greater generality than 'user' is often required. For example, we may wish to express 'anyone running program X may access file Y' or 'if a principal with rights to a file which include **read** issues a command to printer software to print that file then the printer software is "delegated" the right to read that file (but no other files of the principal) until the print command has been carried out'.

- *Validation of imported software*
The access control policies and mechanisms outlined above may be subverted by the injudicious use of unchecked software. If you acquire and run a program, that program runs with all your access rights. It could read, overwrite or delete your files. For this reason it is desirable that the source of software can be authenticated.

These are some of the issues we shall be discussing in more detail in Chapter 7.

2.9.1 An object model for access control

A general protection model is achieved by forming a matrix with rows representing principals, columns representing objects, and entries representing the access rights of the principal to the object. In addition we assume that objects are typed, that the rights are associated with the object type and can be enforced by a type manager, see Figure 2.20.

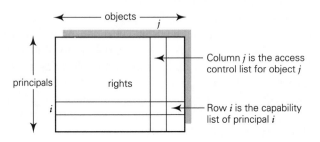

Figure 2.20
An access matrix.

In practice, such an access matrix would be sparse and would be held in a partitioned representation. For example, with each object could be associated a list of the principals with access rights to the object together with their specific rights. This is a list of the non-null entries in the column associated with the object. For objects of type file such a list is known as an **access control list** (**ACL**).

Alternatively, with each principal could be associated a list of the non-null entries of the corresponding row, that is the objects the principal can access together with access rights. Each component of such a list is known as a **capability**.

Both ACLs and capabilities have been used in system designs and will be defined in detail when we study specific object management functions.

2.10 Summary

We need a way to think about complex software systems. The basic functionality of a system can be described in terms of **modular** software structure. By distinguishing between the **interface** and **implementation** of a module it is possible to create abstractions, that is, to focus on what a module does rather than how it does it. A specification of the modules of a system does not tell us how it is executed dynamically, a computational model is also needed.

The concept of **process** was introduced as the means by which dynamic execution of software is achieved. A process performs its computation by invoking the interface operations of modules. A **protocol** defines the correct orderings of operation invocations. An outline of some typical operating systems' modular structure was given and major functions, or **subsystems**, were highlighted. A conventional **closed operating system structure** was compared with an **open** structure based on a **minimal kernel** or **microkernel**. The potential advantages of a microkernel-based system were outlined and we discussed the criteria for deciding what should be included in a microkernel. Existing operating systems' interfaces can be provided above the microkernel so that existing application software can continue to be used.

Although object modelling is well established as a basis for software engineering, for example using the Unified Modelling Language (UML) (Booch *et al.*, 1999), and has been used to design research operating systems, it does not yet pervade operating system design. We saw in outline how each system resource type can be modelled as an object type, thus allowing resources to be named, invoked, protected and shared in a uniform way. We then explored how objects could be used as a basis for distributed systems, typically running above a heterogeneous collection of computers and operating systems. A layer of software (or middleware platform) creates the environment of object naming, location, protection, invocation and sharing.

In this chapter we have deliberately taken a high-level, abstract view of concurrent systems. In the rest of Part I we study the implementation of the abstractions that have been introduced here.

Study questions

S 2.1

What is an interface, and how is it specified?

S 2.2

What is the advantage of separating a module's interface from its implementation?

S 2.3

What is a process? Why is this concept needed?

S 2.4

What is a protocol?

S 2.5

Distinguish between a process and a thread.

S 2.6

What are the two broad functions of an operating system?

S 2.7

What are the resources managed by an operating system?

S 2.8

Who or what are the clients of an operating system?

S 2.9

Early operating systems were monolithic and unstructured. What was the first step in structuring an operating system?

S 2.10

What is a layered structure? What is its chief advantage? What is its chief disadvantage?

S 2.11

What requirements do centralized and distributed object systems have in common?

S 2.12

What is middleware and what is it used for?

S 2.13

Distinguish between authentication and authorization.

S 2.14

What is the difference between encryption and decryption?

Exercises

2.1 What are modules, abstract data types and objects?

2.2 What is a process? What is a multi-threaded process?

2.3 Describe how a program, comprising a number of object code files, is loaded and run by an operating system. Which operating system functions are invoked in order to create the required environment for the program to run?

2.4 (a) What are the main functions of operating systems in general?
     (b) What functions would you expect to be present in operating systems for:
       (i) A process control computer with a sensor for monitoring, an actuator for control and a network connection for reporting to and receiving commands from a control centre?
       (ii) A dedicated, network-based filing machine or 'file server'?
       (iii) A computer dedicated to controlling the communications passing between two networks, that is, a 'gateway' computer?
       (iv) An autonomous personal computer?
       (v) A single-user workstation with services available across a network?
       (vi) A machine dedicated to managing and answering queries on a database?

2.5 (a) What is meant by a closed operating system structure?
     (b) What is a microkernel?
     (c) What are the advantages and disadvantages of closed operating systems and microkernel-based systems?

2.6 Relate the definitions of modules and processes to the structure of operating systems. How might modules be used? How might processes be used?

    In a strict hierarchy of modules a process executing in a module at a given level may invoke only lower-level modules. Is it possible to arrange the operating system functions we have encountered so far into a strict hierarchy? What are the advantages and disadvantages of a layered structure? (Section 10.2 describes the strictly layered structure of the THE operating system and Exercise 10.1 describes the layers of the Venus operating system.)

2.7 List the resource types managed by your local operating system, e.g. files, directories, memory, devices, processes, etc. Consider how they might be implemented as objects. Give the interface operations for each object type and outline the interactions involved in using each object.

2.8 Why is a global naming scheme required for objects within an object-based system? Discuss the pros and cons of naming schemes based on hierarchical names and global identifiers (e.g. of 64 bits). How can such identifiers be constructed so as to be unique?

    Distinguish between access control and concurrency control when a process requests to open an object for use. Distinguish between object handles and object names.

    Discuss the circumstances under which an object can be closed but retained, and deleted.

The hardware interface, I/O and communications

3.1 Overview

The kinds of hardware on which a concurrent system might be built were outlined in Chapter 1. In most application areas we do not have to program devices directly but are likely to use an operating system in each component of the system. An operating system provides a high-level interface to the hardware which abstracts away from the specific details of how each device is programmed. This makes life easier for the programmer, but as designers of concurrent systems we have to take care that nothing crucial is lost in this process: that the interface we use gives us the performance and functionality we require. For example, if a hardware event must have a response within a specified time we need to understand all that can happen in the software system that responds to the event. Some operating system designs make them unable to guarantee to meet timing requirements. For this reason, a concurrent system designer needs to know the basics of how devices are controlled.

Some devices are dedicated to a particular task, such as the terminals allocated to individual users, or sensors and actuators for monitoring or controlling industrial processes. Others, such as disks, printers and network interfaces, are shared among users. Both types are managed by the operating system. We consider the low-level interface between devices and the software which controls them. This study forms the basis on which software design decisions can be taken, in particular, the allocation of processes to modules concerned with device handling. Hardware events are one source of concurrent activity in a system; we need to study the precise mechanisms involved.

When a program is loaded and runs it may contain errors which are detected by the hardware. For example, the arithmetic logic unit (ALU) may detect a division by zero or an illegal address; the address of a data operand may be at an odd byte address when an even one is expected. Whenever such a program runs it will cause the same errors at the same point in the execution. These can be classified as **synchronous** hardware events.

In Chapter 5 we shall see that a program may not all be in main memory. When a 'page' that is not in memory is referenced the hardware signals a 'page fault'. Page faults are synchronous events because they are caused by running programs and must be handled before the program can continue to run.

When a program runs, events may occur in the system that are nothing to do with that program. The disk may signal that it has finished transferring some data and is ready for more work; the network may have delivered a packet of data. Such events are **asynchronous** with program execution and occur at unpredictable times.

These aspects of the interaction of a process with the hardware are considered in detail, as is the system call mechanism through which a user-level process may request use of a device.

The network connection of a computer may be considered at a low level as just another device. However, it is a shared device and computer–computer communication can generate a large volume of data associated with multiple simultaneous process interactions. The communications-handling subsystem is therefore a large concurrent system. The design of communications-handling software is introduced in the later sections of the chapter, although a complete study would require a book in its own right (Comer, 1991; Halsall, 1996; Tanenbaum, 1988).

3.2 Device interfacing

In this section the basics of how devices are controlled by program are given. Figure 3.1 gives an operating system context for all the levels associated with I/O handling.

In Section 2.3 it was pointed out that programs running above the operating system must be prevented from programming devices directly. This section will show how this restriction can be enforced and how users may request input or

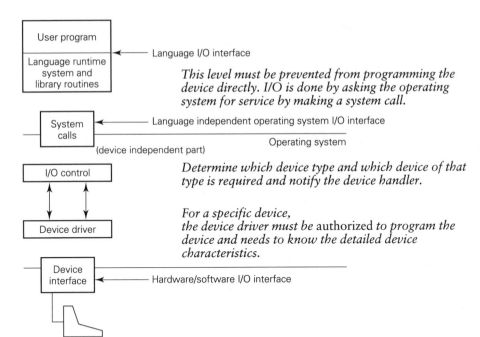

This level must be prevented from programming the device directly. I/O is done by asking the operating system for service by making a system call.

Determine which device type and which device of that type is required and notify the device handler.

For a specific device,
the device driver must be authorized to program the device and needs to know the detailed device characteristics.

Figure 3.1
Device-handling subsystem overview.

output by making a system call, since they are not allowed to program it for themselves (see Section 3.4). Figure 3.1 indicates this difference in privilege between the operating system and the user level. It is clear that when a system call is made a mechanism is needed to change the privilege from user (unprivileged) to system (privileged).

Three interfaces are indicated. The lowest-level interface is with the hardware itself. Only the operating system module concerned with handling the device needs detailed information on its characteristics, for example, the amount of data that is transferred on input or output. The operating system creates a higher-level interface, creating virtual devices that are easier to use than the real hardware. This interface is language independent. Finally, the language libraries offer an I/O interface in the form of a number of procedures that are called for doing I/O. These may differ from language to language and from the operating system's interface. Each language system must invoke the operating system's system call interface on behalf of its programs.

Processes are required to execute these modules. This is discussed in detail in Chapter 4; in particular, Figure 4.1 shows processes allocated to the modules of Figure 3.1.

In Figure 3.1 an interface between the device hardware and the operating system software is shown. Figure 3.2 focuses on this interface and shows a hardware component and a software component. Section 3.2.3 describes one form of hardware interface to a device and Sections 3.2.4–3.2.8 introduce the lowest level of software interface and the mechanism by which it is invoked by hardware.

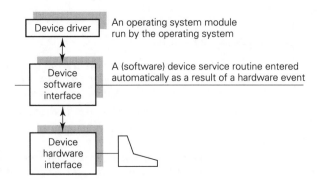

Figure 3.2
Hardware–software
interface.

3.2.1 Processor and device speeds

It is important to realize that devices are, in general, very slow compared with processors. This was always the case, and the gap has widened, since processor speeds have increased faster than device speeds and are likely to continue to do so. Consider a user typing ten characters a second to an editor and suppose the processor executing the editor executes an instruction in a microsecond. The disparity in these speeds becomes more obvious if we scale them up. If we scale one microsecond up to one second then on this scale the user types a character once a day while the processor executes an instruction every second. Current processors would be more likely to be executing a hundred instructions per second on this scale whereas users keep on typing at the same speed. Another way of appreciating the speed of processors is to quantify the number of instructions executed per second. In 1980 a processor would execute about 400 000 instructions per second and in 1990 about ten million. In 2002 a PC may have a processor which operates at a clock frequency of 1.5 GHz and which, with carefully written code, can execute several instructions in each clock cycle; the number of instructions per second is therefore greater than 1500 million. In addition, processors that support simultaneous multi-threading (SMT) are becoming commodity items. A single SMT processor can execute instructions from several threads, switching between them in hardware.

Current workstations and terminals typically have graphical user interfaces which have been made possible by these increases in processor speeds and memory sizes. As you type to an editor which is displaying a page of your text in a window, your screen changes significantly as you type. There is a good deal of processing to be done as a result of the input of a character.

In many concurrent systems disk storage is needed. Although disk density has doubled every three years for the past twenty years, disk access time is limited by the electromechanical nature of the device and only increased by a third between 1980 and 1990. An example illustrates the increase in capacity and performance and decrease in cost:

- In 1963 an 80 megabyte storage system on 32 cartridges cost £100 000. The data rate was 50–100 kilobits per second and it took 50–200 milliseconds to position the heads.

- In 1986 a 765 megabyte storage system on 8 cartridges cost £1000. The data rate was 2 megabits per second and it took 2–35 milliseconds to position the heads.
- In 1992, the HP C3010 had a formatted capacity of 2000 megabytes on 19 surfaces, an average seek time of 11.5 milliseconds, a transfer rate of 10 megabits per second from the disk buffer to a SCSI-2 bus. The cost was US$3.75 per megabyte.
- In 1997 the Seagate Elite 23 disk drive had an unformatted capacity of 29.6 gigabytes and a formatted (512 byte sectors) capacity of 23.4 gigabytes. It had 6880 cylinders, average seek time of 13.2 milliseconds (read) and 14.2 milliseconds (write). It rotated at 5400 revolutions per minute and had an average latency of 5.55 milliseconds. The controller had a 2048 kilobyte cache, the internal transfer rate varied from 86 to 123 megabytes per second and the transfer rate to/from memory varied from 20 to 40 megabits per second. The cost was about 16 pence (25 US cents) per megabyte.
- In 2002, an example of a modern Seagate drive is the BarracudaATA IV which is 80 gigabytes in size, has a maximum burst transfer rate of 100 megabytes per second and costs around £80: £1 (US $1.50) per gigabyte.

Section 3.2.8 shows how disks are programmed.

Many computer systems are network based. Current networks in widespread use, such as Ethernet, typically operate at 10 megabits per second, but 100 megabit through to gigabit networks are becoming available. We shall consider communications handling later in this chapter, but it is clear that an operating system has less time to handle communications devices than peripherals.

For a comprehensive coverage of the characteristics and performance of processors, memory and I/O see Hennessy and Patterson (1996).

3.2.2 CISC and RISC computers

Throughout the 1980s there was a move towards simpler processors. If the instruction set is simple and instructions are of equal length, techniques such as instruction pipelining can more easily be used to achieve high performance. If the processor is simple, the chip fabrication time and therefore time to the marketplace is faster. There may also be space on the chip for cache memory or address translation (see Chapter 5).

When real programs were measured it was found that the complex instructions and addressing modes, designed to support specific data structures, are rarely used by compiler writers. Their complexity implies inflexibility and they are never quite right for the job in hand. The virtual disappearance of assembly language programming means that the machine instruction set need not be high level and attempt to 'bridge the semantic gap' between the programmer and the machine. Compact code is no longer an aim, since current machines have large address spaces, typically 32 bits for a 4 gigabyte address space, and physical memory is cheap.

These arguments have led computer design from **Complex Instruction Set Computers (CISC)**, which were in the mainstream of architectural development until the early 1980s, to the current generation of **Reduced Instruction Set Computers (RISC)**, mentioned in Section 1.3.2. An excellent treatment is given in Hennessy and Patterson (1996). Some aspects of RISC designs are similar in their simplicity to the minicomputers of the 1970s and the early generations of microprocessors. Other aspects, such as the address range, have outstripped early mainframes.

3.2.3 A simple device interface

Figure 3.3 shows a simple device interface which has space to buffer a single character both on input and on output. An interface of this kind would be used for a user's terminal, for some kinds of network connections and for process control systems. In the case of a user terminal, when the user types, the character is transferred into the input buffer and a bit is set in the status register to tell the processor that a character is ready in the buffer for input. On output, the processor needs to know that the output buffer is free to receive a character and

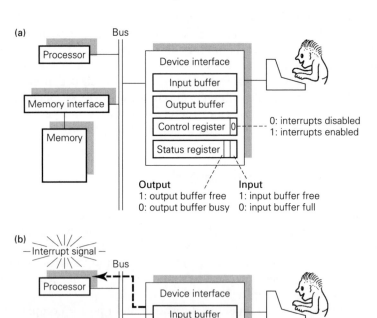

Figure 3.3
A simple device
interface with
(a) interrupts disabled
and (b) interrupts
enabled.

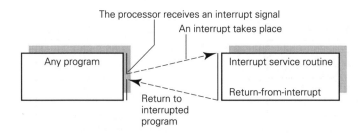

The processor receives an interrupt signal

An interrupt takes place

Any program

Interrupt service routine

Return-from-interrupt

Return to interrupted program

Figure 3.4
An interrupt.

another status bit is used for this purpose. The processor can test these status bits and, by this means, output data at a speed the device can cope with and input data when it becomes available.

3.2.4 Polling and interrupts

Device programming can be done by testing status bits in the interface (Section 3.2.3), in which case the interface sits passively, with the bits indicating the device's status, and the processor must test these bits to determine when to transfer data to the interface on output or from it on input. This is called **polling** the device. The device management subsystem could test each device in turn or perhaps test some devices more frequently than others. This is a very simple and reliable method and could be the best way to handle devices in small systems; an outline of a program of this kind is used as an example in Section 4.15. Polling is a bad method for time-critical systems because an event could occur immediately after its device had been tested and would not be seen until that device was tested again. Also, it is not a good use of processor time to cycle round all the devices, periodically testing which ones are ready for attention.

An alternative is to use **interrupts** if the mechanism is available in the hardware. Figure 3.3(b) shows interrupts enabled in the control register in the device interface. If this is done, the interface will actively signal the processor as soon as data is in the input buffer on input and as soon as the output buffer becomes free for the next item of data on output. This permits the fastest possible response to devices but is more complex to program than polling. We assume that the interface, when sending an interrupt signal to the processor, can identify itself and indicate the priority level that has been assigned to it (see Section 3.2.5).

Now suppose that the processor is fetching and executing instructions from an arbitrary program when it receives an **interrupt signal** from a device. Assuming that handling the device is more important than continuing to execute the program, an **interrupt** should occur from the program to an **interrupt service routine** (see Figure 3.4). It must be possible to resume the interrupted program, and this implies that the program counter (at least) must be saved before it is set up for the interrupt routine. Also, the contents of any processor registers that are used by the interrupt routine must be saved before they are used and subsequently restored. In general, we say that the **processor state** of the interrupted program is saved on the interrupt so that the processor can be used by the interrupt routine. The saved state must be restored by the time the program is resumed.

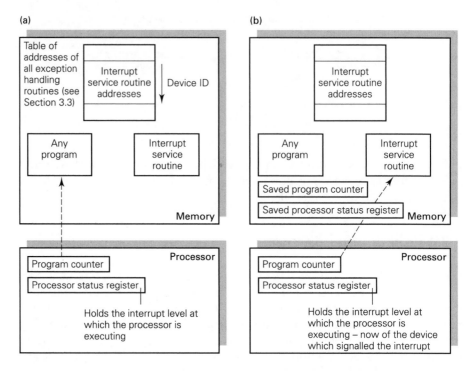

Figure 3.5
The interrupt mechanism.
(a) Before the interrupt is taken.
(b) After the interrupt is taken.

All computers have **hardware** to effect this transfer, and a typical CISC mechanism is described in the following sections and illustrated in Figure 3.5. The program counter (PC) and processor status register (PSR) are saved by hardware. At the end of the routine, assuming we are to return immediately to the interrupted program, a special return instruction will restore both the PC and the PSR. Any other registers that are used by the interrupt service routine are saved at the start of the routine and restored at the end of the routine by software. Note that the hardware mechanism may cause writes to memory in order to store the PC and the PSR.

3.2.5 Interrupt handling: Priorities

Computer systems typically have a large range of device types. Some must be handled with great urgency, for example, a sensor reading from a nuclear reactor which signals a danger level. Others should be handled promptly to keep the system running smoothly, for example, file transfer from disk. We have seen in Section 3.2.1 that a system has no difficulty in keeping up with a human typing characters on a keyboard.

Each source of interrupt signal is therefore assigned a priority. Not only can a normal program be interrupted by the arrival of an interrupt signal, but execution of a service routine for a low-priority interrupt may be interrupted by the arrival of a higher-priority interrupt signal. The processor status register indicates the priority level at which the processor is executing. An interrupt signal with a

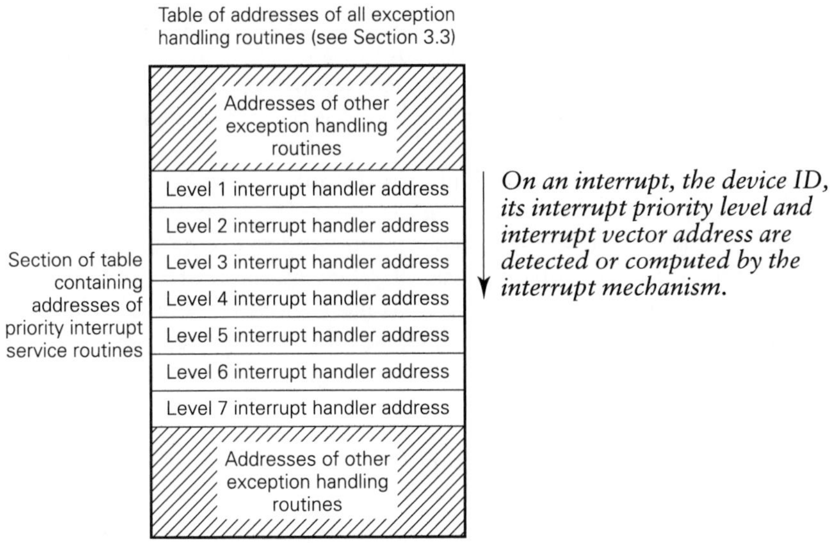

Table of addresses of all exception
handling routines (see Section 3.3)

On an interrupt, the device ID,
its interrupt priority level and
interrupt vector address are
detected or computed by the
interrupt mechanism.

Figure 3.6
Device interrupt
handling and
interrupt vectors.

higher priority causes an interrupt; an interrupt signal with a lower priority is held
pending until the higher-priority interrupt service routine has finished, that is,
until exit from its service routine. Nested interrupts are handled by using a stack
structure; the PC and PSR are stored on a stack each time an interrupt occurs and
restored from the stack when a return from interrupt instruction is executed.

3.2.6 Interrupt vectors

Each device has an associated interrupt service routine. When an interrupt is
to take place (on a priority basis) the address of the correct interrupt routine
must be set up by hardware in the program counter. A dedicated area of main
memory is used to hold these addresses. The device interface identifies itself
when sending an interrupt signal to the processor, and this allows the correct
service routine address to be selected from the table. This table is shown in
outline in Figure 3.5 and Figure 3.6 gives more details.

As well as the addresses of device interrupt service routines the addresses of
all exception-handling routines are held there (see Section 3.3). Notice that,
although the transfer of control from the interrupted program to the interrupt
service routine is carried out by the hardware interrupt-handling mechanism,
this table access is another reference to main memory and adds to the expense of
the mechanism.

3.2.7 The RISC approach to interrupt handling

The exception-handling mechanism described above aims to support the
requirements of operating systems. A good deal of mechanism is provided and
has to be used whenever an exception occurs. A large table in main memory

is indexed on every exception to extract the appropriate exception-handling routine address; the program counter and processor status register are saved on a stack in main memory. The approach described is based on that used in the Motorola 68000 series, the DEC VAX series, the Intel Pentium and other CISC machines.

In the area of exception handling a fresh look at the real requirements of the operating system is in order. It is argued that a fast, simple mechanism may be more appropriate than a very general one, and that complex cases can be handled by software. One obvious way of achieving speed-up is to avoid saving the state in main memory and instead to use processor registers. Another is to avoid accessing main memory to find the address of the exception-handling routine.

Avoiding the saving of state in memory

It is very often the case that the interrupted program is not resumed after the exception is serviced; a fatal error might have been signalled by the exception in which case control passes to a user-level library routine to give an error message and abort the program; or an interrupt may have made a high-priority process runnable and the interrupted process is temporarily suspended. If the state of the interrupted process has been put on a stack in memory it will have to be copied elsewhere in memory (see Chapter 4) rather than set up again in the hardware. It would surely be better for a small amount of state to be saved in registers and copied from there by the exception-handling routine when necessary. Special registers could be provided to hold a small amount of state, such as the interrupted program counter and the previous processor status register.

Avoiding table lookup of an interrupt routine address

Table lookup can be avoided by having a 'first-level interrupt handler': a single exception-handling routine that is executed in response to every exception. Such a routine can determine the cause of the exception by testing values in processor registers, etc. Interrupt decoding is therefore carried out by software instead of by hardware. This first-level interrupt handler may handle a simple exception and return control to the interrupted process with minimum overhead. Alternatively, it may be necessary to pass control to another routine. In this case it might be necessary to enable interrupts selectively; that is, the routine may be executed at some appropriate priority interrupt level. This approach was taken in early computers.

The address of the first-level interrupt handler can be set up in the PC as part of the hardware interrupt mechanism, thus avoiding a table lookup in memory. Also, interrupts will be disabled as part of the hardware interrupt mechanism. If the handling of the exception requires another routine to be called (see above), or processor registers to be used, then state can be saved as necessary. This can be done safely because interrupts are disabled.

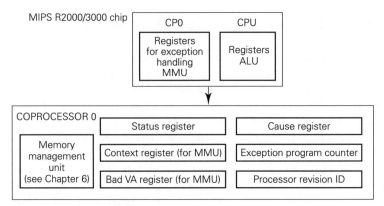

The relevant registers in more detail:

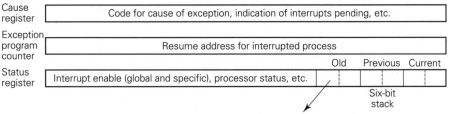

Old, previous and current values of processor status bit and global interrupt disable bit

Figure 3.7
Exception handling in
the MIPS R2000/3000
coprocessor 0.

Figure 3.7 shows the support for exception handling in the on-chip system control coprocessor of the MIPS R2000/3000. The cause, status and exception program counter (EPC) registers are relevant to this discussion and are shown in more detail in the figure. The status register contains a three-level (six-bit) stack; each level has a processor status bit (privileged, unprivileged) and a global interrupt enable/disable bit.

On an exception, the exception-handling mechanism:

• puts the resume address for the interrupted process in the EPC register;
• pushes a new two-bit entry onto the six-bit stack. This sets the processor status to privileged and disables interrupts globally;
• sets up the PC to the address of one of three exception-handling routines. Except on reset and certain memory management exceptions this is the address of a general routine. These addresses can be known to the hardware.

The return from exception (RFE) instruction pops the status stack by two bits. This can follow, and be executed indivisibly with, a transfer of control to the required address: the normal arrangement for pipelined branch instructions.

This discussion has highlighted those aspects associated with making the interrupt mechanism as fast as possible. A complete description of the registers and the handling of specific exceptions for the MIPS processor is given by Kane and Heinrich (1992).

3.2.8 Direct memory access (DMA) devices

A simple interface has been used as an example in the above sections. An interrupt is associated with the transfer of every character. Some device interfaces will transfer a block of data into or out of memory and will interrupt the processor only after the whole transfer is complete. This requires a more complex interface and a simple processor is dedicated to the task of controlling the data transfer. Devices of this kind are called **direct memory access** (**DMA**) devices. This kind of interface is often used in communications: a whole packet of data coming in from the network is placed in memory. Another example is a disk controller.

A disk controller is a simple processor with registers for holding the disk address, memory address and amount of data to be transferred. After this information has been passed to it by a central processor, together with the instruction to proceed with the disk read or write, the disk controller transfers the whole block between disk and main memory without any intervention from the central processor (see Figure 3.8). When the block transfer is complete, the disk controller signals an interrupt. The processor can execute some other program in parallel with the transfer.

During the transfer the disk controller is transferring data to or from memory at the same time as the processor is fetching instructions from memory and reading and writing data operands in memory. The memory controller ensures that only one of them at once is making a memory access. The disk controller may access memory between an instruction fetch and a data access which is part of the instruction execution; this is called **cycle stealing**. DMA slows down the rate at which the processor executes instructions.

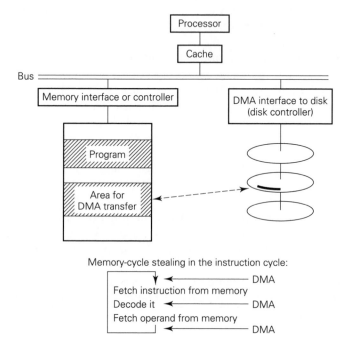

Figure 3.8
Direct memory
access.

A hardware-controlled cache for holding recently used instructions and data (or a separate cache for each) will help to reduce this contention. Instructions and data can be accessed in the cache at the same time as the disk controller accesses main memory. In Chapter 5 we take a closer look at the memory hierarchy in a computer system, including hardware-controlled caches.

Modern disk interfaces have become more sophisticated than that described above. A technique called **scatter-gather** allows the programmer to specify a number of blocks of data to be written to one place on the disk by a single command (gather), or a single area of disk to be read into a number of memory locations (scatter). This is particularly useful when a logically contiguous area is dispersed in the physical memory when paged memory management is used (see Chapter 5). A similar technique is described for a network interface in Section 3.7.

3.2.9 Memory-mapped I/O

In the above sections we have assumed that we can transfer data to a device. There are two approaches to achieving this: by a special set of I/O instructions or by memory-mapped I/O. The latter approach is used in modern machines. The idea is that physical memory addresses are allocated to device interfaces, and input, output, status checking and control are achieved by reading and writing these memory locations. No extra instructions are needed for these purposes. The simple interface described in Section 3.2.3 would have memory addresses assigned for the single-byte input, output, status and control registers.

3.2.10 Timers

Timers are handled among the devices of a computer system. They are available as programmable chips and are almost always used with interrupts enabled, although some programmable timers allow a polling mode of use. Other devices signal an interrupt to indicate that data is ready on input or more data can be output. Timers are used just to generate timing information, usually in the form of interrupts.

A timer interface may be programmed to generate an interrupt after some specified period of time, then do nothing until further instructed. Alternatively, it may be set up to generate interrupts periodically. We can count them and use them, like clock ticks, as a basis for all timing in a system. The rate at which interrupts are generated is programmable and some of the uses that are made of timers require a fine time grain. The range of rates at which timing interrupts can be arranged to occur depends on the specific device and is typically from 1 microsecond to 65 milliseconds.

Examples of the use of timers in a system are as follows:

- *Time of day*
  Systems which perform functions for human users, such as printing and filing, are expected to maintain the correct date and time. This can be based on the clock ticks described above. Typically, the system maintains a count

which is decremented on a timer interrupt. The size of the count is such that it decrements to zero after a second's worth of clock ticks. A time of day counter which is maintained to a one-second granularity from some base value can then be incremented. A 32-bit counter at one-second granularity would overflow after 136 years.

An alternative way of maintaining the time of day is to arrange to receive a signal from an external radio station or satellite. Transmission is typically once a second at an accuracy of the order of a millisecond. This is likely to improve, and processors are likely to have the capacity to receive a more frequent signal in the future (see Chapter 15).

- *Managing the time for which processes run on processors*
  A timer interrupt is a mechanism for stopping a running process.
- *Accounting for CPU usage*
  Clients may be charged for their use of a processor.
- *Providing an alarm clock service for processes*
  Processes can then delay for a specific length of time or until some time of day arrives.
- *For monitoring the system and its clients*
  For example, a profile of the amount of time being spent on various tasks can be built up by noting the value of the PC at regular intervals.

3.3 Exceptions

The above section has introduced device programming and has placed this function within the operating system. The interrupt mechanism is used to transfer control from any running program (inside or outside the operating system) to an interrupt service routine which is part of the operating system. The processor state is set to 'privileged' by the interrupt mechanism and the minimum necessary processor state (the PC and PSR) is saved so that the interrupted program can be resumed later.

The operating system is entered by this means when a device signals that it needs attention. The mechanism can be generalized to be the standard means by which the operating system is entered.

Note that the interrupt signal from the device has, in general, nothing to do with the program that is running when it occurs. Such interrupts occur asynchronously at unpredictable times.

3.3.1 Exceptions caused by a running program

When a program runs it may cause a number of error conditions to be generated in the hardware. All of these conditions may be signalled as interrupts, as described above for devices, and handled by interrupt service routines. The more general terms **exception** and **exception-handling routine** tend to be used to include device and other types of interrupt. Examples are:

- The ALU may detect a division by zero, or two's complement overflow on addition or subtraction.
- The addressing hardware may be given an odd byte address for an instruction fetch when instructions must be aligned on even byte boundaries.
- An illegal bit pattern may be found for an operation code by the instruction decode logic.
- Memory outside the range of the available physical memory may be addressed.

All of these are caused by the program that is running. If the program was restarted, they would occur again at the same point; unlike device interrupts they are predictable. In almost all cases the program cannot continue after the error condition has occurred. The error handling is **synchronous** with the program execution. Device interrupts are **asynchronous** and might or might not be handled immediately they occur, depending on the relative priorities of the running program and the interrupting device.

In Chapter 5 we shall see that a program may not all be in main memory. When part of a program (a 'page') is to be accessed for a data operand or an instruction, the addressing hardware signals that it is not present in memory (a 'page fault' interrupt). This kind of hardware event is caused by the running program, but will not necessarily occur at the same point of every program execution. When the program is run on another occasion, the operating system may have space for more of its pages, or different pages, to be in memory, so the same page faults may not occur. That is, the points at which page faults can occur are predictable to the operating system, but whether they occur or not on a given run depends on which pages are in main memory.

When a page fault does occur it must be handled before the program can continue; that is, the page that is being referenced must be transferred into memory by the operating system. The program execution can then continue from the instruction which caused the page fault. The page fault handling is synchronous with the running program.

Another source of exception associated with a given program is an attention interrupt or break. The user has decided to abort the program run and has pressed the attention key. In this case, the program execution could continue for some time before being aborted. The event is asynchronous.

3.3.2 System (privileged) mode and user (unprivileged) mode

Suppose a call for an operating system service (a system call) is implemented as a simple procedure call. A user process would simply enter the operating system and start to execute system code. The system code might well go on to program devices or change the contents of hardware registers. Assuming the system code is correct there is no problem. Notice, however, that privileged actions are being carried out by a user process. Now suppose that a user process executes similar privileged actions when executing an application program at user level. How can we allow the former but not the latter? That is, how can we prevent a process from executing privileged actions when it is executing an application but allow it to execute privileged actions when executing the operating system?

For this reason, processors are designed to run in at least **two modes** or **states**. In **user mode** certain privileged instructions, such as enabling and disabling interrupts, are forbidden. If code executing with the processor in user mode attempts to execute a privileged operation the processor generates an exception. A privilege violation of this kind is synchronous with program execution. The associated exception-handling routine handles this error. If the processor is executing in **privileged** or **system mode** the execution of the same instruction proceeds without interruption. It is therefore necessary to arrange for operating system code to be executed in the privileged state. We have seen how this is achieved for exception-handling routines: the exception mechanism sets the state to privileged.

It could be argued that in a single-user system there is no need to protect the operating system or hardware from corruption. The user suffers but the program can be debugged and run on a rebooted system. (One hopes that the program errors have not corrupted the filing system!) A similar argument can be applied to dedicated server computers or embedded systems, that is, any system that runs a single application. In these cases the same software runs indefinitely and it may be argued that once this has been developed and tested then the overhead of protection checks is unnecessary. However, large software systems will have residual bugs, and protection checks can help to locate and confine them. Most non-trivial systems benefit from protection from error and malice.

3.3.3 The system call mechanism

When a user requests a service which requires privileged actions to be carried out it is necessary to switch the processor state from user mode to privileged mode. The exception mechanism is usually employed for this purpose: we force a system call to generate an exception. Instructions called **software interrupts** or **traps** are designed specifically for this purpose. The fact that such instructions cause an exception has the side-effect that the processor state is changed to privileged as part of transferring control to the interrupt service routine. The interrupt service routine can then pass control to the required system call procedure.

The mechanism just described is usually the standard method for entering the operating system on a machine where privileged state is used. In this case, a system call is like a procedure call with a change of state; in an unprotected system, a system call is just a procedure call. In general, if the processor has only two states, the system designer must choose which modules should run under privileged state and which need not.

3.3.4 Summary of the use of the exception mechanism

Figure 3.9 shows the table of addresses of exception-handling routines for the Motorola MC68000 processor; the Intel Pentium is similar. This example brings together the various types of exception we have discussed.

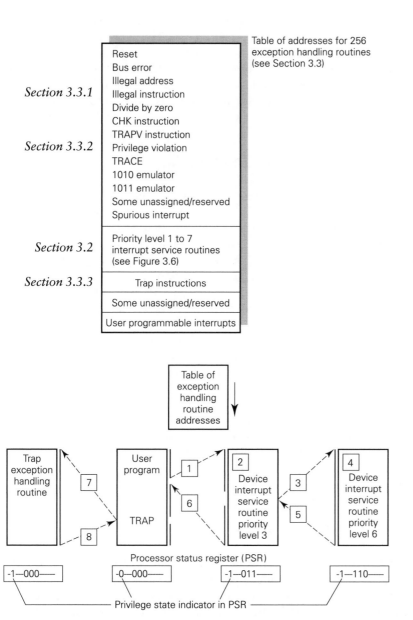

Figure 3.9
Example of exceptions from the Motorola MC68000.

Figure 3.10
An example showing nested interrupts.

Figure 3.10 shows a sequence of events which illustrate nested interrupt handling and trap handling. A user program is running when an interrupt from a device at priority level 3 occurs (1). The service routine for that device is entered (2). As part of the transfer mechanism the PSR and PC of the user program are saved and then set up for the interrupt service routine; the PC is loaded from the table of addresses of interrupt service routines; the status register is set to level 3 and privileged state. Part-way through execution of this interrupt service routine a higher-priority device interrupts (3). Its service routine is executed (4).

This completes and the interrupted PC and processor status are restored to return to the interrupted level 3 routine (5). This completes and we return to the interrupted user program (6). The user program makes a system call and a trap instruction is executed by a library routine (7). The trap service routine is executed. The priority level in the PSR is not changed but the state is set to privileged. The routine completes and control is returned to the interrupted user program (8).

3.3.5 User-level exception handling

In the above discussion we have seen the low-level mechanism for detecting certain errors and the first stage of dealing with the errors in an exception-handling routine. In many cases the error will be fatal and the process will be aborted, but before this happens an error message should be given to an on-line user or written to a log file. This is not a high-priority activity and should not be done by the operating system (and certainly not by an interrupt routine!). Error handling should be done in the context of the user process that caused the error. Error-handling routines are typically provided as part of a programming language library and their addresses are made available to the operating system so that control can be transferred to the correct place when an error occurs. When a process is created and initialized the address of its normal start and the address of an initial error-handling routine are recorded (see Section 4.3.1 and Figure 4.4).

UNIX signals are an example of a mechanism for signalling exceptional conditions. A signal is a flag which is set in the kernel and detected on return to the application. Also, some programming languages have an exception facility to allow users to name certain error conditions and to supply procedures for handling them. The language library can then pass control to the user's routine when appropriate.

3.4 Multiprocessors

The discussion so far has considered only a single processor. We should consider how exceptions and interrupts are managed on multiprocessors.

When a program runs on a processor, any exceptions it causes are signalled to that processor. These include errors, system calls and page faults, all of which are synchronous.

The handling of asynchronous exceptions, such as those caused by interrupts from a peripheral device, will depend on the details of the multiprocessor configuration. An installation may include dedicated devices, such as user terminals, shared devices such as disks, and possibly system management devices, such as an operator console. One option is that each hardware device is allocated to a single processor, which issues all instructions to control that device. Interrupts generated by the device are always signalled to that same processor. A lot of multiprocessor systems are based on this model for I/O.

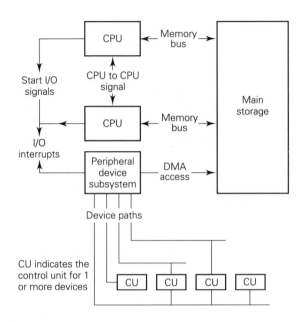

Figure 3.11
IBM's System/370 XA
configuration.

In a shared-memory multiprocessor the action of a DMA device is essentially independent of the processor that initiates a particular transfer. Provided that each processor has a private stack for saving the processor state, an interrupt signalling the end of a DMA transfer may be handled on any processor. A system configured so that shared devices may be controlled by any processor is more flexible than one in which a process requiring access to a given peripheral device must be run on a particular processor.

The IBM System/370 mainframe architecture provides for multiprocessor configurations that share main memory. Each processor has a dedicated page of memory which is used for such purposes as saving the processor state on interrupt, and interrupts may therefore be handled without interference between processors. In the first version of the System/370 architecture introduced in 1970 each peripheral device was allocated to a single processor. As technology advanced the original design was found inadequate in various ways, and in 1982 the System/370 Extended Architecture (XA) became available. There were two major changes for XA, both recognizing that processors at the top end of the range had become limited by the architecture. First, there is a 31-bit addressing mode in addition to the previous standard of 24-bit addresses (see Chapter 5). Secondly, the configuration for peripheral devices was modified so that any processor may control any device (see Figure 3.11). I/O devices are usually configured so that there is more than one path to a shared peripheral, such as a disk drive.

There are other considerations to be taken into account in a multiprocessor system. If a user aborts a program by depressing the escape key, the processor that takes the interrupt must be able to interrupt the processor on which the program is running; there is a requirement for inter-processor interrupts.

We saw in Section 3.2.10 that a timer is a particular kind of device that can be set to generate interrupts. Two types of timing service are needed, one based on the time in the world outside the computer ('real time'), the other measuring the computation time of a given process. The real-time clock in any processor should tick provided the processor is alive, regardless of whether it is performing any computation. The **timer resolution** (the length of a tick) will depend on the processor design. Either the operating system or an application program may require action to be taken at a particular time; it is important that the act of informing the program of the time carries a low overhead. In a uniprocessor system the timer will interrupt the processor on which the program runs. In a multiprocessor system a given processor may take timer interrupts, update various counts in the operating system's data structures and detect whether any time limits have expired. In this case, the processor running a program which needs to take action must be interrupted; an inter-processor interrupt mechanism is again required. Alternatively, each processor may have its own timer, and the interrupt will occur on the processor on which the program runs. In the latter case it will be necessary to synchronize the timers on the various processors, and there should be system support to achieve this.

Timing individual processes in execution is essential in many applications, and it can also be useful when debugging. Most processors have an interval timer which can be read from within an executing process, usually by entering a trap routine. It is also possible to interrupt a process after a specified computation time has elapsed. This interval timing service may or may not be provided by the same clock that maintains the real time.

3.5 User-level input and output

Low-level mechanisms for performing input and output have been described in some detail. Application programs are, in general, not allowed to program at this level, and must ask the operating system to do I/O on their behalf. We now consider this top-down application-driven view of I/O programming, shown in Figure 3.12.

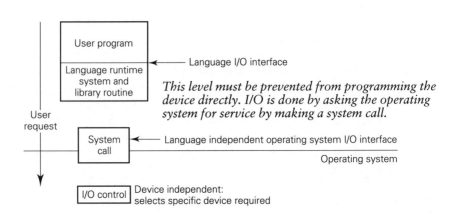

Figure 3.12
Top-down invocation of I/O.

A general point is that I/O statements should be made as general as possible. Ideally, a given program should be written with I/O statements that can be bound to different devices for a given execution. The language-level I/O is in terms of logical devices which can take or deliver arbitrary amounts of data. A stream facility is often provided by languages as well as single character and string I/O. An application can set up a number of named input and output streams and send or deliver arbitrary numbers of bytes to or from them. The operating system interface is used by the language libraries. This is likely to support the input or output of a single character or a string of characters.

3.5.1 Buffers and synchronization

The application level can request input or output of an arbitrary amount of data; the device concerned can transfer a fixed amount. Data buffers are needed between the I/O modules which are invoked by the application (top-down) and those which are executed in response to device events (bottom-up). Figure 3.13 shows the general idea. The top-down software can place the data to be output in one or more buffers. We then need a mechanism for telling the lower levels that there is work to do. Similarly, when a device delivers data it is placed in one or more buffers by the low levels and the high levels must be told there is work to do. We are seeing a requirement for processes to **synchronize** with each other.

There is likely to be a buffer area for user terminals, one for disk blocks, one for network communications, and so on. Figure 3.13 shows the data buffers as abstract data types or objects. We assume interface operations such as *acquire-buffer*, *release-buffer*, *write bytes into buffer* and *read bytes from buffer*. We are not concerned here with the details of buffer space allocation, but rather to draw out the requirement for synchronization between processes.

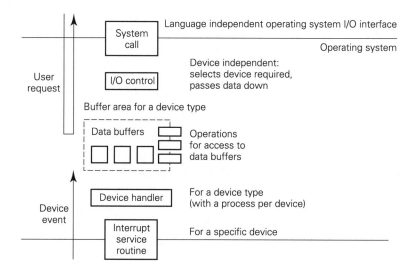

Figure 3.13
I/O buffers.

A general point is that the device handler should be able to start work as soon as possible on a large amount of output, before the top level has put it all into a number of buffers. Similarly, on input the high level may be able to start taking data from a buffer as soon as one is full. Care must then be taken that the processes synchronize their accesses to the buffers. Chapters 9, 10 and 11 discuss this problem in general and solutions are given there.

In the case of characters input from terminals, the device handler must look at each character before deciding whether to put it into a buffer. The character might indicate that the program should be aborted or that output to the screen should be halted until further notice.

3.5.2 Synchronous and asynchronous input and output

When a user-level process makes a request for input or output, the following may be the case:

- The request can be satisfied by a transfer of data from or to a buffer in memory. For example, a previous DMA transfer may have delivered a block of data and the user may request a few bytes at a time. In this case there is no need for the process to be delayed. Control can be returned to it with the data on input, or with the transfer to the device scheduled to take place on output.
- The request cannot be satisfied immediately. For example, the required data may not already be in a buffer in memory and it may be necessary to perform physical device input. On output, the system's policy may be such that a limited amount of buffer space can be allocated to a single process and physical output must be performed before the whole output request can be satisfied.

System designs differ in the options available to the user-level process when a delay is necessary. A **synchronous** I/O policy indicates that the user-level process is blocked when a delay is necessary until the request can be satisfied. An **asynchronous** option means that, if a delay is necessary, control can be returned to the user-level process, which can proceed with its work and pick up the requested input or acknowledgement of output in due course. In some systems, user-level processes can specify whether they require synchronous or asynchronous I/O when they make a request.

The UNIX system offers only synchronous I/O, often referred to as 'blocking system calls'. The IBM System/370 allows the user-level process to select synchronous or asynchronous I/O as required, as does Microsoft's Windows NT.

3.6 Communications management

Distributed systems running on computer networks were introduced in Section 1.1.3 and local area network (LAN) topologies and wide area networks (WANs) were introduced in Section 1.3.7. An operating system for a computer with a network connection must have a communications-handling function.

The network connection of a computer may be considered at a low level as just another device. It has an interface and is handled by device-driving software. The characteristics of the network interface will depend on the network concerned. Each network is designed to deliver packets of data to its attached computers via their network interfaces. Sometimes the packets are of variable size, up to some maximum size, while sometimes the data arrives in fixed size cells. Section 3.7 gives examples of packet sizes and interfaces.

Communications handling differs from the device-handling function we considered above because the network connection is shared and networks are often faster than devices. We considered terminal handling where one user process has one device and there is a duplex connection between them. We considered disk DMA interfaces. In this case many processes share the use of a filing system on a number of disks and there can be several outstanding data transfers in progress, initiated on behalf of different processes. In Section 3.2.1 we saw an example of a disk with a data transfer rate of 2 Mbits per second. It is commonplace for networks to operate at 10 Mbits per second and rates of 100s to 1000s Mbits per second are coming into use. Disk speeds are unable to increase dramatically because of the electromechanical nature of the device.

In the case of communications handling, the network connection is shared. Several local processes can request to communicate with external processes and their requests may be in progress simultaneously. Also, external processes may autonomously request to communicate with local processes. Computer–computer communication can generate a large volume of data associated with these multiple simultaneous process interactions. The communications-handling subsystem is therefore a large concurrent system. It must handle simultaneous inputs and outputs for very large volumes of data. The subjects of data communications, networks and protocols merit complete books, but we need an overview of this function if we are to understand how processes on different computers can cooperate to achieve the goals of a concurrent system. Also, specialized texts on communications do not cover how these systems may be implemented in terms of processes.

In some distributed systems a network connection may be the only peripheral a computer has. In others, a workstation may have a local keyboard and screen, but may use the network for file access. Yet another arrangement is for a workstation to have a local disk and filing system augmented by a network file service. Also, applications may be implemented as concurrent processes spread across a number of computers.

Processes on different machines may need to communicate with each other. A client process may invoke a server function or peer processes may need to exchange information. Figure 3.14 shows the basic requirement, with process A on one machine and process B on another. The *virtual communication*, shown as direct between process A and process B, may in practice be achieved by a system call to the operating system which organizes data transfers across the network: the *real communication* shown in the figure. Section 15.4 describes the socket interface.

Section 15.4

We now look at the low-level aspects of communications networks, those concerned with network interfaces and drivers. We then proceed to the higher levels of communications software in Section 3.8.

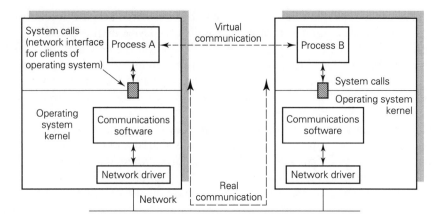

Figure 3.14
Communication
between processes
on different
machines.

 ## 3.7 Communications networks, interfaces and drivers

A given computer might be connected to a local area network (LAN) or a wide area network (WAN). Perhaps the most common (and most general) topology is that of interconnected LANs connected by WANs to form an internetwork. Figure 1.9 shows local networks of workstations and servers with WAN connections. For generality, it also shows some host computers directly attached to the WAN. Some concurrent systems span large-scale or even global networks, for example, electronic mail systems, information retrieval services and the private networks of companies with widely dispersed branches.

A computer's network connection is handled by the operating system in much the same way as a device. The network has an interface and the operating system contains a driver for the interface. Aspects of relevance to the network connection are the method that is used to access the network medium and the interface between the network hardware and the attached computer (see Figure 3.15).

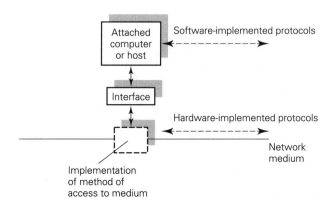

Figure 3.15
Medium, access
method and interface.

Table 3.1 Characteristics of LANs.

Ethernet	10 Mbit s^{-1}	Variable size packets with up to 4 kbytes of data
IEEE 802.4 token bus	10 Mbit s^{-1}	Variable size packets, 96 bytes to 8 kbytes
FDDI token ring	100 Mbit s^{-1}	Variable size packets, typically 96 bytes
Cambridge Ring (CR)	10 Mbit s^{-1}	Fixed cell size with 2 bytes of data
Cambridge Fast Ring (CFR)	100 Mbit s^{-1}	Fixed cell size with 32 bytes of data
Cambridge Backbone Ring (CBR)	1 Gbit s^{-1}	Fixed cell size with 32 bytes of data
Standard ATM	155 Mbit s^{-1}	Fixed cell size with 48 bytes of data

For example, some networks require active connections which participate in the transmission of packets from one network link to the next, whereas in others the network connection is just a passive tap. These issues are not relevant to the concurrent software structures we are considering here. We discuss interfaces briefly in Section 3.7.3.

Above the driver are higher levels of software implementing communications services and protocols. There are system calls to give the operating system's clients an interface to the communications service. The basic structure is similar to that of the I/O subsystem, with communications initiated both top-down and bottom-up and with the requirement for data to be buffered.

Some examples of LAN characteristics are given in Table 3.1. These examples illustrate two major approaches to LAN design: the bus and ring topology. Their access methods and some interfaces for them are described briefly below. A complete description can be found in Hopper *et al.* (1986) and Halsall (1996). Some network interfaces use DMA; they deposit an assembled block of data into main memory then signal an interrupt. Others interrupt the processor every time a packet arrives at the network interface.

We shall not discuss the packet structure in detail. In all cases we assume that the packets that are transmitted onto the network have control information as well as data so that the source and destination of the transmission can be determined by the network hardware and errors can be detected and recovery procedures invoked. Our main concern is the software systems in the attached computers. As network users we need to be aware of the data transmission rates they can sustain and with what guarantees.

3.7.1 Ethernet

Ethernet is a LAN designed at Xerox's Palo Alto Research Center (PARC) (Metcalfe and Boggs, 1976) and a prototype was operational there in 1976. It is a broadcast bus type of network whose medium is a coaxial cable named the 'ether'. The access method (for an attached computer) is **carrier sense multiple**

access with collision detection (CSMA/CD). In this scheme a potential transmitter listens to the communications medium to determine whether there is already a transmission in progress on the network. If the ether is quiet the transmission goes ahead. Since it is possible that another station initiates a transmission at the same time, a packet collision can occur. In order to detect this, each station listens to the transmission of its packet and if corruption is detected the transmission is aborted. To avoid transmissions which have collided being retried in phase, a random back-off period is used before retransmission takes place. This period increases exponentially on repeated collisions.

Ethernets were originally intended for 'office' applications, but became widely used during the 1980s. In practice they work well at light loads, typically 10% of capacity. As processors continue to increase in performance and multiprocessors become more widely used Ethernets will become more heavily loaded. As load increases, so does the chance of contention and the possibility of delay. The network is monopolized while a transfer takes place, which, together with the probabilistic nature of the access mechanism, means that timing guarantees cannot be made for applications that need them.

3.7.2 Ring-based LANs

Several ring-based networks have been developed over the years. One method of controlling access to the ring is to employ a unique circulating **token**. When a computer receives the token from the ring it may delay transmitting it until it has placed its own packet onto the ring. Only one computer may be transmitting at one time. IBM Zurich have developed a token ring (Bux *et al.*, 1982); another is FDDI (fibre distributed data interface) (Burr, 1986; Ross, 1986).

The Cambridge Ring networks are based on the **slotted ring** principle (Hopper and Needham, 1988). The first was operational in 1976 at the University of Cambridge Computer Laboratory. A ring of given length can carry a fixed number of cells, constantly circulating. Each carries a leading bit indicating full or empty. A station assembles a cell it wishes to transmit and inserts it into the first available empty packet. A packet makes a complete circuit of the ring and the destination station copies the cell and marks it as received. Other responses may also be indicated. When the cell returns to its sender, the response is noted and the packet is marked empty and passed on. Notice that the sender may not reuse this packet. This is called an 'anti-hogging' mechanism and ensures that all stations have an equal chance of using the medium. This allows timing guarantees to be made.

If a small fixed packet size is used, a given piece of data to be transferred is split for transmission and reassembled after reception. Software immediately above the interface must handle this; that is, higher-level protocols implemented in software manage the transmission of larger packets (see below). If a larger, variable packet size is used, as in Ethernet, some communications can be achieved by the transfer of a single packet. It will still be necessary to split some 'messages' into packet-sized portions and reassemble them at the destination. This is called 'segmentation and reassembly'.

3.7.3 Examples of network interfaces

Because of the commercial success of Ethernet in a wide variety of applications, a great deal of effort has been expended on producing high-performance interfaces for it. Examples are the DEQNA (DEC, 1986) and LANCE (AMD, 1985) interfaces. Both employ a ring of transmit descriptors and a ring of receive descriptors in main memory. The transmit descriptors indicate buffers containing data to transmit as packets and the receive descriptors indicate buffer space to use for incoming packets. Transmission and reception is done by DMA from and to these buffers defined by the descriptors in the rings. An interrupt may be generated on the emptying or filling of a buffer by the interface. Concurrent access by the interface and the host computer to the descriptor rings could cause errors, and a protocol is employed to ensure correct access. By using large packets and a suitable memory system a host can, in theory, achieve close to 100% utilization of an Ethernet with one of these interfaces.

The Cambridge Fast Ring and Cambridge Backbone Ring are used primarily in a research environment. No interface supporting DMA access has yet been built for the CFR so all data must be moved between the host memory and the interface using processor cycles. The CFR can buffer only one 'cell' of 32 bytes. So far, only a single type of interface (for the VME bus) has been built for the CBR (Greaves *et al.*, 1990). It contains four transmit FIFO buffers and one receive FIFO buffer. Each buffer has a capacity of 256 cells of 32 bytes per cell. It can be programmed to interrupt on every cell received or only when a cell containing an end of frame bit is detected. A version offering DMA has been designed.

3.8 Communications software

A communications **protocol** is a set of rules for controlling communication. It may define a particular, ordered sequence of messages to be used in a communication. The order is agreed by convention between the communicating entities to satisfy their requirements. A simple example, taken from a different context, is:

message: 'Hi beta, this is alpha, are you receiving me? OVER'
reply: 'Yes alpha, this is beta, I'm receiving you. OVER'

The above two messages implement a **connection establishment** protocol.

An example of an **application protocol** (see Figure 3.16) is a client's interaction with a file server, for example:

file-id = **open** (*filename, write-mode*)
data-bytes = **read** (*file-id, byte-range*)
close (*file-id*)

The client must obey certain rules for interacting with the file server. The operations must be invoked in the right order and the correct arguments must be passed. In this example the client must **open** a file before reading it. The

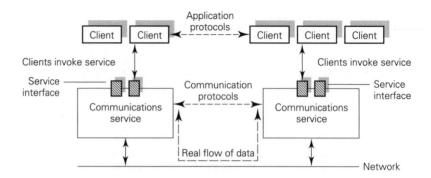

Figure 3.16
Service interface
and protocol.

server replies with a *file-id* for subsequent use by the client. The client passes the *file-id* when it wants to read data from the file.

Communications software implements services and protocols to allow information to be transmitted between computers. A service interface to the communications software is specified so that its clients may indicate which services and protocols they require. Figure 3.16 shows this scheme.

This simple picture does not express the many functions of communications software. The communications service shown in Figure 3.16 must have a great deal of internal structure and is always described in terms of layers with functions associated with each layer. The lowest layer is concerned with the physical network and the highest with applications concerns. The next section gives a standard definition of the various layers of communications functions.

3.8.1 The ISO reference model for Open Systems Interconnection

The International Standards Organization's (ISO) reference model for Open Systems Interconnection (OSI) (see Figure 3.17) provides a framework for discussion and comparison of communications software. Standard protocols and service interfaces have been specified for some of the levels. The reference model is itself a standard: ISO-7498 (see ISO, 1981 and Zimmerman, 1980).

The network architecture shown in Figure 3.17 is deliberately all-embracing and most networks map onto a subset of it. It may represent a network comprising any number of connected LANs and WANs. The two **end systems** indicate a source and sink of communication and the **communications subnet** may comprise any number of intermediate (gateway) computers which cooperate to transfer information between the end systems.

The reference model provides a framework for modular, layered software. Each layer provides a service interface to the layer above and protocols for communicating with the corresponding layer in other systems. Figure 3.18 gives the general idea. Figure 3.19 shows how data to be transmitted is passed down the layers. At each level a header, and possibly a trailer, is added as defined for the particular layer protocol to be used. At the receiving end system each layer strips off its header and trailer and passes the data up to the layer above. The

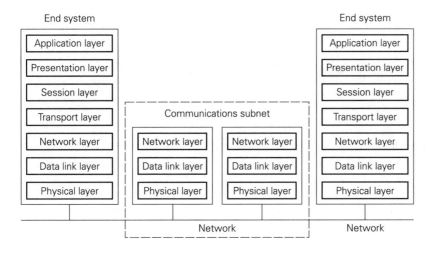

Figure 3.17
The ISO reference model for OSI.

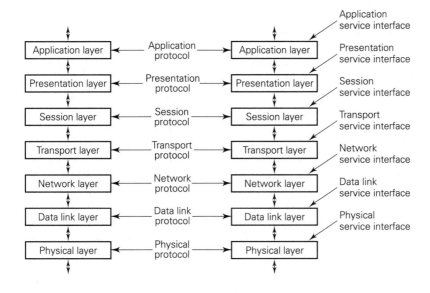

Figure 3.18
Protocols and service interfaces.

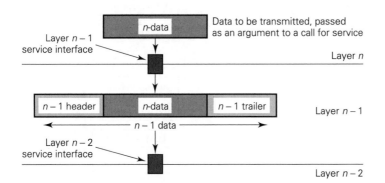

Figure 3.19
Data packaged for transmission by a protocol.

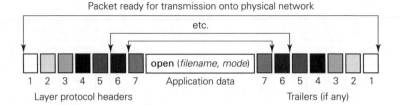

Figure 3.20
Example of data packaged for transmission.

highest level interprets the data according to an application protocol. Figure 3.20 shows a simple example of a small amount of data to be transmitted between two application processes. By the time it has reached the lowest level and is ready for transmission to the network it has accumulated a protocol header from each layer (and possible also a trailer). The figure assumes a network which allows this data to be transmitted as a single packet.

Figure 3.18 shows the protocols between the seven reference model layers and the service interface for each layer. The layers were chosen to give useful abstractions; a brief definition of the function of each layer is given below.

The **physical layer** is concerned with transmitting uninterpreted bits across a communication channel from one computer to another and with managing the connection.

The **data link layer** is mainly concerned with taking a raw transmission facility and turning it into a link that appears to be free from errors.

The **network layer** is concerned with transmitting data from a source to a destination across (possibly a number of heterogeneous) networks. It must determine a route for the data packets and must attempt to avoid congestion in the network by controlling the number of packets transmitted.

The **transport layer** is concerned with transmission from end system to end system. It provides hosts with a standard service. A number of different qualities of service are appropriate to this level. One major distinction is between a **connection-oriented service** and a **connectionless service**. The transport layer is usually the highest level of communication service in the operating system and the session layer provides an interface to the operating system's communication service (see Figure 3.21).

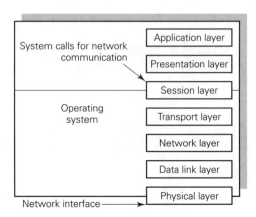

Figure 3.21
ISO reference model layers in a typical operating system.

The **session layer** allows clients of an operating system on one machine to establish and use sessions with clients of an operating system on another machine.

The **presentation layer** is concerned with the representation of data. In the extreme case, the communicating end systems may run on different hardware, with different operating systems and with different implementations of language systems. Even in this case, a standard data representation allows arguments such as strings, integers, etc. to pass from a client to a service. Some more homogeneous examples are considered in Chapter 15.

The **application layer** contains a number of standard protocols that are of general use. The remote procedure call (RPC) protocol discussed in Chapter 15 is an example. We shall study an RPC package that contains application, presentation and session layers. Other examples are file transfer protocols, electronic mail, remote login, remote job entry, virtual terminals and many others. Any service program may define an application protocol that its clients must use when invoking it.

3.8.2 Connection-oriented and connectionless communication

There are two fundamentally different kinds of service that a layer can offer to the layer above it: **connection-oriented** and **connectionless**. In a connectionless service a data item being transmitted by a protocol is sent as a separate unit, unrelated to any previous communication at that level. The data is sent as a so-called **datagram** which contains full addressing information.

A connection-oriented service requires that a connection or **virtual circuit** is set up between the communicating entities. In this case data items are sent along the connection, and are identified only by the virtual circuit concerned and not by full addressing information.

There are variations of both styles of service. In outline, the trade-offs are as follows:

- It takes longer to decode a datagram to determine which process it should be delivered to.
- It takes time to set up and tear down a connection. If a communication consists, for example, of a single request followed by a single reply the overhead of a connection is unnecessary.
- Use of a virtual circuit implies that the computers implementing communications must retain state about the connections that have been set up. Several computers might be involved if communication is taking place across interconnected LANs or WANs. A problem is that if any computer fails, the connections that are routed through it will have to be re-established.

For some applications, such as client–server interactions, connections seem to be unnecessary. We shall see a request–response protocol implemented above a datagram service in Chapter 15. For other applications, such as the transfer of a voice or video stream from a server to a workstation, a connection seems to be essential. The time for each packet to be decoded afresh is likely to be prohibitive.

In the past, connection-oriented services, X.25 for example, were notorious for being heavyweight and therefore inappropriate for a large number of distributed applications. New protocols are now in use which implement lightweight virtual circuits (McAuley, 1989). Techniques that achieve efficiency are:

- The circuit is not set up by a separate connection establishment protocol, including an end-to-end acknowledge before data can be sent along it. As soon as the first hop is ready the data can go.
- A circuit can easily be broken and re-established.
- There is no multiplexing above the datalink level; each application-level process-to-process connection has a separate virtual circuit.

 ## 3.9 Communications handling within and above an operating system

Figure 3.21 gives an example of how the ISO layers might be provided in a typical operating system.

There are a large number of different protocol hierarchies. Taking a local example, the UNIX systems at the University of Cambridge Computer Laboratory are configured with over 20. It is therefore important for operating systems to allow their clients to select the protocol hierarchy they require. Figure 3.22 shows a commonly used protocol hierarchy in relation to the ISO layers in an Ethernet-based UNIX system. Section 15.4 shows how network communications are set up and used in this system.

We have seen the need for synchronization between user-level processes requesting to send or receive data and the hardware carrying out physical I/O.

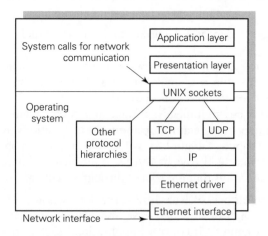

Figure 3.22
The ARPA protocols
in an Ethernet-based
UNIX system.

TCP = Transmission Control Protocol (a connection-oriented transport service)
UDP = User Datagram Protocol (a connectionless transport service)
IP = Internet Protocol (network level)

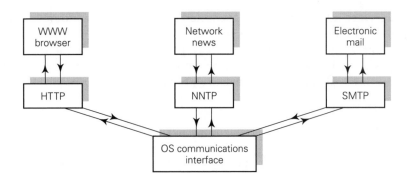

Figure 3.23
Application-specific
protocols.

We also discussed the use of I/O buffers on input and output (see Figure 3.13). Similar synchronization and buffering arrangements are needed for network I/O.

Figure 3.23 shows examples of application-level protocols within an overall communications architecture. The mail application is using a specialized protocol, SMTP (simple mail transfer protocol); the web browser is using HTTP (hypertext transfer protocol). Other examples of special-purpose application protocols are FTP (file-transfer protocol) and NNTP (network news transfer protocol). The details of two general-purpose application-level protocols, RPC (remote procedure call) and Java RMI, will be developed in Chapter 15.

Chapter 15

3.10 Summary

The hardware is one source of events, and therefore of concurrent activity, in a concurrent system. We have seen how the hardware may signal an event, such as the arrival of a unit of data, and how events are handled by software. Hardware events may be classified as those which are caused by (and must be handled synchronously with) a running program and those which are external and may be handled asynchronously.

Some concurrent systems may need to meet timing requirements. For such systems it is necessary to understand how events arrive and the mechanism for handling them. It is also important to realize that, although the hardware may be fast enough to meet timing requirements, software policies could make it impossible to guarantee them. We shall see more of this in Chapter 4. So far, we have seen that an operating system provides a convenient, high-level interface for device handling, and therefore hides the details.

In a concurrent system processes may need to interact with devices and communicate with other processes which may be across a network. The communications subsystem must handle simultaneous requests from local users and interleaved communications data arriving across the network. Other computers are likely to generate more data than local peripherals. Because of this potential volume and complexity, careful modular structuring is required. The most general case is when unlike systems need to communicate, and the ISO OSI standards are designed to address this. The ISO reference model is used to describe and compare all communications software.

In Chapter 4 we see how the processes we introduced as an abstraction in Chapter 2 are implemented by the operating system. We can then study how processes may be used to handle devices and run users' programs.

Exercises

3.1 By looking in Hennessy and Patterson (1996), for example, find out the following:
 (a) The execution times of typical instructions of CISC computers such as the VAX series, the IBM System 370, the Motorola 68 000 series, the Intel 8086 and 80x86 series.
 (b) The execution times of typical instructions of RISC computers such as the Motorola 88 000, the SPARC, the MIPS R4000 and the Intel 860.
 In both cases note the instruction lengths and their functionality.
 Now find out the rate at which networks and peripherals, such as terminals, printers, disks and RAM used as disks, can accept or deliver data and also the unit of data that is accepted or delivered.

3.2 What are the advantages and disadvantages of handling devices by a polling scheme compared with an interrupt-driven approach? In what kinds of system does the application dictate which approach must be taken?

3.3 How many memory accesses are made without and with the RISC exception-handling hardware described in Section 3.2.7? Estimate the total time to achieve the transfer of control from the interrupted program to the exception-handling routine in both cases.

3.4 You have hardware support for seven priority interrupt levels. On what basis would you assign these priorities?

3.5 What is direct memory access (DMA)? How can (a) a single block and (b) several blocks of data be transferred between main memory and a disk or network?

3.6 Processors are usually designed to execute in one of two (or more) privilege states, for example, user and supervisor mode.
 (a) When and how is the state change from user to supervisor mode made?
 (b) When and how is the state change from supervisor to user mode made?
 (c) Which instructions would you expect to be privileged (executable only in supervisor mode)? What is the mechanism for preventing them from being executed in user mode?

3.7 An application should be able to send an arbitrary amount of data to be output to a device. Devices transfer a fixed amount. How is this achieved?

3.8 Error conditions are often detected at a low level in a system, such as in an exception-handling routine. Why should they not be dealt with immediately? Devise a method to allow error handling at user level within the context of the application that caused the error.

3.9 How are exceptions handled in a shared-memory multiprocessor?

3.10 Compare and contrast peripheral I/O and network I/O.

3.11 Define wide area networks and local area networks (see also Section 1.3.8).

3.12 Compare and contrast the Ethernet with a ring-based LAN. Which design type will guarantee bandwidth between connected systems? What kind of applications need such guarantees? Are the guarantees usually made to the application level?

3.13 What is meant by connectionless and connection-oriented communication?

3.14 Which of the ISO layers would you expect to be implemented inside an operating system?

3.15 How do you think the ISO layers might be implemented in terms of the modules and processes introduced in Chapter 2? Try this question again after reading Chapter 4.

4

Support for processes

In the previous chapters we have considered a static description of a software system as a number of modules and the functions of some of the major operating system modules. The concept of 'process' as an active element which causes the modules to be executed dynamically was introduced briefly. We now return to and develop this concept in order to satisfy the requirement, established in Chapter 1, that separate activities should be supported in concurrent systems. This support, as provided by operating systems, is now examined in detail. We show that one function of an operating system is to create the abstraction of a set of concurrent processes. Having created this abstraction, processes may be used to execute both operating system and application modules.

Terminology

Recall that we are using the classical term **process** to indicate an active element in a system. Many current systems denote their practical unit of scheduling as a **thread**. Before Section 4.11 the term thread can be used interchangeably with process for the unit of scheduling. Later sections discuss the implementation of concurrent programs and need to distinguish between the unit of resource allocation (process) and the unit of scheduling (process or thread, depending on whether the system supports multi-threaded processes).

 # 4.1 Use of processes in systems

The designers of early operating systems solved the problems of concurrency and synchronization in an ad hoc way. It was always necessary to support synchronization between programs doing input or output and the corresponding devices, to take account of the great disparity in processor and device speeds. During the 1960s the concept of process came to be used explicitly in operating systems design, for example in Multics (Corbato and Vyssotsky, 1965), THE (Dijkstra, 1968) and RC4000 (Brinch Hansen, 1970).

Section A.2

One aspect of designing a concurrent system is to decide where processes should be used. A natural assignment is to allocate a process wherever there is a source of asynchronous events. In an operating system, for example, a process could be allocated to look after (synchronize with) each hardware device. If a user switches on a terminal and presses the escape key, an operating system process is waiting to respond. In an industrial control system a process could be allocated to each monitoring sensor and controlling actuator.

Another natural allocation of processes is to assign at least one process to each independent unit of work comprising a loaded program, data and library. Such a process will make system calls on the operating system to request service, for example, to request input, output, use of a file, etc.

Figure 4.1 shows two active processes assigned to execute the static modules of Figures 3.12 and 3.13. One executes the user program and makes library and system calls to do I/O; the other programs the device, taking requests from user programs and transferring data to or from the device. We have made an

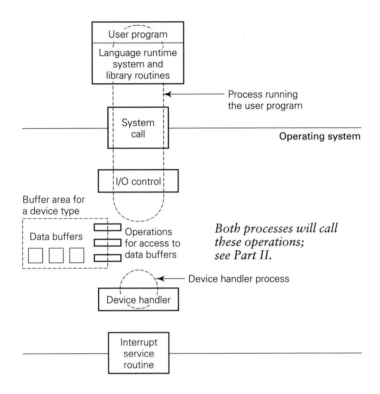

Figure 4.1
Part of a device-
handling subsystem
showing processes.

assumption in the figure: that a user process enters the operating system (with a change of privilege as discussed in Section 3.3.2) and executes the top level of the operating system. This is only one way in which the operating system might be designed (see Section 4.10).

We have assumed that processes exist in a system and have outlined how they might be used. We now focus on how they are supported and managed by the operating system. We assume that there is a process management module within the operating system which 'knows about' a number of processes, such as those handling devices and those executing users' programs.

4.2 Processes and processors

There are often far fewer processors than the processes we should like to use in a system. If this was not the case we could dedicate a processor permanently to each process. When the process has something to do, it executes on its processor; when it has nothing to do its processor idles. In practice, the operating system must perform the function of sharing the real processors among the processes. We shall see that this function can be regarded as creating **virtual processors**, one for each process; that is, the operating system is simulating one processor per process.

In Section 3.2.5 we saw that interrupts from devices may be given a priority ordering and that the handling of a low-priority interrupt is temporarily abandoned

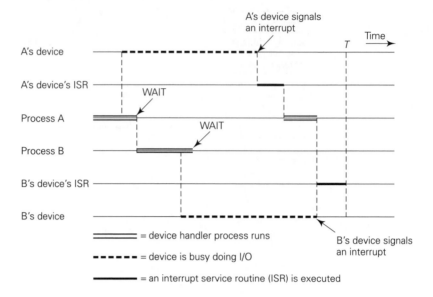

Figure 4.2
Time graph of two
device handler
processes, running
on one processor.

if a high-priority interrupt arrives, and is resumed after the high-priority interrupt
has been handled.

This idea can be applied to processes as well as to the interrupt routines which
are entered by a hardware mechanism. A user process may be busily inverting
a large matrix when an interrupt arrives (and its service routine is executed) to
say that a block of data that was requested from the disk is now in memory and
the disk is free to accept further commands. The disk-handling process should
run as soon as possible (to keep a heavily used resource busy), and then maybe
the matrix program should resume or maybe the data from disk was awaited by
some more important user process which should run in preference to the matrix
program. We assume that the operating system process management function
will implement a policy such as that outlined here.

Consider two processes in detail: Figure 4.2 is a time graph and shows two
device handler processes (such as the one shown in Figure 4.1) sharing a single
processor. It also shows when their respective devices are active and when the
associated interrupt service routines (ISRs) run on the processor. We assume, in
this example, that an ISR does not run as part of any process.

Initially, process A runs, starts its device then gets to a point where it can
do no more until the device completes its activity. It must be possible for the
process to indicate this fact to the process management function, shown here as
WAIT. When a process executes WAIT it changes its state from **running** to
blocked. Process B is then run on the processor, starts its device then WAITs. If
only A and B are available for running then the system becomes idle. In practice,
there may be some other process that can be run. The next event shown in the
graph is that A's device signals an interrupt which is taken by the processor and
A's interrupt service routine is entered. This makes process A able to run again
– its state changes from **blocked** to **runnable** and then to running when it is
selected to run on the processor. While process A is running, B's device signals an

interrupt which is taken by the processor, interrupting process A. B's interrupt service routine is executed and finishes at time T, shown in the graph.

A policy decision must be made over what should happen at time T. In some operating systems, the policy is that process A must resume whatever the relative priorities of A and B are. The justification is that A has not voluntarily executed a WAIT and should be allowed to continue until it does so. This is called **non-preemptive scheduling**: processes only lose control of the processor on a voluntary basis. The UNIX operating system schedules kernel processes (those executing the operating system) in this way. The advantage is simplicity – a process can be assumed to have tidied up its data structures, and not be hogging some valuable resource if it is allowed to finish its current task. The disadvantage is slow response to hardware events. Non-preemptive scheduling is useless if fast response to unpredictable events is required; for example, alarm signals or other events in hard real-time systems.

4.3 Process state

The discussion of Section 4.2 highlights that a process may be in a number of distinct states, illustrated in Figure 4.3:

- running on a processor: RUNNING state;
- able to run on a processor: RUNNABLE state;
- unable to run on a processor because it is awaiting some event and cannot proceed until that event arrives: BLOCKED state.

The transition from running to runnable occurs when the process does not voluntarily give up its processor (by asking to be blocked while waiting for an event to occur) but is forcibly preempted from its processor either because it has used up its allotted time and must make way for another process or because some higher-priority process has become runnable as a result of an interrupt. This approach is known as preemptive scheduling.

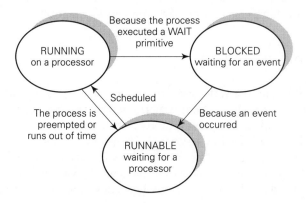

Figure 4.3
States and state transitions of a process.

```
Process ID
Priority (see Section 4.6)
Process state
Events awaited by process
Record of events signalled (see Section 4.4)
Area for saving registers,
     including PC, stack pointer, general-purpose registers
Start address
Exception address (see Section 3.3.5)
Time slice (see Section 4.6.2)
Time left this run
Links for data structures
```

Figure 4.4
A process descriptor.

4.3.1 Saving process state

If a process can be preempted from its processor at any instant, it is the responsibility of the operating system to make sure that it can be resumed in exactly the same state. The contents of the memory allocated to the process will be unchanged but the contents of any processor registers must be saved, since they will be used by the processes which run subsequently.

The operating system keeps a data block, often called a **process descriptor**, for each process that it supports. When a process is preempted or blocks voluntarily, the processor state, which includes the program counter and contents of registers, is saved in the process descriptor. Other information is also held here, such as the process's state (blocked or runnable) and its start address (see Figure 4.4). Information on the memory allocated to the process may be held here in a simple system or elsewhere if large page tables are involved (see Chapter 5). Other information such as that associated with open files and other resources allocated to the process may be kept here or in a second process environment data structure at user level. This kind of information is only needed when the process is running and is quite large and variable in length. Information that must be in the process descriptor is that which is needed when the process is not in main memory (for example, a record of event(s) the process is awaiting). We are now seeing the detailed implementation of the process abstraction.

4.3.2 Context switching

The process of saving the state of a process and setting up the state of another is called **context switching**. The instructions that are executed in performing these operations and the frequency at which context switching happens are an overhead at the lowest level of a system. When we consider alternative ways of supporting communication between processes in Part II we shall consider the context switches that are necessary to implement the various methods. Context switching overhead is relevant to many aspects of system structuring.

4.4 Synchronizing with the hardware: Events and the WAIT operation

We have seen above that the operating system's support for processes must include the provision of a WAIT operation to allow processes to synchronize with the hardware. The term 'event' will be used to include the arrival of an interrupt signal from a device.

This operation might be provided as a WAIT for one specific event, for any one event or for any one of a selected set of events. (The logical possibility of waiting for all of a set of events makes little sense: interrupts need to be processed rapidly.) Possible hardware events are relatively small in number and are known at system design time. This set of possible events can easily be encoded as an integer, representing a bit-map. As shown in Figure 4.4, the process descriptor could encode the reason the process is blocked and the events of interest to this process that have occurred, see below. Figure 4.5 shows one way of implementing process–event synchronization. The assumption here is that it is well known which system processes will wait on which events. An example is a dedicated device handler that synchronizes with a single device (see Figure 4.1). For consistency, Figure 4.5 represents process descriptors as objects, although within most operating systems, a purely procedural, not an object-oriented, approach is taken.

Figure 4.5 shows the process level and the implementation level for a WAIT for a specific event. When the process invokes **OS.WAIT (anEvent)**, control is transferred to the operating system method **WAIT**. The operating system object, **OS** (not shown), in turn invokes **WAIT (anEvent)** on the process descriptor for the current process. Asssuming that the event of interest has not already occurred, the process state is set to *blocked* and the event it is waiting for is recorded in the 'events awaited by process' slot. Some other process is then run. When the event occurs, we assume that a method **SIGNAL (anEvent)** is

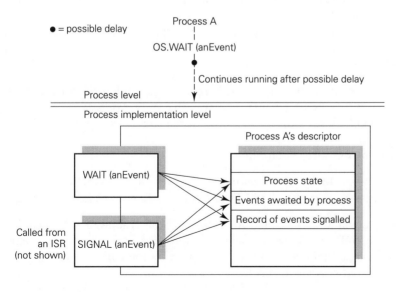

Figure 4.5
Process synchronization with events.

invoked on the process descriptor which causes the process state to be set to *runnable* and the reason for waiting to be removed. The process will be selected to run again in due course. This assumes that the system design is such that a single, well-known process waits for each event so SIGNAL (anEvent) is invoked on the appropriate process descriptor. Section 4.4.2 takes a more general approach.

An event might arrive while the process that would be interested in it is still busy on some previous task, and hasn't yet got around to waiting for it. Another possibility is that the process sets a device in motion, but was preempted from its processor before it could execute OS.WAIT (anEvent) in order to synchronize with the device. It is essential that the operating system should not unset the interrupt and ignore the event if no process is waiting for it. This was a 'feature' of some early operating system designs. In Figure 4.5 the operating system notes that the event has occurred in the 'record of events' slot. This is sometimes called a '**wake-up waiting**'. When the process requests to wait for the event it can continue running and need never enter the blocked state.

4.4.1 Race conditions

Consider the following sequence of events:

A process (via the operating system) executes WAIT (anEvent) on a process descriptor:
The WAIT method checks that the event is not already recorded.
   The hardware signals an interrupt to indicate the event has occurred.
   The interrupt handler invokes SIGNAL (anEvent) on the process descriptor.
      The SIGNAL method checks that the process is not waiting for the event.
      The SIGNAL method records that the event has occurred ('wake-up waiting').
   Interrupt processing terminates and the WAIT method resumes execution.
The WAIT method records the awaited event and sets the process state to BLOCKED.

The sequence of actions recorded here is an example of a '**race condition**'. A race condition exists whenever the relative timing of a set of events affects the outcome. This, as in our example, often indicates a problem that needs solving.

Following our race condition:

- the process is BLOCKED, waiting for the event to be SIGNALLED;
- the event has been SIGNALLED, and is recorded as a 'wake-up waiting'.

The process will wait indefinitely for the event if this is allowed to happen. For this reason the WAIT and SIGNAL process desciptor methods must be implemented as indivisible, **atomic**, or **primitive** operations by some means. We shall discuss how this might be done in Part II.

4.4.2 Event and process objects

The design described above has encoded hardware event information in the process descriptors, assuming that specific processes are dedicated to handling the various events. A more general approach is to separate the event objects from the process descriptors.

An event object comprises an internal data structure representing an event plus methods SIGNAL () and WAIT (), as shown in Figure 4.6. The figure also shows process objects with methods to BLOCK and UNBLOCK a process.

When a process executes OS.WAIT (anEvent), the operating system object OS (not shown) in turn invokes WAIT () on the event object. The process identifier is recorded in the event data structure and the BLOCK () method is invoked on the relevant process descriptor, causing the representation of the process state to be changed from running to blocked. A SCHEDULE method (not shown) could then be called to decide which process to run next. Process scheduling is discussed in the next section.

When an event occurs, the SIGNAL () method is invoked on the event object. If one or more processes are recorded as waiting for the event, one of them (or perhaps all of them, depending on the system policy) can be made runnable by invoking the UNBLOCK () method on the relevant process descriptor object. Again, scheduling is invoked after this. If no process is awaiting the event its occurrence is recorded as a wake-up waiting in the event data structure.

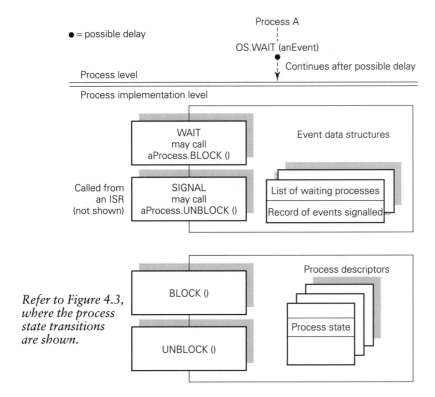

Figure 4.6
Event and process objects.

Windows NT has an object-oriented design with process objects, thread objects and event objects. A process may have the right to use, and have a handle for, an event object in which case any of the process's threads may synchronize with the event via the event operations.

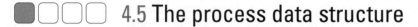

4.5 The process data structure

The operating system must handle many processes and will maintain a data structure holding their descriptors. This could be set up in a number of ways. The aim is that the operating system should be able to choose and run the highest-priority process as quickly as possible. Selecting a process to run on a processor is called process **scheduling**. The selection policy determines which process will be selected and is effected by the **scheduling algorithm**. Setting up a process state in the processor's registers is called **dispatching**. Figure 4.7 shows one possible data structure: an array or table of process descriptors; many alternatives are possible.

4.6 Scheduling: General approaches

When a free processor is available the operating system must select a runnable process (if one exists) to run on it. The **scheduling policy** of the system determines which process is selected.

The mechanisms to effect this policy must be as efficient as possible since they are an overhead on every process, however urgent. The design of the data structures representing processes and the algorithms for inserting and removing processes into and out of them is therefore important. In this section, scheduling

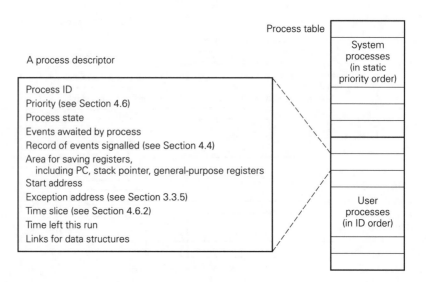

Figure 4.7
A possible process structure.

policies appropriate for meeting the requirements of systems of different types are discussed.

4.6.1 Unary, binary and general scheduling

In certain cases the selection of the next process to run can be simplified.

Unary scheduling: in the case where the system is idle (all processes are blocked, waiting for events) and an event occurs which makes some process runnable then that process is clearly the one that should run. No others need be considered and scheduling can be bypassed.

Binary scheduling: when a process is running it is by definition the most important, highest-priority process. If that process does something to make another process runnable then the choice of which one to run is between the two processes concerned. No others need be considered. Similarly, if an event occurs while a process is running which makes another process runnable, the choice is, again, between the two processes.

General scheduling: when the process that is running terminates or blocks, waiting for some event, a general schedule must be carried out.

4.6.2 Process behaviour and priority

Operating system processes have known function and duration, and in many systems are put into a permanent, **static fixed-priority** ordering. Figure 4.7 gives an example of how the information on processes might be held in a process management module and shows system processes handled separately in this way. They are in fixed-priority order and the operating system's scheduler will first search from the top of the table for a runnable system process.

In some application areas, such as process control, the function and duration of all processes may be known at system design time and it may be appropriate to assign them a static fixed-priority ordering. It may be possible to analyse the timing requirements of all processes and pre-specify a schedule which meets them. This kind of system is discussed further in Section 4.8.

In a multi-user system, the nature of application processes is unknown to the operating system and their behaviour will change during a typical program run, for example, from a data input phase to a processing phase to an output phase. In interactive systems, one user cannot be kept waiting while another indulges in a long bout of number crunching, so a **time slice** is allocated to a process when it begins to run. The process descriptor may indicate the length of the time slice to be allocated to this process and will have a record of the time left to this process on this run. This time must be decremented every time the clock interrupts and when it reaches zero the process is out of time. There may also be some indication of process priority.

Figure 4.7 shows one way of recording all the processes in a system. One or more queues of runnable processes may be chained through the user processes in this table, using the link fields in the process descriptors, as indicated in Figure 4.8. When a process becomes runnable it is added to the end of the appropriate queue.

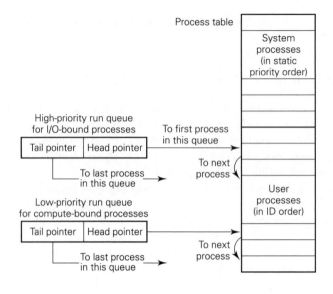

Figure 4.8
Run queues through
the process structure.

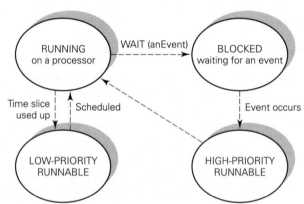

Figure 4.9
Run queues with
priority based on
recent activity.

Processes doing input or output usually become blocked very soon and do not get to the end of their time slices. They may also be using shared system resources, such as the filing system's disks, which should be kept running to the greatest extent possible. Figure 4.9 gives an alternative view of a high-priority and a low-priority run queue. When a process becomes runnable after being blocked it is allocated to the high-priority run queue. If it continues to block before using up its time slice it will always be scheduled from the high-priority queue. If a process runs to the end of its time slice it is moved to the end of the low-priority queue. Only if a high-priority queue is empty is a low-priority queue examined. In practice, processes may stay blocked for long periods (see Section 3.2.1) and the high-priority queue is often empty.

In summary, system processes have highest priority and are scheduled according to a static fixed-priority scheme. User processes which have blocked and have become runnable again are next highest and user processes which run to the end of their time slices are lowest.

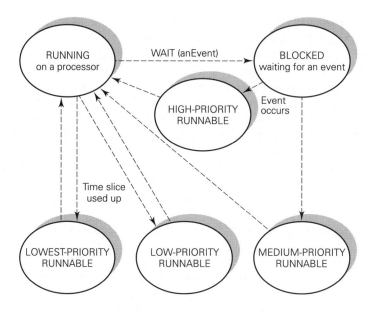

Figure 4.10
More run queues with priority based on recent activity.

Figure 4.10 shows a refinement of this general idea.

- As before, system processes are of highest priority and are handled in static, fixed-priority order. They are not shown in the figure.
- There is a high-priority queue for user processes that blocked, waiting for certain events such as a page fault and are now runnable.
- There is a medium-priority queue for user processes that were blocked, waiting for resources which are less critical for system performance (for example, devices such as dedicated terminals or tape drives), and are now runnable.
- The low- and lowest-priority queues are for processes that use up their time slice. Two queues allow for an allocation of two priority levels for processes when they are not doing I/O. More queues could be used if required by the applications supported by the system. Alternatively, a single queue, ordered according to process priority (instead of first come first served) could be constructed. Process priority may be assigned statically (in response to application requirements) or computed dynamically, depending on recent CPU usage.

The idea of multiple queues can be extended as required in a system, for example, NT has provision for 32 priority levels (16 real time and 16 normal).

4.7 Scheduling for shared-memory multiprocessors

Section 1.3.3 introduced shared-memory multiprocessors and Chapter 3 discussed the allocation of devices to processors and interrupt handling. Chapter 5 describes the memory hierarchy in a computer system, including a hardware-controlled

cache and an address translation unit. In a shared-memory multiprocessor each processor has a separate cache and address translation unit.

A given processor may have a local run queue for the device handlers of any dedicated devices it might have. There are also likely to be one or more global run queues. A possible approach is that a processor, on becoming free, should execute code such that it first examines its local run queue and, if that contains no runnable process, should take a process from the global run queue(s). Note that the global run queues are writeable data structures and adding or removing a process will involve more than one read or write of memory. It must be ensured that these data structures remain correct in the presence of simultaneous attempts to update them. This is important in all systems, but requires particular attention in a multiprocessor. Mechanisms to ensure this are the subject matter of Part II.

In the introductory chapter we saw that an application might best be programmed as a number of concurrent processes. Later in this chapter we consider how the component processes of a concurrent program might be specified and supported by the language runtime system and the operating system. A general point is that an application should be able to indicate to the operating system that it has a number of processes and to give their relative priorities for scheduling purposes. It is then possible to run them simultaneously on the processors of a multiprocessor.

Recall that in Section 3.4 we discussed the need for an inter-processor interrupt. An example of its use is that a process A running on a processor P makes a process runnable which is of lower priority than A but of higher priority than the process which is running on processor Q. An inter-processor interrupt from P to Q can start off the required context switch.

Scheduling algorithms for multiprocessors form an active research area. One approach to process scheduling for shared-memory multiprocessors is to allocate the process at the top of the run queue to the first processor that becomes free. This policy ignores the fact that a process may have run very recently on a particular processor and may have built up useful state in both the cache and the address translation unit. It might have blocked for a high-priority event and be runnable again in a very short time. If a process has been blocked for some time then its state is likely to have been superseded by that of more recent processes. In the case of a page fault, for example, the process should clearly continue to run on the same processor.

It might be appropriate to allow a process to 'busy wait' on a page fault. This will be described in more detail in Chapter 9, but the idea is to keep the process scheduled and running instead of blocking it and doing a context switch to another process. The waiting process might execute in a tight loop, or 'spin', until it is interrupted by the arrival of the required page.

Another factor to take into account is the relationships between groups of processes. If certain processes are designed to work closely together then the ideal arrangement may be for them to be scheduled simultaneously on the multiple processors of the multiprocessor. Bad performance could result from ignoring this kind of relationship; for example, a process runs, then tries to communicate with a partner. The partner is runnable but not scheduled. The first process is blocked and the partner is scheduled on the same processor. It picks up the pertinent information from the first process, acts on it then tries to send back an answer. Its partner is not scheduled, and so on.

The counter-argument is that if the processes are sharing data it is better for them to run on the same processor so that the same cache is used. If they run on separate processors and are sharing writeable data the overhead of keeping the caches coherent will be introduced.

4.8 Process scheduling to meet real-time requirements

Although preemptive scheduling with carefully chosen process priorities may ensure optimum use of resources it may not be sufficient to ensure that a number of processes meet their timing requirements in a real-time system.

Real-time systems were introduced in Section 1.1. There we defined two kinds of real-time process: those which are periodic and carry out some cyclic activity like data sampling and analysis, and those which must respond to unpredictable events in a specified time. A real-time scheduler must ensure that all processes satisfy their timing constraints.

Another example was introduced in the discussion on multimedia workstations in Section 1.1.1. A video and voice stream must be delivered to a workstation so that the voice is synchronized with the moving lips of the person in the picture. Although video generates far more data than voice, and is therefore likely to be managed at higher priority, the voice stream must be allowed a small proportion of time periodically. Conventional scheduling might well allow the voice to fall behind.

It is relatively easy to schedule a number of periodic processes, see below. It is more difficult to incorporate response to unpredictable events. Should the system designer allow for the worst possible case of all events arriving at the same time (or very close together) or take some probabilistic model of when they might arrive and live with a low probability of bursty behaviour?

A model of an aperiodic process is that it becomes ready to run when a particular event occurs, it must then compute for a known length of time and, in competition with other processes, it must complete in some specified time. We assume that the system has process preemption.

Figure 4.11 shows two processes A and B each with a known computation time (work$_A$ and work$_B$) and a known length of time in which the work must be completed. The graph shows this as a **deadline (D)**, **work time (W)** and **slack time (S)** for each process. The first graph in Figure 4.12 shows one possible sequence of events for the two processes. First process A's event occurs and process A is scheduled. Before process A's work is complete, process B's event occurs. The scheduler now has to decide whether to schedule A or B. The scheduler has the information to compute the deadlines of A and B and the remaining slack time of A and B.

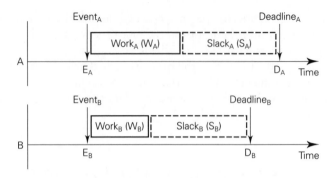

Figure 4.11
Processes in a
real-time system.

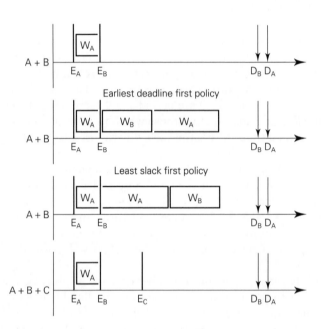

Figure 4.12
Real-time scheduling.

An **earliest deadline first** policy would cause process B to be selected. B then completes before its deadline by the value of its slack time. If a third process then comes along the option of using up some of B's slack time (by delaying B) has been lost.

An alternative strategy is to schedule first the process with the least remaining slack time, provided that they can both meet their deadlines. The third graph of Figure 4.12 shows this **least slack first** policy for A and B. The fourth graph shows the event for a third process C occurring. It is left as an exercise for the reader to compare the two policies with respect to work done and slack time left for A and B at time E_c. We now consider periodic scheduling in more detail, then discuss how dynamic events might be incorporated into the system.

Periodic schedules

A real-time system often consists of a known number of periodic processes. A schedule can be determined when the system is designed, based on the values of the work time of each process and the frequency at which this work must be done (the period). A suitable value for the scheduling period must be chosen and this will be the minimum value of all the processes' frequencies. Designing the schedule then involves creating a list of processes to be run to completion in each scheduling period. Some processes will not need to run every period but, for simplicity, time is usually left for all tasks to execute in every period, that is, some parts of each period will be unused. When the system is designed, enough processing power is put in for this to be possible.

Rate monotonic scheduling

Rate monotonic scheduling (RMS) is a scheduling scheme in which each periodic process is allocated a priority proportional to its frequency. High-frequency processes are assumed to be of higher priority than low-frequency processes. The scheduler selects the highest-priority runnable process and each process runs until its work time is completed for that period. RMS is simple and does not waste processor time to the extent we saw above for the cyclic schedule. It is therefore cheaper to implement. RMS is designed to ensure that, on average, each task will meet its deadline but it does not cope well with overload or with bursty behaviour. Also, the assumption that high frequency indicates high priority may not hold for some types of system.

Combining periodic and aperiodic processes

The earliest deadline first (EDF) and least slack first (LSF) algorithms described above may also be used for periodic processes, the deadline being taken as the end of the current period and the slack computed from this value. If processes are periodic, EDF will tend to execute high-frequency processes in preference to low-frequency ones, depending on the point at which the decision is made. This can cause priority inversion, as discussed for RMS.

This discussion does not take into account that any scheduled process may not be able to run to completion but may be delayed, waiting for a resource. At this point the process's slack time begins to elapse and a new process is scheduled. For a system that can be analysed statically (at design time) it may be possible to compute a bound on the potential delay for each process, taking into account the resources it uses, its priority and the relative priorities of other processes which compete for these resources, see also Section 9.6.2.

Section 9.6.2

The aim here is to introduce the issues that are involved, and some approaches that are taken, to scheduling in real-time systems so that the reader has a basis for evaluating any operating system that is claimed to be 'real time'. It is important to note that the conventional system of the near future will have multimedia capabilities and scheduling will need to move in this direction. Here, the deadlines are not hard, as in many process control systems, and the periodic processes do not exist for the lifetime of the system but arrive dynamically in response to users' requests. It may be that a user has to notify the system in advance that continuous media will be required and book a guaranteed share of processor time, so-called quality-of-service (QoS). In the case of a multi-user video conference it is possible to degrade the picture quality of existing members to free resources for a new member. For further study of real-time systems see Burns and Wellings (1989), Levi and Agrawala (1990), Gomaa (1993), Selic *et al.* (1995), ACM (1996) and Joseph (1996).

4.8.1 System structure and response to events

The ability to meet the requirement for a process to be scheduled in some bounded time after an event occurs is affected by the overall operating system design as well as the specific scheduling algorithm it employs. Some operating systems are executed 'procedurally'; that is, operating system code is executed 'in-process'. When a user process makes a system call it becomes a system process and enters the operating system. Such systems tend to have very few dedicated system processes and much of the work that is done by one process may be on behalf of others.

An example is that in UNIX an interrupt is serviced in the context of whatever process is running when it occurs. Another example from UNIX is when a process waits in the kernel for an event, the event occurs and the process is about to return to user mode to respond to the event. Before returning to user mode the process executes system code to determine whether any process is due to be woken up after asking to be delayed for a certain length of time. A high-priority process could therefore be required to act as an alarm clock for any number of low-priority processes between receiving the event for which it was waiting and responding to it.

This style of system design makes it difficult to compute how quickly a process can be guaranteed to run after an event occurs. There is an indeterminate amount of system code that may be executed as part of any process. The alternative design approach is to have the operating system executed by dedicated processes and to request service from them. System structure is discussed further in Section 4.10 and in Part II.

4.9 Process abstraction and implementation

The above sections have shown the details of how processes may be implemented. Figure 4.13 shows two layers: the high-level process abstraction and the layer supporting the abstraction. The function of the support layer is to provide an environment in which concurrent processes may exist. The support layer can be thought of as being at a low level within an operating system, so

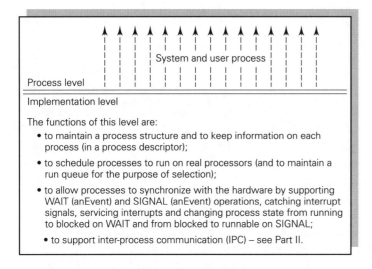

Process level

Implementation level

The functions of this level are:

- to maintain a process structure and to keep information on each process (in a process descriptor);
- to schedule processes to run on real processors (and to maintain a run queue for the purpose of selection);
- to allow processes to synchronize with the hardware by supporting WAIT (anEvent) and SIGNAL (anEvent) operations, catching interrupt signals, servicing interrupts and changing process state from running to blocked on WAIT and from blocked to runnable on SIGNAL;
- to support inter-process communication (IPC) – see Part II.

Figure 4.13
Supporting concurrent processes.

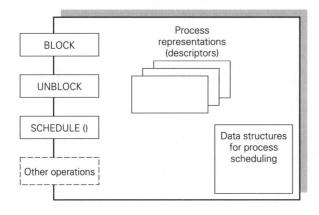

Figure 4.14
Process management module, alternative view.

that processes may be used to execute operating system functions, such as device handlers and the memory management subsystem. Figure 4.14 gives an alternative view of Figure 4.13, showing the process management module as an abstract data type, located within an operating system, see also Figure 4.6. The representation of processes (the various process data structures) is hidden and the interface contains operations on processes.

Figure 4.15 highlights the general idea that a single operation at the process level may be implemented by a method at the level below. The invocation mechanism might be a simple procedure call from within the operating system to the process management module or a system call from an application process running above the operating system. At the process level, the operation appears to be a single indivisible instruction. An operation of this kind is sometimes called a 'primitive': for example, the **WAIT** () method on events could be referred to as a synchronizing primitive. In this case the implementation of the operation must be atomic, to avoid the race conditions discussed in Section 4.4.1. If the

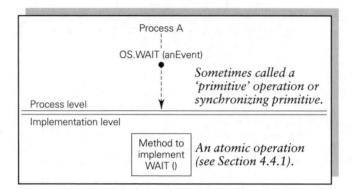

Process A

OS.WAIT (anEvent)

Sometimes called a 'primitive' operation or synchronizing primitive.

Process level

Implementation level

Method to implement WAIT () *An atomic operation (see Section 4.4.1).*

Figure 4.15
Implementation of
operations.

operation invocation blocks the process there will be a delay, indicated in the figure by a blob in the process path, before the process continues.

There has been no indication in the above discussion that the processes supported are other than completely independent of each other. In Chapter 8 the need for processes to communicate will be motivated and mechanisms for achieving inter-process communication (IPC) will be described throughout Part II.

4.10 Operating system structure and placement of processes

We can now put together the notions of static modules of code and their dynamic execution. We shall use an operating system as an example. We have seen how one operating system function is to support processes. We now consider how processes might be used in the implementation of an operating system. Figure 4.16 shows the major components of a traditional, closed operating system and gives a possible placement of processes to achieve dynamic execution of the system. Processes are allocated as follows:

- A single process is allocated to each user-level activity: a user program execution or a command execution. This assumes that each of these activities is a single sequential process. We shall consider concurrent programs in the following sections.
- A process is allocated to handle each device instance. Such a process will wait for and respond to device interrupts and be given work to do by the high level of I/O management (see Sections 3.5 and 4.1). Data will be passed between the high and low levels via buffers (see Section 3.5).
- Some memory management processes are indicated to respond to address translation faults, to allocate main memory to processes, and to move processes into and out of main memory as necessary (see Chapter 5). A process which is concerned with swapping other processes between main memory and backing store must be guaranteed to be resident in main memory itself.

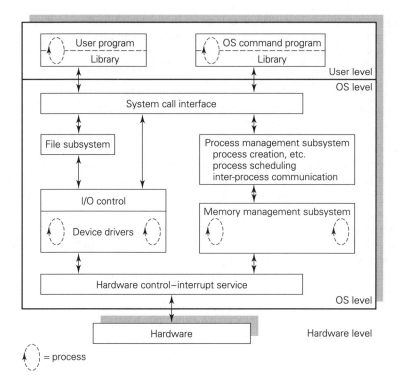

Figure 4.16
Outline of OS modules
with processes.

- Certain modules are shown with no permanent allocation of processes. It is assumed here that the code is executed in the context of the user process as a result of a system call. In this case, a state change from user state (unprivileged) to system state (privileged) is necessary, as discussed in Section 3.3.2.

    Section 8.1 discusses different ways of using processes within a module such as a filing subsystem. An alternative that could have been shown here is a number of permanently allocated processes.
- The process management module cannot itself be implemented as processes (see Section 4.9).

The UNIX operating system takes an extreme position and minimizes the number of processes which are bound to modules. There are no device handler processes and virtually the whole kernel is executed 'in-process'. Interrupt handling is executed in the context of whatever process happens to be running when the interrupt occurs. Exercise 4.10 discusses one aspect of this further.

4.11 Multi-threaded process implementation

In the discussion in Section 4.10 we saw that a number of processes might execute in a single module of the operating system. In the following sections we shall see a number of processes executing a concurrent program at user level.

Section 2.3.2

These are commonly called **user threads** when we are discussing implementation. The user threads share the address space of the application and all the resources allocated to the application by the operating system at runtime, such as memory and open files. We have two separate concepts here:

- the unit of execution (the unit of scheduling by the operating system);
- the unit of resource allocation: memory and other resources with which the unit of execution is associated.

So far, we have shown how processes, the units of execution, can share a processor. The process descriptor contains the processor state, including the program counter. The memory allocated to the process might be recorded in the process descriptor or elsewhere, for example, as a page table associated with the process.

Some operating systems allow user threads to be registered with them as schedulable **kernel threads**. Such operating systems are said to support **multi-threaded processes**. Note that the operating system's thread management must create and maintain a separate descriptor for every such thread since each thread will have its own values of processor registers, including the program counter. The memory management information and other resources, such as open files, will be common to all the threads of the process. The context switching overhead is relatively low since there is no need to change the memory management or other resource information on a context switch.

Some operating systems do not support multi-threaded processes and each process is defined to have a separate address space. Such systems are said to have a **heavyweight process** model because the overhead on a context switch is high. If an operating system is to run on a shared-memory multiprocessor it is important that multi-threaded processes are supported. The separate threads of a process can then be scheduled to run simultaneously if processors are free.

Section 12.9

Most microkernels and recently designed operating systems run on multiprocessors and support multi-threaded processes. There is a great disparity in the terminology used for these concepts; see Table 4.1. Figure 12.13 shows both a process descriptor and a thread descriptor as used in the NT operating system. The process supported by traditional operating systems is equivalent, in this terminology, to an address space with one thread, a task with one thread, a process with one thread, etc.

Table 4.1 Microkernel terminology.

Microkernel	Unit of execution	Unit of resource allocation
Mach	Thread	Task
Chorus	Thread	Actor
Mayflower	Lightweight process (LWP)	Domain
V	Thread	Team
Amoeba	Thread	Cluster
Windows NT	Thread	Process
Sun OS	Lightweight process	Address space

A widely used threads package, specified in IEEE POSIX 1003.4a (pthreads), is described in Section 10.8 and thread packages are discussed in general in Section 4.17. We first look in detail at how threads may be defined and supported within an application.

4.12 Processes in languages, runtime systems and operating systems

Concurrent systems are almost invariably programmed in a high-level language. We now consider how concurrency can be programmed and implemented by runtime systems and operating systems. First, we review relevant runtime system aspects of the execution of a program by a sequential process. Then we consider how concurrency might be supported within a language.

When a sequential programming language is used, one operating system process is created to run the program (Figure 4.17(a)). When a concurrent programming language is used the programmer, explicitly or implicitly, may set up a number of concurrent processes (to be implemented as user threads), see

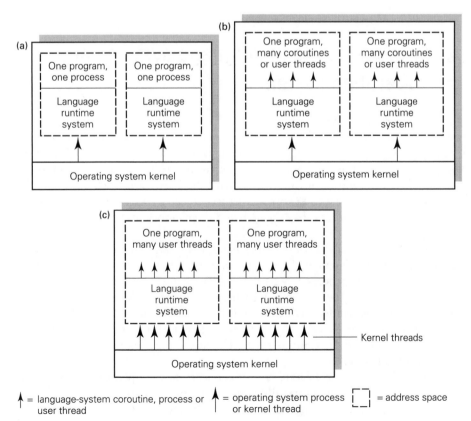

Figure 4.17
Implementation
of concurrent
processes.
(a) Sequential
programming
language.
(b) Concurrent
programming
language without
operating system
support.
(c) Concurrent
programming
languages with
operating system
support for user
threads as kernel
threads.

Figure 4.17(b), (c). If these user threads may be made known to the operating system as kernel threads, through a system call, we have the situation shown in Figure 4.17(c). We saw in Section 4.11 that modern operating systems are likely to support threads as well as processes, that is, **multi-threaded processes**. Processes are then the unit of resource allocation and (kernel) threads the unit of scheduling.

The programs indicated in Figure 4.17(a), (b) and (c) will run as operating system processes, each in a separate address space. If the user threads can be registered with the operating system as kernel threads, they are scheduled independently and can WAIT for synchronous I/O separately. While one blocks, waiting for I/O, another thread of the same process can run. This is essential if the concurrent program is to run on a multiprocessor.

For a real-time system to be able to make timing guarantees it is certainly necessary for threads to be scheduled preemptively and it may, in addition, be necessary for special priority-based or deadline-based scheduling to be used (see Section 4.8).

When designing a concurrent system in a concurrent programming language it is necessary to know about the operating system and hardware on which the system will run. We now explore in more detail how processes are programmed in concurrent programming languages and implemented by their runtime systems.

4.13 Process state in language systems and operating systems

In earlier sections we have defined the state of a process as far as the operating system is concerned, that is, the information stored on a process by the process management module of the operating system. It includes the value of the program counter and the contents of other hardware registers; information about any ongoing interaction of the process with the hardware, such as events the process is waiting for and events of interest to the process that have already occurred; the files a process has opened; and the memory that has been allocated to the process.

A process which is executing a program, originally written in a high-level language, also has a language-level state comprising the values of variables which are accessible to the process at a given time. These are stored in data areas in the memory allocated to the process. One simple arrangement (Figure 4.18) is that a process has a code segment, which includes the runtime support and library code as well as the user-level code, and two data segments, one for the static data and the **heap** and one for the **runtime stack**. The use of these data areas is discussed in more detail below.

This level of the process state is of no concern to the operating system, as it is stored safely in the memory allocated to the process and, unlike processor registers, is not used by any other process. Rather, it is the concern of the

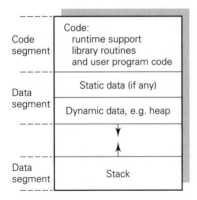

The user-level of the virtual address space of a process.
   The operating system may support three segments, which are used as shown (refer to Chapter 5).

Figure 4.18
A common storage arrangement for a single process.

In a sequential programming language system each program is executed by one operating system process.

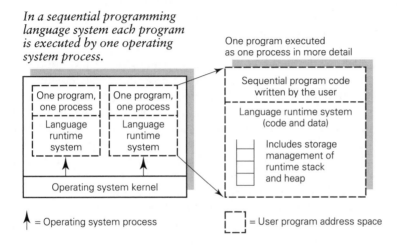

Figure 4.19
One program, one process: runtime system support of user-level program.

runtime system which is responsible for managing the dynamic execution of a program by a process. Figure 4.19 gives an overview; the user-level code runs within a framework provided by the runtime system. The runtime system code manages the storage needed by the user program when it is executed. Note that there is a **single thread of control** within which the runtime system and the user level code is executed. For example, when the program is loaded and the operating system passes control to the process, this is likely to be to the runtime system code in the first instance. When the runtime system has initialized its data structures, etc., it will pass control to the user code. When the user code runs, it calls into the runtime system for service.

We now examine the language-level process state in some detail. It is assumed that the reader is familiar with a high-level sequential language such as Pascal, Modula-3 or Java and has already encountered the basic ideas of language implementation, such as the allocation of storage for variables on a runtime stack. This section revises these ideas and highlights the essentials of the state associated with a process in a language system.

4.13.1 Activation records and the runtime stack

Activation records were originally defined for procedural languages, as described below. The same mechanisms are used in the runtime support for object-oriented languages. 'Procedure call' and 'method invocation' are interchangeable in this section. The main point is to understand the need for a runtime stack.

The programs or modules (or objects) defined in Section 2.1 have a finer-grained structure which may be defined in terms of procedures (or methods). When a procedure is called at runtime it must be allocated storage space for local variables, etc. One function of the language runtime system is to acquire storage space from the operating system (if a data segment needs to grow in size) and to allocate this space as required by the running program.

Programming languages vary over where variable declarations can be made and the degree of nesting of declarations that is allowed. We shall assume for simplicity that storage space is associated with modules and procedures and that procedure declarations are not nested. Chapter 7 of Aho *et al.* (1986) gives a comprehensive treatment of this topic.

At compile time the variables declared in each module or procedure are noted and an **activation record** is created for each procedure which defines the data space that will be needed when the procedure is called. When the module is entered, by procedure call at runtime, a stack frame containing control information and storage space for the variables is set up from the associated activation record. For any procedure activation, storage must be available as follows: for the call parameters before the call; for the return address at call time; and, during the procedure execution, for local variables, any further procedure call parameters and the return parameters for this activation.

At runtime, some specific sequence of module entries and procedure calls is followed and the stack structure reflects this dynamic sequence, as shown in Figure 4.20. The variables become accessible (addressable) by the process when the stack frame containing them is set up.

When the process exits from the procedure by executing a **return** instruction the stack frame associated with that procedure is removed from the stack. The frame pointer is reset to the stack frame of the calling procedure. The calling procedure may pick up return parameters from the stack. Note that all the state associated with the procedure activation is lost on exit from it; indeed, the space on the stack will be reused if the process calls another procedure from its current context.

4.13.2 The heap and garbage collection

The classes described in Section 2.1 maintain the state of their data objects independently of any of the operations being called. A stack structure is therefore not appropriate for the storage of such objects, since stack storage disappears on procedure exit. A data structure called a **heap** is used for the storage of such long-lived objects. A client may create a new object of the type and will receive a reference to the object for use as a parameter for subsequent calls. Object references may be placed on the stack as input and output parameters in the usual way.

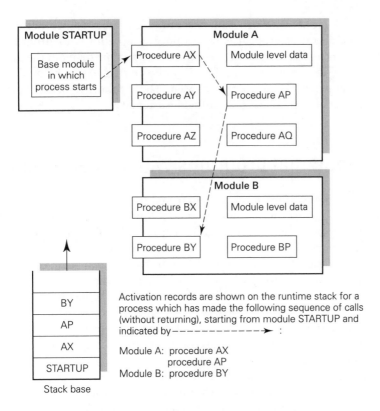

BY

AP

AX

STARTUP

Stack base

Activation records are shown on the runtime stack for a
process which has made the following sequence of calls
(without returning), starting from module STARTUP and
indicated by – – – – – – – – – – – → :

Module A: procedure AX
             procedure AP
Module B: procedure BY

Figure 4.20
Modules, procedures
and the runtime
stack.

It may also be convenient to use a heap for the storage of large objects or
where it is impossible to determine the size of an object at compile time; that
is, if the language allows data structures to be created dynamically and their
size may depend on some runtime calculation or input data. In these cases a
reference to an object may be put on the stack in place of the object itself. The
language CLU took this approach to an extreme in that all data was stored in
the heap and the stack contained only references; the language was said to have
pointer semantics. Java has followed this approach.

Whenever storage space is allocated from the heap there is a problem over
reclaiming it when it has fallen out of use. In some languages it is the responsibility
of the programmer to deallocate unwanted storage. The problem here is that
programmers make errors and may forget to deallocate storage. Storage allocation and deallocation is one of the most common sources of programming errors.
Continuously running programs (that is, systems of some sort) are particularly
susceptible to this form of error, which is called a **storage leak** and is a common
cause of system crashes.

Another example is that storage may be deallocated when there are still references to it. Any use of such a reference is an error.

The alternative policy is that the language system automatically reclaims
storage space by detecting when variables can no longer be reached. This is
called **garbage collection**. It may be carried out synchronously, in which case
execution halts until garbage collection completes, or asynchronously (also called

on-the-fly) in parallel with program execution. There are heated debates in the systems area about whether it is worth putting up with your program going away to (synchronous) garbage-collect from time to time to avoid the possibility of a crash due to a storage leak. This is a choice that has to be made when a system implementation language is chosen. The ideal of efficient, transparent, asynchronous garbage collection is difficult to achieve.

4.14 Sequential programs with system calls

We have seen how a single process, supported by the operating system, is used to execute a single user-level application. This model is assumed in the discussion on language systems presented in Section 4.13. Each user-level process is typically independent of all others and needs only interact with the operating system (by means of system calls). Section 4.4 showed how the operating system allows a process to synchronize with the hardware by means of a WAIT primitive and event signalling. This interaction with the hardware is typically done by an operating system process (that is, a process executing operating system code) acting in response to a request by a user process. In a concurrent system it may also be necessary for user-level processes to synchronize and share information with each other.

In Chapter 1 a range of concurrent systems was described, and an aim of the book is to show how to write software to implement them. For some applications it may be appropriate to use a sequential programming language. Each unit of the concurrent system may be a single sequential process and the operating system may provide **system calls to allow interaction with other processes** in addition to the system calls for requesting operating system service.

The characteristics of the systems for which this approach is appropriate are that the units to be run concurrently are relatively large; the concurrency is **coarse grained** rather than **fine grained**. Also, interactions are likely to be relatively infrequent: perhaps an occasional synchronization rather than frequent cooperation involving extensive use of common information. That is, the processes are likely to be **loosely coupled** rather than **tightly coupled**.

A problem with the approach is portability of the concurrent system. The processes have made use of an operating system interface (a number of system calls) that has been provided to allow interactions between processes. If the system is to be able to run on any other operating system it is necessary for the same interface to be present. Syntactic differences can be allowed for when the code is ported, but semantic differences between operating systems are likely to occur in this area.

We shall revisit this approach after looking at the evolution of concurrent programming languages. Many concurrent systems are built from sequential languages such as C and C++ that have been extended to support concurrency. A standard library package such as **pthreads** provides the extensions. Details are given in Part II; in this chapter we focus on how more than one **thread of control** might be supported in a concurrent program.

4.15 Evolution of concurrency in programming languages

We now explore the support for concurrency that might be provided by a **concurrent programming language**. We take the extreme position that an entire concurrent system is to be written as a single concurrent program. For generality, we take the model that the concurrent system to be programmed is to run above a minimal operating system and explore the resulting requirements on the runtime system and the operating system for different types of application. In practice, some of the examples below are likely to be implemented as special-purpose systems with integrated operating system functions.

4.15.1 Examples

We consider some examples (A–D below) of concurrent systems and attempt to see how they could be programmed as a single concurrent program running above a minimal operating system. An important conclusion that will be drawn is that it is not sufficient to write a concurrent system in a concurrent programming language without knowing how the operating system on which the program is to run supports concurrency.

A A file server is to run on a dedicated uniprocessor machine available to its clients across a network. It takes requests from clients and can be working on a number of requests at the same time. For example, it may need to wait for the disk to be read on behalf of one client, so starts work on behalf of another. Figure 4.21 shows the static modular structure. Refer to Figure 2.13, Chapter 5 and Section 8.1 for background and related information.

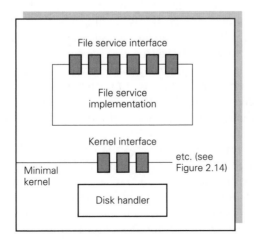

Figure 4.21
A: a dedicated file server.

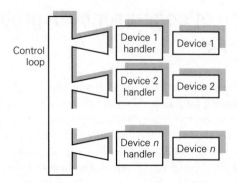

Figure 4.22
B: a device-handling
subsystem.

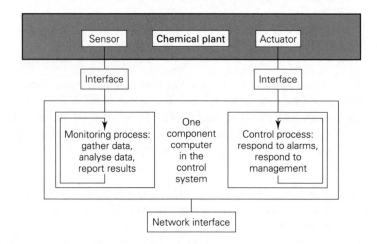

Figure 4.23
C: a chemical plant
controller.

B A simple operating system must control a number of devices, and a device-handling subsystem (Figure 4.22) is to be written in some appropriate programming language. A device handler may finish its immediate task and may need to wait for more data to be input or output. It must not lose track of what it was doing, however. If it was filling a buffer with characters coming in from the network, the buffer and associated counts and pointers should still be there when that device is serviced again.

C Figure 4.23 shows a computerized control system for a chemical plant which carries out periodic data gathering, analysis and feedback, as described in Section 1.1.1. The computer system should also respond to alarm signals which are infrequent and unpredictable, but of very high priority.

D A shared-memory multiprocessor is available and a parallel algorithm is proposed to search for a particular value in a large amount of stored data. Parallel activities should execute code to search a partition of the data, see Section 1.2.1. A management activity is needed to start off the correct number of parallel searches, allocate partitions of the data to them and be ready to receive the result and stop the searches when the result is found.

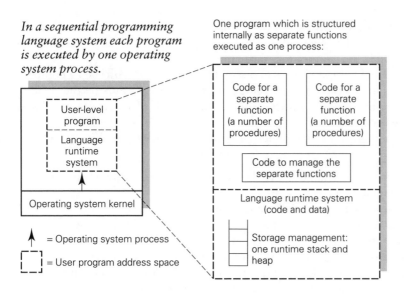

In a sequential programming language system each program is executed by one operating system process.

One program which is structured internally as separate functions executed as one process:

Code for a separate function (a number of procedures)

Code for a separate function (a number of procedures)

Code to manage the separate functions

Language runtime system (code and data)

Storage management: one runtime stack and heap

User-level program

Language runtime system

Operating system kernel

↑ = Operating system process

⌐ ¬
 ⌐ ⌐ = User program address space
L ⌐

Figure 4.24
Sequential language, separate activities in user-level code.

4.15.2 Concurrency from a sequential language

Although many procedures (methods) may be active at any time, because of nested or recursive invocations, there is only one thread of control, one stack and one heap when a program that was written in a sequential programming language is executed (Figure 4.24).

It is therefore difficult, and unnatural, to write independent subsystems (collections of related objects or modules) within a single program or to manage simultaneous activation of such code on behalf of a number of clients. There is no assistance for implementing a subsystem which may get to a point where it must wait for an event, remember where it got to and resume later (as discussed in Section 4.4). In particular, it is not possible to freeze the runtime stack at some point and go back to it later. There is a single runtime stack which is used on behalf of whatever computation succeeds the computation that can no longer run.

It would be extremely tedious to attempt to program A, B or C as a single sequential program and D would revert to a sequential algorithm running on a single processor. At any point where a wait was required, state would have to be saved by the programmer and resumed correctly at the appropriate time. There would be no chance of achieving a fast response to events (which C must have) as there is a single thread of control and the operating system sees only one process. If an interrupt occurs, the state of the process is saved, a wake-up waiting is recorded and the process is resumed. Whatever the desired effect of the interrupt might be within the concurrent program, there is no immediate transfer of control. The program could be written to test from time to time to see which events had happened, using a polling system with interrupts disabled. Alternatively, it could execute a system-provided WAIT (*set of events*) primitive and transfer control accordingly.

It would therefore be out of the question to use such a scheme for C (because timing requirements could not be guaranteed to be met) and highly undesirable for A and B, even if they are to run on a uniprocessor.

It would be impossible to exploit a multiprocessor with such a computational model. Since any internal structuring is transparent outside the program and there is only one thread of control it is only suitable for execution as one process on one processor.

In summary, if separate activities are implemented within a single program written in a sequential programming language:

- There is no assistance from the runtime system or the operating system for managing them as separate activities.
- If one activity must be suspended (because it cannot proceed until some event occurs) and another resumed, the user-level code must manage state saving and (later) restoring.
- There is no possibility of making an immediate response to an event by a transfer of control within the user-level code. After an interrupt, control returns to exactly where it was within the process.

4.15.3 Coroutines

Some programming languages, for example Modula-2 and BCPL, provide **coroutines** for expressing independent subprograms within a single program. The motivation for having a single program with internal coroutines is that data can be shared where appropriate but private data is also supported: each coroutine has its own stack. The language provides instructions to create and delete a coroutine and to allow a coroutine to suspend its execution temporarily but retain its state. Control may be passed explicitly from the suspending coroutine to another. Alternatively, control may be returned to the caller of a coroutine when it suspends. Figure 4.25 gives an overview of how coroutines are supported.

When a coroutine activation is created, the name of the associated code module, the start address and the space required for the stack are specified.

co-id = **coroutine-create**(*name, start address, stack size*);

A stack is initialized and a control block is set up for the coroutine activation which holds the stack pointer and the start address. At this stage, the coroutine is in the suspended state at the main procedure entry point. Later, when the coroutine is suspended, the control block will hold the address at which execution will resume. An identifier *co-id* is returned for use in subsequent references to this coroutine activation.

kill (*co-id*)

frees the space occupied by the activation. The coroutine scheme must specify who can execute **kill**. It is likely that it is illegal for a coroutine to terminate itself, and that one cannot kill a dynamic ancestor. We assume that an **active list** is maintained by the coroutine management system of the dynamic call sequence of coroutines, see below.

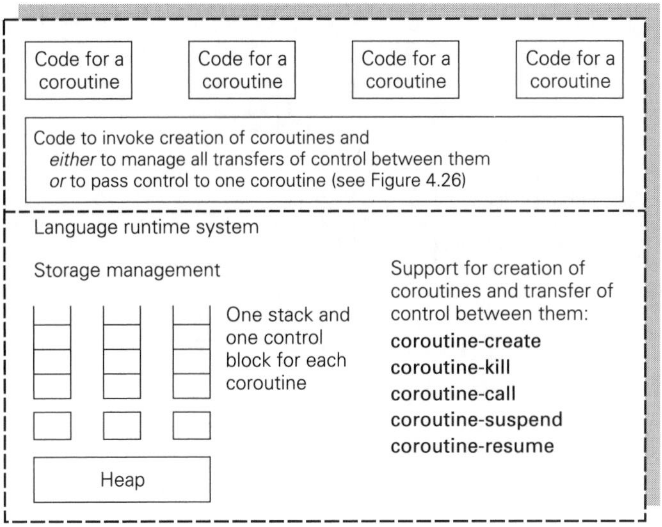

Figure 4.25
Language support for coroutines.

At any time at most one of the coroutine activations can be running. Two types of control flow can be used:

call (*co-id*)   //pass control to the activation *co-id* at the address specified in its control block. *co-id* is deemed to be a child of the caller and is added to the active list.

suspend   //pass control back to the parent of this child on the active list. Remove the executor of **suspend** from the active list.

resume (*co-id*)   // remove the executor of **resume** from the active list, pass control to the activation *co-id* and add it to the active list.

Figure 4.26 shows these alternatives. Note that to use **call** (*co-id*) repeatedly would cause the active list to grow indefinitely. We assume that **suspend** or **resume** is executed when a coroutine cannot proceed until some condition becomes true. Note that this supension is voluntary; that is, the coroutine executes until **suspend**, **resume** or another **call**.

Programming the examples using coroutines

We can program example A by creating a coroutine activation for each client of the file server. The same code may be executed for each client and they may share system data but each will have a separate stack for private data. The arrangement of a main loop which decides which coroutine to call, followed by **suspend** in the coroutine (Figure 4.26(a)), is appropriate for this application provided that immediate response to events is not required and that the operating system offers asynchronous (non-blocking) system calls.

Example B could be programmed using a coroutine scheme. However, there is only one thread of control through the program and the sequence of control is programmed explicitly; that is, the device handlers are called in an order that

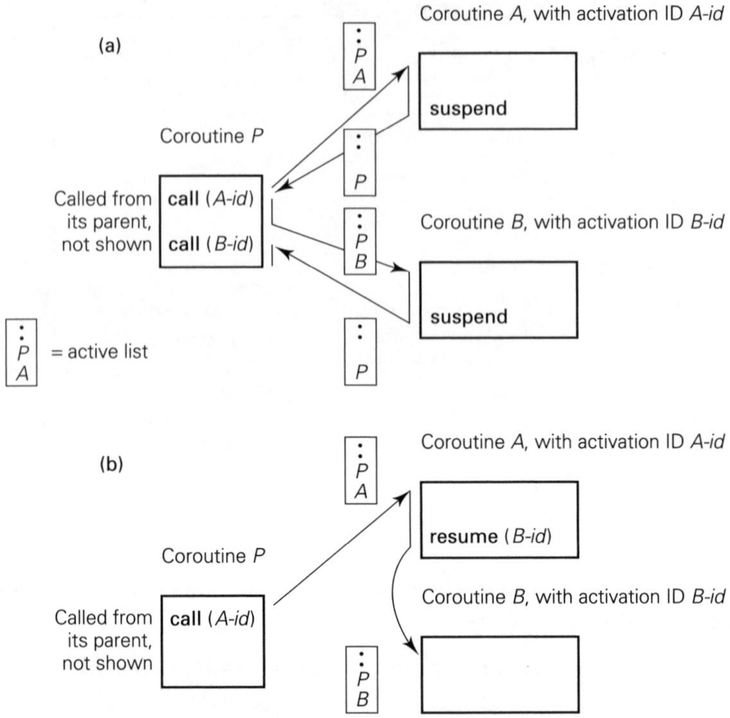

Figure 4.26
Alternatives for management of transfer of control in a coroutine system.
(a) A parent **calls** coroutines in turn, which pass control back to it by **suspend**.
(b) A parent **calls** a coroutine. This resumes a coroutine at the same level which **replaces** it on the active list.

does not depend on whether they have work they can do. Figure 4.27 shows a coroutine associated with each device and a polling loop in which the coroutines associated with the devices are called in turn and the devices are polled from within the coroutines.

Such a scheme could be used with device interrupts disabled. In this case, data could be lost if a device was not polled often enough and a second data item arrived before the first had been detected and transferred from the interface.

If interrupts are enabled, the interrupt service routine for a device could transfer a small amount of data onto the stack associated with the corresponding coroutine or could set a flag to indicate that a block of data had arrived in memory. A ring of buffers can be exploited by some interfaces (Section 3.7.3). After execution of the interrupt service routine, control returns to the interrupted instruction.

It can be arranged that the devices with the shortest critical times or the highest throughput are polled more frequently than other devices. It is impossible to respond instantly to any particular device.

It is impossible to program the monitoring and control activities of example C using coroutines. An interrupt service routine would be entered automatically (Section 3.2) but after that we would return to our predefined sequence of control, no matter how high the priority of the interrupt, since the operating system is aware only of one process and not of its internal coroutine structure. The chemical plant might blow up before we tested to see whether an alarm signal came in. The only way to take effective action on an alarm would be for the

Assuming that a coroutine activation has been created for each device, a polling loop could be implemented as follows:

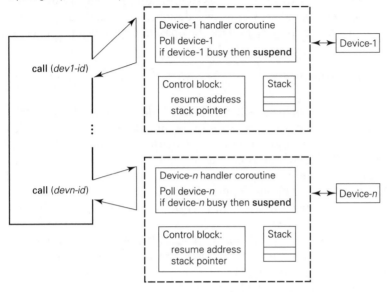

Figure 4.27
Coroutines for a device-handling subsystem.

interrupt service routine to do all the work. This might be appropriate in a crisis situation, but is unsuitable as a general approach for achieving timely response.

A multiprocessor cannot be exploited using coroutines since there is only a single thread of control. D cannot be programmed as a concurrent algorithm to exploit a multiprocessor.

In summary, if separate activities are implemented as coroutines within a single program:

- The runtime system supports creation of coroutine activations, shared and private data and transfer of control between activations.
- The scheduling of the coroutine activations must be implemented in the user-level code. Explicit transfer of control takes place at user level.
- There is a single thread of control. Scheduling of coroutines and execution of coroutines takes place within this single thread.
- There is no possibility of making an immediate response to an event by a transfer of control within the user level code. After an interrupt, control returns to exactly where it was within the process.
- Suspension is voluntary; control stays with a coroutine (except for interrupt and return) until it executes **suspend** or **resume**. It may therefore be assumed that any shared data structure that is accessed by a coroutine is left in a consistent state by it; it cannot be preempted part-way through updating a data structure.
- Transfer of control between coroutine activations involves very little overhead, typically of the order of ten machine instructions. The address for resumption is stored in the control block and the activation list is managed. There is no need to save data.

The Tripos operating system (Richards *et al.*, 1979) was written in BCPL and has a coroutine structure. A filing system (example A) and device handling (example B) were included. Tripos was designed as a single-user system and a single shared address space is used for the operating system and applications.

4.15.4 Processes

Some programming languages, such as Java, Modula-3, Mesa, Concurrent Pascal, Pascal Plus and occam, support processes within a program. Again, as described above for coroutines, a program may be written to contain independent sub-programs. Each subprogram is now executed by a separate application process, or **user thread**, as defined by the runtime system. Like coroutines, each user thread has its own stack, but unlike coroutines, control is managed by an outside agency, the runtime system, and is not programmed explicitly within the subprograms (Figure 4.28).

A user thread may need to wait for a shared application resource (such as a shared data structure) or for another user thread to complete a related activity. A wait operation is provided and will be implemented as a call into the runtime system. Another user thread will then be selected to run.

A major question in system design is the relationship between the user threads, created by the runtime system, and the processes or kernel threads scheduled by the operating system. It might be that the operating system can support only one process for one program. The processes within the program are then managed as user threads by the runtime system which effectively reimplements a scheduler.

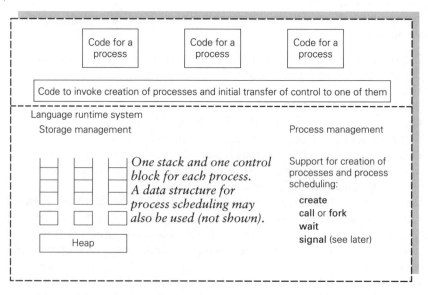

Figure 4.28
Runtime system support for processes.

Terminology: the processes defined in the concurrent programming language are implemented as user threads (termed 'processes' above) by the runtime system.

The runtime system is multiplexing one operating system process among user threads known only to itself.

The scheme is similar to a coroutine scheme, but the application programmer does not have to program the transfer of control between the user threads since their scheduling is provided by the runtime system.

A problem with this scheme is that if any one of the user threads makes a system call to the operating system to do I/O and becomes blocked then no other user thread in the program can run. Recall that an operating system might only provide system calls for I/O which are synchronous (Section 3.5.2). This is operating system dependent; for example, UNIX system calls are synchronous, IBM MVS or Windows NT calls may be synchronous or asynchronous. Even if the user threads were to use the runtime system as an intermediary for the purpose of making a system call, a blocking system call made by the manager will still block the whole process. This is a fundamental problem if the operating system does not support multi-threaded processes.

If the user threads defined in a program may be made known by the runtime system to the operating system they become separately schedulable, operating system processes or **kernel threads**. They are then scheduled by the operating system to run on processors and may run concurrently on the separate processors of a multiprocessor. In Figure 4.28 the runtime system's **create** routine would include an operating system call to create a thread (which would return a thread identifier), its **wait** routine would include a system call to block the thread and its **signal** routine would include a system call to unblock the thread. Each thread may then make operating system calls that block without affecting the others.

Programming the examples using processes

1 *Processes not known to the operating system (user threads only)*
   For A each client's request is handled by a user thread which executes the file service code. In B each device handler is a user thread, as shown in Figure 4.29. The way in which the threads might be used is as discussed above for coroutines.

   The scheme is inadequate for example C, where instant response to an alarm is essential, and for D which requires the user threads to be scheduled to run on separate processors of a multiprocessor. The only difference between coroutines and user threads is that scheduling is provided by the runtime system, whereas coroutine scheduling must be written by the application programmer.

2 *Processes known to the operating system (kernel threads)*
   Now let us suppose that the runtime system registers each user thread with the operating system as a kernel thread, and consider whether C and D can now be programmed. The parallel search activities of D can be programmed as threads which may run on separate processors. For C we have further requirements on the operating system. Suppose the data gathering process is running. An interrupt arrives to indicate that an alarm condition has developed; the interrupt service routine passes control to the

Assuming that a process activation has been created to handle each device, we have:

Process management module in the runtime system

Note that **wait** *passes control to this module and is not a system call to the operating system. Contrast with Figure 4.27.*

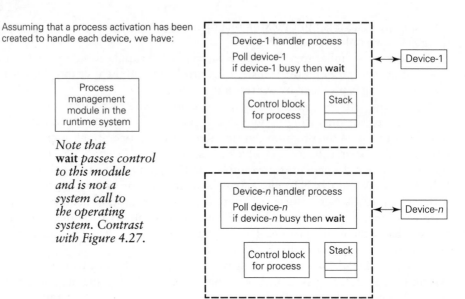

Figure 4.29
Language-level processes (user threads) for a device-handling subsystem.

thread manager to change the state of the control thread from waiting to runnable. It is a high-priority thread and therefore should run immediately, preempting the data gathering and analysis. The operating system must support this.

The scheduling policy of the operating system is therefore crucial. If the scheduling algorithm is **non-preemptive** a thread may continue to run until it blocks. Even if an interrupt occurs and the corresponding interrupt service routine is executed, control passes back to the interrupted thread. The scheduling algorithm is only invoked when the current thread blocks, in spite of the fact that a high-priority thread may have been made runnable. It might be the case that the requirements of A and B could be met with non-preemptive scheduling, but it is essential to have **preemptive scheduling** for C, as described in Section 4.3. Even this may not be sufficient for implementing real-time systems in general, see Section 4.8.

4.15.5 Issues arising

The issues that have been highlighted in the above discussions are:

1 *Blocking, synchronous calls to the operating system*
   If an operating system provides only synchronous system calls and a concurrent program runs as a single operating system process, then no component of the program can run while the operating system regards the process as blocked.
2 *Response to events, the need for preemption*
   A system which does not need rapid response to events may choose to use polling, with interrupts disabled, rather than being event driven.

Suppose we are running with interrupts enabled. Suppose a user thread (which has a kernel thread) invokes **WAIT (anEvent)** on the operating system and is blocked, waiting for the event to occur. When the event occurs, rapid response to it can only be achieved if the thread is scheduled immediately by the operating system, preempting whatever thread was running when the interrupt occurred.

It is important to have a thread dedicated to waiting for any high priority event such as an alarm. Suppose a user thread (which has a kernel thread) is running at user level, and an interrupt indicating an event of interest to it occurs. A record of the event is made (in the thread descriptor or an event data structure) and the thread resumes where it left off. A response to the event can only be made when a **WAIT (anEvent)** invocation is made on the operating system.

3 *Voluntary suspension and integrity of shared data structures*
If a coroutine or user thread can run until it suspends voluntarily (apart from interrupt and return) then it can be arranged that the shared data structures that it accesses are left in a consistent state before it suspends. A simple way of ensuring data integrity is therefore achieved at the expense of prompt response to events.

If a thread can be suspended **at any time** we can no longer make the assumption that data structures are in a **consistent state** on a switch. The concurrent program might run on a multiprocessor, in which case separate threads might access shared data structures at the same time. If the concurrent program runs on a uniprocessor the same problem arises if we have preemptive scheduling.

4 *Thread switching overhead*
There is more overhead on a switch, even between threads of the same process, if the operating system is involved. We saw that a switch between coroutines or between user threads without kernel threads involves very little overhead: a procedure call into the runtime system. A switch between user threads which have kernel threads involves an entry into the operating system, and the saving of state such as the contents of processor registers.

4.16 Specification, implementation and control of processes

4.16.1 Specification, creation and termination

In some languages a special kind of procedure call indicates that a new process should be created to execute the call and should run in parallel with the caller, sharing the address space of the caller. The modular software specification does not indicate which modules will be executed in parallel. Processes are created dynamically to execute the modules of the system. Mesa, Modula-3 and CCLU (see Chapter 15) follow this style.

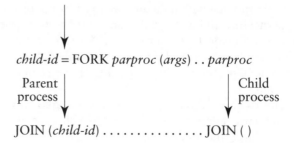

Figure 4.30
Process creation and
termination using
FORK and JOIN.

child-id = FORK *parproc* (*args*) . . *parproc*

Figure 4.30 shows an example of syntax that may be used to create a process to perform a specific function, after which it is deleted: FORK, for procedure call with process creation, and JOIN, for child process deletion and return. Note that the parent and child will need to synchronize at JOIN; that is, one will get there first and must be able to wait for the other. In some cases the child process will need to pass the results of its work to its parent and the parent may need to interact with the child. How this is done is the subject matter of Chapters 9–11. This use of FORK should not be confused with the UNIX **fork** system call which causes a new process, with its own separate address space, to be created by the operating system.

An alternative approach to achieve process creation is to allow a new kind of module to be declared as a process; that is, a process is defined as a syntactic unit in a program. For example, a device driver for devices of a particular type might be programmed in general and specific device drivers for specific devices created as process activations.

> **process** *iodriver* (*dev:device, buffer-size:integer*)
>   // a routine to transfer characters to the device from a buffer on output
>   // a routine to transfer characters from the device to a buffer on input
>   . . .
> **end** *iodriver*   // this specifies a general device driver

We now need to set up a separate process for each device. We assume in this example that this is done at system initialization, that the processes will run indefinitely and are not managed by their creator; a *process-id* is not returned. Process creation is achieved here by what looks like a normal procedure call to the process module. For example:

> *iodriver* (*dev1*, 1000)   // this creates a device handler process for *dev1*
> *iodriver* (*dev2*, 50)   // this creates a device handler process for *dev2*

We now have two device driver processes, each with its own stack and input parameters specifying the name of the device to be handled and a buffer count for data input or output. The processes are created and are candidates for scheduling. When control is passed to such a process it runs from its start address.

A more general scheme, allowing for process management through use of the process identifier, might be as follows:

p1-id = **process-create** (*iodriver*, *dev1*, 1000)   // to create a device handler
                                                          process for *dev1*
p2-id = **process-create** (*iodriver*, *dev2*, 50)   // to create a device handler
                                                          process for *dev2*

Subsequent calls may make use of the returned process id. For example:

kill (*p1-id*)
signal (*p2-id*)

Languages may allow **dynamic process creation** at runtime as in the examples above. The first approach allowed dynamic creation and removal of processes; the second showed specification of a process in a program with dynamic instantiations of it at runtime.

A language system may insist on knowing the number of processes that will run in a given program and may create them statically. occam is an example (Inmos, 1984).

A general classification of styles of concurrent programs is that modules may be passive and processes may call procedures to execute the module code, as in the first example above, or modules may be active and have permanent, internally bound processes, as in the second example above. We shall explore these alternative structures throughout Part II. Section 4.18 describes the approach taken in Java with examples.

4.16.2 Parental control of processes

A design issue is the degree of control or influence a creator (parent) process should have over a process it creates (child). Once a process is created it is likely to be independent of its parent for scheduling purposes and may be able to outlive its parent. If a *child-process-id* is returned when a process activation is created, this can be used to control the process.

If the system has the notion of process **priority** then it is necessary to indicate the priority of a process when it is created. Obviously, safeguards are needed if this is in the hands of normal users and the priority specified is likely to be relative to that of the creator and its other children. The implementor of a concurrent system will have a view of the relative priorities of its component processes.

We have seen in Section 4.16.1 that it might be appropriate for a process to **terminate** on completion of its work and for its parent to receive the results of the work. It might also be necessary or desirable in certain circumstances to **kill** a running process. A debugging process may detect that the system being debugged is acting erroneously and its execution should be terminated. A command interpreter process which has loaded a program and has created a process to execute it may detect, or be told by the operating system, that an error state has arisen in its child; or the human user that started a program execution may abort it. In example D above, a number of processes are searching for a single solution to a problem. As soon as one of them finds the solution all the others should be terminated. There is therefore a general need for external control of running processes, and a mechanism to achieve this should be provided.

Processes known to the operating system can be controlled. The interrupt mechanism starts the removal of control from a running process. For example, a break character typed by the user may be interpreted as a command to abort the current user program execution. The act of typing the character forces an interrupt service and the break character indicates that the process associated with that user should not be restarted from where it was interrupted but should be aborted. In the case of example D an inter-processor interrupt (see Section 3.4) is needed to achieve immediate termination of the searching processes once the result is found.

For application processes which are not known to the operating system (user threads which do not have kernel threads), external control of running processes is more difficult. Each process may need to be programmed to 'check in' with a manager periodically so that it can be stopped.

A universal requirement is the ability to **synchronize** with a created process. The process was created to do work in parallel with the creator. Mechanisms for finding out that the work has been done and for acquiring the results of it are needed. It is often necessary to combine the partial solutions to a problem that have been obtained by parallel processes, for example. This is part of a more general requirement discussed throughout Part II.

4.16.3 Exception handling in programming languages

User-level exception handling was introduced in Section 3.3.5. The idea was that error-handling routines which output error messages to the user or write them to a log should run in the context of the program causing the error rather than as part of the operating system. We saw that a compiler could pass not only the start address of a program to the operating system but also the address of an exception-handling routine. In Section 4.3.1 we saw that the process descriptor could contain such an address.

As well as error routines, typically provided as part of a library, the application may name exceptions and provide handlers for them. This is another means by which transfer of control from one part of a program to another can be achieved as a result of the occurrence of some event or condition. Some programming languages offer an extensive exception-handling facility. Examples are Java, CLU (Liskov *et al.*, 1981), and Modula-3. A simple example of the use of exceptions in Java is given in Section 4.18.

4.16.4 Storage allocation for language-level processes

Section 4.15.4 discussed language-level processes and Figure 4.28 gave a simple representation of a process management module within the language system and a stack associated with every process. We assume that the concurrent program runs in a single address space and that instead of a single 'runtime stack' we now have a number of stacks.

In a system with a storage allocation model, such as that shown in Figure 4.18, it is likely that the process stacks will be allocated in the stack segment and that all processes will share the heap segment. The convenience of an easily extensible single stack growing towards a heap, as used for a sequential program implementation, has been lost with this arrangement. An alternative is to use the heap for the process stacks. In every case a maximum stack size will need to be specified explicitly (or implicitly as a default value) on process creation. If this size is exceeded because of a greater depth of procedure call nesting than foreseen, the multiple stack data structure will have to be adjusted or a new, larger stack allocated for that process in the heap.

Language-level storage allocation schemes will not be studied in depth in this book and for more information the reader should consult, for example, Aho *et al.* (1986).

4.17 Thread package architectures

We have studied, in general terms, how processes and threads are supported by operating systems and language runtime systems. We now look at some specific thread packages. We have established that an operating system may support only one process per address space (Figure 4.17(b)) or it may support many (Figure 4.17(c)). In the latter case we have assumed implicitly that every user thread will be registered as a kernel thread. We now describe and evaluate various alternative approaches. The discussion is based on Pham and Garg (1996).

User threads without kernel threads (Figure 4.17(b))

Thread switching at user level is fast since it does not involve a call into the operating system. Since each application may run with its own copy of the runtime library it may choose the most suitable scheduling policy and is not constrained to use the single policy embedded within the operating system's scheduler. It is difficult to manage time slicing however. If preemptive scheduling is required, the thread library must register with the kernel that it wishes to receive timer signals. The mechanism is that which we have seen for exceptions and is often termed an **upcall**. When the timer interrupt occurs (interrupting some thread), control returns to a routine in the thread library which can then decide whether the thread is out of time.

A major problem that must be solved by the implementors of a user-level threads package is how to deal with blocking system calls; if any thread makes such a call the whole process is deemed by the operating system to be blocked. If the operating system provides non-blocking versions of the blocking system calls, the threads library may use these instead. Since all system calls are made via library routines, the safest approach is to rewrite the blocking system calls. A non-blocking call can be made from the thread library to effectively poll the resource. If the call returns successfully the result can be passed to the calling thread which may continue. If the call returns with a pending status the library may block the calling thread and schedule another one. When the non-blocking call completes, the calling thread may be made runnable again and the result made available to it in the usual way.

Another problem is that the libraries may have been written on the assumption that they are invoked serially by a single thread rather than in parallel by multiple threads. The problems we study in Part II may then occur – of uncontrolled access to shared data structures. We may have to enforce serial execution of sensitive routines.

Also, the operating system may return control to a per-process exception or upcall routine if an error has occurred; we would now like to have per-thread routines for this purpose. This can be solved, with difficulty, by keeping per-thread data on exception handling. The first level of exception handling is always in a general library routine. That routine then determines whether the exception relates to the current thread or some other.

Finally, multiple processors cannot be exploited since the operating system sees only one process.

Examples are DEC's CMA threads, OSF's Distributed Computing Environment (DCE) threads and Xerox PARC's Portable Common Runtime (PCR) system (Weiser *et al.*, 1989).

Kernel threads (Figure 4.17(c))

The problems discussed above do not arise if the user threads are registered with the operating system as kernel threads. A kernel thread is created for each user thread and all scheduling is carried out by the kernel, according to only one scheduling policy. The blocking and unblocking of threads is carried out by the kernel and occurs when the thread waits for I/O, when the event subsequently occurs and makes the thread runnable again, and in response to block and unblock calls from the thread library when thread state changes for application-level reasons.

The main disadvantage of kernel threads is the context switching overhead: all thread switching is carried out via the kernel and typically takes about ten times as long as user-level thread switching. It is likely that the libraries for such operating systems will have been made re-entrant, thus avoiding the problems described above; an exception is the X Windows system. More subtle problems relate to the management of the number of kernel threads each address space may use. So far, we have assumed that kernel threads may be created without limit.

Examples of systems which support kernel threads are Windows NT, MACH, Chorus and OS/2.

User threads multiplexed on kernel threads (Figure 4.31)

It seems like a good idea to combine the two approaches described above to give flexibility and maximum potential performance to the application writer. Figure 4.31 illustrates the approach:

- user threads u_1 and u_2 may run in kernel thread k_1;
- user thread u_3 maps directly onto kernel thread k_2;
- user threads u_4 to u_7 may run in either of kernel threads k_3 or k_4.

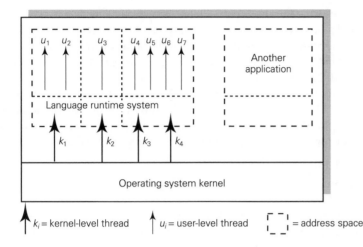

k_i = kernel-level thread u_i = user-level thread   = address space

Figure 4.31
Multiplexing user
threads on kernel
threads.

When making the static assignment of user threads to kernel threads, the application writer must take into account how many processors are available, which threads should run in parallel on separate processors, which threads will potentially make blocking calls and when the efficiency of having only user threads should be exploited. When a kernel thread blocks, none of its user threads can run; user threads that should run on separate CPUs must have different kernel threads and so on.

SunOS provides this scheme, calling kernel threads 'lightweight processes' (LWPs) and user threads just 'threads'.

Scheduler activations

Ideally the application writer should be able to use threads without having to be aware of the distinction between user and kernel threads. This can be achieved if the operating system is designed to interact with user thread libraries to a greater extent than we have seen. So far we have assumed that **create**, **kill**, **block** and **unblock** comprise the operating system's thread interface operations. If, in addition, the operating system notifies the thread library of events relating to its kernel threads then the thread library can deliver a uniform thread abstraction to the application programmer and make correct and efficient use of kernel threads. Moreover, the kernel may ensure that a given number of kernel threads per application are runnable at all times. Research to design and evaluate various schemes can be found in (Anderson *et al.*, 1992; Li, 1993; Barton-Davies *et al.*, 1993). The first of these is as follows:

- The kernel provides a virtual multiprocessor abstraction to each thread library; the number of virtual processors may be changed by the kernel as the application runs.
- The thread library has complete control over which of its threads are running on the virtual processors, termed 'scheduler activations'.

- The kernel informs the thread library of every event affecting it: when a thread blocks or wakes up in the kernel; when the number of scheduler activations allocated to it changes; when a thread is preempted in the kernel. Note that such events are notified at exactly those points where a scheduling decision would normally be taken by the kernel.
- The thread library informs the kernel when it wants more or needs fewer processors. It also informs the kernel of the subset of thread events that might affect processor allocation decisions. The vast majority of user-thread events are not relevant to kernel scheduling (see Part II for more detail).

A scheduler activation has three roles:

- It serves as an execution context for running user threads (exactly as a kernel thread does).
- It notifies the thread library of a kernel event.
- It provides space in the kernel for saving the processor context of the activation's current user thread (when the thread blocks or is preempted).

The crucial difference between scheduler activations and kernel threads is that once an activation's user thread is stopped by the kernel, the thread is never resumed directly by the kernel. Instead, a new scheduler activation is created to notify the thread library that the thread has been stopped. The thread management system then copies the state of the thread from the old activation, tells the kernel that the old activation can be reused and then decides which user thread to run on the processor. By this means, the kernel is able to maintain the invariant that there are always exactly as many running scheduler activations (contexts for running user threads) as there are virtual processors assigned to the address space.

Nemesis

The Nemesis research operating system at the University of Cambridge, UK (Roscoe, 1995; Leslie *et al.*, 1996) uses scheduler activations combined with a priority ordering based on 'earliest deadline first' scheduling to meet the requirement of applications which may include continuous media. The system's structure comprises a minimal microkernel, and the majority of the operating system runs in user space: is 'vertically partitioned'. Each partition is called a scheduling domain and may schedule its internal threads as appropriate. A scheduling domain requests resources as a tuple (p, q) where p is the period and q the resource requirement within p, e.g. (30 ms, 200 µs). The domain scheduler then orders the domains for execution based on an ordering derived from EDF scheduling; other policies are being investigated.

4.18 Java threads and exceptions

In Java, threads are created from a class which either inherits from the class **Thread** or implements the interface **Runnable**. In either case we specify the activity to be carried out by providing a **run** method. In the case of a thread inheriting

```
public class PrintThread1 extends Thread {
    String message;
    public PrintThread1 (String m) {
        message = m;
    }
    public void run () {
        for (int i = 0; i < 100; i++) {
            try {
                this.sleep (100);
            }
            catch (InterruptedException e) {
                System.out.println ("Thread Interrupted in sleep");
            }
            System.out.println (message);
        }
    }
    public static void main (String args[ ]){
        Thread a = new PrintThread1 ("a");
        Thread b = new PrintThread1 ("b");
        a.start ();
        b.start ();
        try {
            a.join ();
        }
        catch (InterruptedException e) {
            System.out.println ("Main method Interrupted whilst joining a");
        }
        try {
            b.join ();
        }
        catch (InterruptedException e) {
            System.out.println ("Main method Interrupted whilst joining b");
        }
        System.out.println ("c");
    }
}
```

Figure 4.32
Specializing Thread.

from the **Thread** class, the **run** method overrides the **run** method of **Thread**, which otherwise has an empty method body. Producing threads via the mechanism of implementing the interface **Runnable** allows us to produce a class which can be used to create threads whilst still being able to inherit from some class other than **Thread**. Java only has single inheritance.

The program in Figure 4.32 explicitly creates two threads, using a thread that specializes **Thread**. The program in Figure 4.33 shows an alternative approach based on extending the **Runnable** interface. In both cases two thread objects are created (in the **main** method), referenced by variables **a** and **b**. The threads are made active by applying the method **start**, this causes the **run** method to execute as a separate thread. These new threads are in addition to a thread that always exists in Java, whose task is to execute the main method.

The behaviour of Java threads varies according to the operating system of the host platform. In particular, on some systems Java threads are scheduled preemptively and on other systems they are non-preemptive.

It is often useful to be able to make a thread delay execution for a period of time. This might be useful for example where a thread controls some animation

```
public class PrintThread2 implements Runnable {
    String message;
    public PrintThread2 (String m) {
        message = m;
    }
    public void run () {
        for (int i = 0; i < 100; i++) {
            try {
                Thread.sleep (100);
            }
            catch (InterruptedException e) {
                System.out.println ("Thread Interrupted in sleep");
            }
            System.out.println (message);
        }
    }
    public static void main (String args[ ]) throws InterruptedException {
        Thread a = new Thread (new PrintThread2("a"));
        Thread b = new Thread (new PrintThread2("b"));
        a.start ();
        b.start ();
        a.join ();
        b.join ();
        System.out.println ("c");
    }
}
```

Figure 4.33
Implementing the
Runnable interface.

in order to ensure that the relevant movements don't happen too quickly. The Java thread class has two **sleep** methods which allow for a delay, the sleep period can be specified in milliseconds or in milliseconds and nanoseconds. Examples of the **sleep** method are illustrated in Figures 4.32 and 4.33. Whilst in Figure 4.33 our **PrintThread2** class does not inherit the method **sleep** from **Thread,** we are still able to make use of the **sleep** method by invoking it as **Thread.sleep ().**

The **sleep** method invocations in Figures 4.32 and 4.33 also illustrate Java's exception-handling mechanism. In Java there are classes to represent exceptions. Exceptions can be dealt with as in Figure 4.32 by using the **try{...} catch () {...}** construct that Java provides. In Figure 4.32, if an exception belonging to class **InterruptedException** occurs whilst the thread is sleeping, the **catch** clause will be executed. Alternatively we can specify that a method should terminate when particular exceptions occur, deferring responsibility to the invoking method. The syntax for this is illustrated in Figure 4.33, where the method **main** is declared as throwing an **InterruptedException.** Java provides classes defining a range of exceptions, and programmers are free to extend the existing hierarchy of these.

A thread can wait for the completion of some thread **t** by applying the **join** method to **t,** i.e. **t.join().** The example uses the **join** method to make the main thread delay its execution until firstly thread **a** terminates and then thread **b** terminates. The **join** method invocation once again illustrates Java's exception-handling mechanism, the details being similar to those described above.

Java threads have priorities associated with them. Threads of higher priority are given preferential treatment over threads of lower priority. A thread's priority can be set using the thread method **setPriority** and determined by using the thread method **getPriority**. The Java threads class provides a number of other methods, some of which we will encounter in later chapters.

4.19 Summary

In Chapter 1 we established the requirements for implementing concurrent systems:

1 Support for separate activities.
2 Support for the management of separate activities.
3 Support for related activities to work together.
4 The ability to meet timing requirements.
5 Support for composite tasks.

At this stage the reader should understand:

- the concept of process;
- how the process abstraction is supported by language runtime systems and operating systems;
- the relationship between these process implementations and the implications of this relationship.

The requirement to support separate activities (1) has therefore been explored in detail. The reader should now be able to think of a software implementation of a concurrent system as a set of concurrent processes.

The requirement for the management of separate activities (2) has been discussed. We have seen how a process activation may be created from a process specification. We have discussed the need for process termination.

The support for the related activities to work together in a concurrent system (3) has been motivated, but has yet to be addressed systematically. We have seen that a coroutine or process scheme where only user threads are implemented may allow simplifying assumptions to be made about the consistency of shared data structures on a coroutine or process switch. This also holds for kernel threads when they are scheduled non-preemptively, but only if the system runs on a uniprocessor. We discuss the problem in general in Part II.

The ability of a concurrent system to meet timing requirements (4) must obviously depend on hardware characteristics. It has been shown that this ability also depends on the support for concurrency provided by the operating system. If this basic level of support is not given, a real-time system cannot be programmed. It is therefore necessary to know whether the operating system schedules its processes preemptively. If not, critical timing requirements cannot be guaranteed to be met. Preemptive scheduling is a necessary condition for timing guarantees to be met, but is by no means sufficient. It is also necessary to know a bound on the time that can be spent executing the operating system. Scheduling algorithms were discussed, both for general-purpose and for real-time systems.

We have explored the options for implementing concurrent systems. Either components are written in sequential programming languages and system calls are provided to support their interaction or a concurrent programming language is used.

In the former case there is a potential portability problem. Concurrent systems developed in this way can only run on operating systems which have compatible system calls for this purpose. Standard library packages have been developed to provide a convenient interface for some programming languages on some operating systems.

In the latter case we have examined the possible relationship between the processes (or coroutines) specified in a concurrent programming language and the processes supported by the operating system. This was shown to be operating system dependent.

The overhead involved in switching between the separate activities of a concurrent system should be taken into account. This is lowest for coroutines and language-only processes, highest for operating system (heavyweight) processes (when each has a separate address space), and intermediate for switching between kernel threads of the same process.

An important issue emerges from the discussion in this chapter. Even if a concurrent system is to be written in a high-level language it is necessary to have knowledge of:

- the relationship between the language runtime system and the operating system;
- details of the operating system support for processes;
- some aspects of the hardware on which the system will run; for example, is it a uniprocessor or a multiprocessor?

Study questions

S 4.1

(a) Give two methods of allocating processes.
(b) What is the purpose of a process management module?

S 4.2

(a) What is a virtual processor?
(b) Why must a process be able to execute a **WAIT (anEvent)** operation?
(c) Distinguish between the process states called *blocked*, *runnable* and *running*.
(d) What is meant by non-preemptive scheduling? Under what circumstances is it useless?

S 4.3

(a) Under what circumstances will a process relinquish a processor?
(b) What is a process descriptor and why is it needed?
(c) What is a context switch?

S 4.4

(a) What actions are taken by the method that implements the **WAIT (anEvent)** operation on process descriptors?
(b) What causes the **SIGNAL ()** operation to be invoked?
(c) What actions are taken by the routine that implements the **SIGNAL ()** operation on events?
(d) Why is a record of events kept in a process's descriptor?
(e) Under what conditions does a race condition occur?
(f) What is an atomic operation? Why must **WAIT ()** and **SIGNAL ()** on events be implemented as atomic operations?

S 4.5

Distinguish between the process level and the process implementation level for the support of concurrent processes.

S 4.6

(a) Distinguish between a lightweight and a heavyweight process.
(b) What is a multi-threaded operating system?

S 4.7

(a) Describe in your own words what is being represented in the three figures shown in Figure 4.17.
(b) Use Figure 4.17 to illustrate what is meant by the statement that processes are the unit of resource allocation.
(c) Why is it necessary to know whether or not language-level processes are known to the operating system?

S 4.8

(a) What three segments are usually found in the memory allocated to a process?
(b) Distinguish between an activation record and a stack frame. What is contained in a stack frame? How long does a stack frame last?

S 4.9

(a) What is a synchronous system call?
(b) What problem is caused if an operating system provides only synchronous system calls, and a concurrent program runs as a single operating system process?
(c) Why must an operating system that supports interrupts allow the preemption of processes?
(d) What problem arises if a process is forcibly suspended, i.e. not voluntarily?

Exercises

4.1 Discuss how you would wish to allocate processes in the systems that were described in the Introduction, for example:
(a) an industrial process control system
(b) a multiaccess (time-sharing) computer
(c) a powerful personal workstation
(d) a transaction processing system
(e) a parallel searching algorithm to run on a shared-memory multiprocessor
(f) a multiphase compiler to run on a shared-memory multiprocessor.

4.2 How would you simulate one processor per process in a uniprocessor and a shared-memory multiprocessor?

4.3 List everything that might be considered part of the state of a process. Which of these items must always be in main memory and which could be swapped out to backing store when the process was not running?

4.4 (a) Design a method of implementing synchronization between a peripheral and a single process which is dedicated to managing it.
(b) Design a method of implementing synchronization between a peripheral and a process which is currently waiting for it to deliver data but is not dedicated to this task.
(c) Design a method of implementing synchronization between any hardware device and one or more processes.

4.5 Design a data structure which implements the representation of the processes known to an operating system. You should consider whether your system has a significant number of dedicated system processes and, if so, whether they will be held separately from user processes. What operations would you expect to provide at the interface of a process management module?

4.6 (a) When does a general schedule need to be carried out in a multi-access system?
(b) How can a process in a multi-access system be scheduled differently when it is in a compute-bound phase from when it is doing input or output?
(c) How many processes would you expect to be active in a single-user workstation, a dedicated gateway computer and a dedicated file server?
(d) How would you expect processes to be scheduled in a multimedia workstation (see Section 1.1)?

4.7 How does scheduling for real-time systems differ from scheduling for multi-access systems?

4.8 What approaches can be taken to scheduling for shared-memory multiprocessor systems?

4.9 Recall the layered communications software described in Chapter 3. Consider the situation when several user processes have made requests for network input or output.
(a) How might the layers be executed by processes?
(b) How might synchronization between user-level processes and the arrival or transmission of data at the network be arranged?
(c) Where might network buffers be located with respect to the ISO layers?
(d) Why would it be a bad idea to have a process execute each of the ISO layers?

4.10 For a given modular operating system structure, what is the minimum set of dedicated, resident system processes that can be used? How does the rest of the operating system get executed in this case?

How would you design to maximize the number of dedicated system processes?

For both of the approaches indicated above, discuss where a separate address space could be used for protection purposes. Assume that the system provides a mechanism for a process to make requests of the operating system. We have studied one such mechanism in Section 3.3.2. We shall expand on this in Part II.

4.11 In what circumstances might it be advantageous to use several threads of control within a single process?

4.12 Section 4.9 introduced a process management module and pointed out that, as this module implements the process abstraction, it cannot itself be implemented in terms of processes.

Within an operating system, the interface operations of the process management module may be called as simple procedures. In Section 4.4, for example, we saw the WAIT () operation on events invoking the BLOCK () operation on processes.

In Section 4.10 it was mentioned that an operating system might be executed by a set of system processes taking users' requests or might instead be executed 'in-process'. For both of these models of execution, discuss how the invocation of process management can be incorporated into the model. (The problem to address is, if you are executing the operating system yourself, what happens when you block yourself?)

4.13 What aspects of the state of a process are of concern to an operating system and a language system?

4.14 Discuss how a sequential programming language can be used to implement a concurrent system. What assistance would you expect from a library package and operating system? What are the advantages and disadvantages of using a concurrent programming language?

4.15 What is the essential difference between coroutines and processes? If a concurrent program is to run on a uniprocessor machine, what advantages are there in using a language which supports processes? When might coroutines offer an advantage?

4.16 What are the potential problems of using a language-level 'threads package' when the operating system sees only one process? Why might such a scheme be inappropriate for a shared-memory multiprocessor?

4.17 What are essential requirements for real-time response to be achieved?

4.18 (a) What is meant by a static specification of processes in a programming language?
  (b) How would you expect a static approach to be reflected in the syntax of a language?
  (c) How can dynamic process creation and deletion be supported in a concurrent programming language?
  (d) How might a parent process determine properties of a child process it creates, such as its name or identifier?
  (e) How might a parent process be given control over a child process once it has been created?

4.19 You are working in an environment where application developers need to be able to use different scheduling algorithms. Which thread architecture would be most suitable and why?

4.20 Are there any disadvantages arising from using only kernel threads in an application?

4.21 Discuss the pros and cons of multiplexed threads compared with scheduler activations.

4.22 Discuss why soft real-time requirements, such as those that involve dynamically arriving continuous media, might best be met with a combination of user-level and kernel-level threads.

Operating system functions: Memory management and file management

In this chapter we give an overview of the operating system functions, memory management and file management. It is assumed that the reader has some knowledge of these topics from experience and prior study. Here, we review the aspects that are essential for an understanding of concurrent and distributed systems programming.

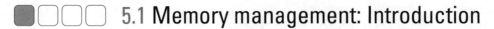

5.1 Memory management: Introduction

Instructions must be in main memory in order to be fetched and executed by a processor. Any data operand referenced by an instruction must be in main memory for the instructions to execute successfully. An operating system function is to allocate memory to processes. As explained in Section 2.4, a command interpreter will take a command to run a program, request memory from the operating system, load files into the memory and cause a process to be created to execute the program. When a process runs, its data structures may need to grow beyond the initial memory allocation and it must be possible for more memory to be requested from the operating system. The operating system must keep track of free physical memory and must record the allocations it has made to each process.

5.2 The memory hierarchy

Figure 5.1 shows a typical computer system's memory hierarchy. There is a trade-off involved in using these storage devices (CPU registers, cache, main memory and disks) which involves size, speed and cost. In Figure 5.1, the closer the storage is to the CPU the more expensive, and therefore smaller, it is. The CPU registers are the fastest and most expensive, therefore smallest store. The instructions and data of an executing program must be in main memory. A large proportion of the machine's instructions transfer data between main memory and CPU registers, or access data in CPU registers. Compiler writers must organize their use to optimize program execution time.

The design of the processor and the hardware-controlled cache are not our concern here but as system designers we need a broad view of current and projected sizes and speeds. An excellent summary is given in Hennessy and Patterson (1996). The **cache** is small and fast compared with main memory and acts as a buffer between the CPU and the memory. It contains a copy of the most recently used memory locations: address and contents are recorded there. Every address reference goes first to the cache. If the desired address is not present we have a **cache miss**. The contents are fetched from main memory into the CPU register indicated in the instruction being executed and a copy is retained in the cache. It is likely that the same location will be used again soon, and, if so, the address will be found in the cache, in which case we have a **cache hit**. If a write occurs, the hardware not only writes to the cache but also generates a **write-through** to main memory.

Figure 5.1
The memory
hierarchy.

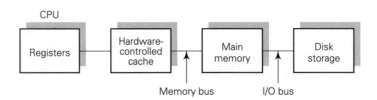

In a uniprocessor operating system the cache can be considered as transparent. The designer of an operating system for a shared-memory multiprocessor needs to know how the processors' caches operate. It might be that more than one processor has the same writeable data value cached, for example. This raises a concurrency control issue, but in hardware design, and we do not consider it further here.

Our expectations of what 'a reasonable amount of main memory' is have changed over the years and will continue to do so, roughly: 1970, 64 kbytes; 1980, 1 Mbyte; 1990, 16 Mbytes; 2000, 512 Mbytes. From a system designer's point of view an important property of main memory is that it is in general volatile; that is, if there is a power failure the information stored there is lost. This is a daunting prospect if one has 512 Mbytes of it! Non-volatile memory is available, but is more expensive than conventional volatile memory. Disk storage, on the other hand, is non-volatile and much system design effort is concerned with writing information safely out to disk to guard against loss of main memory on a crash. We shall return to this topic in Chapter 14, and throughout Part III.

Main memory is used for the code and data of currently executing programs and the system software needed to support them. Disk storage is used for filing systems and as an extension to (overflow for) main memory. It may be that only a small part of a program's total code and data is in use over a small timescale. That part must be in main memory but the currently unused parts may be on disk – in 'swap space'. The operating system must manage the transfers between main memory and disk of program code and data as it falls into and out of use.

5.3 The address space of a process

We shall often use the concept of the address space of a process (the range of addresses available to it). The concept is important for naming (addressing), protection and system structure and we need to examine it in some detail. Some machine language instructions contain addresses, for example:

LOAD a specified processor register with the contents of an address;
STORE the contents of a processor register in an address;
CALL a procedure at some address;
JUMP or BRANCH to an address.

The instructions have an address field which contains a representation of a memory address. The number of bits allocated to an address is an architectural decision. Many early computers' instruction sets had only 16-bit address fields, which allowed only 64 kbytes of memory to be addressed directly. A typical figure is now 32 bits which allows 4 gigabytes (Gbytes) to be addressed. We say that such an architecture gives a **virtual address space** of 4 Gbytes. The amount of physical memory configured into a given computer system is likely to be smaller than this.

The important concept is the virtual address space of a process. An address can be anywhere within the virtual address space, but must be **bound** to a physical memory address before the instruction execution can be carried out.

Object code addresses are produced by system software: a compiler and/or an assembler. Any realistic program should be developed as separate modules which are then linked and loaded into memory. When the compiler or assembler is translating a single module, it does not know (except in very simple systems) where the module will be loaded in the physical memory of the computer. Translators must therefore adopt a convention about the addresses to use in the code they output. Let us assume that translators output code for each module as though it would start from address zero in memory. A linker can take a sequence of such modules and create a single load module by adjusting the (relative) addresses in all but the first module. The addresses in this composite load module are still relative to its start. The basic principle is illustrated well by this simple example, using address zero as the start of a single program module. However, a compiler has the whole virtual address space at its disposal and modern compilers have more elaborate conventions for use of the virtual address space.

We now consider what happens when such a module comes to be loaded into physical main memory. The operating system is responsible for managing memory and we assume that it will give the loader a base address from which to load the module. The important question is whether the loader should adjust all the relative addresses in the module, converting them to absolute physical addresses, before loading it. This is called **static relocation** or **static binding**. If this was done, then once a program was loaded into memory the addresses in it would be fixed and the code or data at these addresses could not be moved in memory. The only flexibility available to an operating system would be to move the program out to backing store and then later move it back into main memory into exactly the same place. Some early IBM systems divided memory into partitions, and programs were allocated to run in a given partition. It would be possible to move a module to a different place in main memory only if the relocation information (the location of relative addresses within the module) was retained with the module and the translation from relative to absolute addresses was carried out by software every time the module was moved.

In a system which is dedicated to a single task, such as monitoring an industrial process or providing a service, it might be the case that once a program is loaded in memory it runs there indefinitely. In this case the static binding of addresses (at load time) just described might be appropriate. All the processes executing in such a system would share the same **physical address space**. They are all using the absolute machine addresses of the available physical memory. They would not be protected from each other, should addressing errors occur, nor would any operating system code be protected from application-level processes, unless some additional hardware was provided (see Section 5.5).

We now consider the possibility of keeping the loaded addresses relative to the start of a program. The advantages of doing this are:

- a given program can run anywhere in physical memory and can be moved around by the operating system;
- it might be possible to protect processes from each other, and the operating system from application processes, by whatever mechanism we employ for isolating the addresses seen by processes.

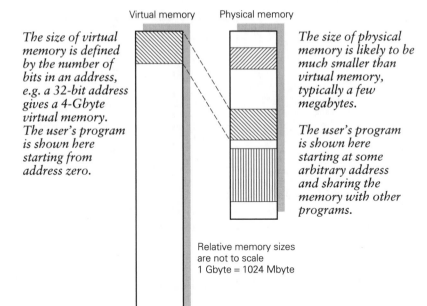

The size of virtual memory is defined by the number of bits in an address, e.g. a 32-bit address gives a 4-Gbyte virtual memory. The user's program is shown here starting from address zero.

The size of physical memory is likely to be much smaller than virtual memory, typically a few megabytes.

The user's program is shown here starting at some arbitrary address and sharing the memory with other programs.

Relative memory sizes are not to scale
1 Gbyte = 1024 Mbyte

Figure 5.2
Virtual and physical memory.

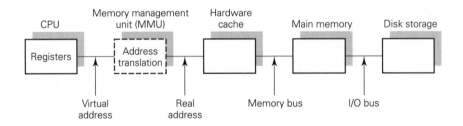

Figure 5.3
Address translation in a memory hierarchy.

To realize these advantages we must have a mechanism to bind the virtual addresses within the loaded instructions to physical addresses when the instructions are executed.

Figure 5.2 illustrates the concept we have just introduced, that of the virtual address space of a process. The process sees a virtual machine in which it has access to a virtual address space starting from address zero. The real machine is shared by a number of processes, and we see the virtual memory of the process occupying a portion of real physical memory. Since this address translation is part of every instruction fetch or data fetch from memory, it has to be integrated closely with the hardware instruction cycle.

Figure 5.3 extends Figure 5.1 to show the memory hierarchy with this additional hardware component, the memory management unit (MMU). In the CPU, the program counter register will contain a virtual address which must be translated to a real address before an instruction is fetched. When the processor decodes an instruction, extracts an address field and computes the address of an operand, this is a virtual address. It must be translated to a real address, dynamically, by hardware at runtime, before it can be used to read or write memory. The memory

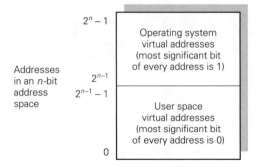

Addresses
in an n-bit
address
space

$2^n - 1$

2^{n-1}
$2^{n-1} - 1$

0

Operating system
virtual addresses
(most significant bit
of every address is 1)

User space
virtual addresses
(most significant bit
of every address is 0)

Figure 5.4
The address space of
a process.

management unit contains an associatively addressed translation table, called a translation lookaside buffer, for this purpose. There are various forms of hardware mechanism which support and extend the basic idea introduced here.

5.4 Layout of a process's virtual address space

Figure 5.4 shows a convention that is often adopted by hardware and operating system designers. The top half of the virtual address space of every process is reserved for the operating system. The bottom half is used for the process's code and data. At the hardware level, it is convenient that virtual addresses which have the value one for their most significant bit are addresses within the operating system. Those with value zero are user-space addresses. Within user space, a compiler will also have conventions for use of the virtual address space. It is unlikely that program code and data and library code will be tightly packed into a contiguous segment, as shown in Figure 5.2. Instead, program code, library code, stack data and heap data will be at widely separated virtual addresses.

The operating system's memory management functionality must include the maintenance of a record of all of these segments of all the executing processes. The OS tables contain the information necessary for the hardware to be set up to translate from virtual to physical addresses at runtime.

5.5 Memory protection and sharing

We saw above that address references into the operating system can be detected. Operating system address references that originate from user space can therefore be trapped, and the program aborted, in order to protect the OS. As we saw in Sections 2.5.1 and 3.3.3, a software interrupt mechanism will be provided for controlled entry into the operating system to make system calls for OS service. The fact that each process has a virtual address space, and virtual address references are mapped to physical addresses by hardware at runtime, provides a method for isolating processes. The mechanism prevents one process from addressing the memory allocated to another so they are protected from corruption by a faulty process.

A general categorization of memory management is into segmentation, paging and a combination of the two. **Segmentation** is a means of structuring a process's address space and of sharing some parts with other processes while keeping other parts private. This allows a single copy of programming language libraries to be shared by any number of processes. **Paging** mechanisms are transparent to the programmer and solely for the purpose of managing physical storage allocation. Here, the process's virtual address space is conceptually divided into pages of fixed length and the main memory is allocated in blocks of the same size. A page that needs to be loaded onto main memory can be placed in any free block. The operating system keeps process page tables to keep track of these allocations and the address translation hardware maps between 'page of process' and 'block of physical memory' at runtime.

In general, all forms of memory management hardware support protection, while segmentation allows portions of the virtual address space to be shared. We leave the details for further study.

5.6 Memory management in system design

Is memory management hardware always needed in a computer system? If the system is very small and simple and needs to be very cheap, such as a handheld or embedded computer, a memory management unit may not be justifiable. In some systems, once software is loaded it remains resident and runs indefinitely. The software may have to be resident in main memory to guarantee real-time response. The system may be dedicated to a specific function and have nothing equivalent to error-prone or malicious user programs. It could be argued that memory management hardware is unnecessary in such cases; there is certainly no need for virtual memory. The protection afforded by memory management hardware is useful, however. The memory management access controls can be set up so that an instruction which causes an illegal attempt to write or transfer control outside the module in which it occurs can be trapped. As software grows in size, this support for debugging will become increasingly important.

In systems where program sizes are unpredictable, programs are loaded dynamically, and the system is shared by several users, the limited size of physical memory can cause problems. In this case virtual memory is essential. It is also desirable that the various independent programs should be protected from each other and the operating system should be protected against them. For efficiency, swap space may be a device or partition of a device that the operating system writes to directly. In some systems, swap space is implemented as a single, large file, accessed via the filing system. Another scheme is to use a single, large, memory-mapped file; see Section 5.13.

Memory mapping (in particular, paging hardware) can be used to avoid the inefficiency of copying data. Examples are: the transfer of data between a network or I/O buffer and the address space of a process; the transfer of data between processes; and the copying of an address space on process creation. Single-user networked workstations are now more common than multi-user systems. Workstation operating systems typically have to deal with only a small number of processes at any time. Memory technology is such that 64-Mbyte units are available at low cost. It might be argued that all software will be able to fit in a main memory of this size and virtual memory techniques will become redundant.

Application program sizes have continued to grow, however, and system software such as graphical user interfaces has become very large. Also, we expect to be able to manipulate large coloured images. It is likely that virtual memory techniques will continue to be needed, but the assumptions on which they are based have changed dramatically. Although disk density has doubled every three years for the past twenty years, disk access time has lagged behind and has only increased by a third in the past ten years. As processor speeds continue to increase, disk access will increasingly be a bottleneck. New technology such as non-volatile RAM or power-backed RAM disks is likely to be used for virtual memory swap space. Perhaps a 'memory server' across a high-speed network will support virtual memory better than a local disk can.

We now consider massive, persistent disk-based storage systems (filing systems) as opposed to the use of disks as an extension to main memory as described above. After that, we consider how file I/O and memory management might be integrated.

5.7 File management: Introduction

Chapter 2 introduced the major subsystems within operating systems. Every component computer in a system has some main memory and at least one device, even if this is only a network connection, so some form of memory management and device management is always needed. Not every system needs file management; a dedicated network gateway, an embedded computer or a node of a process control system are examples of those that do not. Even a workstation might not have a local disk. In this case the user needs assistance in retrieving files from remote file servers across a network.

The relative and projected performance of processors and disks, described in Section 3.2.1, should be borne in mind. I/O will become a bottleneck in future systems and very large main memories will be used to compensate for relatively poor I/O performance; that is, a great deal of information will be cached in main memory, some of which may be non-volatile.

5.8 An overview of filing system functions

Filing systems provide:

- a **storage service**: clients do not need to know about the physical characteristics of disks, or where files have been stored on them. The filing system should take steps not to lose a file that has been entrusted to it, even if there are hardware faults or software crashes.

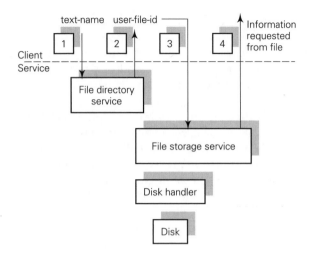

Figure 5.5
A client interaction
with a file service.

- a **directory service**: clients can give convenient text names to files and, by grouping them in directories, show the relationships between them. Clients should also be able to control the sharing of their files with others by specifying who can access a given file and in what way.

Figure 5.5 illustrates a typical interaction between a file service and a client. We shall see later that filing system designs differ, particularly when they are serving a distributed system. Interactions between the component modules of the file service are not shown.

We assume that a file is created with some text name such as exercise1.c or chapter7. The client quotes this name in order to use the file again. In (1) the client calls an operation such as open-file with the text name as an argument. Another argument will specify whether the client wants to read only or read and write the file. The directory service will carry out an **access check** to ensure that this client is **authorized** to access this file in the way specified. The directory service is responsible for translating the text name into a form which enables the file storage service to locate the file on disk; we call this **name resolution**. In order to do this it may need to call on the storage service and the storage service may need to call the disk handler to read the disk.

A filing system stores very large numbers of files, only a few of which are in use at any time. At (2) the filing system is ready for the client to use this file. It will have set up information about the file in its tables in main memory. It returns a **user-file-identifier** (**user-file-id,** or **UFID**) for the client to use in subsequent requests to read or write the file, shown at (3). At (4) the storage service returns the portion of the file that was requested at (3).

Notice that the initial request must give a filename that allows the file to be identified uniquely in the filing system. The user-file-id may be a temporary name for use by the process and might be something like 'my open file number 7'.

A potential problem that arises because files can be shared is concurrent requests for access to the same file. Another function of filing systems is therefore **concurrency control**. A crude approach is based on the argument that many clients can safely read a file at the same time but only one should be allowed to have write access. A filing system could enforce such a policy by noting whether a file has been opened for reading, and if so by how many clients, or for writing, in which case any subsequent requests to read or write would be refused. This is called **mandatory concurrency control**. A file is said to be **locked** for reading or writing.

Current thinking is that this approach is too inflexible. Many applications, such as distributed database management systems, may wish to have write access to different parts of the same file, and it is tedious if the underlying mechanisms enforced by the operating system prevent it. Indeed, the multiple writers are usually multiple instances of the same program in a distributed system and are designed to work together. For this reason, operating systems may now allow simultaneous write access to files. They may, as an optional extra, provide a **locking service** to help the clients cooperate with each other. A client may be able to request a shared lock or an exclusive lock on a file and be told whether locks have already been taken out and, if so, by whom. Clients may also be given an advisory warning on a request to open a file if the file is already open for a potentially conflicting access mode. Filing systems differ in the concurrency control services they offer.

A filing system is a concurrent system since it may have to handle simultaneous requests from clients. Consider a computer dedicated to providing a file service for clients at workstations on a network and assume that a number of clients' requests are outstanding. The server takes a request and starts to work on it. The disk must be read, so, rather than wait for the (electromechanical) disk to deliver the required data, the server starts to work on another request. A filing system will be used as an example of a multi-threaded system component throughout the book. Here we outline the interface and implementation sufficient to motivate such an example. Design details are left for more specialist texts.

5.9 File and directory structure

As far as the file storage service is concerned, the objects it stores (files) are unstructured sequences of bytes. The filing system must be able to identify each file uniquely in the filing system and, to achieve this, will associate an identifier with a given file (we shall call this the **system-file-identifier, SFID**).

A **directory** is a structured object and comprises a list of entries, each of which associates a text name with information on the named object, including its SFID. The directory service will use the storage service to store directories. A directory is therefore given a SFID by the filing system. This is discussed further in Section 5.10, and Figure 5.7 gives an example of a directory object with associated operations.

A very simple filing system could hold the names of all files in a single directory. This was done in some early systems and in some small personal computer systems, but it has the following disadvantages:

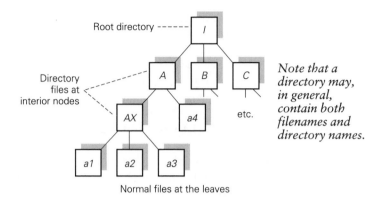

Root directory - - - - - /

Directory files at interior nodes

A   B   C

Note that a directory may, in general, contain both filenames and directory names.

AX   a4   etc.

a1   a2   a3

Normal files at the leaves

Figure 5.6
A filing system.

- The directory would be very large and held on disk. Looking up a given filename in it would take the directory service a long time.
- Different users might use the same text names for their files. Unique text names could be achieved by appending the owner's name to each filename. Grouping each user's files into a separate directory is an obvious rationalization. This would give a two-level hierarchy. This was provided in some early systems such as TOPS10 for the DecSystem 10.
- Users typically store a great deal of information in a filing system and some support for organizing this information is desirable. Convenient grouping within a user's files should be supported for easy location and access control; for example, users should be able to keep files of different types in different directories and group files that they are likely to use together in the same directory.

Therefore, although a directory hierarchy is not essential in theory, it is now provided in practice by most filing systems. Directories are created and named by clients of the filing system through requests to the directory service which in turn invokes the storage service. The filing system keeps a top-level or root directory. Figure 5.6 shows a simple example.

5.9.1 Pathnames and working directories

In a hierarchical filing system, files and directories are named relative to the top-level root directory, that is, the full name of each file and directory is a **pathname** starting from the root. The examples below use / as a separator between components of a pathname, and a pathname starting with / is assumed to start from the root.

/A/AX   is the full pathname of the directory *AX* of Figure 5.6. Directory *AX* is recorded in directory *A* which is recorded in the root directory.

/A/AX/a2   file *a2* of Figure 5.6 is recorded in directory *AX* which is recorded in directory *A* which is recorded in the root directory.

A pathname can be long and tedious to use. Most systems have the concept of a **current** working directory and names can then be relative to this as well as full pathnames. For example the name *a1* can be used for the file */A/AX/a1* if the current working directory of the user has been set to *AX*. When a user logs in there is usually a procedure for establishing an initial working directory.

5.9.2 File sharing: Access rights and links

A major advantage of a generally accessible filing system is that stored objects (files and directories) can be shared. One means of supporting and controlling this sharing is to allow the owner of each object to indicate who may use it and in what way. When a user who is not the owner attempts to access the object, the access rights are checked and access is granted or denied accordingly.

An alternative way to support sharing is to allow new directory entries to be set up to point to existing objects. Such entries are called **links**. The idea is that an authorized sharer can give a new name to the object instead of remembering the owner's pathname. A given object is no longer defined to have a unique pathname and the naming tree becomes a general directed graph. Systems may restrict the use of links so that a link can be set up to a file but not to a directory.

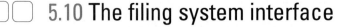

5.10 The filing system interface

The filing system interface will contain operations such as those listed in Tables 5.1 and 5.2. Filing systems differ, however, so these sets of operations should not be considered definitive. The operations are given in general terms because filing system interfaces may differ in syntax.

UFID is used as an abbreviation for the user-file-identifier introduced in Section 5.8 above and illustrated in Figure 5.5. This may or may not be the same as the system-file-identifier, SFID, introduced in Section 5.9. The filing

Table 5.1 Directory service: Operations available to clients of the filing system.

Operation	Arguments	Returns
Create directory	Pathname of directory	Done
Delete directory	Pathname of directory	Done
List directory contents	Pathname of directory	List of directory contents
Set access rights to file or directory	Pathname of file or directory, users/rights specification	Done
Link	Pathname of directory, pathname of file or directory	Done
Create file	Pathname of file	Done
Delete file	Pathname of file	Done
Open file	Pathname of file, read/write	UFID

Table 5.2 File storage service: Operations available to clients of the filing system.

Operation	Arguments	Returns
Read file	UFID, byte-range, where to put bytes in memory	Bytes requested
Write file	UFID, byte-range to write, where to find bytes in memory	Done
Close file	UFID	Done
Position pointer	UFID, position for pointer in bytes	Done

system may return a given user UFIDs 0, 1, 2, 3, etc., for the files currently in use, whereas the SFID is unique within the filing system. We assume that the SFID is for internal use and is a reference to information on the file or directory, including its location in the storage system, see Figure 5.8 below.

Note that when a file or directory is created its name is recorded in a directory: the pathname argument is intended to indicate both the name of the newly created object and the superior directory in which this name is to be recorded. Error returns are not given.

5.10.1 The directory service as type manager

Note that a directory cannot be read and written arbitrarily by clients of the filing system, but can be accessed only through the interface operations on directory objects such as list directory contents and create directory. A directory can therefore be regarded as an example of an abstract data type with associated operations (see below). We can think of the directory service as the owner or type manager of directories which it stores as files on the lower-level storage service. Figure 5.7 gives an example of a directory with associated interface operations. Creating a file or directory includes making an entry for it in a superior directory as well as allocating storage for it. Deleting a file or directory includes removing a directory entry. The operations on directory objects shown in Figure 5.7 are listed in Table 5.3.

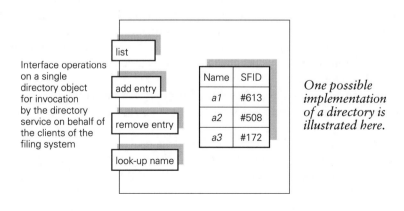

Figure 5.7
A directory object.

Table 5.3 Operations available on the directory objects of Figure 5.7.

Operation	Arguments	Returns
Lookup name in directory (for pathname resolution and access checking, see below and Section 5.11)	Name, pathname of directory	SFID
Add entry to directory (to implement creation of a file or directory)	Name, pathname of directory	Done
Remove entry from directory (to implement deletion of a file or directory)	Name, pathname of directory	Done

5.10.2 The directory service interface

The directory service is concerned with pathname resolution and access checking. Suppose a file is to be opened. To resolve the pathname of the file the directory service must read each component directory in the path in turn in order to locate and read the next component. Section 5.11 gives more information on how this is implemented. The file's entry is looked up in the final directory component and an identifier for the file (UFID) is returned to the client.

The directory service will check whether the user is authorized to carry out the specified operation on a file or directory. The access allowed is set by the owner. The link operation requests a new directory entry to be made for an existing file or directory.

5.10.3 The file service interface

These operations assume that a file has been opened successfully and the user has been given an identifier (UFID) for use in subsequent requests. The arguments for **read** and **write** operations must include the position in the file (byte-range) of the bytes that are to be read and the main memory location for the bytes to be read to or written from. The byte-range in the file is likely to be specified not as start-byte, finish-byte but as start-byte and count. The start position can then be taken as an implicit pointer held by the system which is positioned at the start of the file initially. For sequential file access the user need never worry about positioning the pointer but can just request to read the next n bytes. The operation **position pointer** has been included for use by applications which need random access. This style of operation is convenient in a centralized system but can be a problem in distributed systems. A request might be repeated because of network congestion or server failure and restart. We shall discuss this in Chapters 14 and 15.

The **close** operation tells the system the file is no longer needed, so any data structures it is holding in main memory on the file can be removed after the file and its metadata (information on the file or 'data on the data') are safely recorded on disk.

5.11 The filing system implementation

Filing systems must keep information on each file or directory, such as where it is stored on disk, who may access it and in what way, its time of creation and last access, etc. A typical information block is shown in Figure 5.8.

Different filing systems may store this information in different ways. An important point is that several directory entries (links) may exist for a given file or directory. The method of storing information on the file should ensure that there is only one copy of it. If the information was kept with the directory entry, for example, not only would this make directories large but it would also cause the information to be replicated when links were set up. The information is needed to locate the file or directory on disk, so that part certainly cannot be stored with the file. A common approach is to use a table where each entry is a block of information on a file or directory. We shall call this a **metadata table** because it holds data about the data stored in files and directories. Figure 5.8 shows such a table and Figure 5.9 makes it clear that the files, directories and metadata table recording information on them are all stored permanently on disk.

It is important that the entry on a given file or directory should be located quickly. A good algorithm is needed to convert a SFID into the correct entry in the table. The method used in the UNIX system is a simple index into a table. An alternative is a hashing function.

Figure 5.10 outlines data structures, typical of those used within filing systems, that are held in main memory when a file is in use. The case where two users have opened the same file is illustrated. User A has UFID 3 allocated for the file and user B has UFID 5. The file has a single SFID and a single metadata table entry.

Two main memory filing system data structures are shown. The system open file table has an entry for each sharer of the file. This allows for concurrent sharers of a file to have their own position pointer into it for reading and writing. The active file information table contains entries with information similar to

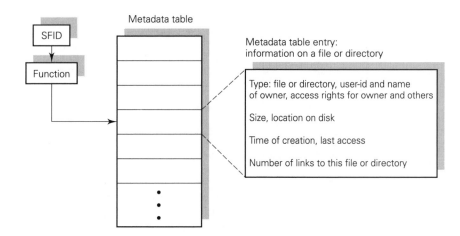

Figure 5.8
A metadata table for a filing system.

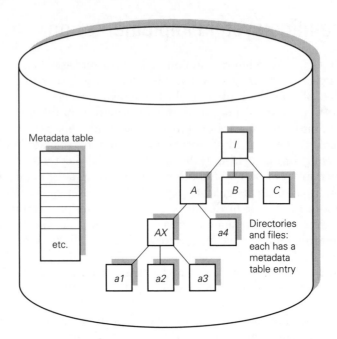

Figure 5.9
A filing system on disk.

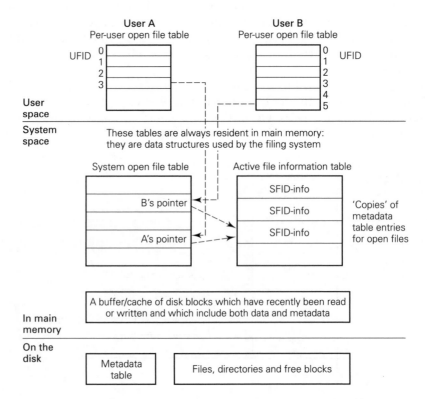

Figure 5.10
Data structures used by a filing system.

that held in the metadata table. Additional information that is likely to be held is the SFID and concurrency control information, that is, whether the file is open for reading or writing and by how many readers and/or writers.

Figure 5.10 also shows a buffer area for disk blocks. Recall Figure 3.13 and Section 3.5.1 where I/O buffering was introduced. It is likely that this buffer area is also used as a cache. Disk access is slow and the system will aim to satisfy as many read requests as possible from the cache.

File systems differ in the semantics of their write operations. A successful write might indicate that the data has been written to disk or might mean only that the data has reached the buffers in (volatile) memory. In this case it would be lost on a power failure. File system policies differ over whether they attempt to write out the write buffers to disk as soon as possible or whether they attempt to avoid physical disk writes by keeping data in memory as long as possible. The advantage of the latter approach is that the data in a disk-block-sized buffer may be changed several times in quick succession by user-level writes of arbitrary byte sequences. Data written out may also be reread from the cache.

Keeping the data in memory allows a fast response to a write request at the risk of data loss and file system inconsistency on a power failure. Another reason to delay a given write is that the disk handler may be able to achieve higher performance if it reorders the writes to allow the arms to sweep across the surface of the disk and back instead of moving back and forth in response to requests in the order that they arrive.

There is scope for using non-volatile memory as a write cache both to achieve secure, asynchronous writes and to improve disk-head scheduling performance.

5.12 Network-based file servers

The previous sections have presented general principles that are relevant to filing systems in general: for single-user workstations, centralized time-sharing systems or distributed systems. We now focus on the special properties of network-based filing systems for distributed systems.

We are not concerned here with how network communication is invoked between the client of the file service and the service. We shall discuss this later in Chapter 15. Neither are we concerned with how a number of file server machines work together to provide a service. That is the concern of a more advanced course on distributed systems such as Tanenbaum and van Steen (2002) or Coulouris *et al.* (2001). Even less are we concerned at this stage with the problem of how to manage more than one copy of a file.

A question we should address is where the functions we have discussed above are provided, that is:

- naming and pathname resolution
- access control
- existence control
- concurrency control.

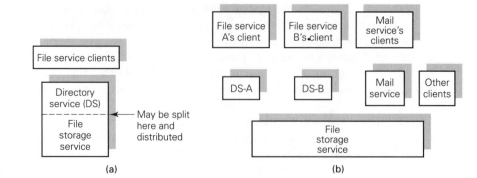

Figure 5.11
Storage service architectures:
(a) closed; (b) open.

5.12.1 Open and closed storage architectures

Figure 5.11 shows two ways in which a network file service can be provided. In the first case, a single file service comprising a directory service and storage service is provided. The only way to use the storage service is through the directory service; we have a closed storage service architecture. This enforces a single naming convention and access control policy on all clients.

Note that, although the architecture is closed, the service components might be distributed; for example, the storage service component might be provided remotely and the directory service in a client workstation, perhaps as a component of a closed operating system. In this case, the user invokes the local directory service which invokes the remote storage service. The user does not interact directly with the storage service.

In the second case we see the service interface at the level of the file storage service; recall the file service interface operations given in Section 5.10. The names used at the interface are SFIDs and not pathnames. This allows a network-based file storage service to support different client operating systems, each with its own directory service. It also allows direct use of the file storage service by clients, such as a mail service. A mail service does not need to use pathnames for messages and, since the mail service is the owner of all messages while they are in transit, it has no need for fine-grained access control. Messages may be taken from and delivered to filing systems by the clients of the mail service. Again, as discussed in Section 2.4, we see an **open architecture** providing a more general and flexible service than a closed one.

5.12.2 The storage service interface

We have argued that the interface of a network-based file service should be at the file storage service level and should be open for general use. Figure 5.12 extends the simple picture of a closed architecture presented in Figure 5.5 so that we can see the implications of separating the directory service from the storage service and of making the storage service interface open. Roughly, we see the directory service dealing with pathnames and the storage service dealing with SFIDs.

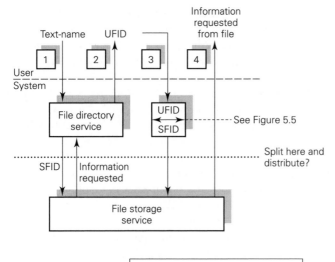

Figure 5.12
Client interaction with a closed file service.

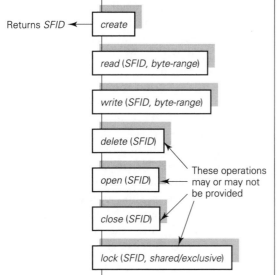

Figure 5.13
The storage service interface.

Figure 5.13 shows a possible interface for a network storage service. Let us assume that the interface that was previously invoked from within a closed file service is now both remote and open to invocation across a network by any client.

5.12.3 Location of function

We should consider the location of filing system functions with this proposed division of functionality.

Naming and **name resolution** is the responsibility of the clients of a storage service defined at this level. As we have discussed above, an open interface allows a number of different naming schemes and access control policies to be supported. Note that a given directory service will store its directories on the storage service. The directory service is the owner of its directories. To resolve a pathname the directory service will need to fetch each component of the pathname in turn from the storage service in order to look up the SFID of the next component in a directory.

The **existence control** function is closely associated with the naming graph. (Recall that an object should be kept in existence if it is accessible from the root of the naming graph.) The storage service level sees only a flat SFID-to-file mapping and has no knowledge of the internal structure of the files (including directories) it stores. This appears to place the existence control function at the directory service level; that is, in an open environment each client of the storage service would have to carry out its own existence control.

This model of the world is not fully general. It does not allow for the possibility that stored objects might be shared by different kinds of client; for example, a file might represent a video clip and be embedded in a mail message. The owner of the file wishes to delete it. Is its SFID still in an active mail message? The Cambridge File Server (Birrell and Needham, 1980) provided both an open interface at the storage service level and support for existence control. This was achieved by maintaining a skeletal naming graph within the storage service. The CFS interface contained no delete operation and asynchronous garbage collection was carried out periodically.

Figure 5.13 shows a delete operation in the storage service interface. Who should be able to invoke this operation? Recall that to delete a file means that a directory entry is to be removed. This interaction is between the directory service and its clients, and the directory service decides whether the material may also be removed. If there is no sharing between different types of client of the storage service each can detect and delete garbage.

An alternative approach is that the storage service ages its objects and can delete (or archive) an object when its time expires. The clients of the service should keep their objects alive by touching them within the defined time period. A touch operation could be provided for this purpose. A directory service, or any service which uses the storage service, can perform this service on behalf of its clients.

Current filing systems tend to make restrictions which simplify these issues. If only files and not directories can be shared, a reference count can be kept with each file. Also, current systems tend not to support the open interface and full generality of sharing we have set up here. Users often work within a closed but distributed environment. Future filing systems will need to support a variety of types of objects, such as voice, video, database, mail, etc., and more general solutions than those currently in use will be needed.

The **concurrency control** function cannot easily be placed at the client level since, even within a single client type, there may be many instances of the client, such as a directory service, and any one might have opened a file. It would be necessary for all the clients which could access a file to communicate to achieve concurrency control. We assume that there is one copy of a given file, and a natural place to implement concurrency control is where the file is stored. The storage service might provide shared and exclusive locks on files, as discussed in

Section 5.8. An alternative is to provide a separate lock service which clients are trusted to use. If the storage service is stateless it cannot provide this service.

The storage service does not know about the internal structure of files and is likely to provide concurrency control at the granularity of whole files. If a client of the storage service, such as a database management system, requires arbitrarily fine-grained concurrency control (that is, locking of components of structured objects), this must be provided above the storage service level, within the client application or in some new service.

In a centralized system **access control** is carried out during pathname resolution, when a file is opened (for reading or writing) or a directory operation is invoked. In a distributed system these access checks must still be carried out during pathname resolution.

In a closed, but distributed, system the clients of the storage service are all instances of the client operating system's directory service; they may be authenticated as such by the system mechanisms. The storage service is said to have a **protected interface**. In an open system the storage service interface can be used directly by a number of different clients. Access control is therefore needed at the storage service level so that the files stored there cannot be read or written by unauthorized clients. We discuss this further in Section 5.12.4.

5.12.4 File identifiers and protection at the storage service level

The network storage service must guarantee to protect the information that is entrusted to it from unauthorized access. We assume that the underlying system provides an authentication service so that the storage service has secure knowledge of who is invoking it. There are two basic approaches to access control.

1 *Access control lists*

The storage service keeps access control information on each file it stores, as described in Section 5.9.2. The owner specifies who may access the file and in what way. Each time a read or write request is made, the storage service checks that the initiator of the request has the access rights required, then uses the SFID to locate the file internally.

Note that the directory service represents directories as files stored on the storage service. (Recall Figure 5.7 and the notion of the directory abstraction and the directory implementation.) Only the directory services may read and write their directories arbitrarily; users of the directory service access directories through their type operations via the directory service. As far as the storage service is concerned, a directory service is the owner of its directories. The directory service needs to implement a higher-level access control policy for its clients.

A general comment on the access list approach is that we may wish to be able to express fine discriminations on who or what may access each file. For example, we may wish to give various groups of people subtly different rights and we may wish to exclude certain individuals who belong to those

Figure 5.14
A typical format for a
capability.

Access rights	Unique identifier within filing system	Check digits

groups from having the group's privilege. Also, a name on an access control list may itself represent a list. If this is so, the mechanism does not scale well, and access list checking could become too great an overhead, particularly if it is carried out every time a file is accessed and not just once and for all when a file is opened.

2 *Capabilities*

In this case, the storage service does not record who may access a file and in what way. Instead, possession of an identifier, of a carefully designed form, is taken as proof of the right to access the file. An identifier that is used in this way is called a file **capability**. Figure 5.14 shows a typical format for a capability.

A capability must not be forgeable; that is, it must not be possible to invent a number and use it to access some arbitrary file. For this reason, capabilities contain sparse random numbers so that if you invent a number of the right length you are very unlikely to hit on one that maps onto a file.

It is possible to encode access rights within capabilities so that the storage service can discriminate read and write access rights, for example. It must be impossible for the user of the capability to change the access rights encoded in it. If you change a capability in any way it must be rejected by the storage service. Section 15.11 discusses capabilities in a more general context and explains how they may be constructed and checked.

We assume that the underlying system is such that it is not possible to eavesdrop on network communication and pick up and use capabilities that are being transmitted.

We have outlined how the functions of a storage service can be provided in a distributed environment. Further study should be carried out in the context of a discussion of distributed systems architecture.

5.13 Integrating virtual memory and storage

5.13.1 File mapping

We have seen files used for persistent storage, and main memory for the storage of running programs and data. The most common programming language abstraction for stored data is the file; files are named and used explicitly in programs.

We have seen in Section 5.11 that the filing system maintains a cache of buffers in main memory and that users' requests are satisfied from those buffers. This means that on a read, data is first written into the system buffers and then copied to the application. On a write, data is copied into system buffers, then written to disk. The efficiency of file input and output could be improved if this copying was avoided. The integration of virtual memory and file I/O is an attractive idea.

Memory management is concerned with the organization of the disk backing store for running programs and with the transfer of pages between main memory and disk. File management is concerned with the organization of the file store and with the transfer of blocks of files between main memory and the disk to satisfy I/O requests. A file comprises a number of disk blocks or disk 'pages'; a segment comprises a number of memory pages. There is obvious scope for the integration of file management and memory management. As well as rationalizing the system design, performance gains should result, since a page is transferred directly into the memory area of a process and not via a system buffer.

Several operating system designs have used this idea (Bensoussan *et al.*, 1972; Lampson and Sproull, 1979; Wilkes and Needham, 1979). The Multics design unified the concepts of file and segment: when a file was opened it was mapped as a segment into the address space of a process. Others have provided an option to map files in virtual memory as well as access them conventionally; for example, UNIX BSD 4.3 specified but did not implement this option, while Sun OS extended and implemented this specification. A file-mapping facility is used as follows:

- Instead of opening a file a process makes a system call to map the file, or part of the file, into its address space. As virtual address spaces are now typically of the order of a gigabyte, this is feasible. The process may specify the virtual addresses where the file should be mapped or the operating system may decide and return the address. The operating system creates appropriate page table entries, marking the pages as not present in memory initially.
- As the file is addressed in memory it is moved in by the memory management mechanisms of the system, such as demand paging. The page table entries are filled in with the physical page base addresses in the usual way.
- The process may specify whether the file is to be mapped private or shared and will indicate the mode of access allowed, such as read, write, execute.

Note that the file store on disk and the backing store for memory management, often an area of the same disk, have been unified. Once the mapping is noted by the operating system, pages may be read directly from the file. Updated pages may be written back to the file. An insertion or deletion in the middle of a file must be handled in both styles of system. The usual approach is to create a new file (see your local editor).

Although several systems in the past have supported file mapping it has not become popular with programmers, who appear to prefer the familiar file abstraction. It is used within the NT executive, for example, for loading a new (binary) program – the program is then paged in as required. The NT filing system and memory management system work together to achieve file mapping. OS/2 (Cook and Rawson, 1988; Kogan and Rawson, 1990), Mach and Chorus (Rashid 1986; Abrossimov *et al.*, 1989a, b) provide memory-mapped files.

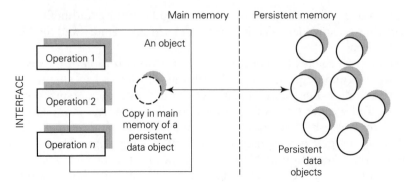

Figure 5.15
Persistent data objects.

Large virtual address spaces make the approach feasible and the gain in efficiency through avoiding copying into and out of buffers is desirable. There are some limitations and potential problems, however:

- The file may be changed in place and paged back to the disk, thus overwriting the original version. System software, such as an editor, may have to take a copy of it before allowing it to be used in mapped mode.
- Management of the virtual address space has to allow for growth in size of mapped files. An object which grows may overflow its allocated space.
- The method assumes a closed, homogeneous world. The bits stored in a file (instruction and data representation) are assumed to be correct for the memory the file is loaded into. This is not the case if a filing system is shared by heterogeneous hardware and software, which is the standard case.

The technique may therefore be useful within a single system or within a cluster of homogeneous workstations. It is not extensible to an open heterogeneous world.

5.13.2 Object mapping

In the previous section we saw that a file could be mapped into the virtual address space of a process. An extension to this idea is often used in object-oriented systems. Modules, abstract data types and objects were introduced in Chapter 2. Recall that a data object can only be accessed through the operations associated with its type; see Figure 5.15.

The following assumptions form the basis of this object-oriented approach to system design:

- Typed objects are defined and used in programming languages.
- An object may be made persistent and stored in persistent storage. It then exists independently of the running program that created it and may be used later by any program that knows its name.
- Each persistent object is identified uniquely in a system.
- Given an object's identifier it can be located in the persistent storage of the system.
- For simplicity, we assume that there is a single copy of a persistent object.

In a system of this kind, programmers may work with a higher-level abstraction for persistent storage than unstructured files: that of typed objects. We shall not study such systems in great detail, but it is interesting to note here that the object abstraction may fit very well with the desire to integrate virtual memory and persistent storage. When a persistent object is to be used by a process it may be mapped into the address space of the process and demand-paged between persistent store and main memory, as described above for files. The assumption of homogeneity should again be noted, as for mapped files. Examples of persistent programming languages and object management systems are PSAlgol (Atkinson *et al.*, 1982; Cockshot *et al.*, 1984), Texas/C++ (Singhal *et al.*, 1992), and E (Richardson *et al.*, 1993).

5.14 Summary

Memory management of some kind is necessary in every component computer of a concurrent system. In some cases it can be very simple, when embedded software runs indefinitely. In other cases demands on memory are dynamic. Even in the case of permanently resident software it is likely that unpredictable demands will be made on data space, for example, for buffer space for packets coming in from a network. Segmentation is a means of structuring a process's address space and of sharing some parts with other processes while keeping other parts private. Paging mechanisms are transparent to the programmer and solely for the purposes of managing physical storage allocation; we have therefore not considered them here.

Memory management is relevant to the concurrent system designer because it is through memory management that processes may share memory. Also, the memory management subsystem is itself a concurrent system. It is invoked on initial program loading to arrange physical storage allocation; it has an interface for client programs which need to expand their data areas during a program run; and it is entered as a result of hardware events such as address faults.

Filing systems may be thought of as a service offered above an operating system kernel rather than a mandatory part of every kernel. Network-based filing systems are common and users' workstations may or may not have local filing systems. Traditional centralized operating systems, however, offer filing system services as part of a resident kernel and some system designs reflect an evolution from centralized to distributed systems.

A filing system is an example of a concurrent system. Many clients may simultaneously have requests outstanding. We shall consider how a filing system may have several client requests in progress simultaneously.

The data structures that a filing system is likely to use have been outlined. We shall study the problems of interference between processes doing work on behalf of different clients simultaneously. We have also considered the data structures held permanently on disk and the data structures held in main memory on currently active files. We shall be concerned with the problems of updates to data structures in main memory being safely written out to disk. We shall also be concerned with the consistency of the data structures held on disk in the presence of concurrency and crashes.

We have studied the basic functions provided by a filing system as part of a storage architecture and have gone on to consider how best these functions might be distributed. An open architecture allows many different types of client to be supported. We outlined how we might build such an open architecture by distributing the functions of a filing system.

The role of disk-based filing systems is likely to change dramatically as processor performance continues to increase relative to disk speed and increasingly large amounts of main memory are used. In the meantime, techniques for improving the efficiency of filing systems will be used.

File input and output is inefficient because data is copied into system buffers and again into user space. We discussed the integration of virtual memory and storage through mapped files. Several operating system designs have used this idea and, in general, programmers have found the storage model presented by this approach rather low level and complex. A current trend is to provide programmers with a model of persistent objects. Objects, rather than files, could then be mapped into the address spaces of processes.

Exercises

5.1 Outline the basic memory management functions of an operating system.

5.2 Describe how copies of instructions and data are held in the various levels of a memory hierarchy: permanent disk storage, backing store for main memory on disk, main memory, cache memory and processor registers. When are transfers of data made between the various levels? In each case, indicate whether the transfer involved is controlled by hardware or the operating system and explain the interface between the hardware and the operating system.

5.3 What is the virtual address space of a process? How large is the virtual address space for address lengths of 16, 24 and 32 bits? How does a separate address space per process protect processes from each other and the operating system from processes?

5.4 What are the advantages and disadvantages of running the operating system in the address space of every process? What are the advantages and disadvantages of running the operating system as a separate process with its own address space? (Bear this question in mind while reading Part II of the book.)

5.5 Which component computers of what types of system would you expect to have local disks with associated disk management software and filing system software?

5.6 What are the advantages and disadvantages of providing filing system software inside and outside the operating system?

5.7 Explain how a directory may be considered as an abstract data type or object.

5.8 How might the modules and processes introduced in Chapter 2 be used to implement a filing system?

5.9 Is a multi-level filing system such as a tree structure essential or just convenient in a multi-user system? How might a two-level system be used?

5.10 How can file sharing be supported in a filing system? What additional problems over normal file sharing are introduced if directory sharing is also allowed?

5.11 In what ways might a filing system provide concurrency control, that is, control of the simultaneous use of a shared file or directory? What are the advantages and disadvantages of the methods you suggest?

5.12 What are the functions of the directory service level and the file storage service level of a filing system?

5.13 File protection is achieved by a combination of authentication and access control (authorization). Describe different kinds of access control policies that you might wish to implement. Discuss how these policies could be implemented.

5.14 Contrast the access control list approach to file protection with the capability approach. Could both methods be combined in a filing system?

5.15 Filing systems often attempt to hold as much current data and metadata as possible in main memory. The advantage is to be able to satisfy clients' read and write requests faster than if a disk had to be read or written. What are the possible dangers of this approach? Which application areas could not tolerate it?

5.16 Take the file service operations given in Section 5.10 and work out a modular design with file service interface operations and nested modules for directory object management and file object management.

6

Fundamentals of distributed systems

6.1 Introduction

Since distributed systems have become commonplace we should take distributed software into account at an early stage in our study of concurrent software design. In Chapter 2 we took an architectural view of how software systems might be structured by decomposition into modules, subsystems and objects and introduced the idea that such components might reside on different computers in a distributed system. Each component of such a system comprises an operating system, with internal modular structure, which in turn supports modular services and applications.

We saw that a distributed system can even be built above different operating systems running on different hardware. A **middleware platform** might run as a service above the heterogeneous operating systems. The idea is to convert the various operating systems' system call interfaces into a higher-level common interface to be used by the higher-level modules of the distributed system.

In Chapter 3 we studied the hardware–software interface and the functionality of communications subsystems within and above operating systems. We therefore have the basic framework in place: that distributed computations can be built at higher levels, making use of communications services.

In Chapter 4 we saw how processes and threads are supported by operating systems and therefore understand in detail how modules are executed dynamically. We now establish a framework for understanding how a **distributed computation** comprising **distributed modules** can be executed dynamically by **distributed processes**.

Chapter 5 is an introduction to two operating system functions, memory management and file management. The former is the concern of each separate computer within a distributed system. File services may be provided in different ways in distributed systems. Each networked computer may or may not have its own file service. In most distributed systems a network-based, shared file service is usually provided.

In this chapter we establish the fundamental properties of distributed systems that distinguish them from centralized systems. For the rest of the book we look first at the general principles of software systems design and then go on to study the special problems of a distributed implementation.

The advent of local area networks in the 1970s provided the motivation for the development of distributed systems. We start this chapter by discussing the evolution of distributed systems, first for a professional, workplace environment and then for more recent personal and home environments.

Terminology

A number of different names are used in the literature to indicate a single component computer system in a distributed system, such as **host, node** or **site**. We shall use the term **node** and also **client** and **server** where appropriate.

⬛⬜⬜⬜ 6.2 Evolution of distributed systems for the workplace

Sections A.2, A.3
⮕

In the 1970s local area network (LAN) communications technology became available, see Chapter 3. The lightweight protocols which exploited the low error rates and high bandwidth made it possible to base distributed systems on frequent interaction between component systems. A number of design trade-offs were explored in research environments. Issues to be decided were what kind of system to put on each user's desk and what to provide as shared services, across the network.

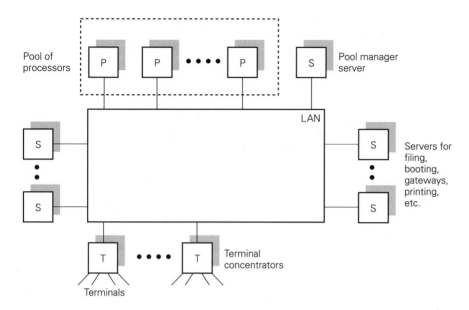

Figure 6.1(a)
Distributed system evolution: Pool of processors plus servers.

Pool of processors plus servers (Figure 6.1(a))

The Cambridge Distributed System was an early example of a distributed computing environment which was in everyday use throughout the 1980s. When it was designed, workstations were expensive so each user was given only a dumb terminal. Work was done by acquiring a processor from a pool and requesting an operating system to be loaded into it. The pool was managed by the Resource Manager (a server) and other servers existed for filing, printing, bootstrapping, serving the time, gateways and authentication.

Diskless workstations plus servers (Figure 6.1(b))

The V system at Stanford (home of the later Stanford University Network which became SUN) provided a diskless workstation on the desk. The idea is that

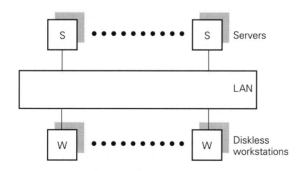

Figure 6.1(b)
Distributed system evolution: Diskless workstations plus servers.

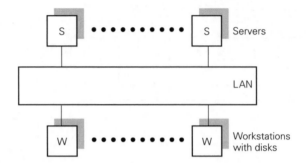

Figure 6.1(c)
Distributed system
evolution:
Workstations plus
servers.

code and data can easily be transferred across the network when required and information which needs to be shared is naturally held in file servers. System software can be held and maintained remote from the end systems. The workstations can be relatively inexpensive.

Workstations plus servers (Figure 6.1(c))

At Xerox PARC, the home of Ethernet, the philosophy was to provide a workstation on the desk, even before this was economically feasible outside a research environment. The idea was to stimulate the development of next-generation software by providing a next-generation environment.

As time went by price/performance trade-offs changed; also workstation software became as complex in functionality as the mainframe software it had replaced. Current workstations can function as time-sharing systems if the owner authorizes remote logins. A shared file service offered by a number of servers has become the conventional way to share data. The system on the desk will probably have local storage but this is likely to be used for system software, temporary storage and space for 'swapping out' programs that are not in immediate use rather than functioning as part of a permanent filing system.

Distributed systems have now grown to global scale. The internet-based World Wide Web is an example of a global information service. There is currently a great deal of interest in creating a **computational grid** for compute-intensive applications, in so-called e-science. Network-based compute servers are to be made available to run scientific applications and scientific databases are to be made available across the net. The intention is that computing should be provided much as electricity is at present. Current problems to be solved are therefore associated with large scale and wide distribution.

6.3 Personal computing

The price/performance ratio of small computers has led to their widespread use as personal and small-business systems. Network access for electronic mail and other internet access such as the World Wide Web has become increasingly popular outside professional computing laboratories and offices. The computer companies are now looking to the profits that may be made from widespread ubiquitous computing, home area networks and the like.

It is interesting to see the trade-offs which were explored for the computing workplace revisited for the home environment. In the mid 1990s the '**network computer**' white paper by Oracle advocated that the end system should be as inexpensive and simple to use as possible and SUN's Javastation is based on a similar approach.

Such systems need a network interface, which adds to their cost. A diskless workstation is proposed, with extra processing and all storage across the network. Environments in which a single application is run continuously can use a simple system of this kind; for example for flight reservation, airport check-in, tax calculation, etc. In the home, an implication of a diskless system is that the user is obliged to transfer all programs and data across the network and their use can therefore be monitored and charged. Gigabyte disks have become available at low cost and thin clients have continued to occupy a special-purpose niche leaving desktops for the home environment.

6.4 Model and software architecture

Whatever the physical architecture of the distributed system to be used we need to establish principles for designing and engineering the distributed software that is to run on it. The following questions raise the basic issues.

1 *Model*
   What are the entities that comprise the distributed system? How do they interoperate? How is their behaviour specified?
2 *Architecture*
   How are the components named, located and protected? What system services are needed by all the applications?
3 *Engineering*
   Is the fact that the system is distributed transparent to the user or the application programmer? How are the non-functional requirements such as high performance, reliability and availability achieved?

We defined a system model in Chapter 2. Components might be modules, abstract data types or objects. When the system is operational the components must be able to interwork. We saw one approach to providing support for this interworking as a middleware platform or layer of software that lies above heterogeneous operating systems and converts their different interfaces to a uniform one. We shall study the details of such platforms later. We shall also study the architectural and engineering issues raised above at a later stage.

First, we set down the fundamental properties of distributed software systems which apply whatever the model and architecture.

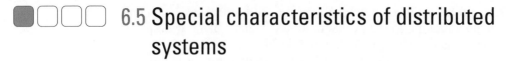

6.5 Special characteristics of distributed systems

The distinguishing characteristics of a distributed system may be summarized as follows:

1 *Concurrency*
   The components of a distributed computation may run at the same time.
2 *Independent failure modes*
   The components of a distributed computation and the network connecting them may fail independently of each other.
3 *No global time*
   We assume that each component of the system has a local clock but the clocks might not record the same time. The hardware on which the clocks are based is not guaranteed to run at precisely the same rate on all components of the system, a feature called **clock drift**.
4 *Communications delay*
   It takes time for the effects of an event at one point in a distributed system to propagate throughout the system.
5 *Inconsistent state*
   Concurrency, failures and communications delay together imply that the view of any state maintained by the distributed computation will not be consistent throughout the system.

We are concerned with property 1, concurrent software design, throughout the book. The details of communications protocols are outside the scope of this book but it is worth noting that an aspect of their design is to take account of the possibility of failure, property 2. We shall take failure into account whenever we consider a distributed implementation of a particular service or algorithm, for example in distributed filing systems and later in general distributed algorithms. Property 4, potential delay, makes the detection of failure quite difficult; the protocol designer has to distinguish between delay, when components are operating slowly, and failure, when something has crashed. Property 5 is a concern of Part III of the book and we postpone an in-depth treatment until then.

For the rest of this chapter we focus on time in distributed systems and discuss how naming schemes, such as those introduced for objects in Chapter 2, can be designed for systems which might be large scale and widely distributed.

6.6 Time in distributed systems

6.6.1 Physical earth time

We should first note that earth time is established only by convention. There is no universal time. Einstein proved that the velocity of light is constant for all observers irrespective of their velocity, see Figure 6.2.

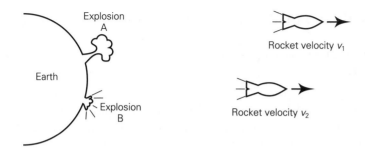

(a) The rockets travelling at different speeds would observe different times for the occurrence of each explosion and different times between the explosions.

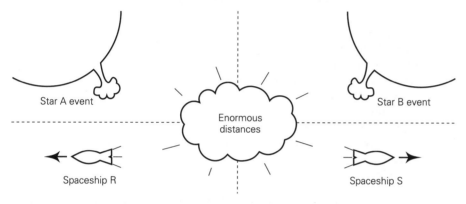

(b) It is possible for spaceship S to observe star B event occurring before star A event while spaceship R observes A before B.

Figure 6.2
Time beyond the earth.

Let us assume that our distributed system is earth based so that we can assume some notion of conventional physical time. Standard earth time is based on the earth's rotation in terms of days and years but accurate values are now derived from an atomically defined caesium clock. This time is (mis)named **Universal Coordinated Time (UTC)**.

It is possible to buy for a computer a device that can receive a UTC signal either from a satellite or from a radio station. Examples of satellite services are **GPS (Global Positioning Service)** and **GEOS (Geostationary Operational Environment Satellite)**. The accuracy of time received from these services varies with atmospheric conditions but is typically 10 ms for radio broadcasts and 0.1 (GEOS) to 1 ms (GPS) for satellite service. It is not possible to equip every computer with a time receiver but those that are equipped may function as time servers to the others.

We can assume that each computer has a programmable timer module based on a quartz crystal oscillator. These devices are programmed to interrupt at some interval, typically 10 ms, see Section 3.2.10. The accuracy of these devices is typically $1/10^6$ (1 second in 11.6 days) and they also vary with temperature, i.e. they are subject to **clock drift**.

We next consider how applications might make use of time. This motivates the need for drifting local clocks to be kept in synchrony with a **network time server** and we then outline how this may be achieved.

6.6.2 Use of time by distributed processes

The following examples cover possibilities of how time might be used in a range of applications.

1 *Resource reservation, such as airline booking*
   We may have a specification such as 'if the resource requests of two transactions may each be satisfied, but there are insufficient resources for both, then the transaction with the earliest time-stamp wins'.
2 *Banking*
   (a) The interest calculation program runs after midnight. All transactions made before midnight are attributed to the previous day.
   (b) Was a credit made to a certain bank account before money was withdrawn from it?
3 *Programming environments*
   Only those files of a related set with time-stamps which indicate they have been edited since the last compilation of the set (for example in a UNIX 'make') will be recompiled.
4 *Share dealing*
   (a) Can it be proved that executive X read certain sensitive information before initiating the transaction to buy or sell some shares?
   (b) The cost of the shares you purchase will be taken to be their value at the time of your transaction.

It should be noted that although we are sometimes concerned with the time at which something happened we are also concerned about the order of events. Bearing in mind clock drift and communications delay, event ordering in distributed systems can be difficult to establish.

6.6.3 Logical time: Event ordering

Figure 6.3 shows three nodes in a distributed system with a time graph for a process running at each node. Events within a single process are defined to be sequential. Let us first consider their behaviour without relating it to physical time. Process X communicates with process Y (by sending a message, say). We can assert that the send in process X happened before the receive in process Y. Process Y subsequently communicates with process Z. We see that communication imposes a partial ordering on events in the system of processes.

Using < for 'happened before' we can assert:

Events in region x_1 < events in the regions y_2 and y_3,
Events in region x_1 < events in region z_2,
Events in region y_1 and y_2 < events in region z_2.

For other regions we 'can't say'. This reasoning must impose constraints on any mechanism for achieving a common view of time in a system of communicating processes.

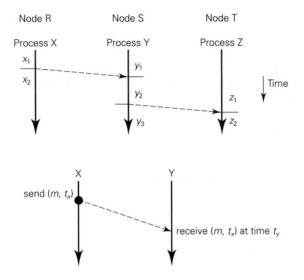

Figure 6.3
Communicating
processes in a
distributed system.

Figure 6.4
Message send and
receive times.

Let us now suppose that the processes each have a local clock which, as we have seen above, may drift. We could use the local clocks to time-stamp events within each process and we could agree a convention for resolving who has won when time-stamps are equal, for example by appending the process-id to the time-stamp. It seems that a total ordering of events in a system is within reach, provided we can ensure that clock drift does not cause the constraints we established above to be violated, for example:

Suppose that process X puts a time-stamp t_x on the message it sends to process Y: send (m, t_x). When process Y receives the message: receive (m, t_x), its own clock reads t_y; see Figure 6.4.

if $t_y > t_x$ all is well,
if $t_y \leq t_x$ we have a violation of the event-ordering constraint.

Process Y could reset its timer to t_x plus one increment and all would be well, except that system time would drift further and further ahead of real time. We would, however, have a total ordering of events in the system.

In the next section we look at how local clocks can be synchronized with standard earth time while maintaining the event-ordering constraints.

6.6.4 Algorithms for clock synchronization

Algorithms for synchronizing with a UTC receiver

First suppose that one computer has a receiver and is functioning as a time server. (At this point you should remember the fundamental properties of distributed systems and ask 'suppose it fails?') The other computers (clients) poll the time server periodically (the period depending on the accuracy required) to ask for the time. The server sends back the time. On receiving the time message from the server, a client may just use this value or may adjust it to allow for communications delay, for example by adding the known minimum delay or by adding half the time since the message was sent.

If the value from the time server is greater than local time the local clock can either be set to it or be adjusted to run a little faster for a short time to build up gradually to this time.

If the value received is less than local time the local clock is drifting ahead of standard time. We may not put it back because of event-ordering constraints but we can adjust the time increments for a period to slow it down, for example from 10 ms to 11 ms.

This algorithm has a single point of failure: the single clock server. For reliability we could have a number of servers, poll them all and use the first reply. For further detail see Cristian (1989a, b).

Algorithms which do not rely on a UTC receiver

If no computer has a receiver the participants may attempt to arrive at an average value of the time shown by their various clocks. One computer may act as coordinator, ask all the machines for their times, compute the average value from their replies and broadcast this to all of them. They can then adjust their clocks as described above. An operator might set the time server manually from time to time. For details see Gusella and Zatti (1989).

Algorithms for large-scale synchronization

The algorithms discussed above rely on all participants contacting a server. Such an approach does not scale to a large number of participants. An example of a large-scale system is the internet in which the **network time protocol (NTP)** achieves clock synchronization to an accuracy of a few tens of milliseconds (Figure 6.5).

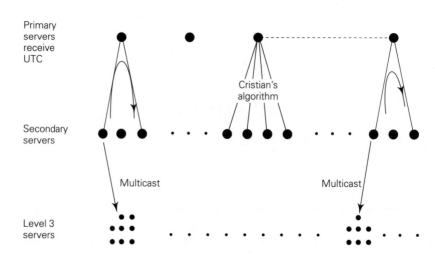

Figure 6.5
Outline of network time protocol (NTP).

A common approach to cope with large numbers is to impose a hierarchy on them. A three-level hierarchy is used by NTP. At the top level are a number of primary servers with UTC receivers. Each of these is responsible for propagating this time down a subtree. At the second level of each subtree are a group of servers which interact with their primary UTC server as described above. Each second-level server then broadcasts its time to the level-3 servers for which it is responsible.

As always in distributed systems we should specify the behaviour under failure. Also, large-scale systems are typically subject to reconfiguration, with nodes joining and leaving the system and this should also be taken into account. These and other refinements of the basic approach are explained in Mills (1991).

6.7 Naming

An operating system maintains a namespace for a single system. Examples of the objects it supports are processes, files and I/O streams. We saw in Chapter 2 that object-based systems are able to use a unified naming scheme for all objects and sketched how this could be defined for a single system. When we consider distributed systems we need to expand namespaces beyond those maintained by a single operating system.

Names are defined in a context. It may be that a distributed system design is based on a homogeneous operating system which supports a distributed object model. Alternatively, we may have to work in a heterogeneous world and devise a naming scheme for the distributed application we wish to build. For example, names may be used only within the context of a distributed file service, mail service, news service or bank account management service. It is useful to model this as a type manager naming objects of that type. In all cases each object named must have a **unique name** within the context in which it is used. We now consider how uniqueness may be achieved.

6.7.1 Creating unique names

Uniqueness may be achieved through so-called **unique identifiers** or by using a hierarchical naming scheme.

Unique identifiers (UIDs)

The namespace is a specified number of bits, so a UID is a number in the range $0 \rightarrow 2^N - 1$ for an N-bit UID. Thirty-two, 64 and 128 bits are typical choices. A UID is never reused and a given bit pattern either refers to the same object at all times or to no object at all.

Hierarchies

Uniqueness is achievable by using a hierarchy as well as a long bit pattern, for example, **puccini.cl.cam.ac.uk** is a unique name for a computer. A manager of the domain **cl** must ensure that **puccini** is unique in that context; the manager of the domain **cam** must ensure that the name **cl** is unique in that context, and so on.

6.7.2 Pure and impure names

A useful distinction is between a pure name which in itself yields no information and an impure name (Needham, 1993).

Pure names

A pure name yields no information such as the location of the named object, or the context in which the name is to be resolved, i.e. looked up. An example is a UID which is interpreted as a flat bit pattern with no internal structure. All we can do with a pure name is compare it with other names of that type, for example in table lookup.

The major problem with pure names is therefore to know where to look them up. It might be that a pure name refers to nothing, but how do we avoid a global search to be sure that no object with that name exists?

Impure names

An impure name yields information and commits the system to maintaining the context in which the name is to be resolved, for example:

puccini.cl.cam.ac.uk (a computer)

jeanb@alexandria.lcs.mit.edu (a registered user)
jmb@cl.cam.ac.uk (a registered user)
    We have examples here of location-dependent names. Note that there
    is no way of telling from the names that they both refer to the same
    person: **jmb** is unique within the domain **cl**; **jeanb** is unique within the
    domain **alexandria**. If Jean Bacon from Cambridge spends some time
    at MIT she is registered separately in both places and must arrange
    manually that any interactions with her Cambridge name are forwarded
    to her MIT name.

host-id, object-id (a form of unique object identifier)
    Here we have an interesting point. It may be that the algorithm used to
    ensure the uniqueness of a UID is to append the host-id at which the
    object was created to a monotonically increasing count at that host.
    It appears at first sight that the object name yields location information.

System policy must determine whether the name is to be treated as a pure or impure name. If pure, the host-id should either be ignored or at most be regarded as just a **hint** about the object's location. If the name is impure we may expect the creating host to keep a record of where any object has moved to.

The major problems with impure names are **object mobility** and the difficulty of restructuring a hierarchical namespace. If an object changes its resolution context by moving to a new location then its name also changes. A hierarchical namespace may be designed to reflect the structure of an organization. It may be desirable to restructure within an organization, by merging departments or creating new ones, or one company may merge with or purchase another. Many names will change if the new structure is to be reflected in the name hierarchy. This problem was tackled in the design of the **Global Names Service** (**GNS**) (Lampson, 1986).

6.7.3 An example: The internet Domain Name Service (DNS)

An outline of this familiar name service (Mockapetris and Dunlap, 1988) will help to introduce the issues of name service provision. In practice, the objects named are computers, mail hosts and domains.

Examples of domain names are:

uk
ac.uk
cam.ac.uk

An example of a computer name is:

puccini.cl.cam.ac.uk

An example of a mail host name is:

swan.cl.cam.ac.uk

The type of the object named is therefore not apparent from the name itself.

Below a notional root are top-level domain names such as:

com (US companies)
edu (US academic institutions)
gov (US government)
net (network management)
org (organizations)
int (international)
uk (the United Kingdom's root)
fr (the root for France)
. . . and so on . . .

Note that the naming scheme has an unfortunate US bias, for example within the UK domain are the nested domains:

ac.uk (UK academic institutions)
co.uk (companies within the UK domain)

and similarly within all countries other than the USA. Although the namespace is badly designed it is impossible for it to be restructured without invalidating huge numbers of existing names, for example for all names that end edu to be renamed to end edu.us.

A domain has a manager but the management role may be delegated to sub-domains. It is the responsibility of the manager of a domain to ensure that unique names are assigned within it.

A directory is a sequence of names, each with an associated list of values (attributes). Users may query DNS to obtain the attributes associated with a given name, for example:

computer-name, location? → IP address
user, mail host? → list of computer names ordered by preference

The DNS namespace is huge. Before 1989 a naming database was held centrally and was downloaded into selected hosts periodically. When the scale of the internet made this approach impossible, DNS was introduced. The domain database is partitioned (as are all large-scale naming databases) into directories and the directories are replicated at suitable locations on the internet.

To resolve a multicomponent name such as puccini.cl.cam.ac.uk:

ac is looked up in the directory for the uk domain
cam is looked up in ac
cl is looked up in cam
puccini is looked up in cl.

If these directories were stored on different computers, four computers would have to be contacted to resolve the name. These directories need not necessarily be held at different locations, i.e. heavily used directories may be stored and replicated strategically to avoid many computers being contacted to resolve a multicomponent name.

As we have seen, name resolution could be a lengthy process and to increase efficiency a resolved name is likely to be cached by your local software. Also, because many users are using DNS simultaneously there is scope for batching queries and responses. Updates are made locally by the domain manager. This makes the local copy of that domain directory up to date but all other copies have become out of date. Changes are propagated to all copies which will be up to date in due course.

In this example (DNS) we have seen:

• the specification (syntax) of unique names within the DNS hierarchical namespace;
• management of the namespace;
• querying the name service;

- partitioning and replicating the naming database because of its large scale;
- name resolution;
- some efficiency tactics.

We now discuss these issues in general terms.

6.7.4 Naming, name services and binding

Name services provide clients with values (attributes) associated with named objects.

Namespace

A namespace is a collection of valid names recognized by a name service, for example:

- a 128-bit UID;
- a pathname in a filing system such as /a/b/c/d in UNIX;
- a DNS multicomponent name such as puccini.cl.cam.ac.uk.

The structure (syntax) of names must be specified.

Naming (management) domain

A naming domain is a namespace for which there exists a single administrative authority for assigning names within it. This authority may **delegate** name assignment for nested subdomains. For example, we have seen within DNS that the manager of the domain ac.uk may delegate management of the subdomain cam.ac.uk.

Directories

The values (attributes) associated with the names for a domain are held in a directory for that domain. The name service is offered by a number of name servers which hold the naming directories and respond to queries.

Binding or name resolution

This is the process of obtaining a value which allows an object to be used; for example, to determine the network address of a named computer or the network addresses of the computers which receive mail (hold the mailbox) for a named individual.

For large-scale systems the naming database is invariably partitioned, replicated and distributed among the name servers, so resolving a multipart name is an iterative process which involves navigation among name servers.

It is good programming practice to bind late and to embed unresolved names, not addresses, in programs.

6.7.5 Attributes stored by name services

A name service maintains an information database. The fundamental requirement is to hold the locations of various types of objects such as users and resources so that they can be contacted or used. A number of attributes may be associated with a given name and a query must specify both the name and which attribute is required.

An alternative form of query, which may or may not be supported by a name service, is the attribute-based query. Here an attribute is supplied and a list of names with that attribute is returned. This is sometimes referred to as a **yellow pages service**, although a naming service may have the functionality of both the white pages (directories) and yellow pages services of the telephone companies. We shall focus on the white pages or directory function.

Name services have typically held the following types of object and associated attributes:

user: login name,
a list of mail hosts for that user, ordered by preference,
authenticator, e.g. password (usually held elsewhere)
computer: architecture, OS, network address, owner
service: list of <network address, version #, access protocol>
group: list of names of members of the group
alias: name
(directory: list of computers which hold that directory)

It may be that, as an optimization to avoid several queries, the network addresses of the mail hosts, etc., are stored and returned on the first query.

The type of **service** listed here is likely to be stable, long lived and widely used, such as a mail service. We shall see later that distributed programs that are short lived and 'private' will tend to use a special-purpose name service for name-to-location mapping.

A design choice is whether a directory should be treated as just another type of named object or whether directories should form a separate structure. In either case, a directory name will resolve to a list of computer names (plus network addresses) which hold that directory.

It may be argued that making a great deal of information freely available is bad for system security. It could be useful for a potential intruder to be able to look up which OS and which version of a given service are running.

Examples of name services include DNS (Mockapetris and Dunlap, 1988), which was described in Section 6.7.3; Grapevine (Birrell *et al.*, 1982), an early classic from Xerox PARC; Clearinghouse (Oppen and Dalal, 1983), also from

Xerox PARC and on which an early ISO directory standard was based; GNS (Lampson, 1986) from DEC; and X.500 (ITU/ISO, 1997). LDAP (Lightweight Directory Access Protocol) (Wahl *et al.*, 1997) is a popular, simplified implementation of the full X.500 directory service. Detailed case studies of these name services may be found in books specializing in distributed systems (Coulouris *et al.*, 2001; Tanenbaum and van Steen, 2002).

6.8 Mobile users, computers and objects

6.8.1 Mobile computers

The use of small computers such as laptops and palmtops has increased over the years and internet-enabled telephones are coming into widespread use. Developments in technology have made it possible to build laptops with substantial processing power and memory and a certain amount of local storage. Increasingly, their owners expect to be able to attach such computers to a network wherever they happen to be. The requirement is then to be able to use their home environment from anywhere in the world as well as access general network-based services. This requirement raises many questions:

- How should a mobile computer be named so that it can be recognized whenever it attaches to a network? The established name services were designed before mobility became a requirement.
- How should a user's home environment, especially files in the filing system, be kept secure but allow authorized remote access, as described above?
- Which services should be used when the computer system is reattached? There may be an instance of a service that is closer than the one in use before the computer was detached.
- If the user was sharing objects with others before detaching, how should the shared objects be restored to a consistent state when the user reattaches? The potential problem is that reading and writing by the sharers of the objects may have continued without restriction during the detached period.

6.8.2 Pervasive computing

Another scenario is that the computing environment is fixed but users may move around. At present the user has to take explicit action by making a connection and logging in from a different system. If she has moved outside her home security domain she may have to make special arrangements to be allowed to login from outside.

In the future, we may live in an environment where computers are ubiquitous or pervasive. We may carry many small devices with us and may encounter myriad small embedded devices. A current example of this style of computing is that a user may wear a locating device such as an **active badge**. A working environment such as an office or university department will contain a network of sensors so that the badges are detected as their wearers move around. The user's computing environment may move with her or she may cause it to transfer to any computer by clicking on her badge at a nearby detector.

This approach can be extended for wide area interworking among a number of geographically separated departments but naming, location and security issues must first be addressed. More generally, we may have active cities where people may find out about their current context (shops or restaurants) or may display the location of a bus or hail a taxi by means of a small personal computing device. Mark Weiser's vision of a future of ubiquitous computing is presented in (Weiser, 1993). The IEEE Computer Society's Pervasive Computing magazine (IEEE, 2002) is devoted exclusively to this topic.

6.9 Summary

The aim of this chapter is to make the reader familiar with the special properties of distributed systems at an early stage in the study of software system design. Most of the readers of this book will be using a networked computer with a window interface as their working environment. Distribution and concurrency are therefore natural properties of everyday systems.

We have looked at time in distributed systems, first emphasizing their fundamental relativistic nature. Current technology allows the clocks of our networked computers to be synchronized at a reasonably fine granularity, but we should be aware that software design may be based on assumptions about time and event ordering.

Object naming was introduced in Chapter 2, first within a single program and then for operating system services. Here we have shown how naming schemes can be designed for large-scale and wide distribution. The next chapter is devoted to security, a topic which has been made crucial by the widespread deployment of distributed systems.

Exercises

6.1   What does a model of a distributed system tell you about? What does the architecture of a distributed system define and what issues are addressed when a system is to be engineered? Into which category, model, architecture or engineering, would you place the following statements:
     (a)   The distributed system comprises distributed objects.
     (b)   Name-to-location mapping is carried out by means of a name service.
     (c)   Name servers are replicated for high availability.
     (d)   Objects may be made persistent and stored in persistent storage.
     (e)   Objects are invoked transparently of whether they are local or remote.

6.2 Criticize the following assertion: 'If every communication is given a time-stamp on being sent then all events in the distributed system can be ordered.'

6.3 Why can it not be assumed that distributed system state will converge after any possible communication delay time has elapsed?

6.4 How does the fact that components of a distributed computation can fail independently of each other affect the way they are programmed? Why does this issue not arise in a centralized implementation?

6.5 What is meant by logical time in a distributed system? If logical time achieves event ordering can it be used without reference to physical time?

6.6 What is the average value of a typical computer's clock drift? What is the accuracy that can be achieved by using NTP (Network Time Protocol)? How would you estimate a value for the time at a computer with a UTC receiver? How would you estimate a value for the time at a computer interacting with a time-server with a UTC receiver?

6.7 How can unique names be defined for a distributed system or application? What is meant by pure and impure names? Why is the DNS namespace hard to change? What queries and responses does DNS support?

6.8 If an IP address is bound to a computer, what difficulties do you foresee for a world with large numbers of mobile computers?

7

Security

In this chapter we consider the security issues associated with the various styles of software interaction we have studied. Centralized software systems, both with single and with multiple users, have **protection** requirements and we discussed in earlier chapters how these can be met. The security concerns in distributed software systems are significantly more severe and they are our main focus here. We first state some of the problems then describe various techniques that together can be brought to their solution. We explain three building blocks that form the basis of most current packages: public key cryptography, private key cryptography and message digest. We explain how trusted certification authorities are used for key generation and management and for authentication.

7.1 Scenarios and security requirements

As a focus for the discussion we describe some common scenarios and discuss the range of security requirements that might be associated with them. We then go on to list the various styles of threat. A system design should have an associated risk analysis where the designers' assumptions of the risks to the system are stated, together with whether they are countered in the design. It should be clear which threats a system is supposed to be able to withstand and which are not addressed.

7.1.1 Client–server interactions

A principal invokes a service. This may be in order to access some object which is managed by the service but to which the principal may have access rights. The service must authorize the access by means of a mechanism such as access control lists or capabilities, as we saw in Section 5.9 for files. Examples of service invocation are accessing one's own file on a file server, buying a flight from a web server (where online payment is involved), ordering goods needed to support a military campaign, accessing a patient's electronic health record, reading stockmarket values and buying shares. Possible requirements are

1 *Mutual authentication*
   The system which supports the interaction must ensure that the principal and the service are mutually authenticated. The service must be assured of the identity of the client and the client must be confident that the intended service is being invoked.
2 *Access control or authorization*
   The service can check that this principal has the necessary rights to carry out the invoked operation on the object, thus ensuring the **confidentiality** of the data. If unauthorized access is allowed, the **integrity** of the data is threatened by any method which can write to the data.
3 *Secure communication*
   No other principal can see the invocation request or result; **confidentiality** is required in the communication.
4 *Non-tampering*
   The request reaches the service as it left the client; the **integrity** of the communication is assured.
5 *Non-repudiation*
   After the service is performed, the client cannot claim that it did not make the request or receive the result. The server cannot claim wrongly that the client did not pay.
6 *No replay*
   A third party cannot acquire a copy of any part of the communication and replay it to ill effect.
7 *No denial of service*
   A malicious third party cannot flood the service or the communication paths to it, thus preventing the legitimate invocation from taking place or degrading the performance.

In a standalone system, such as a personal computer, most of the above requirements are redundant. If such a system is used by more than one person then authentication by password is commonly used to authenticate the principal to the (trusted) system services. In the future, biometrics such as fingerprints or iris recognition may be used. In a distributed system all of the above may be required, depending on the environment and the application. We discuss this further in Section 7.2.

7.1.2 Importing source code and object code

Source code may be provided on disk or from a source across a network. Object code or byte code may be downloaded from another computer across a network. This includes executable email attachments, Java applets to run in client virtual machines, servlets to run in servers and so-called 'mobile agents'. Security requirements may be:

1 *Authenticated source*
   The installer should be confident of the identity of the provider.
2 *Software functionality*
   The software should do what it is supposed to do; it should behave according to its published specification, no more, no less.
3 *Non-tampering*
   The software is not tampered with en route; its **integrity** is maintained.
4 *Non-repudiation*
   The receiver cannot claim, wrongly, not to have received the software.

7.1.3 Connecting home while travelling

The security within an organization may be less stringent than that for external access. It is often the case that people want to access their home-domain computer while travelling. The security requirements may be:

1 *Mutual authentication*
   The remote user and the home system must be securely identified to each other.
2 *Non-tampering*
   The connection request reaches the service as it left the client; its **integrity** is maintained.
3 *Secure communication*
   No other principal can see the connection request or subsequent data transfers; its **confidentiality** is maintained.
4 *No replay*
   A third party cannot successfully replay the connection request.

A primitive connection service might allow a password to be transmitted 'in clear'. This is highly undesirable and could lead to penetration of the home domain by an eavesdropper. The organization may operate within a **firewall** whereby all incoming and outgoing communications are intercepted and vetted. For example, incoming service requests might only be legitimate if their destinations are to web services. The firewall must be able to distinguish legitimate external connection requests.

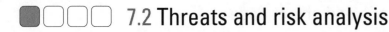 ## 7.2 Threats and risk analysis

The above scenarios have introduced some likely security requirements. We now consider possible threats in more detail, focusing on distributed systems.

- *Masquerade*. A principal may attempt to impersonate someone else. A service may pretend to be some other service. A message may apparently be from a certain IP address when it is in fact from some other address (called **IP spoofing**).
- *Eavesdropping*. A third party may intercept and obtain copies of network traffic. If the message contents are 'in clear' this violates the **confidentiality** of the communication. Other misuses of intercepted messages are covered separately.
- *Tampering with transmitted data*. A message copied by an eavesdropper may be altered and reinjected into the network, thus violating the **integrity** of the message. This is often called a man-in-the-middle attack.
- *Replay*. Messages copied by an eavesdropper may later be replayed. This may assist in masquerade or fraud such as extracting double payment.
- *Unauthorized access*. Some principal gains access to data to which they are not entitled. Not only is **confidentiality** violated but the data is vulnerable to unauthorized change, thus violating its **integrity**.
- *Malicious corruption of stored data*. This may be as a result of a masquerading principal gaining unauthorized access to data. It may also occur when imported software exceeds its specified functionality. The code may be running as a process of some principal and therefore have access to the objects owned by that principal. A **trojan horse** is a software component of this kind.
- *Denial of service*. A denial of service tactic is to flood a network or service with spurious communications, thus denying legitimate use or severely reducing performance. If the attack is from a single source it can be stopped, but attacks are often more sophisticated than this, arranging simultaneous transmissions from many different sorces. **IP spoofing** may also be used to cause an excessive number of reply messages to be sent to some unfortunate network address after messages apparently, but not actually, from that address have been broadcast. Imported software may contain a **virus**. Virus programs may cause an excessive number of processes to be scheduled, an excessive number of emails to be sent, or an excessive number of system management messages to be sent. **Worm** programs are designed to replicate themselves and spread across networked computers. The general pattern is to use up resources, thus denying them to legitimate users.
- *Repudiation*. A principal may deny that some interaction took place in order to avoid payment or to claim ignorance of some item of information.

Once we have a list of possible threats and attacks on a system we can assess the likelihood that each will occur and the damage that would result: a **risk analysis**. Countering security threats costs money, computing resources and performance and a judgement must be made about the appropriate trade-off between these factors for the given system. For example, within a firewall-protected, LAN-based domain, messages might not be encrypted by default, but individuals may choose to encrypt their messages if they wish. A company building with strict control on who enters and where colleagues are well known to each other and trust each other may need little internal security. A hospital may have a community of trusted colleagues but the computer systems are vulnerable to casual access by members of the public who can easily enter.

To address these problems we now study how encryption can be carried out in computer systems and how it can be used. Encryption can be integrated with authentication. Authentication is based on what you are (biometrics) or what you know (a password). A secret encryption key is another example of a secret that you know.

Anderson (2001) gives a comprehensive treatment of how the engineering of distributed systems is and should be approached.

7.3 Approaches to encryption

Encryption has been used for millennia. For an entertaining description, see Singh (1999) which starts with stories of techniques used in military campaigns in classical history and progresses through to computerized methods. Our concern here is encryption for distributed systems and this chapter gives an introduction to basic components which together are used to build secure systems. Schneier (1996) is an encyclopaedic reference on the subject and should be consulted for expansion and further references.

Definitions

A message originates in **plaintext** or **cleartext**. The process of encoding it to make it unreadable in transit is called **encryption** and the process of transforming it back into the original message is called **decryption**. The encoded text is called **ciphertext**. In a computerized system the plaintext is binary data, as is the ciphertext. An **encryption function** operates on plaintext to produce ciphertext and a **decryption function** operates on ciphertext to produce plaintext. A **cryptographic algorithm** or **cipher** is the mathematical function embodied in the encryption and decryption functions as **encryption and decryption algorithms**. All modern encryption algorithms use **keys** which are fixed-length bit-patterns, for example 64 or 128 bits. The range of possible values of a key is called the **keyspace**. A key used to encrypt a message is called an **encryption key** and one used to decrypt a message is called a **decryption key**.

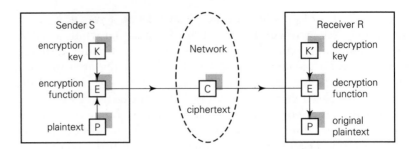

Figure 7.1
Encryption for secure
communication.

Figure 7.1 shows the process pictorially, and in mathematical notation we have:

P = plaintext   C = ciphertext
E = encryption function   D = decryption function
K = encryption key   K' = decryption key

$E_K(P) = C$
$D_{K'}(C) = P$

So that

$D_{K'}(E_K(P)) = P$

7.3.1 Secret key encryption

One of the two general forms of key-based algorithm is based on a shared secret key. In these **symmetric algorithms** the decryption key is equal to or easily derived from the encryption key. Security depends on the secrecy of the key and key distribution is a major concern. Keys are sometimes distributed outside the computer system, perhaps by motorcycle courier. In some environments keys are held in tamper-proof boxes. It also assumes that the sharers of secrets can be trusted not to reveal them deliberately, perhaps to repudiate some communication. We look at protocols based on secret key encryption in Section 7.5 and outline the algorithmic approach in Section 7.4. Note that as well as ensuring the confidentiality and integrity of the transmitted data, the ownership of a secret key can be used to aid authentication; if only two principals know a secret key, their communication is authenticated. Data Encryption Standard (DES) is a symmetric algorithm and is the most widely used encryption algorithm.

7.3.2 Public key encryption

In public key cryptography one key is kept secret (the **private key**) and the other is freely available (the **public key**) and may be distributed widely. As above, the holder of a secret key is trusted to keep it secret. Suppose a message is encrypted with a public key and sent to the holder of the corresponding private key. The sender knows that only the intended receiver, the holder of the private key, can decrypt the message. Now suppose that a message is encrypted with a private key. Anyone who decrypts the message with the public key is assured that the sender

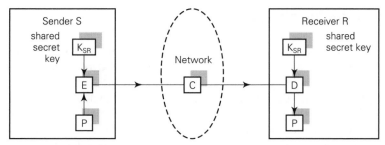

(a) *Only a holder of K_{SR} can read P.*   *Only a holder of K_{SR} could have sent P.*

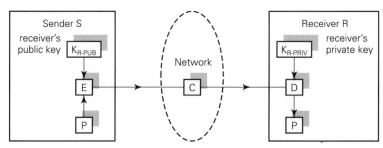

(b) *Only R can read P.*   *Anyone could have sent P.*

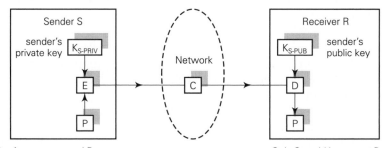

(c) *Anyone can read P.*   *Only S could have sent P.*

Figure 7.2
Secret and public
key encryption.
(a) Secret key
encryption. (b) Public
key encryption:
authenticated
receiver.
(c) Public key
encryption:
authenticated sender.

holds the private key. Note that in both cases, the private key is serving as an authenticator. This technology is useful for authentication as well as for ensuring the confidentiality and integrity of the message. Figure 7.2 summarizes.

An analogy is useful: the distribution of public keys is similar to distributing open padlocks with the same key, or open combination locks with the same combination. Whatever is to be sent is packed in a box and secured by the lock. Only the key or combination holder can open the box. Now suppose that the eventual receiver of the goods wishes to be sure that a particular sender is sending the expected goods (rather than an enemy sending a bomb). The receiver puts his open padlock into a box, secures it with the sender's padlock and sends it to him. The sender opens the box, inserts the gift, secures it with the receiver's padlock and sends it back to him. The receiver opens the box with his key. Here, we have two-way authenticated and secure communication.

7.3.3 One-way functions

We have outlined key-based approaches to computer-based encryption. A different, simpler technique can be used for checking the integrity of data. A one-way function is one that is easy to compute but significantly harder to reverse (invert). However, we are usually not concerned that an attacker might recreate the original text from the output value of a one-way function but rather that two different inputs should not lead to the same output. An example is a one-way hash function which converts an input string to a (usually smaller) fixed-length output string. Alternative names are **message digest, fingerprint, cryptographic checksum, compression function, data integrity check, data authentication code**. Hash functions for ensuring data integrity are designed to make it highly improbable that two different input strings convert to the same hash value. They therefore give us a technique for checking whether a message has been tampered with in transit and, in general, whether two documents are the same.

One-way hash functions may or may not be used with a key. Those without a key can be computed by anybody. A one-way hash function with a key is a function which takes both an input string and a key as input. Only someone with the key can compute the hash value. A hash with a key held by one person only therefore creates a **digital signature** for a document; the person is creating a signature for it that serves the same purpose as a handwritten signature. The keyholder cannot claim not to have signed the document. The remaining question is, how can the digital signature be checked if there is only one person in possession of the key? We shall see in Section 7.5.1 that a trusted third party, a certification authority, can fulfil this role by issuing such keys, by being the second keyholder and by verifying the signature. A second approach is to hash first then encrypt the result with the signer's private key. Anyone can decrypt the signature with the sender's public key then check the hash value by reapplying the digest function to the message that was signed.

We saw another example of the use of a digest function with a secret key in Section 5.12.4 where a server issues a capability giving access rights to an object. The capability is signed with what we called a 'check digits' field. This is generated from the fields of the capability and a secret (a secret key) held by the server. The holder of the capability presents it with each request to access the object. The server recomputes the digest function of the secret, together with the fields of the capability (other than the check digits) and compares the result with the check digits stored in it. If they are the same the access is allowed. If not, the capability has been tampered with and the access request is rejected.

7.4 Algorithms

Cryptographic algorithms traditionally substituted characters for one another or transposed characters. Successful algorithms typically did multiple substitutions or transpositions. Computerized algorithms work on bits instead of characters but the algorithms still employ substitution and transposition.

key	A	B	C	D	E	F	G	H	I	J	K	L	M	N	O	P	Q	R	S	T	U	V	W	X	Y	Z
0	A	B	C	D	E	F	G	H	I	J	K	L	M	N	O	P	Q	R	S	T	U	V	W	X	Y	Z
1	B	C	D	E	F	G	H	I	J	K	L	M	N	O	P	Q	R	S	T	U	V	W	X	Y	Z	A
2	C	D	E	F	G	H	I	J	K	L	M	N	O	P	Q	R	S	T	U	V	W	X	Y	Z	A	B
3	D	E	F	G	H	I	J	K	L	M	N	O	P	Q	R	S	T	U	V	W	X	Y	Z	A	B	C
4	E	F	G	H	I	J	K	L	M	N	O	P	Q	R	S	T	U	V	W	X	Y	Z	A	B	C	D
5	F	G	H	I	J	K	L	M	N	O	P	Q	R	S	T	U	V	W	X	Y	Z	A	B	C	D	E
6	G	H	I	J	K	L	M	N	O	P	Q	R	S	T	U	V	W	X	Y	Z	A	B	C	D	E	F
7	H	I	J	K	L	M	N	O	P	Q	R	S	T	U	V	W	X	Y	Z	A	B	C	D	E	F	G
8	I	J	K	L	M	N	O	P	Q	R	S	T	U	V	W	X	Y	Z	A	B	C	D	E	F	G	H
9	J	K	L	M	N	O	P	Q	R	S	T	U	V	W	X	Y	Z	A	B	C	D	E	F	G	H	I
10	K	L	M	N	O	P	Q	R	S	T	U	V	W	X	Y	Z	A	B	C	D	E	F	G	H	I	J
11	L	M	N	O	P	Q	R	S	T	U	V	W	X	Y	Z	A	B	C	D	E	F	G	H	I	J	K
12	M	N	O	P	Q	R	S	T	U	V	W	X	Y	Z	A	B	C	D	E	F	G	H	I	J	K	L
13	N	O	P	Q	R	S	T	U	V	W	X	Y	Z	A	B	C	D	E	F	G	H	I	J	K	L	M
14	O	P	Q	R	S	T	U	V	W	X	Y	Z	A	B	C	D	E	F	G	H	I	J	K	L	M	N
15	P	Q	R	S	T	U	V	W	X	Y	Z	A	B	C	D	E	F	G	H	I	J	K	L	M	N	O
16	Q	R	S	T	U	V	W	X	Y	Z	A	B	C	D	E	F	G	H	I	J	K	L	M	N	O	P
17	R	S	T	U	V	W	X	Y	Z	A	B	C	D	E	F	G	H	I	J	K	L	M	N	O	P	Q
18	S	T	U	V	W	X	Y	Z	A	B	C	D	E	F	G	H	I	J	K	L	M	N	O	P	Q	R
19	T	U	V	W	X	Y	Z	A	B	C	D	E	F	G	H	I	J	K	L	M	N	O	P	Q	R	S
20	U	V	W	X	Y	Z	A	B	C	D	E	F	G	H	I	J	K	L	M	N	O	P	Q	R	S	T
21	V	W	X	Y	Z	A	B	C	D	E	F	G	H	I	J	K	L	M	N	O	P	Q	R	S	T	U
22	W	X	Y	Z	A	B	C	D	E	F	G	H	I	J	K	L	M	N	O	P	Q	R	S	T	U	V
23	X	Y	Z	A	B	C	D	E	F	G	H	I	J	K	L	M	N	O	P	Q	R	S	T	U	V	W
24	Y	Z	A	B	C	D	E	F	G	H	I	J	K	L	M	N	O	P	Q	R	S	T	U	V	W	X
25	Z	A	B	C	D	E	F	G	H	I	J	K	L	M	N	O	P	Q	R	S	T	U	V	W	X	Y

Figure 7.3
A Vigenère table for our 26-letter alphabet.

7.4.1 Substitution ciphers

In a **simple substitution cipher** each character in the plaintext is replaced by another character to form the ciphertext. Decryption is simply the reverse substitution. In the **Caesar cipher**, each character is replaced by the character three places to its right, mod 26, in the alphabet. In UNIX systems ROT13 replaces each character by that 13 places to the right, mod 26, in the alphabet.

Figure 7.3 shows a Vigenère table for our alphabet of 26 characters; each row gives the encoding scheme for a shift of 'key' places. For example, using a key of five and reading from row 5, CONCURRENT translates to HTSHZWWJSY. For decoding, reading along row 21 (26–5) HTSHZWWJSY translates to CONCURRENT; the decryption key is easily derivable from the encryption key. Substitution ciphers based simply on rotation are trivially easy to break, especially with the aid of a computer; the number of possible keys is the number of letters in the alphabet.

The scheme is made a little more difficult to break by translating first using a codeword then performing the rotation. For example, using the word CODEWORD, and writing it without repeated letters, we have:

A B C D E F G H I J K L M N O P Q R S T U V W X Y Z
C O D E W R A B F G H I J K L M N P Q S T U V X Y Z

The word CONCURRENT first becomes DLJDTPPWKS. It can then be enciphered using a row of the Vigenère table. The codeword must be shared between sender and receiver, giving a key distribution problem. For security it should be changed regularly and this leads to the publication of code books where the 'code for the day' can be looked up. If such a book falls into the hands of the enemy, and is recognized as such, it gives a big step towards breaking the cipher. This happened in the Second World War when the British found the Enigma code book in a captured German submarine. (A recent US film reinvented that particular piece of history by showing the Americans making the discovery.)

Note that in the substitution ciphers above a given letter of the alphabet always translates to the same (different) letter of the alphabet. When this is the case, the properties of the natural language in which the original message is thought to be written can be used to break the cypher. The most commonly occurring letters are known, and their frequencies of occurrence in large pieces of text, as are commonly occurring groups of letters such as TH, RR or ION in English.

Elaborations on this simple approach are as follows. A **homophonic substitution cipher** allows a single character of plaintext to map to one of several characters to form the ciphertext. A **polyalphabetic substitution cipher** uses multiple simple substitution ciphers; the selection depends on the position of the character in the plaintext. In a **polygram substitution cipher** characters are encrypted in groups of fixed size; the encryption algorithm must specify all character combinations and their replacements. Another variation is to use a second piece of (secret) text to encrypt the plaintext in a **running key** cipher.

7.4.2 Transposition ciphers

Here, the letters in the plaintext remain the same but they occur in a different order. An anagram is an example. In a columnar transposition the text is written in rows of fixed length and the ciphertext is read off down columns. The order in which the colums are read is the key of such a cipher. Transposition may be combined with substitution but, since transposition requires a lot of memory and may require messages to be a multiple of the row length, substitution ciphers are more common.

7.4.3 Rotor machines (e.g. Enigma)

In the twentieth century various mechanical devices were invented to automate encryption. A mechanical wheel (rotor) with 26 positions is wired to perform a character substitution; when one character is typed on a keyboard, another is output. For decryption, typing the output character regenerates the input. One

Figure 7.4
An Enigma machine.
Reproduced with
permission from
Volker Steger/
Science Photo
Library.

rotor performs a simple Caesar cipher, so multiple, connected rotors were used. The Enigma machine, used by the Germans in the Second World War, is the most famous example of this style of machine, with some enhancements. A codeword was first transmitted to indicate how the rotors should be initialized for the message to follow. The codebreakers at Bletchley Park in England, among whom was Alan Turing, broke the cipher of Enigma. Bletchley Park is now a museum located a few miles from the Open University. Figure 7.4 shows an Enigma machine.

7.4.4 Encryption by computer

It is beyond the scope of this book to describe cryptographic algorithms and their underlying mathematics. Schneier (1996) gives an excellent overview and many references to sources. We give a brief outline of the approaches taken in some of the widely used algorithms.

Secret or symmetric key algorithms (e.g. DES and IDEA)

The two basic approaches used by secret key algorithms are **stream ciphers** and **block ciphers**. Stream ciphers operate on a single bit at a time; block ciphers operate on groups of bits. An example of a block cipher is DES, which has been an international standard since 1981. Sixty-four-bit blocks of plaintext are encrypted to produce 64-bit blocks of ciphertext. The encryption is based on substitution and permutation, using a key of length 56 bits. The key is extended to 64 bits by including a parity bit for each 8 bits. Only standard arithmetic and logical operations (such as XOR) are used, making it feasible for late 1970s hardware. The process is carried out 16 times (called 16 **rounds**). The repetitive nature of the algorithm makes it suitable for implementation on a special-purpose chip.

The security of the algorithm has been a source of controversy; especially the relatively small key size. Government agencies have the resources to build computers capable of cracking the algorithm and there is speculation as to whether such computers exist. Some DES implementations use triple DES for greater security. Here the plaintext is encrypted with one key, decrypted with a second key and re-encrypted with the first key. For even greater security, three independent keys could be used for three separate encryptions. The choice of algorithm depends on the length of time the data is to remain secret (even data encrypted with a 56-bit key takes significant time for an attacker to recover) and whether the feared attackers are governments.

IDEA (the International Data Encryption Algorithm)

A block cipher to improve on DES was proposed by Xuejia Lai and James Massey (Lai and Massey, 1990) and, with some improvements, became IDEA (the International Data Encryption Algorithm) in 1992. IDEA operates on 64-bit plaintext blocks, 16 bits at a time, using a 128-bit key and employing only algebraic operators (rather than permutations) in eight rounds. These are XOR, addition modulo 2^{16} (addition ignoring overflow) and multiplication modulo 2^{16} (multiplication ignoring overflow). The same algorithm is used for encryption and decryption. IDEA is efficient to implement and is as fast as DES while being more secure.

Public key algorithms (e.g. RSA)

Public key algorithms are based on the theory of large numbers and, in particular, the computational expense of finding their prime factors. As we saw in Section 7.3, keys come in pairs, an encryption and a decryption key, and it must be infeasible to generate one key from the other. The concept was invented by Whitfield Diffie and Martin Helman, and presented in 1976 (Diffie and Helman, 1976), and independently by Ralph Merkle (Merkle, 1978). The first public key algorithms became public at the time that DES was being proposed for standardization and, at that time, they were often seen as competing rather than complementary approaches. The fastest public key algorithms will always be much slower than secret-key algorithms; Schneier (1996) suggests a factor of 1000. Public key cryptography is therefore not used for bulk data encryption. It is typically used for small amounts of data and its use for key distribution solves the problem of how secret keys can be distributed.

Many variants of the basic algorithmic approach have been proposed over the years but RSA (Rivest *et al.*, 1978) is the easiest to implement and most popular. RSA is named after its inventors Ron Rivest, Adi Shamir and Leonard Adleman. The public and private keys are functions of a pair of large prime numbers, which must both remain secret. The RSA algorithm had been invented secretly about four years earlier than 1978. Clifford Cocks was put to work on the problem when he arrived, fresh from studying number theory at Cambridge, at the UK's Government Communications Headquarters (GCHQ) in Cheltenham. His contribution caused a breakthrough in solving the problem, but the work was not allowed to be published.

One-way hash algorithms (e.g. SHA, MD)

Again, there are many one-way hash algorithms. The US National Institute of Standards and Technology (NIST) together with the US National Security Agency (NSA) designed the Secure Hash Algorithm (SHA) for use with the Data Signature Algorithm (DSA). The standard is the Secure Hash Standard (SHS). SHA is an extension of Rivest's MD4 (Message Digest) of 1990. Rivest went on to design MD5 which has some extensions to MD4 in common with SHA. SHA produces a 160-bit hash value.

7.5 Protocols

We now show how the styles of algorithm described above can be used in practice in distributed systems. In order to communicate securely the participants must agree to follow a protocol. A convention has arisen for naming the parties involved in security protocols. When two parties are involved they are called **Alice** and **Bob**. Participants three and four, if they exist, are named **Carol** and **Dave**. We are concerned with various threats and **Eve** is the name of an eavesdropper, **Mallet** is a malicious attacker with computing resources at his disposal and **Trent** is a trusted third party or arbiter. In some cases we will name a **Server**. We give a selection of basic protocols and assume in each case that a cryptosystem has been agreed in advance by the parties involved rather than stating or negotiating it as part of the protocol. Protocols that are used in practice may have to be more complex than the ones in this section to resist a wider range of possible attacks. Section 7.6 describes some that are used in practice.

7.5.1 Secure communication

Secret key

Based on the discussion in Section 7.3 we can attempt to design protocols for secure communication. Using **secret key** cryptography:

1 Alice and Bob agree on a key **KAB**.
2 Alice encrypts her message **M** with the key and sends it to Bob

   Alice → Bob: $E_{KAB}(M) = C$

3 Bob decrypts the message using the key

   Bob: $D_{KAB}(C) = M$

This protocol depends on step 1 being carried out in secret. It also assumes that Alice and Bob trust each other not to disclose the key **KAB**. Although the protocol achieves confidentiality of the communication it is vulnerable to replay attacks and corruption by man-in-the-middle attacks. The message can be signed digitally to ensure its integrity as follows:

1 Alice and Bob agree on a key **KAB**.
2 Alice applies a one-way function to her message $F(M) = H$ and appends the resulting hash value to it **M, H**.
3 Alice encrypts the resulting message with the key and sends it to Bob

   Alice → Bob: $E_{KAB}(M, H) = C$

4 Bob decrypts the message using the key and extracts the hash value,

   Bob: $D_{KAB}(C) = M, H$

   applies the one-way function to the remaining message $F(M) = H'$ and checks the resulting hash value against that transmitted.
   If they agree ($H = H'$) the message arrived as it was sent.

We discuss replay attacks later.

Public key

Using **public-key** cryptography:

1 Bob sends Alice his name and public key

   Bob → Alice: Bob, KB-PUB

2 Alice encrypts her message **M** with Bob's public key **KB-PUB** and sends it to Bob

   Alice → Bob: $E_{KB\text{-}PUB}(M) = C$

3 Bob decrypts Alice's message with his private key **KB-PRIV**

   Bob: $D_{KB\text{-}PRIV}(C) = M$

This apparently solves the problem of secure key distribution in step 1 of the secret key protocol since the key is public and available to anyone. As above, the message may be signed digitally to ensure its integrity and replay attacks will be discussed later. It is, however, vulnerable to substitution; Mallet may substitute his own public key for Bob's, giving:

1 Mallet sends Alice Bob's name and Mallet's public key

> **Mallet → Alice: Bob, KM-PUB**

If Alice does not know Bob's location in advance, or if Mallet is using IP spoofing, Alice may communicate with Mallet, thinking that she is communicating with Bob.

Certification

The solution is to use a **Key Certification Authority** or **Key Distribution Centre** (**KDC**) which is responsible for key management. The KDC holds a **certificate** for each principal comprising its name, public key and any other required information on that principal. The KDC signs this certificate with its own private key. We now have:

1 Alice gets Bob's certificate from the KDC and extracts Bob's public key **KB-PUB** from it. (The interaction between Alice and the KDC is left as an exercise for the reader, as is Alice's verification of the contents of the certificate using the KDC's public key.)
2 Alice uses Bob's public key to encrypt her message and sends it to Bob

> **Alice → Bob: $E_{KB\text{-}PUB}(M) = C$**

3 Bob decrypts Alice's message with his private key **KB-PRIV**

> **Bob: $D_{KB\text{-}PRIV}(C) = M$**

As before, the message may be signed digitally by Alice and we discuss replay attacks later.

Public key cryptography is significantly slower than private key cryptography and in practice is used to secure and distribute keys which are used with symmetric algorithms to secure communication. This is called a **hybrid cryptosystem**. Also, in the public key approach each user has a pair of keys, whereas in the secret key approach a key is needed at least for every pair of users. In practice, a new **session key** is generated for each conversation.

7.5.2 Session keys in hybrid protocols

Using a fresh secret key for each session is obviously more secure than requiring pairs of communicating parties to store and manage secret keys over long periods of time. The time in which replay attacks can be made is limited by the end of the session; we discuss improvements below. In all cases, the message may be signed digitally. We first assume that Alice is capable of generating a session key KAB. A possible protocol is as follows:

1 Alice gets Bob's public key **KB-PUB** from the KDC.
2 Alice generates a random session key, **KAB**, encrypts it using Bob's public key and sends it to Bob

$$\text{Alice} \rightarrow \text{Bob: } E_{\text{KB-PUB}}(\text{KAB}) = C$$

3 Bob decrypts Alice's message using his private key to recover the session key

$$\text{Bob: } D_{\text{KB-PRIV}}(C) = \text{KAB}$$

4 Alice and Bob use the session key **KAB** to encrypt their conversation.

The management of keys is complex. It is argued that users cannot be trusted to generate session keys and this should be done by a secure, trusted server. We therefore introduce a trusted third party Trent into the protocol. Trent's function is both as a certification authority and as a session key generator. Trent's public key is well known.

1 Alice requests a session key from Trent to communicate with Bob.
2 Trent generates a random session key **KAB**. He encrypts two copies, one in Alice's public key and one in Bob's and sends both copies to Alice. Trent also encrypts information about Alice with Bob's public key and sends it to Alice. Trent sends to Alice:

$$\text{Trent} \rightarrow \text{Alice: } E_{\text{KA-PUB}}(\text{KAB}), E_{\text{KB-PUB}}(\text{KAB}), E_{\text{KB-PUB}}(\text{Alice-info})$$

3 Alice decrypts her copy of the session key **KAB**.
4 Alice sends Bob his copy of the session key and her encrypted identity information

$$\text{Alice} \rightarrow \text{Bob: } E_{\text{KB-PUB}}(\text{KAB}), E_{\text{KB-PUB}}(\text{Alice-info})$$

5 Bob decrypts both, retrieves the session key **KAB** and determines who Alice is.
6 Alice and Bob use the session key **KAB** to encrypt their conversation.

7.5.3 Authentication

For authentication Alice traditionally enters a password to prove her identity. If passwords are stored in a computer system for checking, the password file is an obvious target for attackers. However, all that is needed is a mechanism which can tell whether or not this is Alice's password. **One-way functions** of passwords may be stored instead of the passwords, and the following protocol may then be used:

1 Alice enters her password.
2 The computer system performs a one-way function on the password
3 – and checks that the result of the one-way function is the value stored in Alice's record.

Although the one-way function cannot be reversed to recover the passwords the password file is vulnerable to a **dictionary attack** (password guessing). In early UNIX systems, passwords were encrypted like this and the encrypted password file could be copied freely and worked on at leisure by an attacker. Mallet may generate many thousands of possible passwords, apply the known one-way function to them and compare the results with the password file. Any match gives him a password. Stoll (1989) describes a major penetration of this kind.

Salting or seeding

The solution is to concatenate a random bit-string, held securely within the computer system (called a **salt** or **seed**) with the password before applying the one-way function. The longer the salt, the better the security.

Challenge–response

If Alice's password is transmitted across a network in the above protocol it is vulnerable to eavesdropping. Eve may see the login sequence 'in clear' and then impersonate Alice. Public key cryptography can be used as follows:

1 Alice requests login by the server.
2 The server sends Alice a random string **R**.
3 Alice encrypts the string with her private key **KA-PRIV** and sends it back to the server

   Alice → Server: $E_{KA\text{-}PRIV}(R) = C$

4 The server looks up Alice's public key and decrypts the message with it

   Server: $D_{KA\text{-}PUB}(C) = R'$

5 If the decrypted string matches the one it sent to Alice ($R' = R$) the server logs Alice in.

This **challenge–response** interaction ensures that Alice does indeed know the private key associated with her public key. ISO 9798 (ISO/IEC 9798, 1992) is a challenge–response protocol. In the above example, Alice requests to be authenticated by the server. In general, it is a bad idea to use your private key to encrypt something sent to you by an unknown party and return it to them. This could be used against you in many kinds of fraud. In the examples in Section 7.6 we see several alternative approaches to authentication and key exchange.

Authenticating the source of a document: Digital signatures and MACs

We saw in Section 7.3 that the output from a digest function applied to a document, when associated with it, can verify its integrity. We also saw that using a digest function with a key creates a digital signature for the document; only a keyholder could have created the signature. Using **public key cryptography**, Alice signs a message with her private key and sends the message plus the signature to Bob. Bob can check the signature using the well-known digest (hash) function and Alice's public key. Spelling out the protocol, and assuming the hash function to be used is agreed between Alice and Bob, we have:

1 Alice applies the hash function **F** to her message **M**, $F(M) = H$.
2 Alice encrypts the hashed message using her private key **KA-PRIV**

   $$E_{KA\text{-}PRIV}(H)$$

3 Alice appends the hashed encrypted message to the original message as its signature and sends it to Bob, encrypted under Bob's public key **KB-PUB**

   $$E_{KB\text{-}PUB}(M, E_{KA\text{-}PRIV}(H)).$$

4 Bob decrypts the message using his private key, **KB-PRIV**.
5 Bob extracts the signature component and decrypts it using Alice's public key **KA-PUB**.
6 Bob applies the hash function to the message component and checks it against the decrypted signature.

Secret key encryption can also be used for creating and authenticating digital signatures. Only a secret known to Alice alone can be used to generate the equivalent of a handwritten signature. But a secret known to Alice alone could not be verified by anyone but Alice. If only two parties, Alice and Bob, are involved, a secret key shared between them could be used. Alice is then required to trust Bob absolutely; Bob could give away the secret, put words into Alice's document that she did not write, etc. If many parties are involved, allowing them access to Alice's secret key is out of the question so we use a trusted third party: a **certification authority** (**CA**). Alice uses a secret known only to her and the CA; the CA must then verify the document's signature. A possible scenario is as follows:

1 Alice and Trent (the CA) share a secret key **KAT**. One of Trent's functions is to issue such keys and to keep a secure record that this key belongs to Alice.
2 Alice signs a document with a hash function, agreed with Trent, and **KAT**.
3 Alice publishes the signed document in a digital library.
4 Anyone can check with Trent that the document was signed by Alice.
   No one can tamper with the document and put words into Alice's mouth.
   Alice cannot claim she did not write what is in the document.

A name for a digital signature that is created as described above and used to sign a message is a **Message Authentication Code** (**MAC**).

7.5.4 Replay attacks and 'nonces'

We have not yet considered replay attacks explicitly, although the use of session keys instead of long-lived, persistent, secret keys limits the time in which these attacks can be effective. In general, guarding against replay at a short time-granularity adds further complexity to the protocols. The basic idea is to use what is called a 'nonce': a bit string which may be read from a clock or generated by some random number procedure. All parties know that the nonce is to be used only for a single interchange. For example:

1   Alice sends a request to a server, including a nonce **N** with the request before encrypting it with the server's public key

   Alice → Server: $E_{KS\text{-}PUB}(M, N)$

2   The server decrypts the request and recovers the nonce.
3   The server includes the nonce with the reply **M′**, encrypts it with Alice's public key and sends it to Alice

   Server → Alice: $E_{KA\text{-}PUB}(M', N)$

4   Alice decrypts the message, recovers the reply and the nonce, and is assured that this reply is in response to the request she just made.

If Alice receives a replay of the server's reply message she knows it is stale, because she has already had the matching reply. If the server receives a replay of Alice's request message it will be rejected as stale: it has already replied to the message containing that nonce. Nonces add another source of complexity to encrypted communications: they must be detectable as fresh or stale by all parties. One way to achieve such a check is to use a component with an increasing count in the nonce such as a time-stamp. If time is used as a check on freshness, the clock synchronization tolerance must be taken into account and it has been suggested that the clock synchronization protocol could be attacked to create a window of opportunity.

7.6 Examples

In this section we describe some well-known and widely used security protocols and packages. The basic building blocks, discussed in general above, are used as required in these packages and may be thought of as a 'security toolkit'.

7.6.1 X.509 certification

X.509 is the most widely used standard form for certificates (CCITT, 1988b). It was originally designed as part of the X.500 standard (CCITT, 1988a) which addresses the construction of directories of names and attributes for large-scale distributed systems. X.500 defines globally unique names, a topic we discussed in Section 6.7. X.509 certificates have come to be used in cryptography for self-standing certificates. An **X.509 certificate**'s primary role is to bind a public key to information that identifies an individual uniquely. It contains the following information:

Subject	Distinguished name, Public Key
Issuer	Distinguished name, Signature algorithm, Signature
Period of validity	Not before date, Not after date
Administrative information	Version, Serial number
Extended information	

Distinguished name (DN) is the X.500 term for a globally unique name. The subject is the individual or organization, etc., to be certified; the issuer is the certification authority (CA), for example, Verisign. Anyone requiring certification must submit satisfactory evidence of their identity to the CA. All certificates are signed by the CA, using the specified algorithm and anyone using a certificate for authentication should verify the signature. Certificates have a specific period of validity. When a certificate expires it should be removed from the CA's public directory but the CA should keep a copy so that it can resolve any dispute that arises.

If there were a single CA, the procedure, as implied above, would be quite simple. In practice, certificates are signed by different CAs and the CAs themselves are certified (as organizations) with other CAs. A chain of verifications can be needed for two parties to verify each other's certificates.

The extended information field may be used in two ways. Firstly (relating to the owner) to provide additional information on the certificate and its owner. Typically this is application specific. Secondly (relating to the user) to constrain the user of the certificate or to give warnings to anyone using the certificate. There are many problems with X.509, some relating to the absence of the assumed X.500 naming and directory infrastructure. Revocation is another problem that has not been solved. It is assumed that certificate revocation lists (CRLs) will be checked by applications and there is no provision for notification of revocation.

7.6.2 Simple Public Key Infrastructure (SPKI)

X.509 uses distinguished names that are supposed to be globally unique. At the 1996 USENIX Security Symposium, Ellison questioned the need for globally unique names and certification authorities. He argued that global naming is impractical and that instead, names should be made unique by reference to other people and organizations. An analogy in a non-computerized context is that a driving licence, a utility bill or a bank account, each of which contains our name and address, are often accepted as proof of identity.

SPKI was proposed by Ellison and others in 1999 (Ellison *et al.*, 1999). Under SPKI, companies and organizations may manage naming and certification of their employees by supporting sets of publicly available certificates. SPKI supports certificate verification through a chain of certificate providers. Each provider is certified by the next provider in the chain. The process continues until verifiers reach a provider they can trust or until they decide to reject the certificate in question.

7.6.3 Authentication and key exchange

With the advent of distributed systems it became necessary to provide encrypted authentication. For example, the very early Grapevine message delivery system (Birrell *et al.*, 1982), invented at Xerox PARC and used internally by Xerox, provided registration services as well as message delivery. Authentication was originally based on simple password checking. Two of the designers of Grapevine, Roger Needham and Michael Schroeder proposed an authentication protocol in 1978.

Needham–Schroeder (secret key)

The protocol assumes that an authentication server shares a different secret with each of its users. Alice wishes to communicate with Bob:

1 Alice sends a message to Trent comprising her name, Bob's name and some random value **RA**

> Alice → Trent: **Alice, Bob, RA**

2 Trent generates a random session key **KAB**. He encrypts **KAB** and Alice's name using the key **KB** he shares with Bob to form a message **C**

> Trent: E_{KB}(**KAB, Alice**) = **C**

He encrypts **RA**, Bob's name, the key **KAB** and the message **C** using the key **KA** he shares with Alice, and sends her

> Trent → Alice: E_{KA}(**RA, Bob, KAB, C**)

3 Alice decrypts this message and extracts **KAB**. She checks that **RA** is the value she sent Trent in step 1. She then sends Bob the message **C** that Trent encrypted

> Alice → Bob: E_{KB}(**KAB, Alice**)

4 Bob decrypts the message and extracts **KAB**. He generates another random value **RB**, encrypts it with **KAB** and sends it to Alice

> Bob → Alice: E_{KAB}(**RB**)

5 Alice decrypts the message with **KAB**, computes **RB – 1**, encrypts it with **KAB** and sends the message to Bob

> Alice → Bob: E_{KAB}(**RB – 1**)

6 Bob decrypts the message and verifies that it is **RB – 1**.

RA and RB are 'nonces' to guard against replay attacks as we discussed above. Alice knows that Trent's reply is in response to her specific request containing RA. Bob knows that Alice's reply is to his specific request containing RB, and that Alice also knows the key KAB.

The consensus about the security weakness of this protocol is that old session keys are valuable. Any secret that is long lived gives an adversary time to work on cracking the cipher or penetrating where it is stored. Suppose Mallet gets access to an old KAB. He replays step 3 of the protocol, which is the first Bob hears from Alice.

1 Mallet sends Bob a replay of E_{KB}(**KAB, Alice**).
2 Bob extracts **KAB**, generates **RB** and sends to 'Alice' E_{KAB}(**RB**).
3 Mallet intercepts the message, decrypts it with **KAB**, and sends Bob E_{KAB}(**RB − 1**).

Bob now believes he is communicating with Alice. This problem was corrected in several subsequent protocols. The details may be found in Needham and Schroeder (1978).

Kerberos (secret key)

Kerberos was implemented at MIT as part of the Athena project to provide networked computing facilities throughout the MIT campus. Detail of the total system design can be found in Steiner *et al.* (1988). Kerberos version 5, see Kohl and Neuman (1993), is widely used and is part of the OSF Distributed Computing Environment (DCE) and the Windows 2000 operating system. The basic Kerberos version 5 protocol, which again assumes that Trent shares a secret key with each of his users, is as follows:

1 Alice sends her identity and Bob's identity to Trent

> Alice → Trent: (**Alice, Bob**)

2 Trent generates a message with a time-stamp **T**, a lifetime **L**, a random session key **KAB** and Alice's identity. He encrypts this using the key **KB** he shares with Bob. He then encrypts the time-stamp, the lifetime, the session key and Bob's identity using the key **KA** he shares with Alice. He sends to Alice

> Trent → Alice: E_{KA}(**T, L, KAB, Bob**), E_{KB}(**T, L, KAB, Alice**)

3 Alice decrypts the first component and generates a message containing her identity and the time-stamp, encrypted using **KAB**. She sends this to Bob together with the second component from Trent

> Alice → Bob: E_{KAB}(**Alice, T**), E_{KB}(**T, L, KAB, Alice**)

4 Bob decrypts the second component and retrieves **KAB**. He decrypts the first component using **KAB** and computes **T + 1** which he sends to Alice, encrypted using **KAB**

> Bob → Alice: E_{KAB}(**T + 1**)

This protocol is free from the attacks we have discussed so far. A possible weakness is that it assumes that all clocks are synchronized with Trent's. This can be resolved by ensuring that clocks are synchronized to within an interval of a secure time server and checking for replays within that time interval.

7.6.4 Pretty Good Privacy (PGP)

PGP is a public domain encryption program designed by Philip Zimmermann and published in 1992. PGP assumes no key certification authorities. All users use PGP to generate and distribute their own public key. A user can sign another's public key, as a gesture of trust, adding confidence to the key's validity. When someone receives a public key they can examine the list of 'introducers' who have signed it and make an informed decision (or take a calculated risk) on whether to trust the key.

PGP uses RSA for key management and MD5 as a one-way hash function. It uses IDEA (Lai and Massey, 1990) as the symmetric algorithm for data encryption instead of DES. PGP gets an initial random seed from the user's keyboard latency while typing, in generating the random 128-bit IDEA key. Alice sends a message to Bob (as we have seen in our basic building block protocols) as follows:

1 Alice hashes the message using MD5.
2 Alice encrypts the hashed message using RSA and her private key **KA-PRIV**.
3 She appends the hashed, encrypted message to the original message.
4 She compresses (zips) the message.
5 She generates the 128-bit IDEA key **KAI**.
6 She encrypts the compressed message using IDEA with **KAI**. She encrypts **KAI** using Bob's public key **KB-PUB** and appends the result to the encrypted message.
7 She encodes the message as ASCII characters using base-64 and sends it.

To decrypt the message, Bob does as follows:

1 Bob reverses the base-64 encoding.
2 Bob decrypts **KAI** using his private RSA key **KB-PRIV**.
3 Bob uses **KAI** with the IDEA algorithm to decrypt the message.
4 Bob decompresses the message using unzip.
5 Bob can now read the plaintext message (the first component). He can authenticate it by using Alice's public key **KA-PUB** to decrypt the signature (the second component). He now applies MD5 to the first component and checks the result against the decrypted signature (second component).

PGP encrypts the information in message headers as well as in their contents. The only thing an eavesdropper can learn from a message in transit is the intended recipient. Only after the recipient has decrypted the message is it apparent who signed it.

7.6.5 Secure Socket Layer (SSL)

The SSL protocol was developed by the Netscape Corporation in 1996. An extended version of SSL has been adopted as an internet standard as the Transport Layer Security (TLS) protocol. SSL is supported by most web browsers and web servers and is widely used in internet-based commerce. It is designed to work with existing application-level protocols such as HTTP, Telnet, FTP, etc. It is layered between the application and the transport service, which is usually TCP.

SSL is an implementation of authentication and key exchange based on public key cryptography. As such it has similarities with the protocols described in Section 7.5 and in this section. Its unique feature is that it allows negotiation of the particular cryptographic algorithms to be used for key exchange, message content encryption and message digest. We saw that PGP has a fixed selection for these three purposes: RSA, IDEA and MD5. SSL allows the communicating parties to negotiate in order to select the algorithms (the 'cipher suite') they will use from those they each support and approve.

After agreeing on the cipher suite they optionally authenticate each other by exchanging signed, public key certificates in X.509 format. These may be obtained from a Certification Authority or may be generated locally. However this mutual authentication is carried out, at least one public key is needed for the interaction to proceed.

One party then generates a 'pre-master secret' and sends it to the other party encrypted with that party's public key. A pre-master secret is a large random number that is used by both parties to generate two session keys (called 'write keys'). The parties now have a chosen cipher suite, their public and private keys and two shared secret keys. Encrypted communication then proceeds as we have seen in several examples above.

SSL therefore does not depend on the availability of any particular algorithm. It depends only on public key certificates that are acceptable to both parties. Commercial and public domain implementations are widely available in the form of libraries and browser plugins.

7.7 Summary

It is important to explore the security requirements of a distributed software system as part of the design process. Some large research projects have had security cut from their budget on the grounds that it is separable, a specialist field, and can be added later. Retrofitting security may not be possible without major redesign. A risk analysis should therefore be carried out as part of the design process of a distributed system. For example, UK Government edict is that electronic health records will be transferred across networks. Threats may be from journalists, insurance companies, estranged family members. Penetration might be by interested parties walking into hospitals, undetected among legitimate visitors, rather than by wire-tapping heavily encrypted network communication. The human element in security provision may often be the weakest link, and if security measures are complex they will tend to be ignored.

A brief outline of cryptographic algorithms was given, sufficient to convey a general feeling for their complexity and likely performance. We left the details for further study.

We established the basic elements in a security toolkit: secret and public key cryptography and message digest. We saw that public key cryptography is of the order of a thousand times slower than secret key. Practical protocols for other than small amounts of data therefore use public key cryptography to set up the secret keys needed for secret key cryptography. We studied authentication in general, how it might be achieved through the certification of key ownership, and in the context of digital signatures. The simple basic protocols have to be extended to counter various styles of threats and risks such as man-in-the-middle, replay and repudiation.

Finally, we described some examples taken from the literature, from implemented systems and from freely available and widely used packages.

Exercises

7.1   Discuss the severity of the problems associated with authentication and access control for centralized and network-based systems.

7.2   Suppose an eavesdropper captures the complete (unsecured) interaction between a client and each of the following services. Discuss the possible implications.
(a)   Purchase of an item from a web service.
(b)   An interaction with a health advisor (such as the UK's NHS Direct).

7.3   What is meant by a firewall? How can people connect to their computers that are located behind firewalls? How can web services be provided? How can peer-to-peer sharing be provided?

7.4   What are the main problems associated with each of secret key and public key encryption? How are secret and public key encryption commonly used together to achieve the best of both worlds?

7.5   How can encryption keys (initially designed to achieve secure communication) be used for authentication?

7.6   What is meant by a digital signature? How are digital signatures created? How do they support non-repudiation and prevent tampering?

7.7   What is meant by a 'nonce' and what problem does the use of a nonce attempt to solve?

7.8   What is meant by a session key? Why are session keys used? How can a session key be shared securely?

7.9   What is the idea behind SPKI?

7.10 What is the role of certification authorities and services?

Single Concurrent Actions

In Chapter 1 requirements for implementing concurrent systems were established, among which were:

1 Support for distinct activities.
2 Support for management of these activities.
3 Support for correct interaction between these activities.

We have already seen how the first requirement above can be met. Chapter 4 showed how independent activities are supported as operating system processes. If only coarse-grained concurrency is required it might be sufficient for the operating system to support synchronization and sharing of information between processes; a sequential language might be augmented by a number of system calls for this purpose. The problem is that the same system calls might not be available on another operating system; we went on to study how separate activities might be programmed and supported in a high-level language system. If concurrent processes in a language system are to be more than just a structuring convenience it is necessary for the operating system to support multi-threaded processes.

As discussed in Section 2.4 a software system may be described in terms of its functional modules and their interfaces. When we wish to understand its dynamic behaviour we need a model for how the operations of the modules are executed by processes. The set of concurrent processes which comprise a concurrent system cannot be assumed to exist in steady state. We have to consider where they should be placed, how they come into being, how their execution is started and stopped and how and when they are deleted: requirement 2 above. In Chapter 4 we saw alternative mechanisms that might be provided in concurrent programming languages to achieve process creation and deletion. We now go on to explore how these mechanisms can be used.

A concurrent system may be considered as a set of concurrent processes. If the processes are unrelated and never need to interact in any way our problems are over. More typically, the processes need to work together to achieve the goal of the concurrent system: partial solutions to a problem, generated by distinct processes, may need to be combined; a user process may need to request service from a system process. Support for interaction between processes is invariably required. Part II addresses this requirement in detail.

It is helpful to define a framework for considering the problems that can occur when processes execute concurrently. This allows the subject to be presented as simply as possible and in a coherent order. We first study how a 'single action', carried out by a process, can complete correctly without interference from the activities of any other concurrent process.

The notion of a single operation is informal and may be related to the modular structure of systems. A process can read or write a single word of memory without fear of interference from any other process since such a read or write is made indivisible by the hardware. In practice, a programming language variable or a useful data abstraction, such as an array, list or record, cannot be read or written in a single hardware operation. It is the access to such shared abstractions by concurrent processes that is the main concern of Part II; the discussion focuses on the execution of a single operation on a single data abstraction.

First, Chapter 8 establishes a context for this detailed study by taking a high-level view of the software structure of systems. A broad classification can be based on whether processes execute in memory which they share with other processes, in particular, whether shared data objects can be invoked. Alternatively, each process may execute in a separate address space, disjoint from that of all other processes or perhaps sharing only immutable code. In this case processes must cooperate without the benefit of directly addressable shared data objects. The need for both styles of system is justified by a number of examples.

The model of computation underlying Chapters 9 through 13 is that a concurrent program is loaded, proceeds to execute, and builds up state in main memory. The concurrent operations we consider are on data objects in main memory and we do not, at this stage, focus on persistent data that is independent of any running program. At the end of Part II we extend the discussion to consider concurrent invocations of a single operation on persistent data. In this case it is necessary to consider system crashes in which main memory is lost, the concern of Chapter 14.

In Chapter 15 the issues which are peculiar to distributed systems are raised; parts of a distributed computation may fail independently and there is no global, system-wide, common value for time. We again restrict the discussion to the invocation of a single operation on one computer from another.

8

System structure

In Chapter 5 the concept of the virtual address space of a process was introduced and we saw how virtual addresses are mapped onto physical addresses. We also saw that the virtual address space of a process may be divided into segments and that it may be possible for a given segment to be shared by many processes. It is straightforward for the code of a compiler, for example, to be shared by any number of processes while each sharer has a private data segment. We are concerned here with **shared data**.

An important distinction to be made in Part II is whether the processes being considered in a given interaction can access shared data objects directly. They may share an entire address space, and can therefore make use of shared data, as we saw in Chapter 4. They may execute in separate but segmented address spaces in which segments may be shared. If data segments can be shared by processes, again we need to consider how processes should access shared data objects.

If the processes' address spaces are completely disjoint, for example on separate machines, or are such that they cannot share data segments, we must consider how processes can share information without having access to shared data objects. Examples are now given to illustrate that both arrangements have their place in system design.

The concurrent system designer has to decide how to use processes, how many to use and where to place them. Some alternative design possibilities are examined. After this system context is established we go on to explore the support required for process interactions.

8.1 Processes sharing an address space

A file management system might be provided as a subsystem within a closed operating system for a centralized time-sharing system or a personal workstation. Alternatively, it might be provided as a service above a microkernel for local clients or it might run in a dedicated file server machine across a network from its clients.

Examples of possible clients of a file service are: an application process requiring to read or write a data file; a command interpreter, acting in response to a user's command to run a program, initiating its loading into memory from the file store; or a compiler creating an object code file.

We assume that the module which is to implement the service has an interface which offers operations such as **open** a file for reading or writing or **read** or **write** part of an open file, etc.

We can envisage a structure as shown in Figure 8.1 with the following components:

- clients of the service;
- a module concerned with looking up the names of files and checking whether the client making the request is in fact authorized to use the file in the way requested: the **file directory service**;
- a module concerned with locating the required piece of the file on disk, or perhaps in a buffer in main memory if there have already been some operations to read data from the file: the **file storage service**;
- a module concerned with handling the disk and with synchronizing with disk interrupts.

Recall that there is a great deal of system data in main memory recording the location of files and free storage on disk and the transactions in progress (the

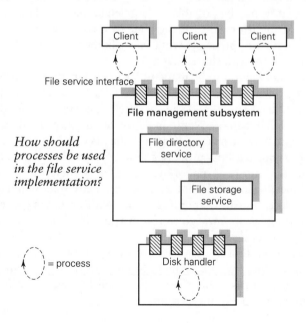

How should processes be used in the file service implementation?

Figure 8.1
A subsystem showing modular structure.

filing system's metadata). We assume that system data in main memory is available as shared data structures to any process which executes the file system code.

8.1.1 Placement of processes within the subsystem

As discussed in Chapter 4 it is natural to place a dedicated process in the disk-handling module. It is natural to place a process (at least one) with each client. The question of interest here is how processes should be located in the intermediate module offering the directory and file storage service. There are a number of options.

1 Use no processes at all. Allow the client processes to enter the service module by calling procedures (invoking methods). Note that if more than one client at once enters the module, problems could occur when they read and write shared system data (see Section 8.7.1). This is the essence of the problem to be solved in Chapters 9, 10 and 11.

2 Use a single file manager process which takes one request for service at a time from a queue of messages. Suppose this process starts to work on behalf of one client. All other clients' requests have to wait until the file manager gets around to them. This is a wholly inappropriate arrangement for a multiprocessor. Even on a uniprocessor, the file manager might find that serving one client involved a delay while waiting for data to be retrieved from disk. It would not be a good idea to keep all the other clients waiting while the (electromechanical) disk rotated. It would be better to start work in parallel on behalf of another client. To do this within a single process it would be necessary to keep track of where it had got to with client 1 while beginning to service client 2. This would effectively reimplement process management and create a multi-threaded server process.

3 Associate a set of dedicated processes with the module. The number could be chosen to reflect the number of processors available or some arbitrary, soft limit. A sensible arrangement would be to have an interface, or listener, process and a set of worker processes to carry out requests. The job of the interface process is to take new requests, one at a time, from a queue of messages requesting service, and to assign a worker process for each. This should be done as quickly as possible so as to free the interface process for handling the next request. The set of worker processes need to share an address space in order to share file system data. This may lead to problems as mentioned in (1) above.

4 Initially, a single process is associated with the module and listens for a request. When one arrives it creates a new process to listen in its place, carries out the request and then terminates. It might be necessary to limit the number of processes that are created and delay some incoming requests. Again, the processes need to share an address space.

We have argued the need for simultaneous execution of the file service code by many processes. Such processes need to access common data structures associated with the file service as well as private data of relevance only to one specific client. The most suitable arrangement is that the processes share an address space. Whether processes enter the (passive) service module by calling the interface procedures or whether there are internally bound processes is a question of system design style. The trade-offs are discussed later.

8.2 Processes in separate address spaces

In many systems there is a requirement for memory protection. In a multi-user system one user must not be allowed to write to or read from another user's memory indiscriminately. Also, in a multi-user system any corruption of the system software affects all users and not just the culprit and there is therefore a stronger protection requirement than in a single-user system. To satisfy this protection requirement it must be possible to control the access a process has to memory, in particular, to be able to prevent write access.

Let us first consider a process running in an address space that is disjoint from that of any other process; that is, it shares no code or data with any other process. Such a process can only fetch and execute an instruction or read or write a data operand from its own address space. This is the case if processes run on separate machines in a distributed system. It may also be arranged in a shared system, if memory protection hardware is available.

Shared code segments

Let us now suppose that memory protection hardware supports a segmented address space and that certain code segments (such as compilers or editors illustrated in Figure 2.10) can have 'execute only' access enforced; that is, any attempt to read or write an address in the segment would cause a protection error. The segment is protected from corruption and it can therefore be shared by many processes. To achieve this sharing the segment must be in each sharer's virtual address space and be mapped onto the same pages of physical memory for each of them. The mechanism is a system convenience to avoid wasting memory on multiple copies of identical, immutable code and is irrelevant to any consideration of a process at an abstract level. We shall consider processes which share user-level code in this way as effectively running in separate address spaces. The issue is whether it is possible for processes to share writeable data segments.

It could be argued that only system code will run in a dedicated server machine, such as a file server, and there is therefore no strong requirement for protection. However, any software may have bugs and memory protection may be useful for containing their effects. The idea is to confine an erroneous process to its own address space by using memory relocation and protection hardware. An error in the communications system should not be able to corrupt the file system, for example. There is no need for communications processes and file server processes to have access to each other's data structures and enforcing this separation by hardware can trap an error before its effects spread around the whole system. We have to pay for protection of this kind by not being able to share memory when it would be convenient, for example, when data read from a file has to be transferred across the network. We shall see how this problem is solved in Chapter 13 and in the case studies in Part IV.

Distributed processes

As mentioned above, an example of processes occupying separate address spaces is when they run on different machines. In this case any communication between them takes place across the network via network hardware interfaces. We assume that a network (device) handler process will be allocated to synchronize with data arriving via the network interface. The network handler will alert a higher-level process that data has been transmitted. As discussed in Chapter 3, we have synchronization between the low-level and high-level communications software and exchange of data by means of a shared buffer.

When a request to synchronize with some local process arrives from a process across the network, a system process implementing a communications protocol will decode the request and decide which local process to signal. We have therefore reduced synchronization between processes on separate machines to synchronization between local processes.

Shared data segments

Memory segmentation schemes often allow only code segments to be shared at user level, as discussed above.

The most general segmentation scheme allows many segments per process with arbitrary sharing. With such a scheme it would be possible for some data areas to be shared (for example, shared system tables and communication areas), but others to be private (for example, work space for a single client). This generality of sharing was a design aim of some early systems such as Multics (Saltzer, 1974), but recent systems have tended to be more restricted.

Section A.2
→

In Part II we are concerned with the problems that can arise when data is shared directly in memory by concurrent processes and with the arrangements that must be made for sharing information when there is no shared memory.

8.3 Sharing the operating system

In order that a process can easily make system calls to request system services, it is often arranged that the operating system code and data occupy the same part of every process's address space, typically one half of it. UNIX is structured in this way, as shown in Figure 8.2. When a process is executing in user mode it

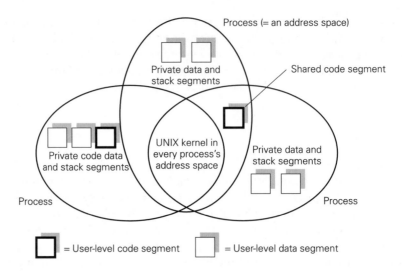

Process (= an address space)

Private data and
stack segments

Shared code segment

Private code data
and stack segments

UNIX kernel in
every process's
address space

Private data and
stack segments

Process

Process

☐ = User-level code segment   ☐ = User-level data segment

Figure 8.2
UNIX structure.

may be separate from all other processes (as in UNIX). When it requests system service by making a system call, it enters a region which is shared with all other processes. Operating system code accesses shared operating system data. When concurrent processes access shared data the problems of interference mentioned in Section 8.1.1 can arise.

Example

Figure 8.3 shows the arrangement of the virtual address space of the MIPS architecture; the Intel Pentium has a similar arrangement. Half the virtual address space is for user code and data, half for the operating system. Much of the operating system must be resident in memory, that is, it must not be swapped out to backing store and need never be moved around in memory once loaded. It is possible to make these parts of the operating system directly mapped onto physical memory, thus avoiding the need for address translation for references to them. The address translation table is a scarce resource since it has room for only 64 entries, and this is a good way of conserving it. There is also provision for some parts of the operating system not to be cached. This is for memory-mapped I/O and data areas used by DMA devices (see Section 3.2).

As discussed in Chapter 5 and above in Section 8.2, if a system supports segmentation it is possible to arrange for arbitrary segments of user-level code or data to be shared. It is common for code to be shared, for example, editors, compilers and libraries. It is less common for a system design to allow data segments to be shared, even if the hardware makes it possible. Figure 8.2 shows the original UNIX design with three segments at user level, one for code (the text segment) and two for data. Although the text segment could be shared, it was not possible to share any data areas. Recent versions of UNIX support shared data.

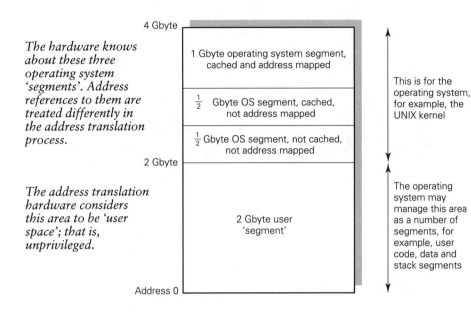

The hardware knows about these three operating system 'segments'. Address references to them are treated differently in the address translation process.

The address translation hardware considers this area to be 'user space'; that is, unprivileged.

4 Gbyte

1 Gbyte operating system segment, cached and address mapped

$\frac{1}{2}$ Gbyte OS segment, cached, not address mapped

$\frac{1}{2}$ Gbyte OS segment, not cached, not address mapped

2 Gbyte

2 Gbyte user 'segment'

Address 0

This is for the operating system, for example, the UNIX kernel

The operating system may manage this area as a number of segments, for example, user code, data and stack segments

Figure 8.3
MIPS architecture virtual address space.

8.4 Summary of process placement in the two models

The above sections have discussed the placement of processes in relation to system structure. Figure 8.4 (a), (b) and (c) illustrates these cases.

Some fundamental points are:

- Processes (often called threads in this context) may share the same address space, as described in Section 8.1 above and illustrated in Figure 8.4(a). Here we have a multi-threaded process (recall Section 4.11). The process is the unit of resource allocation and threads are the unit of execution and scheduling and the active entities which need to communicate.
- Processes may run in separate address spaces on the same machine; see Section 8.2 and Figure 8.4(b). Here we have a heavyweight process model where the process is both the unit of resource allocation and the unit of scheduling and execution.
- User processes may run in separate address spaces on the same machine. System processes on this machine may share an address space. It might be that user processes become system processes when they make system calls and enter the operating system; see Section 8.3 and Figure 8.4(b).
- Processes may run in separate address spaces on different machines; see Section 8.2 and Figure 8.4(c).

To complete the picture, it should be pointed out that a thread of one multi-threaded process may need to be aware of and interact with a thread of another multi-threaded process, as shown in Figure 8.5.

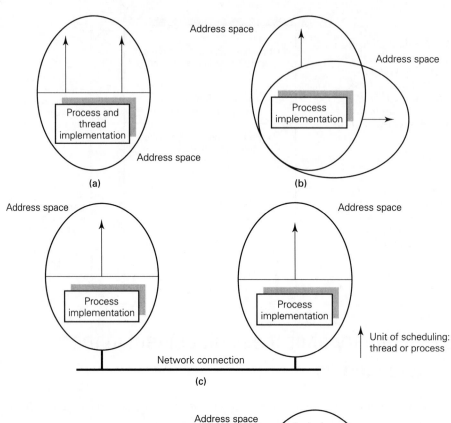

Figure 8.4
Process placement
within systems.
(a) Many processes
(threads) per
address space.
(b) One process
per address space,
same machine.
(c) One process per
address space,
separate machines.

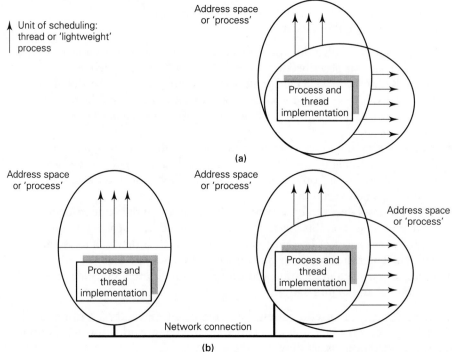

Figure 8.5
Multi-threaded
processes within
systems.

To avoid confusion in terminology we shall continue to discuss **inter-process communication (IPC)** throughout Part II. In systems where threads are the active entities, scheduled by the operating system, it would be more correct to use the term **inter-thread communication**.

8.5 Requirements for process interaction

Bearing these structural points on process placement in mind we now look in more detail at why processes might need to interact and how their interactions might be supported in a system.

1 *Processes may need to cooperate to carry out some task*
Specifically, one process may need to **make a request** for service of some other process and eventually may **wait** for the service to be done. An example from Section 8.1 is a request from a process in the file management module to a disk-handler process to read the disk and to wait for the required data to be available in memory before proceeding.

We have already seen in Section 3.2 that the disk-handler process synchronizes with the disk in a similar way. It issues the commands which cause the required section of the disk to be read into memory, then waits for the DMA transfer to finish. The hardware signals an interrupt when this has happened and the process control module changes the state of the disk handler from blocked to runnable as a result. We have studied synchronization between a process and the hardware; we now have a requirement for synchronization between processes.

It may also arise that one process reaches a point where it must ensure that some other process has carried out a certain task before continuing, for example, that one process has written some data to a file before another process can process it. An example occurs in a pipeline of processes, such as the pipelined compiler shown in Section 1.2. Each processing phase must wait for the previous phase to complete. Another example is that the process requesting I/O must synchronize with and share buffer space with a process-handling device I/O, as shown in Section 3.5.

We are seeing a general requirement for **synchronization**. A process may need to **WAIT** in order to synchronize with some other process, just as a process may need to **WAIT** to synchronize with the hardware.

There is also the associated requirement for **sending a request** or **signalling** that some task has been carried out. When one process **WAIT**s, something should, in due course, cause it to proceed again.

In summary, cooperating processes need to synchronize with each other and to do this need to be able to WAIT for each other and SIGNAL to each other.

This basic requirement is independent of whether they share the same address space.

2 *Processes may* **compete** *for exclusive use of services or resources*
Many clients may make simultaneous requests for some service; several
processes may attempt to use a resource at the same time. The system
implementation must manage this competition; order must be imposed,
making the processes take turns, waiting where necessary, and a choice must
be made between processes making simultaneous demands for resources
which must be used serially.

*Competing processes need to WAIT to acquire a shared resource and
need to be able to SIGNAL to indicate that they have finished with the
resource.*

These two requirements may be summarized as follows:

1 Condition synchronization.
2 Mutual exclusion.

Support for process interaction

Figure 8.6 shows interacting processes, and the implementation of support for the
interactions, in some of the process placement diagrams. The term inter-process

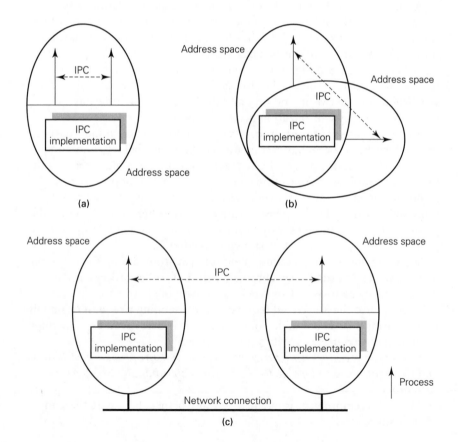

Figure 8.6
Inter-process
communication
(IPC) and its
implementation.

communication (IPC) is used in the figure to include the types of interaction discussed above. We now consider process interactions in more detail.

8.6 Types of process interaction

We have seen how to implement a concurrent system as a set of concurrent processes and have seen a system context for the placement of processes. We have established a requirement for processes to interact in order to cooperate together or compete for resources in order to meet the design goals of the concurrent system.

We now focus on what is interacting with what. There was an implicit assumption that two processes were involved in the interactions described in Section 8.5. If we examine the interactions more closely, we see that in some cases, specific processes are involved in an interaction. An example is a pipeline of processes (see Section 1.2) in which a given process will always need to synchronize with the same processes, those preceding and succeeding it in the pipeline. It may know their names in advance and happily WAIT for or SIGNAL to the appropriate process. In other cases a process may have no idea in advance which processes will require to interact with it and therefore cannot synchronize with specific, named processes.

A general classification of process interaction is described below.

One-to-one

The type of system in which this arrangement is appropriate is one which has a **static configuration** of interactions between individual processes. A process control system where a process reads a sensor or controls an actuator associated with the physical environment is likely to fit this model. These processes send their data to or receive commands from other known management processes. A pipeline structure is another example. The interactions which will take place are known in advance; in particular, the **names** of the processes involved are known.

Any-to-one

The most common example of this type of interaction is multiple clients of a single server. In this case a server process offering the service will accept a request from any potential client process. In a given interaction one client invokes one (possibly well-known) server. The server cannot know which potential client will next invoke it and needs to be able to WAIT for 'anyone' to make a request.

The ability for a system to support this style of interaction in general requires a naming problem to be solved. This is relatively easy for well-known system services: the server process name can be made known in advance to all clients.

One-to-many

This style of communication may be used to notify a set of interested parties that an event has occurred. The term **broadcast** is used if a communication is sent out to 'everyone' and there is usually no record of who has and who has not received it.

A **multicast** implies that a communication is sent to a specific set of recipients. There may (in a reliable multicast) or may not (in an unreliable multicast) be an indication as to whether each individual has received it. In this case the interaction is genuinely 'one-to-many'.

It might be that the system does not support multicast directly and forces the one-to-many interaction to be implemented as a series of one-to-one interactions. This could be very slow if a response from a recipient had to be received before the next one-to-one communication could be made. Protocols have been developed to avoid this cost.

Again, naming is relevant to a discussion of multicast. At the level at which processes are interacting, a group name might be supported to indicate a list of individuals. An example of a slow version of this style of interaction is sending an electronic mail message to a distribution list. In this case the system guarantees to buffer the message until it can be delivered to its recipients.

One-to-many communication may also be used in fault-tolerant systems where a given task must be carried out by more than one process; for example, three processes might compute a result and vote on its value. If one process fails, the other two can still agree on the result.

Any-to- (one of) many

A given service might be provided by a number of anonymous processes. A client needs to request service from any free service process rather than one particular named process. The servers may execute shared service code and data concurrently, as in some of the schemes described in Section 8.1.1, or may run on separate computers in a computer network.

This communication pattern is included for completeness, but it may in practice be reduced to the cases already discussed. The problem may be solved as a naming problem; the required server may be selected by a name lookup (see Chapter 15). Alternatively, a multicast protocol may be used first to request the service. One responding server is selected and we then have one-to-one communication.

Many-to-many via shared data

Finally, as we have seen in Section 8.1, processes may be able to share writeable data. Any number of processes can communicate through a shared data structure.

We shall bear these broad categories in mind in subsequent chapters, although many refinements and alternative methods of implementation exist for each type of interaction.

8.7 A process interaction

We now consider the interactions between processes in more detail, bearing in mind the broad categories of cooperation and competition and the architectural distinction of shared data and no shared data.

8.7.1 Problems when processes share data in memory

If processes share an address space, the system designer may make use of shared data objects to effect cooperation or manage competition for resources. If shared data objects can be written as well as read by concurrent processes, problems can arise.

Consider an airline booking system, for example. The database of flight bookings will be held on disk, but read into main memory for reading and update. Let us consider the data in main memory. Suppose that the seats of a particular flight are marked as free or booked and that each process, acting on behalf of a client, has to find a free seat and book it. If the concurrent processes run on a multiprocessor, or if preemptive scheduling is used, two processes could find the same seat free at the same time and both could proceed to mark it as booked. The problem arises from uncontrolled concurrent access to shared data. (We assume that, even if the airline has an overbooking policy, booking should be implemented in a controlled way and that booking errors should not occur by accident.)

More realistically, booking might proceed on the basis of a count of the number of seats which remain unbooked on a given flight, rather than causing specific seats to be reserved. A booking process might invoke a method to book a seat on a given flight and execute code which includes a statement such as:

if *unbooked-seats* > 0
    then *unbooked-seats* = *unbooked-seats* − 1;

If several processes execute this code simultaneously, overbooking can still occur. First, the value of *unbooked-seats* is read into a processor register (several processes could read the same value), then the value in the register is tested, then (if the value is greater than zero) the decremented value is written to memory.

Figure 8.7(a) shows two processes executing on two processors of a multi-processor. Both read the value of *unbooked-seats* into a register (either from their caches or from main memory) and find the value is 1. There is one seat left! They each proceed to book it.

Figure 8.7(b) shows two processes running on a uniprocessor with preemptive scheduling. Process A reads the value of *unbooked-seats* into a register and is then preempted in favour of Process B. The saved state of process A includes the values stored in the processor registers. Process B reads the value of *unbooked-seats* into a register, finds there is one seat left and books it. When Process A runs again its saved state is set up in the processor registers; it finds there is one seat left and proceeds to book it.

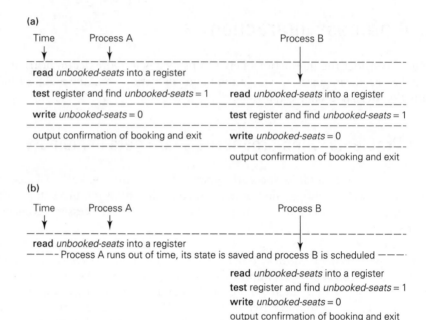

Figure 8.7
Interference between
processes which
share data.
(a) Two processes
running on two
processors of a
multiprocessor.
(b) Two processes
running on a
uniprocessor with
preemptive
scheduling.

The problem arises from uncontrolled access to shared data, but, more specifically, because the implementation of the high-level language statement given above requires several machine language instructions. This is discussed in more detail in Chapter 9.

There are many examples of concurrent systems based on a shared memory model and problems which might arise from shared data. For instance:

- In a process control environment, a count of the amount of material produced might be incremented by many processes which monitor production and decremented by processes which organize the loading and transportation of the material.
- In an operating system, a data structure might be set up to hold requests for service by some system process. In order to make a request, a process must write an entry into the data structure, managing the associated pointers and counts. In order to service a request, the system process must read an entry and manage the associated pointers and counts.

We have focused here on the problem that a single logical operation may not be implemented as a single machine-level operation. In Chapter 14 we return to the example discussed above, of booking a seat, with a different focus. Figure 8.7 showed the statement 'output confirmation of booking and exit'. In practice, this must not be done before the fact that the seat is booked has been safely recorded in persistent memory. If a crash occurs, and main memory is lost, a record of the booking must persist.

8.7.2 Problems when processes do not share data in memory

Here, the problem is how to support the sharing of information, which is necessary if processes are to work together to achieve some goal. A concurrent system in which processes do not share memory requires information to be passed between processes as well as the WAIT–SIGNAL synchronization requirement established in Section 8.5 above. It is possible to support the transfer of data around the system from process to process.

The problems associated with this are:

- **Naming**: the processes involved must know each other's names in order to communicate.

  In a single centralized system we can assume that the operating system will extend the namespaces of the processes it supports so that they can communicate. We return to the need for a system-wide naming scheme in Chapters 12 and 15 when we look in more detail at inter-process communication in distributed systems.

Section 6.7

- The time to copy data between address spaces or to move it across a network.

  Chapter 13 and the case studies in Part IV show how this time can be minimized by using memory management hardware.
- The time to context-switch between processes running in separate address spaces and the number of context switches involved (see Section 4.3.2).

At first sight it appears that no problem of concurrent access to shared data can arise if processes share no memory. However, it might be that a process is managing some data that is of interest to other processes and will carry out operations on it for them on request: the process is encapsulating a data structure. For all the reasons discussed in Section 8.1.1, the process may work on more than one such request simultaneously. We have rediscovered the need for a multi-threaded server process.

8.7.3 Granularity of concurrency

The size of a process, that is, the number of operations it comprises, is system- or application-dependent. For example, it might be appropriate to use a separate process to carry out operations on each element of a vector or array. This is **fine-grained concurrency** and would typically be used to achieve a highly parallel solution on a special-purpose architecture such as a vector or array processor. An example of **coarse-grained concurrency** is the use of one process for each user job in a time-sharing system.

The concurrent systems addressed by this book tend to require processes that fall between these two extremes.

For some concurrent systems, shared memory is highly desirable, so that data structures can be shared, and processes (threads) do not each bear the overhead of separate memory management. In this case it is relatively easy to create new processes dynamically to achieve parallel computation. A new address space, with associated memory management tables, is not needed on process creation and switching between processes does not require a switch between memory management tables.

There is often a limit to the number of processes and threads that an operating system, running on a given hardware configuration, can support. This typically depends on the **space** allocated for process management data structures, memory management tables, etc., and the **time** taken to execute the algorithms which access these data structures.

As we have seen in Chapter 4, many lightweight processes known only to the language system may be multiplexed into a single heavyweight process known to the operating system. Switching between these language-level processes involves less overhead than switching between threads that are known to the operating system.

For some applications, a separate address space per process is mandatory or desirable. Many systems include subsystems of both types.

The concurrent system designer must analyse the application to determine the best decomposition in terms of:

- the number of separate activities;
- the frequency of interaction between them;
- the extent to which they need to access shared information and the granularity of access;
- the need for protection between them;
- the extent to which they need to make potentially blocking system calls.

It is important, for performance and other reasons, to decide where processes known to the operating system must be used, where threads known to the operating system are appropriate and where processes known only to the language system are sufficient. As we established in Chapter 4, it is necessary to know (or choose) the properties of the hardware and the operating system on which the system will run.

8.8 Definition of single concurrent actions

We now attempt to define a 'single' action that might be carried out by a process in a concurrent system. As stated in the introduction to Part II, such a definition must be somewhat arbitrary and is made in order to divide the material to be presented so that we can focus on it in a coherent order. We could define a single action to be a single read of main memory or a single write to main memory.

There is no problem arising from such operations being carried out by concurrent processes, since each operation is guaranteed by the hardware to be indivisible or **atomic**. This definition of a single operation would not help us to focus on the problems associated with concurrent systems.

Rather, we are concerned with a higher-level or logical operation which involves more than one read or write of memory. The examples in Section 8.7 are relevant here. To book a seat is a single logical operation and involves a read, test and write of a count. A request to an operating system process to carry out some service may require a record to be written into a data structure and a pointer to be updated. In these cases we need to execute more than one machine instruction on data in main memory and to exclude other processes from that specific data abstraction until the abstract operation is complete.

The motivation given above is driven by requirement; a top-down view is taken. Andrews (1991) uses the following definition, which focuses on implementation; a bottom-up view is taken to arrive at the same intuition:

> An **atomic action** is a sequence of one or more statements that appears to be indivisible; i.e. no other process can see an intermediate state. A **fine-grained** atomic action is one that can be implemented directly by an indivisible machine instruction. A **coarse-grained** atomic action is a sequence of fine-grained actions that appear to be indivisible.

It is helpful to relate the notion of a single logical operation, or Andrews' coarse-grained atomic action, to the modular structure of systems, and in particular to the abstract data types introduced in Section 2.1.1. A single operation on a data abstraction is the intuition required throughout Part II.

This simple model of a single, logical operation carried out on a data structure in the main memory of a single computer is sufficient for most of Part II. In Chapter 14 system crashes are considered; computer systems crash and main memory can be lost. If you tell a client that a seat is booked then you must have noted the booking in persistent memory or a crash could erase the record that the booking took place. We must therefore consider operations which involve data objects stored in persistent memory.

We extend the definition of an atomic operation to include the property that any permanent effects of a completed atomic operation should survive a crash and that either the entire operation is done or none of it is. If there is a crash part-way through an atomic operation, no intermediate state created by it may persist. We dicuss how this can be achieved in Chapter 14.

In Chapter 15 an operation invocation across a distributed system is discussed. Here again the effects of an operation are visible beyond the main memory of a single system and we have to consider the possibility of crashes in the systems involved and the network connecting them.

Part III considers how several Part II-style operations may be combined into a higher-level operation. An area of concern is multiple related operations within main memory, but the main emphasis in Part III is the problem of multiple related operations on data held in persistent memory (for example, in a database or file store on disk).

Study questions

S 8.1

(a)   In your opinion, which of the four suggested options for locating processes within a file service implementation is the preferable one in a system supporting multiple processes? Explain why. What is the major disadvantage, if any, of your option?

(b)   Assuming that one adopts a solution involving a separate process for every client seeking to use the file service, what might be the best arrangement regarding the processes and their address spaces?

S 8.2

(a)   Under what circumstances is it preferable to have processes in separate address spaces?

(b)   Why does the use of shared code segments allow processes to be viewed as effectively running in separate address spaces?

(c)   In a distributed system do processes share address spaces? How is communication achieved between processes running on separate machines? How is synchronization achieved between distributed processes?

S 8.3

(a)   What are the three varieties of process placement?

(b)   What does IPC mean?

S 8.4

(a)   What are the two basic reasons why processes need to interact?

(b)   What are the two basic operations needed to synchronize the actions of two interacting processes?

S 8.5

(a)   What is the major problem when processes share data in memory?

(b)   Why should a client not be informed that a booking (e.g. for an airline seat) has been made before a record of the booking has been stored in persistent memory?

(c)   What are the problems when communicating processes do not share data in memory?

(d)   Can the problem of concurrent access to shared data arise when processes do not share data in memory?

S 8.6

(a)   What is an atomic action? What is its significance?

(b)   What is the difference between fine-grained and coarse-grained atomic actions?

(c) What mechanism guarantees that fine-grained and coarse-grained atomic actions are atomic?

(d) Define the concept of a single concurrent action.

(e) Atomic actions must appear to be indivisible. What additional requirement is necessary to take into account the possibility of a crash during an atomic operation?

Exercises

8.1 (a) Why is a single process inadequate to implement a dedicated service such as a file server?

(b) Why are multiple processes each in a separate address space inconvenient for such an implementation?

(c) For what kinds of concurrent system would you expect to use a separate address space for each process?

(d) To what extent can memory management techniques be used to achieve the kind of data sharing that is needed in the implementation of a service?

8.2 Consider the file service implementation given in Chapter 5. Which data structures must be accessed on behalf of every client of the service? Which data is private to an individual client? Could memory management techniques, introduced in Chapter 5, be used to achieve shared service code, some shared data and some private data? (Consider the programming language storage allocation scheme outlined in Chapter 4. Assume that each process has a separate stack and that they share a heap.)

8.3 Give examples of interactions between processes that require one-to-one, many-to-one, one-to-many and many-to-many interactions.

For each example other than one-to-one, consider whether you could use a sequence of separate one-to-one interactions or whether you genuinely need an interaction involving many processes simultaneously.

8.4 Give examples of problems that can arise from uncontrolled access by concurrent processes to shared writeable data.

9

Low-level synchronization: Implementation

Concurrent processes need to work together in order to achieve the goals of the concurrent system they comprise. They may need to synchronize and to access common information. We now look at how this requirement for interaction is met. As specified in Section 8.5:

- *Condition synchronization*: Cooperating processes need to synchronize with each other and to do this need to be able to WAIT for each other and SIGNAL to each other.
- *Mutual exclusion*: Competing processes need to WAIT to acquire a shared resource and need to be able to SIGNAL the fact that they have finished with a shared resource.

To avoid the problems that can arise when two or more processes attempt to access a shared data structure, a mechanism must be found that permits only one process to access the shared data at any time. Section 9.1 briefly explores why the event SIGNAL () and WAIT () operations are unsuitable as general synchronization mechanisms. In Section 9.2 we introduce the concept of critical regions: the code which each process executes when accessing a shared item of data. A range of mechanisms can be provided such that only one process at a time is allowed to execute its critical region for a given item of shared data, thus guaranteeing **mutual exclusion;** that is, exclusive access to the shared data. In practice, these mechanisms are built on top of hardware-enforced mechanisms such as forbidding interrupts or certain machine instructions.

For educational and historic interest, Section 9.3 shows how mutual exclusion can be provided, albeit for a fixed number of processes, without hardware support; that is, by software alone. The discussion begins by illustrating the variety of factors that have to be taken into account when devising algorithms that are guaranteed to provide mutual exclusion, and introduces the notions of **entry** and **exit protocols,** which are fragments of code that each process must execute in order to guarantee mutual exclusion. These code fragments come immediately before and after the code of the critical region and correspond to **wait** and **signal**.

In Section 9.4 **semaphores** are introduced, which provide a general software approach to solving the mutual exclusion problem whilst also addressing the synchronization of processes. Semaphores are objects providing **semWait ()** and **semSignal ()** methods. A range of ways in which semaphores can be used is explored in Section 9.5.

In Section 9.6 we consider how semaphores should be implemented. Semaphores can be used for synchronization between processes executing in a shared address space or in separate address spaces. Processes in separate address spaces will be known to the operating system. They may be executing code that was originally written in a sequential programming language, in which case the semaphore operations are likely to be provided as system calls (see Section 4.14).

Processes sharing an address space are likely to be part of a single concurrent program originally written in a high-level, concurrent programming language. The language runtime system will implement them as user threads and, if the operating system supports multi-threaded processes, may make them known to the operating system as kernel threads; see Section 4.12. If the user threads are not registered with the operating system as kernel threads, semaphores will be provided by the language runtime system only to support application-level mutual exclusion and condition synchronization. If they are known to the operating system, semaphores will still be provided by the language runtime system in the first instance. Section 9.6 gives details of how semaphores are implemented and how the runtime system must interact with the operating system.

Chapter 11 shows high-level language constructs that achieve similar effects but are easier for programmers to use. Chapters 12 and 13 focus on synchronization and exchange of information between processes in separate address spaces.

9.1 Process synchronization compared with event signal and wait

Section 4.4 introduced an implementation mechanism which allows a process executing in the operating system to synchronize with a hardware event, typically the arrival of an interrupt signal. In Section 8.5 a requirement was established that a process should be able to synchronize with another process as well as with the hardware.

Chapter 4

We shall first consider whether the familiar WAIT (), SIGNAL () mechanism on events is suitable for process synchronization. Some characteristics of an event synchronization mechanism are:

- In the case of hardware events, a complete list of events of interest may be specified at system design time. We are now moving on to consider general inter-process synchronization 'events'. A system might have a small, static number of processes, but in general we should consider a large number of processes with dynamic process creation.
- When one process synchronizes with one hardware device, simplifying assumptions can be made. It is not necessary to allow for simultaneous execution of WAITs by processes or SIGNALs by the device. The possibility of simultaneous WAIT () and SIGNAL () should be allowed for, but many (uniprocessor) operating systems avoid the possibility of race conditions by forbidding interrupts for a short time while a process executes WAIT ().

These two points, the naming of the processes involved in a communication and the possibility of concurrent use of the mechanism by processes, must be considered when a general inter-process synchronization mechanism is to be designed.

There is usually a requirement for interactions which are more general than one-to-one specifically named processes. One process should be able to WAIT for a SIGNAL from any other process. Also, a number of processes may need to synchronize their accesses to a shared data structure. A given process must WAIT for the data structure to be free if it is in use. Suppose a process has finished its access to the shared data. How should it indicate this to any processes that might be waiting to use it? Again the requirement is for one process to SIGNAL several others which are not known to it. In the next section we see that the solution to the mutual exclusion problem yields a mechanism that can also be used for condition synchronization.

9.2 Mutual exclusion with hardware support

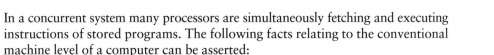

In a concurrent system many processors are simultaneously fetching and executing instructions of stored programs. The following facts relating to the conventional machine level of a computer can be asserted:

- reading a memory location is indivisible or atomic (see Section 8.8);
- writing a memory location is atomic.

There can be arbitrary interleaving of machine instruction execution from concurrent computations and therefore arbitrary interleavings of memory accesses. The possibility should be considered that between any two instructions of one computation, any number of machine instructions of any other concurrent computation could be executed. It should also be noted that a high-level language statement, even a simple increment x++, may be compiled into a number of machine instructions.

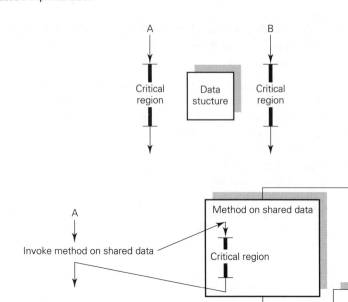

Figure 9.1
Two processes with critical regions for the same data structure.

Figure 9.2
Modular representation of Figure 9.1.

Now consider two processes sharing a data structure. We assume that within each process there is at least one sequence of instructions which accesses the data structure. We also assume that at least one of the processes will write to the data structure and that more than one memory location is written. An example is inserting a new object into a queue: several references must be updated before the data structure reaches a consistent state. Figure 9.1 shows two processes, each with a **critical region** of code for the same data structure. Figure 9.2 gives a more realistic, modular representation of the way operations on shared data would be programmed in practice. Processes A and B invoke methods to operate on the shared data and within these methods are critical regions where the data must be accessed exclusively.

The problem to be solved is how a process can be given exclusive access to a data structure for an arbitrary number of reads and writes. A first attempt at a solution might be to associate a boolean variable with the data structure to indicate whether it is *free* or *busy*. The two processes agree, by convention, that they will test the variable before entering their critical regions associated with the data structure and will only enter if the region is free; Figure 9.3 shows this scheme informally; Figure 9.4(a) shows the scheme in operation for two processes running on a multiprocessor; and Figure 9.4(b) shows two processes preemptively scheduled on a uniprocessor.

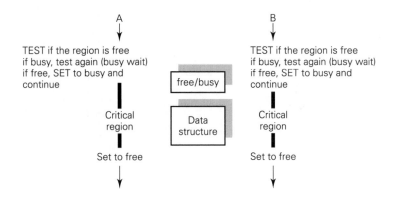

Figure 9.3
Two processes with critical regions for the same data structure: First attempt at control by a boolean.

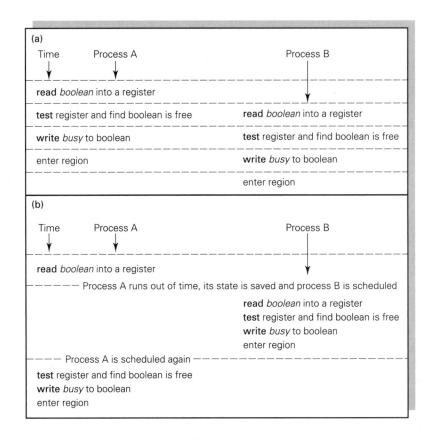

Figure 9.4
Failure to protect a critical region with a boolean. (a) Two processes running on two processors of a multiprocessor. (b) Two processes running on a uniprocessor with preemptive scheduling.

The problem here is that there are several instructions involved in entering the region safely (and several memory accesses) and only a single memory access is atomic. Process A could read the boolean, find the region free, set the boolean to busy using a write instruction and proceed into its critical region. Process B could read the boolean between Process A's read and write, apparently find the data structure free and also proceed to set it to busy and enter its critical region. We are no nearer a solution.

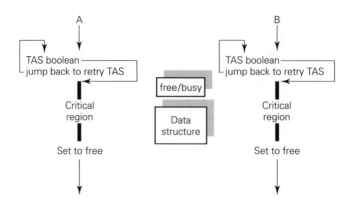

Figure 9.5
Two processes with critical regions for the same data structure: control by indivisible test-and-set of a boolean.

9.2.1 Using hardware to enforce mutual exclusion

Many computers have instructions which perform *read*, *conditional modify* and *write* of a memory location within a single bus cycle; that is, they provide an atomic, conditional update of a memory location. With such an instruction we can implement mutual exclusion on a multiprocessor. One example is a test-and-set (TAS) instruction which is typically of the form:

> TAS BOOLEAN **if** the boolean indicates that the region is free
> **then** set it to indicate busy and skip the next instruction
> **else** execute the next instruction

If the boolean was free it is now set to busy and the process enters its critical region. If the boolean was busy, the next instruction in sequence is executed (see Figures 9.5 and 9.6). The next instruction can simply jump back to try the test and set again, this is called a **busy wait** or **spin lock,** or can jump to some other place where a WAIT which blocks the process is implemented. This is discussed in detail in Section 9.4. Other instructions of this kind include 'increment (or decrement) memory and set condition code' and 'compare and swap'. An example of the use of the latter is given in Section 10.7.4.

A boolean and a TAS instruction may also be used to implement synchronization, as shown in Figure 9.7, but only between two processes. A boolean, to be used as a synchronization flag, is initialized to busy. Process A executes TAS when it needs to synchronize with process B. Process B sets the flag to free. There must only be one possible signaller to set the flag to free since only one signal is recorded.

In uniprocessor systems the technique of **forbidding interrupts** while small sections of critical code are being executed to completion is often used within the operating system. With interrupts disabled, a process will continue to run indefinitely on the single processor. No other process can do anything. This is because the interrupt mechanism is the basis of timing and preemption as well as external device handling. The technique will not work for multiprocessors, since processes are running simultaneously. Ensuring that interrupts are disabled on one processor, to allow one process to run on its processor without interruption, does not prevent another process on a different processor from accessing the same memory locations.

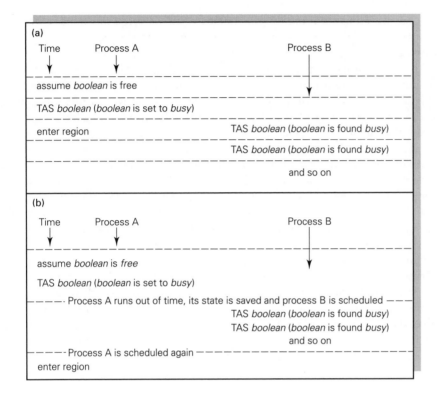

Figure 9.6
Protecting a critical
region with an
atomic test-and-set
instruction.
(a) Two processes
running on two
processors of a
multiprocessor.
(b) Two processes
running on a
uniprocessor with
preemptive
scheduling.

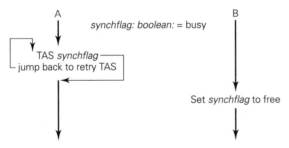

Figure 9.7
Two-process
synchronization
using TAS.

Multiprocessors

If a composite instruction is used in a multiprocessor it is preferable, for performance reasons, that the instruction is such that processes read in the period when they are waiting to enter a critical region and write only once on entry. This is the case in a TAS instruction which reads, tests then writes only if the test is successful, for example, if the critical region is free. This is because each processor is likely to have a hardware-controlled cache (see Section 5.2); a read can take place from the cache alone whereas any value written to data in the cache must be written through to main memory so that all processors can see the up-to-date value. There would be severe performance penalties if several processes were busy waiting on a flag and the busy waiting involved a write to memory. Some composite instructions are defined in the exercises at the end of this chapter.

When a number of processes are busy waiting on the same flag and are scheduled on different processors, each processor's cache will contain a copy of the flag. A test-and-set on a boolean in a cache alone would not, of course, achieve concurrency control. The hardware cache control mechanisms must prevent the use of out-of-date values.

A standard mechanism is that when a memory location is written, all cached entries of that location are invalidated and the new value must be fetched from memory by the next read instruction. A more lightweight mechanism is the 'snoopy cache' designed for the DEC Firefly multiprocessor (Thacker *et al.*, 1987) which is based on the VAX CISC architecture. In this case each cache controller is designed to monitor the memory bus for addresses that it has cached in order to detect whether another processor has written a new value to any of its cached data and, if so, to pick up the updated value.

Section 9.4 describes a general mechanism, the semaphore data type and associated operations, which can be used to support both **synchronization** and **mutual exclusion** and which incorporates the blocking of waiting processes. Although not satisfying all the higher-level requirements established in Section 8.4, it forms the basis of many current implementations and has historic significance. In considering the implementation of semaphores we shall bring together the ideas of Sections 9.1 and 9.2.

Examples of instructions that support mutual exclusion

Current processors typically provide either atomic **compare-and-swap** (**CAS**) or **load linked/store conditional** (**LL/SC**). The simplest instruction for supporting mutual exclusion is a **read-and-clear** operation which can be used as shown in Figure 9.8.

After the **read-and-clear** instruction is executed the destination register contains the value of flag before it was cleared. If the destination register contains zero the data structure was already busy, in use by some other process, but the **read-and-clear** instruction has done no harm. The executing process must not access

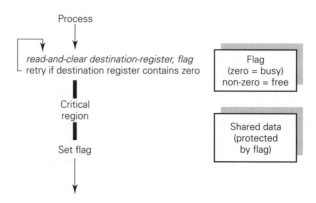

Figure 9.8
Use of read-and-clear to achieve mutual exclusion.

the shared data and must test the flag again. If the destination register contains a value other than zero the data was free and the executing process has claimed the shared data by clearing the flag. The PA-RISC processor provides this instruction. Note that it executes as a single memory to register transfer and is compatible with a load-store architecture. RISC and CISC architectures were discussed in Section 3.2.2.

CAS, compare-and-swap is a more complex instruction than **read-and-clear**. CAS compares the value of flag with some value 'old' and, if they are equal, atomically sets flag to some value 'new'. This instruction requires both a memory read and write and is therefore typical of a CISC rather than a RISC (load-store) architecture. It is provided by IBM/370, IA-32, SPARC, Motorola 68000 architectures and WG94. A simpler register-to-memory swap is provided by the ARM processor.

The general idea of **LL/SC** is to split the read–modify–write idiom of **CAS** into two components. A load-linked (**LL**) from a location by processor i is recorded as 'read by i'. Subsequent invocations of store conditional (**SC**) succeed if and only if it was marked thus by the writing processor and all existing marks by other processors on that location are then cleared. The Alpha, MIPS32 and PowerPC implement variants of this general approach.

In summary, shared data can be accessed under mutual exclusion by:

- forbidding interrupts on a uniprocessor;
- using a hardware-supported instruction.

In practice, we expect to be able to use one of these mechanisms. In the early days of processor design such instructions were not provided and a great deal of work was done on algorithms to ensure mutual exclusion without hardware support. These algorithms are of educational and historic interest and are covered in the following section.

9.3 Mutual exclusion without hardware support

Section 9.2 discussed how processes can achieve mutually exclusive access to shared data. There we emphasized the use of hardware support in the form of composite instructions and discussed the option of forbidding interrupts inside the kernel of a uniprocessor. It must be emphasized that hardware mechanisms are used in practice.

A great deal of research effort was directed towards the mutual exclusion problem before processor designers routinely provided instructions on which mutual exclusion can be built. It was first discussed by Dijkstra (1965), and the Dutch mathematician Dekker was the first to publish a correct algorithm, for two processes. This algorithm was generalized to n-processes by Dijkstra. Subsequently, versions with greater efficiency and alternative algorithms were devised. Two such algorithms are the N-process mutual exclusion protocol of Eisenberg and McGuire (1972) and Lamport's N-process bakery algorithm (1974). We will cover these two algorithms in Sections 9.3.3 and 9.3.4 respectively. Note, however, that these algorithms do not allow for a dynamically changing number of processes.

9.3.1 Requirements

Each process contains a critical region (CR) of code which it may execute any number of times. The phases of a process's execution may be represented as follows:

execute non-critical code
 execute an **entry protocol** for the critical region
  execute the critical region
 execute an **exit protocol** for the critical region
execute non-critical code

The requirements on an algorithm implemented by the entry and exit protocols are as follows:

- The processes may run on a multiprocessor, so we cannot forbid interrupts to achieve mutual exclusion.
- The processors may not have a composite read–modify–write instruction. We must solve the problem by software alone.
- The processes are not identical and no assumption can be made about their relative speeds. It is not satisfactory to arrange that they enter their critical regions in some specific order.
- A process may halt in its non-critical region. This must not affect the other processes. It may not halt in its critical region nor in the entry and exit protocols for it.
- The algorithm must be free from **deadlock** (see Chapter 17). If some processes are attempting to enter their critical region then one of them must eventually succeed.
- The algorithm must be free from **starvation** for every process. If a process commences execution of the entry protocol it must eventually succeed.
- In the absence of contention for the critical region the overhead of executing the entry protocol should be minimal. For simplicity we make the (unsafe) assumption that the hardware does not reorder memory accesses. This is not a safe assumption for modern multiprocessors, but in practice these algorithms are of historical interest only.

9.3.2 Two-process solutions

In order to grasp the key issues involved, we will focus our attention on dealing with the special case where we have just two processes, which we shall name P_0 and P_1. We will show the weaknesses that arise from two over-simplistic algorithms and combine aspects of both approaches in order to produce a correct solution. By studying these examples the reader will get a better feel for the difficulties of writing algorithms that must take into account all the problems posed by concurrent execution.

```
Non-critical code
    // Entry protocol for process P₀
while (turn != 0 ) noOp ();
critical region
    // Exit protocol for P₀
turn = 1
Non-critical code
```

(a)

```
Non-critical code
    // Entry protocol for process P₁
while (turn != 1 ) noOp ();
critical region
    // Exit protocol for P₁
turn = 0
Non-critical code
```

(b)

Figure 9.9
The entry and exit protocols for a two-process system (first attempt): (a) Process P_0; (b) Process P_1.

The approach taken in this section follows that given in Silberschatz *et al.* (2001) and previous editions of that book from 1994. The first two algorithms we present are from Dijkstra (1965). The third algorithm is due to Peterson (1981).

First attempt at a two-process solution

The first attempt, which is not correct, uses a single variable **turn** of type **int**. The idea is that, if **turn == 1** then process P_1 is allowed to enter its critical region, otherwise **turn** will be **0** and process P_0 is allowed to enter its critical region.

Initially, **turn** is set to either **0** or **1** (it does not matter which). The entry and exit protocols for P_0 and P_1 using this scheme are shown in Figure 9.9 using Java notation. The method **noOp** does nothing: it is simply a device to keep the process busy waiting until its turn to enter the critical region arrives. (Note that **!=** means 'does not equal'.) This device is usually referred to as a **busy-waiting loop**.

The entry protocols say that the process P_0 will loop while the value of **turn** is not equal to **0** and the process P_1 will loop while the value of **turn** is not equal to **1**. Depending upon the current value of **turn** these loops either invoke the method **noOp** continually, thereby blocking the process, or are not repeated and permit the process to start the execution of its critical section.

Suppose that **turn** has been initialized to **0** and both processes want to enter their critical regions. This means that P_0 will be able to enter its critical region but P_1 will continue to be blocked by its busy-waiting loop.

Once it has completed executing its critical region, P_0 sets **turn** to **1**, which is a signal to P_1 that it can now enter its critical region. That is, the condition **turn !=1** in P_1's busy-waiting loop is no longer true so the looping stops and P_1 moves to the next instruction which is, of course, the start of its critical region.

This algorithm certainly ensures that only one of the two processes will be in their critical region at any one time. Unfortunately, it has one major flaw: the processes are forced to take turns to enter their critical regions, which means that if the one whose turn is next does not want to enter its critical region (because it is still executing non-critical code), it will prevent the other process from continuing because **turn** is only changed after a process has completed executing its critical section. Thus this scheme fails to ensure that a process that wishes to enter its critical region is guaranteed to do so within a reasonable time. That is, the process is unnecessarily prevented from entering its critical region and may be blocked indefinitely. The term **starvation** is used to describe this situation.

Second attempt at a two-process solution

The first attempt does not retain sufficient information about the state of each process. The second attempt replaces the simple variable **turn** by an array named procphase:

    int [ ] procphase = **new** int [2];

The array has two elements indexed 0 and 1 associated with process P_0 and P_1 respectively. It is helpful at this point to introduce a new piece of notation: P_i. We use it in two ways. Either it stands for any one of the processes when we are *not* concerned with which one, or it stands for a particular process when i is intended to have a specific value. In effect, i acts like a variable. It is common to state the range of values that the subscript i may take. For example, if there were only two processes P_0 and P_1, we would write P_i, i = 0 ... 1. If there were 11 processes we would write P_i, i = 0 ... 10. However, if there were an indefinite number of processes, n of them say, we would write P_i, i = 0 ... n − 1.

In connection with the array **procphase** declared above, there are two processes, P_0 and P_1. There are times when we want to indicate that it does not matter which of the two we are interested in, so we name it P_i (i.e. P_i stands for either P_0 or P_1). However, if having chosen one of the processes P_i, we want to talk about the other process, we will write it as P_j and say that j = 1 − i, where i = 0, 1. For example, when i happens to be 0, then j = 1, but if i = 1, then j = 0. In other words, if P_i represents one of the processes, P_j represents the other.

Returning to the array **procphase** declared above, when the value of **procphase** [i] is 1 (i.e. either one of the slots in the array is 1) it indicates that P_i (the process associated with the ith slot) wants to enter its critical region. And when its value is 0 it indicates that process P_i does not want to enter its critical region. Likewise, when **procphase** [j] is 1 (i.e. the slot associated with the other process) it indicates that process P_j wants to enter its critical region. However, when it is 0 it indicates that it does not want to enter its critical region. Initially, both elements of **procphase** are set to 0 to indicate that neither process wants to enter its critical region.

Figure 9.10 shows the exit and entry protocols for the next attempt.

The idea here is that when a process P_i wants to enter its critical region it signals this fact by setting **procphase** [i] to 1. The process then waits until the other process signals that it no longer wants to be in its critical region (by setting

Figure 9.10

The entry and exit protocols for a two-process system (second attempt).

```
Non-critical code
    // Entry protocol for process Pᵢ
procphase [i] = 1;
while (procphase [j] == 1) noOp();
critical region
    // Exit protocol for process Pᵢ
procphase [i] = 0;
Non-critical code
```

procphase [j] to 0 in its exit protocol). By explicitly stating that it does not want to enter its critical region, one process allows the other to enter its critical region.

Unfortunately, this attempt is also flawed. To see this, we need to keep in mind that the two processes are executing *concurrently* and hence we need to examine what might happen if a particular sequence of events occurs. Suppose, for example, that initially both elements of **procphase** are set to 0 and that P_0 starts executing its entry protocol and sets **procphase** [0] to 1. It could happen that, before P_0 is able to test **procphase** [1], process P_1 begins to execute its entry protocol and sets **procphase** [1] to 1. Now both elements of **procphase** are 1 and therefore both processes will become stuck in their respective loops. Neither process can continue. The word **deadlock** is used to describe this situation in which a process is prevented, for all time, from continuing because it is waiting for an event that will never happen or a resource that will never become free; see Chapter 17 for a general treatment of deadlock.

This is not an unreasonable situation to consider. On a multiprocessor system, the timing of such events is crucial. We could argue that such a situation is so unlikely that it may never arise and therefore need not be considered. But, if this situation does arise, the processes will not be able to continue and the application will cease to function. In other words, the algorithm does not guarantee that processes will never deadlock. If this were to occur in a critical application, disaster might ensue before the problem was discovered. In any case, it is not always clear what should be done if deadlock does occur.

This is not simply a problem with multiprocessors alone. On a uniprocessor the same situation can arise when an interrupt occurs immediately after process P_0 has set **procphase** [0] to 1, and process P_1 is allowed to set **procphase** [1] to 1. Again, both processes will be deadlocked. Our second attempt does not guarantee that deadlock cannot occur.

Third attempt at a two-process solution

The third attempt (an amalgam of the first two) at providing a solution to the two-process mutual exclusion problem does work. In this attempt, two shared variables are used: **procphase**, as before, and **turn** which will be either 0 or 1 and asserts which process will be allowed to enter its critical region next:

```
int [ ] procphase = new int [2];
    // initialize the elements of procphase to zero
procphase [0] = 0;
procphase [1] = 0;
    // initialize turn to 0 (or 1, it does not matter which)
int turn = 0;
```

Figure 9.11 shows the (correct) algorithm. Initially, both elements of **procphase** are set to 0 and **turn** is initialized to either 0 or 1 (it is immaterial which).

Suppose that process P_i wants to enter its critical region. It starts by setting **procphase** [i] to 1 to signal this fact. It then asserts that it is the other process's turn to enter its critical region if it so wishes. Process P_i will be blocked in its

```
Non-critical code
    // Entry protocol for process Pᵢ
    procphase [i] = 1;
    turn = j;
    while (procphase [j] == 1 && turn == j)
        noOp ();
    critical region
    // Exit protocol for process Pᵢ
    procphase [i] = 0;
Non-critical code
```

Figure 9.11
The entry and exit
protocols for a
two-process system
(third attempt).

```
Non-critical code
    // Entry protocol for process P₀
    procphase [0] = 1;
    turn = 1;
    while (procphase [1] == 1 && turn == 1)
        noOp ();
    critical region
    // Exit protocol for P₀
    procphase [0] = 0;
Non-critical code
```

```
Non-critical code
    // Entry protocol for process P₁
    procphase [1] = 1;
    turn = 0;
    while (procphase [0] == 1 && turn == 0)
        noOp ();
    critical region
    // Exit protocol for P₁
    procphase [1] = 0;
Non-critical code
```

Figure 9.12
The entry and exit
protocols shown
side-by-side:
(a) process P_0;
(b) process P_1.

(a)   **(b)**

busy-waiting loop if the other process, P_j, has signalled its wish to enter its critical region (**procphase [j] == 1**) and that it is its turn (**turn == j**) to do so. Otherwise, P_i can enter its critical region. On exit from its critical region, P_i sets **procphase [i]** to 0 to signal that it no longer wants to enter its critical region. It is the presence of the variable **turn** that prevents the two processes becoming deadlocked – by both being in their busy-waiting loops at the same time

It may seem rather odd that having signalled its wish to enter its own critical region, process P_i immediately asserts that it is the other process's turn (**turn = j**). We show below that setting **turn** in this way guarantees mutual exclusion; that is, both processes cannot be in their critical regions at the same time. It is left to the reader to show that the more intuitive way for each process to set **turn** does not guarantee mutual exclusion. To prove that the algorithm as specified in Figure 9.11 guarantees mutual exclusion, we start off by assuming it doesn't. In other words, we make the assumption that somehow both processes are executing their critical regions at the same time, and show that this is an impossible situation and that the initial assumption must therefore be false. To help the reader follow the argument we have shown the code for both processes side-by-side in Figure 9.12. Note that this short demonstration is a standard application of what is called the technique of **proof by contradiction**. This technique assumes the existence of the situation you want to disprove, and then attempts to show that it leads to a contradiction.

If P_0 is in its critical region it must have completed its entry protocol. In particular, it must have completed its busy-waiting loop. This implies that the condition for looping:

procphase [1] == 1 && turn == 1

is no longer true. That is, either procphase [1] == 0, or turn == 0, or possibly both. However, procphase [1] == 1 because the other process P_1 sets this value in its entry protocol (which must have happened because we have assumed that P_1 is also in its critical region). Consequently, it must be that turn == 0.

But the same reasoning applied to P_1 yields the conclusion that turn == 1.

Now it is not possible for turn to be both 0 and 1 at the same time in this protocol. This is because, if P_0 had gone into its critical region first on the basis of turn == 0, turn could not subsequently become 1 to allow P_1 to enter its critical region because only P_0 sets turn to 1 (in its entry protocol) and P_1 has already progressed beyond this point. The same argument applies if P_1 has entered its critical region first. So, the initial assumption must have been wrong. That is, the two processes cannot be in their critical regions at the same time and mutual exclusion is guaranteed.

9.3.3 The *N*-process mutual exclusion protocol of Eisenberg and McGuire (1972)

Let us assume n processes, $P_0, \ldots, P_{n-1}$ which share two variables:

```
int [] procphase = new int [n];
int turn = 0;
```

The elements of the array procphase will take one of the following three values:

public final static int outCr = 0;   // not in critical region or seeking access
public final static int wantCr = 1;   // seeking access to critical region
public final static int claimCr = 2;   // has asserted right to enter critical region

Initially, all entries in the array procphase are set to outCr (no process is in the critical region or seeking entry to it) and turn has some arbitrary value, say turn==0. Figure 9.13 gives an example to illustrate how procphase and turn are used and how they must be manipulated by the entry and exit protocols. In the algorithms i indicates the process identifier and j is a local variable of each process P_i.

The entry protocol for process P_i expresses the intention of entering the critical region by setting procphase[i]=wantCr. If no other process P_k for some k between turn and i (in circular order) has expressed a similar intention, then P_i asserts its right to enter the critical region by setting procphase[i]=claimCr. Provided that P_i is the only process to have asserted its right, it enters the critical region by setting turn=i; if there is contention it restarts the entry protocol.

The exit protocol for process P_i examines the array procphase in the order $i + 1, i + 2, \ldots, n - 1, 0, 1, \ldots, i - 1$. If a process is found which has the value wantCr (or possibly claimCr) in procphase, then turn is set to the identifier of that process. In the example in Figure 9.13, P_2's exit protocol would set turn=3. If every process, other than i itself, has *value* outCr in procphase, then turn remains at value i. Finally, P_i sets its own value in procphase to outCr.

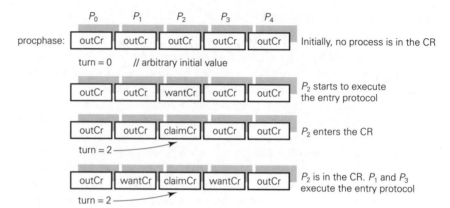

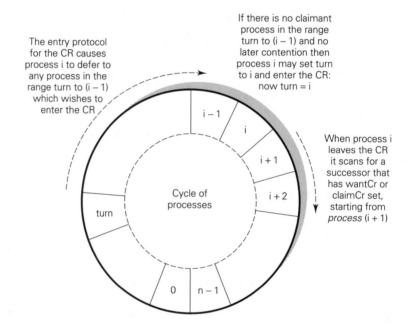

Figure 9.13
An example of the use of procphase and turn by five processes to achieve mutual exclusion.

Figure 9.14
Scanning *n* processes in circular order.

The algorithm depends on scanning the list of processes in circular order (see Figure 9.14). While process P_i is executing the critical region **turn=i**, if at its exit from the critical region no other process has expressed an intention of entering then **turn** remains set to **i**, otherwise P_i sets **turn** to the identifier of the first interested process.

A class implementing the complete algorithm is given below. The following code uses the Java operator %, this is the modulus operator (or mod for short), which returns the remainder after integer division. Thus 7 % 8 is 7 and 8 % 8 is 0.

```
// class to implement Eisenberg and McGuire algorithm

public class EMProtocol {

int n;                              // number of processes
public final static int outCr = 0;   // not in critical region or seeking access
public final static int wantCr = 1;  // seeking access to critical region
public final static int claimCr = 2; // has asserted right to enter critical region

int [] procphase;
int turn = 0;

// set up the protocol for a given number of processes
public EMProtocol(int noProcesses) {
   n = noProcesses;
   procphase = new int [noProcesses];      // elements initialized to 0 (outCr)
}

// entry protocol for process i
public void entry (int i) {
int j;
   do {
       procphase [i] = wantCr;
       j = turn;
       while (j != i){                     // no check if turn==i
       if  (procphase[j] == outCr)
          j = (j+1) % n;
       else j = turn;                       // restart scan
   }
       procphase [i] = claimCr;             // no prior claimant
       j = (i + 1) % n;
       while (procphase[j] != claimCr) j = (j+1) % n;  // contention?
   }
   while( !((j==i) && (turn==i || procphase[turn]==outCr)) );
   turn = i;
}

// exit protocol for process i
public void exit (int i) {
   int j;
   j = (turn +1) % n;                       // turn = i
   while (procphase[j] == outCr) j = (j+1) % n;  // any interest ?
   turn = j;
   procphase[i] = outCr;
   }
}
```

Suppose that a process has finished its turn but has found no successor waiting to enter (see Figure 9.14). Later, process i starts its entry protocol. procphase[i] will be reset to **outCr** only after process i has been through its critical

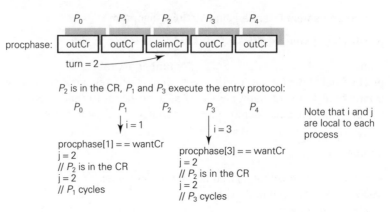

P_2 is in the CR, P_1 and P_3 execute the entry protocol:

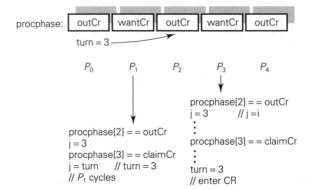

Note that i and j
are local to each
process

Figure 9.15
An example
illustrating the entry
protocol.

region; hence only processes to which process i defers can obtain right of entry before it does. Any such process on exit will detect that process i is waiting to enter, unless some other process intermediate in the cycle is also waiting. At worst, process i will be given its turn after a single critical region execution by each such intermediate process.

In order to understand the entry protocol we shall use an example with five processes and consider some simple cases, followed by parallel execution of the entry protocol.

Figure 9.15 illustrates the case where two processes are waiting to enter the critical region when P_2 exits from it. P_3 detects that P_2 has left the region and that **turn=3**. It therefore proceeds to set **procphase[3]=claimCr** and (eventually) **turn=3**.

The reader should consider what happens if P_1 runs before P_3 after P_2 exits from the critical region.

Figure 9.16 illustrates the case where P_2 exits from the critical region and no processes are waiting to enter. Later P_1 and P_3 execute the entry protocol with instruction execution in parallel as shown in the figure.

The reader should consider:

1 What happens when P_1 and P_3 restart their entry protocols? Why do they not cycle indefinitely as shown in the figure?

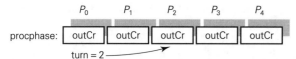

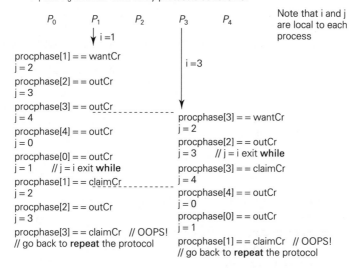

Figure 9.16
Parallel execution of
the entry protocol.

2 What happens if P_2 attempts to re-enter the critical region while P_1 and P_3
   are executing the entry protocol as shown? Recall that **turn** still has value **2**
   when P_2 has finished the exit protocol in this example.
3 What happens if P_0 and P_4 start to execute the entry protocol?
4 How many turns can P_1 have to wait between starting its entry protocol by
   setting **wantCr** and entering its critical region?

9.3.4 The *N*-process bakery algorithm

In 1974 Lamport published an algorithm based on the method used in bakeries,
shoe shops, etc., for achieving service in first come first served order. The idea is
that a process which wishes to enter the critical region takes a ticket and it is
arranged that the processes enter the critical region in the order of the number
on their tickets.

A class implementing the bakery algorithm is as follows:

```
// class to implement bakery algorithm

public class Bakery {

int n;          // number of processes
boolean [] taking;
int [] ticket;
```

Suppose that P_1 has taken a ticket with number 1 and P_4 then takes a ticket with number 2

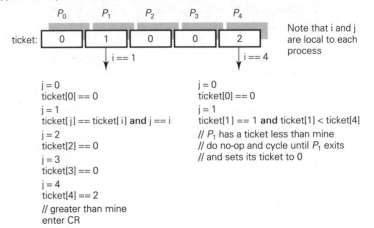

Note that i and j are local to each process

j = 0
ticket[0] == 0
j = 1
ticket[j] == ticket[i] **and** j == i
j = 2
ticket[2] == 0
j = 3
ticket[3] == 0
j = 4
ticket[4] == 2
// greater than mine
enter CR

j = 0
ticket[0] == 0
j = 1
ticket[1] == 1 **and** ticket[1] < ticket[4]
// P_1 has a ticket less than mine
// do no-op and cycle until P_1 exits
// and sets its ticket to 0

Figure 9.17
Parallel execution of
the bakery protocol.

```
// set up the protocol for a given number of processes
public Bakery (int noProcesses) {
    n = noProcesses;
    // taking elements automatically initialized to false
    taking = new boolean [noProcesses];
    // ticket elements automatically initialized to 0
    ticket = new int [noProcesses];

}

// entry protocol for the critical region for process i
public void entry (int i) {
    int j;

    taking[i] = true;
    ticket[i] = max(ticket)+1;
    taking[i] = false;
    for (j= 0; j < n ; j++) {
        while (taking[j]) noOp();
            while (ticket[j] != 0 &&((ticket[j] < ticket[i]) || ((ticket[j] == ticket[i])
                    && j < i)))
                noOp();
    }
}

// exit protocol for the critical region for process i
public void exit (int i) {
    ticket[i] = 0;
}

private void noOp () {
}
```

```
private int max (int [] a) {
    int i,max = 0;
    for (i=0 ; i < a.length; i++)
        if (a[i] > max)
            max = a[i];
    return max;
    }
}
```

9.4 Semaphores

In 1968 Edsger Dijkstra published a paper on the design of a small but carefully structured operating system called THE, which is described in Section 10.2. The design was based on a small, static number of concurrent processes which synchronized with each other and with the hardware by means of a mechanism called a semaphore.

A semaphore is an object with operations **semSignal ()** and **semWait ()**. The attributes of a semaphore are typically an integer and a queue (Figure 9.18). The definitions of the semaphore operations are as follows:

semWait ()   If the value of the semaphore's integer is greater than zero then decrement it and allow the process to continue, else suspend the process (noting that it is blocked on this semaphore).

semSignal ()   If there are no processes waiting on the semaphore then increment the integer; else free one process, which continues at the instruction after its WAIT instruction.

We can envisage semaphores as a class which may be located in the operating system (for semaphores of concern to the operating system) and also in the language runtime system (for semaphores which are not of concern to the operating system); see Section 9.6.3.

We will assume that a semaphore class which implements the interface below is available to us. We will see how we can implement this interface later on. In general, we will require a constructor for any class implementing **Semaphore** which allows an initial integer value to be specified.

```
public interface Semaphore {
    public void semWait();
    public void semSignal();
}
```

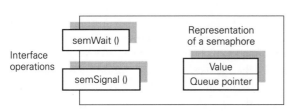

Figure 9.18
A semaphore object.

A typical usage is as follows, to declare a semaphore called *lock* and initialize it to 1:

```
Semaphore lock = new SemaphoreImplementation(1);
```

an example of use of a semaphore:

```
lock.semWait( );
access data
lock.semSignal( );
```

We shall now cover some examples of the ways in which semaphores may be used and then look in more detail at systems implications of their implementation.

 # 9.5 Styles of use of semaphores

Semaphores can be used for a range of purposes. In the following sections we will see that they can be used to achieve (1) mutual exclusion; (2) synchronization of cooperating processes and; (3) management of multiple resource allocation. These different usages are achieved through varying the initial integer value of the semaphore as well as working with different orderings of the **semWait** () and **semSignal** () methods.

9.5.1 Mutual exclusion

A semaphore initialized to 1 may be used to provide exclusive access to a shared resource such as a data structure.

```
MyClass DataStructure // shared data structure
```

```
Semaphore lock = new SemaphoreImplementation(1);
```

To use a semaphore:

```
non-critical instructions
lock.semWait();   // start of critical region
    access shared-data-structure
lock.semSignal(); // end of critical region
non-critical instructions
```

Figure 9.19 shows one possible time sequence for three processes, A, B and C, which access a shared resource. The resource is protected by a semaphore called **lock**, which is initialized to 1. Process A first executes **lock.semWait** () and enters its critical code which accesses the shared resource. While A is in its critical region first B then C attempt to enter their critical regions for the same resource by executing **lock.semWait** (). Figure 9.19 shows the states of the semaphore as these events occur. A then leaves its critical region by executing **lock.semSignal** (). B can then proceed into its critical code and leave it by **lock.semSignal** (), allowing C to execute its critical code.

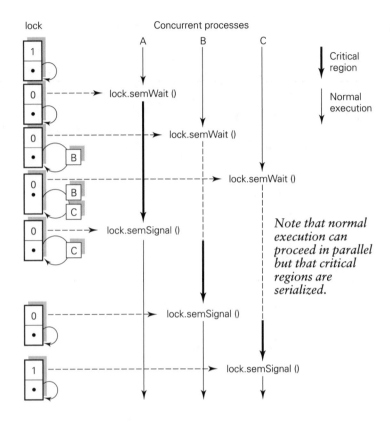

lock Concurrent processes

A B C

Critical region

Normal execution

lock.semWait ()

lock.semWait ()

lock.semWait ()

lock.semSignal ()

lock.semSignal ()

lock.semSignal ()

Note that normal execution can proceed in parallel but that critical regions are serialized.

Figure 9.19
Processes accessing shared data protected by a semaphore.

In general, A, B and C can execute concurrently. Their critical regions with respect to the resource they share have been **serialized** so that only one process accesses the resource at once.

Note that an assumption has been made about the scheduling of processes waiting on the same semaphore, namely that the first process to be queued on **semWait** () will be the first to be freed on **semSignal** (). This is an implementation decision. An alternative implementation is to free all waiting processes and make them execute **semWait** () again when next they are scheduled to run. In this case the scheduling algorithm of the operating system is used to select which process should proceed. Yet another alternative is to implement a scheduling policy for the semaphore queue based on some notion of process priority made available to the semaphore implementation. This is discussed further in Section 9.6.

9.5.2 Condition synchronization

We started the chapter with the requirement that two processes should be able to synchronize their activities. A semaphore can be used for this purpose. Consider two cooperating processes such that when A reaches a certain point it should not proceed until B has performed some task. This synchronization can be

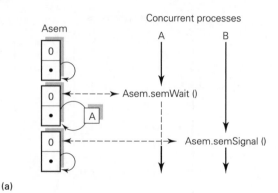

(a)

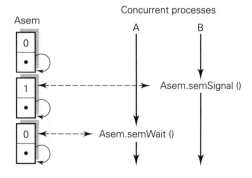

Figure 9.20
Two-process
synchronization:
(a) semWait () before
semSignal ().
(b) semSignal ()
before semWait ().

(b)

achieved by using a semaphore initialized to zero on which A should **semWait ()** at the synchronization point and which B should **semSignal ()**. Figure 9.20 shows the two possible situations that can arise when a process (in this case, A) must wait for another (in this case, B) to finish some task. Part (a) covers the case where A reaches the waiting point *before* B signals it has finished the task. Part (b) shows what would happen if A arrives at its waiting point *after* B has signalled that the task is finished. Notice how in this scenario, one process (A) only executes **semWait ()**, while the other executes **semSignal ()**. This is different from Figure 9.19, where each process first executes a **semWait ()** followed by a **semSignal ()**.

This use of semaphores can be generalized to many signallers of process A's semaphore. Semaphores used in this way have been called private semaphores: only one process may **semWait ()** on the semaphore, while any number may **semSignal ()**.

9.5.3 Multiple instances of a resource

Previously, we have considered the situation in which exclusive access to a resource is required. There are cases where we may wish to allow more than one process to access a resource simultaneously, but want to limit the number of simultaneous accesses. For example, a computer system may have two similar printers and it may not matter which one is used by any particular process. Thus we can think of these printers as a single printing resource that can be accessed by up to two processes at a time. In such an example, an appropriate semaphore would be initialized to 2 to indicate the degree of accessibility of the resource. For mutual exclusion (i.e. single use), a semaphore is initialized to 1.

Every time a process P_i requests access to the resource, and the value of its associated semaphore is greater than zero, the value is *decremented* by 1. When the value of the semaphore reaches zero it is an indication that subsequent attempts to access the resource must be blocked, and the process is queued. When a process releases the resource, a check is made to see whether there are any queued processes. If not, the value of the semaphore is *incremented* by 1; otherwise, one of the queued processes is given access to the resource.

This use of semaphores is based on the idea that, if there are several processes which require access to a resource (more than the resource can accommodate simultaneously), the **semWait ()** operation causes the processes to queue. Whenever a process releases the resource it executes an exit protocol consisting of **semSignal ()**.

Hence access to a resource that must be limited to a fixed number of processes should be programmed with an entry protocol consisting of **lock.semWait ()** and an exit protocol consisting of **lock.semSignal ()** where **lock** is the name of a semaphore that is used to protect the resource. Each such resource will be protected by its own semaphore.

To protect the two-printer service mentioned above we could declare a semaphore named **lock** and initialize it to 2:

```
Semaphore lock = new SemaphoreImplementation(2);
```

and then protect the service by writing:

```
lock.semWait();
    printerService ();
lock.semSignal ();
```

Allocation on demand of multiple instances of a resource can be managed by a semaphore initialized to the number of instances available. A process requests a resource instance by executing **semWait ()** on the associated semaphore. When all the instances have been allocated, any further requesting processes will be blocked when they execute **semWait ()**. When a process has finished using the resource instance allocated to it, it executes **semSignal ()** on the associated semaphore. This method could be used for dynamic allocation of devices to processes, for slots in a shared data structure, etc. Figure 9.21 shows a snapshot of a semaphore class with a number of semaphores in use in the ways described in this section.

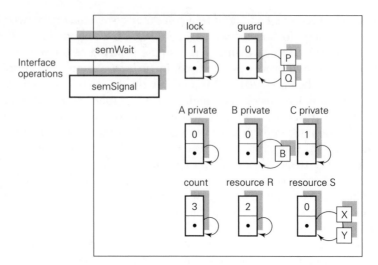

Figure 9.21
A semaphore class
in use.

9.6 Implementation of semaphore operations

Section 9.5 gave an overview of the different ways in which semaphores can be used and showed their representation as data structures. We now focus on how the operations on semaphores are implemented.

The possibility of concurrent invocation of semaphore operations by processes must be considered. This will certainly happen on a multiprocessor and will happen on a uniprocessor unless restrictions are imposed to avoid the possibility.

Approaches to scheduling the queue of processes waiting on a given semaphore are then considered.

There are system design issues concerning where the semaphore class should be located and how it interacts with process management. We first assume that IPC is incorporated together with process management in the operating system and examine the problem of concurrency.

9.6.1 Concurrency in the semaphore implementation

In Section 9.2 the use of an atomic test-and-set instruction on a boolean variable was shown to be sufficient to implement mutual exclusion; that is, to implement a lock on a shared resource. By this means, a data structure can be locked and a number of operations carried out on it without interference from any other process. If the boolean indicates that the shared resource is busy then the process must busy wait until the resource becomes free. Busy waiting may be acceptable on a multiprocessor for short periods of time.

The definition of semaphore operations in Section 9.4 assumes that a process's state can be changed from running to blocked by the operating system if the resource is busy when it executes **semWait** (). Also, the state of some process may be changed from blocked to runnable when the semaphore is signalled. In the former case it is added to the semaphore queue; in the latter it is removed.

The implementation of the operations **semWait ()** and **semSignal ()** on semaphores therefore may involve both changing the value of the semaphore and changing the semaphore queue and process state. These changes must be made within an atomic (indivisible) operation to avoid inconsistency in the system state; all must be carried out or none should be.

In any multiprocessor implementation and any unrestricted uniprocessor implementation, arbitrary numbers of **semWait ()** and **semSignal ()** operations on the same semaphore could occur at the same time.

The requirement for mutually exclusive access to shared data therefore applies to the semaphore implementation. The operations **semWait ()** *and* **semSignal ()** *contain critical regions with respect to the data structure representing the semaphore. But semaphores were introduced to SOLVE the mutual exclusion and synchronization problems!*

It appears that we could be in danger of creating an infinite regression of **semWait ()** operations: the **semWait ()** method which may eventually block the process contains a critical region and a process may therefore have to wait before executing it. How should this latter wait be implemented? Again, the options are:

- Forbid interrupts on a uniprocessor over the **semWait ()** or **semSignal ()** operations.
- Use a test-and-set or equivalent instruction on a (uniprocessor or multiprocessor) together with a boolean. One possibility is that a single boolean can be associated with the module that manages all semaphores. Processes either change the boolean atomically or busy wait on it if another process is executing in the module. This enforces single threaded execution of the whole of semaphore management. Alternatively, a boolean can be associated with each semaphore as shown in Figure 9.22.
- Execute an algorithm which implements a protocol to ensure exclusive access to a given semaphore while the **semWait ()** and **semSignal ()** operations are executed.

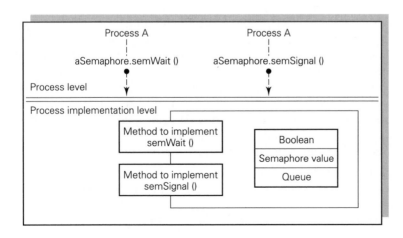

Figure 9.22
Process and implementation level of semaphores.

Having arranged that the **semWait ()** and **semSignal ()** operations are atomic it must be ensured that they will complete once they start, and hopefully without undue delay. Testing and changing the value of a semaphore will not cause delay. Changing the state of the process involves access to the process descriptor, possibly through a call to a separate module to BLOCK or UNBLOCK the process. It might be that the process descriptor is being accessed on behalf of another process, for example, to record the occurrence of a hardware event signal. If we can assume that BLOCK and UNBLOCK are guaranteed to complete in a bounded time (i.e. within some limited period of time) then **semWait ()** and **semSignal ()** can be given similar guarantees.

This is a difficult and crucial area of system design; for example, it must be proved that deadlock cannot occur dynamically as a result of cyclic calls between the semaphore and process classes (see Chapter 17 for further discussion). When we have built atomic and correct **semWait ()** and **semSignal ()** operations which are guaranteed to terminate we can build the rest of the concurrent system above them.

9.6.2 Scheduling the semWait queue, priority inversion and inheritance

Section 9.5.1 indicated that processes waiting on a given semaphore might be scheduled first come first served (FCFS). Two problems can occur:

1 A low-priority process which has acquired a semaphore holds up all processes waiting on it, however high their priorities, until it signals the semaphore. It is scheduled at low priority and may be preempted while holding the semaphore, thus increasing the delay experienced by the waiting processes. This is called **priority inversion**.
2 Low-priority processes may be ahead of high-priority processes in the semaphore's queue.

A simple scheme which solves the second problem for uniprocessors is to free all waiting processes on **semSignal ()**. It must be arranged that each will execute **semWait ()** again. This can be achieved by storing the appropriate value of the program counter in the process descriptor when a process is blocked. The highest-priority process is then the first to be scheduled and the first to acquire the semaphore. The disadvantage is the system overhead in repeatedly blocking and unblocking processes; a given process may have to wait several times before acquiring the semaphore.

This approach does not solve the problem for multiprocessors. In this case a number of the freed processes may be scheduled to run on separate processors and it cannot be guaranteed that the highest-priority process will be the first to execute **semWait ()** and acquire the semaphore.

FCFS scheduling might be appropriate for certain types of system:

- if real-time response is not required;
- if the processes that wait on a given semaphore typically execute at the same priority;
- if semaphore queues are expected to be very short.

A system in which real-time response is required typically allows application processes to be allocated a priority. Process priority could be used to order the semaphore queue and this would solve the second problem. It would be necessary, of course, for the process priority to be made known to the **semWait ()** routine.

The priority inversion problem can be solved by allowing a temporary increase in priority to a process while it is holding a semaphore. Its priority should become that of the highest-priority waiting process; it can be said that it runs at the priority of the 'head waiter'. This is called **priority inheritance**. A process runs at an **effective priority** which is the greater of its assigned priority and its inherited priority.

Process (or thread) scheduling for real-time systems and for multiprocessors is an active area of research. In a real-time system the time taken to respond to an event must be bounded. A process may be delayed while waiting for a resource which is protected by a semaphore. It is important to be able to bound this delay.

Some real-time systems may be analysed statically when the system is designed. In this case it is known which processes use which resources. For a given semaphore it is therefore known which processes may acquire it and, in particular, the highest-priority process that may ever acquire it. This is called the **priority ceiling** of the semaphore. The **priority ceiling protocol** (Goodenough and Sha, 1988) may be used to bound the delay of a process in such a system. The protocol limits the delay which results from waiting for lower-priority processes to a maximum of one critical section of one lower-priority process. The basic idea is that, even if a semaphore is free, it may only be acquired by a process if all the other semaphores that are currently held by processes have lower-priority ceilings than the priority of this process. A summary of this area may be found in Davari and Sha (1992).

Section 4.8

9.6.3 Location of IPC implementation and process (thread) management

In this section we need to distinguish between processes that are created as *user threads* and managed only by the user-level runtime system and the user threads that the runtime system makes known to the operating system as *kernel threads*. Recall Figures 4.17, 4.28 and 4.31 and the related discussion. Figures 9.23 and 9.24 illustrate the location of IPC and process (thread) management in the two cases. Here, we are not concerned with the synchronization of kernel threads over access to operating system data structures (when user threads make system calls and execute operating system code). Rather, we are concerned with the synchronization of user threads over user-level data structures.

A user thread which requires to access a shared resource, or needs to synchronize with another user thread, can call the **semSignal ()** and **semWait ()** operations in the semaphore class in the runtime system. If the semaphore value indicates that the shared resource is free the user thread executing **semWait ()** can continue; there is no call to block the thread.

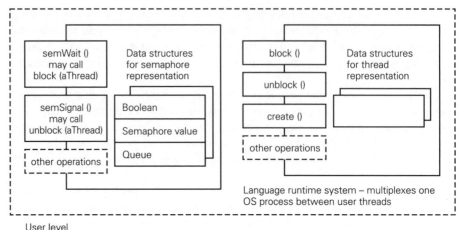

Figure 9.23
Semaphore and user-thread management.

User level

Operating system level – the OS sees only one process

If the resource is busy then the thread must be noted as waiting for the resource in IPC management, then blocked, and another thread must be scheduled. In the Figure 9.23 scenario the blocking and scheduling is done in the user-level runtime system and the operating system is not involved. The single application process that the operating system sees has remained runnable throughout the switches from user thread, to IPC, to process management, to user thread. In the Figure 9.24 scenario the operating system must be called to block the kernel thread corresponding to the blocked user thread.

When a user thread executes **semSignal ()**, if there is no waiting thread the semaphore value is incremented and there is no call to process management. If processes are waiting on the semaphore, one is selected and removed from the semaphore queue and a call is made to unblock it. In the Figure 9.23 scenario this call is to user-level process management. In the Figure 9.24 scenario this call is to the operating system. In both cases the signalled thread's status is changed from blocked to runnable.

The above discussion has assumed that one kernel thread is created for each user thread. As we saw in Section 4.17, thread packages may use more complex arrangements than one-to-one, but the basic scenarios are as discussed above.

9.7 Summary

We started with the requirement for synchronization between processes to achieve both condition synchronization and mutual exclusion. Chapter 4 has shown how a process can synchronize with hardware events and we took this as a starting point. Operations such as WAIT and SIGNAL on processes were considered and were shown to be inadequate as the basis for a general IPC scheme.

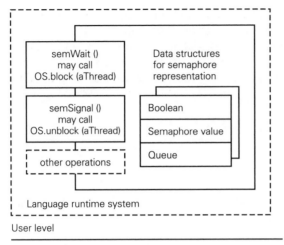

User level

Operating system level – the OS sees a multi-threaded process

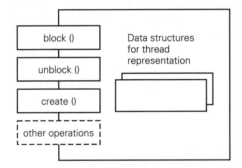

Figure 9.24
Semaphore and
kernel-thread
management.

We studied how to enforce exclusive access to shared data, that is, how to make the operations on the shared data atomic. We defined critical regions within processes and specified that a process must obey an entry protocol before executing critical code and an exit protocol on leaving. We considered hardware-supported implementations of these protocols. A composite instruction can be used both on a uniprocessor and a multiprocessor; forbidding interrupts for a short time while a flag is tested and set can only be used on a uniprocessor. Modern software exploits the availability of hardware-provided instructions which support concurrency control. However, we studied algorithms for ensuring mutual exclusion between a known number of processes for their historic and educational interest. These algorithms are a good illustration that concurrent programming is difficult. Concurrency control lies at the heart of our software systems and its correctness is crucial to their operation.

We defined semaphores and found that their **semWait** () and **semSignal** () operations could be used with greater flexibility and generality than the process-based WAIT and SIGNAL operations discussed in Section 9.1. We saw semaphores used not only for synchronization between two processes but also for synchronization between a single waiting process and many signalling processes, to guard shared data and to manage resources. In these latter two cases many processes can wait on a semaphore. The semaphore acts as an indirect name between processes and allows more general patterns of synchronization than one-to-one (named process to named process). Semaphores can be used for synchronization both when processes share and do not share data.

Study questions

S 9.1

(a) How are the semaphore operations **semWait ()** and **semSignal ()** used by:
  (i)   cooperating processes?
  (ii) competing processes?
(b) Interacting processes use the **semWait ()** and **semSignal ()** operations provided by either the language runtime system or the operating system. Which would it be in the following situations?
  (i)   The processes have separate address spaces.
  (ii) The processes share an address space.
(c) What are the two main requirements of an inter-process synchronization mechanism that the event mechanism does not support?

S 9.2

(a) What is a critical region?
(b) What is meant by the term mutual exclusion?
(c) In general, why is a simple boolean variable not able to ensure mutual exclusion?
(d) How is mutual exclusion guaranteed on a uniprocessor without preemptive scheduling?
(e) How does a hardware test-and-set instruction help in ensuring mutual exclusion?
(f) How can interrupts be used to protect critical regions on a uniprocessor? Why should this mechanism only be used with small sections of critical code? Why will this technique not work for multiprocessors?

S 9.3

(a) Section 9.3 is about algorithms which ensure mutually exclusive access to shared data in a multiprocessor system without support for concurrency. For each process in such a system having a critical region, what phases of execution are assumed?
(b) Distinguish between an entry protocol and an exit protocol.
(c) Why may a process halt (i.e. stop indefinitely) in a non-critical region but must not be allowed to halt in its critical region, nor in its entry or exit protocol?

(d) In an entry protocol, what effect does the following statement have?

while (turn != 0) noOp ()

Explain the reason why this loop invokes a method that performs no actions.

(e) What is meant by the term starvation?

(f) What are the requirements that any software solution to the mutual exclusion problem should satisfy?

S 9.4

What is a semaphore, and how is it implemented?

S 9.5

(a) In Section 9.5.1, we made the statement that 'In general, A, B and C can execute concurrently. *Their critical regions with respect to the resource they share have been **serialized*** [our italics] so that only one process accesses the resource at once.' What is meant by the italicized part of this quote?

(b) If there are several processes waiting to access a resource that is protected by a semaphore and the resource becomes free, explain how the next process to gain access to it is chosen.

(c) What are the three different approaches to the scheduling of processes waiting on the same semaphore?

(d) Figure 9.20 shows two processes synchronizing their actions. In (a) process A is forced to wait until process B signals that it has reached a specific point in its computation. In (b) neither process waits: explain why. Explain the value to which the semaphore must be initialized for this scheme to work.

(e) In what three ways can semaphores be used?

S 9.6

What is the major difficulty in implementing semaphores, and what are the options for solving it?

Exercises

9.1 Support for synchronization between processes and hardware was described in Section 4.4. Concurrent processes also need to synchronize with each other. Discuss the approach of extending the methods described for process–hardware synchronization to encompass process–process synchronization. What kinds of interaction could, and could not, be supported by the designs you devise?

9.2   Examine the processor handbooks of your local machines. Explore any composite instruction definitions with a view to using them to implement semaphore operations, in particular, **semWait** ().

You may find composite instructions in the instruction sets, such as:

TAS   (test-and-set a variable)

INC   (increment a value and set a condition code register)

CAS   *Register1, Register2, Memory* (compare and swap: if the contents of *Register1* and *Memory* are the same then *Memory* is overwritten by the contents of *Register2*. If they are not the same then *Register1* is overwritten by *Memory*. A condition code is set to indicate which of these took place.)

(a)   Write the entry and exit protocols for a critical region using each of the above instructions.

(b)   Show how the instructions may be used to achieve condition synchronization so that a process may delay until a condition becomes true.

You may assume that processes cooperate: that some other process which exits from the critical region or makes the desired condition true will take action to inform the delayed process.

9.3   This exercise examines the first, second and third attempts at a two-process solution to the mutual exclusion problem devised in Section 9.3.2.

(a)   Use the proof by contradiction technique to show that the first attempt guarantees mutual exclusion.

(b)   Can starvation of one or other of the processes occur in the second attempt? Explain your answer.

(c)   Show that the two processes cannot deadlock in the third attempt.

9.4   The **semSignal** () and **semWait** () operations, provided as primitives by a kernel, are defined to be atomic. Discuss how this atomicity can be implemented. Consider the following cases:

(a)   hardware which provides a test-and-set or other composite instruction;

(b)   a uniprocessor, both when a composite instruction is available and when none is available;

(c)   a multiprocessor with no composite instruction.

9.5   The semaphore operations can be described as follows.

```
public void semWait () {
  if (value > 0)
     value = value – 1;
  else {
     add this process to the semaphore queue;
     block the process;
  }
}
```

```
public void semSignal () {
    if (queue.isEmptyQueue ())
        value = value + 1;
    else
        remove a process from the semaphore queue;
        enable the process to continue its execution;
    }
}
```

Show that, if the **semWait ()** and **semSignal ()** operations are not executed atomically, mutual exclusion can be violated.

9.6   In Section 9.6 we discussed the implementation of semaphore operations. Section 9.6.1 concluded: 'This is a difficult and crucial area of system design . . . When we have built atomic and correct semWait () and semSignal () operations which are guaranteed to terminate we can build the rest of the concurrent system above them.' Discuss how the algorithms presented here could be used to implement atomic **semWait ()** and **semSignal ()** in the kernel of a multiprocessor based on hardware without support for concurrency control. Is the overhead involved in executing the algorithms acceptable for this purpose? Is the overhead acceptable for implementing user-level semaphore operations?

9.7   This exercise involves some general questions on the Eisenberg–McGuire algorithm of Section 9.3.3.
      Can you argue (informally) that the algorithm preserves mutual exclusion?
      Is it the case that once a process has expressed an interest in entering the critical region it will not be delayed indefinitely? (Is the algorithm free from starvation?)
      If several processes want to enter the critical region will one of them succeed eventually? Is the algorithm free from deadlock?
      What is the overhead of executing the algorithm in the absence of contention? Express the number of tests made as a function of n.

9.8   Figure 9.17 gives a simple example. Work through this case and complete the entry protocol for P_4. If P_4 completes its exit protocol, what will be the value of the ticket taken by the next process to enter the critical region?
      Under what circumstances will the values of the tickets increase indefinitely? Is this likely to be a problem?
      Notice that it is possible for processes to have tickets with the same value. How does the entry protocol ensure that only one process at a time enters the critical region?
      Can you argue (informally) that the algorithm preserves mutual exclusion?
      Is it the case that once a process has expressed an interest in entering the critical region it will not be delayed indefinitely? (Is the algorithm free from starvation?)

If several processes want to enter the critical region will one of them succeed eventually?

Is the algorithm free from deadlock?

What is the overhead of executing the algorithm in the absence of contention? Express the number of tests made as a function of n.

9.9 Compare the Eisenberg–McGuire and bakery algorithms with respect to scheduling of processes (order of entry into the critical region), overhead, ease of comprehension and programming. Consider how each behaves under heavy contention.

10

Low-level synchronization: Algorithms

10.1 Introduction

In the previous chapter we studied how to implement synchronization primitives for a single computer system with multiple processors. We now show how those primitives may be used to solve concurrent programming problems; we shall need to use several semaphores, for example. On analysing the requirements for solutions we shall investigate:

- which data structures are shared and writeable and must therefore be accessed under mutual exclusion;
- how to manage the waiting for access and the waking up of waiting processes;
- how to manage different categories of processes;
- how to allow several processes to read at the same time while achieving exclusive access for a writing process.

The chapter ends with a more substantial case study (with exercises) to give the reader the opportunity to use the techniques that have been introduced.

The essential problem of Part II is how to make a single operation on shared data atomic and how to make the primitives that achieve this atomicity available to programmers. In this chapter we are starting to move into the realm of complex problems, for example when different categories of process are introduced: readers, writers, producers and consumers of data. We defer a full discussion of fully general concurrent systems until Part III where we consider multiple shared data structures accessed by concurrent processes where the data may be transient or persistent.

As mentioned in Section 9.4 semaphores were designed initially for the THE system and we now examine its structure and see how semaphores were used in it. Note that all processes inhabit a common shared memory.

10.2 An example of semaphores in system design: the THE system

In the THE system, Dijkstra *et al.* designed a hierarchy of virtual resources managed by a strictly layered system of processes. A brief outline of its structure is as follows; see also Figures 10.1 and 10.2. The lowest level, level 0, creates virtual processors. Above this, processes exist and may communicate using a semaphore mechanism. The rest of the system may be written using these concurrency constructs. All interrupts enter at this level, and all but the clock interrupt are handled at higher levels. At level 1, one process provides a one-level

Level 4 (user processes)	Five user processes
Level 3 (one process for each physical device)	Creates virtual devices Synchronizes with device interrupts Synchronizes with the memory manager and console process Synchronizes with requests from higher levels
Level 2 (one process)	The console process Synchronizes with console interrupts Synchronizes with requests from higher levels
Level 1 (one process)	Creates virtual memory Synchronizes with drum interrupts Synchronizes with requests from higher levels
Level 0	Creates virtual processors Provides semaphore for IPC Handles clock interrupt Acknowledges other interrupts which are serviced at higher levels

Figure 10.1
Structure of THE.

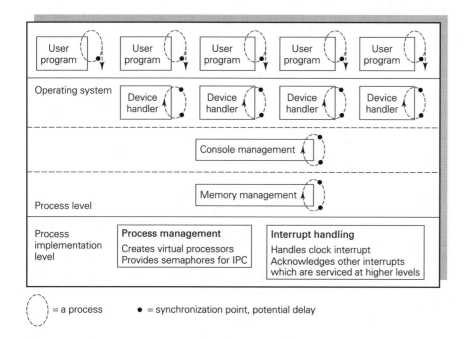

Figure 10.2
Structure of THE, showing process placement.

virtual store. It synchronizes with drum interrupts and with requests for store from higher-level processes. At level 2, one process provides virtual consoles for higher-level processes and synchronizes with their requests. It also synchronizes with console interrupts and the memory manager process. At level 3, a separate process manages each physical device. Each process synchronizes with its device's interrupts, with the memory and console manager processes, and with higher-level processes over I/O requests. At level 4, the highest, reside five user processes. In all cases where data is passed, producer–consumer style message buffering must be used, controlled by semaphores as described in Section 10.3.

In Chapter 2, modular system structure was introduced. A strictly layered system structure is a particular form of modularization. Each layer provides an abstract interface for processes at higher levels to invoke. The system can be proved correct from the 'bottom up' because processes at a given level cannot invoke operations at higher levels, so there is no problem of circular dependencies between modules.

The problems introduced by a strictly layered design are due to the sacrifice of flexibility to achieve layering. In the THE design, for example, the console manager can invoke memory management but not vice versa. The memory manager is not able to output a message to the operator's console. If memory had been placed above the console in the design this would have been possible, but in this case the console process would not have been able to request memory for I/O buffers (Dijkstra, 1968).

The Venus operating system (Liskov, 1972) was another strictly layered design which used semaphores as the basic synchronization mechanism (see Exercise 10.1). Although strict layering makes it easier to reason about the behaviour of a system it is difficult in practice to choose the ordering of the layers, and most systems do not follow this model.

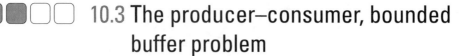

10.3 The producer–consumer, bounded buffer problem

10.3.1 Use of buffers

In Section 3.5 we saw the need for **synchronization** and **data exchange** between user-level processes requesting I/O and device handlers taking output or delivering input. A user-level process should be able to make a request for an arbitrary amount of data to be output or input. The device takes or delivers a fixed amount. A data buffer allows these device-dependent characteristics to be hidden from the user level. It also allows irregular bursts of user-level processing or device activity to be smoothed out. A process engaging in a burst of activity can continue until the buffer is full.

The synchronization conditions on accesses to the buffer are as follows. If a user-level process requests input and the buffer is empty it must block until input arrives. If a device handler process finds there is no more data in the buffer for output it must block until more data arrives. If a fixed amount of space is allocated for the buffer, the user-level process must be blocked when it has filled the buffer on output until the handler has freed some space. Similarly, the device must be stopped on input until the user-level process has freed some buffer space by reading from the buffer. Access to the buffer data structure to read or write will require more than a single memory access, so atomic read and write operations must be implemented (as critical regions for example).

Terminology: There is ambiguity in the way the term 'buffer' is used in the literature and in system design. In the main example in this section we shall discuss a single 'buffer' with a number of 'slots'. An alternative use of the term buffer is to indicate a single block of data in a 'pool of buffers'. This latter usage is often found in I/O, communication and file buffer management schemes.

There are many uses for buffers between processes. A possible use of the cyclic buffer structure we shall discuss in this section is to hold requests for filenames to be spooled to a printer. A server process takes requests from the buffer and organizes the printing of the files. Any process which invokes this service (by a system call) causes a request to be entered into the buffer. We are implementing a queue of requests in an array of fixed size.

In general, buffers may be used between user-level processes according to the needs of the application: between system-level processes or between user-level and system-level processes.

Buffers might be implemented in a number of different ways. In this section we study a **cyclic** or **bounded buffer** implementation (a classic problem in the literature on concurrency).

An *N*-slot circular array – represented by a linear array.

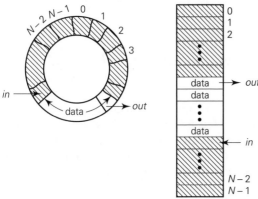

A five-slot circular array in different stages of use

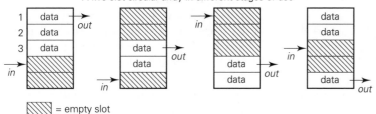

 = empty slot

Figure 10.3
A circular array with
two cursors.

10.3.2 Definition of a cyclic or bounded buffer

A cyclic (or bounded) buffer is a data structure with many of the characteristics
of an array. That is, it is a fixed collection of N data items, indexed from 0 to
N − 1 such that, when a cursor (an integer variable containing an index value)
that currently refers to the last item is incremented, it moves back to index 0.
This kind of structure is sometimes referred to as a circular array, as pictured in
Figure 10.3, which shows:

- the index values ranging from 0 to N − 1;
- some slots are occupied by data items (indicated by **data**); others are empty,
  indicated by shading;
- two cursors (variables holding a valid index value) named **in** and **out**, the
  purposes of which are, respectively, to indicate the first available empty slot
  and the next data item that can be taken from the buffer.

If you were to implement a circular array in Java, you would begin by creating
an array (here we have a buffer with five elements):

```
static final int BufferSize = 5;          // constant holding size of the buffer
Object [ ] buffer = new Object [BufferSize]; // new Object array referenced
                                          // by 'buffer'
```

together with two cursors:

```
int in = 0;
int out = 0;
```

The cursors can be incremented by writing, for example,

```
in = (in + 1) % BufferSize;
```

The operator %, called the modulus operator (or mod for short), returns the remainder after integer division. Thus 8 % 5 is 3 and 10 % 5 is 0. Hence, if **in** is less than 4 given that an array in Java runs from 0 to (**arraysize** − 1), the expression (**in** + 1) % **BufferSize** simply results in 1 being added to **in**; but when **in** is 4, the expression yields 0, which achieves the necessary behaviour for a cursor using a Java array.

We now study the management of a cyclic buffer and, in particular, the concurrency control that is necessary for its correct use.

A producer process continually adds new items to the buffer, each new item being placed at the position referenced by the cursor **in**. However if the buffer is full the producer process must be blocked when it attempts to add an item. The blocked process should be allowed to complete its operation when space becomes available. After adding an item the producer increments cursor **in**. A consumer process continually removes items from the buffer. After removing an item the consumer increments the cursor **out**. If the buffer is empty a process which attempts to take something out of it is blocked. When a fresh item becomes available, the consumer should be allowed to resume operation.

The algorithms given below focus on the problems associated with access to such a buffer by concurrent processes. We consider two general problems:

1 A single producer process sends information, in blocks of a specified fixed size, to a single consumer process.
2 A single circular buffer is used between a number of producer processes and a number of consumer processes.

10.3.3 Algorithm for a single producer and a single consumer

Figure 10.4 gives a high-level view of a solution to the single producer, single consumer problem. The problem would be programmed in practice in a modular style by defining a buffer class. This general scheme is shown in Figure 10.5. The processes must synchronize over the state of the buffer. The producer must delay if the buffer is full and the consumer must delay if the buffer is empty.

Figure 10.6 illustrates a solution in outline, and below we give the complete code using two semaphores, **items** and **spaces**; **items** is initialized to 0 indicating there are no items in the buffer initially, **spaces** is initialized to **BufferSize**, the number of slots in the buffer. Each time the producer inserts an item it executes **items.semSignal()**, thus incrementing the item resource count managed

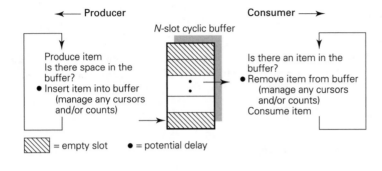

Figure 10.4
Producer–consumer outline.

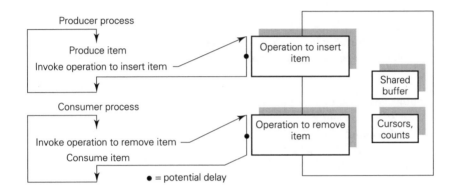

Figure 10.5
Modular representation of the producer–consumer problem.

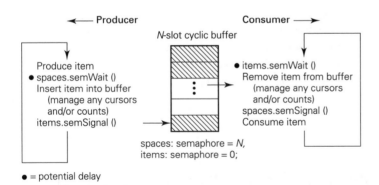

Figure 10.6
Single producer, single consumer.

by the **items** semaphore. Each time the consumer removes an item it executes **spaces.semSignal()**, incrementing the space resource count managed by the **spaces** semaphore. When the buffer is empty, **items** has value zero and the consumer will block on **items.semWait()**. When the buffer is full, **spaces** has value zero and the producer will block on **spaces.semWait()**. Note that for a single producer and single consumer the buffer is not accessed under mutual exclusion since they are accessing different parts of the buffer (using different cursors). The synchronization of the processes ensures that they block before attempting to access the same slot in the buffer.

```
import Semaphore.*;

public class Buffer {
    static final int BufferSize = 5;           // constant holding size of the buffer
    Object [] buffer = new Object [BufferSize]; // new Object array referenced
                                                // by 'buffer'

    int in;
    int out;
    Semaphore items, spaces;

    public Buffer() {
        in = 0;
        out = 0;
        items = new SemaphoreImplementation(0);
        spaces = new SemaphoreImplementation (BufferSize);
    }

    public void insert (Object item) {
        spaces.semWait();
            buffer[in] = item;
            in = (in+1) % BufferSize;
        items.semSignal();
    }

    public Object remove () {
        Object item;
        items.semWait();
            item = buffer[out];
            out = (out+1) % BufferSize;
        spaces.semSignal();
        return item;
    }
}
```

10.3.4 Algorithm for more than one producer or consumer

Figure 10.7 illustrates a solution in outline, and below we give the complete code for a solution for many producers and a single consumer. The many producers must access the buffer under mutual exclusion as they are using the same cursor to insert items. For many producers and many consumers, the consumer code must be similarly extended to enforce exclusive access to the buffer between consumers. One producer and one consumer could access the buffer concurrently, provided producers and consumers use different guard semaphores, such as pguard and cguard.

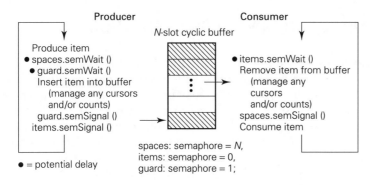

Figure 10.7
Multiple producers,
single consumer.

```
import Semaphore.*;

public class Buffer {
static final int BufferSize = 5;          // constant holding size of the buffer
Object [] buffer = new Object [BufferSize]; // new Object array referenced
                                            // by 'buffer'

int in;
int out;
Semaphore items, spaces, guard;

    public Buffer() {
        in = 0;
        out = 0;
        items = new SemaphoreImplementation(0);
        spaces = new SemaphoreImplementation (BufferSize);
        guard = new SemaphoreImplementation (1);
    }

    public void insert (Object item) {
        spaces.semWait();
        guard.semWait();
            buffer[in] = item;
            in = (in+1) % BufferSize;
        guard.semSignal();
        items.semSignal();
    }

    public Object remove () {
        Object item;
        items.semWait();
            item = buffer[out];
            out = (out+1) % BufferSize;
        spaces.semSignal();
        return item;
    }
}
```

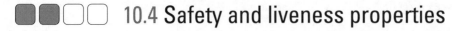

10.4 Safety and liveness properties

We have begun to move from the definition of basic mechanisms for synchronization and mutual exclusion to the design of concurrent algorithms. This book does not cover the theory of concurrency but an outline of the factors relevant to proofs of correctness of concurrent programs is in order. The following discussion is taken from Andrews (1991) where the topic is studied in depth.

A property of a program is an attribute that is true of every possible history of that program. There are two fundamental properties: **safety** and **liveness**. A safety property asserts that nothing bad happens during execution; a liveness property asserts that something good eventually happens. In sequential programs the key safety property is that the final state is correct; the key liveness property is that the program terminates.

For concurrent programs we have argued intuitively the need for **mutual exclusion**; this is a safety property. Another is **absence of deadlock**, which occurs when processes are waiting for conditions that can never be satisfied.

We study the problem of deadlock in systems and concurrent programs in Chapter 17. In Section 17.5, the dining philosophers problem, a classic concurrent programming problem posed by Dijkstra, is introduced. It illustrates the danger of deadlock occurring in concurrent systems, especially when n processes each execute an identical program. Exercise 17.5 suggests approaches to solving the problem.

An example of a liveness property of a concurrent program is that a process that is waiting (for a shared resource or to synchronize with another process) will eventually be signalled and be able to proceed.

The scheduling policy of the operating system has an effect on liveness properties in that it selects which runnable process should next run on a processor. Liveness properties depend on **fairness** which is concerned with guaranteeing that a process will get the chance to proceed regardless of how other processes behave. **Starvation** is when a runnable process is overlooked indefinitely by the scheduler: although it is able to proceed in theory, in practice it is never chosen.

It is beyond the scope of this book to prove the safety and liveness properties of the concurrent programs we develop. It should be noted that concurrent programs are notoriously difficult for humans to reason about; further study on proofs of correctness is highly desirable for anyone who is to work in this area professionally.

10.5 The multiple readers, single writer problem

A style of competition between processes which is more complex than simple mutual exclusion arises when many processes may be allowed to read a resource simultaneously (since they make no change to it) but writers must have exclusive access. Any solution to this problem must make an assumption about relative priorities. Here we shall assume that as soon as a writer wishes to write, all

Structure of code executed by readers   Structure of code executed by writers

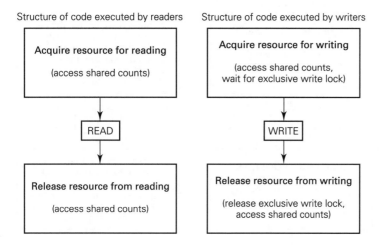

Figure 10.8
Structure of code
executed by readers
and writers.

current readers are allowed to finish reading but any subsequent request to read is held up. This priority scheme is appropriate when it is important that readers read information which is as up to date as possible.

Semaphores are used to manage the situation where processes need to block:

- Semaphore R = **new** SemaphoreImplementation (0) is used to count outstanding requests to read when a writer is writing and readers are blocked on R;
- Semaphore W = **new** SemaphoreImplementation (0) is used to count outstanding requests to write when readers are reading and writers are blocked on W;
- Semaphore WGUARD = **new** SemaphoreImplementation (1) is used to enforce exclusive access by writers;
- Semaphore CGUARD = **new** SemaphoreImplementation (1) is used to enforce exclusive access to the various counts which keep track of how many readers and writers are active:
  - ar   is the count of active readers
  - rr   is the count of active readers which are also reading (i.e. reading readers)
  - aw   is the count of active writers
  - ww   is the count of active writers who have proceeded to the writing phase (i.e. writing writers), but only one of them can actually be writing at once.

Figures 10.8 and 10.9 show the basic structure of the code which must be executed by reader processes and writer processes. To acquire or release the resource, shared counts must be accessed under mutual exclusion. The fact that writers must write under mutual exclusion is indicated. Figure 10.11 shows this code structured in a more realistic modular fashion.

Figure 10.10 gives the algorithm in detail. Priority is given to waiting writers over waiting readers, since active readers only go on to become reading readers if there are no active writers. The various counts are accessed under mutual

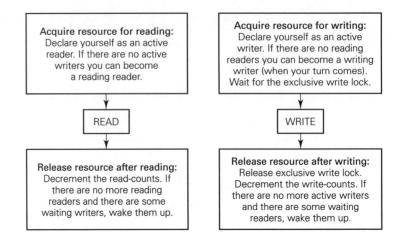

Figure 10.9
Code executed by
readers and writers
in more detail.

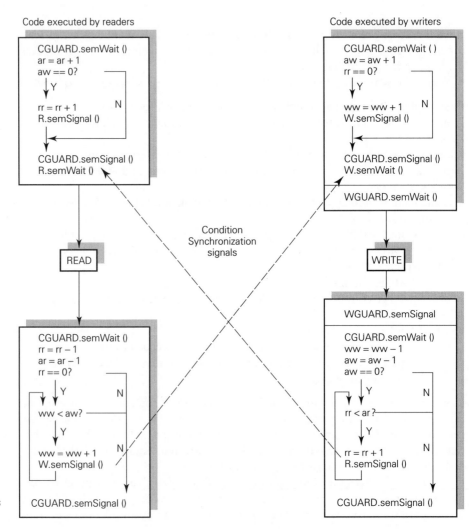

Figure 10.10
Algorithm for readers
and writers.

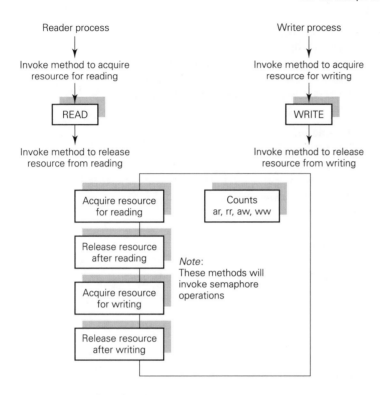

Figure 10.11
Modular structure for readers and writers.

exclusion, protected by the semaphore **CGUARD**. Processes wait to read or write on semaphores **R** or **W** respectively. The complexity of the code derives from the management of these two semaphores. **R** and **W** are given 'wake-up-waiting' signals in the acquire procedures if there are no active writers (for **R**) or no running readers (for **W**). Releasing the resource may involve sending synchronizing signals to waiting readers and writers; the last reading reader wakes up any waiting writers, the last active writer wakes up waiting readers.

Figure 10.11 shows a modular structure for the solution. The resource is managed using a class with methods to acquire and release it for reading and writing. All delay involved in waiting on semaphores is hidden within this class.

We now give the code for a Java class to implement the above approach to the readers and writers problem:

```
import Semaphore.*;

public class RWProtocol {

Semaphore  R,           // outstanding read requests
           W,           // outstanding write requests
           WGUARD,      // exclusive write access
           CGUARD;      // exclusive access to counts
int ar = 0,             // active readers
    rr = 0,             // reading readers
    aw = 0,             // active writers
    ww = 0;             // writing writers
```

```
public RWProtocol() {
    R = new SemaphoreImplementation (0);
    W = new SemaphoreImplementation (0);
    WGUARD = new SemaphoreImplementation (1);
    CGUARD = new SemaphoreImplementation (1);
}

public void readAcquire() {
    CGUARD.semWait ();
    ar = ar + 1;
    // acquire read access if no active writers otherwise
    // will have to wait on R
    if (aw == 0) {
        rr = rr + 1;
        R.semSignal ();
    }
    CGUARD.semSignal();
    R.semWait();
}

public void readRelease() {
    CGUARD.semWait ();
    rr = rr - 1;
    ar = ar - 1;
    // if no longer ANY reading readers, make all active writers
    // writing writers
    if (rr == 0) {
        while (ww < aw) {
            ww = ww + 1;
            W.semSignal();
        }
    }
    CGUARD.semSignal();
}

public void writeAcquire() {
    CGUARD.semWait ();
    aw = aw + 1;
    // become a writing writer if no reading readers otherwise
    // will have to wait on W
    if (rr == 0) {
        ww = ww + 1;
        W.semSignal ();
    }
    CGUARD.semSignal();
    W.semWait();
    // even though now a writing writer, still need to ensure
    // we write under mutual exclusion
    WGUARD.semWait();
}
```

```
public void writeRelease( ) {
    WGUARD.semSignal( );
    CGUARD.semWait ( );
    ww = ww − 1;
    aw = aw − 1;
    // if no longer ANY writing writers, make all active readers
    // reading readers
    if (aw == 0) {
        while (rr < ar) {
            rr = rr + 1;
            R.semSignal( );
        }
    }
    CGUARD.semSignal( );
  }
}
```

10.6 Limitations of semaphores

In Section 9.1 we started by considering a synchronization facility such as WAIT() and SIGNAL() on events. We have now seen that semaphores provide more generality and flexibility than a one-to-one (named-process to named-process) scheme. semWait () can be used by many processes to wait for one or more signalling processes. semSignal () can be used by many processes to signal one waiting process. We have shown examples of how semaphores can be used to solve a range of realistic problems of concurrent systems.

Suppose the semaphore type was available in a language as the only basis for IPC. We should consider some of the concepts which are lacking in semaphore operations that might be important, at least for some types of concurrent system. Typical problems with the use of semaphores are:

- Their use is not enforced, but is by convention only. It is easy to make mistakes in semaphore programming. It is not easy to remember which semaphore is associated with which data structure, process or resource. It is easy to forget to use semWait () and accidentally access unprotected shared data, or to forget to use semSignal () and leave a data structure locked indefinitely.
- The operations do not allow a test for busy without a commitment to blocking. An alternative to waiting on the semaphore might be preferable. We shall see that creating a new process so that one process may continue processing while the other waits is a standard solution which avoids this restriction.
- It is not possible to specify a set of semaphores as an argument list to a semWait () operation. If this were possible, alternative orderings of actions could be programmed according to the current state of arrival of signals. Such a facility would be difficult to implement and would introduce overhead. Again, process creation might solve the problem.

- The time for which a process is blocked on a semaphore is not limited, in the definition we have used here. A process blocks indefinitely until released by a signal.
- There is no means by which one process can control another using semaphores without the cooperation of the controlled process.
- If semaphores are the only IPC mechanism available and it is necessary to pass information between processes, in addition to simple synchronization processes must share (part of) their address space in order to access shared writeable data directly. A scheme such as producer–consumer buffering is required. The semaphore value could be used to convey minimal information but is not available to processes.

In general, if concurrency is to be made available to application programmers, it is desirable to enforce modularity and correct use of concurrency constructs wherever possible. This is the subject of the next chapter.

 ## 10.7 Eventcounts and sequencers

The data types **eventcount** and **sequencer** have been proposed (Reed and Kanodia, 1979) as an alternative to semaphores. The operations on them are designed for any combination of concurrent execution. The notion of counts of event occurrences, increasing indefinitely from the time the system is started, is used. The fact that the 32nd and 33rd occurrences of a given event are distinguished feels better, intuitively, for a multiprocessor implementation than, for example, semaphore values 1 (event 32 occurs), 0 (handled), 1 (event 33 occurs), 0 (handled), or 1 (event 32 occurs), 2 (event 33 occurs), 1 (event 32 handled), 0 (event 33 handled). Also, the values of these counts are made available to processes through the operations defined on them, and these values can be used by processes, for example, to order their actions.

Eventcounts can be represented by positive integers, initialized to zero, and have the following methods defined on them:

advance()   increment by one and return the new value;
read ()   return the current value;
await (int value) delay the executing process until *the value of the event* is greater than or equal to **value**.

In using the values returned by **advance** () and **read** (), processes must take into account concurrent use by other processes.

Sequencers are used for ordering the actions of concurrent processes. Sequencers may be represented by positive integers, initialized to zero. There is a single operation available on them:

ticket ()   return the current value of and increment by one.

Examples are now given to show the distinct uses of eventcounts and sequencers.

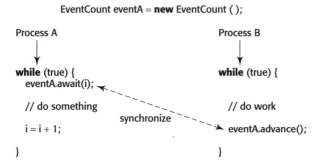

Figure 10.12
Synchronization using
an eventcount.

10.7.1 Use of eventcounts for synchronization

A process specifies which occurrence of an event it is waiting for, rather than just the next event of that type. We therefore introduce a local count i within the process for this purpose (Figure 10.12).

10.7.2 Use of a sequencer to enforce mutual exclusion

Figure 10.13 shows a process competing with others to use a resource protected by the eventcount **GUARD**. The approach is analogous with taking a ticket when you enter a bakery or shoe shop. Customers are served in the order of the number on their ticket. The process first acquires a ticket, which in this example is stored in its local variable **myturn**. It then attempts to enter its critical region by executing **GUARD.await (myturn)**. The critical region of this process is executed after those of processes with lower values returned by **turns.ticket ()**, that is, the order of execution of critical regions is determined by the values returned by **turns.ticket ()**.

```
EventCount GUARD = new EventCount ();   // initially 0
Sequencer turns = new Sequencer ();     // initially 0
int myturn;

Process
   |
   v
myturn = turns.ticket();
GUARD.await(myturn);

// critical region

GUARD.advance ();
   |
   v
```

Figure 10.13
Mutual exclusion
using a sequencer
and an eventcount.

```
public class Buffer {
    static final int BufferSize = 5;            // constant holding size of the buffer
    Object [] buffer = new Object [BufferSize]; // new Object array referenced
                                                // by 'buffer'

    EventCount in, out;
    int i;
    public Buffer() {
        i = 0;
        in = new EventCount ();
        out = new Eventcount ();
    }
    public void insert (Object item) {
        for (int i=1; true ; i++) {
            out.await (i – BufferSize);
            buffer[i % BufferSize] = item;
            in.advance ();
        }
    }
    public Object remove () {
        Object item;
        for (int i=1; true ; i++) {
            in.await (i);
            item = buffer[i % BufferSize];
            out.advance ();
        }
    }
}
```

Figure 10.14
Single producer,
single consumer with
eventcounts.

10.7.3 Producer–consumer, bounded buffer with eventcounts and sequencers

For a single producer and a single consumer all that is needed is synchronization. The producer must delay when the buffer is full; the consumer must delay when it is empty. They may access the buffer at the same time since the solution to the synchronization problem ensures that the consumer does not read the ith item until the producer has written it and the producer does not write into the ith slot until the consumer has read the $i–N$th item from it.

Figure 10.14 outlines the solution. The eventcounts **in** and **out** count the items put in by the producer and taken out by the consumer.

When there are multiple producers and consumers, a sequencer **tp** must be used to order the accesses to the buffer of producers and one **tc** for that of consumers. Figure 10.15 outlines the solution.

10.7.4 Implementation of eventcounts and sequencers

The **advance ()** and **ticket ()** operations must be implemented to allow any number of concurrent executions. The simple way to do this is to use a suitable instruction along the lines of a 'test-and-set' (TAS) described in Section 9.2.1, that is, one

```
public class Buffer2 {
    static final int BufferSize = 5;                // constant holding size of the buffer
    Object [] buffer = new Object [BufferSize];     // new Object array referenced
                                                    // by 'buffer'

    EventCount in, out;
    Sequencer tp, tc;
    int myturn;
    public Buffer2() {
        myturn = 0;
        in = new EventCount ();
        out = new Eventcount ();
        tp = new Sequencer ();
        tc = new Sequencer ();
    }
    public void insert (Object item) {
        for (int i=1; true ; i++) {
            myturn = tp.ticket ();
            in.await(myturn);
            out.await (myturn – BufferSize + 1);
            buffer[myturn % BufferSize] = item;
            in.advance ();
        }
    }
    public Object remove () {
        Object item;
        for (int i=1; true ; i++) {
            myturn = tc.ticket ();
            out.await(myturn);
            in.await (myturn+1);
            item = buffer[myturn % BufferSize];
            out.advance ();
        }
    }
}
```

Figure 10.15
Multiple producers
and consumers with
eventcounts and
sequencers.

which offers a read–modify–write bus cycle. An example is a compare-and-swap (CAS) instruction. For example:

CAS *Register1, Register2, Memory*

If the contents of *Register1* and *Memory* are the same then *Memory* is overwritten by the contents of *Register2*. If they are not the same then *Register1* is overwritten by *Memory*. A condition code is set to indicate which of these took place.

This is used to implement a secure increment, assuming *Memory* contains the value to be incremented, as follows:

1 Read *Memory* into *Register1*.
2 Write *Register1*+1 into *Register2*.
3 Execute CAS.

If no other processes have written to *Memory* it will be as it was when it was read into *Register1* and will have been incremented by the CAS.

If *Memory* has been written since it was read into *Register1* the swap will not take place and the new value of *Memory* will be in *Register1*, ready for a retry.

10.7.5 Discussion of eventcounts and sequencers

Eventcounts and sequencers were designed with multiprocessor implementations in mind. Reed and Kanodia (1979) give further examples and alternative implementations. The fact that the operations can be executed concurrently is an important property. The fact that the values are strictly increasing helps both in implementing and using them correctly. Another advantage of the operations is that a process could be given the right to read an eventcount but not to write it.

However, a process must be trusted to provide the correct value as the argument for the **await** () operation. It is in the interest of cooperating processes to do so, but competing processes might attempt to jump the queue by using a lower value than that returned by a **ticket** () operation or an error could result in a wrong value being passed. Another problem is the potential delay or deadlock if a process acquires a ticket and then delays or terminates before executing the associated **await** ().

Eventcounts and sequencers are, like semaphores, low-level concurrency control operations and are subject to similar difficulties to those listed for semaphores in Section 10.6. There is a great deal of experience in the use of semaphores in systems but, as yet, little experience with eventcounts and sequencers.

 ## 10.8 POSIX threads

IEEE set up the POSIX committee to specify a standard UNIX core. Applications that run above a POSIX compliant UNIX should run above any other. POSIX has been adopted widely and here we focus on the threads package and its support for synchronization. More detail may be found in the IEEE POSIX 1003.4a (**pthread**) standard. An example of a specific implementation is DECthreads, Digital's Multi-threading Run-Time Library for OSF/1.

Section 4.11

POSIX threads execute within (and share) a single address space. **Mutexes** and **condition variables**, see below, are provided for synchronization.

10.8.1 Objects, handles and attributes

An object, such as a thread, mutex, condition variable, queue or attributes object, is referred to via a handle which is returned when the object is created.

Threads, mutexes and condition variables have associated attributes objects. A thread's attributes object contains the thread's scheduling inheritance, scheduling policy, scheduling priority, stack size and stack guard size. A thread may be created with default values for these attributes or the creator may specify them. It is also possible to change some attributes after thread execution starts. The **inherit scheduling** attribute specifies whether a newly created thread inherits the scheduling attributes (scheduling priority and policy) of the creating thread (the default) or uses the scheduling attributes stored in the attributes object. The

scheduling policy attribute describes how the thread is scheduled for execution relative to the other threads in the program. The **scheduling priority** attribute specifies the execution priority of a thread. The **stacksize** attribute is the minimum size (in bytes) of the memory required for a thread's stack. The **guardsize** attribute is the minimum size (in bytes) of the guard area for the stack of a thread (a reserved area designed to help prevent or detect overflow of the thread's stack).

Section 2.6

10.8.2 Synchronization

Threads may synchronize by executing wait and signal operations on synchronization objects. A thread may also wait for a specific thread to complete its execution using **pthread_join**. When the specified thread terminates, the joining thread is unblocked and continues its execution.

Two synchronization objects are provided: the **mutex** (a binary semaphore) and the **condition variable**. Condition variables are used to build higher-level functionality similar to that of monitors, which we shall study in Chapter 11. The operations provided allow the programmer to avoid mandatory blocking on a locked mutex and to delimit the blocked time on a condition variable.

Mutexes

A mutex (mutual exclusion) is an object that multiple threads use to ensure the integrity of a shared resource that they access, most commonly shared data, by allowing only one thread to access it at a time. A mutex has two states: locked and unlocked. For each piece of shared data, all threads accessing that data must use the same mutex: each thread locks the mutex before it accesses the shared data and unlocks the mutex when it has finished accessing that data. If the mutex is locked by another thread, the thread requesting the lock either waits for the mutex to be unlocked or returns, depending on the lock routine called.

Each mutex must be created by **pthread_mutex_init**. On creation an attributes object, including the mutex type (fast, recursive or non-recursive) may be specified.

- A **fast mutex** (the default) is locked exactly once by a thread. If a thread attempts to lock the mutex again without first unlocking it, the thread will wait for itself to release the lock and will deadlock.
- A **recursive mutex** can be locked more than once by a given thread without causing a deadlock. A recursive mutex is useful if a thread needs exclusive access to a piece of data, and it needs to call another routine (or itself) that needs exclusive access to the data.
- A **non-recursive mutex** is locked exactly once by a thread, like a fast mutex. If a thread tries to lock the mutex again without first unlocking it, the thread receives an error. Also, if a thread other than the owner tries to unlock a non-recursive mutex, an error is returned. Non-recursive mutexes are useful during development and debugging and can be replaced by fast mutexes when the code is put into production use.

The **mutex synchronization operations** are:

pthread_mutex_lock
If the mutex is locked, the thread waits for the mutex to become available.

pthread_mutex_trylock
This returns immediately with a boolean value indicating whether or not it was able to lock the mutex. Based on this return value, the calling thread can take appropriate action.

pthread_mutex_unlock
When a thread has finished accessing a piece of shared data, it unlocks the associated mutex by calling **pthread_mutex_unlock**. If another thread is waiting on the mutex, it is placed in the ready state. If more than one thread is waiting on the mutex, the scheduling policy and the scheduling priority determine which thread is readied, and the next running thread that requests it locks the mutex. The mutex is not automatically granted to the first waiter. If the unlocking thread attempts to relock the mutex before the first waiter gets a chance to run, the unlocking thread will succeed in relocking the mutex, and the first waiter may be forced to reblock.

Condition variables

A condition variable allows a thread to block its own execution until some shared data reaches a particular state. A condition variable is a synchronization object used in conjunction with a mutex. A mutex controls access to shared data; a condition variable allows threads to wait for that data to enter a defined state. The state is defined by a boolean expression called a predicate.

Cooperating threads check the predicate and wait on the condition variable. For example, in the producer–consumer program (Section 10.3) consumers could wait on a condition variable called work-to-do. When a producer thread produces an item, it signals the work-to-do condition variable.

A condition variable is used for tasks with coarse granularity; a thread can wait on a condition variable for long periods. A mutex is used for synchronization with fine granularity and should be held only for short periods of time.

It is essential to associate a mutex with a condition variable. A thread locks the mutex for some shared data and then checks whether or not the shared data is in the proper state. If it is not in the proper state, the thread waits on the appropriate condition variable. Waiting on the condition variable automatically unlocks the mutex. It is essential that the mutex be unlocked because another thread needs to acquire the mutex in order to put the data in the state required by the waiting thread. When the thread that acquires the mutex puts the data in the appropriate state, it wakes a waiting thread by signalling the condition variable. One thread comes out of its wait state with the mutex locked (the thread relocks the mutex before returning from the wait); other threads waiting on the condition variable remain blocked.

It is important to evaluate the predicate in a while loop. This ensures that the program will check the predicate after it returns from the condition wait and guards against the predicate becoming false again as the waiting thread completes the wait.

pthread_cond_wait
Causes a thread to wait for a condition variable to be signalled or broadcast.

pthread_cond_timedwait
Causes a thread to wait for a specified period of time for a condition variable to be signalled or broadcast.

pthread_cond_signal
Wakes one thread that is waiting on a condition variable.

pthread_cond_broadcast.
Wakes all threads that are waiting on a condition variable.

10.8.3 pthread operations summary

Table 10.1 gives each pthread operation with a short description of its functionality. The discussion above has set the context and should allow most of the descriptions to be understood. A global lock is provided by the OSF/1 package because some library routines that are called from the pthreads package are not designed to be executed concurrently.

Section 4.17

Table 10.1 A summary of pthread operations.

Operation	Function
pthread_attr_create	Creates a thread attributes object
pthread_attr_delete	Deletes a thread attributes object
pthread_attr_getguardsize	Obtains the guardsize attribute of the specified thread attributes object
pthread_attr_getinheritsched	Obtains the inherit scheduling attribute of the specified thread attributes object
pthread_attr_getprio	Obtains the scheduling priority attribute of the specified thread attributes object
pthread_attr_getsched	Obtains the scheduling policy attribute of the specified thread attributes object
pthread_attr_getstacksize	Obtains the stacksize attribute of the specified thread attributes object
pthread_attr_setguardsize	Changes the guardsize attribute of thread creation
pthread_attr_setinheritsched	Changes the inherit scheduling attribute of the specified thread attributes object
pthread_attr_setprio	Changes the scheduling priority attribute of thread creation
pthread_attr_setsched	Changes the scheduling policy attribute of thread creation
pthread_attr_setstacksize	Changes the stacksize attribute of thread creation

Table 10.1 (*continued*)

Operation	Function
pthread_cancel	Allows a thread to request that it or another thread terminate execution
pthread_cleanup_pop	Removes the cleanup handler at the top of the cleanup stack and optionally executes it
pthread_cleanup_push	Establishes a cleanup handler to be executed when the thread exits or is cancelled
pthread_condattr_create	Creates a condition variable attributes object that can be used to specify the attributes of condition variables when they are created
pthread_condattr_delete	Deletes a condition variable attributes object
pthread_cond_broadcast	Wakes all threads that are waiting on a condition variable
pthread_cond_destroy	Deletes a condition variable
pthread_cond_init	Creates a condition variable
pthread_cond_signal	Wakes one thread that is waiting on a condition variable
pthread_cond_signal_int	Wakes one thread that is waiting on a condition variable. This routine can only be called from interrupt level
pthread_cond_timedwait	Causes a thread to wait for a condition variable to be signalled or broadcast for a specified period of time
pthread_cond_wait	Causes a thread to wait for a condition variable to be signalled or broadcast
pthread_create	Creates a thread object and thread
pthread_delay	Causes a thread to wait for a specified period of time before continuing execution
pthread_detach	Marks a thread object for deletion
pthread_equal	Compares one thread identifier to another thread identifier
pthread_exit	Terminates the calling thread
pthread_get_expiration	Obtains a value representing a desired expiration time
pthread_getprio	Obtains the current priority of a thread
pthread_getscheduler	Obtains the current scheduling policy of a thread
pthread_getspecific	Obtains the per-thread context associated with the specified key
pthread_join	Causes the calling thread to wait for the termination of a specified thread
pthread_keycreate	Generates a unique per-thread context key value
pthread_lock_global	Locks a global mutex if the global mutex is unlocked. If the global mutex is locked, causes the thread to wait for the global mutex to become available
pthread_mutexattr_create	Creates a mutex attributes object that is used to specify the attributes of mutexes when they are created
pthread_mutexattr_delete	Deletes a mutex attributes object
pthread_mutexattr_getkind	Obtains the mutex type attribute used when a mutex is created
pthread_mutexattr_setkind	Specifies the mutex type attribute that is used when a mutex is created
pthread_mutex_destroy	Deletes a mutex
pthread_mutex_init	Creates a mutex
pthread_mutex_lock	Locks an unlocked mutex. If the mutex is locked, causes the thread to wait for the mutex to become available

Table 10.1 (*continued*)

Operation	Function
pthread_mutex_trylock	Locks a mutex. If the mutex is already locked, the calling thread does not wait for the mutex to become available
pthread_mutex_unlock	Unlocks a mutex
pthread_once	Calls an initialization routine that can be executed by only one thread, a single time
pthread_self	Obtains the identifier of the current thread
pthread_setasynccancel	Enables or disables the current thread's asynchronous cancellability
pthread_setcancel	Enables or disables the current thread's general cancellability
pthread_setprio	Changes the current priority of a thread
pthread_setscheduler	Changes the current scheduling policy and priority of a thread
pthread_setspecific	Sets the per-thread context associated with the specified key for the current thread
pthread_testcancel	Requests delivery of a pending cancel to the current thread
pthread_unlock_global	Unlocks a global mutex
pthread_yield	Notifies the scheduler that the current thread is willing to release its processor to other threads of the same or higher priority

10.9 Summary

We have used the basic mechanisms of Chapter 9 to solve a number of problems that arise in systems design. First, we assumed that the data to be passed between processes comprises fixed-size records and we designed a cyclic buffer with space for a number of records. We discussed how to achieve mutually exclusive access to the buffer and how the two categories of process, those that put a record in and those that take a record out, synchronize their activities. Another problem tackled was how several readers could be allowed to read shared data while writers could be given exclusive access. Eventcounts and sequencers were introduced as an alternative to semaphores and the problems were reprogrammed using them.

We noted that a study of concurrent algorithms as such should include formal proofs of correctness. We outlined how such proofs might be approached and recommended formal study for anyone to be involved professionally with concurrent program design. More general algorithms involving persistent and distributed data are considered in Part III.

We explored the problems that can arise if semaphores are the only mechanism provided for concurrent programming. Programmers can easily make mistakes when using them and even the most rudimentary support for ensuring correct use is absent. We explore how a compiler might assist in the next chapter.

Finally an overview of the pthreads package from the POSIX standard was given. Extra operations have been provided compared with those for semaphores so that mandatory and indefinite blocking can be avoided. There is also flexibility in how a signal is implemented: the programmer may specify whether all blocked threads should be unblocked or just one. We did not explore the support for thread priority in detail. We saw limited assistance for preventing deadlock in the provision of recursive and non-recursive mutexes as well as fast mutexes. Correct concurrent programs, involving condition variables and mutexes, are difficult to achieve. In the next chapter we shall see how the functionality achievable by using condition variables and their associated mutex has been provided in various programming languages.

10.10 Case study with exercises: Management of a disk block cache

10.10.1 Disk read and write and the requirement for buffers and a cache

We shall assume a conventional file I/O model rather than files mapped into virtual memory. A **read** or **write** request from a client of a filing system typically specifies a byte sequence. Let us assume that such a request has been converted by the filing system into a request to read or write a subsequence of bytes from or to some disk block. In practice a requested byte sequence may span more than one disk block, but we can generalize to this from the single block case.

It is necessary to have **buffers** to hold blocks of information on their way to or from the disk. The client program requires a subsequence of a block, DMA transfers between disk and memory deliver a block. We therefore assume a pool of disk buffers is available, each one with a data area large enough to hold a disk block and a header to hold information about the block. A block could be delivered directly into user space, but for several reasons it is more usual for the filing system to maintain a pool of buffers.

Once a disk block is read into a buffer for some client program, a number of read requests might be satisfied from that buffer. Having read from a buffer, the client may wish to change the data and write it back. The filing system may detect that the disk block needed for the write is still available in a buffer. Also, files can be shared, so it is possible that read and write requests from any client program might be satisfied from a buffer already in memory. We are moving towards using our pool of buffers as a **cache**.

Case study exercise

10.10.1   What are the advantages and disadvantages of having a system-maintained cache of disk blocks in volatile main memory?

In more detail, on a client **read** or **write**:

- The cache is searched to see if the required block is already there. If so the request is carried out via the cache. Note that when a cache block has been modified by a **write** the data on disk is no longer up to date, and the cached block must at some point be written to disk.

On a **read**:

- If the required block is not in the cache a free buffer must be acquired and filled by a disk read.

On a **write**:

- If the required block is not already in the cache a free buffer must be acquired. If that block of the file already exists it must be read from disk so that the subsequence of bytes may be written into it, to change some existing bytes or to append to the end of a previously written area. If the block does not already exist it is sufficient to acquire a new buffer.

Having outlined the client requirements we now focus on the buffer management that is needed to satisfy them.

10.10.2 Allocated and free buffers

As a first attempt at buffer management let us propose:

- An *available* list which contains buffers that do not hold any valid data. When a new buffer is needed it is taken from the head of this list. When a buffer is no longer required it is put back at the head of the list. This requires only a singly linked list data structure. We extend this definition after the discussion below.
- An *in-use* data structure which provides access to buffers which hold valid data. Whenever a client issues **read** or **write** this structure must be searched to determine whether the disk block is in the cache, so access must be efficient. A simple solution is to use an open hash table: we hash on the disk block number to find the bucket that would contain the buffer. Hash table slots use little memory compared with a disk buffer, so it is fair to assume that there are about as many buckets as buffers. On this assumption it is efficient to organize each bucket as a simple list.

In the previous section we argued that the buffer should be used as a cache for data on disk, and we do not release buffers as soon as each transfer is complete. In this case, we must decide on a policy for recovering blocks that are *in-use*. An obvious case is when a file is closed by a client and no other client has the file open. Any of its buffers *in-use* can be added to the *available* list. Any that contain new data must first be written out to disk.

We also have to solve the problem of what to do if there are no free buffers when we need one. A reasonable strategy is to attempt to find buffers that have fallen out of use. We can implement an approximate 'least recently used (LRU)' policy over all the blocks in the buffer pool. It is proposed that the *available* list should be defined as follows:

- Any free block and any buffer that is allocated but not locked should not be on the *available* list. The hash lists of the *in-use* data structure contain buffers that are both *locked* and *unlocked*. They also contain blocks that have fallen out of use in the cache, for example when a file is closed, but have not yet been reassigned. When a buffer is locked for use by some process it is detached from the *available* list. When a buffer is no longer required by any process and is unlocked it may be replaced in the *available* list, at the *head* if it does not hold valid disk data, at the *tail* if it does. When a new buffer is needed it is taken from the *head* of the *available* list; it will either be free, or it should be LRU.

To implement such a policy requires that we organize the *available* list as a doubly linked list. We must be able to determine the status of the data held in the buffer from information kept in the header. It may be that the data in a buffer in the *available* list has not been written out to disk. This must be done before the buffer can be reused, and the write to disk is initiated. In the meantime we continue the scan from the head of the list in search of a buffer that can be used immediately.

10.10.3 The structure of a buffer

A disk buffer comprises a header and a data field which is sufficiently large to hold a disk block. A disk block is identified uniquely by the identifier of a filing system and its number within that filing system. This information is held in the buffer header. We shall use a simple integer to identify each block in the examples.

Figure 10.16 shows the contents of a buffer header. The disk block held in the buffer is identified; two pointers link the buffer in the *available* list, and a further one indicates the next buffer in the same bucket of the *in-use* data structure.

The status field indicates the current status of the buffer. Several of these conditions may hold at a given time:

- The buffer is *locked* (so that a change to the header and/or data can be made). The *lock* operation must be atomic.
- The buffer contains valid data. It could be that the buffer is allocated to a certain block but the block has yet to be read into it.

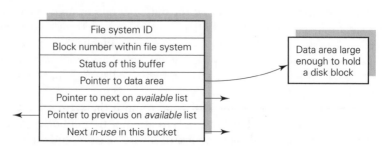

Figure 10.16
A disk buffer header.

| File system ID |
| Block number within file system |
| Status of this buffer |
| Pointer to data area |
| Pointer to next on *available* list |
| Pointer to previous on *available* list |
| Next *in-use* in this bucket |

Data area large enough to hold a disk block

- The data area must be written to disk before the buffer is reused. This is sometimes referred to as a 'dirty' condition; the data has been changed since being read from disk.
- The buffer's data area is in the process of being written to disk or read from disk by a DMA transfer.
- A process is waiting to use this buffer.

In general, processes should be able to WAIT for a specific buffer or for any, as appropriate, and must be SIGNALled when a buffer is *unlocked*.

Case study exercise

10.10.2   Outline the procedure for reading data into a newly acquired buffer. Assume that a process has found a free buffer. What information should it record in the header, and in what order, to achieve a read without interference? Can you ensure that two processes do not acquire a buffer for the same block at the same time?

10.10.4 Outline of the algorithms for buffer access

Figure 10.17 shows the overall data structure. Once a buffer has been allocated for a specific disk block it is added to the list of blocks *in-use* in the appropriate bucket. If the data it holds becomes invalid (for example, if it is part of a file that is deleted) then it is moved to the head of the *available* list. Otherwise it will be removed from the *in-use* data structure only if the buffer is acquired for real-location under the LRU strategy.

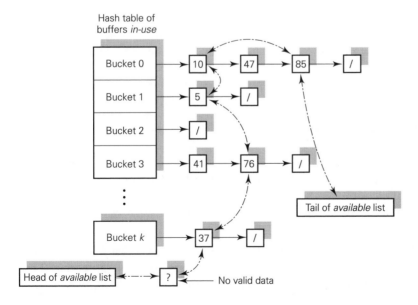

Figure 10.17
An example of hash queues of buffers allocated to blocks.

The following situations might arise when a buffer is to be accessed:

1 The block is *in-use* and is not *locked*. The process may *lock* the buffer, detach it from the *available* list and proceed to use it.
2 The block is *in-use* but is *locked*. The process must WAIT for this specific buffer.
3 The block is not *in-use* and the *available* list is not empty. Provided that the buffer does not contain *dirty* data, the process may use the buffer at the head of the *available* list. The buffer is removed from the *available* list and reassigned within the *in-use* data structure.

　　If the data is dirty, the buffer must be written out to disk. This is initiated and the process continues its search of the available list.
4 The block is not *in-use* and no free buffer is found in the *available* list. The process must WAIT for any buffer.

Event handling: WAIT and SIGNAL

Alternative policies for managing processes waiting for one specific or any buffer are as follows:

(a) When a buffer is unlocked:
　(i) If there are processes waiting for this specific buffer, select one of them and SIGNAL to it. It awakens and proceeds to use the buffer.
　or
　(ii) If there are processes waiting for this specific buffer, awaken all of them. The scheduling algorithm of the system determines which process acquires the buffer.
　　If there are no processes waiting for this buffer but there are processes waiting for any buffer, awaken one (i) or all (ii) of them as above.
(b) When a buffer is unlocked: awaken all processes that are waiting for this specific buffer or for any buffer.

　The choice of policy depends on the mechanisms available for waiting for events and signalling events. It may be that it is only possible to specify 'waiting for a buffer'. In this case, every process waiting for a specific buffer which is not the one that has become unlocked will also be awakened.

Concurrent execution

We assume a multi-threaded file server or procedural execution of file service codes by user processes. It is therefore possible that the algorithms for accessing the buffer pool are executed concurrently. We have implied a degree of concurrency control in the above discussion. The following issues are relevant to concurrent execution of the algorithms:

• A *lock* in the buffer header is provided so that only one process at once may use a given buffer. That is, exclusive access is assumed, rather than a multiple reader, single writer policy. The *lock* operation must be *atomic*.

- The *in-use* data structure and the *available* list are shared, writeable data structures. It is necessary to ensure that they are manipulated under mutual exclusion.
- An interrupt might occur at any time to indicate that a DMA transfer between a buffer and disk is complete. The interrupt may free a waiting process at a time when the cache is being accessed by some other process.

The exercises below invite further consideration of these issues.

Case study exercises

10.10.3 Sketch the event handling mechanisms that are needed to support policies (a) and (b) above.

10.10.4 Evaluate the policies, taking into account the possibilities of unfair scheduling and starvation.

10.10.5 We have discussed the implementation of the *in-use* and *available* shared writeable data structures. Define interfaces for these data objects. Specify the concurrency control requirements on execution of the interface operations.

10.10.6 A file may be open either for reading only or for reading and writing. In the former case access at file level is shared, and it seems reasonable to allow simultaneous read access to a buffer which holds a block of that file. Outline how this facility could be incorporated into the buffer design and the access algorithms.

10.10.7 (a) Outline a design for a buffer management module. What is the interface of this module? Assuming that multi-threaded execution is supported, where can concurrent execution be allowed and where must single threading be enforced? What happens when a process must WAIT within the module?

 (b) Consider any race conditions that may arise because of concurrent execution of the buffer management module. Assume that any process may run out of time or be preempted from its processor at any time.

 (c) Consider the possibility that, at any time, an interrupt may occur which may free a waiting process. Suppose that the system's scheduling policy is such that it is possible that this process may run immediately, preempting some process that was accessing the cache. Describe in detail when and how this could cause problems.

 (d) When a process runs again after waiting for a specific buffer does it need to retest the buffer identifier before proceeding to use it? Can errors occur if a process proceeds, when it is awakened, on the assumption that it now has a specific buffer?

10.10.8 (a) In the design outlined above buffers are written to disk only when a file is closed, unless the buffer reaches the head of the *available* list and is detected as *dirty* when required for reassignment. What are the advantages and disadvantages of this policy?

(b) Sketch an alternative design in which a separate *scribe* process is responsible for writing all cache buffers to disk. When any file is closed a message is sent to the *scribe*, which in addition scans the *available* list from head to tail looking for dirty buffers. What should be done when some other process issues a **read** or **write** request for a buffer while the *scribe* is writing it to disk? What steps might be taken to reduce contention of this kind?

Study questions

S 10.1

(a) Section 10.1 identifies two problems involving concurrent access to shared data. What are they?
(b) What different categories of process are identified?

S 10.2

(a) What is a buffer? What are buffers used for?
(b) What are the synchronization conditions on access to a cyclic buffer?
(c) In the cyclic buffer shown in Figure 10.3, what do the cursors *in* and *out* point to? To what values would you initialize these cursors?
(d) In the Java code given for solving the single producer, single consumer problem, what functions do the semaphores **spaces** and **items** each perform? To what values are these semaphores initialized?
(e) For a single consumer and single producer the buffer is not accessed under mutual exclusion since they are accessing different parts of the buffer (i.e. using different pointers). Why, then, are semaphores used?
(f) In the Java code given for solving the single producer, single consumer problem, can the producer and the consumer access the buffer concurrently? Is there a problem?
(g) In the situation involving many producers and one consumer, what problem arises and how is it solved?

S 10.3

(a) Distinguish between the safety and liveness properties of a program.
(b) In a sequential program name the key safety property and the key liveness property.
(c) In concurrent programs, are mutual exclusion and the absence of deadlock safety or liveness properties?

(d) Distinguish between fairness and starvation. What sort of property is starvation?

(e) Complete the summary table given below by allocating the following to one or more of the entries in the table.
- (i)   termination
- (ii)   correct final state
- (iii) mutual exclusion
- (iv)   absence of starvation
- (v)   absence of deadlock.

Type of program	Safety properties	Liveness properties
Sequential programs (including an individual process)		
Concurrent programs (i.e. many processes executing together)		

S 10.4

In the multiple readers, single writer problem, what priority scheme is conventionally chosen? How many writers can there be in this problem? How many readers can be reading concurrently?

S 10.5

(a) How can the misuse of semaphores lead to problems with safety and liveness?

(b) Give an example of a situation where one process might wish to control another. Why is it not possible with semaphores to enable this to happen without the cooperation of the controlled process?

(c) The semaphore operations do not allow a test for busy without a commitment to blocking. Why is this a problem? What is the standard solution to this problem? Why is it a problem if the time for which a process is blocked on a semaphore is unlimited?

Exercises

10.1 What are the problems of designing a system with a strict hierarchical structure? What are the advantages?

The Venus operating system (Liskov, 1972) had the following levels (bottom-up): 0: hardware; 1: instruction interpreter; 2: CPU scheduling; 3: I/O channels; 4: virtual memory; 5: device drivers and schedulers; 6: user processes. Does this choice of layers solve the problems discussed for THE in Section 10.2?

10.2 A buffer object manager is to be implemented. Buffers are to be managed as a pool of fixed-sized objects. A producer process first acquires an empty buffer, then performs a number of write operations into it until it is full. A consumer process first acquires a full buffer then performs a number of reads from it until it is empty.

Each object has a header part, for holding information on the use of the buffer (such as a count and a pointer), for links so that the buffers can be chained, etc., and a body part for holding data. A chain of empty buffer objects and a chain of full buffer objects are to be maintained. The object manager detects when a buffer becomes full.

Interface operations are proposed as follows:

buffer =	*pool.acquire-empty-buffer* ()	// executed by producers
buffer =	*pool.acquire-full-buffer* ()	// executed by consumers
return-code =	*buffer.write-buffer* (*bytes*)	// executed by producers
bytes =	*buffer.read-buffer* (*byte-count*)	// executed by consumers
	buffer.free-buffer ()	// executed by consumers

Discuss the following:

(a) use of the proposed interface operations and possible modifications;
(b) the information that might usefully be kept in each buffer header;
(c) how a full buffer, on writing, and an empty buffer, on reading, should be detected and indicated to the invoker;
(d) how exclusive access to a buffer object might be ensured;
(e) how the various chains might be updated correctly, secure from concurrent access;
(f) how the scheme compares with a cyclic buffer (see Section 10.3) for concurrent accesses by producers and consumers.

10.3 (a) In the Java code for a producer given in Section 10.3.4, is there any significance in executing **spaces.semWait( )** before **guard.semWait( )**?

(b) Write down, in the manner of the code in Section 10.3.4, the consumer's algorithm when there are several consumers (assume that there are several producers).

10.4 The classic **sleeping barber** problem is given in Exercise 11.10. Consider solving this problem using semaphores. Assume that you are given the following shared variables:

```
static final int chairs = 20;
int waiting = 0;       // shows customers waiting – can be checked to see
                       // whether a new customer should wait or go away

Semaphore guard = new SemaphoreImplementation(1);
                       // guards critical region to update variable 'waiting'

Semaphore customers = new SemaphoreImplementation(0);
                       // provides count of customers and barber must
                       // wait if value is 0
```

```
Semaphore barber = new SemaphoreImplementation(1);
                            // provides mutual exclusion to barber (value is 1
                            // when barber is available to cut, and 0 when
                            // barber is cutting)
```

and the following customer process:

```
guard.semWait();                // wait to access variable 'waiting'
if (waiting < chairs) {
    waiting = waiting + 1;
    customers.semSignal(); // increase the count of customers
    guard.semSignal();         // give up exclusive lock on 'waiting'
    barber.semWait();          // wait for the barber to be free – queue as though
}                                   // waiting on chairs
else
    guard.semSignal();         // customer effectively goes away because
                                    // no chairs available
```

Provide the code that executes the barber process.

10.5 The classic dining philosophers problem is described in Section 17.5 and Exercise 17.5. Attempt the suggested solutions using semaphores.

IPC with shared memory

Throughout this chapter processes are assumed to be executing in a shared address space and therefore are able to share data.

When discussing the limitations of semaphores (Section 10.6), the difficulties in programming low-level synchronization primitives correctly was highlighted. In this chapter we investigate different ways in which support can be given to the programmer. In particular, we describe how the low-level operations, described in Chapter 10, can be made available through a high-level language. That is, the compiler of a high-level language can enforce restrictions on the access to shared data and the correct entering and exiting of critical regions. Clearly, for the compiler to be able to offer this kind of assistance, the programmer needs to specify:

- which data is shared by processes in the program;
- which semaphore (for example) is associated with which shared data;
- where the critical regions for accessing the shared data are located in the program.

The compiler could then check and enforce that:

- shared data is only accessed from within a critical region;
- critical regions are entered and left correctly by processes.

In the following sections we shall see different programming constructs which help the programmer organize the shared data and the processes acting on it, thus ensuring correct use of the low-level primitive operations.

 # 11.1 Critical regions in programming languages

We discussed earlier the general concept of the **critical region**, as that section of code where shared data is accessed. Here we show a possible implementation of the concept. A critical region construct requires syntax such as the following to be added to the high-level language:

- declaring a data type to be **shared**, such as:

    shared DataType someSharedData

- a **region** declaration such as:

    region (someSharedData) { ....}

For each shared data declaration the compiler could create a semaphore, for example **crSem**. Then, at the start of any critical region construct for that data it could insert a **crSem.semWait()** operation and a **crSem.semSignal()** at the end. If the Java syntax included this facility, it would look like the code in Figure 11.1.

Guarding access to shared data is one requirement of the constructs provided for programming a concurrent system. This is an example of arbitration between processes competing for a resource. Assistance is also needed for cooperation between processes. An example is synchronizing over the state of a shared resource (condition synchronization). A producer process cannot put data into a shared buffer if it is full and needs a mechanism to allow it to **wait()** until there is space in the buffer and to allow consumer processes access to the buffer, in order to make space there, while it is waiting.

During the evolution of concurrent programming languages (see Brinch Hansen, 1973b), a proposal for this kind of synchronizing primitive, in addition to the critical region constructs described above, was for **conditional critical regions** with an associated **(condition).await()** primitive. In the form proposed this was difficult to implement since **(condition)** could be any conditional expression, for example, **(count > 0).await()**. It is difficult to establish whether the many conditions involving programming language variables awaited by processes have become true.

```
shared DataType someSharedData
//Here the compiler creates a semaphore, for example, crSem, and initializes it to 1.
//It is associated with someSharedData
        .
        .
        .

region (someSharedData) {
    //compiler inserts crSem.semWait();
        .
        .
    //compiler inserts crSem.semSignal();
}
```

Figure 11.1
Critical region construct.

v is declared as a **shared** record with two integer fields:
aw (active writers) and rr (reading readers) both initially 0.
writelock is declared as a **shared** boolean.

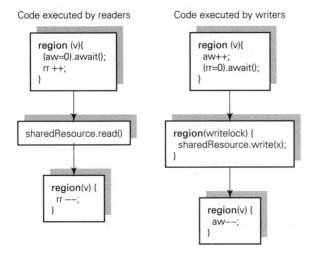

Code executed by readers

```
region (v){
    (aw=0).await();
    rr ++;
}
```

```
sharedResource.read()
```

```
region(v) {
    rr --;
}
```

Code executed by writers

```
region (v){
    aw++;
    (rr=0).await();
}
```

```
region(writelock) {
    sharedResource.write(x);
}
```

```
region(v) {
    aw--;
}
```

Figure 11.2
Algorithm for readers
and writers using
conditional critical
regions. (The problem
is described in
Section 10.5.)

Figure 11.2 shows a solution for the readers and writers problem using conditional critical regions. An active writer is one that is either waiting to access or accessing the shared data. A reading reader is a reader that is currently accessing the shared data.

In the code executed by writers, once a writer has completed its execution of the first critical region it cannot gain access to the shared resource if a previous writer has access, that is, mutual exclusion to the shared resource is required. One might think that the region in which this is done should begin with something similar to:

region (sharedResource) { ... }

where **sharedResource** had been declared as:

shared DataTypeSharedResource sharedResource

Instead, the actual writing to **sharedResource** is within a region associated with a boolean variable named **writelock**. The reason is that it would be usual to insist that, having declared some data as shared, the data should only be accessed within a critical region. In this example, this would be inappropriate for the *readers*, as several readers are allowed to read at the same time. Therefore, in order to ensure mutual exclusion for writers, an additional shared boolean, **writelock,** has been introduced to prevent more than one writer at a time accessing **sharedResource**. In this sense, the boolean is providing a lock on the shared data although there is no need for any manipulation of it.

Notice that the solution in Figure 11.2 is much simpler (for the programmer) than the semaphore solution given in Figure 10.10, although similar in structure. The programmer has only to be concerned with when to **await()**. When to unblock (wake up) a process is the problem of the implementation.

An implementation of such a primitive would have the overhead of re-evaluation of the conditions on which processes were waiting each time any process left a critical region in which the shared data might have been changed. This is an unacceptable overhead, in general, in a part of the system which should be efficient. An alternative synchronizing primitive was provided in the context of monitors, as shown in the next section, but this brought back the requirement on the programmer to manage explicit signalling.

11.2 Monitors

The critical region construct, in itself, has no way of enforcing modularity and a program might be structured as shown in Figure 11.3. That is, critical region statements performing operations on the shared data, may be dispersed throughout the program. Therefore, if one wanted to check how a particular piece of shared data is used, the programmer would have to go through the entire program to find all the critical regions related to that shared data.

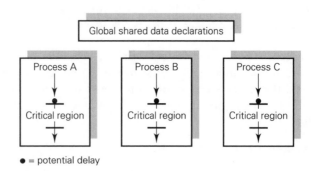

| Global shared data declarations |

| Process A | Process B | Process C |
| Critical region | Critical region | Critical region |

● = potential delay

or, showing two processes coded in Java:

```
Program
data declarations:
data1

procA {
    ⋮
CR (data1) { }
    ⋮

}

procB {
    ⋮
CR (data1) { }
    ⋮

CR (data1) { }
    ⋮

}
```

Figure 11.3
Possible program structure with conditional critical regions.

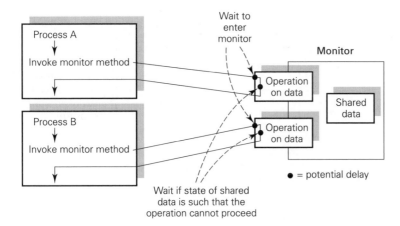

Figure 11.4
Enforced program structure with monitors.

A solution to this problem is to use a monitor, where a monitor has the structure of an abstract data object. In a monitor the shared data and the operations manipulating it are encapsulated. As in object-oriented programming, this ensures that there is no uncontrolled access to the data, since it is only accessible through a well-defined interface. In addition, the monitor implementation must ensure that several processes wishing to access the same shared data at the same time are prevented from doing so; that is, the monitor operations are executed under mutual exclusion. This is illustrated in Figure 11.4. Compared with Figure 11.3, the critical region statements in the program have been replaced by calls to monitor procedures. The monitor implementation must ensure that only one process is active in the monitor at any time. As Figure 11.4 shows, there is therefore a potential delay for mutual exclusion and a commitment to wait, if necessary, on calling a monitor procedure. To implement this mutual exclusion the compiler associates a synchronization mechanism (for example, a semaphore) with each monitor. Any call to a monitor procedure would involve a **wait()** on this synchronization mechanism and return (exit the procedure) would include a **signal()** on it.

Mutual exclusion is not sufficient for programming concurrent systems. In most of the problems solved in Chapter 10, for example, condition synchronization is also needed (the resource may be busy when you want to acquire it; the buffer may be full when you want to put something into it). This is provided in most monitor-based systems by a new type of variable called a **condition variable**. The programmer declares the condition variables that are needed by the application and the monitor implementation manages them as synchronization queues (see below). The operations on condition variables are again, **wait()** and **signal()**. A process may delay itself by executing conditionVariableName.wait(). It is freed subsequently by some other process executing conditionVariableName.signal(). Figure 11.5 shows a typical structure of a simple monitor procedure. On entry, the process tests whether it can proceed to operate on the shared data or whether it must wait for some condition on the data to be satisfied (for example, for the buffer to have a space for inserting an item).

Section 10.8 ⟵

The definition of condition variables used in this chapter follows those given in the original monitor proposals (Hoare, 1974; Brinch Hansen, 1973a, b).

Monitor procedure

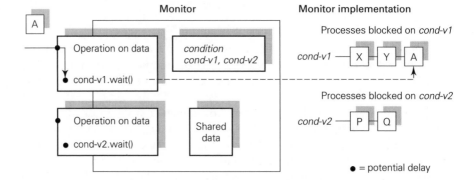

Figure 11.5
Condition
synchronization
under exclusion in a
monitor procedure.

- Enter: now have mutual exclusion

  Can I proceed to operate on the shared data or must I block?

  proceed | • conditionVariableName.wait() ↘ block

  Note that wait( ) *releases the exclusion on the monitor.*

  Operate on the shared data

  Exit: release mutual exclusion and return

• = potential delay (on entry) and delay on wait()

Figure 11.6
Condition variable
queues.

Monitor

A

Operation on data

cond-v1.wait()

Operation on data

cond-v2.wait()

condition
cond-v1, cond-v2

Shared
data

Monitor implementation

Processes blocked on *cond-v1*

cond-v1 — X — Y — A

Processes blocked on *cond-v2*

cond-v2 — P — Q

• = potential delay

Whereas a semaphore is implemented as an integer and a queue, a condition variable is implemented only as a queue. That is, a condition variable does not have a value, it has 'no state', and the **wait( )** operation always queues the executing process. The definition of **signal( )** is that if there are any waiting processes then one of them is freed. If there are no waiting processes there is no effect.

It is possible to use this simple definition because the **signal( )** and **wait( )** operations on condition variables take place within monitors under mutual exclusion. It is therefore possible for a process, under the protection of guaranteed exclusive access, to test the value of some variable, say **count**, referring to a count of items in a buffer, and to decide to block itself on the basis of the value of the variable, as shown in Figure 11.5. Note that there are two types of variables here, a normal variable which has a value (e.g. **count**), and a condition variable which is a queue. No other process can be accessing the **count** variable at the same time nor signalling the condition variable between the test and the **wait( )**. That is, the fact that only one process is active in a monitor at any time ensures that there are no race conditions.

A process must not be allowed to block while holding a monitor lock. If a process must wait for condition synchronization the implementation must free the monitor for use by other processes and queue the process on the condition variable, as shown in Figure 11.6 where process A finds it has to wait for condition **cond-v1** to become true, and is therefore added to the back of the queue for the condition variable **cond-v1**. Whatever synchronization mechanism was

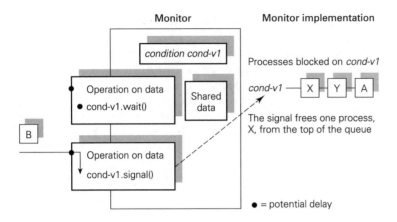

Figure 11.7
Signalling a condition variable.

used by the compiler to implement exclusive access to the monitor must now be signalled so that another process is allowed to enter the monitor.

In some monitor implementations semaphores are used as the synchronization mechanism to enforce mutual exclusion and the compiler inserts the appropriate semaphore operations in the code. We could thus view the monitor as a 'higher' level construction, which is easier to use for the programmer.

Figure 11.7 is another snapshot of the same monitor showing process A now on the queue for condition variable **cond-v1** and process B signalling that variable. The discussion continues in Section 11.2.2 after Java monitors have been introduced.

11.2.1 Monitors in Java: Java's synchronization mechanism

In this section we discuss how monitors are provided in Java. Given that Java is an object-oriented language, some of the monitor issues discussed, i.e. the encapsulation of shared data, and the controlled access to data through monitor operations, come quite naturally to any class defined in Java. What is required though, is to ensure that the operations (or methods) of an object execute under mutual exclusion, as well as some way of implementing condition synchronization. We will see that the monitor mechanisms are available through the use of the following Java primitives: **synchronized**, wait(), and notify() or notifyAll(). By using the example of a simple Account object which has a debit and credit method, we will show how these primitives can be used to construct monitors which enforce mutual exclusion and enable condition synchronization.

Methods used with threads and the Java thread life-cycle

First of all, recall that in Java, separate (lightweight) processes are created as objects of type **Thread** (or more accurately, as objects of a user-defined class that extends **Thread**). A new process (or thread) is created by invoking the **start** method of an object of such a class. This process will execute the run method for that object.

The traditional Java application programming interfaces (APIs) do not provide a mechanism for terminating threads explicitly. Instead, applications are expected to use threads in a cooperative manner in which each thread performs periodic tests of whether it should exit. The Thread class provides two methods which are conventionally used for this purpose. Invoking t1.interrupt() on a thread t1 requests that thread to exit. The target thread does not usually notice the request automatically, but is expected to make regular calls to Thread.isInterrupted() and to exit should that method ever return true. As we will see below, if the target thread is blocked when it is interrupted then, for most operations, it is made runnable again and the operation fails with an instance of InterruptedException.

Why does Java not allow threads to be terminated explicitly? One reason is that supporting uncontrolled termination would make it impossible to write most data structures in a way that is safe for concurrent use: a thread may be terminated part-way through an update to the data structure. The cooperative model allows an interrupted thread to continue until it has reached a safe point to exit.

Here follows a summary of some of the methods that can be used to manage Java threads and to change their state. Note that not all the methods summarized here belong to the class Thread: the final three methods are from class Object and can only be used on the objects that threads are accessing via **synchronized** methods.

- start, which when applied to a thread launches it and calls the thread's run method;
- isAlive, which when applied to a thread returns true if the thread has been started and has not yet terminated;
- sleep, which causes the calling thread to sleep for a number of milliseconds specified by the argument. This is a static method, affecting only the caller, and so it is invoked directly on the Thread class rather than on a particular object;
- join, which suspends the calling thread until the target thread finishes. For example, t1.join () suspends the thread in which this call is made until t1 completes. This method throws an exception of type InterruptedException if the calling thread is interrupted while waiting;
- yield, which when applied to a thread causes it to give up control to other threads of the same priority;
- setPriority, which takes an argument and when applied to a thread resets its priority to the value of the argument;
- getPriority, which when applied to a thread returns its priority;
- wait, which is a method of the class Object that, when invoked on an object inside a synchronized method of that object, causes the calling thread to release the lock it holds on the object, to become blocked and to be added to a set of threads waiting on the object. This method throws an exception of type InterruptedException if the calling thread is interrupted while waiting;

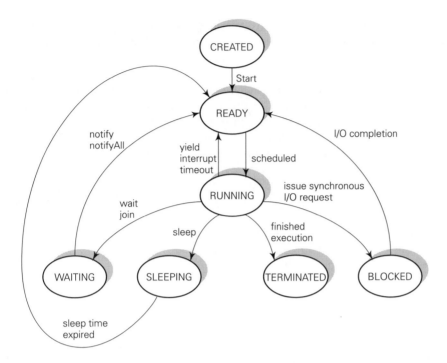

Figure 11.8
The life-cycle of a thread.

- **notify**, which is a method of the class **Object** that, when invoked on an object inside a **synchronized** method of that object, causes an indeterminate thread (if there is one) currently waiting on the object to be made runnable again;
- **notifyAll**, which is similar to **notify** except that it causes all the threads (if any) waiting on the object to be made runnable again.

The operating system is responsible for looking after (i.e. creating, scheduling and eventually destroying) threads. In a manner similar to the diagram of the state transitions of processes in Figure 4.3, a diagram of the life-cycle of threads can be constructed, which shows the result of executing the various methods listed above that change the state of a thread. In Figure 11.8, the ovals represent the states that a thread can be in and the arrowed lines show the 'event' that causes a thread to move from one state to another. (Notice that the term 'READY' also means 'RUNNABLE'.)

Note in Figure 11.8 that the **yield** and **interrupt** methods (coming from the RUNNING state) both cause one thread to stop running and another thread to move from the READY state to the RUNNING state. Figure 11.8 is based on Figure 15.1 of Dietel and Dietel (2002).

Java critical regions: **synchronized** methods

If we want a thread that will access a shared resource to execute under mutual exclusion, then we need to declare the methods that access the shared data as **synchronized**. Once a thread has gained access to a **synchronized** method, it will finish the method before any other thread is allowed access to that *or any other* **synchronized** *method for that object*. Any thread that must wait is placed in a **wait set** (this is not a queue, because it is not ordered) associated with that object.

An object with one or more **synchronized** methods acts as a *monitor* on all or part of its data, provided that this data is accessed via the **synchronized** methods alone. Methods in the interface of an object that are not **synchronized** may be invoked by another process *at the same time* as a **synchronized** method is being executed. Therefore, for an object to act as a monitor, the data accessed by its **synchronized** methods *must not* be accessed by its non-**synchronized** methods. Looking at it another way, an object can be thought of as locked as far as **synchronized** methods are concerned but not locked with regard to methods that are **non-synchronized**.

If we refer back to Figure 11.4, then by declaring the methods (shown as operations on data in the figure) as **synchronized**, we have defined Java syntax for 'wait to enter', with possible delay for mutual exclusion.

Java condition synchronization: **wait** and **notify**

We discussed conditional critical regions and condition variables earlier; these are both associated with achieving condition synchronization, where a thread cannot continue until some condition, set by another thread, becomes true. At the time that the thread finds that it cannot continue, it will be executing a **synchronized** method belonging to a particular object and will call the method **wait** on this object (inherited from the class **Object**) from within this method. This causes the thread to be placed in the wait set associated with the object, and is therefore equivalent to the object having a single condition variable. Note that this 'conditional' wait set is *not* the same as the one on which threads are placed if they cannot get access to the **synchronized** method itself. In terms of Figure 11.4, this conditional wait set is associated with the second 'blob' for potential delay in the monitor.

When a thread is waiting on a condition, it will only be able to proceed when the condition changes. Clearly for this to happen, the data upon which the condition is based must change in some way. For example, if the condition involves an empty buffer, then the condition will change when an element is added to the buffer. Since the thread that has been caused to wait, because the buffer is empty, cannot do anything to change the buffer's state (it is not running), one or more other threads must be responsible for the change. Such threads must be made to execute either a **notify** or a **notifyAll** (both inherited from the class **Object**) when they change the buffer's state. The method **notify** causes an arbitrarily chosen thread in the wait set to become runnable again. The method **notifyAll** causes all threads in the wait set to be scheduled for execution.

In other words, the **wait** method makes the current thread block until it is made runnable (or ready) by another thread executing **notify** (or **notifyAll**) inside a **synchronized** method. When this runnable thread (or possibly more than one thread in the case where **notifyAll** is called) is once again scheduled to run, it must once again 'compete' for the **synchronized** method it was executing when it was forced to wait on the condition. However, once it has regained exclusive access to this **synchronized** method, it will resume at the point immediately after its call to **wait**. By incorporating this **wait** call in a suitable **while** loop that tests whether the condition is true, the thread can be made to retest the condition before it is allowed to enter into the critical region.

When should a program use **notify** and when should it use **notifyAll**? The former can be used when exactly one thread out of those waiting on a condition should become runnable and it does not matter which is chosen; for example in the resource allocation class in Section 11.2.3. The latter should be used either when multiple threads should become runnable or when the choice of exactly which thread is resumed is important: it will cause *all* of the threads waiting on the condition to be resumed and each can then acquire access to the **synchronized** method and, by executing the next iteration of the enclosing **while** loop, test whether to continue or whether to invoke **wait** again. The buffer class in Section 11.2.4 must use **notifyAll**.

Note that the **wait** method throws an exception of type **InterruptedException** if the calling thread is interrupted while waiting. The call to **wait** must therefore either be used within a **try** statement that handles the exception or, more usually, it must propagate the exception to a point at which it may be handled. The exception is usually used to indicate that the calling thread should exit. Both **wait** and **notify** must be used within **synchronized** methods, since they can only be used in relation to locked objects, otherwise an **IllegalMonitorStateException** will be thrown.

The **wait** method comes in two varieties. One has no parameters and simply causes a thread to wait indefinitely. Another has a single parameter, an integer representing the maximum length of time (in milliseconds) for which a thread is prepared to be blocked. This is known as a **timeout**. The caller cannot automatically distinguish between a **wait** operation that times out and one that completes normally; if such a distinction is important then it must be made explicitly based on the values of the fields of the object in question.

Java monitors: An example

We now look at the concrete example of an **Account** class, which has **debit** and **credit** methods that update the balance of the account. As in Chapter 2, this example uses in-memory data structures to represent accounts and is not intended to be a realistic banking application. First of all, we look at the issue of enforcing mutual exclusion, as in Figure 11.9.

Assume that an object of the class **Account** may be accessed by many threads all trying to either debit or credit the account. Notice that the two methods **debit** and **credit** have been declared as **synchronized**. The reason is that **balance** must be updated under conditions of mutual exclusion. This means that a thread wishing to execute the **debit** method, for example on an account object, must not be allowed to do so if some other thread is executing either a **debit** or a **credit** method on the same account object.

Figure 11.9
A simple Account
class.

```
public class Account {
    protected int balance;
    public synchronized void debit (int a) { balance = balance − a; }
    public synchronized void credit (int a) { balance = balance + a; }
    }
}
```

Figure 11.10
Account class
with condition
synchronization.

```
class Account {
    protected int balance = 0;

    public Account(int anAmount) {
        balance = anAmount;
    }

    public synchronized void debit(int anAmount)
                                    throws InterruptedException {
        while (balance < anAmount)
            wait();
        balance = balance − anAmount;
    }

    public synchronized void credit (int anAmount) {
        balance = balance + anAmount;
        notifyAll();
    }
}
```

Where might condition synchronization fit into such an example? Assume, for simplicity, that a debit can only succeed if the balance of the account is greater than or equal to the actual argument associated with the **debit** call. In practice, such a call would result in a failure return but here, as an illustrative example, we program the class **Account** so that, if a thread executing **debit** finds that the debit amount exceeds the balance, it is made to wait.

The **debit** method shown in Figure 11.10 will ensure that when a thread executing the method finds the debit amount is too large, it (the thread) will be put in the conditional wait set. Notice that the method must be declared to propagate **InterruptedException** because that may be thrown within the call to **wait** if the thread is interrupted. The alternative would be to enclose the **wait** within a **try** statement and to discard the exception: however, that would prevent cooperative thread termination.

How will the conditionally waiting thread ever be made runnable again? The answer is that some other thread that causes the waiting condition to change must execute a **notify** or a **notifyAll**. This is of course the thread that executes **credit**, as this might change the condition by making the balance large enough to accommodate the debit that caused the waiting thread to block. Figure 11.10 shows that having increased the balance, the credit method is made to call **notifyAll** (). This will have the effect of making any conditionally waiting threads runnable (an indeterminate one will be chosen if there are many threads waiting, and nothing will happen if no threads are waiting). If **notify** () had been used, then only one conditionally waiting thread would have been made runnable.

```
//A class providing threads that are initialized with an account and an amount
//and will debit the account by this amount when run

public class debitTransaction extends Thread {
    Account acct;
    int amount;

    public debitTransaction(Account a, int x) {acct = a; amount = x; }

    public void run(){
        try {
            acct.debit (amount);
        } catch (InterruptedException e) {
            System.out.println ("Thread interrupted: exiting without performing debit");
        }
    }
}
```

```
//A class providing threads that are initialized with an account and an amount
//and will credit the account by this amount when run

public class creditTransaction extends Thread {
    Account acct;
    int amount;

    public creditTransaction(Account a, int x) { acct = a; amount = x; }
    public void run(){ acct.credit(amount); }
}
```

```
//A class providing the main method that creates an account and different
//threads to credit and debit the account

public class testTransactions {

    public static void main(String[] args) {
        Account acct = new Account(2000);
        Thread dt1 = new debitTransaction (acct, 3000);
        Thread ct1 = new creditTransaction (acct, 500);
        Thread ct2 = new creditTransaction (acct, 600);

        //launch the threads
        dt1.start();
        ct1.start();
        ct2.start();
    }
}
```

Figure 11.11
Classes providing
threads which use
the Account class.

Finally, in Figure 11.11 we see the classes that use the debit and credit methods from the Account class, by creating separate threads.

The scenario provided by the class testTransactions in Figure 11.11 allows us to follow step-by-step what would happen to the balance of account acct, given that three threads are trying to access it. Assuming that thread dt1 will be the first to execute, the following will happen:

- dt1 would call the debit method and because there are no other threads using the debit or the credit method on the account, dt1 would be granted access to it.

- The **debit** method is called with an argument of 3000.
- However, because the **balance** of the account is only 2000, the call to **wait( )** would be made and the thread **dt1** would be put in the conditional wait set.
- One of the **creditTransactions** threads would then be scheduled, given exclusive access to the **credit** method, and credit the account.
- Before completing, the **credit** method would call **notifyAll( )**, which would cause **dt1** to be made runnable again.
- If **dt1** were scheduled, it would continue from where it left off when it called **wait( )** previously, that is, it will check the condition in the **while** loop. It would find that the balance was still not enough and again be conditionally queued.
- The other **creditTransaction** thread would then be scheduled, and after crediting the balance, would also call **notifyAll( )**.
- **dt1** would be made runnable again and scheduled. This time the balance exceeds 3000 and it would succeed in debiting the account.

Note that the example in Figures 11.10 and 11.11 for the implementation of **Account** is very simple and does not claim to be a practical approach to debiting an account that has insufficient funds in it; the blocking behaviour would be unacceptable in practice. Also observe that only the **debit** operation can block and so it is only the **debitTransaction** class that must handle **InterruptedException**.

11.2.2 Some further issues relating to monitors

It is essential that a process should leave the monitor data in a consistent state before executing **condition.wait( )**. It might be desirable to enforce that a process can only read (and not write) the monitor data before executing **wait( )**. Alternatively, software support might be possible to ensure that the data is in a consistent state by allowing an invariant to be associated with the shared data and for assertions that the invariant is satisfied to be checked at every monitor exit point. This opens up the field of how to prove programs correct, which is outside the scope of this book.

The implementation of **signal( )** has a potential problem, as shown in Figure 11.7. The signalling process, process B in the figure, is active inside the monitor and a process freed from a condition queue, process X in the figure, is potentially active inside the monitor. By definition, only one process can be active inside a monitor at any time. One solution is to enforce that a **signal( )** is immediately followed by (or combined with) exit from the procedure (and monitor); that is, the signalling process is forced to leave the monitor. A compiler could check for and implement this. If this method is not used, one of the processes must be delayed temporarily and resume execution in the monitor later.

Let us suppose that the signaller, B, is allowed to continue and the signalled process, X, must wait. One way of achieving this without a separate mechanism is to transfer the signalled process from the condition variable queue on which it is waiting to the head of the queue of processes waiting to enter the monitor. The saved process state would ensure that the process would continue execution from the correct point when next scheduled. We are assuming that the queue to enter the monitor is scheduled first come first served, so that no other process can overtake this one, enter the monitor and possibly invalidate the condition. This may not always be the case, for example if priority inheritance is in use (see Section 9.6.2). The monitor operations must be such that the signaller exits without making the condition that it previously signalled false.

If instead the signalled process X runs, the signalling process B may be put at the head of the monitor wait queue. In this case there is no problem about the condition signalled remaining true but the monitor data must be in a consistent state before a **signal** () is executed. The waiting process has already had this constraint imposed upon it before executing **wait** ().

The approach in Java is as follows. Every **Object** has a lock, and by declaring methods as **synchronized** the effect is that only the thread that holds the object's lock is allowed to execute. When a thread calls **notify()** or **notifyAll()** an arbitrarily chosen thread, say T, from the wait set is scheduled to execute. However, T will not be able to start executing until the thread invoking the **notify()** method has given up its hold on the lock of the object. It is even possible that the thread T from the wait set might not be able to get hold of the object's lock, because another process got hold of it first. The process with the lock will be allowed to execute. For a detailed discussion of Java's locking mechanism, see Lea (1999). For a discussion of pthreads (POSIX threads) see Section 10.8.

The above discussion indicates that the monitor mechanisms must be implemented with great care; also, that the programmer of the monitor procedures must be aware of the constraints imposed by the mechanisms.

11.2.3 Single resource allocator

In Chapter 9 a single semaphore, initialized to 1, was used to allocate a single resource. Processes execute **wait()** on that semaphore to reserve the resource and **signal()** on that semaphore to release it. If monitors are the only concurrency construct available, a single resource allocator would be built as a monitor with operations to reserve and release the resource. The shared data encapsulated by the monitor is in this case a boolean **busy**, initialized to **false**, representing the state of the resource: free or allocated. A condition variable **free** is declared and is used to allow processes to **wait()** if the resource is already assigned to some other process. On releasing the resource, a process must both set **busy** to **false** and execute **free.signal()**. Figure 11.12 outlines the monitor and shows a process making use of it.

A Java implementation of the monitor shown in Figure 11.12 could be as shown in Figure 11.13, where the queueing on condition variable **free** is replaced by calls to **wait()** and **notify()** within **synchronized** methods.

Note that in this example the resource itself is not encapsulated by the monitor, only the variable **busy** which records whether the resource is currently in use. It is therefore still up to the programmer to make sure that the entry and

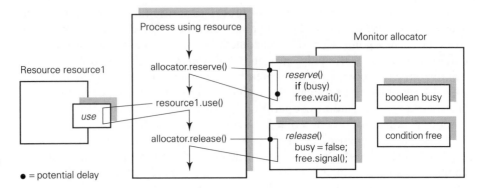

Figure 11.12
Monitor to allocate a
single resource.

● = potential delay

```
public class Allocator {
protected boolean busy = false;

    public Allocator(boolean used) {
    busy = used;
    }
    public synchronized void reserve() throws InterruptedException{
    while (busy)
        wait();
    busy = true;
    }

    public synchronized void release(){
    busy = false;
    notify();
    }
}
```

Figure 11.13
Java implementation
for monitor to allocate
a single resource.

exit protocols are used before and after use of the resource. This is different
from the **Account** example we saw earlier, where the **balance** was encapsulated.

11.2.4 Bounded buffer manager

The semaphore solution to the producer–consumer, bounded buffer management problem is given in Section 10.3. The shared buffer together with associated
counts and pointers may be encapsulated in a monitor. Notice that exclusive
access to the buffer is always enforced by the monitor, even if there is only one
producer process and one consumer process.

Synchronization over the state of the buffer is needed. A producer process
needs to **wait()** if the buffer is full and a consumer process needs to **wait()** if the
buffer is empty. Two condition variables, **notFull** and **notEmpty**, are therefore
used. Figure 11.14 outlines the monitor structure and call sequences.

The monitor with its operations **put** and **get** as represented in Figure 11.14,
can be implemented in Java as shown in Figure 11.15. Note again that there
are no condition variables, but that the calls to the **wait()** and **notify()** methods
have the same effect. It is also interesting to note that in Java it is not possible

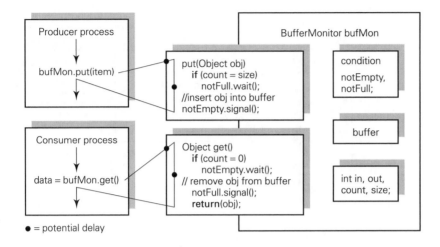

Figure 11.14
Monitor to manage a bounded buffer.

● = potential delay

```
public class BufferMonitor {

    private Object[] buf;          //the buffer, declared as an array of objects
    private int in = 0;            //index of the next place where an item can be added
    private int out = 0;           //index of the next item that can be removed
    private int count = 0;         //count of the number of items in the buffer
    private int size = 5;          //number of slots in the buffer

    public BufferMonitor( ) {
        buf = new Object[5];       //actual buffer can hold 5 objects
    }

    public synchronized void put(Object obj) throws InterruptedException {
                                   // implement conditional synchronization
        while (count==size) {
            wait( );
        }
        buf[in] = obj;             //place object into buffer at index 'in'
        + + count;                 //increment count of number of items in buffer
        in = (in + 1) % size;      //increment index 'in'
        notifyAll( );              //update of shared data completed
    }

    public synchronized Object get( ) throws InterruptedException {
                                   //implement conditional synchronization
        while (count==0) {
            wait( );
        }
        Object obj = buf[out];     //get object from buffer at index 'out'
        buf[out] = null;
        - - count;                 //decrement number of items in buffer
        out = (out + 1) % size;    //increment index 'out'
        notifyAll( );              //update of shared data completed
        return (obj);
    }
}
```

Figure 11.15
Java implementation of monitor to manage a bounded buffer.

to indicate exactly *which* condition variable needs to be signalled, i.e. there is no **notEmpty.signal()**, but a more crude **notify** or **notifyAll**. It is therefore necessary to place the **wait()** method within a **while** loop, rather than an **if** statement, to verify that it is correct for the current thread to continue.

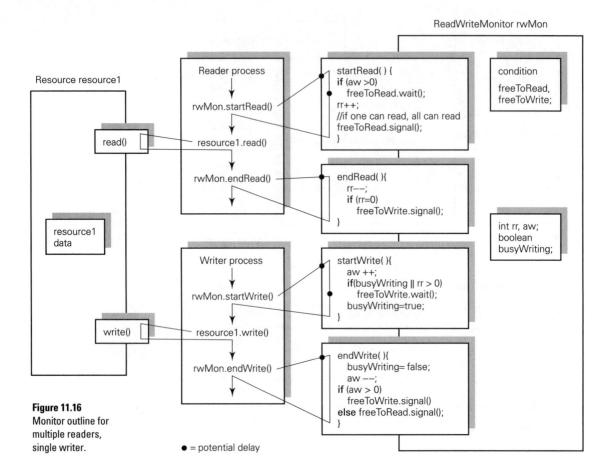

Figure 11.16
Monitor outline for multiple readers, single writer.

● = potential delay

11.2.5 Multiple readers, single writer

The readers and writers problem is described in Section 10.5 and a semaphore solution is given there. In Figure 11.2 the solution was presented using the critical region construct. In Figure 11.16 we now see the procedures required in a monitor solution. In this case the resource to be read or written is not part of the monitor data since the monitor would enforce exclusive access, preventing multiple simultaneous reads. This was also discussed in relation to the need for the variable **writelock** in Figure 11.2. In many ways, the use made of the monitor is similar to that given in Figure 11.12 for the single resource allocator, in that the monitor operations are essentially the entry and exit protocols for the protected region, and it is still the programmer's responsibility to remember to use these protocols. The data that is being encapsulated by this monitor are the variables that keep track of the number of active readers and writers and whether the resource is currently being accessed.

A reader process calls **startRead**. This may involve delay getting into the monitor because another process is currently executing one of the monitor operations, and a possible further delay on the condition variable, because a writing process is waiting for or using the resource. When all active writers have finished, reader processes read the resource together. After each reader has finished reading it calls **endRead** (which, as always, may involve delay getting into the monitor). The last reader to call **endRead** signals a waiting writer. Writer processes call **startWrite** (which may involve delay getting into the monitor and delay getting the resource). They then write the resource (one at a time is enforced by the monitor) and call **endWrite** (which may involve delay getting into the monitor).

The readers and writers problem has variants which require different priority schemes. If writing is relatively infrequent or it is very important that the information read is up to date then priority should be given to a new writer which should write as soon as all current readers have finished reading. This is implemented in the solution given in Figure 11.16. If writing is frequent and old data is better than no data for readers then a scheme which allows waiting readers in after one writer finishes may be preferable. The choice depends on the application requirements.

In the solution in Figure 11.16, when a writer finishes writing, and if there are no other writers waiting to write, it wakes up one waiting reader by **freeToRead.signal( )**. Readers may all read together, however, so that a reader wakes up another reader before leaving the **startRead** procedure. Each reader wakes up one more reader until no more are waiting.

An invariant on the monitor is

if busyWriting **then** rr = 0

The invariant expresses the condition that when **busyWriting** is true (i.e. when a writer has exclusive access to the shared resource), the variable **rr** (that shows the number of reading readers) must be zero. In other words, there must be no reading readers while writing is in progress. The invariant has thus captured an important part of the semantics (i.e. rules governing the operation) of this particular monitor. If the language in which the monitor is written allows the programmer to express this invariant, and the runtime system checks it, first, when the monitor is initialized, and thereafter whenever a monitor operation completes its execution, this will contribute to the correct working of the monitor.

11.2.6 Discussion of monitors

Exclusion: monitors are a crude concurrency mechanism, enforcing a restriction that whole operations on shared data are executed under exclusion. If monitors are the only available concurrency construct it can happen that programmers define shared data abstractions unnaturally in order to make the exclusive operations as small as possible. As we have seen in the examples above, we can arrange that the shared data is the condition data only, rather than the condition data plus the shared resource, if we wish to allow controlled simultaneous access to a resource (for example, multiple readers, single writer). In the language Mesa the exclusion requirement was alleviated to some extent by only enforcing atomic execution of those procedures explicitly declared as **mutex**. This allows operations such as 'read the size of the buffer' to be invoked concurrently with monitor operations. As we saw above, this was followed in the design of Java.

Synchronization over the state of the resource occurs within a mutually exclusive operation, in contrast with the flexibility available in semaphore programs. This allows simplifying assumptions to be made by the implementation. There is no need to allow for wake-up waiting signals and a process is always blocked when it executes **wait( )** on a condition.

The language CCLU was developed at the University of Cambridge Computer Laboratory, UK (Bacon and Hamilton, 1987) from CLU (Liskov *et al.*, 1981) and originally provided monitors. CCLU was intended for use as a systems programming language and, for this purpose, monitors were found to decrease performance unacceptably in some circumstances. The language was redesigned to retain its modular structure based on abstract data types but to use critical regions within the operations when exclusive access to data objects was needed.

As with semaphores, a process calling a monitor procedure is committed to wait if the monitor is in use and then wait if the resource managed by the monitor is not available. If the language provides dynamic process creation, for example by means of a FORK primitive which creates a child process to run in parallel with the parent process, a child can be created to call the monitor operation and the parent can proceed in parallel. This is discussed further in the next chapter and illustrated in Figure 12.7.

Section 9.6.2 discussed how processes waiting on a semaphore might be scheduled. The same arguments apply to processes waiting to enter a monitor. Priority inversion might happen if a low-priority process is executing in a monitor and higher-priority processes are waiting. Priority inheritance could be used to solve this problem; that is, the monitor code could be executed at the priority of the highest-priority waiter.

In Java, we are not dealing with queues, but with wait sets, from which a thread is arbitrarily chosen when **notify( )** is used. When **notifyAll( )** is used all the threads in the wait set are unblocked and the operating system's scheduling algorithm then takes over. This allows the threads' priorities to be taken into account at the expense of imposing repeated blocking and unblocking overhead. For a full discussion of these issues see Lea (1999).

11.3 Synchronization at the granularity of operations

In Chapter 10 we programmed a cyclic buffer between many producers and many consumers. In the solution, producers first checked whether a slot was free, and consumers whether an item was available; then exclusive access to the buffer was ensured among producers or among consumers. One producer and one consumer could access different parts of the buffer at the same time.

The development from critical regions to conditional critical regions and then to monitors combined concurrency control and encapsulation. In order to carry out an operation on a shared object a process first calls a monitor procedure, which may involve a delay, waiting to enter the monitor. Once inside the monitor the process may again be delayed if the state of the shared data is such that it cannot proceed. The operations on the condition variables used for this purpose are low-level primitives, equivalent to event or semaphore operations, and just as difficult to program correctly. Also, by putting synchronization over the state of the shared data inside the monitor procedure the need for a convention has been reintroduced. The convention of ensuring that the data is in a consistent state before a **wait()** on a condition variable is executed must be observed. There might also be a convention that **signal()** must immediately precede exit from the monitor, as discussed in Section 11.2.

An attractive idea is to allow an operation on an object to go ahead only if the object is in a state such that the operation can complete. For example, a call to put an item in a buffer should only start if there is an empty slot. Thus, a delay before starting to execute the operation would replace both a delay to enter a monitor and a synchronization delay within it. We now explore two approaches to achieving this: path expressions and active objects.

11.3.1 Path expressions

It is possible to specify the order in which operations may be invoked on an object in the form of a **path expression** (Campbell and Haberman, 1974). The language Path Pascal (Campbell and Kolstad, 1980) used this approach. A path expression involves only the names of the operations. The default is that they are not executed under mutual exclusion, so the path expression must express this requirement. The code of the operations no longer has to express synchronization constraints.

path *name1*, *name2*, *name3* **end**   // the separator is a comma(,),

indicates that *name1*, *name2* and *name3* may be executed in any order and any number of instances of each may be executed together.

path *first*; *second*; *third* **end**   // the separator is a semicolon(;) ;

indicates that one execution of *first* must complete before each execution of a *second* can start, and similarly for *second* and *third*. Concurrent executions of *first*, *second* and *third* are allowed provided that this restriction is followed.

path 2:(*device-type-handler*) **end**

restricts the number of concurrent executions to 2.

path 1:(*op1*, *op2*, *op3*) **end**

means that only one of the three operations can be active at any time. They are critical regions for the same single resource (managed by a monitor-like structure).

path 1:(*op1*), 1:(*op2*) **end**

indicates that a maximum of one *op1* and one *op2* can execute concurrently.

path setup; [*spooler*] **end**

[ ] are used to indicate that when one instance of spooler has started, any number of other instances can start.

path 6:(5:(*op1*), 4:(*op2*)) **end**

indicates that as many as five invocations of *op1* can proceed together and as many as four of *op2*, provided that the limit of six invocations is not exceeded.

For an *N*-slot buffer we can write:

path N:(1:(*insert*); 1:(*remove*)) **end**

which indicates that inserts are mutually exclusive, *removes* are mutually exclusive, each *remove* must be preceded by an *insert* and the number of completed *inserts* is never more than N times the number of completed *removes*.

Because the code of the operations no longer expresses synchronization constraints we cannot express synchronization that depends on input parameters or the state of a monitor. For example, we may wish an input parameter to indicate the priority of the caller and use this value to order processes waiting to invoke a certain operation. Path expressions are therefore less flexible than conventional monitors for many problems.

As monitors are passive structures the code associated with a path expression must be executed by the caller. Only one process at once may execute this code. More concurrency could be achieved if, instead, an active process managing a monitor-like structure could decide which operations could go ahead.

11.3.2 Active objects

An **active object** is a monitor-like structure (encapsulating shared data) with an internally-bound process. In a normal monitor, which is a passive structure, the code for a client of the monitor will include procedure/method calls to the monitor operations. All the code that is necessary to ensure mutual exclusion and condition synchronization will be part of the monitor procedures being called. As a result, the system will ensure that the concurrent processes executing such code are managed according to the rules of the monitor. For an active object executable code is produced which is executed by the process associated with the object.

This process may carry out a number of functions. First, it can be made aware of outstanding calls from clients and can actively schedule these calls. It can therefore implement the synchronization at the granularity of operations we are discussing in this section. Secondly, it can execute the operations on behalf of the clients, although in the most widely known implementation of active objects, Ada, it is not defined (so is left to the implementation) whether the caller or called process executes the called procedure/method. Thirdly, it can execute some of the housekeeping tasks associated with the monitor operations, such as updating buffer pointers and counts. This means that the time during which the client process is waiting for the operation to be carried out on its behalf can be reduced, thus freeing it to enable it to get on with other tasks. (This point is only significant for a shared memory system that runs on a multiprocessor since, in a uniprocessor implementation, it has no impact on efficiency to shuffle tasks between processes.)

This style of concurrency control for shared-memory systems is based on Dijkstra's **guarded commands** (Dijkstra, 1975). A scheme of this general kind (but without the assumption of shared memory) was proposed by Brinch Hansen (1978) for a language called Distributed Processes. The implementation of a procedure call, or method invocation, other than within a single address space is a large subject which we discuss in Chapters 12, 13 and 15. Ada (Welsh and Lister, 1981) implements this method of concurrency control for shared memory systems (where the processes inhabit a single address space).

An example of an active object in the form of an Ada task will shortly be shown.

Non-deterministic selection

Conventional if statements and switch (or case) statements are used to select between two or more courses of action. Each option is selected on the basis of a boolean (in the case of an if statement) or the value of a variable (in the case of a switch statement). Such constructs are said to be **deterministic** because, given the current state of the variables involved in the boolean condition or switch variable, it can be determined precisely which action is to be performed. However, if a situation arose in which the choice of action was immaterial, that is, any of the courses of action would be acceptable, then a new programming construct would be required to express this need for a **non-deterministic** (random) choice to be made. Such a structure is available in the programming language Ada. This is known as the **select** statement and has the following syntax.

```
select
    when <condition1>
        ...
or
    when <condition2>
        ...
or
    when <condition3>
        ...
end select;
```

The **select** statement has any number of **when** parts, each of which has an associated condition known as a **guard**. If a guard is true, the associated set of actions could be executed. However, it is possible for more than one guard to be true simultaneously and a choice of which associated actions must be made. In the **select** statement, the choice is made non-deterministically, that is, the runtime system makes the choice and the programmer is not aware of the choice that is made.

Note that Java does not have an equivalent mechanism although Chapter 4 of Lea (1999) discusses how a form of guarded wait can be programmed.

The bounded buffer task in Ada

The Ada programming language combines synchronization and mutual exclusion into one mechanism known as the **rendezvous**. Two processes exchange information by performing a rendezvous. One of the processes, known as the client, calls an **entry** defined by the other process, known as the server. An entry is similar to a procedure (method) but has some additional properties. For example, if the name of a server is **buffer-manager**, and one of the services is named **insert**, an entry call by a client will have the form:

```
buffer-manager.insert (ch);
```

The server responds to an entry call by executing an **accept** statement which is similar to the body of a procedure (method). It has the form:

```
accept insert (c: in character) do   // c is a formal input argument of type character
   // some code
end insert;
```

When the client has made an entry call and the server has accepted the call by starting the execution of the corresponding **accept** statement, the two tasks are synchronized and the rendezvous begins.

If the server is not ready to accept the entry call, the client must wait. If no client wishes to make an entry call and the server reaches an **accept** statement, the server will wait. Both the client and the server wait for the duration of the rendezvous, that is, while the code forming the body of the **accept** statement is being executed (Ada does not specify who executes this code).

Data, including the results of executing the **accept** statement, can be transferred between the client and server as arguments to the entry call.

Once the code in the body of the **accept** statement has finished, the rendezvous is complete and the two processes (the client and the server) proceed independently of one another.

In Ada, a process (actually known as a **task**) is defined in two parts: a task specification (similar to an interface) and a task body (the implementation of the task specification). To get a feel for the structure of an Ada **task,** here is the implementation of the producer–consumer problem. First, the definition of the producer and consumer tasks:

```
task producer;            // a task specification
task body producer is     // a task body
   c: character;          // a local variable
begin
   loop
      produce (c);
      buffer-manager.insert (c);
   end loop;
end producer;
task consumer;            // a task specification
task body consumer is
   c: character;
begin
   loop
      buffer-manager.remove (c);
      consume (c);
   end loop;
end consumer;
```

Both the **producer** and **consumer** execute indefinite loops (the code between the keywords **loop** and **end loop**). The former produces a single character and then passes it to a **buffer-manager** process to place it in the buffer. The **consumer** asks the **buffer-manager** for a character which it then 'consumes'.

The **buffer-manager** acts as a monitor on the buffer but is also a task (process) in its own right. The specification of the **buffer-manager** is:

```
task buffer-manager is
   entry insert (c: in character);
   entry remove (c: out character);
end buffer-manager;
```

Thus the task **buffer-manager** has two entries named **insert** and **remove.** The corresponding implementation of **buffer-manager** is:

```
task body buffer-manager is
   buffer-size: constant := 2560;            // initializes an integer constant
   buffer: array (1..buffer-size) of character;
   count: INTEGER range 0..buffer-size := 0; // initializes an integer variable that
                                             must
                                             // always remain in the range 0 to
                                             buffer-size
   inptr, outptr: INTEGER range 1..buffer-size := 1;
```

```
            begin
               loop
                  select
                     when count < buffer-size = >          // guard (is there space in the
                                                           buffer?)
                                                           // = > is a single symbol that can be
                                                           read as 'then'

                        accept insert (ch: in CHAR) do
                           buffer (inptr) := ch;            // := is the assignment symbol
                        end insert;
                        inptr := inptr mod buffer_size + 1;  // mod is equivalent to Java's %
                                                           operation

                        count := count + 1;
                  or
                     when count > 0 = >                    // guard (is there an item in the
                                                           buffer?)

                        accept remove (ch; out CHAR) do
                           ch := buffer (outptr);
                        end insert;
                        outptr := outptr mod buffer-size + 1;
                        count := count − 1;
                  end select;
               end loop;
            end buffer-manager;
```

In this implementation, the buffer is an array of character values whose size is specified by the constant **buffer-size** (2560). In Ada it is possible to specify the range of values that an integer variable is restricted to using a **range** expression. For example, the number of items in the buffer is recorded in the variable **count**, which can take any integer value in the range from **0** to **buffer-size** inclusive; initially, it is set to 0. The indexes **in** and **out** are also restricted to a range and are initialized to 1.

The **buffer-manager** task executes as follows. When it first starts, it immediately encounters a **loop** statement, which means that it will repeat the body of the loop indefinitely. It then executes the **select** statement which selects from the entry calls with the guards. Suppose it selects a call to the first **accept** statement:

```
accept insert (c: in char) do
   buffer (inptr) := char
end insert;
```

The server makes a rendezvous with a calling producer. When this occurs, the argument (a character) provided by the producer is copied to the formal argument of the **accept** statement, and the body of the **accept** statement is executed. This consists of placing the character into an appropriate place in the buffer. Once the body of the **accept** statement has been completed, the producer can continue its execution as can the server which executes the remainder of the chosen part of the **select** statement:

```
inptr := inptr mod buffer-size + 1;
count := count + 1;
```

and then it repeats the loop.

The Ada active object mechanism, the **rendezvous**, has the following characteristics.

When select is not used:

- The server waits at a rendezvous for a client to make an entry call.
- The client waits when it reaches its call to the server, if the latter is busy (i.e. has not reached the corresponding **accept** statement).
- The server will deal with only one client at a time, that is, only one rendezvous can occur at a time (guaranteeing mutual exclusion).
- The client can pass data to the server as an argument to the entry call.
- The server can pass data to the client as an argument to the entry call.

Once the rendezvous is complete (i.e. the execution of the **accept** statement is complete), both the client and the server are free to continue with their own tasks.

When select is used to achieve condition synchronization at the granularity of operations:

- Each accept statement is preceded (guarded) by a condition and a call is only accepted if its condition is true.
- At a select statement the server makes a nondeterministic selection between such calls.

11.4 Summary

We aim to make system issues clear and then discuss how they may be programmed. We have established the areas of systems where the model of processes sharing memory is appropriate: at the application level, where lightweight processes share an address space, and at the implementation level for any type of system. Chapters 9, 10 and 11 followed the development of concurrency constructs in high-level languages for shared-memory-based systems.

We have discussed the critical region construct, as one of the earlier forms of concurrency support. Its advantage is that the compiler supports the programmer by adding entry and exit protocols. However, it lacks modularization.

A monitor protects a single shared data object, by encapsulating the data and the operations acting on it. Essentially, the concept of the critical region is implemented through monitor operations which are mutually exclusive. It was shown that in Java the mechanisms of the monitor can be implemented through the primitives: **synchronized, notify(), notifyAll()** and **wait()**. In Java, a lock is associated with each object, and only the thread that holds the object's lock is able to execute. We considered synchronization at the granularity of whole operations. The motivation is to avoid a wait for exclusive access to shared data followed by another wait if the shared data is in a state such that the desired operation cannot proceed (for example, the buffer is full). Path expressions have been suggested to achieve this for passive structures such as monitors. Active objects can achieve the effect by executing some form of guarded command. It was shown how the rendezvous mechanism in Ada combines synchronization with mutual exclusion. We now return to system architecture and trace the development of support for concurrency when processes do not share memory.

Study questions

S 11.1

In addition to marking the beginning and end of a critical region, what other information must be supplied to the programming construct that delineates a critical region? Explain.

S 11.2

In the solution to the multiple readers, single writer problem given in Figure 11.2, where, and for what purpose, are the conditional critical region constructs used? What is the **writelock** variable used for?

S 11.3

Compared with the semaphore solution, what is the main advantage of the conditional critical region solution to the multiple readers, single writer problem?

S 11.4

What is the structure of a monitor? How does a monitor deal with shared data? What rules do the operations of a monitor obey?

S 11.5

What replaces a critical region when monitors are used?

S 11.6

When a monitor operation is invoked, why is the calling process not guaranteed immediate access to this operation?

S 11.7

What happens if, during the call of a monitor operation, a process is blocked on some condition variable?

S 11.8

Why is it essential that a process should leave the monitor in a consistent state before executing a **(condition).wait( )**? What is meant by this statement?

S 11.9

Why does making a method **synchronized** not ensure mutual exclusion? How can the synchronization mechanism ensure mutual exclusion?

S 11.10

In Figure 11.12, why has the shared boolean **busy** been introduced? In other words, why is the condition variable **free** not the only variable that is necessary?

S 11.11

In Figure 11.10, the **wait** call has been put inside a **while** loop that tests the condition. Explain why a simple **if** statement such as

```
if (anAmount > balance) {
    wait ();
}
```

would not have been appropriate.

S 11.12

Suppose that a reader has been granted access to the readers/writer monitor shown in Figure 11.16, and begins to execute the procedure **startRead**. Describe the execution of **startRead**.

S 11.13

What is the attraction of allowing an operation on an object to go ahead only if the object is in a state such that the operation can complete?

Exercises

11.1 How would a compiler use semaphores to implement critical regions in a concurrent programming language?

11.2 Why is it inefficient to implement condition synchronization within a critical region using an expression involving programming language variables?

11.3 Rewrite the readers and writers solution using conditional critical regions to include writers waiting to write in the first critical region for writers.

11.4 In Hoare (1974) it was proposed that the scheduling of processes waiting on a condition variable in a monitor could be priority based rather than just first come first served: a 'scheduled wait'. Syntax such as wait(*condition-name, priority*) could be used to indicate the ordering of waiting processes on a condition queue.

Using this construct, write an **alarmclock** monitor with methods
wakeMe(int n) and tick( ). The tick( ) method is invoked on a timer
interrupt at regular intervals to maintain a value of system time.
The wakeMe method is to allow a process to request that it should
be blocked for a number of units of time and then woken up again.
The process's 'priority' is to be used to order the time at which the
process is awakened.

11.5   The process priority described above for Exercise 11.4 can also be used
to wake up processes in a suitable order for writing to the cylinders of a
disk. Assume that a sweep or 'elevator' algorithm is to be used to control
the disk heads: that is, the heads are to move across the surface to the
outermost required cylinder in one direction then are to move back in
the opposite direction. The heads sweep smoothly across the surfaces
and back, stopping at cylinders en route for processes to make data
transfers.

Write a monitor with a method to request that the heads be moved
to a given cylinder and to block the invoking process until its required
cylinder is reached, and a method that is called by a process after it has
finished making a data transfer to a given cylinder.

11.6   Rewrite the readers and writers monitor operations to give priority
to waiting readers over waiting writers. The application is such that
it is better to read stale data quickly than to wait for up-to-date
data.

11.7   Sketch pseudo-code for the monitor examples given in Java for single
resource allocation, producer–consumer and readers–writers, using the
traditional monitor facility where any number of condition variables can
be used. Compare your solutions with those in Java for convenience and
clarity for the programmer and implementer.

11.8   Why is 'synchronization at the level of operations' desirable? How might
this approach be supported in a concurrent programming language?
Consider the cases of both passive modules (or objects) and active
modules (or objects).

11.9   Discuss how dynamic process creation can be used to avoid unnecessary
delay in a monitor-based system.

11.10   The **sleeping barber** problem. (We assume that the barber and his
customers are male.)

A barber provides a hair-cutting service. He has a shop with two
doors, an entrance and an exit. He spends his time serving customers
one at a time. When none is in the shop, the barber sleeps in the
barber's chair.

When a customer arrives and finds the barber sleeping, the customer
awakens the barber and sits in the barber's chair to receive his haircut.
After the cut is done, the barber sees the customer out through the
exit door.

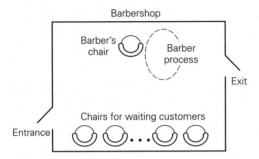

Barbershop

Barber's chair

Barber process

Exit

Chairs for waiting customers

Entrance

Figure 11.17
The sleeping barber problem.

If the barber is busy when a customer arrives, the customer waits in one of the chairs provided for the purpose. If all the chairs are full he goes away.

After serving a customer the barber looks to see if any are waiting and if so proceeds to serve one of them. Otherwise, he sleeps again in his chair.

Write a solution to the problem for the barber process and the customer processes.

Notice that the problem is set up with a single (active) server process and many client processes. The clients rendezvous with the barber who cuts their hair while they sit. The barber can sweep up after each customer has left.

We could envisage a do-it-yourself barbershop with a single pair of scissors and book of instructions. The clients would take it in turns to use these shared resources then sweep up before leaving. This would model a monitor-like approach to having a service done.

We could also envisage a number of equivalent barbers offering the service in the shop, each with a barber's chair but with a single queue of waiting customers. If the solution is to be written in a language which provides active objects, such as the Ada tasks described briefly in Section 11.3.2, the problem is trivial. The barber provides a single operation **cutHair** which customers call. No **select** statement is needed (because there is only one operation) and the **accept** statement takes a waiting customer, if any, for service. The language implementation does all the work.

If we are to solve the problem, as set, in a language which provides only monitors, or semaphores, we have to program the client and server process's rendezvous using only these tools. A solution might start from the following:

a monitor **barberShop**
exported methods **getHaircut** which clients call and **getNextCustomer** which the barber calls
various condition variables such as **barberAvailable**.

The problem as formulated above is not matched exactly by a solution along these lines. It would be necessary to specify that the barber entered the shop to see if there were waiting customers and, if not, left the shop and slept in a back room until signalled (by a bell ringing perhaps). Andrews (1991) gives several alternative solutions.

11.11 The following code fragment is a first (wrong) attempt to implement the startRead operation for the readers and writers problem.

```
CGUARD.semWait ()
ar = ar+1
if (aw != 0) {R.semWait () } // wait until all writers have finished
rr == rr + 1
CGUARD.semSignal
```

Its logic appears to be the same as that for the implementations we have seen in this chapter for conditional critical regions and monitors. Why is it wrong?

12

IPC and system structure

12.1 Styles of inter-process communication

The general theme of Part II is inter-process communication (IPC). In Chapter 8, Part II was introduced by considering system structure and the placement of processes within systems. We saw that it is often desirable for processes to share memory. For example, a server of many clients is implemented most conveniently as multiple server processes (or threads) sharing an address space.

Chapters 9, 10 and 11 developed the inter-process communication primitives that processes sharing memory might use when programmed in a high-level language. The underlying system primitives may be based on semaphores, event queues or eventcounts and sequencers, but the high-level language programmer need not be aware of them. The compiler can create and initialize any required semaphores, for example, and can include semaphore operations at the beginning and end of modular constructs such as critical regions or monitor procedures. The development we followed through Chapter 11 is outlined in Figure 12.1, on the left.

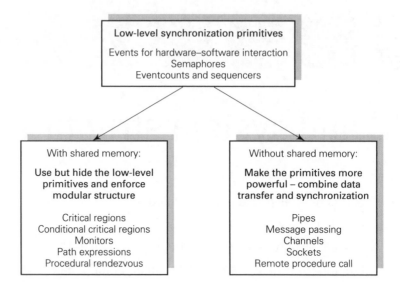

Figure 12.1
Examples of IPC
primitives.

Processes which comprise a concurrent system yet which run in separate address spaces, sharing no data, still need access to common information in order to work together or compete for resources; that is, IPC is also required for systems of processes with no shared memory. Two approaches to sharing information are as follows:

- Data is passed from process to process; an example of this style of process cooperation is a pipeline of processes (see Section 1.2.2).
- The common information is managed by a process. In this case the managing process will carry out operations on the data it encapsulates on request from other processes. This is called the client–server model.

In both approaches the IPC mechanism must support the transfer of data between processes which share no memory. In the first approach, the data itself is passed around. In the second approach a request must be passed to the server which contains information on which operation is to be invoked on which server-managed data item. We discuss these approaches throughout the chapter.

IPC primitives that may be provided in systems without shared memory are also outlined in Figure 12.1 (on the right). Primitives for both shared-memory and no-shared-memory systems must provide synchronization. Synchronization is all that is provided by the low-level primitives taken as the starting point in Figure 12.1. In systems with shared memory, processes can synchronize their access to shared data by using these low-level primitives, although, as we have seen, higher-level constructs are safer and easier to use. In systems without shared memory, the IPC primitives must not only support synchronization, but also support data transfer.

One of the simplest forms of cross-address-space IPC is a **pipe** or **synchronized byte stream**: one process can send bytes in an unstructured stream into the pipe, another can read bytes from the pipe. If an attempt is made to read more bytes than have been written into the pipe, the reading process is blocked until more bytes are available. Note that this method conveys no information about the structure of the byte stream nor of the data types that are being transmitted between the processes. The applications which use the mechanism can, of course, interpret the byte stream as structured, typed data. For example, if data is transmitted in the form of file or device I/O through a library stream package, then at the application level this data could be interpreted as a stream of records, each with typed fields. However, the byte stream mechanism does not provide support for this.

Another form, **message passing**, is more akin to transferring information in the form of typed arguments on a procedure call. A **message** is constructed with a header indicating the destination of the information and a body containing the arguments. There may or may not be support for type checking the arguments, as we shall see in Chapter 13. A pipe is an example of connection-oriented communication between two processes; once the pipe is set up any number of writes and reads can be made to it. Message passing is an example of connectionless communication; each message needs to be addressed to its intended recipient. We first encountered connection-oriented and connectionless communication in Section 3.8.2.

An issue to consider, as with shared-memory primitives, is the assistance that can be provided to the programmer within a high-level language, and this will be covered in Chapters 13 and 15. The rest of this chapter is concerned with the system structures and system design issues associated with the two styles (shared memory and no shared memory) of IPC.

12.2 Procedural system structure

A typical design approach for a system of concurrent processes which share memory is shown in Figure 12.2. A process is associated with each source of asynchronous events, in this example an application and a device. The application process outputs data to the device by means of a buffer manager, in the form of a monitor. A dedicated system process handles the device. It invokes a monitor method to acquire a unit of data of the correct size, waits on the 'device free' event, and transfers the data to the device. The scenario is that shown in Figure 4.1 where the application process has called down into the operating system (thus acquiring system status temporarily) to do some output. The application process, the device handler process and the I/O buffer (managed by a monitor for concurrency control) share the same address space.

The application's monitor method invocation m1.insert(data) is synchronous. When this line of code is executed, the process enters the monitor, and only when it has completed the monitor method will the next line of code in the application program be executed (as represented by the downward arrow). It may take a while to complete this monitor method, because there are two potential sources of delay: one on trying to enter the monitor (represented by the first 'blob'), the second on the condition variable (represented by the second 'blob'). For systems programming, such as the I/O example illustrated in Figure 12.2, it is important that these synchronization delays are very short.

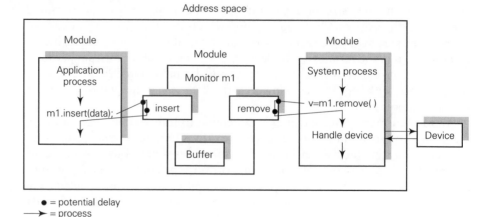

Address space

Figure 12.2
Procedural system
structure (in shared
address space).

● = potential delay
⟶ = process

How processes are used and how they communicate with each other is an important design issue. In particular, we can see that the monitors are passive structures and that the active processes thread their way through them, by calling procedures, to get those things done which involve cooperation or competition with other processes.

12.3 System structure and IPC without shared memory

In the model of system structure where there is no shared memory, each process runs in a separate address space. There is no shared data and we cannot therefore build passive structures independent of processes to encapsulate shared data. The IPC implementation in the operating system must provide a mechanism for a process to send some data to another process and for the intended recipient to synchronize with its arrival. For example, in Figure 12.3, a client process will send a request for an operation to be done on its behalf by a server process and, in due course, will wait for the result to come back, or an acknowledgement that the request has been carried out. In the figure, possible synchronization delays are shown, as usual, by a blob. The processes are actually delayed when they WAIT for a message before it is sent. Conversely, if a message is sent before the recipient executes WAIT, the message must be buffered in the operating system as part of the message transport service. Then, when the recipient executes WAIT the message is delivered to it from the buffer.

Note that we have seen exactly these synchronization scenarios for semaphore operations; see Figure 9.20. Figure 9.22 showed the process level and implementation level for the semaphore operations SIGNAL and WAIT. We have a similar situation for the process and implementation levels of message passing with the addition of message buffer management in the message service.

Section 9.6
◀

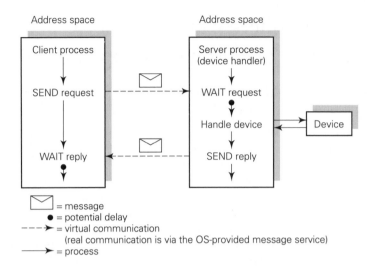

Figure 12.3
System structure with
no shared memory.

Figure 12.3 shows the same functionality as Figure 12.2, but now for a system without shared memory.

12.4 Systems where shared-memory communication is appropriate

It may be appropriate for a programmer to write a concurrent program in a language which provides shared-memory IPC for the following systems:

- An unprotected system such as those implemented for many PCs. All processes and the operating system run in a single shared address space or may use the real, unmapped addresses of the machine.
- A system in which the language runtime system functions as a simple operating system. This is the case in many real-time process control and embedded control systems.
- A system in which multi-threading is provided by the language runtime system only or where multi-threaded processes are known to the operating system. An example is a server serving simultaneous clients.
- The program may implement a subsystem within an operating system. As we saw in Sections 1.4 and 8.3, many calls from user-level processes may be in the process of being serviced by the operating system at a given time. An operating system is a multi-threaded server at a coarse grain, as are its subsystems at a finer grain. The program may run on a uniprocessor or a shared-memory multiprocessor and a given program may exhibit very different behaviour and performance in these different environments. The programmer should be aware of this. We give examples from operating system structures in Section 12.9.

12.5 Systems where shared-memory communication is not appropriate

Some areas where the programmer may find shared memory undesirable or impossible to use are as follows:

- In protected systems, such as multi-user systems, where processes run in separate address spaces, see Section 12.9 for examples. This includes client–server communication above a microkernel.
- Between processes on different computers, such as within certain process control systems or general-purpose network-based systems.
- In systems where it is desirable to retain flexibility over where processes are loaded. Here, it is assumed that we want to defer the decision of which processes to load into which computers until system configuration time. Processes which use shared-memory IPC are constrained to be loaded into the same computer. IPC which does not rely on shared memory can be used between processes on the same machine or on different machines.
- In systems which have a process migration facility to achieve load balancing. The idea of a process migration facility is to keep open the option of moving a process from one machine to another when the system is running. Shared-memory IPC would prevent this, as it assumes that processes reside on the same machine, sharing the same address space.

12.6 Overview of inter-process communication

Shared-memory mechanisms for IPC were the concern of Chapter 11. IPC for systems with no shared memory has been introduced here and is discussed in more detail in Chapter 13. Figure 12.4 gives a high-level view of both styles of mechanism: parts (a) and (b) show the two basic approaches to shared-memory (shared-address-space) IPC we discussed in Chapter 11; (c) and (d) show two different approaches to cross-address-space **message passing** for systems with no shared memory; (c) is the asynchronous or buffered message passing introduced above.

The IPC implementation must support the transfer of information and the synchronization of the processes involved in the transfer. Figure 12.4(a) and (b) show two approaches to shared memory IPC. In both cases the initiating process invokes a method; the transfer of information is in the form of call and return parameters. In (a) the invocation is to a passive module, a monitor. Section 11.2 and Figure 11.5 show the detail of how the possible synchronization delays are managed. In (b) the invocation is to an active module where the internally bound process selects a call to accept. Section 11.3.2 gave the detail of how synchronization delays are managed.

Message passing is the topic of Chapter 13 and in this chapter we are concerned with architectural issues, contrasting IPC within and across address

(a)

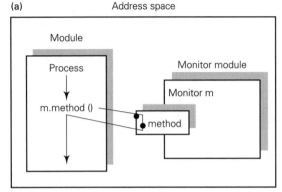

Procedural (passive: monitor structure)

(b)

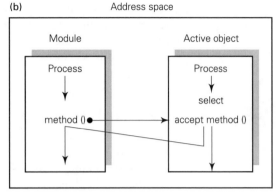

Procedural (active: rendezvous)

(c)

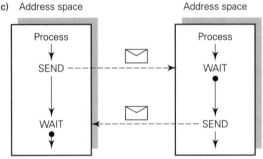

Message passing (asynchronous or buffered)

(d)

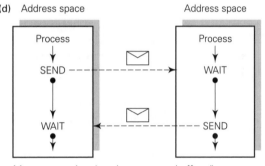

Message passing: (synchronous or unbuffered)

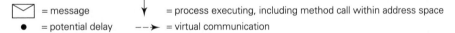

= message   = process executing, including method call within address space

= potential delay   --→ = virtual communication

Figure 12.4
Summary of
high-level IPC
mechanisms.

spaces. In (c) the asynchronous or buffered message passing which was introduced in Section 12.3 is illustrated. A sending process is not delayed and the
system must buffer information in transit if the receiver is not ready for it.
In Figure 12.4(d) we see synchronous or unbuffered message passing where the
communicating processes must both reach their synchronization points, the
SEND and WAIT instructions, in order for the information to be passed directly
from sender to receiver. There is therefore potential delay on both SEND and
WAIT operations.

Note that Figure 12.4(a) and (b) illustrate synchronous method invocation;
that is, the caller/invoker cannot carry out processing in parallel with the call. In
(a) this is natural since the caller process moves from module to module to
achieve its goals, synchronizing with other callers of monitor methods when
necessary. In (b) the Ada rendezvous is illustrated, which is based on Dijkstra's
guarded commands (Dijkstra, 1975). Although, as in (a), the invoker and the
invoked active object inhabit the same address space, in (b) it seems less obvious
that the invocation has to be synchronous, and block the caller, since another
process is available to take and execute the call. Nevertheless, the invocation is
synchronous and the Ada specification does not indicate whether caller or called

process should execute the invoked operation. We shall see in Chapter 15 that remote procedure call (RPC) provides cross-address-space procedure call. In this case the call and return arguments are packaged into messages to be transported between address spaces.

12.7 Duality of system structures

A question which comes to mind is whether the functionality provided by same-address-space and separate-address-space system designs differ fundamentally. Are there some things you can do in one type of system but not in the other?

Lauer and Needham (1978) claim that the two basic system structures are duals: that any problem that can be solved in a shared-memory system has a dual solution in a non-shared-memory system, and vice versa. We shall see that the argument holds but only if certain process management and IPC primitives are available.

The example we consider is that of a buffer management function, which can either be implemented through a monitor in a shared-memory system, or as a managing process using message passing in a non-shared-memory system. Figures 12.5 and 12.6 illustrate one way of achieving this (dual) functionality in the two different system structures. In Figure 12.6 we see how a message can be sent to request invocation of a particular method on the data. If the receiving process is not yet ready to receive the request, there will be a delay. This potential delay is mirrored in Figure 12.5 by the delay that might occur when trying to enter the monitor.

There is a second potential delay (as indicated by the second 'blob' in the monitor method invocation) which represents possible waiting *inside* the monitor on the condition variable, either (for a producer) because there is no room to add further items, or (for a consumer) because there are no items to be removed. The placing of the blocked process on the condition variable's queue allows

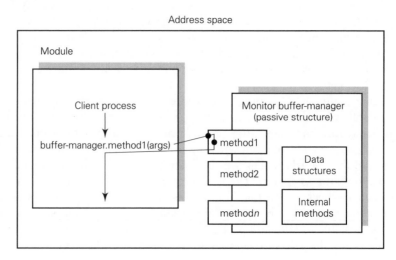

Figure 12.5
Procedural sytem structure.

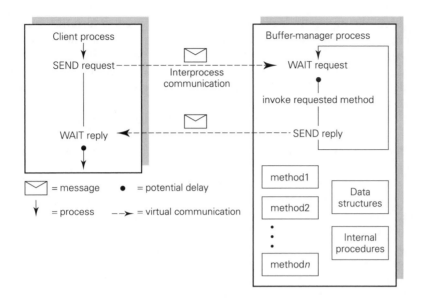

Figure 12.6
Dual functionality using a managing process and message passing.

another process to enter the monitor to do some work on the buffer. This type of waiting on the condition variable is mirrored in Figure 12.6 by the managing process finding that it cannot proceed further, again because there may be no room to add further items, or there are no items to be removed. Here, the manager will suspend work on behalf of the current caller, take another message if one exists and start work in response.

A difference apparent from the figures is that the calling process in the procedural system is committed to wait in the monitor, if necessary, and does not have the option of carrying out processing in parallel. However, this option can be made available to the process through a FORK primitive (see Sections 4.16 and 11.2.6 and Figure 12.7). The parent process forks a child process to make the call to the monitor procedure. The child may be delayed in the monitor but the parent can get on with other work in parallel. The parent can synchronize with

Sections 4.16, 11.2.4

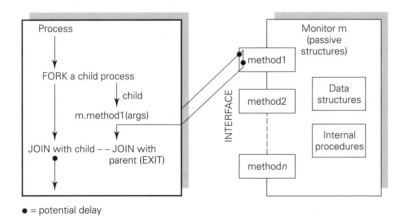

Figure 12.7
Forking a child to make a call.

the child to obtain the result of the monitor call by executing a JOIN primitive. Assuming that the sole purpose of the child was to make the monitor call, it can now terminate by executing EXIT. This scheme is feasible because processes are 'lightweight'. They share the address space of the parent and require only a small descriptor and a stack. If the FORK primitive is not available we cannot have a complete duality mapping.

Exercise 12.4 invites the reader to work out the duality mapping for a shared memory system, where synchronization is at the granularity of whole operations, with a message passing system, again taking a buffer manager as the example.

The point to emphasize is that there is no intrinsic reason for preferring shared-memory or no-shared-memory based systems. The same functions can be provided in each in equivalent structures and the same degee of concurrency can be achieved. There may be implementation-dependent factors to consider, which affect performance, such as: to what extent the operating system is invoked to get some operation done or how many context switches are involved.

The style of working may be constrained by the hardware that has been purchased for a system or the software that must be used. If the primitives described above are available there is functional equivalence between the two styles.

 ## 12.8 Naming

Within a single concurrent program running in a shared address space we can assume that the processes know the names of the procedures to call in order to access shared data, and the semaphores or condition variables to use for synchronization. We can also assume that how to invoke operating system service is well known, for example, through the specification of a system call interface.

Section 6.7

For IPC between processes in separate address spaces to take place, a process initiating communication must know the name of the destination of the communication. Let us first assume that the processes are running in separate address spaces on the same machine. The machine has a single operating system which has full knowledge of all the processes it supports and their attributes. We can assume that system services, such as mail, which run above the operating system, also have well-known names. The operating system is able to map the name to the appropriate object to be used for IPC.

If a concurrent application is to run as a number of separate processes on the same machine it is necessary for each process to know the name of the others. When a process is created, by requesting that a named file should be loaded and a process created to execute the loaded program, the process's name (identifier) is returned by the operating system to the creator. The creator of the processes of the concurrent application may make the names available to all components.

Within a single machine, we can assume that the operating system will manage any namespaces that are relevant to more than a single address space. The operating system can be seen to be extending the address space of a single process by making names available to it to be used for communication.

We defer considering the problem of naming for cross-machine IPC until Section 15.11. The issue was discussed in general terms in Chapter 6.

12.9 Process and IPC support in operating systems

Concurrency control was first studied in the context of operating system design because operating systems were the first multi-threaded servers. Operating systems may have many system calls in progress simultaneously and system data may need to be read and written to service these calls. We first look at the decisions that were taken when UNIX was first designed in the early 1970s, based on assumptions that were reasonable at the time but which soon came to be seen as over-restrictive. IPC was acknowledged as the weakest part of UNIX version 7. We then consider Microsoft's NT which was designed twenty years later.

12.9.1 UNIX version 7

The UNIX process structure was described briefly in Section 8.3. Each process runs in a separate address space, but the UNIX kernel occupies part of every process's address space. When a process makes a system call and enters the kernel its status changes from user mode to system mode and it begins to execute kernel code, as shown in Figure 12.8. A process is quite likely to wait for an event while in the kernel or to access some system data structure. At any time a number of user mode processes may have entered the kernel and be executing it as system processes. The shared-memory methods of IPC discussed in Chapters 9, 10 and 11 are relevant here; that is, UNIX processes cannot share data when they are in user mode but they can share data when they are in system mode.

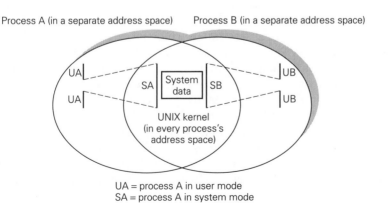

Figure 12.8
Processes in UNIX, system-mode communication.

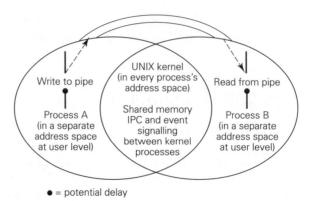

Figure 12.9
Processes in UNIX, user-mode communication.

System processes are scheduled non-preemptively in UNIX. If an interrupt occurs when a process is executing in the kernel the interrupt service routine is executed in the context of that process and control is always returned to the interrupted process, however urgent or important the event may be. It can continue to run until it voluntarily chooses to wait for an event. In UNIX event wait is called **sleep** and event signal is called **wakeup**. It may also forbid interrupts for a short time if it is about to access a data structure that could also be accessed by an interrupt service routine. Note that there are no semaphores in the UNIX kernel, forbidding interrupts is used instead. Many of the problems discussed in Chapters 9, 10 and 11 are avoided and the kernel design is kept simple. The price to be paid for this simplicity is that UNIX cannot guarantee real-time response to events and cannot run on a multiprocessor.

Processes executing in user mode in UNIX may need to cooperate over some task. Figure 12.9 illustrates the IPC facility provided for these processes which share no memory. Two processes may arrange to have a 'pipe' set up between them. A pipe is a synchronized byte stream: one process writes bytes into the pipe and the other takes them out. If the pipe is empty, the reader is delayed. If the pipe has become too 'full' for the system to hold it conveniently in main memory, the writer is delayed. There is no support for separating the byte stream into separate, structured communication. The facility is described in more detail in Section 13.3.

Finally, the writer of an application which is to run under UNIX may wish to use concurrent processes but may wish them to share data structures: the typical requirement for implementing a server process with many clients. In this case a coroutine or process package may be used as described in Section 4.15 and illustrated in Figure 12.10. Many lightweight processes or 'threads' are supported at user level but the underlying operating system sees only one process for scheduling, blocking, waking up, etc. A disadvantage of this arrangement is that if a blocking system call is made, that is, the process sleeps, waiting for an event, no thread may run in the application: as far as the operating system is concerned, the process is blocked. Again, a multiprocessor could not be exploited.

Sections 4.15, 4.17

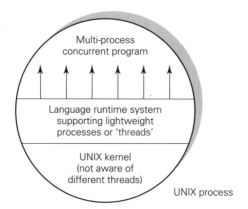

Figure 12.10
Multi-threading over
UNIX.

A summary of the problems of early UNIX are:

- The kernel cannot run on a multiprocessor because it uses the technique of forbidding interrupts to implement critical regions. This can only be solved by a complete rewrite of the kernel.
- UNIX is unsuitable for implementing multi-threaded servers. This is because each process runs in a separate address space, processes cannot share data and system calls are synchronous. If a thread package is used (multiplexing a single process) any thread might block for I/O, thus blocking the whole process.
- It is impossible to make any guarantees on response time to events because non-preemptive scheduling is used.
- Only pipes are provided for IPC.

There have been some rewrites of the UNIX kernel for multiprocessor and real-time systems, for example SunOS 5.0 which introduced semaphores. The two most widely used versions of UNIX are Berkeley's BSD 4.3 and UNIX System V. Both offer a wide range of IPC mechanisms to user-level processes including same-machine message passing and shared-memory regions, with semaphores to protect shared data structures. The UNIX system call interface is emulated by a number of microkernels, for example, Mach and CHORUS.

12.9.2 NT

In 1988 Microsoft decided to design and build an operating system for the 1990s. An operating system has a long development period, is long-lived and should therefore be portable to new technology (NT) as it becomes available. MS-DOS was designed for hardware and modes of use that were rapidly becoming restrictive, if not obsolete; that is, unprotected, single-user operation on 8- and 16-bit architectures. OS/2 had attempted to be broader in scope but was written in assembler for a uniprocessor CISC architecture (Intel 80286), and could not evolve to take advantage of the new RISC processors. Also, experience from OS developments such as Mach and other microkernels was becoming available to be taken into account.

Models used in the NT design

We have seen various operational models in the course of this book. Those used in the NT design are as follows:

- **Client–server model**. Although the NT executive is not a minimal microkernel it is intended that many substantial services should be provided above it rather than within it. For example, Win32 runs as a server process above rather than within the privileged executive. The NT executive provides standard mechanisms (invoked by trap-implemented system calls in the usual way) for passing service calls and replies between client and server processes.
- **Object model**. This forms the basis of the internal NT design. Resources managed by NT are implemented as objects and are manipulated by general object services. This gives a uniform approach to tracking resource usage, to protection and to sharing. Processes, threads, files, memory, events and many other familiar OS entities are implemented as objects.
- **Symmetric multiprocessing**. All software, including the NT executive can run on any available processor. The threads of a process can run simultaneously and priority-based preemption is implemented.

NT structure

Figure 12.11 shows a privileged executive (running in system mode) and a set of non-privileged servers called protected subsystems (running in user mode). The protected subsystems such as Win32, OS/2, MS-DOS and POSIX are server processes which realize environments for their respective client processes; NT is typically used through a user-mode GUI. Client and server processes run in their own address spaces. A client's request for service is executed by a thread in the server.

Executive components

- The object manager creates and deletes executive objects. A system call to create any specific type of executive object results in a call from the component of the executive that manages objects of that type to the object manager to create the object. Object management is the uniform underlying mechanism for the representation and management of resources and the object manager is involved in all generic operations.
- The security reference monitor provides runtime protection for objects and, being involved in object manipulation, can audit their use.
- The process manager is responsible for processes and threads. An NT process must be created with one thread to start with, since a thread is the unit of scheduling in NT; more threads may be created as the process progresses.
- The local procedure call facility (LPC) supports client–server communication.

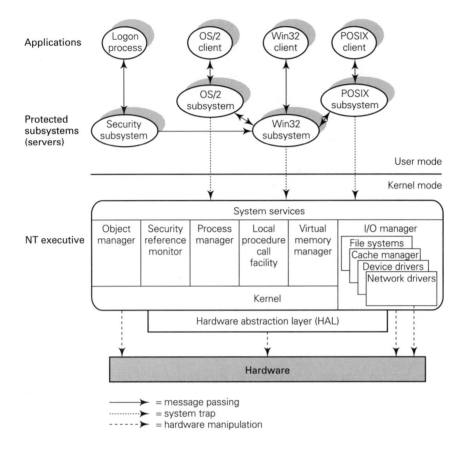

Applications: Logon process, OS/2 client, Win32 client, POSIX client

Protected subsystems (servers): Security subsystem, OS/2 subsystem, Win32 subsystem, POSIX subsystem

User mode

Kernel mode

NT executive:

System services

Object manager	Security reference monitor	Process manager	Local procedure call facility	Virtual memory manager	I/O manager
					File systems
					Cache manager
					Device drivers
					Network drivers

Kernel

Hardware abstraction layer (HAL)

Hardware

⟶ = message passing
⋯⋯▶ = system trap
- - - ▶ = hardware manipulation

Figure 12.11
Windows NT block diagram.

- The virtual memory manager provides a protected address space for each process (shared by its threads) and supports paging.
- The I/O system provides device-independent I/O and manages file and network buffers.
- The kernel handles interrupts in the first instance and schedules threads, for multiple processors on multiprocessor architectures. It also provides certain low-level objects on which the executive objects are built; that is, certain object data structures are maintained by the kernel and are manipulated by calls from the executive on the internal kernel interface.
- The hardware abstraction layer builds on the disparate I/O interfaces, interrupt controllers and multiprocessor communication mechanisms to create a uniform abstract interface to any hardware.

Login: illustrating processes, threads and IPC

Figure 12.12 shows how processes, threads, client–server communication and system calls are used to achieve login and process creation for two users A and B. The login server, the security subsystem and the Win32 subsystems are processes.

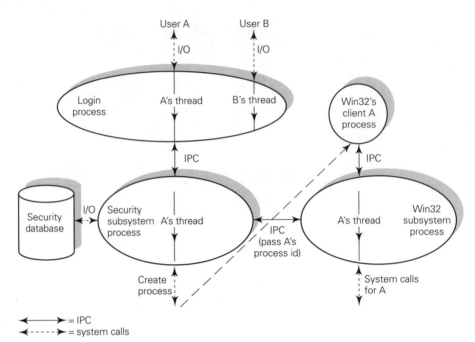

Figure 12.12
Logging in as a client
of Win32.

First, threads are created by the login process to interact with users A and B. Let us now consider user A only. A's thread in the login process uses NT-executive-supported IPC to send A's login information to the security subsystem. A thread is created by the security subsystem to deal with this request. This thread checks A's supplied password against its record in the security database and, if all is well, makes a system call to create a process for user A. A security access token is attached to user A's process at this stage. The security system then calls the Win32 server, using IPC, to inform it of this newly-created process which is to be managed by Win32. The same is happening independently for user B.

Processes, threads and concurrency control

A process is an executable program which defines initial code and data. It has a private address space and system resources such as semaphores and communications ports that the operating system allocates to the process as the program executes. A process must have at least one thread since a thread is the unit of scheduling by the NT kernel.

A process executing in user (unprivileged) mode invokes operating system services by making system calls. Via the familiar trap mechanism (Section 3.3) its mode is changed to system (privileged) as it enters and executes the operating system and is returned to user mode on its return.

NT processes are objects, so are manipulated using object management services; see Figure 12.13(a). The access token attribute is that of the user represented by this process. Notice that the process has a base priority used for the

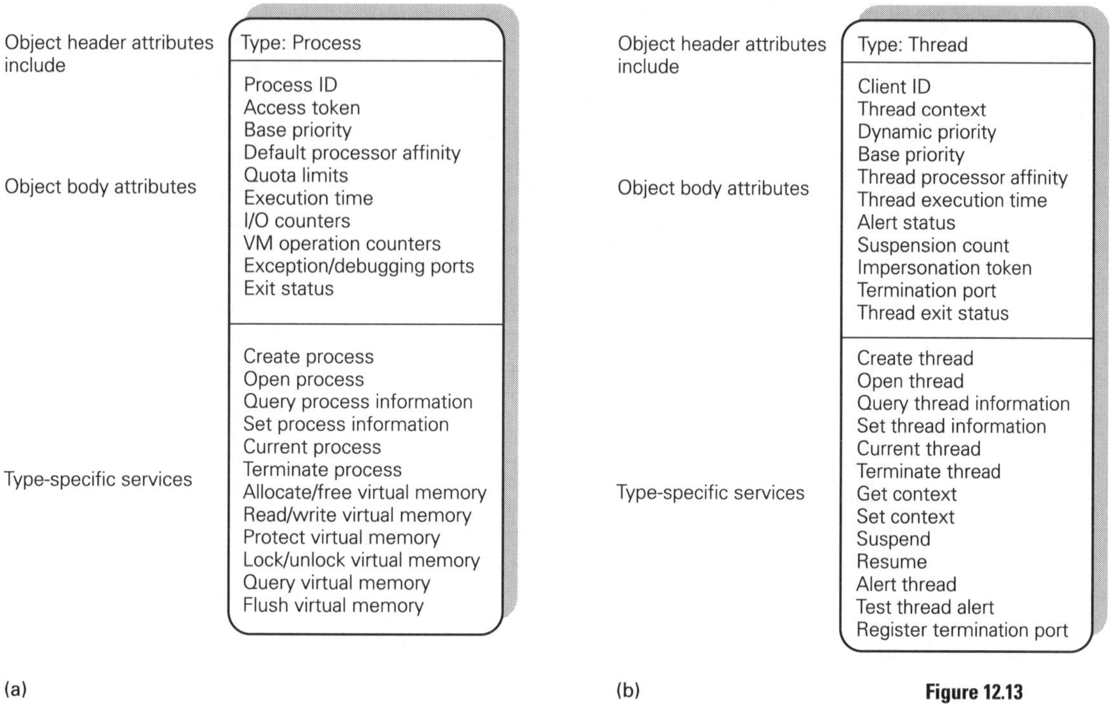

Object header attributes include	Type: Process
Object body attributes	Process ID Access token Base priority Default processor affinity Quota limits Execution time I/O counters VM operation counters Exception/debugging ports Exit status
Type-specific services	Create process Open process Query process information Set process information Current process Terminate process Allocate/free virtual memory Read/write virtual memory Protect virtual memory Lock/unlock virtual memory Query virtual memory Flush virtual memory

Object header attributes include	Type: Thread
Object body attributes	Client ID Thread context Dynamic priority Base priority Thread processor affinity Thread execution time Alert status Suspension count Impersonation token Termination port Thread exit status
Type-specific services	Create thread Open thread Query thread information Set thread information Current thread Terminate thread Get context Set context Suspend Resume Alert thread Test thread alert Register termination port

(a)

(b)

Figure 12.13
(a) Process object;
(b) thread object.

scheduling of its threads and a default processor affinity which indicates the set of processors on which the threads of this process can run. The quota limits specify maximum useable amounts of paged and non-paged system memory, paging file space and processor time. The total CPU time and resources used by the process are accounted in execution time, I/O counters and virtual memory operation counters.

A process can create multiple threads to execute within its address space and both process objects and thread objects have built-in synchronization capabilities. Once a thread has been created it is managed independently of its parent process. Figure 12.13(a) shows a typical process and its resources. Figure 12.13(b) shows a thread object. The client ID identifies the thread uniquely; this is needed when it makes service calls, for example. The thread context includes the thread's register dump and execution status.

Thread synchronization

We are familiar (Section 4.4; Chapters 8 and 9) with the requirement for threads to synchronize their activities by waiting for events and signalling their occurrence. In NT synchronization is implemented within the overall object framework. **Synchronization objects** are executive objects with which a thread can synchronize and include process, thread, file, event, event-pair, semaphore, timer and mutant objects. The last five of these exist solely for synchronization purposes.

Table 12.1 Thread synchronization for object types.

Object type	Set to signalled state when:	Effect on waiting threads
Process	last thread terminates	All released
Thread	thread terminates	All released
File	I/O operation completes	All released
Event	a thread sets (signals) the event	All released
Event-pair	dedicated client or server thread sets the event	Other dedicated thread released
Semaphore	count drops to zero	All released
Timer	set time arrives or interval expires	All released
Mutant	thread releases the mutant	One thread released

At any time a synchronization object is in one of two states: **signalled** or **non-signalled**. These states are defined differently for different objects as shown in Table 12.1. A thread may synchronize with one or a number of objects and may indicate that it will wait only for a specified time. It achieves this by invoking a WAIT service provided by the object manager and passing one or more object handles as parameters. For example, a file object is set to the signalled state when a requested I/O operation on it completes. A thread waiting on the file handle is then released from its wait state and can continue.

Asynchronous I/O calls

We have often seen the problems associated with synchronous I/O, particularly when associated with single-threaded applications. The application must block until the I/O completes, even though processing could continue in parallel with the relatively slow device operation. NT supports asynchronous I/O as well as synchronous: the application need only specify 'overlapped' mode. Services that are likely to involve lengthy I/O operations are asynchronous by default: about one-third of the native NT services. The underlying I/O system is implemented completely asynchronously, whether the caller is using synchronous or asynchronous mode.

Care must be taken to use asynchronous I/O correctly; in particular a thread must avoid accessing data which is simultaneously being used in an I/O transfer. The calling thread must synchronize its execution with completion of the I/O request, by executing WAIT on the file handle associated with the I/O.

Execution of asynchronous I/O by system threads

We have seen that, in general, the executive is executed procedurally when user-level threads make system calls into the NT executive. We now see that when I/O is asynchronous, the thread may return to user level leaving the I/O call still to be serviced. NT has a special system process which initializes the operating system and lives through its lifetime. This process has several worker threads which wait to execute requests on behalf of drivers and other executive components. If a file system or network driver needs a thread to perform asynchronous work, it queues a work item to the system process. A thread in the process is awakened to perform the necessary operations.

NT summary

NT has a well-defined modular structure although the privileged executive is by no means a minimal microkernel. It contains a great deal of functionality, including the filing system, although I/O drivers can be loaded dynamically. The fact that NT provides protected address spaces allows protected subsystems to be built and prevents interference between them. Also, the executive is protected from the systems running above it. In these features we have long-established software technology.

More novel aspects of the design include:

- the generic use of objects throughout the system, including within the executive;
- multi-threaded processes with threads as the unit of scheduling by the kernel;
- asynchronous (non-blocking) I/O with asynchronous notification of completion;
- preemptive, priority-based scheduling, including both fixed-priority, real-time processes and variable-priority processes. This scheduling is implemented both for user-level processes and for execution of the executive;
- (associated with the previous point) the provision of synchronization and mutual exclusion, including for kernel-mode processes;
- multiprocessor operation (possible because of the last two features);

The power and capacity of the modern PC has made it potentially able to support a virtually unlimited range of applications. The first generation of PC operating systems lacked almost all of the design features necessary to support advanced applications and it was essential to replace them. The NT design is based on good practice established over many years. It avoids the problems noted above in the UNIX design (of twenty years earlier), which modern UNIX systems have also solved.

12.10 Summary

In Chapter 8 we considered system structures based on shared memory and no shared memory and established where each type of structure might occur in a concurrent system. We considered how processes should be placed and used in both kinds of system. In this chapter we have taken the same theme and have extended the discussion to inter-process communication.

We have seen that any task that can be accomplished using the IPC facilities of one style of system can also be accomplished with the IPC facilities of the other style of system. This has been called the **duality** property of the two styles of system structure when a mapping between specific primitives is applied.

We have already studied how concurrent processes can use shared data to achieve their goals. In Chapters 9, 10 and 11 a number of different concurrency facilities that have been used in programming languages and operating systems were studied. In this chapter an outline of IPC without shared memory was given. In the next chapter we study this topic in detail.

We considered briefly the issue of naming in a concurrent system. Within a single computer the operating system was seen to extend the namespace of the processes it supports to allow them to communicate. Naming in distributed systems in general is considered in Chapter 6, and for IPC in Chapter 15.

Finally, we saw how processes and IPC were supported in 1970 in UNIX version 7 and in 1990 in NT.

Study questions

S 12.1

What is a synchronized byte stream? What is the main problem in using byte streams for IPC?

S 12.2

What are the essential differences between the shared-memory design shown in Figure 12.2 and the message passing design shown in Figure 12.3?

S 12.3

What sorts of system are appropriate for shared-memory communication?

S 12.4

What sorts of system are appropriate for non-shared-memory communication?

S 12.5

In Figure 12.4, what are the essential differences between the mechanisms labelled (c) and (d) that use message passing in a non-shared-memory environment?

S 12.6

In asynchronous message passing, why must messages be buffered?

S 12.7

In synchronous message passing, why are messages not buffered?

S 12.8

What are the differences between the use of a monitor and the use of a process for IPC in a shared-memory system as illustrated in Figure 12.4?

S 12.9

Is there any intrinsic reason for preferring shared-memory over non-shared-memory based systems?

S 12.10

In an asynchronous message passing system, the process that sends a message can continue processing in parallel with the process that receives the message. How can the same functionality be provided in a procedural (shared-memory) system?

Exercises

12.1   To what extent can processes which run in separate address spaces make use of kernel-provided semaphores to support their cooperation? To what extent can processes which share an address space or part of an address space make use of this facility?

12.2   How would you expect a user-level process to request a service from an operating system in a procedural system and in a non-procedural system? How might the hardware constrain or support the choice of system structure? When do context switches take place in both cases?

12.3   Explain all the possible causes of the potential delay shown (as blobs) in Figure 12.4(a), (b), (c) and (d). Which delays are to achieve mutual exclusion and which are for condition synchronization?

12.4   (a)   What is meant by the assertion that shared-memory (shared-address-space) systems and systems without shared memory may be viewed as duals of each other?
    (b)   Give the duality mapping of: monitor, monitor procedure, condition synchronization on a condition variable in a monitor, process, monitor procedure call, dynamic process creation.
    (c)   Outline how the monitors given as examples in Chapter 11, including the exercises, may be rewritten as processes. (Details of how to do this are given in the next chapter.)
    (d)   Work out the duality mapping for a shared-memory system where synchronization is at the level of whole operations with a message passing system. Use a buffer manager as an example, as in Section 12.7.

12.5   Contrast the process models of, and support for IPC in, version 7 UNIX and NT. What lessons were learned between 1970 and 1990, as illustrated by these two designs?

13

IPC without shared memory

13.1 Introduction

It is often necessary for processes to access common information in order to achieve the goals of the concurrent system they comprise. If processes do not share any part of their address spaces, in particular writeable data space, some other approach must be taken. In this chapter we first discuss alternative approaches to providing cross-address-space IPC in general terms, without reference to implementation. Many of the mechanisms are suited to distributed implementation and this major topic is left for Chapter 15. In this chapter, when implementation is discussed, it relates to IPC within a single computer.

A first attempt at a solution might be to put the common data in a file and allow access to the file by a number of processes. This approach has been used successfully in many applications, but is shown in Section 13.2 to be inadequate as the only system mechanism for concurrent processes to share information.

The UNIX operating system supports pipes between processes, as outlined in Section 12.9. The mechanism is designed to support the pipeline model of computing; a pipe is an unstructured, synchronized byte stream between two processes. It is not able to support many-to-one, client–server interactions, which are often required. Details are given below in Section 13.3.

Cross-address-space message passing is the main topic of this chapter and it is covered in general terms, applicable to both centralized and distributed implementations. It is important because distributed implementations are a natural extension to cross-address-space IPC on a single computer. Message passing may be asynchronous, where messages are buffered by the message passing mechanism, or synchronous, where no buffering is provided. In practice, buffering is likely to be implemented at the application level if a synchronous system is used.

Support for process interactions which are more general than one-to-one may be provided by message passing systems. Alternative approaches are presented and evaluated in Section 13.5. Group naming schemes and indirection through named channels or mailboxes are included.

The implementation of asynchronous message passing within a single computer is covered. The details of integrating IPC with communications services to give a distributed implementation are left until Chapter 15. A potential efficiency problem is the need to copy data between address spaces. Methods of avoiding this are discussed. In practice, message passing is likely to be used in distributed systems and the mechanism will then be integrated with communications services. This aspect of an implementation is deferred until Chapter 15.

Synchronization with the hardware by event signalling was covered in Section 4.4. If a system is to be based on message passing then event signalling can be unified with message passing, as shown in Section 13.7.

Integration of message passing into a programming language may be achieved by providing primitives to send and receive a message. Instead, a higher level of abstraction might be created. The novel approach, used in the occam programming language, of making message passing look like an assignment which is distributed between two processes is described in Section 13.8.1. Although occam programs might reside on a single transputer, they are also intended to be written for systems comprising many transputers. The Linda high-level abstraction of a shared-memory-like tuple space is also described. Here, we apparently have content-addressable messages.

The premise of this chapter is that processes do not share writeable data. We shall assume, in the first instance, that processes are single-threaded rather than multi-threaded. Multi-threaded processes are considered in Section 13.9.

13.2 Use of files for common data

Processes do not need to share memory in order to be able to access shared files. File access is slow, however, compared with accessing data in main memory. This method of sharing information is therefore only appropriate where high-speed inter-process interaction is not required. A pipelined compiler is likely to use this method of sharing information. In this case the concurrency is coarse grained: a great deal of work is done in each phase and the output is naturally placed in a temporary file. All that is required as an IPC mechanism is a means by which the phases can synchronize.

Some operating systems only provide for a file to be open for exclusive writing or shared reading. Again, this is appropriate for coarse-grained interactions. For example, a process opens a file for writing, writes data to it then closes the file. Other processes may read it concurrently with each other. We have seen how an operating system could implement such a 'multiple readers, single writer interlock' by a semaphore program in Section 10.5 and by a monitor in Section 11.2.5. This method of sharing information could involve long delays, but this might not be important if the waiting process had nothing else to do, such as in a pipeline of processes. In other applications simultaneous write sharing might be a natural way for the application to operate.

Other operating systems provide advisory locking of files and issue a warning if a lock is requested which conflicts with an existing lock. Applications are allowed to ignore such warnings.

It might be that a large amount of data is located in a file and that a number of processes are to cooperate over processing it. In this case, the application could require that all the cooperating processes should have the file open for writing simultaneously. The application ensures that they will each process a different part of the data in the file and therefore will not interfere with each other. For this reason, operating systems designers now tend to provide **shared locks** and **exclusive locks** rather than **read locks** and **write locks** (see also Chapter 5). It is usually left to the application software to organize correct use of the files although system storage services could support fine-grained concurrency control.

An alternative scheme to allow concurrent write sharing is for a data management subsystem to be implemented above the operating system. This client of the operating system would itself have many higher-level clients. It would manage files on their behalf and would cause data to be moved between disk and main memory in response to their requests. The function of such a subsystem is to manage requests for data from application processes and to ensure that reads and writes to the data do not interfere. It might also provide a higher-level view of the data, superimposing type information on the data, which the operating system stores and interprets only as a sequence of bytes.

Persistent programming languages and database management systems provide this kind of service. Here, the clients may be humans waiting for information, in which case there is all the time in the world (at the level of machine instruction execution time) to satisfy the request. The database management system does, however, have to handle concurrent requests from clients and ensure the correctness both of the stored data (the database) and the information output to clients. This topic is covered in Part III.

Part II is concerned with high-speed, relatively fine-grained inter-process interactions that cannot be achieved through file I/O. A mechanism for moving information between running processes is required.

 ## 13.3 UNIX pipes

We have seen that access to normal files is too slow for them to be used as a general mechanism for inter-process communication. The pipe in UNIX is designed to be used like a file but implemented to allow more efficient transfer of information between two processes. When a file is opened by a process a small integer file identifier is returned by the system for subsequent use when reading or writing the file. For example:

file-id = **open** (*filename, access required*)
[*bytes*] = **read** (*file-id, byte-range-within-file*)
write (*file-id, number and location in memory of bytes to write to file, where to write bytes in file*)

A pipe is created by a special system call, but a normal file identifier is returned to the creating process. This identifier may be made available to another process as described below and the pipe is subsequently read or written, in the same way as shown for files, by means of this ID. The processes must be programmed so that one writes to the pipe and the other reads from it.

write ((*pipe*)*file-id, number and location in memory of bytes to be written to pipe*)
[*bytes*] = **read** ((*pipe*)*file-id, number of bytes to be read*)

The implementation ensures that a pipe stays in main memory rather than being written out to disk. For this reason there is a notional, system-dependent, maximum size for a pipe. When the pipe contains this number of unread bytes the writing process is blocked on any further attempt to write until the reading process removes some bytes. The reading process is blocked if it attempts to read from an empty file. A pipe may therefore be seen as a **synchronized byte stream** between two processes.

An obvious difference between a pipe and a file is that there is no notion of selecting where to read from or write to in a pipe. One reads the next bytes that arrive, or writes some more bytes to the pipe. The pipe is therefore a stream of bytes flowing from one process to another, whereas a file is a sequence of bytes. There is no operating system support for any structuring of the information represented by the bytes of the file or the bytes passed in the pipe.

A process is created in UNIX by means of a **fork** system call which causes a new address space to be created. The address space of the parent is replicated for the child. Any files the parent has opened, or pipes the parent has created, become available to its children. The children can be programmed to communicate via the pipes they inherit. The processes which may use a pipe are therefore the children, grandchildren or descendants in general, of the process that created the pipe. Figure 13.1 gives an example of a pipe in use by two processes.

The pipe mechanism described above has been criticized as too restrictive in that processes must have a common ancestor in order to use a pipe for communication. For this reason, some later versions of UNIX have introduced named pipes. In this case a text name with the same structure as a normal filename is associated with a pipe. Such a pipe has a permanent existence in the UNIX

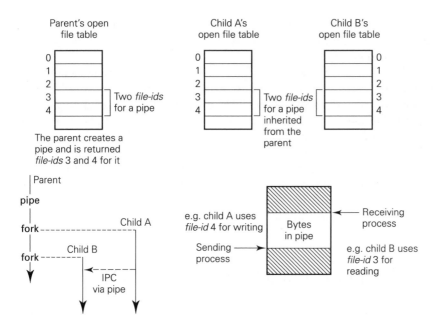

Figure 13.1
A UNIX pipe.

namespace and can be opened and used by processes under the same access control policies that exist for files. There is no longer the requirement for a family relationship between the processes.

13.3.1 Use of pipes by UNIX: Command composition

As indicated by the name 'pipe', the model of concurrent programming that the UNIX designers had in mind was the pipeline of processes. Applications programs may create and use pipes as described above. The system programs which implement UNIX commands are written so that the output from any command may be piped as input to another. Commands may be composed into sophisticated programs.

For example, a text file could be piped to a program which removes punctuation and creates a list of words as output. This could be piped to a program which sorts the words into alphabetical order. This could be piped to a program to remove adjacent identical words. This could be piped to a program to compare the words with those in a dictionary file and to remove words that match the dictionary. The remaining words could be output to the user's terminal: we have a spelling checker.

13.3.2 Evaluation of the pipe mechanism

There is no system support for structuring the byte stream into separate packets of information. Processes using a pipe may, of course, implement application-level protocols, above the pipe mechanism, to control their interaction. It would be possible in theory for many descendants of a common ancestor to use the same pipe, for example if they agreed to use fixed length messages, but it would be difficult to program in practice.

A pipe tends to be used as a one-way, one-to-one IPC mechanism, to support pipelines of processes. Two pipes are needed to support two-way communication between two processes. Although a process can set up a number of pipes it is impossible to test whether one pipe is empty and, if so, to read from another. One is committed to block if one reads from an empty pipe.

Section 8.6 discussed the types of process interactions that are required in systems. Pipes do not support the (one of) many-to-one interactions needed to implement a server with many potential clients. Nor do they support one-to-many or many-to-many interactions.

We now proceed to study a more general and flexible IPC mechanism.

13.4 Asynchronous message passing

Message passing as an IPC mechanism has been in use since the late 1960s, at the same time that Dijkstra used the semaphore mechanism in the single-address-space THE operating system. Examples of the use of this mechanism within a single computer are the MU5 design at Manchester University (Morris and Detlefsen, 1969; Morris and Ibett, 1979) and the operating system for the RC4000 (Brinch Hansen, 1970). Message passing was used in distributed systems from their earliest days, as a natural mechanism for cross-address-space IPC when the address spaces are on different computers. In this chapter we study message passing in general terms, both for centralized and distributed implementations. In Chapter 15 we consider its integration with communications services.

Section A.2

→

A typical message is shown in Figure 13.2. The system makes use of the message header in order to deliver the message to the correct destination. The contents of the message, the message body, are of no concern to the message transport system. The contents must be agreed between sender(s) and receiver(s). Application protocols associated with specific process interactions determine how messages should be structured by a sender in order to be interpreted correctly by the receiver.

The message body comprises fields that contain typed data such as is passed as arguments on procedure call.

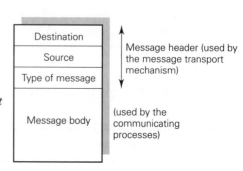

Figure 13.2
A typical message.

The source of the message is likely to be inserted, or at least checked, by the system. This is a kind of security check, as it prevents one process masquerading as another as the source of a message and means that we can be sure that the message was sent by the specified process. Figure 13.2 shows a field in the message header for 'type of message'. This might be used to indicate whether the message is an initial request for some service or a reply to some previous request; it might be used to indicate the priority of the message; or it might be a subaddress within the destination process indicating a particular service required. The header may contain additional fields to those shown, particularly if a message must be transported across a network (see Chapter 15). There has been an implicit assumption here that the source and destination fields of the message will each indicate a single process. This might be the case, but a more general and flexible scheme is often desirable, as discussed below.

Figure 13.3 gives an outline of a message passing mechanism. Process A wishes to send a message to process B. We assume that each knows an appropriate name for the other. Process A builds up the message then executes the SEND primitive with parameters indicating to whom the message should be delivered and the address at which the message can be found (in a data structure in process A's address space). Process B reaches the point in its code where it needs to synchronize with and receive data from process A and executes WAIT (or perhaps RECEIVE) with parameters indicating from whom the message is expected and the address (in process B's address space) where the message should be put. This assumes that:

- each knows the identity of the other;
- it is appropriate for the sender to specify a single recipient;
- it is appropriate for the receiver to specify a single sender;
- there is an agreement between them on the size of the message and its contents (an **application protocol**). We shall see that language-level type checking could be helpful here.

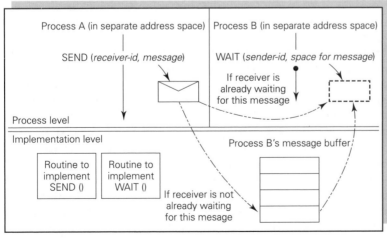

● = potential delay

Figure 13.3
A message passing system.

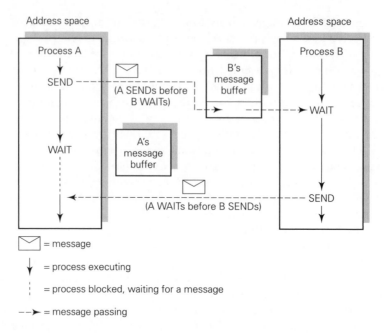

Figure 13.4
Synchronization delay in a message passing system.

We also assume that (in asynchronous message passing) the sending process is not delayed on SEND; that is, there is no reason why its state should be changed from runnable to blocked. This implies that the message passing implementation must buffer messages, as shown in Figure 13.3, in the case when the destination process has not yet executed a WAIT for that message. The message acts as a wake-up waiting signal as well as passing data. A process which executes WAIT will have its state changed to blocked if there is no appropriate message waiting for it in its message buffer. When a message arrives subsequently it is delivered to the process, assuming that it satisfies the conditions specified in the WAIT primitive, and the process becomes runnable again. Figure 13.4 illustrates this synchronization delay in more detail using the representation of Chapter 12.

The above discussion implies that the message is copied from the sender's address space into the receiver's address space, if necessary via a buffer maintained by the message passing service. Message passing primitives support both synchronization and data transfer. It is argued that, even in a system structure based on shared memory, processes synchronize in order to exchange information and that supporting both in the low-level system primitives allows complex buffer management at the process level to be avoided. The counter-argument is that complex buffer management must then be done in the implementation, which is an overhead on all processes. If processes cannot access shared data structures, a system mechanism must be provided to pass data between them. Section 13.6 discusses the implementation of asynchronous message passing in more detail, and Section 13.7 discusses synchronous message passing.

13.5 Variations on basic message passing

A message passing service may be provided with variations on the scheme described above, in order to satisfy the requirements of the systems which will use it. The reasons for these variations include the following. Note that the process address spaces may be on the same or on different computers.

- The communicating parties may not know, or need to know, each other's names (Sections 13.5.1, 13.5.4, 13.5.5).
- A process may need to be able to send a message to more than one process (Section 13.5.6).
- Support for discriminating between different messages that arrive for a process is desirable (Sections 13.5.2, 13.5.3).
- Processes may not want to commit to an indefinite WAIT for a single, specific message (Sections 13.5.2, 13.5.3, 13.5.8).
- Messages may become out of date in certain environments (Section 13.5.9).
- It may be appropriate for a reply to a message to be sent to some process other than the sender (Section 13.5.7).

13.5.1 Receiving from 'anyone'

In the message passing scheme outlined above we assumed that communication was one-to-one. It is often reasonable to assume that the sender knows the identity of the receiver (the receiver may be a well-known system service), but in many applications a process may wish to receive messages 'from anybody' in order to participate in many-to-one communication (see Section 8.6). The implementation should provide a means for a potential receiver process to specify 'from anybody', either as a default if no sender is specified or as a distinguished identifier. An alternative is to use indirection so that messages are sent and received via what have variously been called channels, ports or mailboxes (see later subsections).

13.5.2 Request and reply primitives

The message system may distinguish between requests and replies and this could be reflected in the message passing primitives. For example:

```
SEND-REQUEST   (receiver-id, message)
WAIT-REQUEST   (sender-id, space for message)
SEND-REPLY     (original-sender-id, reply-message)
WAIT-REPLY     (original-receiver-id, space for reply-message)
```

A typical interaction is illustrated in Figure 13.5. After sending the request the sender process is free to carry on working in parallel with the receiver until it needs to synchronize with the reply. It has been suggested that it might be better to enforce that the SEND-REQUEST, WAIT-REPLY primitives should be

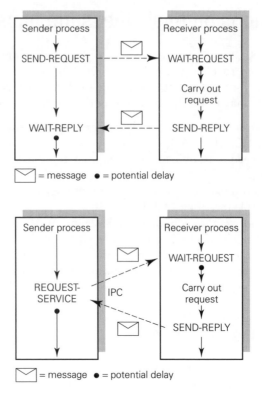

Figure 13.5
Message-based
client–server
interaction.

Figure 13.6
Alternative message-
based client–server
interaction.

used as an indivisible pair, perhaps provided to the user as a single REQUEST-SERVICE primitive. This would prevent the complexity of parallel operation and would avoid context switching overhead in the common case where the sender has nothing to do in parallel with the service being carried out and immediately blocks, waiting for the reply, when scheduled, as shown in Figure 13.6.

There is an obvious dual with a procedural system here, as discussed in Section 12.7, in that REQUEST-SERVICE corresponds to a procedure call. This is the only mechanism provided in the Amoeba message passing kernel (Tanenbaum *et al.*, 1990). The designers argue that any communication they require can be built from these primitives and that having a single simple mechanism imposes minimum overhead.

If processes are single threaded, the requesting process blocks until a reply is returned. If processes are multi-threaded, and threads can be created dynamically, a new thread may be created to make the request for service. We reconsider this option in Chapter 15 in the context of distributed systems.

13.5.3 Multiple ports per process

We have seen above that the primitives provided may allow a process to distinguish between request and reply messages. Let us assume a system design that does not use a single REQUEST-SERVICE primitive (which is a composite of

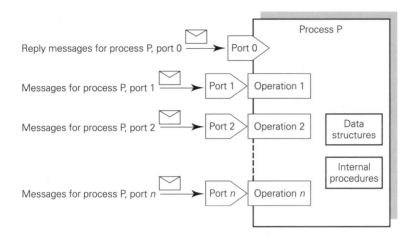

Figure 13.7
Example showing use
of ports for message
selection.

SEND-REQUEST and WAIT-REPLY) and that a process may continue after
SEND-REQUEST. Such a process may reach a point where it can either start on
some new work, by taking a new message (if any) using WAIT-REQUEST, or can
take the reply (if any) to its previous request for service using WAIT-REPLY.
Suppose the process executes WAIT-REPLY and blocks until the reply arrives.
A new request message might be available and work could proceed on it. It
seems desirable that a process should be able to test whether a message of a
given type is available (that is, 'poll' its message buffer(s)) before committing to
a WAIT. If such a facility is not available, we do not have the flexibility we need
and may as well use the composite REQUEST-SERVICE.

Extending the idea of allowing a process to select precisely which messages it
is prepared to receive and in what order it will receive them, it may be possible
for a process to specify a number of **ports** on which it will receive messages.
With this facility, a port could be associated with each of the functions a process
provides as a service to other processes and a port could be allocated to receive
replies to requests this process has made, as shown in Figure 13.7. With this
scheme we have come very close to the dual model discussed in Section 12.7.
Each function offered on a port of a service process is the dual of a procedure
exported by a monitor in a procedural system.

Again, unnecessary blocking must be avoided. This may be achieved either by
allowing a process to poll its ports, in order to test for waiting messages, or by
supporting the ability to specify a set of ports on which it is prepared to receive a
message. A priority ordering may be possible, or a non-deterministic selection may
be made from the ports with messages available. This is equivalent to a process
(task) in Ada selecting which of its entry calls it is able to accept (see Section 11.3.2).

13.5.4 Input ports, output ports and channels

Within a given module a message may be sent to a local entity (named as a local
program variable), which may be called an output port or a channel within a
given language. Only at configuration time is it specified which other process's

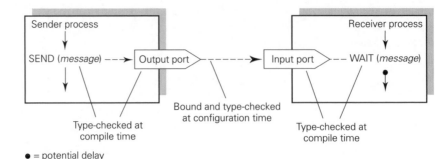

Figure 13.8
Input ports and output ports.

input port is associated with this output port or which other process is to receive from this channel. Such a scheme gives greater flexibility when a large system is to evolve. Reconfiguration can be carried out without changing the internal code of the modules concerned.

Such a scheme also allows type checking to be extended to cross-address-space communication. An output port could be declared as accepting a particular type of message structure and any SEND to that port could be type-checked against the port declaration. For example, a message would typically be declared as a record with appropriately typed fields: a string for a name, an integer for a size, etc. An output port would typically be a structure such as an array of such records. An input port could similarly be typed and messages received from it type-checked against it. Thus type checking of messages against input and output ports is achieved statically at compile time.

At configuration time, a configuration language could be used in which one or more typed output ports could be bound to a typed input port and type checking could again be carried out. This scheme is used in the CONIC system developed at Imperial College, UK (Sloman and Kramer, 1987). Figure 13.8 illustrates the basic idea with a binding of a single output port to a single input port. Figure 13.9 shows a many-to-one binding.

13.5.5 Global ports

A free-standing entity called a **global port** or **mailbox** may be used to achieve (one of) many-to-(one of) many communication. Figure 13.10 illustrates the basic idea. Any number of processes may send to it and receive from it. Such an object can be used so that equivalent server processes may take request-for-work messages from it. A new server can easily be introduced or a crashed server removed. The same effect is achieved as with many-to-many producer–consumer buffering using a monitor (see Section 11.2.4), or programmed with semaphores (see Section 10.3). In the case of a global port the system is supporting a named object which is known to many processes. Naming schemes for global objects are discussed in Chapters 6 and 15.

The Intel iAPX432 hardware supported global ports for process dispatching as well as for inter-process message passing. An idle processor could look for a

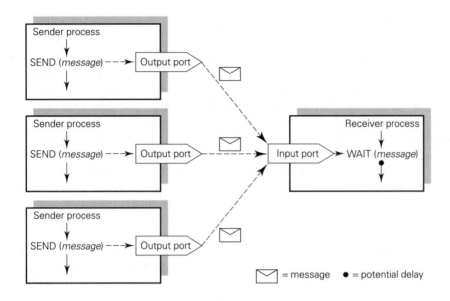

Figure 13.9
Many output ports bound to one input port.

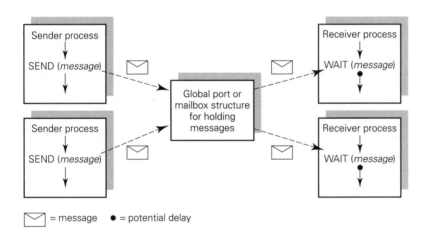

Figure 13.10
A global port.

runnable process at a dispatching port. If none was found the processor could wait there. Similarly, a runnable process could look for a free processor at a dispatching port. If none was available the process was added to the run queue implemented there.

The cross-address-space type checking described in Section 13.5.4 could be extended to global ports if each named global port was defined to accept messages of some specific type. Compile-time type checking of messages against the typed input and output ports of a single process could be carried out as before. A separate configuration phase could bind processes' ports to global ports after checking for type consistency.

13.5.6 Broadcast and multicast

Input ports, output ports, channels and global ports were introduced so that inter-process interactions other than one-to-one could be supported. They can all be viewed as introducing **indirect naming**. A message is sent to an intermediate, named object rather than to some specific process.

It is possible to achieve 'from anyone' (many-to-one) or 'to everyone' (broadcast) without introducing this indirection, simply by using a special name in the message header. What is achieved by channels, etc., is the ability to **receive** messages from a specific group of processes, selected at system configuration time. What is achieved by global ports is the ability to **send** to a group of anonymous, identical processes. Global ports also support the ability to receive messages from 'anyone', or from a selected group, depending on how the name of the global port is used and controlled.

An alternative approach is to support the naming of groups of processes in a system as well as individual processes. The semantics of sending to a group name and receiving from a group name must be defined very carefully. In the previous discussion a send to a global port implied that one anonymous process would take the message and process it. This is a common requirement: for example, when a set of like servers offer a service. A different requirement is indicated by the term **multicast**. In this case the message should be sent to *every* process in the group. Figure 13.11 illustrates this distinction. The Isis system at Cornell University (Birman, 1985) and the V system at Stanford (Cheriton, 1984; Cheriton and Zwaenpoel, 1985) both have multicast as a basic primitive. Other systems have implemented an efficient multicast without group naming, for example, the Coda file system at Carnegie-Mellon University (Satyanarayanan *et al.*, 1990).

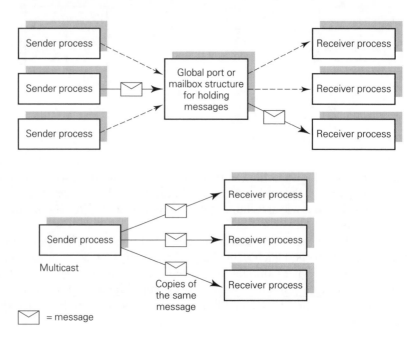

Figure 13.11
Global port contrasted with multicast.

13.5.7 Message forwarding

Message forwarding is more appropriate for distributed systems, but is mentioned here for completeness. A message may be delivered to a process which is one of a set of processes offering the required service but which no longer has the object required. An example is that a file may have migrated from the file server which created it to some other file server. Any request associated with the file may, for a time, still be delivered to the birthplace of the file.

On receiving the request and detecting that the required object has moved, the original destination process wishes to forward the request to the correct destination but to have the reply sent to the original sender. If such a forwarding service is not offered, a great deal of data could retrace the path of the original request in the reverse direction. Message forwarding can be useful, but is not so crucial, in a centralized system.

13.5.8 Specifying WAIT time

It might be appropriate to WAIT for a specified time only for a message rather than commit to an indefinite wait. Again, this facility is important in a distributed system, where a destination machine might have crashed or the network might be down or congested.

If such a timeout facility is available it can be used to poll for a message on a given port (using a zero timeout), or to enforce crisis times for event handling and to take action if some deadline is not met. The general point is that a timing facility can be put to good use, particularly in a hard real-time system.

13.5.9 Discarding out-of-date messages

It might be that a message contains information that should be superseded by a later message. A large industrial process could be monitored by many sensors, or some object's position could be tracked. In such cases, time would be wasted if an early message was received and processed when a more recent message was already available.

A method of achieving this is to support the declaration of input ports of finite size. A port of size 1 would thus hold only the most recent message of that type, previous messages being discarded.

13.6 Implementation of asynchronous message passing

If asynchronous message passing is used in a distributed system it must be integrated with communications services; we cover this topic in Chapter 15. In both centralized and distributed implementations buffer management is an issue.

In a shared-memory system, processes manage their own data transfers through producer–consumer buffering, supported by underlying mechanisms which bear little implementation overhead. The processes have to do more work for themselves to achieve IPC but only the processes involved in the IPC are affected by this overhead (the overhead is in the context of the processes using the mechanism).

In a system with no shared memory, messages may need to be copied twice: from process address space to system buffer, then from system buffer into destination process address space. There may be several context switches. All processes in the system are affected by this overhead and not just the processes involved in the IPC. More processor cycles are spent executing the underlying system if a complex message buffer has to be managed.

If a single large message buffer is used it is a shared data structure and synchronized access to it must be implemented using one of the methods explained in Chapters 9, 10 and 11. Shared-memory techniques are necessary in the implementation of no-shared-memory techniques!

Operating system designers attempt to make the resident kernel data structures fixed in length. For example, there is likely to be a maximum number of processes the operating system can manage, each one represented by a fixed length descriptor. Space can therefore be allocated statically to the process structure.

In the design of the data structures for a message passing system the following must be considered:

1 *Messages*
  What do messages look like? Early systems had fixed length messages and there is still likely to be a maximum message size for data that is passed by value; for example, the Chorus limit is 64 kbytes. It is unacceptable to make such a restriction visible at the user level. Messages at the language level should be variable length and typed, allowing type checking against a channel or port.
2 *Message buffers*
  What form do the message buffers take? Fixed or variable length slots may be used.

  Early systems had many restrictions, such as a maximum number of messages outstanding (sent but not received) from any one process, in order to control the space used. Mach and Conic employ a scheme of this kind, but each process message buffer is specified as having a maximum size. A buffer slot used for a request message was sometimes reserved for the associated reply message to avoid contention (Brinch Hansen, 1970).

  The amount of memory required is less of a problem now than in early systems which had both a small virtual address space and a small amount of physical memory. Current systems use a great deal of buffer space for communications messages as well as messages between local processes. Communications protocols are designed to take account of lost messages: if there is no space a message can be discarded and a reliable protocol will detect this and resend the message.

An alternative to a large shared system buffer is to keep messages in the address space of processes, for example, in output ports. Problems here are that this part of the process address space should not be swapped out to disk and that the process should not be able to change a message after sending it. Copy-on-write memory management can be used here (see below). If messages are held at the process level it is easy to acquire more memory for the data structures which hold them by making a system call. If messages are held in a buffer in the kernel, the space allocated for this purpose may become exhausted.

3 *Memory management techniques*

Can memory management techniques be used in order to transfer large amounts of data between processes without copying? Within a single system a segment name could be passed in a message and the segment could be mapped out of the sender's address space and into the receiver's. Alternatively, the segment could be mapped into both address spaces and the processes could synchronize their accesses to it by the shared memory techniques described in Chapters 9, 10 and 11. This was available in the UK GEC 4000 series in the 1970s.

Another possible scheme is for the system to manage a number of pages which can be mapped into the address spaces of processes. In advance of creating a message a process asks the system for a page or pages. These pages are temporarily mapped into the sender's address space while the message is created. On SEND, the pages are unmapped from the sender and mapped into the receiver's address space. This technique is an efficient means of sending data to a network interface for transfer to a remote machine as well as for cross-address-space inter-process communication.

Copy-on-write techniques may be used to implement message passing. For example, when a message is sent its pages may be mapped copy-on-write in both the sender's and the receiver's address space. The physical pages are not copied. If either process makes a write access to a message page a new physical copy of that page is made and each process is then given read/write access to a separate copy of the page.

13.7 Synchronous message passing

A message system in which the sender is delayed on SEND until the receiver executes WAIT avoids the overhead of message buffer management. Such a system is outlined in Figure 13.12. The message is copied once (or mapped) from sender to receiver when they have synchronized. The behaviour of such a system is easier to analyse since synchronizations are explicit. Figure 13.13 illustrates possible synchronization delay for Figure 12.4(d).

In practice, explicit synchronization is not feasible in all process interactions. For example, an important system service process must not be committed to wait in order to send a reply to one of its many client processes. The client cannot be relied on to be waiting for the reply. A device handler, for example, must get

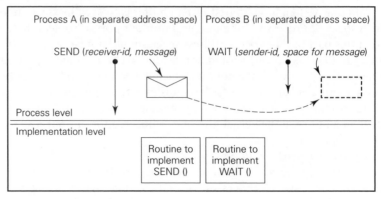

Figure 13.12
Implementation of synchronous message passing.

● = potential delay

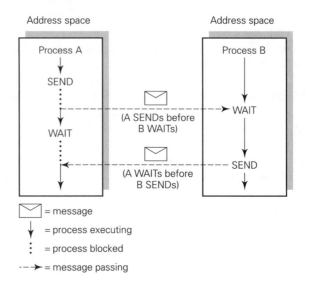

Figure 13.13
Synchronization in synchronous message passing.

✉ = message
↓ = process executing
⋮ = process blocked
--→ = message passing

rid of its data quickly in order to be free to respond to the device. It cannot wait for a high-level client to ask for the data.

Processes with the sole function of managing buffers are often built to avoid this synchronization delay in synchronous systems. We have removed message buffering from the message passing service only to find it rebuilt at the process level. The advantage of this is that the kernel has less overhead than in asynchronous systems and the time taken to manage message buffers is used only by those processes that need them, thus avoiding system overhead for others. See Exercise 13.4 for an alternative approach.

An outline for a buffer management scheme is given in Figure 13.14. Clients interact with the server through an interface process which manages two buffers, one for requests to the server, one for replies from the server. The interface process answers to a well-known system name for the service. Although the interface process must synchronize with the server process and its clients it never commits itself to synchronization with a specific process, and takes any incoming

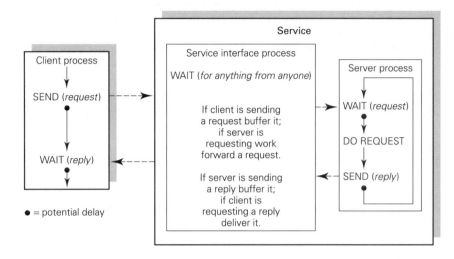

Figure 13.14
Server buffering
in a synchronous
message passing
system.

message. It might be possible for server messages to be given priority over client messages in the primitives provided, as discussed above in Section 13.5. Since the real service is carried out by a process which is anonymous to its clients, this scheme could be used to allow a number of server processes to perform the service, each taking work from the interface process.

13.8 Message passing in programming languages

So far we have concentrated on the implementation and interface of the message passing system rather than on a high-level language view of message passing.

Software that is to run in a single address space is likely to be developed as separate modules and to require linking, often into a single load module. The linking phase involves type checking of the parameters for inter-module calls. When processes execute in a single address space their presence and interactions need not be visible at linking and loading time since the data passed between processes is type-checked as part of the normal module linkage procedure. In shared-memory systems, this data is just procedure call arguments.

In a system where processes run in separate address spaces, the load module for each one will be created as described above. The data passed in the bodies of messages in this case passes between address spaces and we should consider whether it is type-checked.

Recall that the input ports and output ports of CONIC, described above in Section 13.5.4, were assumed to be declared in the CONIC programming language. A message sent to or received from a port is type-checked against the port declaration. A configuration language is used to set up links between ports which must be of the same type. Type checking of the data contained in messages is therefore done both at compile time and at configuration time. Chapter 15 discusses this issue for cross-machine IPC.

Message passing can be incorporated in a high-level language directly, in the form of any of the variations of the SEND and WAIT primitives we have discussed above. We now consider two approaches which give the programmer different abstractions for message passing.

13.8.1 occam channels for synchronous communication

The concurrent programming language occam is based on synchronous communication, and processes do not share memory. occam evolved from the earlier language specification and formalism CSP (Communicating Sequential Processes) (Hoare, 1978). In CSP, named processes are the source and destination of a communication. In occam, communication takes place via a named channel.

In occam, IPC is equivalent to assignment from one process to another. An assignment statement

variable := *expression*

is distributed between two processes: one holds the variable, the other evaluates the expression. The value of the expression is communicated along a channel known to both processes.

Destination process   **Source process**
channel ? *variable*   *channel* ! *expression*

For example, $x := y+z$ could be distributed as:

channelA ? *x   channelA* ! *y+z*

These three kinds of statement (input, output and assignment) may be composed sequentially or in parallel using SEQ and PAR respectively. A small example is as follows (see Figure 13.15).

Declare a non-terminating procedure which takes a value from channel *source* and outputs its square on channel *sink*:

```
PROC square (CHAN source, sink)=
   WHILE TRUE
     VAR x:
     SEQ
       source ? x
       sink ! x × x
```

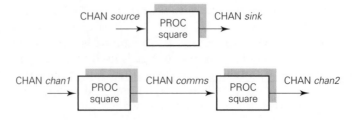

Figure 13.15
occam example.

and use the procedure, for example to create a pipeline:

CHAN *comms*:
   PAR
     square (*chan1*, *comms*)
     square (*comms*, *chan2*)

occam is intended to be a simple language with few constructs, after the philosophy of William of Occam. It is often called a high-level assembler for the transputer rather than a high-level language. It enforces a static declaration of processes and is therefore applicable to embedded systems rather than general-purpose systems. Many examples can be found in Dowsing (1988), Burns (1988) and Inmos (1984).

13.8.2 The Linda abstraction

Linda was developed in the early 1980s (Gelernter, 1985) as a concurrent programming model which aims to give a high-level, abstract view of IPC. Linda is not a complete new programming language, but a set of primitives that may be used to augment a sequential programming language, such as C, C++ or Fortran. Carriero and Gelernter (1989) evaluate Linda in comparison with other concurrent programming paradigms and give examples and references on its use. Andrews (1991) includes Linda in his overview of concurrent programming languages.

In message passing systems, the message passing mechanism is only concerned with the message header, and not the internal structure of the message (see Section 13.4). The header is used to indicate the destination(s) of the message. In Linda, tuples are used instead of messages to communicate information between processes.

A **tuple** is a series of typed fields. Unlike messages, tuples are data objects within the programming language. An example is:

('*tag*', 15.01, 17, '*a string*')

where each field is either an expression or a formal parameter of the form ? *var*, where *var* is a local variable in the executing process. The '*tag*' field is a string literal which is used to distinguish between tuples.

Tuples do not need to have a recipient's name appended as part of a header (following system-defined rules), but instead are deposited into and extracted from 'tuple space' (TS). Depositing a tuple into TS is a non-blocking operation.

A process that wishes to 'receive' a tuple does not need to know who sent it. TS is logically shared by all processes and tuples are received by an **associative search mechanism**; that is, a process can extract a tuple by giving a template of what it requires to have matched in the various fields, as illustrated below. The application programmer can decide, for example, whether one process or any process of a given type or any process that knows about a particular tag in a field of a tuple, etc., should pick up the message. A receiver blocks if there are no matching tuples.

Tuples exist independently of the processes that created them and a multi-tuple data structure in TS may have been created by many processes.

The Linda primitives are:

out   causes a tuple to be generated and deposited into TS;

in   removes from TS a tuple that matches a specified template;

rd   reads a tuple that matches a specified template but does not remove it from TS;

eval causes a new process to be created. The process executes an assigned routine and, on termination, generates a tuple in TS.

For example, the tuple generated by:

out (*'tag'*, 15.01, 17, *'a string'*)

can be read by:

rd (*'tag'*, ? *f*, ? *i*, *'a string'*)

where *f* is a real variable and *i* is an integer variable in the executing process.

The **eval** primitive can be used by a parent to offload work onto a child and later to pick up the result in the form of a tuple. Alternatively, a child can be created in order to generate a tuple to communicate with some other process.

Exercise 13.9 invites the reader to compose a client–server interaction using the Linda primitives. In this case a server must be concerned with who deposited a tuple to make a request for service in order to return a reply tuple.

More examples can be found in the Bibliography but the flavour tends to be of small-scale computations rather than large-scale systems.

Potential problems are in the following areas:

- Naming in the form of simple, unstructured strings is used to discriminate between tuples.
- Protection is a potential problem in that all processes share TS. Any process can read or extract any tuple it can match. This is acceptable within a small-scale application but not for programming a general system, where processes do not necessarily trust each other.
- Efficient implementation is difficult to achieve, even in a centralized system. The implementation needs to be concerned with the contents of the various fields of the tuples and not just a message header, as in a message system. The distinction between a message header, of concern to the system, and a message body, of concern to the application, is clean at the IPC implementation level if inflexible to the applications above it.
- It is not clear how distributed implementation of a global shared TS abstraction would be achieved.

13.9 Multi-threading in clients and servers

When we considered shared-memory-based IPC in Chapter 11 we found that the possibility of dynamic process creation should be taken into account. A child can be created to invoke the service (by procedure call) and the parent can, later, synchronize with the child to receive the results. The parent process can carry out work in parallel. The same arguments apply in message passing systems if multi-threaded processes are supported and threads may be created dynamically. A child may be created to invoke a service (by message passing) and the parent can continue with work in parallel. This may make simple message passing primitives feasible which are too inflexible for use by single-threaded processes.

A common requirement in system design is the server that can serve many clients simultaneously; the example of a file server was taken in Chapters 4 and 8. Even if such a server receives requests for service in the form of messages, we have the same need for multiple internal threads of control: the work for one client may come to a temporary halt and work should proceed on behalf of another. All such threads may need to access the same system data structures and the shared-memory model of lightweight thread creation and access to shared data by shared-memory techniques is desirable within the server.

Multi-threading may be used to solve the problem described above in Section 13.8; in a synchronous message passing environment a heavily used system server must not be delayed, waiting for a client to synchronize in order to receive a reply. With multi-threading, the server can create a thread to handle each reply, even if a separate thread has not been used to serve each client.

A system design should therefore support shared-memory techniques as well as cross-address-space message passing.

Further reading on the implementation and use of threads may be found in Anderson *et al.* (1992), Birrell (1991), McJones and Swart (1987), Nelson (1991) and Pham and Garg (1996). Ousterhout *et al.* (1980) are early in discussing the requirements for threads.

13.10 Summary

Asynchronous message passing was motivated as a general mechanism suitable for cross-address-space IPC. A number of variations in the primitives and in the detailed design and use of messages were described. Various naming schemes for the sources and destinations of messages were also considered.

Implementation was discussed in some detail. The overhead introduced into the system by buffer management and message copying can be alleviated by the use of memory mapping. Alternatively, by using ports associated with the particular processes concerned in a message exchange, the space and time overhead may be allocated to the processes using the facility.

Synchronous message passing avoids copying messages into system buffers at the expense of delaying the sender of a message as well as the receiver. Buffering processes have to be implemented to avoid important server processes being delayed, waiting for less important client processes. A synchronous system is easier to model mathematically than an asynchronous one.

The Linda approach was introduced briefly and compared with message passing. Although the Linda primitives may be convenient and flexible for the writers of concurrent applications, there are many systems issues, such as naming, protection and distribution, to be addressed before Linda can be considered as a basis for concurrent systems in general.

Message passing is a general mechanism which can be implemented with many subtle variations to satisfy the specific requirements of the system that is to use it. It can be incorporated into the programming language level and, in this case, type checking of the message contents can be carried out with the same generality as in the languages for shared-memory systems. Flexiblity in system development can be offered in that the binding of modules to machines can be deferred until configuration time or even until runtime.

In a system based on message passing we still need multi-threaded server processes which can work on behalf of many clients simultaneously. The internal implementation of such a server is best done in terms of shared-memory-based communication; a system should support both shared-memory and message-based IPC. The availability of multi-threaded processes affects the choice of message passing primitives. Simple primitives may suffice in a system with multi-threaded processes and dynamic process creation, whereas more complex primitives might be required to do the same job in a single-threaded environment.

Message passing extends naturally to distributed systems and many of the examples given here have been taken from distributed operating systems. To discuss distributed message passing properly we need to consider how network communication is used. Also, processes may fail independently of each other in distributed systems. These issues are addressed in Chapter 15.

Study questions

S 13.1

What is an application protocol, and where is it used?

S 13.2

What parameters do the SEND and WAIT primitives usually have? What are the purposes of the parameters?

S 13.3

What mechanism is used to enable asynchronous message passing (in which the sender is not blocked on SEND)?

Exercises

13.1 Contrast the UNIX pipe facility for same-machine, cross-address-space IPC with message passing.

13.2 Suggest ways in which memory management hardware could be used for passing large messages between processes in separate address spaces.

Consider both the case when the message is available to both sender and receiver after the message is sent and the case when the send involves only a transfer from one address space to another. Which semantics do you think should be the default and why?

13.3 Suggest two ways in which the handling of message passing between processes may be unified with process–device interactions.

13.4 What problems do you think would arise if synchronous message passing was used to implement interactions between client processes and heavily used servers?
   (a) How might multi-threading be used in the server to solve this problem?
   (b) How might a separate process be used to solve the problem?
   (c) What are the advantages and disadvantages of (a) and (b)?

13.5 How can language-level type checking be included in a message passing system?

13.6 In what ways can the naming of a specific destination process be avoided in a message system design? Why is this desirable?

13.7 What is meant by multicast? What kind of naming service would be needed to support multicast?

13.8 Why might it be important to be able to specify a limit on the time that one is prepared to wait for a message?

13.9 Use the Linda primitives introduced in Section 13.8.2 to program the interaction between a single centralized file server and its many clients. Generalize your solution to many file servers offering a file service.

Crash resilience and persistent data

14.1 Crashes

Part II is concerned with the execution of a single action by one process concurrently with and without interference from the execution of related actions by other processes. So far we have not considered that a system might crash at any time. In this chapter we consider this problem in relation to the execution of such a single concurrent action. In Part III higher-level actions comprising multiple lower-level actions are considered. Figure 14.1 shows an operation invocation. We are not concerned with the means by which the invocation takes place, for example, by procedure call or by message passing.

We also assume that the action of invoking the operation takes place in the same machine as the execution of the invoked operation. In this case a crash causing the loss of the contents of main memory causes all the computations to

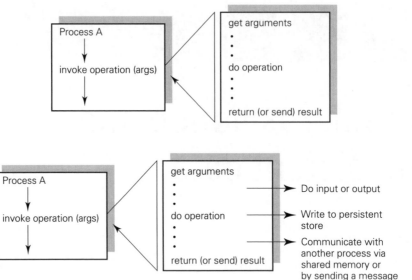

Figure 14.1
An operation
invocation.

Figure 14.2
An operation
invocation with
externally visible
effects.

fail together. Invocation from one machine of an operation on another machine will be considered in the next chapter.

Figure 14.2 shows that a single operation invocation might have **externally visible effects**. It might read input, do output, cause a write to **persistent storage** or communicate with another process. A crash might happen after one or more of these effects have occurred but before the end of the operation. What, if anything, should the system do before the invocation is repeated? From the point of view of this chapter we shall consider that communication with another process brings us into the management of sets of related actions and will leave that issue for Part III. We shall therefore consider only those externally visible actions of concern to this process.

For example, take a transaction processing (TP) system, which involves large persistent stores (e.g. databases), which may be accessed concurrently by many transactions (i.e. client requests) on the database. Suppose a client of such a TP system invokes a *credit* operation on a bank account, as part of an electronic funds transfer, and the system replies 'done' if the credit has been performed correctly or 'not done' if there is some error such as an unknown account name. There are two externally visible effects: the updated value of the account and the response to the user. In this example these effects are related: if you tell your client you have done an operation you must first have recorded its results in persistent memory.

14.2 A model of a crash

A simple model of a crash will be taken initially, a **fail–stop** model. We shall assume that a crash happens at some instant rather than over a period of time. It results in the instantaneous loss of volatile state: the processor registers, the cache and memory management unit, and the (volatile) main memory. Any changes that have been made to persistent state, for example in any non-volatile memory and disk-based storage, are assumed to be correct, but may be incomplete. By making this simplifying assumption we avoid considering how incorrect system software may behave before finally causing a crash. In Section 14.7 we take a more realistic look at the likely behaviour of failing software.

Schlichting and Schneider (1983) discuss the fail–stop model. For further reading, Lamport *et al.* (1982) present an approach to reasoning about failing distributed systems which has become the classic 'Byzantine Generals Problem'.

14.3 Crash resilience or failure transparency

If a program runs on a single machine and a failure occurs we assume that all the memory is lost; that is, all the data structures of the program are lost. If no externally visible effects have been caused by the program it is as though it had never run and it can simply be restarted. In practice, every program will eventually perform output or cause some change of permanent state or communicate an intermediate result. If a crash occurs during a program run and after such an externally visible action, we consider how to restart after the crash.

An aspect of system design is the extent to which an application is offered support to recover from system crashes. Another name for crash resilience is **crash** or **failure transparency**. In this chapter methods of achieving crash resilience are outlined. A general point is that there is a high overhead associated with these methods and some applications will not require them. Crash resilience should therefore, in most systems, be an optional extra rather than being imposed on every application.

14.4 Idempotent (repeatable) operations

In certain simple cases it is possible to ensure that an operation can be repeated without causing any errors or inconsistencies. When deciding how certain operations should be specified, for example the form their arguments should take, it may be possible to choose an idempotent implementation. For example, the repeatable method of writing a sequence of bytes to the end of a file is to specify the precise byte position at which the new bytes should be written and make this an argument of an 'append' operation. If an append operation is relative to a system-maintained pointer, the bytes could be written more than once if the operation was repeated. It is not always possible to achieve repeatable operations.

This point becomes more important in distributed systems, when a congested network may cause a reply message saying 'operation done' to be greatly delayed or lost. The invoker does not know this and repeats the request when the operation requested has already been carried out.

14.5 Atomic operations on persistent objects

The concept of an atomic operation is necessary for a systematic approach to analysing and solving the problem of making an operation repeatable. An atomic operation invocation is defined as follows:

- if it terminates normally then all its effects are made permanent;
- else it has no effect at all.

Note that this definition (which focuses on crash resilience) does not take into account the fact that the persistent data being accessed might be shared with other processes (that is, concurrency control is also needed). In this case we should add:

- if the operation accesses a shared data object, its invocation does not interfere with other operation invocations on the same data object.

It is essential to provide atomic operation invocations in some transaction processing systems, as argued in Section 1.1.2. They are called **transactions**, that is, the term transaction implies atomicity. Examples are banking and airline booking systems.

A programming language which supports atomic operations will provide a means of defining the start and end of a given transaction. If the operation completes successfully it is said to **commit** (and its effects are guaranteed to be permanent); if it does not complete it **aborts**. The system must make sure that all the effects of an aborted transaction are undone, as though it had never run. The result of an invocation, commit or abort, is usually notified to the invoking client (a human user or other software).

Suppose, again, that a client of a TP system invokes a *credit* operation on a bank account as part of an electronic funds transfer, and the system replies 'done' if the credit has been performed correctly or 'not done' if there has been some error such as an unknown account name. Suppose the system crashes after the invocation has started but before 'done' or 'not done' is sent to the client. The record in persistent store of the value of the bank account might or might not reflect the credit.

If *credit* is an atomic operation then the invocation which did not complete correctly must be undone; effectively it never happened. When the system comes up again the client repeats the operation. This invocation updates the account correctly and 'done' is received by the client. There is no possibility of multiple, and therefore incorrect, credits (or debits). Also, once the client has received 'done' the credit must persist, even if there is a head crash on the disk on which the account is stored.

General points are therefore:

- Computer systems crash, data in main memory is lost.
- If the system tells a client (human user or software) that an atomic operation has been done then the changes made by it must have been recorded in persistent store.

14.5.1 Volatile, persistent and stable storage

We established above that an atomic operation must write its results to persistent store before it commits. We also emphasized that this record must persist, even if there is a medium failure such as a bad block or a head crash which destroys the surface of a disk. For this reason an abstraction called **stable storage** has been established.

A single write to persistent store does not guarantee that the information written will persist. In practice, the information is typically written to at least two independent places in persistent store, so that if one copy is lost the other can be used. The phrase 'write to stable storage' is used as a shorthand for such a replicated write.

14.6 Implementation of atomic operations

Figure 14.3 illustrates the essentials for implementing an atomic operation on a persistent object. When the execution causes a write to persistent store, both the old value and the new value of the data must be recorded in some form, together with the identifier of the transaction that carried out the update. This is so that if a crash occurs before the operation completes, the old value can be restored. This is sometimes referred to as **rolling back** the state recorded in persistent store or **undoing** the operation.

This is a very general outline of atomic operations. In the context of Part II, a single operation invocation could be defined as involving only a single read, modify and write of a persistent object, and rolling back seems unnecessary at first sight.

However, if a crash occurs after the operation's single write to disk and before the operation returns, the invocation could be repeated. The final state recorded in persistent store could be affected by the first, abortive invocation, as in the *credit* example of Section 14.1.

Could rolling back be avoided? Input could be recorded and reused. Depending on the application, any output might be done again if the operation is repeated, or the output that has been carried out may be recorded and repeats avoided.

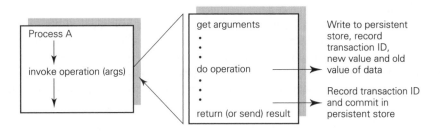

Figure 14.3
A potentially atomic operation invocation.

A great deal of overhead is associated with implementing atomic operations. The persistent store may be disk, in which case each write would require an acknowledged disk transfer. In some operating systems, for example UNIX, an apparent write to disk is merely a transfer into a cache in main memory and this would clearly not be good enough to implement atomic operations.

There are two basic approaches which may be used to support rollback: these are logging and shadowing.

14.6.1 Logging

When logging is used the persistent store is changed (updated in place) and a record is kept in a log. The log entry must contain an identifier for the transaction, the old data value and the new data value. The log will contain a number of records for each transaction, for example, a record indicating a new transaction, a number of update records and an end of transaction (or commit) record.

After a crash the log is processed in order to restore the persistent store to a consistent state. Any partially executed transaction can be undone; that is, the persistent store is rolled back to its state at the start of the transaction using the old values recorded in the log.

Section 20.4

An important practical point is that the log must be written to persistent store before the data in the persistent store is changed. If these operations were carried out in the reverse order, a crash could occur before the log was written and after the data was changed and the old data values would be lost. The log must therefore be a **write-ahead log**.

Details of algorithms for log processing are considered further in Chapter 20.

14.6.2 Shadowing

An alternative mechanism is to leave the persistent data unchanged until the transaction is committed but to build up a shadow data structure which will replace it on successful termination (when the transaction is committed).

An essential technique here is to make the final switch between the old and new data structures achievable in a single operation, for example by changing one pointer. A crash can then occur only before or after the switch and not in the middle.

The implementation of shadowing may be built at the level of disk pages: a **shadow paging** mechanism. This is because the disk is written in units of fixed-sized blocks or pages. This technique can be used in filing systems where the data structures kept by the file storage service (which themselves are stored in disk pages) map the disk pages in use for storing files, directories and so on.

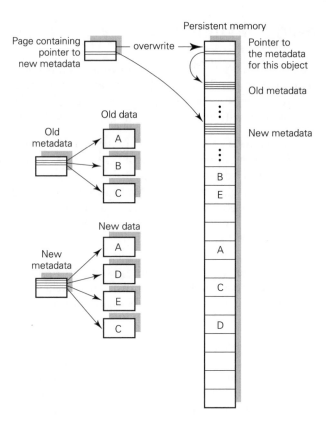

Figure 14.4
An example
illustrating shadow
paging.

Figure 14.4 gives an example of one way in which a shadow paging scheme might be used. Here we see a representation of an old and new version of a given object. The figure shows the stage at which all the object's data is safely written to the disk, as are the pages containing the old and new version of the metadata. The figure illustrates a scheme where a certain disk block contains a mapping from an object's name to the location of its metadata. The change from the old version of the object to the new one is achieved by overwriting this block with one containing the new pointer.

We can make the simple assumption that the write of a single disk block is atomic. Either the new block is written, in which case we have switched to the new version of the object, or it isn't, in which case we still have the old version. If we are not prepared to make this assumption and there is a crash during the write of this page we can read it back on restart and examine the pointer. If the crash took place before this pointer was transferred we still have the old version; if afterwards, we have the new version. This assumes that writing a single pointer is atomic.

An alternative scheme is that the object's name maps onto a particular metadata location on disk. In this case, having written the data pages to disk, we can overwrite the old metadata with the new.

14.7 Non-volatile memory

Non-volatile RAM (NVRAM) costs about four times as much as normal RAM and has become available in increasingly large units, currently up to about 10 megabytes. A cheaper alternative is battery-backed RAM. There are many potential uses for non-volatile memory, for example:

- for caching data in a file storage service. This allows fast response to write requests, but gives the assurance that the data is stored securely, normally achieved by an acknowledged write out to disk;
- to hold the file service's data structures. When a change is made it need not be written out immediately, to achieve consistency of the stored filing system;
- to accumulate requests for writes to disk and to order them for use by an efficient disk-arm scheduling algorithm;
- if NVRAM is available to high levels of system software which have knowledge of the semantics of data at a fine granularity, then shadowing can be implemented at a finer granularity than disk pages. When the new data structure is complete it can be written to the disks of the storage service in its entirety.

A good discussion of the options and technology is given in Baker *et al.* (1992).

In practice, a system may not fail in the fail–stop manner described in Section 14.2. Wild addresses might be generated while the system is failing, causing writes to areas of memory that were not intended. This behaviour might cause the data we are carefully preserving in non-volatile memory to be corrupted. Also, we may be taking advantage of the availability of NVRAM to hold more data in main memory and deliberately delaying its write to disk. Have we made our system more vulnerable to this kind of failure behaviour by using NVRAM?

Because a very specific protocol has to be followed for writing to disk it is unlikely that failing software will write all over the disk by accident. In this respect, NVRAM is more vulnerable than disk.

Recall from Chapter 5 that filing systems may keep data in a volatile cache in memory. In some systems data may not be written out as soon as possible, but may be kept in memory until the buffer space it occupies is needed. Also, the filing system's metadata is changed in volatile main memory before being written out to disk. There is therefore the possibility that failing software might corrupt these items before they are written out. This is equally true for volatile and non-volatile memory, although we are likely to keep more data in memory for longer if we have NVRAM. To achieve crash resilience we should not only store this data in NVRAM, but also protect the NVRAM from corruption. If this is possible we shall have achieved both better response to write requests and better protection of data and metadata through using NVRAM.

One approach to protecting NVRAM is to require a simple protocol to be followed in order to write to it (Needham *et al.*, 1986). Another is to use memory management hardware to protect it. It is unlikely that failing software would accidentally change the memory management tables correctly and give itself access to NVRAM by accident.

14.8 A single operation on persistent data

For most of Part II we have considered the case where the data structures accessed by concurrent processes reside in main memory. In order to consider the effects of crashes we have started to look at the externally visible effects of operations. We have therefore begun to focus on persistent store. Figure 14.5 shows an operation (specified as part of a module's interface) operating on persistent data. An example is an implementation of an airline booking system, as used in Section 8.7.1, where we focused on the value in main memory of the variable *unbooked-seats*. In fact, the information on a particular flight would be retrieved from persistent memory before being tested and updated in main memory:

if *unbooked-seats* > 0
    then *unbooked-seats* = *unbooked-seats* − 1;

The result would then be written back to persistent memory. The single operation therefore involves a read, modify, and write of persistent memory.

An obvious concern is whether another concurrent process could access the same data object in persistent store at the same time. In the next section we consider one approach to solving this problem. The basic model there is that an application-level service, such as a DBMS, manages the persistent data of the application. We assume that any service of this kind is likely to be multi-threaded; that is, several threads will be executing the service code at a given time, on behalf of different clients.

The persistent data is assumed to be stored in files and the operating system provides file-level concurrency control (see Sections 5.8, 5.12.3). The application service reads any required data from the relevant files into main memory. The application service is therefore in a position to carry out any fine-grained concurrency control that is required; that is, a given data object which is stored as a component of an OS file may be locked by and within the application service on behalf of a client.

In general, a concurrent program may need to access persistent data objects that are stored within operating system files. Let us first assume that the program is seen by the operating system as a single, possibly multi-threaded, process. The

Sections 5.8, 5.12.3 ←

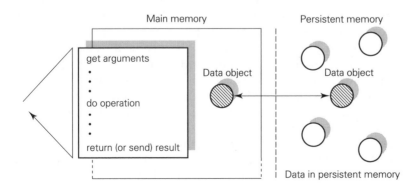

Figure 14.5
An operation on persistent data.

OS sees the process as the unit of resource allocation and will allow any thread of that process to open the files to which it has access rights. The situation is as described above for an application service.

If the concurrent system comprises several (heavyweight) processes, these are seen as separate units of resource allocation by the operating system. The access rights associated with OS files may be set up so that any of the processes comprising the application may read, write and so on. It is the responsibility of the concurrent system developer to organize any required sharing of data objects stored in these files.

The next section highlights the points raised in this discussion. A concurrent system may need to access persistent data stored within OS files and may need to implement atomic operations. Its developer must know in detail how certain functions of the operating system on which it will run are provided.

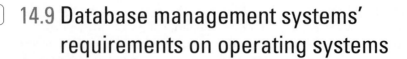

14.9 Database management systems' requirements on operating systems

When a concurrent system which must provide transactions (such as a DBMS) is implemented above a general-purpose OS, the following must be considered:

- the file buffer management policy of the OS;
- the concurrency control facilities provided by the OS.

When the DBMS makes a file-write request, and the OS says 'done', the data must have been written to persistent memory. It is not sufficient for the data to get as far as an OS buffer in volatile main memory. A crash could occur and the data could be lost. In the meantime, the DBMS has told its client that the operation is committed and has no means of effecting this.

As we saw in Chapter 5, a file management system provides facilities for its clients to specify who can use a given file and in what way. Assuming that several users have write access to a given file and are running processes simultaneously, there could be simultaneous requests to open the same file for writing. If the file system has **mandatory concurrency control** (see Section 5.8), then a multiple reader, single writer policy might be enforced, making concurrent write access, or simultaneous read and write access, impossible. The first process to open the file for writing has exclusive access to all of it.

In a centralized system this might work well enough. A client of the filing system that wished to manage a database (the client is a DBMS), and make it available to its own users in turn, would own the files holding the data and would take out a write lock on them. It would then take concurrent requests from users and manage any sharing of small parts of the data. Figure 14.6 shows such a centralized DBMS.

It might be difficult to implement a distributed DBMS in this way, since the several DBMS components would be perceived by the operating system as competing rather than cooperating users of its files. If the filing system has a more

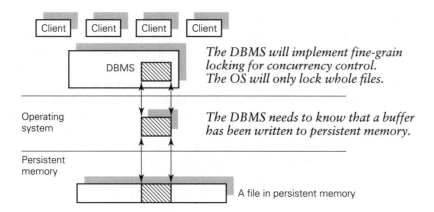

The DBMS *will implement fine-grain locking for concurrency control. The OS will only lock whole files.*

The DBMS *needs to know that a buffer has been written to persistent memory.*

A file in persistent memory

Figure 14.6
A DBMS using an operating system.

enlightened concurrency control policy it might allow its clients to build systems in which concurrent write access is allowed. Operations which lock files might be provided separate from the normal file operations. Shared locks and exclusive locks could be provided without any association with reads and writes. Distributed DBMS components could take out a shared lock and cooperate to ensure that concurrent clients did not access the same part of the data at the same time.

Operating systems may support shared or exclusive locks on whole files, but do not support fine-granularity locking on small portions of files. This is done by the DBMS.

Database management systems are discussed in greater detail in Part III.

14.10 Summary

Computer systems crash and main memory is lost on a crash. If a single operation invocation takes place in the main memory of a single computer and has no externally visible effects then there is no need for crash resilience. If the operation has written to a persistent object we have to decide what to do if there is a crash before it completes. We should design operations to be **idempotent** (repeatable) if it is possible to do so, but this is not always possible.

We defined **atomic operations** on persistent objects as a basis for studying the more general case. An atomic operation either completes successfully, in which case its results are guaranteed to persist, or the system state is restored as though the operation had never been invoked. If you tell a client an operation is done (by output, which is one form of externally visible effect of an operation) then its results must first have been written to persistent memory.

There is a great deal of overhead associated with supporting atomic operations on persistent objects. The system must be able to undo an incomplete operation. Approaches to achieving this were outlined, but more detail will be given in Part III.

We considered what is meant by a 'single operation' on persistent data. In Section 8.8 a read–modify–write sequence of operations on data in main memory was shown to comprise a single operation, such as 'book a seat'. The point made there was that several reads and writes of data in main memory may be necessary to achieve a change to a data object. The additional point made in this chapter is that unless the result of the operation is recorded in persistent memory a crash might destroy any record that the operation ever took place (even though the client has been notified that the seat is booked). Computers crash, so we must use persistent store to implement atomic operations on persistent data.

Access to persistent data is likely to be via an operating system and concurrent write sharing of OS files (introduced in Chapter 5) was revisited. The DBMS will manage fine-grained component locking within a file whereas the OS is concerned only with whole file locking. If atomic operations are to be supported, the DBMS must know when data has been written to persistent memory by the OS.

The final chapter of Part II discusses a single operation invoked from a remote machine. In this case it is necessary to consider the possibility that either the invoking system or the system containing the invoked operation might crash at any time.

Study questions

S 14.1

What is an externally visible effect? Explain, giving an example, why such effects are significant when a crash occurs.

S 14.2

What is the fail–stop model of a crash? Why is such a model inadequate?

S 14.3

If a program runs on a single machine, a failure occurs and no externally visible effects have been caused, the program can simply be restarted. Why?

S 14.4

What is an atomic operation invocation on a persistent object in a concurrent setting?

S 14.5

For crash resilience, what must be done when an atomic operation aborts?

S 14.6

In logging, what might happen if log information is written to the persistent store after the data updated by the atomic operation is written there?

S 14.7

What is shadowing? What essential feature is required to ensure that shadowing is implemented successfully?

S 14.8

A DBMS will normally 'sit on top' of an operating system. What is the main problem that occurs in this situation?

S 14.9

If an operating system supports mandatory concurrency control, what difficulty occurs in the implementation of a distributed DBMS? What might be an answer to this problem?

Exercises

14.1 (a) How do you think an operating system which has bugs and is about to crash might behave differently from the fail–stop model described in Section 14.2?

(b) Why is it unlikely that an operating system that is about to crash will write all over the disks it manages?

(c) Is it more likely that an operating system that is about to crash will write all over main memory? Note that such erroneous writes may be to non-volatile memory that is being used as a cache for data and metadata waiting to be written to disk. How could it be made less likely that a non-volatile cache would be corrupted in this way?

14.2 Define 'idempotent operation' and 'atomic operation'. Give examples of operations that can and cannot be made idempotent. How can an operation that cannot be made idempotent be made atomic? Consider objects that reside only in memory and objects that reside in persistent memory.

14.3 How would you support atomic operations in a system which updates persistent data values 'in place'; that is, the new values overwrite the old values in the persistent store?

14.4 What is meant by a shadow copy of a portion of a filing system?

15

Distributed IPC

15.1 Introduction

In Chapter 2 we set up a context of modular software. In Chapter 6 we studied distributed systems in general terms, introducing the model of a distributed software system, its architecture and how it might be engineered. In Chapter 12 we explored IPC and system structure, contrasting the style of system design where processes inhabit separate address spaces, and IPC is via cross-address-space message passing, with that where processes share an address space and synchronize their activities via monitors. We saw that in general terms the functionality that can be built with one style of system design can also be built with the other. Chapter 24 gives a broad coverage of the design of middleware and currently available middleware systems. In this chapter we will discuss some of the issues that arise when a modular software system is distributed over several computers and the active processes that execute it need to interoperate.

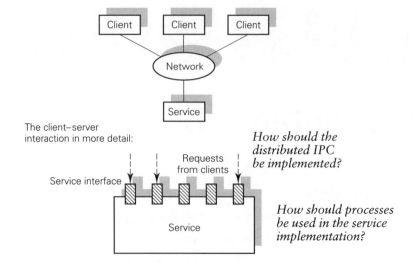

Section 8.1

Figure 15.1
Client–server
interaction in a
distributed system.

Figure 15.1 gives the general context of a number of clients invoking a service across a network. The questions that arise from the figure are:

- How should the service be implemented in terms of concurrent processes? Ideally, for a substantial service, we should like to use a multi-threaded process with threads that are known to the operating system.
- How should the distributed service invocation be implemented? In previous chapters we have studied methods of service invocation without specifically relating them to a centralized or distributed implementation. We now focus on distributed IPC.
- How is the IPC integrated with the lower levels of communications service provided by the operating system?

In this chapter we attempt to answer all of these questions.

15.2 Special characteristics of distributed systems

In Section 6.5 we discussed the fundamental properties of distributed computations: concurrent execution of their components, independent failure modes, lack of global time and inconsistent state. The issue of main concern in this chapter is that a component of a distributed computation may fail while other components continue to run, or a component may be unreachable because of a connection failure. In a centralized implementation the whole system fails together.

In a distributed system a process on one node may invoke an operation on another which, in turn, may invoke an operation on a third node, as shown in Figure 15.2 Any one of these nodes may crash independently of the others

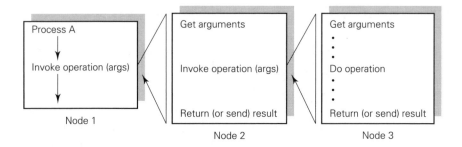

Figure 15.2
A nested invocation.

at any stage in the invocations. Also, the network connections between the nodes may fail while the nodes continue to run. When programming distributed software it is therefore necessary to allow for the fact that a call to a remote system may never return, if the system or connection has failed, or may take a long time if the system or connection is congested.

15.3 Distributed IPC: Message passing

15.3.1 Distributing IPC

Figure 12.4 summarizes the styles of inter-process communication mechanism that can be used for operation invocation. Chapter 11 discussed in detail the shared-address-space mechanisms illustrated in parts (a) and (b) of the figure and Chapter 13 expanded on parts (c) and (d). It is easy to see how to distribute the cross-address-space IPC of Figure12.4(c) and (d): the address spaces of the communicating processes may naturally reside on separate computers and the messages that pass between them must be sent via network communications services.

In this book we do not attempt to distribute Figure 12.4(a) and (b) directly, although it is possible to create the illusion of a single large address space spanning several computers. A number of 'distributed shared memory' (DSM) systems have been built by research teams; an internet search will yield a large number of projects. Instead, as well as distributed message passing, we will study the more general remote procedure call (RPC) mechanism which has led to international middleware standards and products. For RPC we assume an address space, on one computer, for the calling process and another address space, on a different computer, for a process managing the called procedure. The procedure call and return arguments are packaged into messages by the RPC service, which exists on every computer hosting the distributed system, and the messages are sent via cross-network communication. Details of RPC, including the handling of failures, are given in Section 15.7.

A design decision for a distributed IPC scheme is whether the fact that processes are distributed is transparent to the application, by which we mean that a process which communicates with another process does not have to know whether it is on the same machine or not. If distribution transparency is not

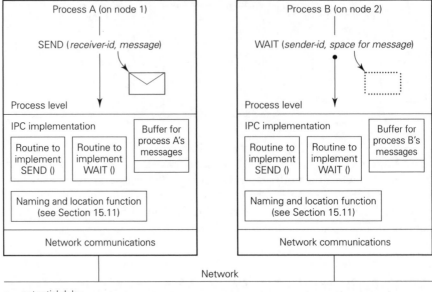

Figure 15.3
Distributed message
passing.

• = potential delay

provided another design decision relates to location transparency; that is, whether the location (host address) of the recipient of IPC must be known by the sender. The example in Section 15.5 illustrates a scheme which is not location transparent. We now consider how a distribution-transparent message passing mechanism might be designed.

15.3.2 Distributed, asynchronous message passing

Figure 13.3 shows asynchronous, cross-address-space message passing on a single node, indicating an implementation level with routines to effect the SEND and WAIT primitives and a data structure for buffering the messages sent to process B. In a single node we can assume that the IPC implementation knows the name of the destination of any message and can deliver the message. We now develop a distributed message passing system, starting from this centralized design.

Figure 15.3 shows one approach to implementing distributed asynchronous message passing. The IPC management function is extended to invoke network communication. Process A now runs on node 1 and SENDs a message to process B which is on node 2. Process B WAITs for a message from process A. We assume that the IPC implementation on node 1 can detect that process B is not a local process and either knows or can find out that process B resides on node 2. There are several ways in which this **naming and location function** can be provided in a distributed system, and we return to the topic in Section 15.11.

The implementation of a SEND message on node 1 can invoke network communication software to transmit the message to node 2. The network communication software on node 2 can receive the message from the network, and

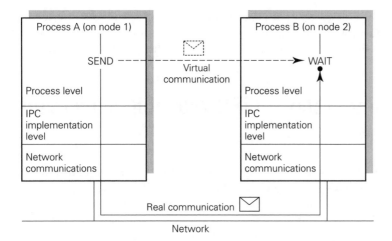

Figure 15.4
Virtual and real communication paths.

pass it to the IPC mechanism for delivery to the message buffer of process B. Figure 15.4 gives a higher-level view of the same procedure, showing virtual communication at the process level being implemented by real communication through the supporting levels and across the network. Recall that network communications software was discussed briefly in Chapter 3.

The basic approach illustrated here may be used to distribute any form of IPC transparently to the application. Here we have assumed that the kernel IPC implementation determines that a communication is to a non-local process and itself takes action to locate the destination. An alternative approach is used in the Accent and Mach kernels, where the kernel detects a non-local communication and passes the message to a local process which is responsible for all network communication, the *NetServer* process. The basic idea is illustrated in Figure 15.5. The IPC implementation now handles only local communication and the *NetServer* process acts as an indirection for remote communication. An advantage of this approach is that the kernel is kept simple. A disadvantage is the extra context switching and message passing between user-level processes

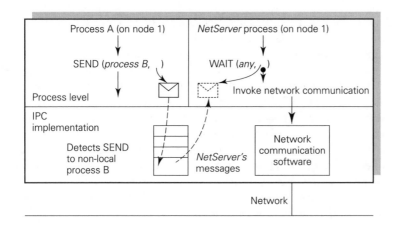

Figure 15.5
Using a process to handle remote communication.

(A and the *NetServer*) that is needed to send a message to a non-local process. Incoming messages are passed by the communications software to the *NetServer* process, which can use a local SEND to deliver them to their intended destination.

15.4 Integration of IPC with communications

15.4.1 IPC above sockets

A socket is the operating system provided interface to communications services. In this section we see the system calls that any IPC support package, for example **java.net,** makes on behalf of the distributed system programmer. An example of Java socket programming is given in Section 15.5. In later sections we see how higher levels of abstraction are provided for the programmer.

The basic concepts at the operating system interface for integrating IPC with communications software are:

- **socket**: an endpoint of communication;
- **domain**: within which sockets are named and communication takes place. A socket operates in a single domain and the address format of the socket depends on that domain. Each domain employs a single protocol suite.

Many domains are possible, for example, the internet domain (AF-INET) in which protocols such as TCP and UDP over IP are used (see Section 3.9). The address formats are internet addresses comprising a 32-bit host identifier and a 32-bit port identifier.

There are several types of socket. Each type may or may not be implemented in a given communication domain. Our Java socket example uses the stream socket.

- A **stream socket** provides a reliable duplex data stream, a 'virtual circuit' in communications terminology. There are no record boundaries within the byte stream. In the UNIX domain a pipe may be implemented as a pair of sockets of this type (two communication endpoints). In the INET domain the TCP protocol supports this socket type.
- A **sequenced packet socket** is used in the NS domain, supported by the sequenced packet protocol. These sockets are like stream sockets but, in addition, record boundaries are provided.
- A **datagram socket** will transfer a message of variable size in either direction. This is an unreliable datagram service; that is, there is no guarantee that the order of sending will be preserved on receipt and a datagram might be lost. This type is supported by UDP (the user datagram protocol) in the internet domain.
- A **reliably delivered message socket** is defined to provide a reliable datagram service and guarantees delivery of a message.
- A **raw socket** allows direct access by processes to the protocols that support the other socket types. This is intended for use in developing new protocols. For example, a new protocol suite to support lightweight connections (a service between streams and datagrams) for multimedia working could be developed above the Ethernet protocol.

A socket is used via a descriptor which is created by:

socket-descriptor = **socket** (*domain, socket type, protocol*)

The newly created socket must have a name for another process to use it, for example, a port number.

bind (*socket-descriptor, pointer to name, length of name in bytes*)

The **close** system call closes a connection and destroys a socket, whereas the **shutdown** call allows one direction of the duplex connection to be closed. There are other calls such as **getsockname, getsockopt** and **setsockopt**.

We now look at how connection-oriented communication may be set up. We first show a connection between two processes and then show how a server may have simultaneous connections to a number of clients. After that we show how connectionless communication can be set up using sockets.

Pairwise connection

Two processes which wish to communicate must each create sockets and bind names to them. To establish connection:

connect (*socket-descriptor, pointer to name, length of name in bytes*)

indicates a local descriptor and remote socket name. When both processes have executed **connect** the communication can proceed.

An example of a one-to-one communication is as follows:

ProcessA:
    sA-id = **socket** (*AF-INET, stream, default-TCP*)
        bind (*sA-id, <A-socket-name>*)

ProcessB:
    sB-id = **socket** (*AF-INET, stream, default-TCP*)
        bind (*sB-id, <B-socket-name>*)

ProcessA:
        connect (*sA-id, <B-socket-name>*)

ProcessB:
        connect (*sB-id, <A-socket-name>*)

Client–server interaction via connection-oriented communication

In the case of a client–server interaction, the clients will know the name of the server, for example, a well-known port number, but not vice versa. Two additional system calls are provided:

listen (*socket-descriptor, queue-length*)

which the server executes to tell the kernel that it is ready to accept calls for service. It also indicates how many requests the kernel should allow to accumulate.

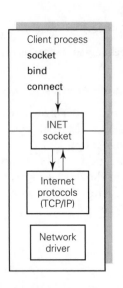

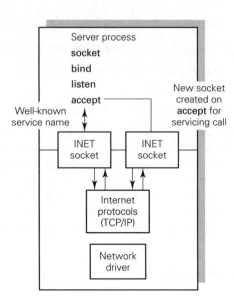

Figure 15.6
Client–server
interaction using
sockets.

new-socket-descriptor = **accept** (*socket-descriptor*)

which allows the server to take a single request for connection from a client. A new socket is created for that client.

An example of a client–server interaction is as follows:

Client processC:
    sC-id = **socket** (*AF-INET, stream, default-TCP*)
        bind (*sC-id, <Client-socket-name>*)

Server processS:
    sS-id = **socket** (*AF-INET, stream, default-TCP*)
        bind (*sS-id, <Server-socket-name>*)

ProcessC:
        connect (*sC-id, <Server-socket-name>*)

ProcessS:
        listen (*sS-id, <queue-length>*)

    sN-id = **accept** (*sS-id*)

Figure 15.6 shows a client–server interaction. The server creates and binds a name to a socket to function as the 'well-known' address of the service. A client **connects** to that well-known name. An example of such a name is port 80 at the host's IP address on which web services conventionally listen.

Connectionless communication

For connectionless communication, datagram sockets are used as follows:

$$byte\text{-}count = \textbf{sendto} \ (socket \ descriptor, \ data\text{-}buffer\text{-}pointer \ and \ length,$$
$$address\text{-}buffer\text{-}pointer \ and \ length)$$
$$byte\text{-}count = \textbf{recvfrom} \ (socket \ descriptor, \ data\text{-}buffer\text{-}pointer \ and \ length,$$
$$address\text{-}buffer\text{-}pointer \ and \ length)$$

The number of bytes transferred is returned in each case. The address buffer contains the destination address, for example the host IP address and the port number, on **sendto** and the source address is supplied by the system on **recvfrom**.

Any style of process interaction can be built above connectionless communication. For **client–server** programming it avoids the restriction on the number of clients a server may handle simultaneously. Nevertheless, connections are often set up for the purpose of a single client–server, request–response interaction, after which they are torn down; the example in Section 15.5 is like this. A well-known example is given in Chapter 23 where we see the HTTP protocol built above TCP connections.

15.5 Java's sockets and streams

In this section we give an example of client–server programming in Java over connection-oriented communication. We see how the java.net package supports the development of such systems; the full detail of connection management, as described above in Section 15.4, is done on behalf of the programmer. The programmer is aware of the socket abstraction but is shielded from some of the detail of socket programming.

Figure 15.7 shows a client and server program (application) executing on two different **host machines**, communicating with each other via layers of standard networking software and a physical connection. Note that for each host machine, the other machine will be considered a **remote machine** (or remote host). The server's **name** is a port name plus its host name (either a name under which the machine is registered in the DNS or an IP address that has been assigned to it). This name is bound to the server's socket and a two-way connection is set up between client and server, as decribed in Section 15.4. The connection provides an input and output stream for both client and server to enable data to be transferred between them. Figure 15.11 gives a high-level view.

We will now discuss a very simple client–server system from the world of bank accounts, in which clients can receive information about the latest rate of interest. In this system:

- the server, which runs indefinitely, called InterestRateServer waits for a client to connect, and then sends it the current interest rate obtained from an object of the class InterestRate. The server is a simple sequential server and does not create separate threads to deal with different clients; each interaction is very short.
- a client connects to the InterestRateServer, reads the message it receives back from the server and prints it to the screen. Note that the client does not send an explicit request to the server: the server is programmed to react to the setting up of the connection. After the interest rate is sent the connection is closed by the server.

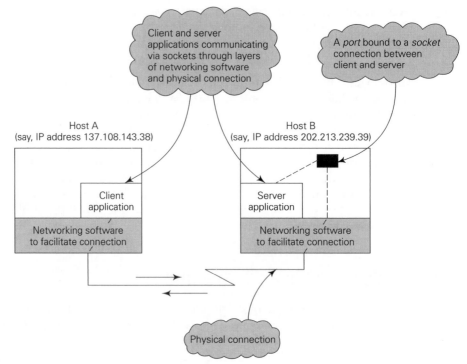

Figure 15.7
An abstract
architecture for a
client–server system.

Figure 15.8
Code for
InterestRateServer,
using sockets.

```
import java.net.*;
public class InterestRateServer {
//...
//...
static final public int portNumber = 4200;
InterestRate currentRate = new InterestRate(5.5);

    public InterestRateServer()throws IOException {
        ServerSocket server = new ServerSocket(portNumber);
        while (true) {
            Socket sock = server.accept();
            OutputStreamWriter out =
                new OutputStreamWriter(sock.getOutputStream());
            String message ="Current Interest Rate ="+ currentRate.getCurrentRate() ";
            out.write(message);
            out.close();
        }
    }
}
```

The code for the server and the client is provided in Figures 15.8 and 15.9 respectively. In Figure 15.10 we show the code for the class **InterestRate** in this client–server system. Note that this is a very simplified example, and that in a real banking system matters would be organized very differently.

The computers on which the client and server reside have been excluded from Figure 15.11 since the focus is on the connection being made between the client

```
import java.net.*;
public class InterestRateClient {
//...
//...
    static final public int portNumber = 4200;

    public InterestRateClient( )throws IOException {
        Socket sock = new Socket(InetAddress.getByName("202.213.239.39"), portNumber);
        Reader isread = new InputStreamReader(sock.getInputStream());
        BufferedReader input = new BufferedReader(isread);
        System.out.println("message is " + input.readLine());
    }
}
```

Figure 15.9
Code for
InterestRateClient,
using sockets.

```
public class InterestRate {

    double currentRate = 0;

    public InterestRate(double cr) {
        currentRate = cr;
    }

    public void setCurrentRate (double sr) {
        currentRate = sr;
    }

    public double getCurrentRate (){
        return currentRate;
    }
}
```

Figure 15.10
Class InterestRate.

and server programs. The figure shows pictorially how the client and server are connected by 'plugging' together (joining) their respective sockets. It also indicates the way in which the message is sent from the server to the client via the two shaded streams (i.e. the output stream of the server's socket and the input stream of the client's socket). Section 15.4 has already introduced the system calls associated with sockets. Exercise 15.5 invites the reader to explore how an application-level abstraction of socket connection is implemented by calls to the client and server's operating systems.

Each program has a socket and each socket is associated with two streams: one for output and the other for input. In Figure 15.11, the server is shown using its socket's output stream (shaded) to write the message. The client, in turn, uses its socket's input stream (shaded) to read the message. The client then outputs this message to the screen (not shown).

When the server sends a message to the client (or vice versa), you should think of it as a two-stage process. The server uses its *output* stream to send the message to a sink (not shown in Figure 15.11). The client in turn must use its *input* stream to fetch the message from this sink (which, for the client, is now a source). This sink/source can be thought of as a 'pigeon-hole' or 'mailbox' into which the server drops a message and from which the client retrieves it.

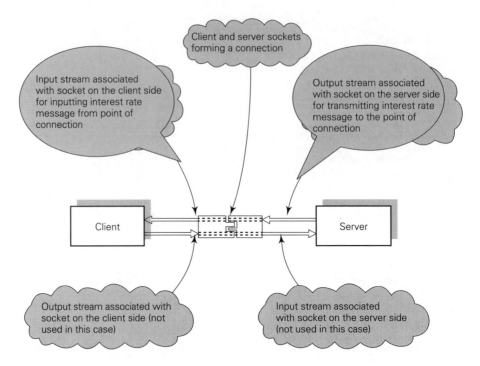

Figure 15.11
Abstract view of
connection between
client and server.

Communication in the opposite direction will work in exactly the same way, but with a *separate* pigeon-hole. All the details needed to implement such a model are, of course, hidden from the programmer.

15.5.1 The java.net package

The **java.net** package is relatively large, and here only a few of the classes will be examined, those used for building connection-oriented, client–server systems. It is interesting to compare these Java classes with the socket system calls provided by the operating system and described in Section 15.4. The **InterestRate** client–server system relies on **Socket**, **ServerSocket**, and **InetAddress**. A few additional remarks about these classes should be helpful.

- **InetAddress**
  An object of this class is used to represent an internet address.
  It has no public constructors. Instead it uses **public static** methods that return an internet address when used anywhere in a program. The method **getByName (String host)**, returns an **InetAddress** object representing the address of the host specified by name. Note that this method throws **UnknownHostException** if the name presented to it cannot be resolved to an internet address; it must be used within a suitable **try** statement.
- **Socket**
  An object of this class is used to establish a **connection** (sometimes referred to as a **socket connection**) between client and server processes. Its constructor

methods (it has more than one) associate a new socket (sometimes referred to as a **connection socket**) with a specified host (IP address) and host port. The client and the server must each construct a socket, so that the connection can be thought of as being made by these two sockets joining together.

In Java, a socket object is also associated with both an input and an output stream to enable data to be communicated via the connection. This means that the client process, say, can send data to the server via the output stream associated with the client's socket, which the server can receive via the input stream associated with the server's socket, and vice versa.

- ServerSocket

  An object of this class (not to be confused with the class **Socket**) is used by a server to 'listen' for connection requests from clients, and then establish a socket connection with each client. A **ServerSocket** object must be associated with a port (in Figures 15.8 and 15.9 this is 4200) where it can listen for a request using the method **accept ()**. The method **accept ()** has a dual function: it not only listens for a client request, but when this is received, returns a socket (of type **Socket**) for the server, which is connected to the client's socket. Note that **accept ()** throws an exception and therefore must be called within a **try** statement.

It is easy to confuse the various terms associated with the above classes, in particular, a **ServerSocket** object with the server's **Socket** object. The former does not have input and output streams: its role is to provide the facilities to listen for a client's request and then to create the server's **Socket** object, which is connected to the client's **Socket** object.

15.5.2 The **InterestRate** client (Figure 15.9)

To connect to the **InterestRateServer** shown in Figure 15.8, the client program shown in Figure 15.9 attempts to create a connection socket associated with the host (with IP address "202.213.239.39", assuming that that is the server's IP address) at port 4200. If there is a server 'listening' at this port to accept the request, the input stream associated with this socket will be used as the basis for inputting the server's interest rate message, and outputting it to the terminal.

15.5.3 The client–server mechanism and asynchronous message passing

The example above has shown how a distributed, client–server architecture can be built using asynchronous message passing, similar to Figure 12.4(c). We gave a simple example in which only a single message passes: that from the server to the client. Also, the message passing was built above connection-oriented communication, with sockets as communication endpoints and input and output streams at the client and server. A connection must be set up between each client and the server.

If a connection is set up for a single request–response interaction, after which it is closed, this is a heavyweight mechanism. In general, once a connection is set up it can be used for any number of interactions. It is a design issue whether a server can support long-lasting connections to all its clients, depending on the number of clients and the nature of the service. Connectionless communication is an alternative, as discussed in Section 15.4.

Once a connection is set up the communication along it is asynchronous: a sending process can write data at any time without checking the status of the receiver, and does not have to wait for the response until it is ready. The receiving process may be doing some other task at the moment the data is transmitted, and may read the message later when it is ready to do so. Although we do not see it explicitly, the socket mechanism provides for message buffering at the recipient. The server must indicate how many outstanding client calls are to be buffered as part of connection set up. Notice that the server's name, the port and host IP address, is location dependent.

15.6 Distributed programming paradigms

15.6.1 Synchronous and asynchronous communication

An advantage of the asynchronous communication style is that when a process makes a remote service request it is not blocked, but it can continue with other processing in parallel until it requires a reply message. A disadvantage of this style of communication is that it is difficult to get right, and prone to errors especially when implemented above connectionless communication, unlike the above example. In the following sections we will discuss synchronous communication, where the process that invokes the method is blocked, as in a local method invocation. This is generally considered to be easier to use as it is at a higher level of abstraction, akin to method invocation in a programming language.

As shown in Chapter 8, however, we can have the best of both worlds if we have a FORK primitive available: that is, the ability to create a new process dynamically. A child process can be forked to make the remote invocation and WAIT for the result, after which it can synchronize with its parent in the usual way to pass the result. The parent can proceed with parallel work which might include forking more children to make more remote invocations. Note that it is necessary for the application to run on a kernel which supports multi-threaded processes to achieve concurrent execution of the parent with the blocked child. This is because if the kernel does not support multi-threaded processes, and one of the threads (i.e. a child process) belonging to a parent process were to block for remote communication, the operating system would consider the parent process (including all its threads) to be blocked as well.

Section 4.17

A way of viewing this model is that concurrency and distribution issues have been separated. Concurrency has been achieved by having two processes: the parent and the child it creates using the FORK primitive. Distributed programming is carried out by the child forked for the purpose.

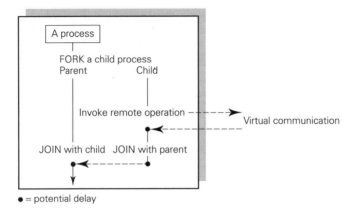

Figure 15.12
Forking a child to make a synchronous call.

15.6.2 Procedural versus message passing style

The processes involved in a remote invocation are certainly running in separate address spaces as they are on different machines. One might therefore assume that message passing of some kind would be the best programming model for distributed IPC. We have just argued, however, that a synchronous model is preferable for manageable remote communication. This could be achieved by enforcing that a SEND request is immediately followed by a WAIT reply, perhaps by inventing a single primitive which combines them. This is done in the Amoeba distributed operating system and is the only communication paradigm supported in that system.

An alternative is to remain within the procedural system structure, and to support a procedure call to a *remote* procedure. In a local procedure call (or method invocation) the calling process passes data to the procedure via the procedure's arguments, the procedure is then executed, and the results are passed back to the caller, which then continues its execution. In a remote procedure call, the call is made to a procedure located on a machine that is different (remote) from the machine from which the call was made, yet the arguments can be type-checked as before. This is an attractive notion, since procedural programming languages are in widespread use. A facility for distributed sequential programming could be offered by this means for those users who do not have a requirement for concurrent programming but who need to make use of remote services. It can be incorporated into a concurrent programming language, as outlined above in Section 15.6.1.

A further attraction of such remote procedure call (RPC) systems, is that they provide the programmer with a higher-level mechanism, which is much easier to use. Compared with the use of sockets and unstructured data streams, or even asynchronous message passing, a call to a method or procedure which happens to be remote is much less problematic.

For these reasons a great deal of effort has been directed towards RPC systems. Several became available as products as early as the 1980s, such as Xerox Courier and Sun RPC. Some, such as ANSA (1989), led to standards to run above a wide variety of operating system and communications services (ISO, 1992). Others were part of research projects and were integrated into high-level language systems, such as CCLU RPC, developed at Cambridge University, UK (Bacon and Hamilton, 1987). More recently, emerging from within the object-oriented paradigm, Java's Remote Method Invocation (RMI) mechanism is becoming increasingly popular in business and industry.

15.7 Remote procedure call (RPC)

An RPC system consists of a communications protocol, which typically sits on top of a transport-level service, such as the ARPA (TCP-UDP)/IP hierarchy, and language-level routines concerned with assembling the data to be passed by the protocol. It is also necessary to provide a mechanism for binding remote procedure names to network addresses. This is the requirement for a naming and location function that we saw when we distributed a message passing system in Section 15.3.1. An overview of a typical RPC system will now be given, followed by a discussion of alternative ways in which this service might be provided.

15.7.1 An RPC system

Figure 15.13 outlines system components that are invoked when a remote procedure call is made. Binding remote procedure names to addresses is not shown. A request–reply–acknowledge (RRA) protocol is assumed. An alternative is request–acknowledge–reply–acknowledge (RARA). In the former case it is assumed that the reply is likely to come back sufficiently quickly to function as an acknowledgement of the request.

Before looking at the details of Figure 15.13, we note that the system structure is similar to that described for Figure 12.4(b), but now in a distributed context. That is, the calling process (located on one machine) has to wait until the

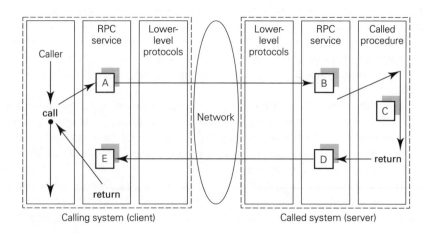

Figure 15.13
An RPC system.

response from the procedure call comes back (from the process on the other machine), before it can continue processing. Given that the system structure is now distributed, the possibility of delay has increased, as the procedure call may experience all kinds of network problems.

First the operation of the RPC protocol when client, server and network are performing well will be described. In this case a procedure call is made which is detected (by some means, which will be discussed in Section 15.8) to be a remote procedure call. Arguments are specified as usual. Control passes to point A in the diagram.

At point A:

- the arguments are packed into a data structure suitable for transfer across the network as a message or packet;
- an RPC identifier is generated for this call;
- a timer is set.

The data is then passed to lower protocol levels for transportation across the network. Typically, this is done by making a system call into the kernel, as described in Section 15.4. At the called system the lower levels deliver it up to the RPC service level.

At point B:

- the arguments are unpacked from the network buffer data structure in a form suitable for making a local procedure call;
- the RPC identifier is noted.

The call is then made to the required remote procedure, which is executed at C. The return from the procedure is to the calling environment in the RPC system, point D.

At point D:

- the return arguments are packed into a network buffer;
- another timer is set.

On arrival at the calling system's RPC service level, point E:

- the return arguments are unpacked;
- the timer set at point A is disabled;
- an acknowledgement is sent for this RPC ID (the timer at D can then be disabled).

15.7.2 The RPC protocol with network or server congestion

The systems involved in the RPC may be performing badly or the network may be congested or suffer a transient failure, causing the timers at A or D to expire. The RPC service level at the calling system, point A, may retry the call a few times without involving the application level. If the problem was network congestion the request may or may not have got through to the called system, depending on the service offered by the lower-level protocols. The RPC ID is used by the called system to detect a repeated call. If the call is still in progress it need take no action. If a reply has been sent it can be resent in case of loss. The actions described here can be called 'EXACTLY ONCE RPC semantics' in the absence of node crashes or prolonged network failure. That is, EXACTLY ONCE RPC semantics ensures that, in the absence of failures, a request is carried out once and only once. It is the nature of distributed systems that failures can occur and sometimes it is impossible to make remote calls. In this case an exception return is made.

In some RPC systems the user is given a choice of RPC semantics. 'AT MOST ONCE semantics' means that as soon as the timeout at A expires, control is returned to the application level. The protocol does not retry, although the application level is likely to do so. If the application repeats the call, several copies of the same message may arrive at the called system, but with different identifiers and therefore not detectable by the RPC service as the same. The application has caused this situation and must deal with any repeated replies and any effects at the server.

15.7.3 The RPC protocol with node crash and restart

In a local procedure call, caller and called procedures crash together. In a remote procedure call the following possibilities must be considered (the node containing the call is referred to as the client, that containing the called procedure, the server).

Client failure (see Figure 15.14)

The client may fail after sending the request. The remote call will go ahead (termed an **orphan**), as will any further related calls that it may make (more orphans), but the timer at D will expire and no acknowledgement will be received on prompting. The server, and other invoked servers, may have made permanent state changes as a result of the call. Some server operations can be made repeatable (idempotent), recall Section 14.4.

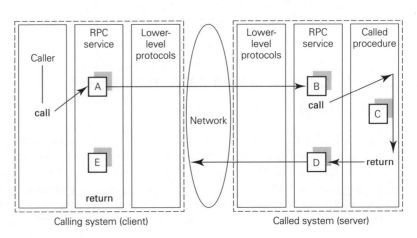

Figure 15.14
Client crash.

The application-level client, on being restarted, may repeat the same call but the repeat cannot be detected as such by the RPC service and a new ID will be generated.

Most RPC systems aim to provide an efficient communication facility and make no attempt to exterminate orphans. Software at higher levels may provide atomic transactions with checkpointing and rollback facilities, as discussed in Chapter 14. The performance penalties associated with such a service can be high and should not be made mandatory for all applications.

Server failure (see Figure 15.15)

The server may fail before the call is received or at some point during the call (in all cases the client timeout at A will expire):

- after the RPC service receives the call but before the call to the remote procedure is made, point B;
- during the remote procedure invocation, C;
- after the remote procedure invocation but before the result is sent, D.

In all cases the client might repeat the call when the server restarts. In cases C and D this could cause problems since the server could have made permanent state changes before crashing. Again, most RPC systems do not attempt to handle rolling back state changes associated with incomplete RPCs before accepting further calls. To do this it would be necessary for the RPC service to retain RPC IDs through crashes. Some form of stable storage could be used or a time-stamp could be included in the ID so that the server could distinguish pre- and post-crash calls and could undo incomplete pre-crash calls.

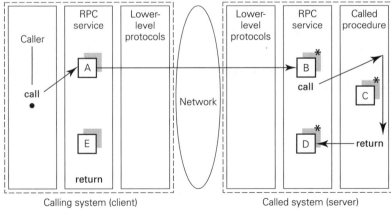

Figure 15.15
Example of a server crash.

✱ = points at which server might crash

15.7.4 An example: CCLU RPC call semantics

The CCLU RPC programmer has a choice of call semantics. The default is the lightweight MAYBE:

t: *a_type* = **call** *a_remote_proc* (*<args>*)

If the alternative 'reliable' EXACTLY ONCE (in the absence of node crashes) is required, the keyword **zealously** is appended to the call. For example:

call *logger* ('kernel running low on heap') **zealously**

The keyword **timeout**, followed by an integer expression representing a time in milliseconds, may be appended to any remote call. For MAYBE calls, this represents the time after which the call should be abandoned. For EXACTLY ONCE calls it represents the recommended interval between retries.

If an error occurs during execution of a remote call, the RPC will signal either the *hard_error* or *soft_error* exception, together with an error code. *soft_error* is only signalled by the MAYBE call mechanism and indicates that an error has occurred, such as a timeout or apparent congestion at the remote node, but that a retry may succeed. *hard_error* is signalled by both the MAYBE and EXACTLY ONCE options and indicates that an apparently unrecoverable error has occurred, for example, failure to contact the server node or denial by the server node that the called *a_remote_proc* is to be found there.

An exception handler for the MAYBE protocol would have the form:

begin
    .
    t: *a_type* = **call** *a_remote_proc* (*<args>*) **timeout** 2000
    .

end except
    when *problem* (*p: problem*):
    ... // exception signalled by the remote procedure
    when *hard_error* (*why: int*):
    ... // not worth retrying
    when *soft_error* (*why: int*):
    ... // worth retrying a few times
    end

where *problem* is an exception signalled by the remote procedure, for example, because of an incorrect argument value. An example of a remote procedure declaration which includes this exception is given in Section 15.8.1.

15.7.5 RPC and the ISO reference model

Communications protocols were introduced in Chapter 3. Section 3. 9 showed a typical division of the ISO layers between an operating system and the applications it supports. The transport level and below were located in the operating system. Similarly, in Figures 15.13, 15.14 and 15.15 the lower-level protocols are assumed to be those at transport level and below. The discussion above has

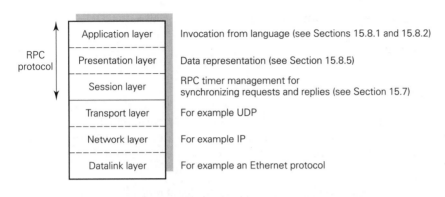

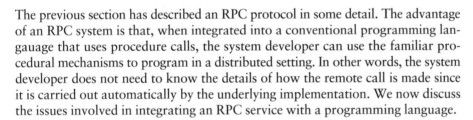

Figure 15.16
RPC in relation to the
ISO reference model
for OSI.

assumed that the RPC protocol is built on an unreliable transport service such as ARPA's UDP rather than a reliable connection-oriented protocol such as TCP. Figure 15.16 shows an RPC protocol in relation to the ISO layers.

The RPC protocol described above has provided a **session-level service**: client and server were synchronized for request, reply and acknowledgement by the use of timers. We now go on to consider the application and presentation levels associated with RPC.

15.8 RPC–language integration

The previous section has described an RPC protocol in some detail. The advantage of an RPC system is that, when integrated into a conventional programming language that uses procedure calls, the system developer can use the familiar procedural mechanisms to program in a distributed setting. In other words, the system developer does not need to know the details of how the remote call is made since it is carried out automatically by the underlying implementation. We now discuss the issues involved in integrating an RPC service with a programming language.

15.8.1 Distribution transparency

A design issue is the extent to which the fact that some procedures are remote is made transparent to the application. One approach is to acknowledge that remote calls are likely to take substantially longer than local ones and that parts of a distributed program may fail separately. It may be argued that distribution transparency should not be a goal. In this case changes can be made to the language, in the syntax for procedure declaration and call, to distinguish procedures that may be called by remote processes and indicate when they are being invoked.

The non-transparent approach

An example of the **non-transparent** approach taken in CCLU is as follows. The definition of a procedure which may be called from a remote node contains the keyword **remoteproc** replacing **proc** in the header. Other aspects remain the same.

a_remote_proc = **remoteproc** (*<args>*)
   returns (*a_type*)
   signals (*problem*)

   .

   .

end *a_remote_proc*

A new syntax, the call expression, is used for performing RPCs. The keyword **call** precedes the invoked procedure's name and a number of control keywords (**resignal, zealously, timeout, at**) may follow the invocation's arguments; for example:

v : a_type = **call** *a_remote_proc* (*<args>*) **resignal** *problem*

where *problem* is an exception signalled by the remote procedure, shown in the procedure declaration. (A CLU procedure, both when returning normally and signalling an exception, may return an arbitrary number of results of arbitrary type.)

The transparent approach

The **transparent** approach means that the compiler (or a preprocessor) must detect any call to a non-local procedure. Such a procedure may be remote or non-existent, indicating an error. In order to determine which is the case it is necessary to support a naming service in which procedures available for remote call are registered and can be looked up. For each remote procedure called, a **stub** (sometimes called a **proxy**) is generated so that a local call can be made to it, as shown in Figure 15.17. Thus the RPC support level is called transparently at runtime.

The functions carried out by the stub are required by both transparent and non-transparent RPC systems. The only difference is that when transparency is

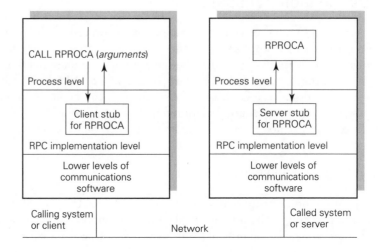

Figure 15.17
Implementation of
transparent RPC.

needed the stub is called as a local procedure with the same name as the remote procedure. The stub controls the assembling of arguments (more on this is given below) and invokes the RPC protocol.

Even if **transparency** is achieved to this extent the call semantics for remote procedures may have to be more restricted than local calls. Some potential problems with **transparent semantics** are as follows:

- What would it mean to pass a reference parameter? In practice, RPC systems have implemented call by copy. (A brief discussion of the way object references are handled in object-oriented systems is given in Section 15.8.3.)

    If the language is such that several concurrent processes may have pointers to an object, and a reference to the object is passed as an argument in a local procedure call, all processes see any change that procedure makes. If the object is copied as an argument for a remote procedure, and the remote procedure changes the object, this is not seen by the local processes. Nor is any change made by a local process during the RPC seen by the remote process. The semantics of the language have been changed by the introduction of RPC.
- Should a call argument that is changed by the remote procedure be passed back as well as the results?

A question that is separate from transparency issues concerns large objects. It might be that only a small part of the object is used by the called procedure. In a local environment a reference parameter would typically be used in these circumstances. Should the whole object be copied and shipped across to the remote node or should it be fetched piecemeal on demand? RPC systems have tended to implement the former, but see below for object systems.

15.8.2 Argument marshalling

Figure 15.18 shows the general approach to packing, flattening or '**marshalling**' **arguments** into a form suitable for transmission via a network buffer. The arguments are data objects that reside in the calling process's stack and heap (see Chapter 4). They must be copied into a data structure that the transmission system handles as a flat byte sequence. Any internal cross-references must be preserved so that the data can be restored at the called node. This is **call by copy semantics**. Pointers (main memory addresses) within the objects must therefore be translated into pointers that are meaningful within the buffer. Any data object that is pointed to more than once need only be copied once into the buffer.

As well as the built-in data types of a language, programmers can generate their own types. Should the language allow such **user-defined types** to be passed as arguments and, if so, how does the system know how to pack them? Many RPC systems only allow the built-in system types to be transported. The Cambridge CCLU system allowed almost all types, including user-defined types, to be passed as RPC arguments. This is possible because each user-defined type can be broken down successively until its component system types are reached, and the system has library routines for marshalling the language's built-in types.

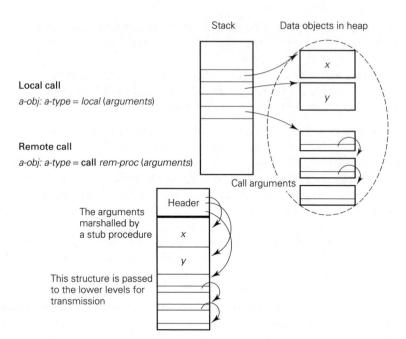

Figure 15.18
Arguments for
local and remote
procedures.

When user-defined types which are to be passed as RPC arguments are declared in CCLU, the user must include a marshal and an unmarshal operation for each such type. All that is necessary is to decompose the type into lower-level components on marshalling and compose it on unmarshalling. An example of an abstract data type (a cluster) *thing* with an internal representation in terms of lower-level types (**rep**) and marshal and unmarshal operations is as follows:

```
thing = cluster ...   // abstract data type thing
    rep =             // the representation of thing in terms of lower-level
                      // (eventually built-in) types and type constructors
        record [v: thing_value,
                l: lock
                       ]
        .
        .
    marshal = proc ( t: thing )          // how to marshal thing for RPC
            returns ( thing_value )
        .
        .
        end marshal;
    unmarshal = proc ( tv: thing_value )  // how to unmarshal on return
            returns ( thing )
        .
        .
        end unmarshal
end thing;
```

15.8.3 Object-oriented systems

So far, we have followed a client–server model, in which objects are created and named by a server and stay within the address space of the server. The server carries out operations on the objects in response to requests from clients. In the more general object model, objects are named globally (system-wide) and are invoked directly; that is, operations are carried out on them directly rather than via a server. Ideally, objects should be able to migrate from node to node but in current middleware object names are location dependent, see Chapter 24.

Chapter 24 →

It is relevant to the discussion in Section 15.8.1 to note that object names are meaningful globally and therefore can be passed as references. It is no longer necessary to make a copy of an object which has a global name in order to pass it as an argument.

Suppose that an object-oriented (OO) system contains an object repository for storing typed objects. Suppose that a process at one node in the system invokes an object which is not in use elsewhere. Typically, that object is mapped into the address space of the invoking process. This involves converting the representation of the object into the form expected by the language system from the form in which it was stored. (Preparing a data object for storage is similar to marshalling it as an RPC argument; see Section 15.8.2.) In addition, the type operations of the object must be associated with it. They are no longer provided by a managing server.

If a process at another node in the system invokes this object, several approaches are possible:

- Only one process has an object mapped. The process which has the object mapped acts as object manager and accepts RPCs to invoke operations on the object. This was done in the Comandos system (Balter *et al.*, 1993).
- Any number of processes may have an object mapped. These copies of the object are regarded as cached copies of the persistent object and a cache coherency protocol is followed by the processes. There must be a policy on how the processes may use the object. It may be that only one at a time may write to the object, or concurrent writes to different parts of the object may be allowed.

This short discussion is included to show that there have been more recent approaches to passing object references than the call by copy semantics described in Section 15.8.2. Also, it should be noted that RPC may still be used within an object-oriented system, as we shall see when discussing Java's RMI in Section 15.9. A case study on the Object Management Group's (OMG) common object request broker architecture (CORBA) is given in Chapter 24.

15.8.4 Type checking and consistency checking

A language may have static, compile-time type checking, in particular of procedure call arguments. Can this be extended for an RPC system? To do so it is necessary to have a specification of any procedure which can be called remotely available for the compiler to look up. A name server or library might be used (see Section 15.11). Many systems have the concept of an interface specification where an interface contains a number of procedures.

A final point concerns the engineering and maintenance of large systems. Any component of a distributed system might be changed and recompiled. It might be that a call to a remote procedure becomes out of date and inconsistent with the new version of the procedure. This can be checked by identifying the version of the remote procedure specification that a given call was type-checked against, keeping this identification with the call and having the system check it at runtime.

15.8.5 Data representation for a heterogeneous environment

The above discussion is based on the implicit assumption that the client and server are written in the same language and run on nodes which use the same internal data representations. We have packed the RPC arguments in the client node and expect the bits to mean the same when they arrive at the server node. This may not always be the case, particularly in large-scale distributed systems. At the lowest level of built-in language data types, from which other types are constructed, we may find differences:

- Integers may be represented differently. In CCLU one bit is used to distinguish between pointers and data. CCLU integers are therefore 31 bits in length, in two's complement representation, instead of the usual 32.
- The floating point formats may differ for different hardware floating point units.
- Characters may be represented differently: although most systems use the ASCII code, some may use Unicode.
- Strings are stored in words in a different order on different machines. For example, using a 32-bit word, the string 'Gulliver's Travels' could be stored either as:
  - Gulliver's Travels (with so-called big-endian byte ordering), or as
  - lluGreviT s'evar sl (with little-endian byte ordering).

If a filename is to be transferred from a client to a file server in a heterogeneous world, the presentation layer must be able to carry out byte reordering when necessary.

A number of external data representations have been defined, for example, Sun's XDR (eXternal Data Representation), Xerox's Courier, and the ISO standard, Abstract Syntax Notation 1 (ASN.1) (ISO, 1986). The idea is to encode a standard set of data types in a way that can be recognized by all systems. Since we are not concerned here with large-scale heterogeneous systems we shall leave this topic for further study.

15.9 Java's RMI: RPC in a distributed object model

The object model of IPC exploits the object-oriented paradigm in which objects invoke the methods of other objects, including those residing on remote machines. Java provides the facilities to implement the object model through a mechanism called **remote method invocation** (RMI). In this section we will discuss the object model through the RMI facilities (contained mainly in the **java.rmi** package) and show how they can be used to develop a simple system based on the object model. We will thus see an example of an RPC system of distributed IPC.

15.9.1 RMI and the general object model

Section 15.5 discussed how Java's streams and sockets can be used to build a client–server model of distributed IPC. The clients are processes (running programs) which reside on one or more host computers, and are able to communicate with a server process running a Java program on its host (which in general is different from the client hosts). The communication between clients and server in this model takes place to a port of the server with client and server sockets as communication endpoints. The messages that make up the communication take the form of streams of data. An application protocol must be established between client and server so that the server knows how to respond to these messages. This means that the messages from the client are not method invocations in the OO sense, but rather a stream of data that must be interpreted by the server before it can invoke methods on the objects it manages.

In the OO paradigm, a client object invokes an object located on a (remote) server host. In fact, the execution of the method takes place on the remote host where the remote object resides. The difference between a client–server model as described above and the OO paradigm might seem slight but it is significant. It is a non-trivial task to program the setting up of communication between clients and a server involving the creation of socket connections and the use of input and output streams. Consider how much easier it would have been in the **InterestRate** example discussed in Section 15.5, if the application programmer could simply have invoked an object of type **InterestRate** (even though it was a remote object). This is what the RMI mechanism seeks to achieve, so that developers can remain within the object-oriented paradigm rather than having to concern themselves with sending messages using streams.

Conceptually, what we want to achieve through RMI is represented in Figure 15.19. This shows a client process made up of many communicating local objects. The local object **O3** is shown invoking the remote object **remO**. The three objects named **O1**, **O2** and **O3** have been created as part of the client process running on Host A (indicated by the dotted lines that associate the client process with the three objects) whereas **remO** has been created as part of the server process running on the remote host, Host B (as shown by the dotted line from the server process). The arrows between objects indicate the direction in which one

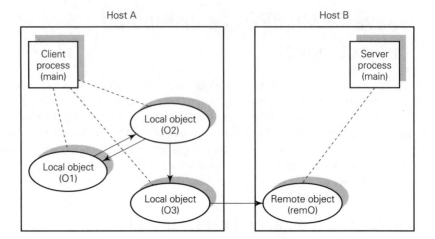

Figure 15.19
A client process
composed of a set
of communicating
objects.

or more method calls are being made. For example, in the figure, object O2
is shown as calling a method or methods of object O3. Note that, although the
direction of the method call is shown as flowing in one direction (in this case
from O2 to O3) the data flow between the objects is likely to be bidirectional, with
input data flowing from O2 to O3, and return data resulting from the call flowing
from O3 to O2; as is always the case in (synchronous) method invocation.

15.9.2 RMI mechanisms

The conceptual view shown in Figure 15.19 brings up the following questions
about the implementation:

1 How are the remote objects created and named?
2 How do the clients learn the names and locations of remote objects?
3 How are invocations made from a local object to a remote object?

The answer to these questions involves a number of mechanisms, some of which
the developer needs to be aware of and others that go on 'below the surface'. An
overall view of these mechanisms is shown in Figure 15.20, where all the new
objects needed for implementing Figure 15.19 are shown *unshaded*, and the
mechanisms not visible at the application level are shown in the shaded areas.
The virtual communications between components are shown dashed (not to be
confused with the dotted lines associating objects with each process); they indicate that, as far as the application is concerned, invocations are made *directly*
on the objects at the other end of the link. However, the implementation of
these virtual communication links by means of real communication links will be
via layers that are not visible to the application. Note that there is a strong
resemblance with Figure 15.17, where we discussed the issue of RPC being
transparent or not.

Figure 15.21 extends Figure 15.20 to show the mechanism by which a client
can discover where a remote object is located: the RMI registry. The registry is a
Java program that keeps a record of where remote objects are kept (it is informed

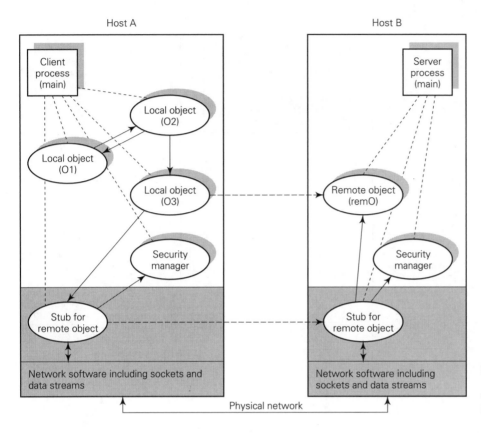

Host A   Host B

Figure 15.20
Implementation
view of the model
in Figure 15.19.

by the server) so that clients can access this information. In general, the registry can be on a third host. In Figure 15.21, one of the application objects (**O1**) of the client process is shown as calling (shown as a virtual method call since it is to a remote machine) the RMI registry in order to obtain a reference to the remote object **remO**.

Figure 15.21 is best explained by showing how it answers the three questions posed above.

1 Before a remote object can be created:
  (a) its operations must be specified in an interface which extends the interface **Remote** from the **java.rmi** package;
  (b) the remote object's class, **RemObjImpl** say, must then be defined by implementing this interface and extending the class **UnicastRemoteObject** (in the **java.rmi.server** package).

For a discussion on interfaces and their implementation as used in Java, see Sections 2.2.2 and 2.2.3. An object of the class **RemObjImpl**, **remO** say, can then be declared and created. To make **remO** available to clients, it must be registered in an **RMI registry** using a string name as an identifier. This registry can either be located on the same host as the remote object or, as shown in Figure 15.21, on another host.

2 Clients find out about remote objects by looking in the RMI registry, where each server will have placed information about the remote objects it has

Host A   Host B

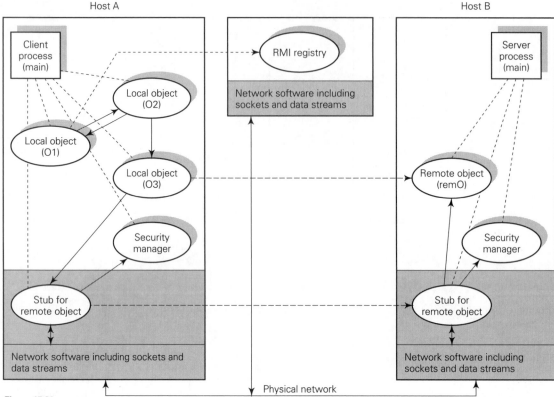

Figure 15.21
RMI registry.

created. The RMI registry is itself a remote server-object. Typically, the RMI registry is accessed via the methods of the **Naming** class. To find a remote object, the developer of a client application must know:

(a)   the location of the RMI registry;

(b)   the string name of **remO**.

In order to obtain a reference to **remO**, the client application can invoke an operation on the RMI registry using the string name as a key. Provided **remO** is in the registry under this name, a reference to it will be returned.

3 In fact, the reference which is returned by the RMI registry is to a **stub** object, a copy of which must be placed on both the client's machine and the server's machine. On the client host, this stub object acts as a **proxy** for the remote object, and the method invocations that the client thinks it is making on the remote object are in fact calls to the stub. The stub on the client, in turn, communicates with a similar stub object on the remote machine. It is the stub on the server's machine that then communicates the call to the remote object itself. One of the important tasks of stubs is to marshal and unmarshal the arguments in the remote call and the return value sent back by the remote object. The stubs use Java's client–server mechanism involving sockets and input and output streams but this is invisible to the developers of the client and server processes.

In Figure 15.21, objects called **security managers** are shown. Similar to the security systems that control applets, RMI security managers control what remote objects and their clients can do.

15.9.3 RMI: An example

We shall now see an example of RMI through the construction of a simple system, again based on the InterestRate example discussed in Section15.5, where a client can be informed of the latest interest rate. Given that we are working on exactly the same problem, it should be possible to draw some clear comparisons between the client–server approach as built in Section 15.5, and the RMI approach.

In the previous section (under point 1) it was outlined that when using remote objects, we need to separate the object into its interface and the implementation of that interface. The idea is that a client (a user of a remote object) needs only to know about the interface of the remote object's class whereas the server (the implementor of the remote object) needs to know about both the interface and the implementation of the class.

The class InterestRate, as shown in Figure 15.10, can be rewritten as shown in Figures 15.22 and 15.23.

The stub classes that a client uses to access a particular server must usually be generated using facilities provided by the development environment. The exact way in which this is done varies between systems, but usually a tool such as

```
import java.rmi.*;

public interface InterestRate extends Remote{
public void setCurrentRate (double sr) throws RemoteException;
public double getCurrentRate() throws RemoteException;
}
```

Figure 15.22
The interface for class InterestRate.

```
import java.rmi.*;
import java.rmi.server.*;

public class InterestRateImpl extends UnicastRemoteObject implements InterestRate {

    double currentRate = 0;

    public InterestRateImpl(double cr) throws RemoteException{
        currentRate = cr;
    }

    public void setCurrentRate (double sr) throws RemoteException {
        currentRate = sr;
    }

    public double getCurrentRate () throws RemoteException{
        return currentRate;
    }
}
```

Figure 15.23
The implementation for Remote Object InterestRate.

```
import java.rmi.*;
public class InterestRateServer {
    public static void main(String[] args) {
        InterestRateServer irs = new InterestRateServer();
    }
    public InterestRateServer() {
        try {
            InterestRate ir = new InterestRateImpl (5.5);
            Naming.rebind ("rmi://aServerName/CurrentInterestRate", ir);
            System.out.println("Remote object registered");
        }
        catch (Exception e) {System.out.println("Trouble: " + e);}
    }
}
```

Figure 15.24
The server registers
the remote object
with the RMI registry.

```
import java.rmi.*;
public class InterestRateClient {
    public InterestRate ir;
    public InterestRateClient() {
        try{
        ir = (InterestRate)
            Naming.lookup("rmi://aServerName/CurrentInterestRate");
        System.out.println("Current Interest Rate = " + ir.getCurrentRate());
        }
        catch (Exception e) {System.out.println(e);}
    }
    public static void main(String[] args) {
        InterestRateClient irc = new InterestRateClient();
    }
}
```

Figure 15.25
Client can look up
remote object in RMI
registry, and use it.

rmic must be used. The next step is to ensure that the remote object is created and registered with the RMI registry. This is the task of the server, as shown in Figure 15.24. In particular the line:

Naming.rebind ("rmi://aServerName/CurrentInterestRate", ir);

has the effect of registering the object **ir**, under the string name **CurrentInterestRate**, at the location specified. Here we have used an example URL, **aServerName**, for the host name.

On the client side we can see how the remote object can be found through the RMI registry, as shown in Figure 15.25.

When looking for a remote object, the client program must know what the string name is by which the object is known. Here this is **CurrentInterestRate**. It must also know where the RMI registry is located, in this case on the local machine. Having found the object, the client can use it as if it were on the local machine, and invoke its methods. The line starting with **System.out.println** is very important in that it contains **ir.getCurrentRate()**, which is a clear example of a method invocation on an object that is remote.

15.9.4 Comparison of RMI with stream and socket programming

RMI is at a higher level of abstraction than socket-level programming. It enables the details of sockets and data streams to be hidden. Although we have not explicitly mentioned it, RMI uses a hidden multi-threading system that would otherwise have to be implemented in a socket layer.

RMI clients can invoke a server method directly but socket-level programming allows only values to be passed that must then be decoded and turned into a method call by the server. This decoding is performed automatically by RMI stubs (marshalling).

RMI programs are much easier to maintain than socket-level programs. An RMI server can be modified or moved to another host without the need to change the client application (apart from resetting the URL for locating the server).

RMI is implemented using socket-level programming. Socket-level programming is low level and prone to error, and RMI should be used in preference. This is similar to the relationship between semaphores and higher-level constructs such as monitors.

The RMI mechanism supports the idea of callbacks in which the server invokes methods on the client. This facility enables interactive distributed applications to be developed. The equivalent behaviour can be built using message passing; most easily if the message passing is built above connectionless communication. If a client–server system is built using streams and sockets then complex interaction protocols between the client and server are difficult to program. However, both synchronous and asynchronous communication can be programmed using streams and sockets, whereas RMI is synchronous.

15.10 Critique of synchronous invocation

We argued in Section 15.6 that a blocking primitive is more manageable than a non-blocking one for implementing remote operation invocation. Two such primitives, RPC and RMI, were discussed in detail. We saw how to implement an RPC and an RMI, both of which are synchronous, blocking calls.

An implementation issue is the number of calls (RPCs or RMIs) that can be in progress at any time from different threads of a given process. It is important that a number of processes on a machine should be able to initiate calls and, in particular, that several threads of the same process should be able to initiate calls to the same destination. Figure 15.26 shows a common scenario which illustrates this issue. Server A is employing several threads to service requests from different clients. Server A may itself need to invoke the service of another server, server B. It must be possible for one thread on server A to initiate a call to server B and, while that call is in progress, another thread on server A should be able to initiate another call to server B.

We have seen that distributed procedure call or method invocation is easy to program, being an extension to conventional programming languages. A system

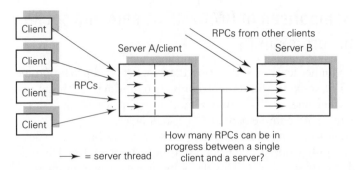

Figure 15.26
Clients, servers
and RPCs.

design issue is whether this synchronous call (RPC or RMI) paradigm is sufficient to meet the communications needs of applications. We have seen that a blocking call is typically implemented, by the lower level service, as message passing: a call is turned into a message from caller to called, the reply is a message from called to caller. Synchronous communication can therefore be built above asynchronous message passing.

Some have argued that a simple, efficient RPC or RMI protocol can be used as a basis for all requirements. Others feel that a selection should be available. Examples of alternative styles of communication are:

- A simple message-send for event notification with no requirement for a reply. Many application areas are emerging where event notification is the main requirement, including mobile and pervasive computing.
- A stream protocol (based on a connection between source and destination) for users at terminals, general input and output, and transport of bulk data, including real-time voice and video.
- A version of RPC (**asynchronous RPC**) which asks the server to carry out the operation but to keep the result for the client to pick up later. An example taken from the ANSA system is given in the next section. The client continues as soon as the invocation has been made. The client may proceed with local work or may do more asynchronous RPCs. If these are to the same server it may be important for the application that they are carried out in the same order in which they were sent. This proposal does not apply naturally to RMI.

Some systems have a real-time requirement for the transfer of massive amounts of data, for example, multimedia systems with real-time voice and video. It is unlikely that RPC will be sufficient for this purpose. RPC requires all the data to be received before the operation commences and is likely to have some maximum data size well below that of a typical video stream. Also, the overhead of marshalling is not needed for this kind of data. We do not want the RPC system to interpret a video stream as a byte sequence and to marshal the carefully counted bytes, one at a time into a buffer. We have typically obtained a block of data from a file or an on-line device and we want it sent uninterpreted (and fast).

Further reading on RPC may be found in Bershad *et al.* (1990) and Birrell and Nelson (1986). Chapter 24 surveys middleware and we see that many standards and packages that started from synchronous object invocation have seen the need to offer a wider range of services.

15.11 Naming, location and binding

So far we have assumed that a process that wishes to engage in communication with a remote process is able to name the destination of the communication. For a single centralized system we assume that the operating system knows the names of all processes and any associated communications endpoints such as ports. A process that wishes to engage in IPC will do so via the operating system. Chapter 6 discussed naming in distributed systems in general terms and a case study (DNS) for objects such as users, mail lists and machines was studied. Here we are concerned with supporting distributed programming where the objects concerned are more dynamic, being associated with currently active processes. One example of a small-scale, distributed programming system was given in Section 15.5, including use of the Java RMI registry. Here we discuss the issues in general terms.

There are a number of issues to be addressed for IPC in a system which might be large scale and widely distributed.

- What entities are to be named?
- What do names look like?
- How does a potential user of a named entity find out the name of that entity in order to use it?
- When is a name bound to a network address?
- Is the communication controlled? (Who is allowed to invoke a given object?)

We shall use the term 'object' in the following sections to indicate anything that might be named in distributed programming, for example, service, process, port, persistent data object, etc. Chapter 24 gives examples of the use of some of the methods outlined below in current middleware.

15.11.1 Naming the objects used in IPC

A convention is needed so that any object in a distributed system can be named unambiguously. A simple scheme that comes to mind is as follows.

Assume that each node has a unique network address. A naming scheme for objects, for example processes, is to name each object by (*node number, object number at that node*). Although this scheme is often used it is inflexible because an object is permanently bound to a node. If the node crashes or if it is desirable to move the object to another node, its name must be changed and all interested parties notified. This example establishes the desirability of a **global naming scheme** comprising **location-independent names**.

Now suppose that we decide to name objects by simple integers that are unique system-wide and location independent. Access control is a possible problem here. Anyone might send a message to process number 123 to request a service or invoke an operation on data object number 456. This could be solved by keeping a list with each object of the processes that are allowed to access it, like the access control lists used for files. This would allow the object to reject an unauthorized access, but would not stop communications being sent to it.

Sections 2.7, 6.7

Figure 15.27
An example of a capability and checking procedure.

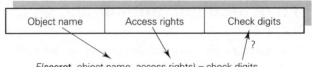

An alternative to using access control lists stored with objects is to use a special kind of name that includes access rights, called a **capability** or protected name. Figure 15.27 gives an example. A number of different capability schemes have been used in distributed systems. The idea is that possession of a capability is taken to be proof that the possessor has the rights indicated in the capability to the object named in it. Possession of a capability has often been likened to having a ticket for a concert. If you can present a ticket, you can go in. The capability can be used any number of times, however (so it is more like a season ticket).

What is to stop the possessor of a capability changing the name of the object or the rights stored in it? These are protected by encryption techniques; one scheme is as follows. When an object is created, a **secret** (random number) is generated and stored with the object. An encryption function, such as a one-way function, is available to the object storage service. When a capability is issued, the object name, rights and the secret are put through the encryption function and the resulting number is stored in the capability as check digits (Figure 15.27). When the capability is presented, with a request to use the object, the object name and rights from the capability and the stored secret are put through the encryption function. The resulting number is checked against that in the capability. If the capability has been changed in any way, the check fails.

This scheme allows the object name and access rights to be represented 'in clear' in the capability, that is, without encryption at the application level. This scheme can be used for file capabilities which include access rights (see Section 5.12.4). Another example is to control communication. Suppose that all communication is addressed to ports which are named and protected by capabilities. A process must have the 'send right' to send a message to a port. The communications implementation can reject a request to send a message to a port if the send right is not present in the capability presented. This prevents erroneous processes flooding the network with messages; we assume that erroneous (typically looping) processes do not accidentally give themselves send rights as well as carrying out spurious sends. But a malicious process can add a send right to the capability and the communications software cannot invalidate it without having access to the secret asociated with the port. A scheme of this kind is used in the Accent and Mach kernels.

15.11.2 Locating named objects

In the previous section we motivated the need for a global naming scheme for various kinds of objects in a distributed system.

Let us suppose that an application process wishes to become a client of a system service and that the application program was written with a name for the service such as 'mail-service'. Before the communication can take place, the communications software must know an address at which the required service is currently being offered. It is also likely that the communication must be addressed to a process number or port number at that network address.

How can this information be obtained? For a centralized system the operating system was assumed to manage names and extend the namespaces of the processes it supports in order to allow them to communicate (Section 12.8). The following possibilities come to mind for a distributed system:

- Every kernel maintains information on all the local objects that can be invoked from other nodes. Each kernel builds a table of all remote objects that can be invoked by local processes. The latter would be too large in practice. It would also be impossible to keep so many copies of naming data consistent, and out-of-date locations would have to be handled.

- Every kernel maintains information on all the local objects that can be invoked from other nodes. When a kernel is asked for IPC with a remote object, it locates the object by interacting with other kernels in the system, asking which one of them has the object. It is allowed to cache the locations of the objects it finds in this way.

  Some systems use methods like this, for example, the Amoeba operating system and the port mapper for SUN RPC. There is a danger that cached locations can become out of date and such values are used only as 'hints'. That is, the kernel is prepared for failure of communication based on a hint, in which case it will request the location of the required object afresh.

- Every kernel maintains information on all the local objects that can be invoked from other nodes. Each message is passed around the system in a logical ring. The kernel for which the destination object is local passes the message to that destination.

  This method was used in a very early distributed system experiment (Farber *et al.*, 1973). It does not scale to a reasonably large number of system components.

- A user-level process at each node maintains information on the local objects that can be invoked from other nodes. These processes interact with each other to locate any required object, as described above for kernels. They are requested to do so by processes attempting remote communication.

- A **name service** is designed for the system. When a service is loaded at a given node it sends its name, location and any other information necessary for using it to the name service. When a client wishes to invoke the service, the information necessary for communication with the service may be looked up in the name service. Figure 15.28 gives the general idea. The location of the name service is assumed to be well known. It can be made available to systems on initial load.

Many distributed systems use a name service. In a large-scale system the name service is likely to be offered by a number of servers. CDCS (Needham and Herbert, 1982), Grapevine (Birrell *et al.*, 1982), Clearinghouse (Oppen and Dalal, 1983), DNS (Mockapetris and Dunlap, 1988), the DEC GNS (Lampson, 1986) and ANSA (1989) (see below), are examples. Many have greater functionality

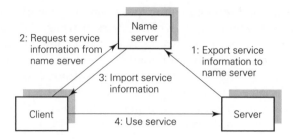

Section 6.7

Figure 15.28
A name server in a
distributed system.

than described above. They may be involved in authentication of principals and registration of groups, for example. Further reading on naming may be found in Saltzer (1979; 1982) and Needham (1993).

15.11.3 The ANSA trader

For a full description of the ANSA Advanced Network Systems Architecture, see ANSA (1989). An example is given here to illustrate the programmer's view of how a name server, ANSA's 'interface trader', might be used for distributed programming.

ANSA have defined a Distributed Programming Language, DPL, which, as well as a conventional range of data types, includes the types *Interface* and *InterfaceRef*. DPL provides a framework in which a conventional language (typically C) is embedded and is used for programming clients and servers.

Suppose the code of a **service**, the *green service*, is to be loaded into a **server** computer and made available for use by clients. An interface specification for *green* with operations *lime* and *jade* is written in an interface definition language (IDL) and made available in an IDL file, for example:

```
green : INTERFACE =
begin
    lime : OPERATION (arguments) RETURNS (arguments);
    jade : OPERATION (arguments) RETURNS (arguments);
end.
```

The server must export the interface of the *green* service to the interface trader. To do this it uses an interface reference for the trader, *traderRef*, and is returned an interface reference, *green_exportRef*, for subsequent use.

```
!   USE green
!   DECLARE [green_exportRef]: green SERVER ansa_interfaceRef
    green_exportRef;
!   [green_exportRef] := traderRef$EXPORT("green","/ANSA/services",
                            \"NAME'green"',NTHREADS)
```

The server may use the interface reference to withdraw the interface from the trader or change it. Any outstanding interface reference to that interface held by a client would then become invalid (see Section 15.8.4).

! *traderRef $withdraw (green_exportRef)*

A **client** which knows about and wishes to use the *green* service (its public name is *green*) will first import the green interface from the trader:

! USE *green*
! DECLARE [*green_importRef*]: *green* CLIENT *ansa_interfaceRef*
  green_importRef;
! [*green_exportRef*] := *traderRef$IMPORT("green","/ANSA/services",*
  \"NAME'green"')

The interface reference returned by the import request to the trader can then be used to invoke the operations of the *green* interface at the server.

! [*result*] := *green_importRef $ lime (arguments)*

It is also possible to initiate an operation asynchronously and pick up the result later by using a *voucher* data type.

voucher v;
! [*v*] := *green_importRef $ lime (arguments)*
! [*result*] := *green_importRef $REDEEM (v)*

A preprocessor replaces the statements which are preceded by ! with calls to the runtime system to marshal arguments and invoke communications software.

15.12 Summary of Part II

We have considered how an operation that is invoked on a data object as part of a concurrent system may be guaranteed to occur without interference from other concurrent actions. A number of methods of implementing this are available. They fall into two basic categories depending on whether the potentially interfering processes access data objects in shared memory. This formed the basis of Chapters 8 to 13. At this stage we had not considered the possibility that a system might crash at any time, causing main memory to be lost. Chapter 14 introduced crash resilience for a single system for a single operation invocation.

Chapter 15 has shown how the inter-process communication mechanisms discussed in Chapters 8 to 13 might be distributed. We saw how IPC software and network communications software might be integrated. Once an invocation arrives from a remote system, the techniques for achieving non-interference with other invocations, both local and remote, are as described in Chapters 8 to 13. Crash resilience was included in the discussion since distributed systems are such that parts of a program can survive crashes of other parts. It is therefore important for the programmer to be aware of the possibility of crashes. A brief introduction to the naming and location infrastructure required to support IPC in a distributed system was given. Having mastered the material necessary for understanding single concurrent actions we now proceed to

Part III in which higher-level actions comprising a number of lower-level actions are considered.

Study questions

S 15.1

Why is the failure of the system even more of a problem in a distributed system than in a centralized one?

S 15.2

Describe what a port and what a socket are. What is the difference between them?

S 15.3

Describe how the connection between a client and server is made. How do a client and server communicate, once this connection is set up?

S 15.4

How can asynchronous communication be implemented in a system that uses blocking primitives and hence synchronous communication?

S 15.5

In Figure 15.13, at point A, an RPC identifier is generated and a timer is set. Why are these two actions taken?

S 15.6

Distinguish between 'exactly once' RPC semantics and 'at most once' semantics.

S 15.7

What is an orphan? What problems can arise when an orphan is created? Why can the use of RPC identifiers not be used to overcome these problems? What actions can be taken to overcome these problems?

S 15.8

Why is RPC communication not particularly well suited to real-time systems requiring massive amounts of data to be transferred (e.g. video streams)?

S 15.9

What are the essential steps in creating an RMI system?

Exercises

15.1 Compare and contrast a client–server model of distributed computation with an object model. Could a pipeline be said to adhere to either model? How would you implement a pipelined compiler in a world based on client–server interactions or object invocations?

15.2 How can the components of a distributed system agree on a value to use for system time? Under what circumstances might such a value be needed?

15.3 A process on node A invokes an operation on node B in a distributed system. How might the fact that the nodes, and the network connecting them, may fail independently of each other be taken into account in the design of the distributed invocation at the application level and at the communications level? Can you think of examples where it is desirable that the clocks at node A and node B should be kept in synchronization?

15.4 (a) For the styles of IPC studied in Part II, explain how the mechanism might be expanded for inter-node IPC.

     (b) Consider how the network communication software and the local IPC support might be integrated.

     (c) Focus on the naming schemes that are used by the centralized IPC mechanisms. Consider the problem of naming when the mechanisms are extended for distributed IPC. When might the name of a remote operation be bound to a network address? How could this binding be supported at kernel, local service, or dedicated remote service level?

15.5 Figure 15.11 gives a high-level view of a connection between a client and a server using sockets. Sketch an implementation-oriented view along the lines of Figures 3.14 and 15.6 and outline the operating system calls that are needed to set up and use a socket connection.

15.6 Security involves both authentication and access control (when you invoke a remote operation you should be able to prove that you are who you say you are (authentication) and there should be a check that you are authorized to invoke that operation on that object (access control)). Consider how both of these functions are supported in a centralized, time-sharing system and in a single-user workstation. What infrastructure would be needed to support these functions in a distributed system?

15.7 (a) How can compile-time type checking be supported in an RPC system?

     (b) How can an RPC system check that you are not attempting to call a remote procedure that has been changed and recompiled since your program was compiled and type-checked against it?

15.8 Can RPC be used in a heterogeneous environment?

15.9 How could you contrive to program an application in which massive amounts of data are to be transferred according to a 'stream' paradigm in a system which supports only RPC for distributed IPC? You may assume that multi-threaded processes and dynamic thread creation are available.

15.10 Is distribution transparency fully achievable in an RPC system? What software components can be used to provide this illusion? How could the independent failure modes of system components be handled in an RPC system where distribution transparency was a design aim?

15.11 Is it desirable that an RPC system should provide support for client, network and server crash and restart? Distinguish between 'exactly once' semantics in the absence of crashes and restarts and in their presence. What are the implications on the application level of providing universal 'exactly once' semantics? What are the likely implications on the performance of all RPCs?

15.12 Extend the Java example in Section 15.15 as follows:
(a) Make the client send an initial message to the server requesting the current interest rate, to which the server responds.

(b) Make the server send a further message to notify the client every time the interest rate changes.

15.13 Discuss how programming in Java at the level of streams and sockets compares with using Java RMI.

Concurrent Composite Actions

The issues addressed in Part II are associated with the correct execution of a single abstract operation by a sequential process which executes as part of a concurrent system of processes. We now assume this problem solved by means of the techniques described in Part II and move on to compose higher-level abstract operations. The notion of a 'high-level' operation is, again, an informal one and can be thought of as an abstract operation consisting of a number of lower-level abstract operations.

An operation hierarchy may be located entirely within the main memory of a single computer; it may span the main memories of computers in a distributed system; it may span main memory and persistent memory of a single computer; or it may span main memory and persistent memory throughout a distributed system. Chapter 16 gives examples from systems and applications.

Chapter 16 motivates concurrent execution of composite operations as desirable to give good system performance, such as fast response to clients. The potential problems of concurrent execution are introduced.

One of the problems that arises when processes must compete for exclusive access to a number of resources or objects is that deadlock could occur. Processes may hold on to objects while waiting for other objects, held by other processes, to become free. In certain circumstances a set of processes can reach a situation where they will wait indefinitely unless the system is designed to recognize or prevent the problem. This is discussed in Chapter 17.

Chapter 18 is concerned with the fact that a system crash could occur part-way through a composite operation. In some application areas users require that either the whole operation is done or none of it is done. The definition of an atomic operation, first discussed in Chapter 14, is developed as a basis for study of systems which support this all or nothing style of composite operation execution.

Chapters 19 and 20 are concerned with methods for implementing atomic composite operations. It is necessary to be able to put the system state back to its value prior to the start of such an operation. If the system can do this it can recover from crashes. The same mechanisms can also be used to control concurrent execution of atomic operations: if interference has happened, act as though the system had crashed!

The treatment given applies equally to centralized and distributed systems. Chapter 21 discusses techniques specific to distributed systems.

Finally, Chapter 22 takes a general view of computations with distributed components.

16

Decomposable abstract operations

16.1 Composite operations

Figures 16.1 and 16.2 show composite operation invocations: first, a simple nested invocation; then a general hierarchy of operations. We are no longer concerned with the detailed mechanism for invocation of the operations and protection of the data objects operated on. We assume that each operation is part of a concurrent system and will therefore have concurrency control associated with its invocation as discussed in Part II.

Figure 16.1 shows a simple nested operation invocation in some detail. Figure 16.2 shows a high-level operation comprising a hierarchy of operations. The top-level operation (0) is invoked. Its execution involves the invocation of two operations (1 and 2), each of which involves the execution of two further operations (1.1, 1.2 and 2.1, 2.2).

The problem we address in Part III is the correct execution of general abstract operations, which decompose into suboperations, in the presence of concurrency or crashes.

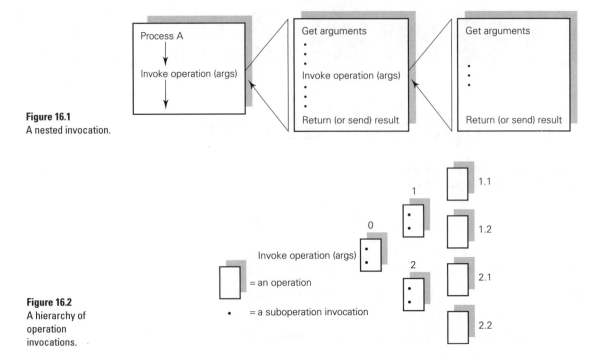

Figure 16.1
A nested invocation.

Figure 16.2
A hierarchy of
operation
invocations.

⬤⬤⬤◯ ## 16.2 Composite operations in main memory

Consider a number of processes sharing an address space and assume that a number of monitors (or objects with synchronized methods) are available to them as the means by which shared data is protected or shared resources are allocated exclusively. The specification of the operations may be such that a process may acquire a monitor (or object) lock, then, while executing an operation of the monitor (or a synchronized method), make a nested call to another monitor (or object) (Figure 16.3). Process A has invoked operation *W*, assumed to be a monitor operation (or synchronized method), and has made a nested invocation of operation *Y* in another monitor. Process B has invoked *X* and made a nested invocation of *Z*, at which point both hold two monitor (or object) locks. At this point process A invokes *Z* and process B invokes *Y* and both will wait indefinitely unless there is system intervention. This is an example of a situation called **deadlock** which is the subject matter of Chapter 17.

Figure 16.3 also shows process C attempting to invoke *X*. The issue of whether process B should continue to hold the lock of the monitor (or object) containing *X* while making a nested invocation of *Z* must be addressed.

The situation shown in the figure is not exclusively the problem of shared-memory-based systems which use monitors (or synchronized objects) for concurrency control. The objects involved could be located in main memory throughout a distributed system and invoked by remote procedure call or remote method invocation.

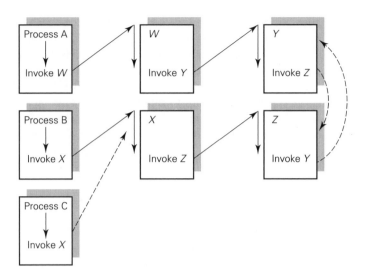

Figure 16.3
Concurrent invocation in main memory.

16.3 Composite operations involving main memory and persistent memory

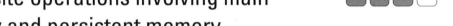

Examples of areas in which composite operations involve both main memory and persistent memory are database management systems and operating systems. Both have to handle multiple simultaneous activities.

16.3.1 Examples from operating systems

Many examples of composite operations arise within the file management subsystem of an operating system. In order to satisfy a request to write a sequence of bytes to a file an operating system might have to send more than one write request to the disk manager. A crash could occur between these associated writes.

Certain file operations require associated directory operations, as outlined in Chapter 5. When a file is deleted, the disk blocks it occupies may be made free (if there are no other paths to it) and its directory entry and metadata should be removed. A crash could occur at any time, including between these operations. If the operations were carried out in the order indicated above, the directory entry and metadata could remain, but blocks of the file would be on the free list. A number of difficulties might then arise. The disk blocks which had comprised the file might be allocated to some other, newly created file. The file system has become inconsistent (and incorrect). An important part of file system design is to avoid or detect and correct inconsistencies, particularly after a crash has occurred.

Another example is that creation of a new file has an associated directory operation to add a new entry to a directory. Disk blocks might be acquired for the file, but a crash might occur before the directory entry is made. The blocks might be lost to the filing system unless action is taken to detect this.

In a file management subsystem we are concerned with the transfer of data and metadata between main memory and persistent memory. There are many examples where a change is made to a file, such as extending it with new blocks, and these changes are recorded in file system tables in main memory. Suppose that at the time of the change the data blocks are written to disk and the new disk blocks used are recorded in tables in main memory. This metadata must also be written to disk for the persistent store to be in a consistent state, but a crash could occur at any time. Care must be taken in the file system design and in crash recovery procedures that the file system can be restored to a consistent state, with minimum loss of data. In this example consistency could be achieved after a crash by detecting that the newly written blocks are not recorded as part of any file and returning them to the free list. The unfortunate user would have to repeat the work.

These examples have emphasized that a crash can occur between the component operations of a logical operation at a higher level. Concurrent execution of component operations can have similar effects, and we shall see that it can be advantageous to consider possible actions to guard against the effects of crashes, together with those for concurrency control.

16.3.2 An example from a database system

An example of a high-level operation is to transfer a sum of money from one bank account to another:

transfer (account-A, account-B, £1000)

Two separate operations have to be invoked to achieve this. One is to access the source account, *account-A*, in order to read that there is sufficient money in there and to write the debited amount back as the new value of the account, a typical Part II-style operation. The second is to credit the destination account, *account-B*, with its updated value, another Part II-style operation.

The constituent low-level operations are therefore:

debit (account-A, £1000)
credit (account-B, £1000)

The techniques of Part II ensure that each of these separate operations can be done correctly, but do not address their composition into a correct, single high-level operation.

 ## 16.4 Concurrent execution of composite operations

There is scope for concurrency in the execution of high-level, composite operation invocations.

1 Several high-level operations, invoked by different processes, could be run in parallel, their lower-level operations being interleaved.
2 It might be possible to invoke the suboperations of a single high-level operation in parallel.

Method 2 cannot be carried out automatically without regard to the semantics of the computation. It might be the case that some of the operations have to be invoked in a specific order. For example, *debit* might only be allowed after a *check-balance* operation but *credit* and *debit* can be carried out in parallel.

Current database programming languages tend to specify a strict sequence of operations. It can be argued, as with imperative programming languages, that the sequencing is often overspecified. To move to parallel execution of the operations of a single transaction, which is desirable for multiprocessor or distributed execution, it would be necessary to specify and enforce any necessary orderings on the operations.

Method 1 provides more obvious scope for automatic provision of concurrency. Resource contention problems are likely to arise.

16.4.1 Desirability of concurrent execution

Before looking at mechanisms for achieving concurrency we should consider whether concurrent execution is a goal worth striving for at the expense of additional complexity in the system. One approach to supporting high-level operations would be to regard them as indivisible: to acquire exclusive use of all the objects needed for the entire set of constituent operations and then to carry out the high-level operation. There are several drawbacks to such an approach:

• It could take a long time to acquire all the objects required, introducing unpredictability of service and (possibly indefinite) delay.
• All the objects would be held for the duration of all the constituent operations. This would prevent other processes from using them, even when the objects were idle and no errors could result from their use.
• A number of logically distinct operations are effectively being combined into a single large operation. Knowledge of all the objects invoked in suboperations is needed at the outermost level.
• Deadlock could occur if the objects were acquired piecemeal (as discussed below and in Chapter 17).

In applications where it is unlikely that two processes would require simultaneous access to the same resource, either because of light use or because accesses are known to be scattered widely across a large data space, this might be a suitable approach. An example is personal data in a social security, medical or taxation database. The same individual is unlikely to be the target of multiple simultaneous queries.

In a heavily used system with frequent contention the performance could be unacceptably slow and we should aim to achieve a higher degree of concurrency. Good performance while serving multiple clients is a sufficiently widespread goal that it is important to strive for maximum concurrency in many systems.

It is worth studying the techniques for achieving concurrent execution of composite operations in order to be able to decide whether and how to provide for it in a given system design. The mechanisms that are needed for crash resilience (failure transparency) are similar to those for some methods of concurrency control, and it is desirable to consider both together.

16.5 Potential problems

We shall use the simple example of Section 16.3.2 to illustrate the problems that can occur during concurrent execution of composite operations and some approaches to their solution. Suppose:

> **process P** executes *transfer* (*account-A*, *account-B*, £1000)
> **process Q** executes *transfer* (*account-B*, *account-A*, £200)

In more detail:

> P: *debit* (*account-A*, £1000);   *credit* (*account-B*, £1000)
> Q: *debit* (*account-B*, £200);   *credit* (*account-A*, £200)

Showing more detail of a possible implementation for **P** (**Q** is similar):

> P: *debit* (*account-A*, £1000);
>   read the value of *account-A*
>   check whether the debit can be made (value ≥ £1000), if not give an error response, otherwise write the debited value as the new value of *account-A*
> P: *credit* (*account-B*, £1000);
>   read the value of *account-B*,
>   add £1000 to the value,
>   write the new value into *account-B*

16.5.1 Uncontrolled interleaving of suboperations

Figure 16.4 shows a hierarchical decomposition for the transfer operation down to the granularity of treating individual read and write operations on account records as separate operations. Consider the possible consequences of having no concurrency control whatsoever. The following sequence of operations could occur:

> Q: complete the whole *debit* operation on *account-B*
> P: read the value of *account-A*
> Q: read the value of *account-A*
> P: check value ≥ £1000 and write back the original value minus £1000
> Q: write back the original value plus £200
> P: credit *account-B* with £1000

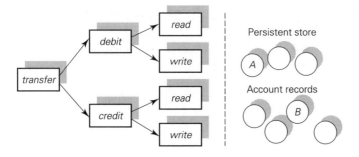

Figure 16.4
A possible hierarchy
of operations for
'transfer'.

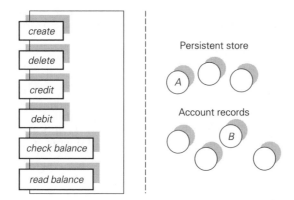

Figure 16.5
Account objects.

The debit of £1000 made by process **P** to account *A* has been lost, overwritten by process **Q**'s credit to the original value of the account. This illustrates that the *debit* and *credit* operations should be treated as abstract operations, indivisible in the sense of Part II. Their implementation in terms of individual reads and writes should not be visible to the client of the transaction system. The reads and writes to persistent store can be thought of in the same way as the individual reads and writes to main memory in Section 8.7.1. The data object *account-A* can be considered as an abstract data type with operations which include *debit* and *credit*, as shown in Figure 16.5. We assume that a mechanism such as a **lock** on a data object is available to implement exclusive access to an object for those operations which require it.

We shall develop a model along these lines in Chapter 18. Much database concurrency control theory in the past has been presented in terms of *read* and *write* operations only, but current thinking is that object orientation, taking into account the semantics of the operations, is a better approach. Returning to our simple example, this does not solve all our problems because interleaving operations at this level can also lead to incorrect results, as shown in the next example.

16.5.2 Visibility of the effects of suboperations

Suppose process **R** is calculating the sum of the values of accounts *A* and *B*, and consider the following interleavings:

P: *debit (account-A, £1000)*;
R: *read-balance (account-A)*;
R: *read-balance (account-B)*;
P: *credit (account-B, £1000)*;

In this case, each of the suboperations of the *transfer* operation is carried out correctly by process **P** but the value computed by process **R** for the sum of accounts *A* and *B* is incorrect. The problem arises because another process has been allowed to see the accounts affected by the *transfer* operation between its two suboperations. This is a Part III problem. Its solution is addressed in Chapters 18 and 19.

16.5.3 Deadlock

If we attempt to solve the problem of Section 16.5.1 by allowing accounts to be 'locked' we could have the following interleaving of operations:

P: *lock (account-A)*;
P: *debit (account-A, £1000)*;
Q: *lock (account-B)*;
Q: *debit (account-B, £200)*;
P: *lock (account-B)*

This can't be done as **Q** already holds the lock on *account-B*. Let us assume that process **P** is obliged to wait for the lock, for example on a condition variable in a monitor.

Q: *lock (account-A)*

This can't be done as **P** already holds the lock on *account-A*. Let us assume that process **Q** is obliged to wait for the lock.

Chapter 17

If this situation is allowed to arise, processes **P** and **Q** will wait indefinitely. They are said to be **deadlocked**. This is a Part III problem. Its solution is addressed in Chapter 17.

16.6 Crashes

In Chapter 14 we considered the effects of crashes and mechanisms that would provide crash resilience for a single operation invocation. Figure 16.6 reiterates the basic approach. In Chapter 15 we considered an operation on one host

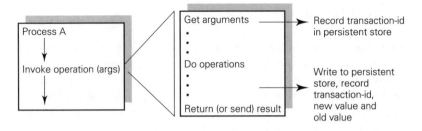

Figure 16.6
A potentially atomic operation invocation.

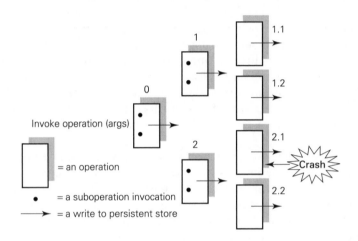

Figure 16.7
A crash during hierarchical operation invocation.

being invoked from another host in a distributed system and considered the possibility of crashes both in the invoking and invoked systems. We now generalize these ideas.

Suppose, in the simple example introduced in Section 16.5 above, that a crash occurs after the *debit* operation, which must have written its result to persistent store in order to complete, but before the *credit* operation. The fact that a transfer operation was in progress was lost, with main memory, in the crash and £1000 has been lost from the recorded values in persistent store. A system design clearly needs to take account of such a possibility.

Figure 16.7 shows the more general case of a composite operation, indicating that any component operation may involve a write to persistent memory. Suppose that a crash occurs, as indicated, during operation 2.1. We have seen from Chapter 14 how that operation might be rolled back and restarted. We now have to consider what to do about operations 1, 1.1 and 1.2, which apparently completed successfully although the crash occurred during operation 0, the high-level invoking operation. Chapters 18 and 19 consider these issues. We should also consider a distributed implementation of such a composite operation. In this case the nodes on which the operations execute need to cooperate. This is considered in Chapter 21.

 ## 16.7 Summary

We defined composite abstract operations and looked at some examples. In some cases, concurrent execution of the component operations of high-level operations is desirable and in others it cannot be avoided. This can lead to problems. In Part III we will study these problems and possible solutions to them.

The general problem that can arise as a result of the uncontrolled concurrent execution of component operations is that the system state can become incorrect. A related problem is that output may be incorrect (Section 16.5.2), even if the persistent state subsequently becomes consistent. A naive attempt to avoid these problems through locking all required resources for exclusive use can lead to bad system performance; locking piecemeal can lead to deadlock.

Incorrect system state might result from a crash part-way through a single composite operation or through uncontrolled concurrent execution of composite operations. A system must at least be able to detect that this has happened. Minimal action is to restore a consistent version of the state, possibly involving loss of information, and to warn the users affected that this has occurred. This is acceptable for some systems, typically filing systems for general-purpose operating systems.

Some systems, such as transaction processing systems, guarantee to their clients that, once a transaction is complete, its results will not be lost whatever happens. Crashes can occur, and not only must a consistent version of the system state be restored but that state must contain the results of all completed transactions. The mechanisms that must be used to achieve crash resilience without loss of the information that has been guaranteed to persist might also be used for concurrency control. It is therefore desirable to consider concurrency control and crash resilience together.

The topic of dynamic object allocation and deadlock is covered in the next chapter in some detail as general background for the specific methods discussed in later chapters.

Study questions

S 16.1

What is the essence of a composite operation?

S 16.2

In Figure 16.3, deadlock occurs because operation Y is waiting to invoke operation Z while operation Z is waiting to invoke operation Y. How has this situation arisen and why do operations Y and Z have to wait?

S 16.3

Assuming that operations W and X in Figure 16.3 are associated with different monitors, what would happen if W invoked X and X invoked W?

S 16.4

In Figure 16.3, what happens when process C attempts to invoke operation X while X is already executing (on behalf of process B)? Is this always desirable?

S 16.5

Other than by incorrect programming, how might a file system become inconsistent?

S 16.6

A crash occurring between the component operations (suboperations) of a single high-level logical operation (composite operation) is one reason why persistent data may become inconsistent. What is another?

S 16.7

Concurrent execution of composite operations means that the suboperations of one may become interleaved with the suboperations of another, causing interference. Why is making a composite operation indivisible, so that this interleaving cannot take place, undesirable?

S 16.8

What is the primary goal for using concurrency?

S 16.9

In the example of Section 16.5, assume that *account-A* and *account-B* both start off with £1000. What would the balance of the two accounts be if:

(a)   process P is completed before process Q starts;
(b)   process Q is completed before process P starts;

and both processes complete their actions?

S 16.10

For the sequence of operations given in Section 16.5.1, what are the resulting balances of the two accounts (assuming that, as the final operation, process P completes the whole credit operation on *account-B*)?

S 16.11

Suppose that you and a friend are having tea together and that you both take sugar in your tea. On the table there is a single sugar bowl and a single spoon. Assuming that the sugar bowl has to be picked up to take spoonfuls, describe a situation in which deadlock occurs. In what ways might you ensure that deadlock would not occur in this situation?

S 16.12

What is the essential difference between crashes in the case of composite operations and crashes in the case of single operations?

Exercises

16.1 What problems might occur if the suboperations of a single high-level operation are started off in parallel (for example, for running on a shared-memory multiprocessor)? Give examples. Why is it difficult to automate this approach?

16.2 Find out about the consistency checks your local operating system runs on its filing system on restarting after a crash or shutdown (an example is UNIX's fsck maintenance tool). Is it possible for users to lose data? If so, how are they informed of this possibility? Why is this approach not possible in a transaction processing system?

16.3 To what extent is it desirable to run the suboperations of different high-level operations in parallel? What are the possible problems arising from uncontrolled concurrency? (Give examples of incorrect output and incorrect system state.) What are the possible consequences of attempting to solve these problems?

16.4 What are the possible effects of a crash part-way through a single composite operation? What mechanisms must be in place to allow for the possibility of a crash at any time in a transaction processing (TP) system? Are these mechanisms suitable for handling concurrent execution of composite operations as well?

16.5 Why is it important, when designing a TP system, to have estimates of the likely level of load on the system and the probability that requests for simultaneous access to the same data items will occur?

16.6 Consider how you would set up an object model for a TP system. What are possible disadvantages of treating read and write as operations on data objects?

17

Resource allocation and deadlock

17.1 Requirements for dynamic allocation

We shall use the term 'object' to include resources of all kinds, including data objects, devices, etc. In Chapter 16 some of the problems associated with concurrent execution of composite operations were introduced. A basic problem was shown to be how to maintain consistent values across a number of distinct objects when a high-level operation may involve related lower-level operations performed sequentially on distinct objects.

An obvious starting point for solving such problems is to support exclusive use of objects by processes. This was studied in Part II, where several methods for achieving mutual exclusion of processes from shared objects were described.

Object allocation is a common requirement in concurrent systems. Physical resource management is a major function of **operating systems** and many of the managed resources must be allocated dynamically. Typical of these are disk space for users' files, buffer space in memory for disk buffers, disk space for spoolers, physical memory, tape drives and other devices which are neither spooled nor allocated statically. Certain data objects must also be managed by operating systems. Entries in fixed-length data structures, such as the central process table in UNIX, must be allocated and recovered; a new process can only be created if a free slot can be allocated. **Database management systems** have to handle requests from multiple simultaneous users to interrogate and update permanently stored data objects. **Communications protocols** require buffer space in memory for incoming and outgoing packets. It is far more common for 'loss of data' to occur through lack of buffer space when systems are congested than through errors on the wire.

17.2 Deadlock

A simple example of deadlock was given in Section 16.5. In that case, process **P** had locked object *A* for exclusive use and went on to request object *B*. Process **Q** had already locked object *B*. Deadlock occurs when process **Q** proceeds to request object *A*.

Figure 17.1 illustrates this problem. It shows the progress of processes **P** and **Q** when they are scheduled to run on a single processor, that is, only one at a time can run. Their behaviour is that each acquires one object and, while still holding it, requests the other. Paths i, j, k, l, m, n illustrate different possible dynamic behaviours of the two processes. In i and j, process **P** acquires both *A* and *B* before process **Q** requests *B*. In k and l, process **Q** acquires both *B* and *A* before process **P** requests *A*. In paths m and n deadlock becomes inevitable *for the particular dynamic behaviour exhibited in this example* when **P** gets *A* and **Q** gets *B*.

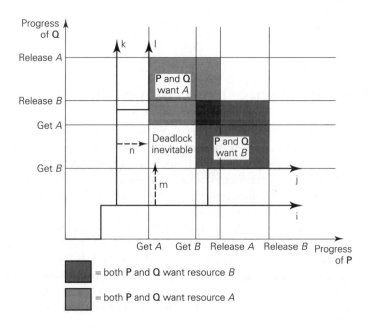

Figure 17.1
Two processes using
two resources
(objects).

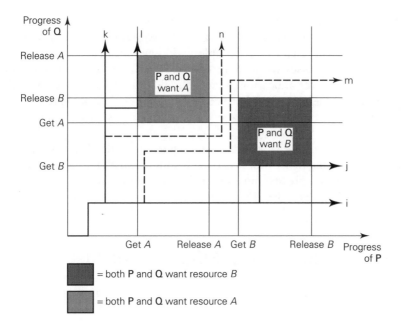

Figure 17.2
Two processes using two objects without deadlock.

We cannot assume that an object management system knows the semantics of the particular application. The dynamic behaviour might have been as illustrated in Figure 17.2. In this case, both processes require both *A* and *B* but process **P** releases *A* before acquiring *B*. The processes may be delayed, waiting for objects, during some dynamic patterns of resource scheduling, but deadlock cannot happen.

17.3 Livelock and starvation

Before proceeding to further investigation of the problem of deadlock it should be pointed out that processes need not necessarily be in the blocked state for there to be no possibility of progress. An example is busy waiting on a condition that can never become true. The process loops, testing the condition indefinitely. This condition is sometimes referred to as 'livelock'.

Communications protocols must be analysed to make sure they do not degenerate into an indefinite 'ping-pong' behaviour when systems are congested. If communication is attempted between two congested systems, packets are likely to be discarded at both ends because buffer space is exhausted. The congestion is worsened by resending messages, replies, acknowledgements and negative acknowledgements, and care must be taken that an indefinite loop is not entered (Lai, 1982).

A more subtle form of a near deadlock state is due to resource starvation. A process may have large resource requirements and may be overlooked repeatedly because it is easier for the resource management system to schedule other processes with smaller resource requirements. It can happen that every time some of the resources the starved process wants become available they are given to some other process which can then complete. This is because system throughput looks good if processes with small requirements are scheduled and complete. The system's resource allocation policies should ensure that processes with large resource requirements are not starved, although it is reasonable to expect them to wait for longer before being scheduled than processes with small resource requirements.

An example from databases is that certain portions of the data may be hot-spots: in demand by many processes. Process scheduling must take this possibility into account and a given process must not be held up unduly for this reason.

Zöbel (1983) gives a classifying bibliography for the deadlock problem.

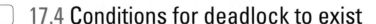 # 17.4 Conditions for deadlock to exist

If all of the following conditions are true at some time in a system then deadlock exists at that time (Coffman *et al.*, 1971).

1 *A resource request can be refused*
   The system's concurrency control policy is such that objects can be acquired for exclusive use or some specific shared use. It is possible for a process to be refused access to an object on the grounds that some other process has acquired it for exclusive use. It is possible for a process to be refused access to an object on the grounds that a group of processes have acquired shared access to it for a specific purpose. An example is that a process may request exclusive access to an object in order to write to it but is refused because the object is currently locked for shared reading.

2 *Hold while waiting*
   A process is allowed to hold objects while requesting further objects. The process is blocked if the request cannot be satisfied. The assumption is that the process will wait for the resource until it becomes available.

3 *No preemption*
   Objects cannot be recovered from processes. A process may acquire an object, use it and release it.

4 *Circular wait*
   A cycle of processes exists such that each process holds an object that is being requested by the next process in the cycle and that request has been refused.

The processes in the cycle are deadlocked. Other processes may be able to continue but the system is degraded by the objects held by the deadlocked processes. If a process makes a request that must be refused for an object that is involved in the cycle, that process will also wait indefinitely. Further cycles could occur if a process in a cycle can have outstanding object requests that are not part of the original cycle. This would not be possible if a process had to acquire objects one at a time and was blocked as soon as a request could not be satisfied.

17.4.1 Deadlock prevention

All of conditions 1 to 4 above must hold for deadlock to exist. Conditions 1 to 3 are policy statements. Condition 4 is a statement about a particular dynamic behaviour of a set of processes. It might be possible to preclude some of the conditions through system policies.

1 *A resource request can be refused*
   Any concurrency control policy provided by a system to assist the applications that run above it should be as flexible as possible.

   An example can be taken from the concurrency control that might be provided as part of a file service by an operating system. Exclusive *write locks* and shared *read locks* were once thought to be what an operating system should provide. They are now seen to be insufficiently flexible: they force a particular view of the world on every application. Some applications may wish to have concurrent write sharing of files. For example, instances of a database management system may wish to provide their own fine-grained concurrency control to access different parts of a file at the same time. The operating system should allow them all to have the file open for writing. The provision of an exclusive lock and a shared lock could be provided so that the owners of the objects are assisted in using the object correctly in a way appropriate for the application.

   Whenever concurrency control is provided, in order to ensure that the values of objects are correct, it is possible that a request to use an object in some way will be refused.

2 *Hold while waiting*
   It may be possible to make a process acquire all the objects it needs at one time. This decreases utilization of, possibly scarce, objects. It may also be counter to the aim of a clean modular structure as discussed in Section 16.3. If a computation has deeply nested invocations then the outermost level would have to be aware of all the objects used at all levels.

   It may not always be possible, for example, if a requirement for an object results from computations based on other objects.

3 *No preemption*
   It may be possible to preempt an object and roll back the process holding it to the point at which it acquired the object that is now required by another process. This could be made transparent to the application. A policy decision is whether this should take place after deadlock is detected or at other times, such as when a process holds objects and fails to acquire another or when a high-priority process needs an object that a lower-priority process holds. This is a heavyweight mechanism and affects many aspects of program and system design. Detecting deadlock and aborting and restarting some processes might be simpler.

4 *Circular wait*
   In certain applications it might be possible to require processes to request objects in a defined order. This would be less wasteful of system resources than acquiring all objects at once. This is feasible for some types of objects

that are allocated; for example, a program may reasonably be required to request input devices before output devices.

An alternative is to enforce an ordering on the processes making the requests. The method of time-stamp ordering for concurrency control in database systems is deadlock free for this reason (see Section 19.5).

One method of solving the problem illustrated in Section 17.5 is to force processes to order their requests for resources so as to make a cycle impossible.

We use these techniques whenever we can in designing systems. We have to trade off the overhead of detecting and recovering from deadlock against the decreased resource utilization or extra complexity arising from the above policies. Knowledge of the likely behaviour of the applications to be supported should determine the policies to adopt.

17.5 The dining philosophers problem

The discussion above is equally appropriate to resource allocation by operating systems and data object management by a DBMS. The following example demonstrates its applicability to a small concurrent program.

This problem was posed by Dijkstra (1965) and is a classic of concurrent programming:

> Five (male) philosophers spend their lives thinking and eating. The philosophers share a common circular table surrounded by five chairs, each belonging to one philosopher. In the centre of the table there is a bowl of spaghetti, and the table is laid with five forks, as shown in Figure 17.3. When a philosopher thinks, he does not interact with other philosophers. From time to time, a philosopher gets hungry. In order to eat he must try to pick up the two forks that are closest (and are shared with his left and right neighbours), but may only pick up one fork at a time. He cannot pick up a fork already held by a neighbour. When a hungry philosopher has both his forks at the same time, he eats without releasing them, and when he has finished eating, he puts down both forks and starts thinking again.

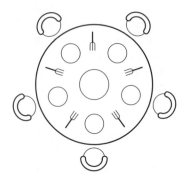

Figure 17.3
The dining philosophers problem.

The conditions for deadlock are set up in the problem: a philosopher acquires each fork exclusively; he must acquire one fork then hold it while waiting to acquire the second; a fork cannot be taken from a philosopher once he has picked it up. It may be possible, depending on the specification of the philosopher processes, for a cycle to occur when they execute dynamically, in which each philosopher has acquired one fork and is waiting to acquire a second: the final condition that must hold for deadlock to exist in a system.

This is illustrated by a first attempt at a solution, which is subject to deadlock. Semaphores are used for fork management:

var *fork:array*[0..4] **of** *semaphore*;

where all the elements of array *fork* are initialized to 1. Philosopher *i* may then be specified as:

```
repeat
    WAIT (fork[i]);
    WAIT (fork[i + 1 mod 5]);
    eat
    SIGNAL (fork[i]);
    SIGNAL (fork[i + 1 mod 5]);
    think
until false;
```

The problem arises because each philosopher process executes an identical program. One approach is to break the symmetry: make one of the philosophers, or each philosopher with an odd identifier, pick up his forks in the opposite order to the others, thus avoiding the possibility of a cycle. Another is to introduce a separate fork manager module which implements deadlock avoidance as described in Section 17.8 below: a general, and therefore heavyweight, solution. Exercise 17.5 outlines some approaches to solving the problem.

Although the problem is posed to explore the dangers of symmetric behaviour, it extends those we discussed in Part II because two specific shared resources must be acquired before the *eat* operation can be done. At a high level a philosopher could be specified as EAT; THINK but EAT is not a single Part II-style operation. The high-level EAT operation comprises five lower-level operations: *acquire fork*; *acquire fork*; *eat*; *release fork*; *release fork*.

17.6 Object allocation graphs

Figure 17.4 shows a graphical notation for describing object allocations and requests. The graph shows object types R1 and R2. The dots inside the R1 and R2 boxes indicate the number of objects of that type that exist. The directed edge from the single instance of R1 to process P indicates that P holds that

Figure 17.4
Notation for resource allocation and request.

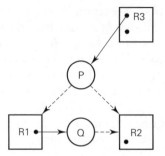

Figure 17.5
A resource allocation
graph.

object. The (dashed) directed edge from P to the object type R2 indicates that P is requesting an object of type R2. P is therefore in the blocked state. If a cycle exists in such a graph and there is only one object of each of the object types involved in the cycle then deadlock exists (this is the definition of deadlock). If there is more than one object of each type a cycle is a necessary but not sufficient condition for deadlock to exist. Examples of object types which may have multiple instances are the tape readers and printers that are allocated by a resource management module of an operating system.

A directed graph of this kind can be used as a basis for object management; for resource allocation by an operating system; for data management by a DBMS, etc. The components of the graph are the set of processes which either hold or are requesting resources; the set of object types with an indication of the number of instances of each type; and a set of edges indicating allocations and requests, as described above.

Figure 17.5 shows an example of an allocation graph. Deadlock does not exist at present, but an allocation decision has to be made: there is one instance of resource type R2 and two processes are requesting it. Figure 17.6(a) shows the graph if the object of type R2 is given to Q. Deadlock does not exist. Figure 17.6(b) shows the graph if the object of type R2 is given to P. A cycle has been created. Because there is only one object of each of types R1 and R2 deadlock exists. Figure 17.6(c) and (d) show a similar problem except that this time there are two instances of objects of type R2. In (c) a cycle exists but there is no deadlock. Although both objects of type R2 are allocated, process T is not deadlocked: it may complete and release its object. In (d) we see process P with both instances of R2. In this case there is deadlock.

We now consider data structures for holding object allocation and request information and algorithms for detecting deadlock in a system.

17.7 Data structures and algorithms for deadlock detection

We assume a subsystem that is responsible for allocating certain objects and detecting deadlock. The object types to be managed and the number of instances of each type must be specified and the subsystem must record which

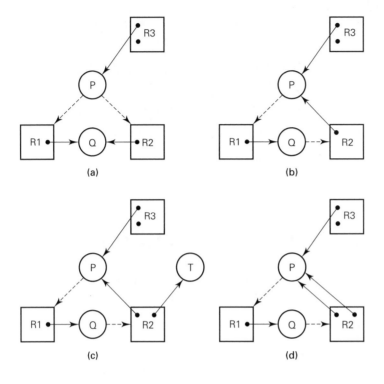

Figure 17.6
(a) Object of type R2 allocated to Q.
(b) Object of type R2 allocated to P.
(c) A cycle but no deadlock.
(d) A cycle with deadlock.

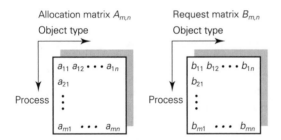

Objects in the system being managed = $R_n = (r_1, r_2, \ldots r_n)$, the number of type i is r_i.

Objects available = $V_n = (v_1, v_2, \ldots v_n)$, the number left of type i is v_i.

V_n can be computed from the total objects in the system, R_n minus the objects allocated.

Figure 17.7
Data structures for object management.

are allocated and which are available. A matrix of processes against allocated objects is a suitable data structure to hold the object allocation information. Let us call it an **allocation matrix** A where a_{ij} is the number of objects of type j allocated to process i. A **request matrix** B of the same structure is suitable for holding outstanding requests by processes for objects (see Figure 17.7). We require an algorithm to detect deadlock by processing these allocation and request matrices.

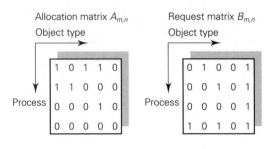

Allocation matrix $A_{m,n}$

Request matrix $B_{m,n}$

Objects in system = $R = (2, 1, 1, 2, 1)$

Objects available = $V = (0, 0, 0, 0, 1)$

Figure 17.8
Example of deadlock detection.

17.7.1 An algorithm for deadlock detection

The algorithm below marks the rows of the allocation matrix A corresponding to processes which are not part of a deadlocked set.

1 Mark all null rows of A. (A process holding no objects cannot be part of a deadlocked cycle of processes.)
2 Initialize a working vector $W = V$, the available objects.
3 Search for an unmarked row, say row i, such that $B_i \leq W$ (the objects that process i is requesting are 'available' in W). If none is found terminate the algorithm.
4 Set $W = W + A_i$ and mark row i. Return to step 3.

When the algorithm terminates, unmarked rows correspond to deadlocked processes.

The algorithm merely detects whether deadlock exists. If the object requests of a process can be satisfied it is not part of a deadlocked cycle and the objects it holds are not under contention by the deadlocked set of processes. The algorithm therefore adds them to the working pool of available objects for the purposes of the algorithm. The physical justification for this is that the process could complete its work and free its objects.

In terms of the corresponding resource allocation graph, the algorithm marks processes that are not part of a deadlocked set. If step 3 finds a process whose resource requests can be satisfied, step 4 removes the edges of the graph associated with the process; that is, its requests are assumed to be granted and the objects it holds become available for allocation.

17.7.2 Example

Figure 17.8 shows an example of a snapshot of object allocation and request at some instant.

On running the algorithm we have:

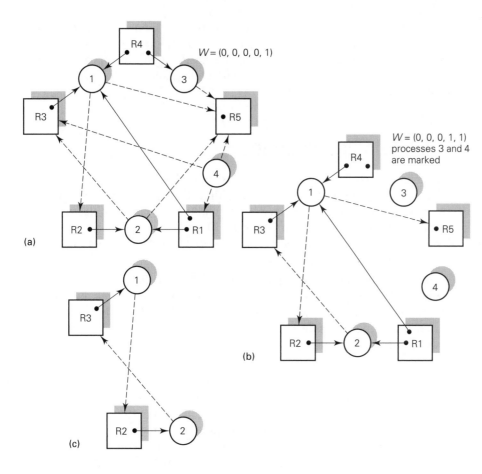

Figure 17.9
Graphs for the example in Section 17.7.2. (a) The graph at the start of the algorithm. (b) The graph when the algorithm terminates. (c) The cycle.

Initialize $W = (0, 0, 0, 0, 1)$
Mark row 4 (process 4 has no allocated objects)
Mark row 3 (process 3's requests can be satisfied from W and process 3's objects are added to W):
    $W = (0, 0, 0, 1, 1)$
Terminate
Rows 1 and 2 are unmarked, so processes 1 and 2 are deadlocked.

Figure 17.9(a) shows the resource allocation graph for this example. Figure 17.9(b) shows the effect of running the algorithm on (a copy of) the graph and (c) shows the cycle of deadlocked processes.

17.7.3 Action on detection of deadlock

The simplest action is to abort all the deadlocked processes, freeing all their objects. This could require a complete restart of these processes or a rollback to a checkpoint before the objects were acquired if the system supports this. An alternative is to abort the processes selectively, but this would require the dead-lock detection algorithm to be run again, at least for the remaining processes that might still be deadlocked. Another alternative is to preempt the objects over which the deadlocked processes are contending one by one, but again the algorithm would have to be rerun.

17.8 Deadlock avoidance

It may be feasible for a process to specify its total object requirements before it runs. This information could be used by the allocation subsystem. Let us assume that a third matrix is now available, $C_{m,n}$, giving the maximum object require-ments of each process as shown in Figure 17.10.

For any given request for objects that it is possible to satisfy from the objects available, the allocator can test whether

> if this allocation is made (construct A', a hypothetical allocation matrix for testing) and all the processes then request their maximum number of objects (construct B', a hypothetical request matrix) would deadlock then exist? (Run the detection algorithm given above on A' and B'.) If deadlock would not exist then it is safe to grant the request being tested.

This is a worst-case analysis since it is unlikely that all the processes would immediately request objects up to their maximum entitlement. It avoids the overhead of recovering from deadlock at the expense of holding an extra matrix C and constructing A' and B' before running the algorithm. It also requires this procedure to be carried out for each set of requests that might be granted. This is a matter for judgement. It might be possible to satisfy all outstanding requests, but in testing this allocation the chances of finding a potentially deadlocked state would be higher than for a more modest allocation. The safest way to proceed is to try to satisfy one process at a time. Figure 17.11 gives an example with matrices A, B and C at some instance in a system. Figure 17.12 shows the constructed matrices A' and B', supposing that process 1's request was satisfied, and the effect of running the deadlock detection algorithm on A' and B'. In this case, satisfying process 1's request would move the system to a state where deadlock did not exist and deadlock could not occur on any subsequent request: a **safe state**.

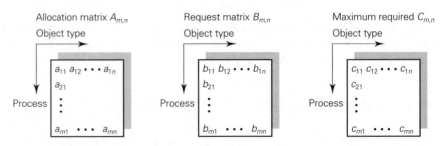

Figure 17.10
Data structures for
deadlock avoidance.

Objects in the system $= R = (r_1, r_2, \dots r_n)$

Objects available for allocation $= V = (v_1, v_2, \dots v_n)$

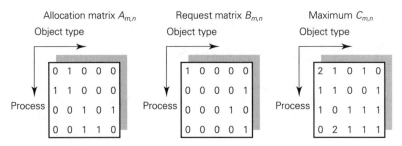

Total objects in system = R = (2, 3, 2, 1, 2)

Total objects available = V = (1, 1, 0, 0, 1)

Figure 17.11
An example for deadlock avoidance.

Try satisfying process 1's request. Construct A' and B' as follows:

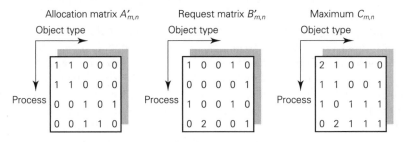

Objects in system = R = (2, 3, 2, 1, 2)

Objects available = V' = (0, 1, 0, 0, 1)

Construct $W = V'$ initially = (0, 1, 0, 0, 1)
Mark row 2
   W = (1, 2, 0, 0, 1)
Mark row 4
   W = (1, 2, 1, 1, 1)
Mark row 1
   W = (2, 3, 1, 1, 1)
Mark row 3
   W = (2, 3, 2, 1, 2)

There would be no deadlock: it is safe to grant the request

Figure 17.12
The deadlock avoidance algorithm for the example in Figure 17.11.

17.8.1 Problems of deadlock avoidance

The avoidance procedure aims to ensure that the system moves from one safe state to another on each object allocation. It could happen, however, that the algorithm finds no allocation which is guaranteed to be safe; that is, deadlock could occur when a subsequent request was made. In practice, some object allocation might have to be made eventually and the risk of deadlock run.

To carry out this form of deadlock avoidance procedure would therefore not only involve a significant overhead but could not be used in all circumstances. A fallback procedure would be needed in case of failure to find a safe state to move to. The system could then move to an unsafe state, in the terms of the algorithm.

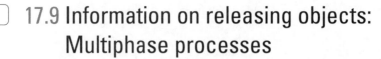

17.9 Information on releasing objects: Multiphase processes

We have seen that making information on total object requirements of processes available to the object management subsystem could allow deadlock to be avoided rather than merely detected dynamically. There are reservations, however, that the avoidance algorithm is over-cautious. It takes no account of the fact that a process might release an object at some time before it terminates. If this information could be given to the object management subsystem, a more realistic model of the system could be maintained and used by a deadlock avoidance algorithm.

In order to bring in the notion of piecemeal acquiring and releasing of objects by processes we need the concept of steps in the progress of a sequential process. At the start of each step a process requests or releases one or more objects. The object management subsystem now knows the precise behaviour of the set of processes under its control. It would be possible, in theory, to schedule a combination of process steps so that the system proceeds through a sequence of safe states, a system state being defined as a step from each process being managed.

The computational overhead of such an algorithm is likely to be large and the approach is unlikely to be applicable to many application areas. The model of a distinct set of processes to be run from start to completion is not always appropriate. Some processes may run indefinitely, possibly in a cyclic fashion; some processes may terminate; new processes may be created dynamically. One area in which the model has been applied successfully is in job scheduling by operating systems. Here it may often be the case that a process will require a few resources in a specific order. It is not applicable to the scheduling of large numbers of short transactions.

17.10 Distributed deadlocks

The resources that are allocated dynamically may reside at different nodes of a distributed system. Requests for use of a resource may come from a source outside its home node. We have seen the possible mechanisms for making such requests in Chapter 15; for example a message or RPC requesting a resource may be pended by the resource manager until the resource becomes free, thus blocking the requesting thread.

In the discussion so far in this chapter we have assumed that global knowledge of the allocation of resources and requests for their use is available to algorithms for deadlock detection or avoidance. This can be made the case in a distributed system if we implement a **centralized resource allocator**. All requests have to go to this one service and it must be told when resources are freed. This centralized approach does not scale: the resource allocator could become a system bottleneck. The resource allocator is also a single point of failure in the system. If it fails, no process may acquire or release resources, even though the processes and resources are on operational nodes.

We saw that one way to prevent deadlock is to assign an integer value to each resource and to enforce that acquisition of resources by processes is in increasing order of their identifiers, thus avoiding cycles. This approach can be used in a distributed system, without the need for a central resource allocator, if the resources are assigned unique system-wide identifiers. All we need to know is that the process does not already hold a resource with a higher identifier, which can be determined locally. As we discussed above, this approach is not ideal for capturing the semantics of applications: most resources do not naturally fall into a sequential order.

A similar approach is to prevent cycles by using the process identifier, or a time-stamp issued to the process, to determine whether a process should be allowed to wait for a resource to become available or whether it should be aborted if it fails to acquire a resource. We shall study this approach, which is called time-stamp ordering (TSO), in Chapter 19 in the context of database transactions.

A pragmatic approach is to abort a waiting process after it has waited for a resource for some specified time.

17.10.1 Distributed deadlock detection

Let us now assume a resource manager (RM) at each node. The RMs have to maintain information:

- about local processes and resources as before;
- about requests made by local processes for remote resources that are waiting to be satisfied;
- about local resources allocated to remote processes.

One possibility is to make each RM attempt to keep a graph representing every process and every resource in the distributed system. This approach does not scale for large systems: it involves more data and more messages than the centralized approach. If the graphs are to be kept consistent we have a bottleneck at every node instead of a single central bottleneck.

We therefore require each RM to maintain a partial graph. All remote processes requesting local resources can be represented as a single process P_{rem} pointing to the local resources concerned. All remote resources being waited for can be represented by a single resource R_{rem} with the waiting local processes pointing to it, see Figure 17.13. We have extended the local resource allocation and request matrices by one row (one process) and one column (one resource).

Cycle detection can then be carried out as before for deadlock detection on each node's partial graph. If there are no cycles, all is well. If there is a cycle, the node must communicate with the other RMs to determine whether it represents a real deadlock. Figure 17.14 shows a simplified resource wait graph which shows only processes that are waiting on each other. We see a cycle distributed over several nodes.

The communication between the RMs follows the path of the possible cycle. In Figure 17.14, suppose the RM at node A detects that a cycle is possible. It

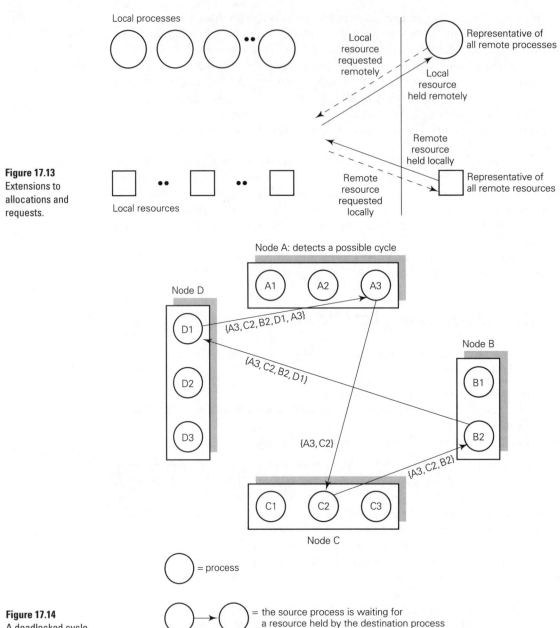

Figure 17.13
Extensions to allocations and requests.

Figure 17.14
A deadlocked cycle of distributed processes.

sends a message to the RM at node C because a process at node A is waiting on the resources held by a process at node C. The message {A3,C2} indicates this. The RM at node C finds that C2 is waiting on a process at node B, B2, so passes the information {A3, C2, B2} on to node B. Node B finds that the process in question is waiting on a resource held by a process at node D and sends

{A3, C2, B2, D1} to node D. Finally, node D communicates {A3, C2, B2, D1, A3} to the RM at node A. The RM at node A receives this communication, notes that the cycle is complete and takes action on the deadlock that exists.

17.11 Summary

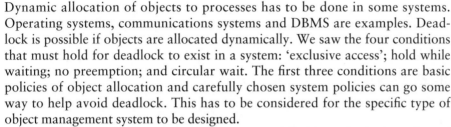

Dynamic allocation of objects to processes has to be done in some systems. Operating systems, communications systems and DBMS are examples. Deadlock is possible if objects are allocated dynamically. We saw the four conditions that must hold for deadlock to exist in a system: 'exclusive access'; hold while waiting; no preemption; and circular wait. The first three conditions are basic policies of object allocation and carefully chosen system policies can go some way to help avoid deadlock. This has to be considered for the specific type of object management system to be designed.

The allocation of objects to processes was modelled by a directed graph, and a cycle in an allocation graph was shown to be a necessary condition for deadlock to exist. It is also a sufficient condition if there is only one object of the object types involved in the cycle. Data structures were shown that could be used to record object allocation and availability and outstanding requests. Simple algorithms for deadlock detection and avoidance were given and discussed. These algorithms could be refined for use in specific systems.

The reader is now aware of a broad range of approaches that can be considered when resources are allocated dynamically. This material will be drawn on as a basis for subsequent chapters. It will also be extended, for example, to allow for shared locks as well as exclusive locks. We shall also consider the use of time-stamps for deadlock avoidance.

The flavour of the discussion in this chapter has been that deadlock is a rare and serious business. We shall see in later chapters that it could be expedient and desirable to provide an *abort* operation. If the ability to abort is available it can be built into many aspects of system design, including deadlock management.

Study questions

S 17.1

What is the basic problem with concurrent execution of composite operations?

S 17.2

Give an example of deadlock that is not related to a computer system.

S 17.3

If you were in your car waiting at traffic lights and the lights failed in such a way that all lights were on red, would that constitute a deadlocked situation?

S 17.4

Describe in detail what happens on path n in Figure 17.1 and why deadlock becomes inevitable.

S 17.5

Suppose that two processes, P and Q, are executing at the same time. If process P wants resource A and then, later, resource B (i.e. it wants both A and B at the same time), but process Q wants resource B and then, later, resource A (i.e. it too wants both A and B at the same time), must deadlock ensue?

S 17.6

Distinguish between deadlock and livelock.

S 17.7

What is starvation and what causes it?

S 17.8

Explain how each of the four conditions that must exist for deadlock to occur apply to path n in Figure 17.1 when deadlock has occurred.

S 17.9

How can deadlock be prevented?

S 17.10

(a)   What is a centralized resource allocator?
(b)   What is the basis on which such an allocator works?
(c)   Why is a centralized mechanism not a good idea?

S 17.11

(a)   What is the most pragmatic approach to deadlock prevention in a distributed system?
(b)   Which of the conditions for deadlock is being avoided by this pragmatic approach?

S 17.12

Describe how a local resource allocation graph held by a local resource manager takes account of requests for, and allocations of, resources on other nodes.

S 17.13

If a local resource manager in a system using the distributed deadlock detection algorithm as described detects a cycle that includes either the representative of remote processes or the representative of remote resources, what does it do?

S 17.14

If, in a system using the distributed deadlock detection algorithm, a node discovers that one of its processes, having a resource that a previous node is waiting for, is not itself waiting for a resource on another node, what should happen?

Exercises

17.1 Consider a wide range of examples of objects or resources that are allocated by a system to meet the demands of the application or applications that it runs. Consider the extent to which these demands are predictable in advance. Consider real-time systems, multi-user (distributed) operating systems, database management systems, etc.

17.2 What are deadlock, livelock and starvation? Give examples.

17.3 (a) What are the four conditions that must hold for deadlock to exist in an object allocation system? Which of these are system policies? Which is concerned with a specific sequence of events that happens to have occurred?

(b) Is it possible to ensure that any of these conditions can be guaranteed not to hold?

17.4 Consider the following alternative specifications of the resource requirements of a process. In each case the process makes requests dynamically for the objects it needs.
(a) No resource requirements are specified in advance.
(b) The total resource requirements are specified.
(c) The order in which the resources are required is specified.
(d) The order in which resources are acquired and released is specified.
Discuss how these levels of information on resource requirements could be used to handle the possibility of deadlock. What are the trade-offs involved in deciding on the amount of information to hold and the amount of processing to be done on it?

17.5 Devise the following solutions to the dining philosophers problem of Section 17.5:
(a) Take the semaphore program given in Section 17.5 as a starting point. Explore the use of an additional semaphore to achieve mutual exclusion, either to ensure that both forks are picked up at once or to simulate a room which the philosophers enter one at a time to eat. Adapt this latter solution to allow four philosophers at once to enter the room.
(b) Write semaphore programs which break the symmetry. Let odd-numbered philosophers pick up their forks left then right and even-numbered philosophers right then left. An alternative is that just one philosopher picks up his forks in the opposite order.

(c) Write the monitor 'solution' that is equivalent to our first attempt, given in Section 17.5, that is susceptible to deadlock.

(d) Write a solution that simulates a room in which the philosophers eat one at a time.

(e) Write a monitor solution that allocates forks so that only four philosophers at once may be attempting to eat.

(f) Write a monitor solution such that philosophers request both forks at once.

(g) The above solutions are specific to this problem. Explore the use of the general approaches to deadlock detection and avoidance described in this chapter. For example, a fork allocator monitor could run a deadlock detection algorithm whenever it could not satisfy a request for a fork. Or each process might register a claim for the total resources it might ever require before starting to run its algorithm. A fork allocator might run a deadlock avoidance algorithm. Note the length of these solutions.

17.6 Investigate the possibility of deadlock in the scenario described in Section 4.4.2 and illustrated in Figure 4.6.

Transactions

18.1 Introduction

In Chapter 8 we defined an atomic operation on data in main memory. In Chapter 14 we extended the definition of atomicity for a single operation on data in persistent memory, and showed how to make such an operation crash-resilient. In this chapter we extend the discussion to composite operations on persistent data. From Chapter 14, a single operation on persistent data is **atomic** if:

- When it terminates normally all its externally visible effects are made permanent (this is the property of **durability**), else it has no effect at all.
- If the operation accesses a shared data object, its invocation does not interfere with other operation invocations on the same data object. We shall extend this concept into the property of **isolation**.

If a crash occurs during the execution of an operation that has been defined to be atomic, in a system which supports atomic operations, then the system can be rolled back to the state it was in before the atomic operation was invoked and the operation can be restarted.

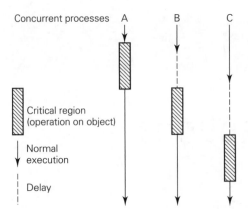

Concurrent processes A B C

Critical region
(operation on object)

Normal
execution

Delay

Figure 18.1
Serialization of
conflicting operations
on one object.

In Part II it was shown that mechanisms such as semaphores and monitors make a Single Logical Action (SLA) *strictly* indivisible. While a process is executing an SLA, no other process may see or access the data objects the process is working with. What this means is that SLAs must run serially, i.e. one after the other. Serial execution, by definition, guarantees indivisibility. This is shown in Figure 18.1.

In Part III we consider composite operations. We could, if we wished, make composite operations (also known as transactions) appear indivisible, simply by running them serially. Figure 18.2 shows a composite operation, comprising related, potentially interfering, operations on different objects, executed by three processes. In this case the composite operation is serialized as a single operation.

However, as discussed in Chapter 16, composite operations may be quite lengthy, and imposing such strict indivisibility would be inefficient. We normally therefore allow composite operations to run concurrently, but use mechanisms that make them *appear* indivisible, i.e. give the impression of running serially, even though the suboperations that make up the composite operation may actually be interleaved, as shown in Figure 18.3. Notice that the conflicting operations on individual objects are still serialized and take place in the same order within the composite operation for a given process.

In this chapter we address the question of how to make transactions *appear* indivisible, while allowing the suboperations of transactions to be interleaved. We must also ensure consistent system state.

 18.2 Transaction specification and programming

It is useful to extend the concept of atomic operation to include composite operations. We assume that it is the composite operation that has meaning to whatever application invoked it; the suboperations are related and all or none

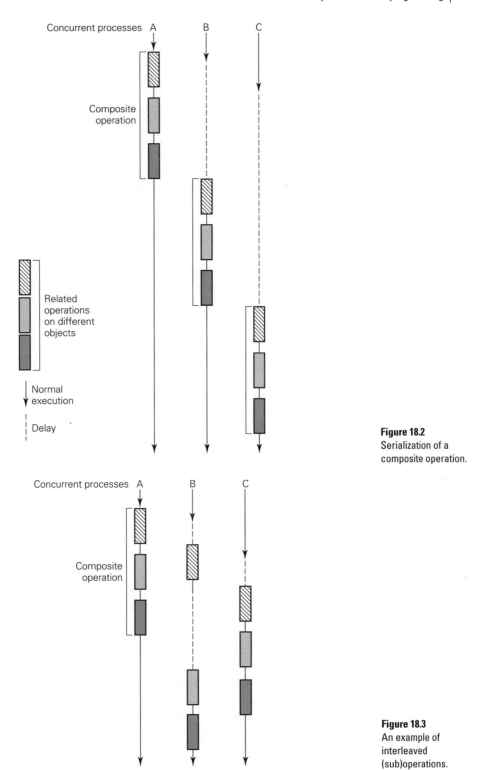

Concurrent processes A   B   C

Composite
operation

Related
operations
on different
objects

Normal
execution

Delay

Figure 18.2
Serialization of a
composite operation.

Concurrent processes A   B   C

Composite
operation

Figure 18.3
An example of
interleaved
(sub)operations.

of them must be carried out. Recall the operation hierarchy of Section 16.1 and Figures 16.4 and 16.7. It is the operation at the outermost level shown in the figures that is meaningful to the application; the application may not even be aware of the suboperations carried out by the system. In a banking system, for example, to credit an account with an amount, to debit an account with an amount, or to transfer an amount from one account to another are all operations that need to be atomic. Assuming that, at the start of processing, the system is in a consistent state, then successfully carrying out a meaningful atomic operation (or transaction) takes the system into another consistent state. We use the term **transaction** to indicate a meaningful atomic operation, that may or may not be composite. In general, a meaningful composite operation may reside at any level in an operation hierarchy. Also, a transaction at a given level may form part of a transaction at a higher level. We do not consider such nested transactions.

This chapter establishes a basis for studying how transactions may be implemented with concurrent execution and in the presence of crashes.

The example from Chapter 16, of a *transfer* transaction, might be programmed in some application-level language as follows:

begin transaction
transfer (account-A, account-B, £1000)
end transaction;

This implies that *transfer* is defined as a transaction and available to the high-level language programmer. At a lower level, within a library or the transaction management system, *transfer* could be expanded in terms of the operations on bank account objects. Using **start**, **commit** and **abort** operations, as well as the operations on bank account objects, a transfer from one account to another could be defined as a transaction as follows.

```
startTransaction();              // creates necessary system information
if(accountA.read-balance ≥ 1000 {
    accountA.debit(1000);
    accountB.credit(1000);
    commitTransaction();         //guarantees debit and credit are durable
}
else{
    System.out.println("Not enough in accountA for transfer");
    abortTransaction();          //guarantees all effects (if any) are undone
}
```

The start of the transaction is indicated by **startTransaction()**. Successful termination is called **commitment** and a successful transaction is assumed to terminate with a **commit** operation. After a successful **commit** operation, the changes that the transaction has made to the system state are guaranteed to persist. This is the **durability** property of transactions.

We discuss in Section 18.9 whether commitment is also the point at which those changes are allowed to become visible to other transactions. If this is the case then the transaction is said to have the property of **isolation**. It might be desirable in an implementation to make them visible earlier, thus achieving greater concurrency, but the effect on long-term system state must be as though the property of isolation was enforced.

A transaction management system must be **crash-resilient** in order to enforce the property of **atomicity** of transactions: either all or none of the operations of a transaction are carried out (see Section 16.6). If a transaction has not been committed it cannot be assumed that all its operations are complete. When the system restarts after a crash it must be able to roll back (undo) the effects of any transactions that were uncommitted at the time of the crash. This is called **aborting** a transaction. A transaction is defined to end with a **commit** or an **abort** operation.

If such a procedure is available for achieving crash resilience it may also be used for **concurrency control** by the management system. Once the possibility of undoing the effects of operations exists in a system we can, optimistically, attempt to achieve greater concurrency than is strictly safe and solve any problems that arise by undoing the effects of the operations that have turned out to be wrong.

The **abort** operation can also be made available to the application level. A transaction may then be coded to read values from a database and, depending on the values, proceed to further processing or abort, requiring any previous operations to be undone. An example is that a **check-balance** operation might find that there is insufficient money in an account to proceed with a **debit** operation.

It is convenient to use a concise notation for transactions and their operations. We assume that a transaction is given a unique identifying number i when it starts and that this number is associated with all its operations. In later examples we refer to the transaction as a whole as T_i, its start as S_i, a **commit** operation as C_i and an **abort** operation as A_i. The operations within the transaction will be named appropriately, such as debit$_i$ (account-A, £1000).

We shall use the example of bank account objects again in the next sections where the operations are discussed in more detail. For more complex transactions the application level may require to interact with the transaction manager and it is returned the transaction identifier for this purpose.

18.3 The definition of serializability and consistency

We defined a transaction as a (possibly composite) atomic operation that is meaningful to the application level: a transaction relates to some given level in an operation hierarchy. A transaction therefore causes the system to move from one consistent state at this level to another. If the possibility of crashes is ignored in the first instance, a **consistent system state** can be maintained by executing transactions **serially**.

If one process's transaction is executed to completion before any other can start there is no possibility of interference between them. We would then have made the transaction a single Part II-style indivisible operation (Figure 18.2).

Such a procedure (single threading of all, even unrelated, transactions) could be bad for system performance, as argued in Chapter 16, and serial execution of all transactions could not be contemplated for a multiprocessor or distributed system. We must therefore consider concurrent execution of transactions.

During concurrent execution of composite operations, suboperation executions are interleaved (see, for example, Figure 18.3). In some cases (hopefully in most cases), different transactions will access unrelated objects. An example is when transactions are associated with the data held about individuals, such as in a social security or tax-related database. The database is massive and processing is likely to be widely scattered across it.

The idea that consistent system state is maintained by serial execution of transactions is fundamental. This leads to the following **definition of serializability**:

If a specific interleaving of the suboperations of concurrent transactions can be shown to be equivalent to some serial execution of those transactions, then we know that the system state will be consistent, given that particular concurrent execution of the transactions.

Further discussion can be found in Korth *et al.* (1990).

An example illustrates the point. Consider two transactions *I* and *T*, each consisting of several operations (as defined in Section 18.6.) as follows:

Transaction *I*:
    add-interest-to-balance (account-A)
    add-interest-to-balance (account-B)

Transaction *T*:
    debit (account-A, 1000)
    credit (account-B, 1000)

A serial schedule of the operations of the transactions may be achieved in two ways (the start and commit operations are not shown here):

I before *T*	*T* before *I*
I: add-interest-to-balance (account-A)	*T*: debit (account-A, 1000)
I: add-interest-to-balance (account-B)	*T*: credit (account-B, 1000)
T: debit (account-A, 1000)	*I*: add-interest-to-balance (account-A)
T: credit (account-B, 1000)	*I*: add-interest-to-balance (account-B)

For example, suppose (to make the arithmetic simple and emphasize the point) that interest is computed at the (very high) rate of 0.1% per day and suppose account A stands at £10,000, and account B at £20,000. Then, after executing the *I* before *T* schedule, account A will hold £9010 and account B £21,020. The schedule *T* before *I* will result in account A holding £9009 and account B £21,021. The two sets of solutions are both valid, because in both cases a consistent system state is maintained.

Now consider two possible interleaved executions of the same transactions *I* and *T*:

Interleaved execution: schedule 1	Interleaved execution: schedule 2
I: add-interest-to-balance (account-A)	*T*: debit (account-A, 1000)
T: debit (account-A, 1000)	*I*: add-interest-to-balance (account-A)
I: add-interest-to-balance (account-B)	*I*: add-interest-to-balance (account-B)
T: credit (account-B, 1000)	*T*: credit (account-B, 1000)

If we assume the accounts hold the same amounts as before, and that the same interest rate applies, then the results after executing the suboperations in the order of schedule 1 are that account A holds £9010 and account B holds £21,020, whereas after schedule 2 account A holds £9010 and account B £21,021. The results for the interleaved execution of schedule 1 are identical to the *I* before *T* schedule, and thus constitute a consistent state. On the other hand, after executing suboperations in the order suggested by schedule 2, A holds £9009 and B holds £21,020. The system would be in an inconsistent state as £1 has gone missing. The problem arises because transaction *I* is seeing an inconsistent state.

By comparing the end results of an interleaved execution with the end results for a serial execution we can establish whether a system is still in a consistent state, and whether the schedule of interleaved operations can be considered to be **serializable**. In Section 18.6.2 we study how to achieve concurrent execution of transactions whilst ensuring that no transaction sees an inconsistent system state.

To summarize the above discussion, we can informally rephrase the earlier **definition of serializability** as follows:

Suppose two concurrently executing transactions S and T interleave their operations in some schedule. This schedule of operations will be serializable if it produces the same result as some serial execution of the same transactions S and T.

18.4 The ACID properties of transactions

Putting together the points made in the discussion above, a transaction may be defined as having the following properties:

Atomicity   Either all or none of the transaction's operations are performed.

Consistency   A transaction transforms the system from one consistent state to another.

Isolation   An incomplete transaction cannot reveal its result to other transactions before it is committed.

Durability   Once a transaction is committed the system must guarantee that the results of its operations will persist, even if there are subsequent system failures.

Note that these properties relate to the definition of transactions and do not imply particular methods of implementation. The effect on system state of running transactions is as defined by these properties.

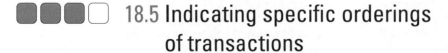

18.5 Indicating specific orderings of transactions

We assume a transaction management system with clients who may simultaneously submit a number of transactions. The system is at liberty to execute their operations in any order provided that a serializable execution is achieved, since a serializable execution of a set of transactions is defined to be correct. All serial executions are assumed by the system to be equally acceptable to the application.

If the semantics of the application require one transaction to be carried out after another they must not be submitted to a transaction management system at the same time. For example, it might be that a user must transfer money from a savings account to a current account before transferring money from the current account to some external account to make a payment. If they are submitted together, the management system may execute them concurrently and the suboperations may be scheduled in any order. The user may be told there are insufficient funds for the transfer.

This is a crude method of specifying dependencies between transactions. In Section 18.7 we explore how dependencies between the operations of transactions might be expressed, with a view to achieving a serializable execution of a number of transactions. Within a single transaction we assume that any two operations on the same object will be carried out in the order specified in the transaction. Unrelated operations may be carried out in any order, thus allowing for parallel execution in a multiprocessor environment.

18.6 A system model for transaction processing

Figure 18.4 shows the example of an abstract data object (a bank account) which we used in Section 16.5. We now use the same example to study serializability. Each data object has an associated set of operations, in this case:

- *create* a new account;
- *delete* an existing account;
- *read-balance* takes an account name as argument and returns the balance of the account;
- *check-balance* takes an account name and a value as arguments and returns true if the balance of the account is greater than or equal to the argument value, else it returns false;

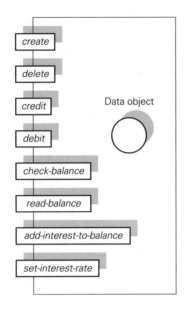

Data object

Figure 18.4
An account object.

- *credit* takes an account name and a value as arguments and adds the argument value to the balance. Note that the value of the balance is not output to the client;
- *debit* takes an account name and a value as arguments and subtracts the argument value from the balance. Note that the value of the balance is not output to the client.

   It is assumed here that the client is responsible for checking the balance before doing a debit. For example, the transfer transaction would contain:

   if *check-balance (account-A, £1000)* **then** *debit (account-A, £1000)* . . .

- *set-interest-rate (r%)* is used to set the daily interest rate to a given percentage;
- *add-interest-to-balance* is run daily by the system administration (probably at 3 a.m., when, although cashpoints are available, not many people will be around doing transactions). This operation computes the interest accrued to the account, based on its value at midnight, and adds the interest to the balance.

18.6.1 Non-commutative (conflicting) pairs of operations

In order to establish serializability, it is important to specify which pairs of operations on a given object do not commute. Operations *A* and *B* are **commutative** if, from any initial state, executing *A* then *B* results in the same object state and external output values as executing *B* then *A*; the order of execution does not matter. We use the term **conflicting** as equivalent to **non-commutative**, relating to a pair of operations.

For a given object it must therefore be specified which pairs of operations conflict. Note that it is necessary to include in the pairs each operation with itself. An example of an operation which does not commute with itself is *write*. This operation stores a given value at some location, typically on a disk drive. For example:

- the order: *write* (x, 100); *write* (x, 200) results in the final value 200 for x;
- the order: *write* (x, 200); *write* (x, 100) results in the final value 100 for x.

Any operation that stores a value and, in doing so, replaces what was there previously does not commute with itself. Assignment is another example.

In the case of the bank account object:

credit and *debit* are commutative (the final value of the account is the same whatever the order of execution and there is no external output);

credit and *credit* are commutative, as are *debit* and *debit*;

read-balance and *credit* are not commutative (the value read and output for the balance is different depending on whether it is executed before or after the credit operation; the final value of the account is the same whatever the order of execution);

read-balance and *debit* are not commutative;

read-balance and *read-balance* are commutative, as are *check-balance* and *check-balance*;

check-balance and *credit* are not commutative;

check-balance and *debit* are not commutative;

set-interest-rate and *set-interest-rate* are not commutative (the final value of the interest rate depends on the order of execution of two *set-interest-rate* operations if their arguments are different);

add-interest-to-balance conflicts with credit and debit because the value computed for the interest is different depending on whether the *credit* or *debit* was done before or after *add-interest-to-balance*. It conflicts with *read-balance* and *check-balance* with respect to the value of the account output.

For example, suppose that interest is again computed at the rate of 0.1% per day and suppose account A stands at £10,000:

credit (*account-A*, £5000)	$A = £15,000$
add-interest-to-balance (*account-A*)	$A = £15,015$

If the operations are executed in the other order:

add-interest-to-balance (*account-A*)	$A = £10,010$
credit (*account-A*, £5000)	$A = £15,010$

The final state is different: the operations conflict.

18.6.2 Condition for serializability

We use this model, defining objects and indicating which of their operations are non-commutative (conflicting), with the following assumptions:

- Objects are identified uniquely in a system.
- The operations are executed without interference (in the sense of Part II); that is, the operations we are considering here are at the finest granularity of decomposition visible to the client.
- There is a single clock associated with the object which is used to indicate the time at which operations take place and therefore their order.
- The object records the time at which each operation invocation takes place with the transaction identifier (see Section 18.2) of the transaction that executed the operation.

It is therefore possible, for any pair of transactions, to determine the order of execution of their operations (in particular the conflicting pairs of operations) on a given object which they both invoke.

In Section 18.3 we presented the fundamental idea that consistency is maintained when transactions are run in *some* serial order. It follows that, if two transactions are interleaved, consistency will be maintained if the result is *equivalent* to the transactions having been run in some serial order. This can be thought of as a *definition* of what serializability means. The question now arises as to how one can ensure that two interleaved transactions are serializable. This is answered by the **condition for serializability** (Weihl, 1984; 1989):

> For **serializability** of two transactions it is necessary and sufficient
> for the order of their invocations of all conflicting pairs of operations
> to be the same for all the objects which are invoked by both
> transactions.

We use this condition as the basis for our study of concurrent execution of transactions. In the next section we generalize from pairwise serializability to serializability of a number of transactions. Note that the condition holds for a distributed system where there can be no assumption of global time. All that is needed is time local to each object.

Herlihy (1990) takes a more general view of conflict and further work is reported in Badrinath and Ramamritham (1992), and Guerni *et al.* (1995).

Example

Consider again (see Section 18.3) the example of two transactions I and T. We saw four possible schedules of suboperations for these transactions. The first two were serial:

I before *T*	*T* before *I*
I: add-interest-to-balance (account-A)	*T*: debit (account-A, 1000)
I: add-interest-to-balance (account-B)	*T*: credit (account-B, 1000)
T: debit (account-A, 1000)	*I*: add-interest-to-balance (account-A)
T: credit (account-B, 1000)	*I*: add-interest-to-balance (account-B)

the third and fourth were interleaved:

Interleaved execution: schedule 1	*Interleaved execution: schedule 2*
I: add-interest-to-balance (account-A)	*T*: debit (account-A, 1000)
T: debit (account-A, 1000)	*I*: add-interest-to-balance (account-A)
I: add-interest-to-balance (account-B)	*I*: add-interest-to-balance (account-B)
T: credit (account-B, 1000)	*T*: credit (account-B, 1000)

The conflicting pairs of operations in these transactions are:

> add-interest-to-balance (account-A) with debit (account-A, 1000)
> add-interest-to-balance (account-B) with credit (account-B, 1000)

In the first serial schedule, labelled *I* before *T*, we find that for the conflicting pair of operations on object *account-A*, that is the add-interest-to balance and the debit operation, the order of execution is *I* followed by *T*. The next conflicting pair of operations, now on object *account-B*, the add-interest-to-balance and credit operations, are also executed in the order first *I* then *T*. So for both pairs of conflicting operations, *the order of execution is the same at all objects involved in both transactions*, and thus the condition for serializability holds, and this is a serializable schedule.

For the schedule labelled *T* before *I*, we find that all the conflicting pairs of operations on all the objects involved in the transaction (*account-A* and *account-B*) are executed in the order first *T* then *I*, and this schedule of operations is therefore also serializable.

It should come as no surprise that a serial schedule is serializable! After all, in a serial schedule first all operations belonging to one transaction are executed, followed by the operations of the next transaction, and thus the conflicting pairs of operations are, by definition, executed in the same order at all the objects common to the transactions. It is more challenging to see if the condition for serializability can hold for an interleaved schedule of operations.

In the interleaved schedule 1, the order of the conflicting pairs of operations on both objects involved (*account-A* and *account-B*) is first *I*, then *T* and thus this schedule will leave the system in a consistent state. However, in schedule 2, the order at object *account-A* is first *T* then *I*, for the conflicting pair:

> add-interest-to-balance (account-A) with debit (account-A, 1000)

and the order at object *account-B* is first *I* then *T* for the conflicting pair:

add-interest-to-balance (account-B) with **credit (account-B, 1000)**

The interleaved schedule 2 therefore has different orderings at the two objects invoked in the transactions by their conflicting pairs of operations, and the schedule does not meet the condition for serializability. In Section 18.3 we were already able to make observations about the inconsistent system state using the *definition* of serializability (by comparing the final values for *account-A* and *account-B* with those they would have if the transactions were executed in some serial order). We now have an explanation for our earlier observation in the form of the *condition* for serializability.

18.7 Dependency graphs for transactions

In this section we develop a graphical representation for schedules of operations of transactions. Any necessary ordering of the operations within a transaction is indicated in its graph. Figure 18.5 shows the transactions *Sum* and *Transfer* where *Transfer* is as used in the previous sections, and *Sum* is defined as follows:

```
read-balance(account-A);
read-balance(account-B);
print(account-A + account-B).
```

Note that the **print(account-A + account B)** statement is shorthand for 'add the balances of the two accounts, found as the result of performing **read-balance(account-A)** and **read-balance(account-B)**'.

Taking the *Sum* transaction as an example, *start* comes first, the *read-balance* operations may take place in either order or in parallel (on a multiprocessor) but must precede the *print* operation, and finally there comes the *commit* operation.

In the next examples we use a more concise notation for the purposes of discussion: *P* and *Q* for objects and *W, X, Y, Z* for operations. Figure 18.6 specifies two transactions, both of which access objects *P* and *Q*. The operations *W* and *X* on object *P* are conflicting, as are operations *Y* and *Z* on object *Q*. In practice, an object is likely to have many operations but we consider a minimal example in order to highlight the issues. We focus on pairs of conflicting operations in order to explore the condition for serializability given in Section 18.6.2. The

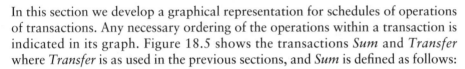

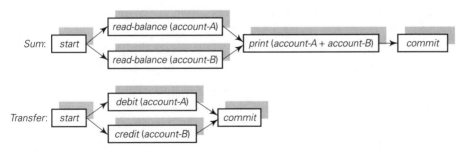

Figure 18.5
Graphical representation of the *Sum* and *Transfer* transactions.

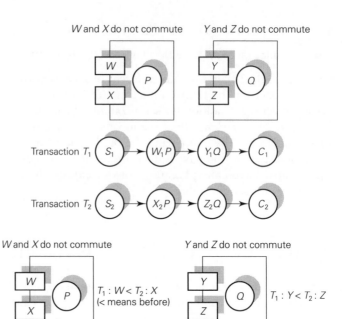

Figure 18.6
A specification of
two transactions.

Figure 18.7
A serializable
schedule of the
transactions'
operations.

graphs show the operations within each transaction in serial order for simplicity. Our concern is to explore how concurrent transactions may be represented.

Figure 18.7 shows a serializable execution of the operations of the two transactions:

T_1 invokes W on P before T_2 invokes X on P (object P: T_1 before T_2)
T_1 invokes Y on Q before T_2 invokes Z on Q (object Q: T_1 before T_2)

That is, the order of pairs of conflicting operations is the same for all the objects which are invoked by both transactions. In the graph this is represented by the two downward arrows, where the direction of the arrow (in both cases from T_1 to T_2) indicates that there is an ordering $T_1 < T_2$.

Figure 18.8 shows a non-serializable execution of the operations of the two transactions:

T_1 invokes W on P before T_2 invokes X on P (object P: T_1 before T_2)
T_2 invokes Z on Q before T_1 invokes Y on Q (object Q: T_2 before T_1)

In this case, the pair of conflicting operations on P (W, X) is invoked in the order T_1 then T_2. The pair of conflicting operations on Q (Z, Y) is invoked in the order T_2 then T_1. There is no ordering of the transactions that is consistent with the order of operations at both objects.

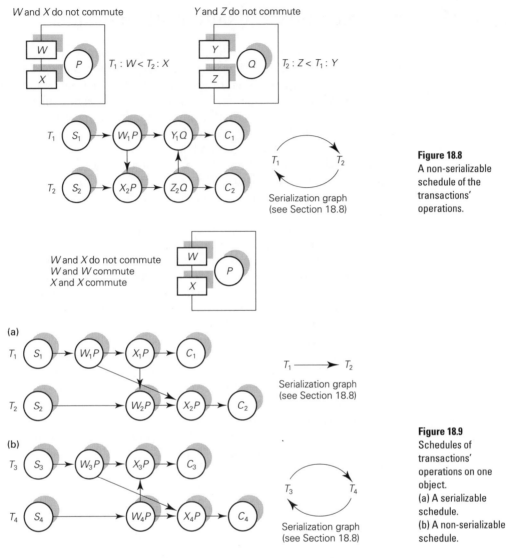

Figure 18.8
A non-serializable schedule of the transactions' operations.

Figure 18.9
Schedules of transactions' operations on one object.
(a) A serializable schedule.
(b) A non-serializable schedule.

Figure 18.9 gives an example involving a single object. Since operation W is invoked by both transactions it is necessary to know whether W commutes with W and, similarly, whether X commutes with X. We specify that W commutes with W and X commutes with X, and so we need only consider the single pair of conflicting operations W and X.

(a) T_1 invokes W on P before T_2 invokes X on P (object P: T_1 before T_2)
  T_1 invokes X on P before T_2 invokes W on P (object P: T_1 before T_2).

The schedule is not only serializable but is, in this case, serial.

(b) T_3 invokes W on P before T_4 invokes X on P (object P: T_3 before T_4)
  T_4 invokes W on P before T_3 invokes X on P (object P: T_4 before T_3).

The schedule is not serializable.

18.8 Histories and serialization graphs

A history is a data structure which represents a concurrent execution of a set of transactions. The directed graphs of Figures 18.7, 18.8 and 18.9 are simple examples: they show the operations within the transactions, and the order of invocation of conflicting pairs of operations by different transactions. Note that the order of invocation of all conflicting pairs of operations on all objects must be shown in the history. Figure 18.10 gives a representation of a history in which the details of the objects and operations involved are not shown.

A **serializable history** represents a serializable execution of the transactions. That is, there is a serial ordering of the transactions in which all conflicting pairs of operations at each object are invoked in the same order as in the given history.

An object is a witness to an order dependency between two transactions if they have invoked a conflicting pair of operations at that object. A **serialization graph** is a directed graph that shows only transaction identifiers and dependencies between transactions; the vertices of the graph are the transactions T_i, and there is an edge $T_i \rightarrow T_j$ if and only if some object is a witness to that order dependency. For example, $T_1 \rightarrow T_2$ is the transaction graph for the history in Figure 18.7. The serialization graph for T_1, T_2 and T_3 is shown in Figure 18.10. A transaction history is serializable if and only if its serialization graph is acyclic.

Figure 18.11 gives examples of possible serialization graphs for four transactions. In both (a) and (b) every pair of transactions has conflicting operations executed in the same order (there is at most one edge between each pair of transactions). In Figure 18.11(b) the serialization graph has a cycle and the history represented by the serialization graph is not serializable.

In general we must ascertain whether a given schedule of the operations within a set of transactions is serializable. We require a total ordering of the set of transactions that is consistent with the schedule:

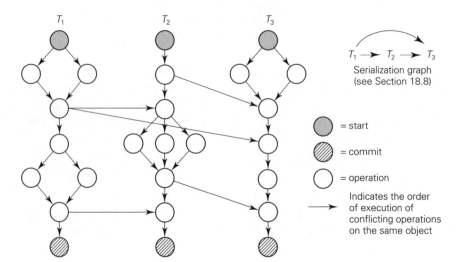

Figure 18.10
An example of a serializable history of three transactions.

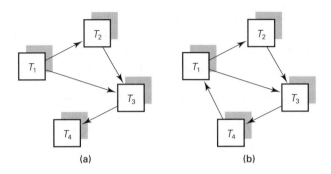

Figure 18.11
Examples of
serialization graphs.
(a) A serialization
graph for a
serializable history.
(b) A serialization
graph for a non-
serializable history.

- Each object knows which pairs of its operations conflict.
- Each object knows which transactions have invoked conflicting operations: it is a witness to an order dependency between them.
- Provided that the order dependencies are consistent both at each given object and between objects then an ordering is determined for each pair of transactions involved. If not, then there is a cycle in the serialization graph, say $T_1 \rightarrow T_2 \rightarrow T_1$ as in Figure 18.8, and the transaction history cannot be serializable. This information can be assembled for all the objects invoked by the set of transactions, giving rise to the serialization graph.
- To find a total ordering of the set of transactions that is consistent with the pairwise order dependencies requires a topological sort of the serialization graph. This can be done if and only if the graph is acyclic (Aho *et al.*, 1983).

We can justify the result informally based on simple cases; for example suppose three transactions T_1, T_2 and T_3 operate on a common object A, invoking operations which conflict. The object A is witness to a single serial ordering of the transactions and a cycle is impossible. Suppose there is no object common to T_1, T_2 and T_3 but T_1 and T_2 invoke conflicting operations on A, T_2 and T_3 on B and T_3 and T_1 on C, as shown in Figure 18.12. The six possible serial orders of the transactions are shown in the figure and none is consistent with a cycle in the serialization graph such as $T_1 \rightarrow T_2 \rightarrow T_3 \rightarrow T_1$.

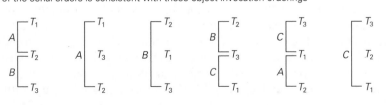

Figure 18.12
Investigation
of cycles in a
serialization graph.

Now consider cycles with respect to the implementation of transactions and suppose that the property of isolation is enforced; that is, a transaction must seize all the objects it invokes and no other transaction can see the results of its invocations until after it commits. In this case a serial order is imposed by the order in which the transactions acquire objects: a cycle is impossible. If isolation is not enforced and the invocations on A, B and C were to go ahead in parallel we would create a cycle of transactions each unable to commit until the previous transaction in the cycle had committed. This must be prevented.

Suppose that a TP system maintains a serialization graph of the transactions in progress. A new transaction is submitted and the system attempts to execute it concurrently with the ongoing transactions. Any proposed schedule of the operations of the new transaction can be tested by creating a serialization graph which is the original one extended with the operations of the new transaction. A schedule can be rejected if the serialization graph thus extended has a cycle.

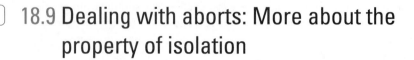

18.9 Dealing with aborts: More about the property of isolation

The theory outlined above does not take into account that the operations of a transaction might be undone due to an *abort* termination. It must be possible to return the system to a consistent state as though the transaction had not taken place. The following problems could arise through concurrent execution of transactions, even if a serializable schedule of suboperations had been devised. It is demonstrated that serializability is necessary but not sufficient for correct concurrent operation.

18.9.1 Cascading aborts

Figure 18.13 shows a serializable schedule of the transactions T_1 and T_2 used above in Section 18.7. This time, T_1 happens to abort.

Suppose that the transaction scheduler, having noted the order of operations for a serializable transaction, had, in order to achieve maximum concurrency, allowed T_2 to execute operation X on object P as soon as T_1 had completed operation W and similarly for object Q. T_2 may have seen state or performed output that is now incorrect because T_1 has aborted and T_2 must also be aborted.

In general, aborting one transaction could lead to the need to abort a number of related transactions, called **cascading aborts**. This behaviour might degrade system performance so badly that it could be advisable to ensure that any state seen by a transaction has been written by a committed transaction. In other words, the effects of the suboperations of a transaction are not made visible to other transactions until the transaction commits, thus enforcing the property of **isolation** in the implementation. A schedule of operation invocations which enforces this property is called a **strict** schedule. This approach would cause difficulties in

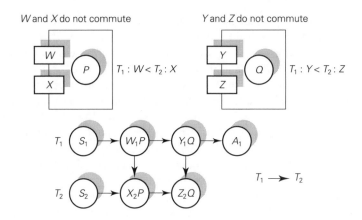

Figure 18.13
Example of cascading abort.

systems where transactions could be long and contention was likely, and could be deemed unnecessary if crashes and aborts are unlikely to happen.

18.9.2 The ability to recover state

The discussion here is in general terms. In the next chapter specific methods for achieving correct (serializable) executions of transactions are described. Some of the scenarios given below as examples might not in practice be allowed to arise, or some of the theoretically possible system actions might be deemed too expensive to implement.

If abort is supported it must be possible to return the system to a consistent state, as though the aborted transaction had not taken place. Consider the following interleaving of operations within a concurrent execution of transactions T_1 and T_2. The operations involved, several credit operations on bank accounts, are commutative so there is no problem with serializability. Suppose that initially $A = £5000$ and $B = £8000$.

$start_1$
$credit_1 (account\text{-}A, £1000)$ $A = £6000$
$credit_1 (account\text{-}B, £500)$ $B = £8500$
$start_2$
$credit_2 (account\text{-}A, £200)$ $A = £6200$
$abort_1$ $(A = £5200$ $B = £8000$ should be achieved)
$credit_2 (account\text{-}B, £600)$ $B = £8600$
$abort_2$ $(A = £5000$ $B = £8000$ should be achieved)

This example schedule is not strict, that is, it violates the property of isolation. If this is the case, greater care must be taken on abort or on crash recovery than merely restoring each object's state to that prior to the aborted operation. When T_1 aborts, T_2 has already done another *credit* operation on *account-A*. The value of *account-A* cannot simply be put back to that prior to $credit_1 (account\text{-}A, £1000)$. Neither can we take no action at all; T_2 goes on to abort. We cannot then put the value of *account-A* back to what it was prior to $credit_2 (account\text{-}A, £200)$ (this was the value after the credit by T_1 which has already aborted). If we had discarded the value prior to T_1's invocation the original state would be irrecoverable. Fortunately, we assume that a record of invocations is kept with the object and we have higher-level semantics than merely a record of state changes.

We assume that every operation has an **inverse** or **undo** operation. When a transaction aborts, each of its invocations must be undone. For a given object, if there have been no conflicting invocations since the one that is to be undone then we simply apply the *undo* operation to the current state (the order of invocation of commutative operations is irrelevant). In this example, the inverse of *credit* is *debit*. When T_1 aborts we can simply *debit* (*account-A*, £1000) and remove the record of the original invocation from the object.

If there has been a conflicting invocation since the invocation we require to abort then we must undo all the invocations back to the conflicting operation. After we have undone that, we can perform the undo to achieve the abort we require, then we must do the subsequent operations again. The following example illustrates this; *interest* is used as a shorthand for *add-interest-to-balance* and a (very high) daily interest rate of 0.1% is again assumed for simplicity. The point is that we cannot simply apply the inverse of *credit*$_1$ when T_1 aborts, for example: this would leave the account with the value £7008 which is incorrect. Note also that even though non-strict operations are allowed to go ahead, transactions which invoke them might be delayed when they request to commit because they have seen uncommitted state. Suppose that initially $A = £5000$.

start$_1$		
credit$_1$	(*account-A*, £1000)	$A = £6000$
start$_2$		
credit$_2$	(*account-A*, £2000)	$A = £8000$
start$_3$		
interest$_3$	(*account-A*)	$A = £8008$
commit$_3$	delay commit?	
start$_4$		
credit$_4$	(*account-A*, £1000)	$A = £9008$
commit$_4$	delay commit?	
abort$_1$		

        undo *credit*$_4$ (*account-A*, £1000) $A = £8008$
        undo *interest*$_3$ (*account-A*) $A = £8000$
        (note there is no need to undo and redo *credit*$_2$ (*account-A*, £2000) because credits commute)
        undo *credit*$_1$ (*account-A*, £1000) $A = £7000$
        redo *interest*$_3$ (*account-A*) $A = £7007$
        redo *credit*$_4$ (*account-A*, £1000) $A = £8007$

abort$_2$

        undo *credit*$_4$ (*account-A*, £1000) $A = £7007$
        undo *interest*$_3$ (*account-A*) $A = £7000$
        undo *credit*$_2$ (*account-A*, £2000) $A = £5000$
        redo *interest*$_3$ (*account-A*) $A = £5005$
        redo *credit*$_4$ (*account-A*, £1000) $A = £7005$

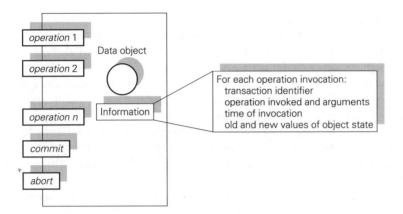

Figure 18.14
An object used in a
transaction system.

This is a complex procedure and is the penalty to be paid for relaxing the property of isolation in an implementation and allowing non-strict conflicting operations to be invoked. In general, we assume a strict execution of operations to avoid this complexity, although as stated above, strictness may not be realistic in some systems. A strict execution can be enforced if each object delays any request to invoke an operation which conflicts with an uncommitted operation. An object must then be told when a transaction that has invoked it commits: this is assumed to be through a commit operation in the object's interface.

commit (transaction-id)

would cause all state changes resulting in invocations on the object by the transaction to be made permanent and visible to other transactions.

We return to this topic in later chapters in the context of specific methods of concurrency control. In the meantime, let us assume that each object holds information on the operations that have been invoked on it which includes the transaction identifier of the invoker and the time of the invocation (Figure 18.14). It should be emphasized that this is a theoretical starting point: all relevant information is assumed to be held. It would not be possible in a practical implementation to hold an indefinite history with every object, and optimizations would have to be made. We assume that each object has a commit operation and an abort operation.

18.10 Summary

We have extended the definition given in Chapter 14, of an atomic operation invocation in the presence of crashes, to cover atomic composite operation invocations (transactions) in the presence of concurrent transactions and crashes. The ACID (Atomicity, Consistency, Isolation, Durability) properties of transactions were motivated and discussed.

A system model to be used as a basis for reasoning about all aspects of transaction processing was introduced. The model focuses on the operations of a single object and generalizes naturally to distributed objects. Conflicting operations were defined to be those which do not commute; that is, the order in which they are executed affects the final state of the object, or the value output by an operation.

We have assumed that each object will hold information on operation invocations that have been made on it, in particular, the time of the invocation and the identifier of the invoking transaction. The order of invocation of all operations on an object can therefore be determined. We shall see how this information might be used for concurrency control and recovery purposes in later chapters. An introductory treatment of serializability was given here, based on this model.

We considered the pros and cons of relaxing the property of isolation of atomic transactions in an implementation, that is, allowing non-strict executions. In this case a transaction is able to see system state (values of objects) written by uncommitted transactions. The motivation is to allow greater concurrency, but the price to be paid is greater complexity. Cascading aborts can occur and the recovery of previous correct system state might involve a complex procedure of undoing and redoing operations. A strict execution (in which the property of isolation is enforced in the implementation) seems to be desirable to avoid this complexity. It may not be feasible to enforce strictness in practice if long transactions are common, failure is unlikely (crashes or application requested abort) and contention is likely.

Study questions

S 18.1

What is the property of durability?

S 18.2

What is the property of isolation?

S 18.3

In Figure 18.2, how has the problem of conflicting operations on several objects been overcome?

S 18.4

How does the situation shown in Figure 18.3 differ from that shown in Figure 18.2? Why is this allowable? What essential features of Figure 18.2 are retained by Figure 18.3?

S 18.5

If a transaction has not been committed (perhaps because of a system crash), what cannot be assumed and what must happen?

S 18.6

What is meant by aborting a transaction and why might this operation be made available at the application level?

S 18.7

How is a transaction identified at the application level?

S 18.8

During concurrent execution of composite operations, suboperation executions are interleaved. In such a scenario, how can we be assured that a consistent system state is maintained?

S 18.9

What is a serial schedule of transactions?

S 18.10

What is the main assumption made by a transaction management system with regard to the order of processing of transactions?

S 18.11

Define the term *commutative*. What is meant by *conflicting* operations?

S 18.12

In Figure 18.7 what information is conveyed by the serialization graph?

S 18.13

What does a serialization graph with a cycle represent?

Exercises

18.1 How can a serial execution of a composite operation be guaranteed? What is a serializable execution of a composite operation?

18.2 In a TP system a client submits a transaction, which is done and acknowledged to the client. What must the system guarantee when that acknowledgement is given?

18.3 What are the ACID properties of atomic transactions and how can they be ensured under concurrency and crashes?

18.4 Relate the system model based on object invocation given in Section 18.6 to the discussion of Section 15.11 on object naming, location and invocation.

18.5 How does the graph which represents the history of a set of transactions being executed differ from a serialization graph? What property of the serialization graph must hold for the transactions that it represents to be serializable?

18.6 Why might the decision to abort one transaction lead to the need to abort another? Could this happen if the property of isolation of atomic transactions was enforced at all times?

18.7 Give some practical examples of conflicting operations on an object.

18.8 Assume that every operation on an object has an inverse or undo operation. Assume that a number of operations have taken place on an object. When can an undo operation simply be applied to the current state of an object, even if there have been operations on the object since the one that must be undone?

18.9 We have used an object model with object operation semantics to define conflicting operations and serializability. Some earlier studies, for example Bernstein *et al.* (1987), were based only on read–write semantics where:
read and read do not conflict
read and write conflict
write and write conflict.
Which of the operations of the object shown in Figure 18.4 would conflict using read–write semantics but not using object operation semantics?

19

Concurrency control

19.1 Introduction

The main concern of this chapter is how concurrent execution of transactions can be implemented. Crash resilience, although related, is covered in the next chapter. The conceptual model based on objects, which was developed in Chapter 18, will be used again here.

A natural approach to concurrency control is to lock the objects involved in a composite operation (transaction). We shall show that locking can achieve serializability of the operations of transactions but that deadlock has to be considered. An alternative to locking is to associate a time-stamp with each transaction and to use this as a basis for enforcing one particular serializable order of execution of the operations of transactions. The methods used for concurrency control are considered in the light of the possibility that conflict may be very unlikely and having a great deal of mechanism in place to resolve it could be misplaced effort. Optimistic concurrency control may be the most suitable method for some application areas and is the final approach we consider.

First, we establish that the concurrent invocation of composite operations in main memory is subject to some of the problems that we have studied in relation to transaction systems. Then we focus on transaction processing systems (where persistent memory must be used).

19.2 Concurrent composite operations in main memory only

Assume that a concurrent program has been developed in a modular fashion. We assume that each shared data abstraction is implemented as an abstract data type, as shown in Figure 19.1, and a data object is locked for exclusive use while any of its operations is invoked. Section 11.2 showed how this might be implemented for a single operation.

The problems of uncontrolled concurrent invocation of composite operations, discussed already in Part III, are relevant to this model. Assume in Figure 19.1 that objects A and B are operated on by one concurrent process; that is, a meaningful, high-level operation comprises both an operation on object A and an operation on object B. Similarly, another composite operation invoked by another process involves both object B and object C. We have already seen that incorrect values can result from inappropriate interleavings of the suboperations of composite operations. This is equally true for data objects in main memory and in persistent memory.

19.2.1 Objects in the main memory of a single computer

We established the properties of transactions in Chapter 18: atomicity, consistency, isolation and durability (ACID). It is helpful to consider these properties for concurrent invocation of composite operations in main memory only; that is, when no suboperation of a composite operation writes to persistent store. We first consider a program running in the main memory of a single computer.

Atomicity   If there is a crash during a composite operation, all the effects of suboperations are lost. If there is no crash the composite operation will complete. Atomicity holds without any special need for enforcement.

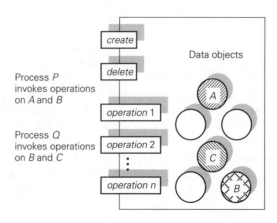

Figure 19.1
Related operations on data objects in main memory.

Consistency   We assume that a composite (high-level) operation has meaning. Invocation of a single composite operation takes the state managed by the program from one consistent value to another. We are not concerned with crashes since all state in main memory is lost on a crash. Consistency must be enforced in the presence of concurrent invocations.

Isolation   The results of the suboperations of a composite operation should not be revealed until the operation completes. Isolation should be enforced.

Durability   If a program runs in the main memory of a single computer and a crash occurs during a composite operation invocation, all the main memory is lost. Durability is not relevant.

The properties of consistency and isolation are relevant to the correct execution of programs which contain composite operation invocations. Control of **concurrent execution of composite operations** is the central issue.

The concurrency control methods for transactions that are discussed later in this chapter might also be applicable to data in main memory only. Since locking has been the approach taken throughout Part II to ensure the correct execution of a single operation, we first consider this method briefly.

A simple example based on Figure 19.1, showing that deadlock must be considered, is as follows:

process P invokes an operation on A (thus locking A);
process Q invokes an operation on B (thus locking B);
the operation on A invokes an operation on B and P is delayed;
the operation on B invokes an operation on A and Q is delayed;
processes P and Q are deadlocked.

An alternative object management scheme is to provide separate *lock* and *unlock* operations. Deadlock can then arise when locks are acquired piecemeal. Section 16.2 set up a similar problem in a monitor-based program. The dining philosophers problem discussed in Section 17.5 is another example.

19.2.2 Objects in main memory in a distributed system

We now consider briefly concurrent invocations of composite operations involving objects which are located throughout the main memory of computers comprising a distributed system. We assume that there is a single copy of each object.

A given composite operation is invoked at a single node: let us call it the managing node. For any object which is not located at that node a remote invocation must be carried out. Chapter 15 showed that this might be done by a remote procedure call or by message passing. Any node or any network connection may be subject to congestion or may fail. As we discussed in Chapter 15, the protocol implementing the invocation will indicate this by returning an exception. Because the distributed program accesses data objects in main memory only, we need not be concerned, on an exception, with changes that might have been made to persistent state by a suboperation invocation. By definition, there are none. Again, the major issue is concurrency control; in more detail:

Atomicity   A number of distributed objects are invoked. If the result of every remote invocation is returned to the managing node and the local operations are also done then the composite operation is known by the manager to be complete.

               If any result is not returned (after retries by the underlying protocol) then the composite operation has failed. The significance of this depends on the application. It may be that the distributed program has to be abandoned. It may be that the program can proceed by making use of an alternative to the operation that failed.

Consistency   We assume that a composite operation has meaning. Invocation of a single composite operation takes the (distributed) state managed by the program from one consistent value to another. Consistency must be enforced in the presence of concurrent invocations and partial failures.

Isolation   The results of the suboperations of a composite operation should not be revealed until the operation completes. Isolation should be enforced.

Durability   If composite operations are invoked in main memory only, durability is not relevant.

Again, our main concern is to achieve consistency through enforcing isolation by some means of concurrency control. If locking is employed then, as above, we must allow for the possibility of deadlock.

19.2.3 Systematic approaches to concurrent program development

Some approaches to solving these problems in the context of a concurrent program are as follows:

1 Incorporate a transaction specification into the programming language. For example:

     start transaction
     invoke *operation* 1 on object *A*
     invoke *operation* n on object *B*
     end transaction;

The objects may or may not be persistent and may or may not be in a single local memory. This pushes the problem down into the transaction implementation. Most of this chapter is concerned with how transactions, which might be specified in this way, can be implemented.

2 Use formal techniques of program analysis to ensure that the software system is deadlock free.

3 Incorporate a general object manager in the program. Data structures and algorithms such as those described in Chapter 17 to detect or avoid deadlock could be used by the manager.

Section 10.4

4 When designing the concurrent program, take into account the possibility of deadlock and avoid calls between operations that could lead to cycles (a systematic rather than formal approach).

For a given program the order in which locks are acquired could be specified statically in order to avoid cycles. In cases where large data objects are broken down into smaller components so that an operation on the containing object involves a nested call to the contained object this is easily achieved; the reverse direction of call is not required. Also, it may be possible to lock only the component concerned and not the whole containing object. In general it is difficult to avoid the possibility of cycles, and a systematic, informal approach is highly susceptible to error. Small problems, such as the dining philosophers example (Section 17.5), can be solved specifically.

5 Consider other methods of concurrency control than locking, such as time-stamp ordering (see below).

We now proceed to concurrency control in systems which support transactions on persistent data.

19.3 Structure of transaction management systems

Figure 19.2 outlines the components of an instance of a transaction processing system (TPS) in a single computer. In Chapter 21 we shall consider distributed transaction processing explicitly although much of the discussion in this chapter is relevant to distributed systems. Clients submit transactions to the TPS, which may start work on them concurrently. The transaction manager is responsible for validating the clients' submissions and for passing the component operations of the transactions to the scheduler (we assume here that the objects to be invoked are in the local database). The scheduler will use some strategy to achieve a serializable schedule of the operations of the transactions in progress. This is the main concern of the rest of this chapter.

The data objects in persistent memory will be transferred into main memory for operation invocation and new values will be written back. This is the concern of the data manager and is discussed in the next chapter.

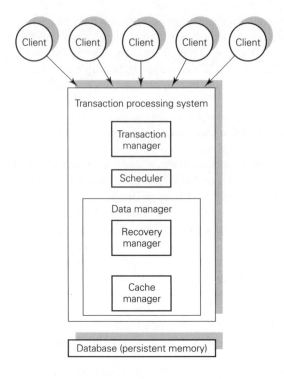

Figure 19.2
A transaction
processing system.

 ## 19.4 Concurrency control through locking

We assume a manager for each object, as discussed in Chapter 18. Figure 19.3 shows an object which is now assumed to have a *lock* and *unlock* operation as well as those previously discussed. We assume that an object can be locked and only the holder of the lock can invoke an operation on the object. Locking a single object does not solve the problems introduced in Chapter 16 since the essence of the problem is how to carry out related operations on distinct objects. A number of locks are needed for a composite operation.

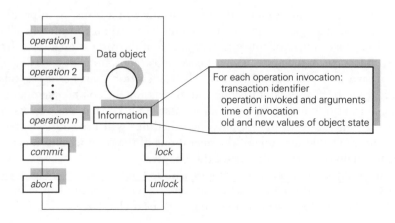

Figure 19.3
An object used in a
transaction system.

We assume that the objects are located in persistent memory in a database and are accessed through a management system (a DBMS or TP system). We assume that each instance of the management system will contain a transaction scheduler and possibly a lock manager, responsible for deadlock detection or avoidance as well. Let us assume for now that the transaction scheduler will issue *lock* and *unlock* operation invocations as well as those discussed previously. A possible strategy is to lock all the objects required by a transaction at its start and to release them on *commit* or *abort*. Can we achieve better concurrency behaviour than this?

19.4.1 Two-phase locking (2PL)

In two-phase locking, locks can be acquired for a transaction as they are needed. The constraint which defines two-phase locking is that no lock can be released until all locks have been acquired. A transaction therefore has a phase during which it builds up the number of locks it holds until it reaches its total requirement.

In the general form of two-phase locking, a transaction can release locks piecemeal as it finishes with the associated objects. If atomic transactions are to be supported with the property of isolation (that the effects of a transaction are not visible to other transactions before commit), a safe procedure is to release all locks on commit. This is called **strict two-phase locking**. Allowing visibility earlier allows more concurrency at the risk of cascading aborts and state which is difficult to recover, as discussed in Section 18.9.

Two-phase locking guarantees that all conflicting pairs of operations of two transactions are scheduled in the same order and thus enforces a serializable schedule of transactions. This is reasonably intuitive, but we will discuss it further after looking at an example.

It is possible for a lock request to fail because the object is locked already. In this case the transaction may be blocked for a time in the hope that the transaction holding the lock will complete and release the lock. It is possible for deadlock to occur, as shown below.

19.4.2 An example of two-phase locking

Figure 19.4 is the example used in Section 16.5.2 to illustrate the problem of inconsistent retrieval. T_1 is the *transfer* transaction which first *debits* (D) A then *credits* (CR) B. For conciseness we shall not show a balance check here. T_2 is a transaction which sums the values of A and B using *read-balance* (R). *Lock* (L) and *unlock* (U) operations have been inserted. When T_1 and T_2 are run concurrently, any of the following can happen:

1. T_2 locks A before T_1 locks A. T_2 proceeds to lock B and calculates and outputs $A + B$. T_1 is delayed when it attempts to lock A. A serializable schedule $T_2 \rightarrow T_1$ is achieved.
2. T_1 locks A before T_2 locks A. T_1 proceeds to lock B. T_2 is delayed when it attempts to lock A or B. A serializable schedule $T_1 \rightarrow T_2$ is achieved.
3. T_1 locks A before T_2 locks A. T_2 locks B. Deadlock is inevitable.

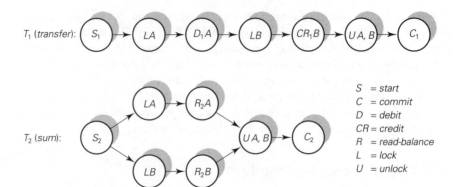

Figure 19.4
Two transactions
including *lock* and
unlock operations.

S = start
C = commit
D = debit
CR = credit
R = read-balance
L = lock
U = unlock

Two-phase locking ensures that a non-serializable schedule of the operations of transactions cannot occur. The method is subject to deadlock, but the occurrence of deadlock means that a non-serializable schedule has been attempted and prevented.

Discussion

Suppose two transactions have a pair of conflicting operations on object A, and another pair on object B. A particular ordering of the conflicting operations is determined as soon as one of the transactions locks one of the objects. It cannot release the object until it has locked the other object (the two-phase locking rule) which it may or may not succeed in doing. If it succeeds, it has acquired locks on both objects over which there is conflict. If it fails because the other transaction has locked the other object, deadlock is inevitable. This argument generalizes to any number of objects. It is not quite so obvious that it generalizes to any number of transactions.

We have established that two-phase locking enforces that the conflicting operations of every pair of transactions are scheduled in the same order. It remains to argue that a cycle involving a number of transactions (see Section 18.8) is not possible. The intuition here is that if T_1 is 'before' T_2 (in the sense of Section 18.8: the operations in T_1 of all conflicting pairs are scheduled before the conflicting operations in T_2) and T_2 is before T_3, then T_1 must be before T_3: the **before** relation is transitive. At this stage we are considering a centralized system, with a single value of time, rather than a distributed one, so events can be ordered.

19.4.3 Semantic locking

The above discussion has assumed that an object is locked for exclusive use before an operation is invoked on it. For some operations, such as *read-balance*, any number of invocations could take place concurrently without interference. We could at least refine the system's locking policy to allow for shared locks and exclusive locks to be taken out.

In this case **lock conversion** might be required in some circumstances. A transaction might read a large number of object values and on that basis decide which object to update. The shared lock on the object to be updated would be converted to an exclusive lock and the shared locks on all the other objects could be released, at the time allowed by the two-phase rule. Deadlock could arise if two transactions holding a given shared lock both required to convert it to an exclusive lock.

By regarding each object as a separate entity there is maximum possible scope for indicating which operations can be executed concurrently and which cannot. Locking could be associated with each operation on an object and not provided as a separate operation. An invocation starts and a check of any degree of sophistication could be computed to determine whether to go ahead or consider the object locked against this invoker at this time and with this current object state.

19.4.4 Deadlock in two-phase locking

Allowing the objects required by a transaction to be locked separately rather than all together and allowing processes to hold their current objects while requesting further locks (the definition of two-phase locking) can lead to deadlock. That is, the rules of two-phase locking set up the conditions which make deadlock possible: (1) exclusive allocation (in the sense that a request for a resource can be refused); (2) resource hold while waiting; and (3) no preemption, (see Section 17.4). An example specifically associated with two-phase locking was given in Section 19.4.2, where a cycle of processes holding some locks and waiting for others was demonstrated. Concurrency control based on two-phase locking must therefore have provision for dealing with deadlock.

The ability to *abort* a transaction is likely to be in place for crash resilience (see Chapter 20) and application requirements. Deadlock detection followed by abortion of the deadlocked transactions is likely to be a better design option than deadlock avoidance, which involves a greater overhead. Algorithms for deadlock detection and avoidance are given in Chapter 17. A simple alternative to maintaining complex data structures and running an algorithm on them for deadlock detection is to **time out** requests for locks and to abort transactions with timed-out lock requests.

A general point is that if the ability to abort is essential in a system design for reasons other than recovery from deadlock (for crash resilience or because the applications require it) then deadlock becomes a problem that is relatively easy to deal with without introducing excessive overhead. The overhead of supporting abort was already there!

19.5 Time-stamp ordering (TSO)

We are aiming to run transactions concurrently and to produce a serializable execution of their operations. An alternative approach to locking for achieving this is to associate a time-stamp with each transaction. One serializable order is then imposed on the operations: that of the time-stamps of the transactions they comprise. Assume initially that the time-stamp is the time of the start of the transaction and is recorded at the invoked object with every operation that transaction invokes. We have already assumed that an object is able to record such information.

Recall from Section 18.6.2 that for **serializability** of two transactions it is necessary and sufficient for the order of their invocations of all non-commutative (conflicting) pairs of operations to be the same for all the objects which are invoked by both transactions. Suppose a transaction invokes an operation. Suppose a second transaction attempts to invoke an operation that conflicts with it. If the time-stamp of the second transaction is later than (>) that of the first transaction then the operation can go ahead. If the time-stamp of the second transaction is earlier than (<) that of the first it is deemed TOO LATE and is rejected (the requesting transaction is aborted and restarted with a new, later, time-stamp). If this is enforced for all conflicting pairs of operations at every object then we have a serializable schedule of the operations of the concurrent transactions.

This approach enforces one particular serializable order on the operations of the concurrent transactions: that of the transactions' time-stamps. It is therefore more susceptible to transaction abort and restart than a method which allows any serializable ordering. This sacrifice of flexibility can be justified on the following grounds:

- the implementation is simple and efficient, thus improving system performance for all transactions;
- the information recorded for concurrency control is associated only with each object and is not held or processed centrally;
- objects are not 'locked' for longer than the duration of a single operation, unlike two-phase locking, thus giving more potential for concurrent access to objects (but see Section 19.5.1 for a discussion of strictness in time-stamp ordering).

Let us consider implementation through the simple example used above in Section 19.4.2 and illustrated here in Figure 19.5. Assume the time-stamps indicate $T_1 < T_2$. Assume that objects A and B record the time-stamps of the transactions which carried out potentially conflicting pairs of operations (*debit* (D) and *read-balance* (R) are non-commutative, as are *credit* (CR) and *read-balance*). Consider

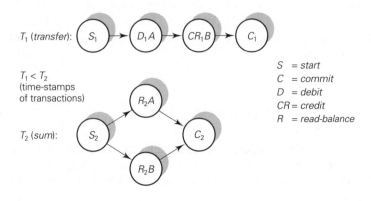

Figure 19.5
Two transactions with time-stamp ordering.

the following examples of orderings of the operations of T_1 and T_2 and the corresponding actions taken by objects A and B:

1. D_1A, R_2A, R_2B, CR_1B FAILS because it conflicts with R_2B which has a higher recorded time-stamp (of T_2); T_1 is aborted.
2. R_2A, R_2B, D_1A FAILS because it conflicts with R_2A which has a higher recorded time-stamp. T_1 is aborted, even though the order $T_2 < T_1$ is serializable.

The method is simple to implement. There is no need to keep central allocation information nor to maintain a resource-wait graph and to run algorithms for deadlock detection or avoidance on it. Transactions are serialized in the order that they were submitted for execution. This means that any other serializable ordering, although correct, will fail, as in 2 above.

An early transaction fails when it attempts to invoke an operation on an object on which a later transaction has already carried out a conflicting operation. Abortion could therefore be a common occurrence if contention was likely. If contention is unlikely, the method incurs little overhead.

The following examples illustrate that the definition of conflicting behaviour must be considered carefully. Suppose a transaction to read a large number of items, process them and write a value depending on all the values read (the account to be credited is that with the lowest balance) was run concurrently with transactions, each of which updates one of the values read. Figure 19.6 illustrates the point with a small number of objects.

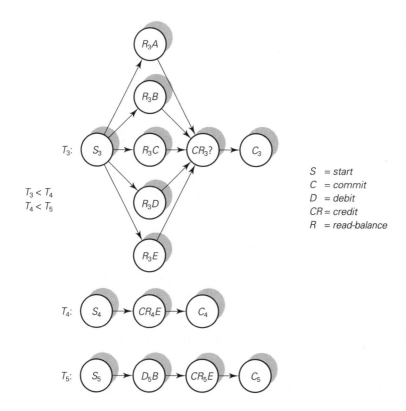

S = start
C = commit
D = debit
CR = credit
R = read-balance

Figure 19.6
More examples of time-stamp ordering.

1. R_3A, R_3B, R_3C, R_3D, CR_4E, R_3E: this fails because R_3E conflicts with CR_4E which has a higher recorded time-stamp. The semantics of the transaction indicate that it need not, since although the value read by T_3 relates to the state after T_4 has run, rather than before, it is not incorrect; in fact it is more relevant. Forcing serialization in the order $T_3 > T_4$ happens to be unnecessary in this case but we can only say this because we know the intention of T_3 is to invoke a credit on whichever of objects A, B, C, D and E has the lowest value.

2. R_3A, R_3B, D_5B, R_3C, R_3D, R_3E, CR_5E is allowed. Suppose T_5 has transferred £1000 from B to E. The values seen by T_3 are correct because B is read before the debit and E is read before the credit.

Two-phase locking was shown to limit concurrency more than might be strictly necessary, but delivered correct results. Time-stamp ordering may achieve a higher degree of concurrency because an object is available unless an operation is being invoked on it (but see the next section). We have seen that a large number of aborts could be made necessary by the particular serialization enforced and that no simple general definition of conflicting operations would allow us to be more flexible than this. The simple description given here has used the time of the start of a transaction as its time-stamp; it might be more appropriate to use the time of its first invocation of an operation which belongs to a conflicting pair. Refinements of the basic scheme are discussed further in Bernstein *et al.* (1987).

Time-stamp ordering can be a simple and effective scheme when conflicts are unlikely. The fact that the decision on whether an operation on an object can go ahead is made on the basis only of information recorded with the object itself makes it a suitable method for a distributed system. We shall discuss this further in Chapter 21.

19.5.1 Cascading aborts and recovery of state

Time-stamp ordering, as described above, does not enforce the property of isolation and is therefore subject to cascading aborts and complex recovery of object state as discussed in Section 18.9. Recall that it is necessary to be able to *undo* and *redo* operations.

If isolation (strict execution) is to be enforced in the implementation, an additional mechanism to that described above is needed. A transaction scheduler together with the individual object managers could achieve this. An object could ensure that a *commit* operation had been invoked for a given transaction before allowing any operation of any conflicting pair of operations to go ahead for another transaction with a later time-stamp.

Note that this does not introduce the possibility of deadlock. Circular wait is prevented by the time-stamp ordering of invocations; that is, a cycle of transactions cannot occur such that each has invoked an operation and is waiting for another transaction to commit before invoking another operation.

Strict time-stamp ordering introduces the requirement for atomic commitment. Assume that a given transaction has invoked, on a number of objects, operations which belong to conflicting pairs. All the objects must agree whether the transaction is to commit or abort. That is, all or none of the objects invoked by the transaction must commit the state changes effected by the transaction. This is not difficult to achieve in a centralized system in the absence of failures. In practice, crashes must be anticipated and distributed implementations may be necessary. Chapters 20 and 21 consider these problems.

19.6 Optimistic concurrency control (OCC)

Optimistic schemes for concurrency control are based on the premise that conflict is unlikely. We should therefore be careful to avoid heavyweight concurrency control mechanisms but we must still ensure a serializable execution. OCC also aims to achieve high availability of objects. The idea is to minimize delay at transaction start. OCC is therefore appropriate for certain application areas where these conditions and requirements hold; that is, for applications which need a transaction system, but where it is unusual for different transactions to touch the same object, and which need real-time response.

For example, suppose my medical record is being updated by the hospital administration some time after my admission to hospital. Suppose that my surgeon finds that she needs immediate access to the details of my medication or history during my operation, but unfortunately, my record is locked for writing by the administrator. Clearly, there should be instant access to my record by the surgeon and the fact that the most recent update about my admission to hospital will not be included in the version available does not matter.

The strategy of OCC is to apply no changes to persistent memory during the execution of transactions. When a transaction requests *commit* its history is validated to determine whether it can be serialized along with transactions that have already been accepted. Recall Section 18.6 on serializability and Section 18.8 on histories and serialization graphs. Once a serial order of validated transactions is established, updates are applied in that order to objects in persistent memory.

The update of persistent memory must be such that in any state read from an object either all or none of the changes at that object associated with a given transaction are visible.

During transaction execution invocations are made on workspace copies, **shadow copies,** of objects. Figure 19.7 shows an object with a shadow for use by transaction T_1. Notice that **isolation** is a side-effect of OCC. No other transaction may see the updates being made by a given transaction to its shadow copies. Each object's shadow copy has a well-defined version, which is the identifier of the transaction (with associated time-stamp) whose updates have most recently been applied to the object in persistent memory. Let us also assume that a time-stamp is recorded with the transaction identifier and that the time-stamp is the time when the transaction is validated and its updates are guaranteed.

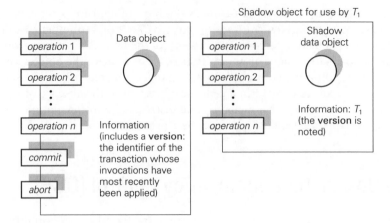

Figure 19.7
An object with a
shadow.

Each transaction undergoes three phases:

1. **Execution (read):** The transaction executes to completion (*commit* or *abort*) shadow copies of data objects.
2. **Validation:** Following *commit* the execution schedule is checked to ensure serializability.
3. **Update (write):** Update invocations are applied to objects in persistent memory in serial order, transaction by transaction. It is the responsibility of the update manager to ensure that all updates succeed. The update manager will know at any time those transactions for which updates have succeeded. It can therefore be asserted that the updates up to those of some transaction have succeeded, see Figure 19.8.

For valid execution each transaction must interact with a consistent set of shadow copies. One (heavyweight) way of achieving this is to ensure that updates are applied atomically across all objects participating in a transaction, using an atomic commitment protocol such as two-phase commit (see Section 21.9) in a distributed system. Validation can take place at each object as part of the first phase of the protocol, with update taking place only if all objects can accept the transaction. Recall that a transaction is defined to take the system from one consistent state to another. We can then make sure that a set of shadows taken at the start of a transaction is consistent; that is, we must also assume that taking a set of shadows is made atomic.

There are objections to this approach:

- The enforcement of update atomicity using a protocol such as two-phase commit reduces concurrency and is bad for performance in general. That is, there is overhead in using such an algorithm which penalizes all clients of the system. Also, specific transactions will not experience high availability of objects if they are held for the atomic commitment of some other transaction.
- At the start of transaction execution we may not know what shadows are required. Even if we enforce atomic commitment this does not help unless all shadows are taken 'at the same time'.

Validated transaction	Time-stamp	Objects and updates	All updates acknowledged
| | | |	| | | |	| | | |	| | | |
P	t_i	A, B, C, D, E	YES
Q	t_{i+1}	B, C, E, F	YES
R	t_{i+2}	B, C, D	YES
S	t_{i+3}	A, C, E	

Object versions:

Object	Version before S's update	Version after S's update
A	P, t_i	S, t_{i+3}
B	R, t_{i+2}	R, t_{i+2}
C	R, t_{i+2}	S, t_{i+3}
D	R, t_{i+2}	R, t_{i+2}
E	Q, t_{i+1}	S, t_{i+3}
F	Q, t_{i+1}	Q, t_{i+1}

Figure 19.8
Single-threading through commit and object versions.

- More importantly, there is a mismatch of philosophy. OCC is postulated on the assumption that interference between transactions is unlikely. It is not worth going to a lot of trouble to ensure that it does not occur. The approach we are objecting to is highly pessimistic rather than optimistic!

We should therefore abandon the requirement that we take a consistent set of shadows at transaction start thus avoiding the machinery to achieve this. We can then delay making a shadow copy of an object until an operation is invoked on it, noting the object's version so that it can be checked by the validator. There is then the risk that execution will proceed using inconsistent shadows (see Figure 19.9), but this risk applies also to other schemes that aim for high concurrency, such as allowing non-strict execution in a two-phase locking approach. As in these schemes we risk rejection when we attempt to commit. We can achieve high concurrency only if we are prepared to risk abort.

The execution of the transaction continues, invoking shadow objects until either

abort: the shadow objects are simply discarded

or

commit: the validator is called.

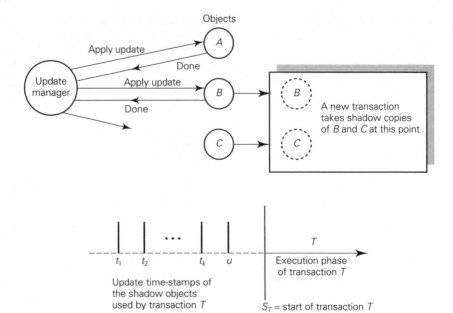

Figure 19.9
Inconsistent
shadow objects.

Figure 19.10
Checking for a
consistent state.

The validator has knowledge of all transactions whose validation or update phases overlap execution of the transaction that is to be checked. When a transaction involves an operation on a shadow object there may be transactions with outstanding updates guaranteed for that object. The validator must ensure that there has been no conflict. The information used by the validator might be extended to take into account transactions that have started to execute since this one, but we shall not consider this possibility further.

Two conditions need to be checked by the validator. If either cannot be met the transaction must be aborted.

1. *The execution must be based on a consistent system state*

   The versions of the shadow objects are available. The requirement is that these versions were all current at some particular transaction time-stamp.

   Figure 19.10 shows a possible scenario. Suppose that at the start S_T of transaction T the earliest unacknowledged time-stamp is u, and that during T's execution phase shadow copies are made whose version time-stamps are (in some order) $t_1, t_2, \ldots t_k$. If all time-stamps $t_1, t_2, \ldots t_k$ are earlier than u, then certainly all versions were current at the latest of the time-stamps recorded, say t_k.

   If interference is low it is likely that all updates to the objects involved will have been acknowledged before the transaction starts, and also that no further updates occur during the execution phase. Even if this precise scenario is not followed it is quite possible for the set of shadows to be consistent.

   If shadow validation succeeds then the execution is based on a time-stamp at which all the shadow versions were consistent. Let us call this the **base time-stamp**.

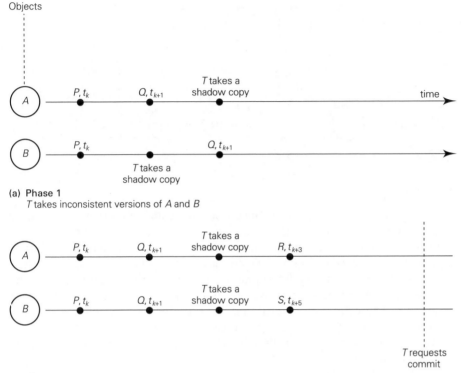

Objects

(a) Phase 1
  T takes inconsistent versions of *A* and *B*

(b) Phase 2
  (i)   shadow copies are consistent
  (ii) updates have since been committed at objects invoked by *T*. If any conflict with *T*'s operations, *T* is aborted, otherwise *T* is assigned an update time-stamp and its updates are queued for application

Figure 19.11
The two phases of validation.

2. *The transactions must be serializable*
   The transactions with which the given transaction must be reconciled are those validated for update with a time-stamp later than the base time-stamp, whether or not their updates have been applied. Recall that once a transaction is validated its updates are guaranteed, and that updates are applied in time-stamp order at each object.
   The requirement is that an ordering of these transactions can be found in which serial update is meaningful; that is, that the final system state reflected after the (serial) update of the set of transactions must be consistent with all of their execution phases, performed concurrently. Recall Sections 18.6 and 18.8. Although the definitions of conflict needed can be based on non-commutativity this is unnecessarily restrictive, as we shall see in an example.
   Figure 19.11 illustrates this two-phase validation.

   Provided that both conditions are met, the transaction can be accepted and recorded as validated. This establishes its position in the queue of validated transactions that are waiting to update. In simple cases object update is just a matter of copying a shadow object back into persistent memory. In other cases

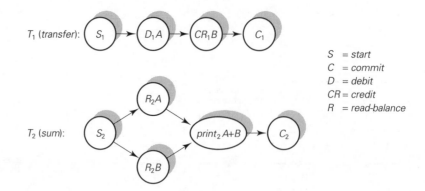

S = start
C = commit
D = debit
CR = credit
R = read-balance

Figure 19.12
The *transfer* and *sum*
example.

it may be necessary to reapply the operations of a transaction to a version more recent than the original shadow.

OCC has very different properties from time-stamp ordering. In the latter, transactions are scheduled in a predetermined order, usually that of transaction start. In OCC the order is determined at validation time, and in theory the validator is free to insert the current transaction at any position in the queue for update. The validation algorithm could therefore become quite elaborate, but it is probably not worth going to great lengths in an attempt to optimize. OCC is suitable only if there is little interference between transactions, and the hope is that simple validation will normally succeed.

Examples

We now consider two simple examples. In the first a consistent set of shadows is assumed. In the second only one object is involved. The examples illustrate the OCC approach and highlight some of the issues. Bear in mind that, in practice, we cannot automatically assume that the shadows are consistent and this must be checked at validation (condition 1 above).

First, consider the example we have often used, of concurrent *transfer* and *sum* transactions (see Figure 19.12), and suppose that both transactions are using shadows of the same values of A and B. Note that *sum* is a read-only transaction. It might be argued on the basis of this example that there is no point in taking shadows for a read-only transaction. The counter-argument is that a number of reads might be required from a large object and taking a shadow ensures that the reads are performed on the same version of the object. We shall make the assumption that shadows are taken when an object is first invoked, either for reading or writing.

The *sum* transaction uses its shadow values of A and B quite independently of what the *transfer* transaction is doing to its shadow values of A and B. In Section 18.6 we considered *read-balance* and *credit* (or *debit*) to be non-commutative. If consistent shadow copies are taken by both transactions this is no longer relevant. In fact, if the shadows used by a read-only transaction represent a consistent system state then that transaction cannot fail. If we allow the possibility that the shadows used by a transaction do not represent a consistent state then it can be rejected when it attempts to *commit*. A problem here is that the transaction may have performed output based on inconsistent object values. This problem is not exclusive to systems which use OCC. Whatever concurrency control scheme is used in a system there must be a policy on how to deal with aborted transactions that have performed output.

If we assume each transaction is working on a consistent set of shadows we need only be concerned with operations that are non-commutative with respect to state changes at the object. Values output by the transaction relate to a consistent version of the system state and cause no problems. The *sum* transaction will therefore be validated as correct at *commit*, whenever this is requested. It has not changed the value of A or B.

It is interesting to note that the values output by a number of transactions that are working on the same version of system state are not the same as those that would be output by a serial execution of those transactions on the persistent state: they execute in parallel on the same version. The transactions are forced to *commit* in some serial order.

When the *transfer* transaction requests *commit*, the operations it has done on A and B are **validated**. The information recorded at the persistent objects and their shadows is sufficient for the *commit* to be validated as correct or rejected. Suppose *transfer* has invoked an operation on A or B which belongs to a conflicting pair. If some other transaction has committed (since the shadow was taken for *transfer*) the result of an invocation of the conflicting operation of that pair, then *transfer* must be aborted. The validation phase checks this for all the operations that the transaction requesting *commit* has invoked on all objects.

Figure 19.13 shows transaction *abort* and restart when non-commutative *credit* and *add-interest-to-balance* operations are invoked on the same value of a bank account. Exercise 19.8 gives another example. The validation phase

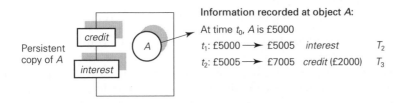

Information recorded at object A:

At time t_0, A is £5000

t_1: £5000 ⟶ £5005   *interest* T_2

t_2: £5005 ⟶ £7005   *credit* (£2000) T_3

T_1	A = £5000	*credit* (£2000)	A = £7000 takes place in shadow taken at t_0
T_2	A = £5000	*interest*	A = £5005 takes place in shadow taken at t_0
T_2	requests *commit*; validated and committed at time t_1.		

Information is recorded at the persistent copy of A. A = £5005.

T_1 Requests *commit*.

REJECTED at validation because *credit* does not commute with *interest* which has been committed since T_1's shadow copy was taken. The transaction is aborted and restarted as T_3.

T_3 A = £5005   *credit* (£2000)   A = £7005 takes place in shadow taken at t_1

T_3 requests *commit*; validated and committed at time t_2.

Information is recorded at the persistent copy of A. A = £7005.

Figure 19.13
Example showing
abort and restart.

indicates whether *commit* is possible and the *commit* phase must ensure the correct persistent values, taking into account changes that have been committed since the shadows were taken.

In the example, T_1 invokes *credit* (£2000) on a shadow copy of *account-A*, changing its value from £5000 to £7000. A shadow copy taken from the same persistent object value has *add-interest-to-balance* invoked by T_2, changing its value from £5000 to £5005. This latter transaction T_2 is first to *commit* and the persistent value of *account-A* is updated to £5005. T_1 now requests *commit*. Because *credit* and *add-interest-to-balance* are defined to be *non-commutative*, and therefore conflicting, the *commit* is rejected. The transaction is restarted as T_3 with a shadow of *account-A* with value £5005. The *credit* (£2000) is performed at the shadow, giving £7005 for the value, and this value is then committed at the persistent copy of the object.

Notice that when transaction T_1 requests *commit* and is rejected, applying the *credit* operation at that stage at the persistent copy of the object would yield £7005! The requirement for commutativity appears to be too strong for a case such as this. Commutativity enforces that the same result is obtained whatever the order of execution of a pair of transactions. As soon as one transaction has committed, the serialization order is defined. If the rejected transaction is aborted and restarted it is from the system state committed by the first. They are no longer running in parallel. Ideally, this should be taken into account when T_1 requests *commit*.

If invocations are carried out on shadow copies which do not conflict with subsequent updates at the persistent object, the invocations can be reapplied to the object on *commit*. For example, suppose a shadow copy of *account-A* was credited by £1000, changing its value from £4000 to £5000. Suppose at *commit*, other transactions have caused the balance to reach the value £8000 by invoking operations that commute with *credit*. The *credit* operation is redone at the object giving a balance of £9000.

Generalizing from these examples, when a transaction requests *commit* and after a consistent starting point has been ascertained (condition 1):

- The validation phase uses the information recorded with each persistent object involved and its shadow to check whether any non-commutative pairs of operations have been invoked on the object by this transaction and any other that has committed since this transaction took its shadows. As noted above, this definition of conflict may be too restrictive. See Herlihy, 1990; Badrinath and Ramamritham, 1992; Wong and Agrawal, 1993; Guerni *et al.*, 1995 for further reading.
- If the validation phase is successful, the transaction is committed. This may involve redoing (at the persistent copy of the objects) the operations that have changed the values of shadow objects. This can be done because the validation phase has rejected the *commit* if any of the invocations of the transaction do not commute with committed invocations.
- If the validation phase is not successful the transaction is aborted.

Optimistic concurrency control allows every operation invocation to go ahead without the overhead of locking or time-stamp checking: it achieves high object availability. The fact that shadows are taken and work proceeds without delay makes this method suitable for applications in which timing guarantees are required and in which conflict is rare. The overhead occurs when *commit* is requested. The validation phase uses the information stored locally at each object. If all the objects invoked by a transaction indicate that *commit* is possible then the updates can go ahead.

Optimistic concurrency control operates on a first come (to *commit*) first served basis. If there are several shadows of an object, the state of the first to *commit* becomes the new object state. If contention is rare the method works well. If the application is such that transactions might invoke heavily used objects (data 'hot-spots') they are likely to be aborted and restarted without regard to fairness or priority of the transaction. The method should probably not be used if this is likely to occur.

19.7 Summary

We have been concerned with methods of implementing transactions in the presence of concurrency and, in particular, with ensuring the property of serializability for correct execution. Three approaches were considered: locking, time-stamping and optimistic concurrency control.

The object model set up in Chapter 18 was used again here. To implement the locking methods of concurrency control the object was extended with *lock* and *unlock* operations. These were assumed to be invoked by a transaction manager or other agency with knowledge of all the locks held and requested by a transaction. Deadlock detection was shown to be necessary.

Two-phase locking guarantees a serializable schedule of the operation invocations of concurrent transactions. The penalty is the overhead of deadlock management. Also, objects are locked for longer than is necessary for their invocations. If the property of isolation is enforced in the implementation, locks are held until *commit*. This is called strict two-phase locking and avoids cascading aborts and complex procedures for recovering previously committed object values (at the cost of reduced concurrency).

When time-stamping is used for concurrency control, the decision to accept or reject an operation invocation is made at the object. One specific serialized order is achieved, that of the time-stamps of the transactions, and this can lead to correct transactions being rejected. A strict execution schedule can be enforced by delaying an invocation until the transaction that previously invoked an operation of a conflicting pair has committed. This cannot cause deadlock because the invocations are in time-stamp order at every object, so a circular wait is impossible.

Optimistic concurrency control minimizes the delay involved in invoking objects: each transaction works on a shadow copy of each object it invokes. It might be appropriate for the shadows to reside in the user's workstation. The shadows could be guaranteed (at heavy cost) to be taken from committed system state and therefore represent a consistent version of it. The property of isolation is manifest in such an implementation. In practice, such an approach is heavyweight and against the optimistic philosophy of the method.

There is no concurrency control until a transaction requests *commit*. A validation phase then takes place to determine whether the persistent values of the objects can be updated from the shadow copies. It may be necessary to redo operations at the persistent objects on *commit*.

The method is suitable for systems where contention is unlikely since, if no conflicting operations have been committed since the shadows were taken, *commit* is very simple. *Abort* is always very simple since it merely involves discarding the shadow objects. If contention occurs, and abortion is necessary, there is no provision for fairness in transaction scheduling. Commitment occurs on a first-come first-served basis.

The delay involved before work can start on the objects used by a transaction is minimized in optimistic concurrency control; shadows can be taken without delay and work can commence. For this reason the method is suitable for systems with a real-time requirement or where timing guarantees must be made.

Most practical systems are based on strict two-phase locking. Time-stamp ordering is based only on information stored at each object. It is probably more suited to distributed systems than a locking approach. We shall explore this in Chapter 21. The optimistic approach, unlike time-stamp ordering, allows work to be carried out which may later have to be discarded. It does, however, allow greater flexibility in the serialization order of transactions. Performance may degrade badly as contention increases in a system using OCC.

Study questions

S 19.1

What are the three approaches to concurrency control mentioned in Section 19.1?

S 19.2

What is meant by locking for exclusive use?

S 19.3

If objects reside in the main memory of a single computer, which of the ACID properties of transactions require no special action to be taken, and why?

S 19.4

What is the main issue that arises when locks are used as the means of concurrency control for objects that reside in main memory?

S 19.5

With regard to the ACID properties of transactions, what is the main difference between objects in the main memory of a single computer and objects in the main memories of a distributed system?

S 19.6

How can the problems of deadlock due to locking be overcome in a transaction management system?

S 19.7

What is the alternative to the use of locks for concurrency control?

S 19.8

Describe the components of the transaction processing system (TPS) shown in Figure 19.2.

S 19.9

What is a lock on an object?

S 19.10

Describe two-phase locking (2PL). What is the major constraint that defines two-phase locking?

S 19.11

What is the advantage of strict two-phase locking?

S 19.12

What does 2PL guarantee? Explain.

S 19.13

If deadlock occurs when 2PL is in use, what has happened?

S 19.14

What is a shared lock?

S 19.15

What is lock conversion, and what problem can arise when it is used?

S 19.16

Which is the better policy for dealing with deadlock in 2PL: deadlock detection or deadlock avoidance?

S 19.17

If an *abort* operation is available, what is a simple alternative to deadlock detection?

S 19.18

What is time-stamp ordering (TSO)? How is it used to obtain a serializable execution of transactions?

S 19.19

What are the advantages of TSO?

S 19.20

What is the main disadvantage of TSO?

S 19.21

Why does TSO not enforce the property of isolation? How can isolation be achieved when TSO is in use?

Exercises

19.1   (a)   Why is the provision of *lock* and *unlock* operations not sufficient to ensure serializability of composite operation invocations?

      (b)   Why does two-phase locking (2PL) ensure serializability?

      (c)   Why is 2PL subject to deadlock? (Consider the four conditions for deadlock to exist, given in Section 17.4.)

      (d)   Why does 2PL not guard against cascading aborts?

      (e)   In what way does strict two-phase locking guard against cascading aborts?

19.2   (a)   Why might the start time of a transaction not be the best time to use for its time-stamp?

      (b)   Given the time-stamps of two committed transactions, can you always draw their serialization graphs? Does time-stamp ordering restrict concurrency more than locking? Discuss.

      (c)   Compare the overhead of implementing locking with that of time-stamp ordering.

19.3   Why are cascading aborts possible in a system with time-stamp-based concurrency control? What extra mechanism could prevent it?

19.4   Is concurrency control based on time-stamp ordering (TSO) (or strict time-stamp ordering) subject to deadlock?

19.5   Why is optimistic concurrency control (OCC) potentially appropriate for use in real-time systems? Why is it potentially good for systems where contention is rare?

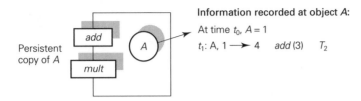

Information recorded at object A:

At time t_0, $A = 1$

t_1: A, $1 \longrightarrow 4$ add (3) T_2

T_1	$A = 1$ add (2)	$A = 3$	takes place in shadow taken at t_0
T_2	$A = 1$ add (3)	$A = 4$	takes place in shadow taken at t_0
T_3	$A = 1$ mult (2)	$A = 2$	takes place in shadow taken at t_0

T_2 requests *commit*; validated and committed at time t_1.
Information is recorded at the persistent copy of A. $A = 4$.

T_3 Requests *commit*

T_1 Requests *commit*

Figure 19.14
Example involving non-commutative operations.

19.6 (a) What is involved in aborting a transaction in a system which uses OCC?

(b) Describe the validation and commitment phases of an OCC scheme. Consider the case where the objects to be committed have had updates committed since the shadow copies were taken. Consider the cases where the updates are the result of operations which do and do not belong to conflicting pairs. What actions should be taken in both these cases?

19.7 Suppose that two transactions use copies of the same objects under an OCC scheme. Suppose that both transactions generate output and are both committed. Does the output reflect a serial ordering of the transactions? Does it matter?

19.8 Consider the example shown in Figure 19.14. What happens when T_3 requests *commit*? What happens when T_1 then requests *commit*?

19.9 A particular application is known to comprise almost entirely read-only transactions. Discuss the three approaches to concurrency control for such a system.

19.10 For a particular application, transactions are either read-only or have a phase in which they read and compute followed by a phase in which they write their results back to the database. Discuss the three approaches to concurrency control for this application.

19.11 In OCC we defined the version number of an object as the time-stamp of the transaction whose validated invocations were most recently applied to the object. The transaction's time-stamp is therefore that of its commit time instead of its start time. Contrast TSO and OCC with respect to the time-stamps allocated to transactions and the schedules that are allowed to execute.

20

Recovery

20.1 Requirements for recovery

There are a number of reasons why recovery procedures are required in a system which supports atomic transactions:

1. *System crash*
   The contents of main memory are lost, perhaps because of a power failure, but persistent store is not affected. This kind of system crash was discussed in Chapter 14 and a fail–stop model was assumed for simplicity. Any transaction in progress (that has not completed commit processing) will be affected by the loss of data structures in main memory and must be aborted. The effects of any committed transaction must persist and the system software must be designed to ensure this.

2. *Media failure*
   For example, a disk head crash. Part of the database will be lost and it must be possible to restore it. If transactions in progress are using that part of the persistent store they must be aborted and the persistent state prior to the transactions must be recoverable. There must be more than one copy of all persistent data, including any system management data. If the system

guarantees to retain the state resulting from every committed transaction then two independent copies must be written during commit processing.

We assume that a **dump** of all the database is taken periodically, for example overnight, as part of normal operating system file backup procedures. The database application is responsible for recording all subsequent changes.

3. *Transaction abort*

An *abort* operation may be available to the transaction programmer. A transaction might not be able to complete for some application-level reason, such as insufficient money in an account to continue with a transfer operation.

A transaction management system may be designed to use *abort* followed by restart of the transaction to solve problems such as deadlock, as discussed in previous chapters. This type of failure can be transparent to the user except that it might detect slower than expected performance.

In general, the transaction is taken to be the unit of recovery.

Figure 19.2 showed the components of a transaction processing system. The concern of this chapter is the data management module which includes the **cache manager** and the **recovery manager**. The cache manager is responsible for moving information between main memory and persistent memory. The recovery manager is responsible for carrying out recovery procedures after a crash.

20.2 The object model, object state and recovery

Throughout Part III we have used an object model for reasoning about atomic transactions. In this chapter we focus on object state and how and when it is recorded in persistent memory. Clients of a TP system are not concerned with object state explicitly, but with the results of operation invocations. The TPS implementation must ensure that the states of the objects comprising the system together present a consistent system state to its clients.

In Section 18.9 we assumed that an object records all relevant information on the operations that are invoked on it, for example, the transaction identifier and time of invocation. In Chapter 19 this was used for concurrency control. We assumed, as a theoretical starting point, that a complete history of invocations is held by every object. In theory, an object's state is defined as a sequence of invocations on an object starting from a *create* operation. In theory, any state can be recovered by starting again from the initial state on *create* and performing some required sequence of invocations, for example, to exclude an operation of an aborted transaction. In practice, this procedure would take too much time and space and a suitable optimization must be devised.

A basis for such an optimization is that an object may make a **checkpoint** of its state. It may even record its state before and after every invocation that changes its state. We justify this recording of state as follows: if it is impossible to distinguish between an object state derived from the application of the invocations which comprise its history and the recorded value, then recording that value is a valid optimization. Practical implementations are based on recording object state, while theoretical models are based on histories of invocations. In this chapter we are concerned with implementation issues, but we must be able to reason about the behaviour and correctness of our implementations.

If we base our recovery procedures on recorded state *instead of* a history of invocations we should consider whether we have lost the ability to recover some required previous state. By dispensing with the full history and recording state we have introduced a requirement that operations should be UNDO-able. We can no longer reason from a basis of invocations (forwards) from *create* so must be able to go backwards from some recorded value of state; that is, starting from a value of state, it should be possible to UNDO an operation to recover the state previous to its invocation. In Chapter 19 we assumed that any operation could be undone; that is, every operation has a corresponding UNDO operation. If this is the case, the UNDO operations may form the basis of recovery; any transaction can be aborted by undoing its operations.

20.3 Concurrency, crashes and the properties of transactions

The ACID properties of transactions must be guaranteed by a TPS in the presence of concurrency and unpredictable failures.

Atomicity   Either all or none of the transaction's operations are performed. This must be ensured by the recovery manager. A crash may occur part-way through a transaction and the invocations of any incomplete transactions must be undone.

Consistency   A transaction transforms the system from one consistent state to another. This is achieved through concurrency control, provided that atomicity is guaranteed by the recovery manager in the presence of crashes.

Isolation   An incomplete transaction cannot reveal its result to other transactions before it is committed. This is achieved through concurrency control.

Durability   Once a transaction is committed the system must guarantee that the results of its operations will persist, even if there are subsequent system failures.
              This is the responsibility of the recovery manager, based on general data management policies. As we discussed in Chapter 14, the system can make the probability of losing information arbitrarily small by replicating its storage. We used the 'stable storage' abstraction to indicate this.

We have used the concept of system state comprising the state of all objects in the system. We now proceed to discuss the implementation of recovery. We shall assume that objects record their state (as discussed above) and the terms 'object value' and 'object state' are used in this practical sense.

20.4 Logging and shadowing for crash resilience

Two basic approaches to achieving crash resilience were outlined in Chapter 14: logging and shadowing. Our concern there was to make a single invocation atomic in the presence of crashes. In Part III we have moved on to transactions comprising a number of related invocations and should reconsider the approaches from this perspective.

- **Logging**: Persistent object values are updated in place and all changes are recorded in a log. The method is based on recorded state and a fundamental assumption is that it is possible to undo an invocation at an object. This is necessary when a crash occurs part-way through a transaction. The pre-crash invocations of the uncommitted transaction must be undone. We shall explore this approach in more detail in the next section.
- **Shadowing**: Persistent object values are not updated in place. The new and old values of each object comprising a transaction are maintained in persistent store and a switch is made from old to new values on *commit*.

    Note that this requires *commit* to be atomic over all the objects involved in a transaction. The objects must participate in a protocol and a single point of decision is necessary for transaction *commit*. If a crash occurs during *commit*, the objects participating in *commit* must be able to find out the decision for the whole transaction and act accordingly.

    We shall study an atomic commitment protocol in Chapter 21. In that chapter we are concerned with distributed objects and partial failures of (components of) a system. In this chapter we focus on centralized systems where the whole TPS is assumed to fail when main memory is lost. Our concern here is to be able to ensure the consistency of the persistent memory on restart after a failure.

In both cases, the aim is to record securely the values before and after operation invocations. The difference is in implementation detail.

An alternative approach is to **defer invocations** until *commit*. Recall our discussion of optimistic concurrency control (Section 19.6) where invocations which have been carried out on shadow copies are first validated, then committed at the database. The approach might be used more generally, depending on the requirements of applications. It might, however, be impossible to defer invocation of operations for some transactions, for example, if they require intermediate results in order to proceed with their computations.

An extension of this approach is explored in the context of distributed systems in Yahalom (1991). We leave this for further reading and consider use of a recovery log in more detail.

20.5 Use of a recovery log

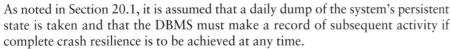

As noted in Section 20.1, it is assumed that a daily dump of the system's persistent state is taken and that the DBMS must make a record of subsequent activity if complete crash resilience is to be achieved at any time.

An outline of the general approach is that, on an invocation, the object value is updated in persistent store and a record of the invocation is made in a log. We have already assumed that every object keeps information (for concurrency control purposes) of the kind we require to be logged and we can require objects to write log records. In order to achieve a recoverable state we must consider when the update to persistent object state is made and when the corresponding log record is written to persistent store (see Section 20.5.1). Points to bear in mind which relate to an efficient implementation are as follows:

- Writing to a log is efficient: it requires an append to a file and involves records from all active transactions.
- Writing values of objects to persistent store is inefficient: the objects are likely to be scattered throughout the database. We should take care not to require object values to be updated in place at a very fine time grain. A long queue of updates can be ordered to exploit an efficient disk arm scheduling algorithm, for example. Also, object values written by committed transactions may be read from the cache in main memory.

20.5.1 Log records and their use in recovery

We require an object to write a log record for all the invocations on it. Depending on the use that is to be made of the log, it might only be necessary to log the invocations that have changed object state. A log record might take the following general form:

Transaction id, object id, operation, arguments, state prior to invocation, state after invocation

We also assume that *start*, *commit* and *abort* are recorded in the log with the appropriate transaction identifier.

If a failure of any kind occurs the log can be used in the recovery procedure by the recovery manager. We assume that the log is written to stable storage so that if a medium failure causes one copy of the log to be lost another copy exists.

The effects of any transaction that committed before the failure must persist and the recovery manager can use the log to ensure this. If a transaction has not committed at the time of the failure it must be aborted and any changes made to object values in the database by any of its operations must be undone by the recovery manager.

If a transaction has simply to be aborted as in case 3 of Section 20.1, its operations can be undone using the information in the log. If a medium failure occurs (case 2) the database can be reloaded from the latest dump. The recovery manager can then REDO the operations of all committed transactions since the time of the dump and UNDO the effects of any uncommitted transaction.

20.5.2 Log write-ahead

Two distinct actions are associated with effecting an invocation of a transaction:

1. Update the value of an object in the persistent store.
2. Write the log record of the change to persistent store.

A failure could occur at any time including between the two actions. Once the object value is changed its previous value is lost. The log record contains both the old value and the new value.

- The log record must be written to persistent store before the object value is changed.

When a transaction *commits*, the system guarantees that the changes it has made to the database become permanent.

- It is necessary for all the log records of a transaction to be written out to the log before *commit* is completed.

Note that we need not insist that all the object values are written to persistent store on *commit*. There is sufficient information in the log records to update the object values if a failure occurs. The point made above, that it could be inefficient to write out object values on the *commit* of every transaction, is relevant here.

20.5.3 Checkpoints and the checkpoint procedure

It can be seen from the above that the log is very large. Processing a large log might be tolerable on media failure but transaction abort must be efficient, and recovery after a crash should be reasonably fast. A **checkpoint** is therefore taken at 'small' time intervals, for example, every five minutes or after a specified number of items have been logged.

A checkpoint procedure would be as follows:

1. Force-write any log records in main storage out to the actual log on persistent store.
2. Force-write a 'checkpoint record' to the log which contains a list of all the transactions which are active at the time of the checkpoint and the address within the log of each transaction's most recent log record.
3. Force-write any database updates which are still in memory (in database buffers) out to persistent store.
4. Write the address of the checkpoint record within the log into a 'restart file'.

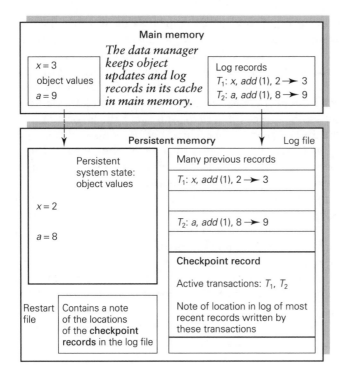

Figure 20.1
A recovery log with a checkpoint record.

It must be possible to know that data has been written out to disk. Figure 20.1 shows that data objects are initially invoked in main memory and log records are initially written in main memory. It also shows the log file and restart file in persistent memory. The figure shows a snapshot after 2 and before 3 in the above list. The log records and checkpoint record have been written but the database updates have not yet been made. Not only does the DBMS cache data in main memory (to avoid many writes to disk of small items of data), but the operating system on which the DBMS runs may also cache data in memory. It is essential that an operating system over which a DBMS runs should allow an application to request that data is written out to persistent store and should acknowledge that this has been done.

20.6 Idempotent undo and redo operations

A transaction can make a number of different types of change to a database, for example:

- delete an existing object;
- create a new object;
- invoke an operation which changes an object's state.

A crash might occur at any time, including in the middle of undoing or redoing invocations during failure recovery. No assumptions should therefore be made about whether the object has its old or new value and the UNDO and REDO operations must be made idempotent (repeatable) by some means.

We have made the simplifying assumption in this chapter that an object's state before and after an invocation is recorded in the log record associated with the invocation. If this is the case, an idempotent UNDO operation can simply set the object value to that before the invocation, and an idempotent REDO operation can set the object value to the state after the invocation.

It could be argued that a more general approach should be taken which is closer to our abstract object model. In some application areas object state is large and recording pre- and post-invocation state might take up an excessive amount of space. Perhaps we should instead expect each object to specify an undo operation for every operation. In the case of the bank account object, for example, a *debit* operation undoes a *credit* operation. Unfortunately, *debit* and *credit* are not idempotent and one would be very pleased, or very angry, depending on which was executed repeatedly on one's bank account object.

In general, operations and their inverses are not idempotent. A recovery procedure based on log records without both pre- and post-invocation state would have to use other techniques to achieve atomic invocation of UNDO and REDO in the presence of crashes.

For simplicity, we shall continue to use our state-based implementation model, which gives us idempotent UNDO and REDO.

20.7 Transaction states on a failure

In Figure 20.2 a checkpoint is taken at time t_c and the system fails at time t_f.

T_1 has already committed at the time of the checkpoint. All its log records will have been written to the log on commit. Any remaining changes to data items will be written out at the time of the checkpoint. T_1 will not be recorded as active in the checkpoint and no recovery action is needed.

T_2 was recorded as active at the time of the checkpoint. Its log records and database updates at that time are written out. T_2 commits before the crash. All its log records are written out before commit completes. T_2 must be REDONE by the recovery procedure since it has committed.

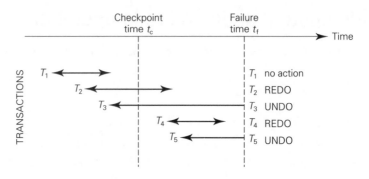

Figure 20.2
Transaction categories for recovery.

T_3 was recorded as active at the time of the checkpoint. Its log records and database updates at that time are written out. T_3 is still in progress at the time of the crash. It must be UNDONE because it is incomplete. The log records are the basis for this.

T_4 was not recorded as active at the time of the checkpoint. It has completed commit processing, however, and must therefore be REDONE since all the changes it made are guaranteed to persist. All its log records were written out on commit.

T_5 was not recorded as active at the time of the checkpoint. T_5 is still in progress at the time of the crash. It must be UNDONE because it is incomplete. The log records are the basis for this.

20.8 An algorithm for recovery
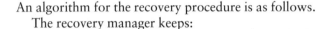

An algorithm for the recovery procedure is as follows.
The recovery manager keeps:

- an UNDO LIST which initially contains all the transactions listed as active in the checkpoint record;
- a REDO LIST which is initially empty.

It searches forwards from the checkpoint record to the end of the log (that is, the most recently written record at the time of failure):

- if it finds a START TRANSACTION record it adds that transaction to the UNDO LIST;
- if it finds a COMMIT record it moves that transaction from the UNDO LIST to the REDO LIST.

It then works backwards through the log from its end,

- UNDOing transactions on the UNDO LIST.

Finally, it works forwards again from the checkpoint record to the end of the log,

- REDOing transactions on the REDO LIST.

An example of the recovery log for T_1 to T_5 above is shown in Figure 20.3. It is assumed that the transactions have the property of isolation and their executions are strict. The columns of the table indicate a partial ordering of the operations and the associated writing of log records; for example, T_3 cannot access x until after T_2 has committed. For conciseness the operations invoked and their arguments are not shown. The figure shows only the object states before and after each invocation.

At the checkpoint, T_2 and T_3 are recorded as active. After the crash, at the start of the recovery procedure:

UNDO LIST = T_2, T_3
REDO LIST is empty

			Checkpoint time t_c				Failure time t_f
T_2	S_2	$x, 2 \rightarrow 3$	$y, 3 \rightarrow 4$	$z, 6 \rightarrow 7$	C_2			
T_3			S_3	$a, 2 \rightarrow 4$	$b, 5 \rightarrow 7$		$x, 3 \rightarrow 5$	
T_4					S_4	$c, 3 \rightarrow 4$	$z, 7 \rightarrow 8$	C_2
T_5						S_5		$z, 8 \rightarrow 9$

Figure 20.3
Example of a recovery log.

After searching forwards through the log to the end:

UNDO LIST $= T_3, T_5$ (T_2 is removed, T_4 is added then removed)
REDO LIST $= T_2, T_4$

While working back through the log from the end to the checkpoint, UNDOing transactions on the UNDO list (T_3, T_5) the following data values are established:

$z = 8$ (T_5), $x = 3$ and $b = 5$ (T_3)

The checkpoint record can then be used to locate the most recent record of an operation invoked by T_3 and to complete the UNDOing of T_3.

While working forwards through the log from the checkpoint to the end, REDOing transactions on the REDO list (T_2, T_4) the following data values are established:

$z = 7$ (T_2), $c = 4$ and $z = 8$ (T_4)

Note that these operations are repeatable, allowing for a crash during the recovery procedure. The previous value of each data item does not matter.

20.9 Location databases for mobile objects

Users and their computers may be mobile. Technology such as wireless networks and high bandwidth wireless ATM networks have opened up design issues for systems to accommodate mobility, for example:

- It should be possible to plug a computer into any network and to continue working as normal. This may involve locating files and accessing services such as mail and news.
- It should be possible for a mobile user to make use of the network-based computers located wherever he or she might be.
- As a user moves around a work environment, relevant environment objects might move with the user. This is a more futuristic scenario; for example, you are taking part in a multimedia conference. You wear a locator object such as an active badge and when you move to another room you are detected there. Your display migrates to a convenient workstation in your new location and the camera, microphone and speaker there are used instead of those in your original location.

Section 26.12
➡

A location database is needed to support mobility; the information held there changes as people, and other objects labelled with locator devices, move around. For this style of database the recovery procedure described in this chapter is inappropriate. It is better to rebuild the location information from badge readings than to restore the pre-crash state which is out of date. Availability of the location service is important and a lengthy recovery procedure will keep it inaccessible. Traditional commercial databases contain integrated, heavyweight recovery and a new approach is needed to support mobility.

20.10 **Summary**

Any system which supports atomic operations must be able to recover from failures of all kinds at any time. In Part II we studied single atomic operations; in Part III we are studying atomic composite operations (transactions).

Throughout Part III we have used a general object model for reasoning about transactions. In theory, object state may be regarded as the result of a sequence of invocations starting from *create*. In theory, any state can be recovered by starting again from *create* and making any required sequence of invocations. In practice, our recovery procedures have to be efficient and have to allow for a crash at any time. We took a simple, state-based model for recovery in which object state was assumed to be recorded before and after an invocation. This allows any operation to be undone and redone, and these UNDO and REDO operations are idempotent.

When a transaction has committed, its effects must be guaranteed to persist. In this chapter we studied one specific system implementation of recovery based on a recovery log. The approach here is to update the database in place and to record all the changes that have been made in a recovery log.

The method is efficient because the log records of all transactions are appended to one place on the disk, the log file. Since log records must be guaranteed to have reached the disk before a transaction is acknowledged as committed, log writes must take place on a fine time grain. Database updates can be done on a coarser time grain and any transaction which needs the committed object values can read them from main memory buffers. The state of all objects affected by committed transactions can be computed from the log if a crash occurs before the object values are updated. Gleeson (1989) makes the following point:

> Once the log records of committed transactions are written to persistent store, the persistent store may be regarded as in a consistent state. When all object values are updated from the log, the persistent store is restored to not only a consistent state but a canonical state.

All this is based on the assumption that the operating system allows the DBMS application to force writes out to the physical disk or to some other form of persistent memory. Many operating systems cache data in main memory until they need the buffer space that it occupies. A TP application cannot be built on an operating system with such semantics.

Our main area of concern is concurrency control. Although crash recovery is not central to this study, the implementation of concurrency control and crash recovery are often inextricably related. Date (1983) and Bernstein *et al.* (1987) are recommended for further reading.

Exercises

20.1 Consider a TP system crash, in which main memory is lost at the following times:
  (a) A transaction has completed some but not all of its operations.
  (b) A client has received acknowledgement that a transaction has committed.
  (c) The system has decided to commit a transaction and has recorded the fact on stable storage, but there is a crash before the client can receive the acknowledgement of commit.
  Discuss what the system must do on restart for each of these cases. Consider for each case where the data values that have been or are about to be committed might be stored. What is it essential for the TP system to know? Why might a conventional operating system not make this information available?

20.2 A recovery log is very large and it may be used for transaction abort as well as crash recovery. How can a periodic checkpoint procedure help to manage this complex process?

20.3 Why must undo and redo operations be idempotent?

20.4 Consider a TP system based on the bank account objects used as an example in Section 18.6 and shown in Figure 20.4. For each operation define an undo operation.

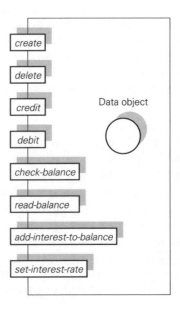

Figure 20.4
An account object.

Suppose that a recovery log record contains:

Transaction id, object id, operation, arguments, state prior to invocation

Define recovery procedures for transactions in all the states shown in Figure 20.2 when a crash occurs. Consider the possibility of a crash during the recovery procedures.

20.5 Redesign the recovery algorithm of Section 20.8 for a non-strict execution schedule (where cascading aborts must be allowed for).

21

Distributed transactions

21.1 An object model for distributed systems

In Section 18.6 a model of objects was set up as a basis for studying transaction processing systems. We now consider this model with specific reference to distributed systems. Figure 21.1 is given here for completeness. We assume each object is invoked through operations appropriate to its type. The figure also shows some object management operations such as *commit*, *abort*, *lock* and *unlock* which may be needed for practical implementation of a transaction processing system (TPS).

The assumptions stated in Section 18.6.2 were as follows:

- Objects are identified uniquely in a system.
- The operations are executed atomically (in the sense of Part II); that is, the operations we are considering here are at the finest granularity of decomposition.
- There is a single clock associated with the object which is used to indicate the time at which operation invocations take place and therefore their order.
- The object records the time at which each operation invocation takes place and the transaction identifier of the transaction that executed the operation.

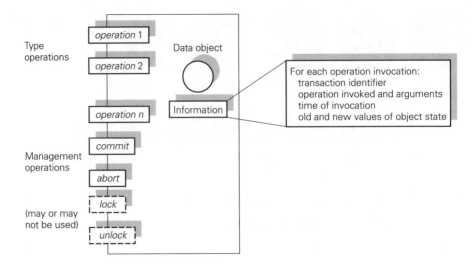

Figure 21.1
An object in a
distributed
transaction system.

The model is appropriate for a distributed system. We now consider object invocation in the context of a distributed TPS.

21.2 Distributed transaction processing

Figure 21.2 shows two instances of the transaction processing system described in Section 19.3 such as would occur at two nodes in a distributed TPS. The following points and assumptions are relevant to an implementation of a distributed TPS, extending the assumptions about objects stated above:

- A client submits a transaction at one node only, which we shall call the **coordinating node**.
- A given object resides at one and only one node; that is, we assume there is no object replication. An object invocation takes place at this **home node**.
- There are mechanisms for locating an object, given its unique identifier.

The TPS instances comprising the distributed TPS must cooperate. A client submits a transaction to one TPS. The transaction manager identifies and locates the objects invoked by the transaction. Local object invocations are passed to the local scheduler; remote object invocations are passed to the (scheduler of the) appropriate remote TPS.

A TPS must therefore handle both transaction requests from local clients and requests from remote TPSs to invoke operations on its local objects. For this latter type of request we assume initially that the TPS does not have a specification of the whole transaction. The scheduler at each node is passed operations which come from both local and remote transaction submissions. As before, the scheduler is at liberty to invoke the operations in any order, subject to the concurrency control algorithm it implements.

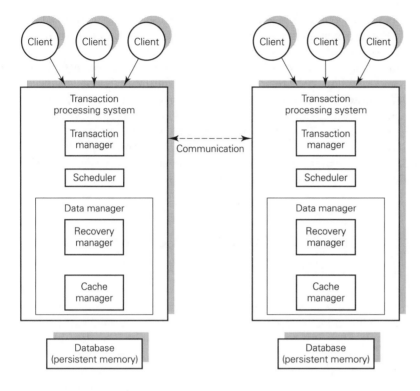

Figure 21.2
A distributed
transaction
processing system.

We must consider:

- **Concurrency control**: how a serializable schedule is achieved in a distributed
  TPS. The methods introduced in Chapter 19 (locking, time-stamping and
  optimistic concurrency control) will be reconsidered for a distributed system.
- **Commitment**: the transaction manager at a single node receives a client request
  for a transaction and initiates local and remote operation invocations. It must
  be notified of the results of attempted invocations: whether an invocation
  was accepted and done, or rejected, or perhaps that a *lock* request has been
  outstanding for some specified timeout period, depending on the method used
  to achieve concurrency control. Assuming that all the transaction's invocations
  (at all the nodes) have been notified as 'done' to the initiating transaction
  manager the transaction must then be committed. We shall study how this
  can be achieved in a distributed system in the presence of partial failures.

As in Chapter 19 we shall assume that the property of isolation is enforced: a
transaction can only see committed object values.

21.3 Communication

The above discussion assumes communication between TPS instances. In some
cases specific application protocols are needed, for example, an atomic commitment
protocol. Application protocols are implemented above general communications

protocols such as remote procedure call (Section 15.7) or some form of message passing. Specific examples are a clock synchronization protocol (Section 6.6.4) and a two-phase commit protocol (Section 21.8).

Communications protocols are designed to allow for the possibilities of congestion and failure of the network and the communicating nodes. The mechanism used is the timeout (see Section 15.7). If a timeout expires the protocol may immediately inform the higher level which invoked it or may retry a few times to allow for congestion. We shall assume the latter here for simplicity. The higher level may therefore receive a 'success' notification or an exception, indicating a failure. The application protocol must be designed on this basis, as we shall see in Section 21.8, for atomic commitment in the presence of failures.

21.4 Concurrency control: Two-phase locking (2PL)

In Section 19.4 two-phase locking was shown to enforce a serializable order on the object invocations of transactions. Each object is assumed to have *lock* and *unlock* operations (see Figure 21.1). We should consider how the two phases, of acquiring and releasing locks, can be implemented in a distributed system. In a centralized system the transaction manager knows when locks on all the objects of a transaction have been acquired and the operations done. The *unlock* operation can then be invoked on all the objects.

Section 19.4

In a distributed system, all the schedulers involved in a transaction must inform the transaction manager at the coordinating node that the requested locking and invocation of objects is done. Only then can the *unlock* operations be sent back to the schedulers concerned. Notice that use of a protocol of this kind prevents timing problems. The phases are defined at one node: the coordinating node of the transaction. For a strict execution that enforces the property of isolation in the implementation, the locks are not released until the transaction is committed.

The method is subject to deadlock, and we assumed in Chapter 19 that deadlock detection and recovery would be carried out by a component of a (centralized) TPS.

This component (let us call it the lock manager) maintains information on the objects that have been locked by transactions and the outstanding lock requests. The implicit assumption in Chapter 19 was that all the objects concerned were local to the TPS, so that complete information on all transactions was available. A deadlock detection algorithm could be run and action taken, such as aborting some or all of the deadlocked transactions.

In a distributed TPS the lock manager at any node can maintain the same information as described above for invocations by local transactions. It can be told about requests for remote invocations by local transactions. It can also know about the requests for local invocations by remote transactions. What it does not know is the remote locks held by these remote transactions and their outstanding requests, and so on until the transitive closure of locks and requests is computed. This information is needed for deadlock (cycle) detection and was discussed in Section 17.10.

Section 17.10

The overhead of two-phase locking is large, particularly when extended for use in a distributed system. Each node must maintain a great deal of information to detect and recover from deadlock, and the method scales badly. In practice a simpler approach based on timeout might be adopted. If a transaction fails to acquire a lock in a given time it is aborted and all the locks it holds are therefore freed.

21.5 Concurrency control: Time-stamp ordering (TSO)

Time-stamp ordering was described in Section 19.5. Each transaction is given a unique time-stamp and their executions are serialized in the order of their time-stamps. In the general model, each object maintains information on its invocations. In time-stamp ordering, the operation invoked and the time-stamp of the invoking transaction are recorded at the object. The object knows which pairs of its operations conflict.

Section 19.5

Assume that one operation of a conflicting pair has been carried out (and committed) at an object and the information described above has been recorded. Assume that a subsequent request for the other operation of the conflicting pair is made. If the transaction time-stamp associated with the request is later than that recorded, the invocation goes ahead and is recorded. If it is less, the invoking transaction must be aborted and may be restarted with a new time-stamp.

The major advantage of this method for a distributed implementation of concurrency control is that only information held at each object is used to achieve serialization. Contrast this with the overhead described above for the distributed deadlock detection associated with distributed two-phase locking.

At first sight it seems that there might be a problem associated with time in using the method in a distributed TPS. In a centralized system the time-stamps have a serial order because they are generated from a single clock. In a distributed system a system-wide ordering of time-stamps is needed for correct serialization of transactions. This is quite easy to achieve. The essential requirement for correctness is that every object takes the same decision about the relative order of two time-stamps. First, suppose that we use the local time of the coordinating node of the transaction for the time-stamp. Except for the case of identically equal times, these values could be used to achieve a correct serializable execution. To deal with the case of equal times we just need a system-wide policy to achieve the arbitration. The node identifiers could be used, for example.

Although this method of generating and using time-stamps achieves correctness it favours nodes with fast-running clocks when arbitration between equal times is needed.

 ## 21.6 Optimistic concurrency control (OCC)

The premise on which the use of OCC is based is that conflict is unlikely to happen. It is also assumed that transactions require high availability of objects, such as in systems which have some degree of real-time requirement. A transaction is allowed to proceed without delay on shadow copies of objects. No changes are applied to persistent object states until the transaction requests *commit*. The transaction is then validated in order to ascertain whether its shadow copies represent a consistent system state and whether its history is serializable with the histories of transactions that have already been validated. Once a transaction is validated, its updates are guaranteed to be made. If the validation fails, the transaction is aborted. This simply involves discarding its shadows. It might then restart with new shadows.

Section 19.6

In Section 19.6 we argued that it would be pessimistic, rather than optimistic, to ensure at transaction start that the shadow copies of objects used by the transaction during the **execution phase** represent a consistent system state. To achieve this consistency we should have to sacrifice guaranteed high availability of objects since an object might be held during commit of some transaction when required by another. It would be necessary to enforce atomic commitment over all the objects invoked by a transaction and to take shadow copies of all the objects needed by a transaction atomically. Section 21.8 shows how atomic commitment can be carried out in a distributed system. This is too heavyweight when we optimistically assume that conflict is unlikely. Also it is not always possible to know at transaction start all the objects that will be needed by a transaction.

As in time-stamp ordering, the decision on whether a transaction may *commit* is based on information recorded at each object. The decision is made during the **validation phase**, after a transaction requests commit. Objects vote independently to *accept* or *reject* the transaction, and this aspect of OCC is therefore appropriate for a distributed system. There is a need to ensure that the local contexts for validation at the objects participating in a transaction are consistent.

The discussion of Section 19.6 was equally applicable to a centralized and a distributed implementation. An essential requirement in a distributed system is that transactions are validated for update in a well-defined serial order. Decisions on validation must be communicated to the participating objects atomically, and we shall sketch a protocol to achieve this in Section 21.9.

In Section 19.6 we required that in the **update phase** of a transaction update invocations are applied to objects in persistent memory in serial order, transaction by transaction. It is the responsibility of the update manager to ensure that all updates succeed. The update manager will know at any time those transactions for which updates have succeeded. It can therefore be asserted that the updates up to those of some transaction have succeeded.

This places a requirement on the underlying communications system used for making remote object invocations. There are issues specific to a distributed implementation that are associated with the independent failure modes of its components. It is necessary to assume that the invocations are made at the object in the order they are sent by the update manager and that these invocations are acknowledged to the update manager. We require that messages are not lost without notification and are not received in a different order from that in which they are sent. This can be achieved by selecting an appropriate communications protocol.

21.7 Commit and abort in a distributed system

Let us assume in the case of 2PL and TSO that the transaction manager at the coordinating node has received a request to *commit* a transaction. We have to ensure:

Atomicity   Either all nodes commit the changes or none do, and any other transaction perceives the changes made at every node or those at none.

Isolation   The effects of the transaction are not made visible until all nodes have made an irrevocable decision to commit or abort.

We have set up the conditions that no scheduler will refuse to *commit* the transaction on correctness grounds. In 2PL and TSO we have avoided this possibility by only allowing serializable invocations to take place. For these pessimistic methods there are two remaining issues to consider:

- Nodes or network connections might fail during *commit*.
- Other nodes may be attempting to carry out distributed commit at the same time and this might involve an intersecting set of objects.

Atomic commitment protocols address these issues. The two-phase commit protocol is discussed in Section 21.8.

In 2PL and TSO we can ensure isolation by holding locks until after *commit* (see Sections 19.4.1 and 19.5.1), thus guaranteeing *strictness*. If strictness is enforced we can assume that all the objects that were invoked by the transaction to be committed are available to the *commit* procedure for it. To achieve this we have introduced a possible additional delay when an object is invoked in 2PL and TSO. Once again we are restricting concurrency (object availability) in order to ensure that transactions see a consistent system state.

In the case of OCC we have made no attempt to ensure the correctness of an executing transaction, preventing harmful consequences by invoking operations on shadow objects. After an executing transaction has issued *commit* we have to ensure during validation:

Consistency   The execution has been based on shadow objects derived from a consistent system state, and there has been no interference at any object from transactions executing concurrently.

We have argued against the atomic commitment of updates for OCC, but its use has definite advantages. Herlihy (1990) proves the correctness of OCC algorithms that are based on a two-phase protocol for update in which validation is performed at each object during the first phase. In this paper he also shows that optimistic and pessimistic methods can be mixed on a per-object basis. Should we wish to enforce strictness (execution based on consistent system state only) for OCC it would be necessary not only to commit updates atomically but also to take the shadow copies needed by a transaction atomically. The drawback of this in a distributed system is that it can greatly reduce object availability, which was one of the goals when OCC was introduced.

On the other hand, we have to ensure a serializable execution, which means that a consistent serial order of committed transactions must be established system-wide. Global consistency is enforced during validation, and locks held during this phase relate only to the process of validation, not to the objects themselves. Once a transaction has its updates guaranteed these can be applied asynchronously at the participating objects, and executing transactions merely read whatever version the object has reached when creating a shadow object. Objects are therefore available except at the moment of version change. The drawback is loss of strictness, with the result that a transaction may be rejected simply because its shadow objects were inconsistent. Since transactions always execute to completion there can be a considerable waste of system resources. A protocol for atomic validation is described in Section 21.9.

We shall now look at a widely used atomic commitment protocol: two-phase commit (2PC). Other such protocols have been defined which vary with respect to the failures they can tolerate and the number of communications that are needed. Further reading on the topic may be found in Bernstein *et al.* (1987), Ceri and Pelagatti (1984) and Bell and Grimson (1992).

21.8 Atomic commitment: The two-phase commit (2PC) protocol

Section 22.3

We assume a number of participating nodes and a commit manager at the co-ordinating node of the transaction (see Figure 21.3(a)). Each participating node 'votes' for *commit* or *abort* of the transaction. Ultimately, all the nodes must make the same decision and the purpose of the protocol is to ensure this. The two phases involved are, broadly:

Phase 1:   the commit manager requests and assembles the 'votes' for *commit* or *abort* of the transaction from each participating node;

Phase 2:   the commit manager decides to *commit* or *abort*, on the basis of the votes, and propagates the decision to the participating nodes.

Showing more detail of the steps involved:

1 The commit manager sends a request to each participating node for its vote.
2 Each node either votes *commit* and awaits further instructions, or votes *abort* and stops (exits from the algorithm). Note that a *commit* vote indicates that both the new value of the data object and the old value are stored safely in stable storage so that the node has the ability to *commit* or *abort*.

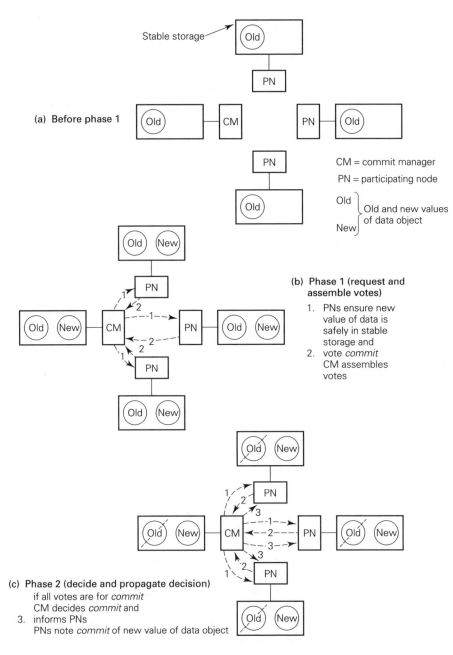

(a) Before phase 1

Stable storage

CM = commit manager

PN = participating node

Old ⎫
New ⎭ Old and new values of data object

(b) Phase 1 (request and assemble votes)

1. PNs ensure new value of data is safely in stable storage and
2. vote *commit*
   CM assembles votes

(c) Phase 2 (decide and propagate decision)
   if all votes are for *commit*
   CM decides *commit* and
3. informs PNs
   PNs note *commit* of new value of data object

Figure 21.3
The two-phase commit protocol when all nodes vote *commit*.

3 The commit manager receives the votes and adds its own vote. If all the votes are to *commit* it decides *commit* and sends *commit* to every participating node. If any vote is *abort* it decides *abort* and sends *abort* to all the nodes that voted *commit* (the others have already stopped). The commit manager stops.

4 The participating nodes that voted *commit* are awaiting notification of the decision. They receive this notification, decide accordingly and stop.

We assume that the decision indicated in step 3 above is permanent, guaranteed to persist; there is a point of decision in the algorithm at the commit manager.

We must consider how the protocol might handle congestion and failures in the nodes and connections involved. As discussed in Section 21.3 above, the two-phase commit protocol is an application protocol which is implemented above lower-level protocols. Each communication involved in two-phase commit will have a success indication or an exception returned from the level below. We shall assume that the lower levels have made allowance for congestion (by retrying after timeouts) and that an exception indicates a failure of some kind. The protocol must be designed on this basis. Bear in mind that a decision cannot be reversed: once a decision is made, failure recovery procedures must ensure it is implemented.

Suppose that an RPC from the coordinating node to each participating node is used to implement steps 1 (request for vote) and 2 (reply with vote). A failure of any one of these RPCs is assumed to indicate a failure of that participating node. The vote from that node might have been *abort*; an *abort* vote is the only safe assumption, so the transaction is aborted.

Suppose that step 3 (send the decision to nodes that voted *commit*) is also implemented by RPC, the reply indicating just an acknowledgement of receipt. A failure of any one of these RPCs indicates that the decision to *commit* or *abort* may still need to be effected at that node. The decision cannot be changed; it has been made and put into effect at the management node and at the nodes which have received the decision from the manager. Recovery from failure at any node must therefore involve terminating correctly any two-phase commit that was in progress when the node failed and sufficient information must be stored in persistent storage to make this possible. On restarting, the node could ask the manager for the decision. The manager knows that node failed and can expect the request.

The above discussion has outlined how failure resilience might be approached in two-phase commit if one or more of the participating nodes fail. The manager might also fail:

1 After sending requests for votes but before deciding. All the participating nodes that voted *commit* will time out (at the two-phase commit level) waiting for a decision.
2 After deciding (and recording the decision in persistent store) but before sending the decision to any participating nodes. All the participating nodes that voted *commit* will time out waiting for a decision.
3 After deciding (and recording the decision in persistent store) and after sending the decision to some but not all participating nodes. Some of the participating nodes that voted *commit* will time out waiting for the decision.

Any one participating node which times out cannot distinguish between these three possibilities. So far we have assumed that the participating nodes know about the manager but not about each other. It would be easy to add a list of participating nodes to the request for vote. Any node that timed out could attempt to find out the decision from the other nodes. Bell and Grimson (1992) and Bernstein *et al.* (1987) give detailed termination protocols for 2PC and also discuss three-phase commit (3PC) protocols.

21.9 Two-phase validation for OCC

We assume a number of participating nodes and a validation manager at the coordinating node of each transaction (see Figure 21.4). In addition there is a single logical agent in the system, the update manager, which is responsible for the queue of transactions that have been validated for update. Each transaction involves a number of participating objects, and each object votes independently *accept* or *reject* on whether there has been conflict. In addition, any object that votes to accept a transaction notifies the validation manager of the version time-stamp of the shadow object that was created for the execution phase.

Section 19.6 ⬅

In the figure, transaction T is being validated by validation manager 2, the participating objects being A, D and X. Another transaction involving objects C and X has just issued *commit*, and validation manager 3 is to validate it. Two-phase validation has much the same general structure as the two-phase commit protocol described in Section 21.8, but there are two important differences. First, an object may be involved in several transactions concurrently: one transaction may issue commit when the object is already participating in the validation phase of some other transaction. It would be possible to block the newly requested validation, but such a policy would run the risk of deadlock. A better approach is to ask the validation manager to try again later if the object's vote is still of interest. Secondly, if all participants vote *accept* at the first phase and the transaction is validated successfully, they do not need to apply the updates during the second phase. Instead the validation manager applies to the update manager for a time-stamp for the transaction, and at this point the serialization order is determined. This interaction is atomic. The validation

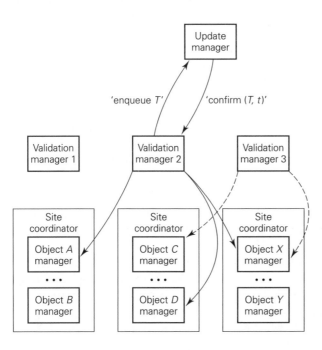

Figure 21.4
Distributed validation for OCC.

manager must then inform each participating object of the decision, so that any subsequent validation takes place in a consistent context.

Interaction between the validation manager and participating objects follows the general pattern shown in Figure 21.3, but the details of the protocol must take account of the above differences. The two phases involved are, broadly:

Phase 1: the validation manager requests and assembles the 'votes' for *accept* or *reject* of the transaction from each participating object, except those that say *busy*;

Phase 2: the validation manager decides to *commit*, *reject* or *retry*, on the basis of the votes, taking account of shadow object consistency. If the decision is *commit* it applies to the update manager for a time-stamp. The decision is propagated to participating objects.

Considering the steps involved in more detail:

1 The validation manager sends a request to each participating object for its vote on the transaction execution.
2 Any object that is performing validation of some other transaction replies *busy* and awaits further information. Other objects either vote *accept* (indicating the shadow object version time-stamp) and await further instructions, or vote *reject*, record rejection locally and discard the shadow object. Objects that vote *reject* need not be contacted further.
3 The validation manager receives the responses and determines what action to take.

   If any vote is *reject* it decides *reject* and sends *reject* to all the objects that replied *accept* or *busy* (the others have already stopped).

   Otherwise, if any vote is *busy* it asks all the objects to suspend validation for a subsequent *retry*. Objects which voted *accept* are then free to validate other transactions. The validation manager will retry after a suitable interval. Objects which voted *accept* originally may then vote *reject*.

   If all the votes are *accept* the validation manager decides whether to *commit* on the basis of shadow object consistency. If the versions were inconsistent (see Section 19.6), it decides *reject* and sends *reject* to all the objects; the validation manager stops.
4 If the decision is *commit*, the validation manager applies to the update manager for a time-stamp for the transaction. The decision is propagated to all participating objects, together with the time-stamp. The validation manager stops.

The point of decision in the above algorithm occurs when the update manager issues a time-stamp for the transaction. At that point all participating objects have voted *accept* in a two-phase protocol, and they must be prepared to apply updates at some later stage.

It is worth considering the extent to which concurrent execution is sacrificed, and the consequences for object availability. First, the interaction to obtain a time-stamp from the update manager is atomic, and requests must be serviced by a single queue manager. Secondly, when a validation manager receives a *busy* reply from an object it abandons the attempt to validate for a while. Objects will service only one request to validate at a time. Both of these restrictions apply to the **validation phase** of a transaction. The *busy* reply may increase the chance that a transaction is rejected, thus wasting system resources. On the other hand there are no bad implications for object availability at the **execution phase,** since updates are applied locally at each object during the **update phase,** without a protocol that involves external sites. Shadow objects can therefore be created except when a request is received during a change of object version (essentially a rename operation).

This discussion has not considered how the protocol might handle congestion and failures in the nodes and connections involved. Two-phase validation, like two-phase commit, is an application protocol which is implemented above lower-level protocols. The considerations outlined in Section 21.8 apply equally here.

21.10 Summary

We considered multiple cooperating instances of the TPS described in Chapter 19 and reiterated, in the context of a distributed system, the general object model that was set up in Chapter 18.

Much of the discussion of concurrency control in Chapter 19 was equally applicable to distributed systems. In this chapter a short discussion on each method highlighted the points specific to distributed systems. There is as yet little practical experience of distributed implementations.

Two-phase locking has the overhead of deadlock detection which is more complex and imposes greater overhead in a distributed system than in a centralized one. A simple timeout approach, in which a transaction that does not succeed in acquiring a lock in a given time is aborted and restarted, is preferable.

Time-stamp ordering has the advantage that information held locally at an object is the basis on which an invocation is accepted or rejected so the method is potentially good for distributed systems. The absence of system-wide time is not a problem provided that there is a policy which ensures that all objects reach the same decision on the relative order of any two transaction time-stamps.

Optimistic methods are also potentially well suited to distributed systems. Operations are invoked on copies of all the objects involved in a transaction and the results of the transaction are incorporated into the database when it requests *commit*. In OCC the order in which transactions' updates are made at each object is determined by the update manager. A time-stamp, issued by the update manager, is associated with the transaction and the updates are made in time-stamp order at each object.

For simplicity, we assumed in 2PL and TSO that strictness was enforced in the implementation of the transaction executions. Greater concurrency might be achieved at the expense of greater complexity by relaxing strictness. We argued that atomic commitment and taking shadow copies atomically would reflect a pessimistic, rather than optimistic, approach and is therefore unsuitable for OCC.

We discussed atomic commitment for 2PL and TSO. The independent failure modes of the components of distributed systems are relevant here. The same decision on transaction *commit* or *abort* must be made for all objects invoked by the transaction. A two-phase commit protocol was described and discussed in some detail. Finally, we discussed a two-phase validation protocol for OCC. In this case, the single point of decision on whether the transaction is to be committed is when the update manager issues the transaction time-stamp. Updates are then guaranteed to be made in time-stamp order at each object.

Study questions

S 21.1

In addition to the operations appropriate to its type, what further operations can be applied to an object in a transaction processing system?

S 21.2

In a TPS, what information is stored with each object for each operation invocation?

S 21.3

What assumptions are made about a distributed TPS?

S 21.4

What must each node in a distributed TPS be able to do? What functions does the local transaction manager perform? What coordinates activities at each node?

S 21.5

What are the two major issues that must be addressed in a distributed TPS?

S 21.6

What is meant, in a distributed TPS, by saying that, 'the property of isolation is enforced'?

S 21.7

At what level are application protocols implemented?

S 21.8

Give an example of an application protocol in a TPS.

S 21.9

What are communications protocols used for?

Exercises

21.1 In what ways do distributed systems differ from centralized ones?

21.2 How can the components of a distributed system agree on a basis for establishing system time? Under what circumstances might system time be needed?

21.3 Relate the object model in Section 21.1 and the distributed TPS of Section 21.2 with the discussion on the implementation of naming, binding, locating and invoking objects of Section 15.11.

First, consider the component TPSs as a distributed application that a client may wish to invoke. The components may be named as a set of application servers. The objects they manage are named internally by the TPS. This is the client–server model.

A more general object model might support global naming and invocation of the data objects. How might this be managed in a system?

21.4 Describe the operation of a distributed TPS from the point at which a client submits a transaction to a single component of the TPS.

21.5 Why are the time-stamp ordering (TSO) and optimistic concurrency control (OCC) approaches to concurrency control potentially more suitable for distributed implementation than two-phase locking? How can 2PL be simplified?

21.6 What is involved in the validation phase of OCC in a distributed system?

21.7 (a) Why is a complex protocol required to *commit* a transaction atomically in a distributed TPS?
    (b) What happens in the two-phase commit protocol if the transaction manager fails? Discuss its failure at all relevant stages in the protocol.
    (c) Suppose a participant fails after voting for *commit* of a transaction. What should it do on restart?
    What are the advantages and disadvantages of letting the nodes participating in a two-phase commit know about each other?

22

Distributed computations

22.1 Introduction

In this chapter we focus on the special problems associated with designing algorithms which are implemented with distributed components. Many are useful building blocks for designing distributed systems.

Chapter 6 introduced the fundamental properties of distributed computations: concurrent execution of components, independent failure modes of components, communications delay, potential inconsistency of data and absence of a single timeframe.

Here, we shall assume that the nodes involved have clocks that are synchronized as described in Chapter 6. Some of the algorithms we consider will make use of locally issued time-stamps, using process identifiers to arbitrate between requests with equal time-stamps. We shall be concerned with the fact that any component of a computation, or any connection path, may fail at any time. It is often impossible to tell which of these has happened. The situation is made worse by the possibility of comunications delay. It may be that timeouts result from heavily loaded networks or servers rather than failures. We took account of this for a simple request–response protocol in Chapter 15. The higher-level components we consider in this chapter are built above such communications.

We have already taken a preliminary look at some distributed algorithms, but without a full discussion of failure implications. In Chapter 5 we saw that clients of distributed filing systems are likely to maintain a cache of files or blocks of files for their users. Maintenance of cache consistency requires a distributed algorithm. In the approaches we studied, the file server played a central role. In

Chapter 17 we considered how distributed deadlock detection might be carried out. Again, we omitted to discuss the failure modes of the various approaches.

Chapter 21 covered distributed transactions and we studied an atomic commitment protocol: two-phase commit. We assumed a known group of processes were to reach consensus on whether to commit or abort a result. In this chapter we extend the discussion to the composition of the group and the election of a coordinator by a group of processes.

Naming was introduced in Chapter 6 as a fundamental issue underlying all system design. We saw that the data held by name servers should be highly available and that a trade-off may have to be made between availability and consistency of data. Implementation approaches are discussed here.

22.2 Process groups

Many algorithms assume that a certain number of components are participating, indeed the algorithm may make use of the number of processes involved and their identities. Before such an algorithm commences we need to have a means of controlling group membership. Typical primitives for managing groups are as follows:

```
create   (group-name, <list-of-processes>)
kill     (group-name)
join     (group-name, process)
leave    (group-name, process)
```

The system may provide a 'group server' to which all these requests must be sent or it may be that join and leave may be sent to any member of the group. It would of course be necessary for a process to have the necessary access privilege to be able to kill a group.

It is necessary to specify whether communication involving groups is closed or open. For example, a distributed algorithm may be such that a process must be a member of the group in order to participate in the algorithm. Alternatively, a group of servers may exist to carry out a service, in which case the service is invoked by a message from a process outside the group to any member of it.

We shall consider cases where the group has no internal structure and the algorithms are fully distributed. Alternatively, we shall study algorithms in which the group is structured and a leader acts as coordinator.

Any process may fail at any time. A crashed process is deemed to have left any group of which it is a member and must rejoin on restarting. The group control algorithms must be robust under failure, for example on failure of a process during leave and join. Failure of a group leader is considered in the next section.

Systems concerned with fault tolerance may be built above a group abstraction. For example, the processes of a group might each compute and vote on the result of a computation. Communication is likely to be based on a **reliable multi-cast** protocol where any message is guaranteed to be delivered to every member of the group. ISIS is an example of such a system, see Birman and Joseph (1987) and Birman (1993).

22.2.1 Leadership election

The coordinator of an algorithm may in some cases be any member of a group. For example, the group members may each be maintaining a data replica and any member that receives an external request to update the data will act as coordinator of the update, see Section 22.3.

If there is no obvious initiator then a leader may be 'elected'. Let us assume:

- each process has a unique ID known to all members;
- the process with the highest ID is the leader;
- any process may fail at any time.

The BULLY election algorithm

One election algorithm that has been proposed is called BULLY. All processes behave as follows:

- P notices there is no reply from the coordinator.
- P sends an **elect** message to all processes with higher IDs.
- If any reply then P exits.
- If there are no replies then P wins, obtains any state needed to function as leader then sends a **coordinator** message to all processes.
- On receipt of an **elect** message a process must both reply to the sender and start an election if it is not already holding one.

Notice that there can be concurrent elections in progress, see Figure 22.1(ii), and that the algorithm can involve a large number of messages. Also, it is not specified how long a process should wait before deciding that no reply has come

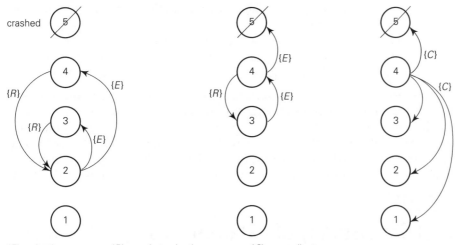

{E} = election message {R} = reply to election message {C} = coordinator message

(i) Process 2 holds an election, receives replies so exits

(ii) Processes 3 and 4 hold elections after receiving {E} from 2

(iii) Process 4 sends {C} to all processes

Figure 22.1
Election algorithm: BULLY.

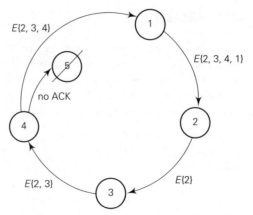

$E\{2, 3, 4\}$

$E\{2, 3, 4, 1\}$

no ACK

$E\{2, 3\}$

$E\{2\}$

Figure 22.2
Election algorithm:
RING.

(i) Process 2 holds an election

back and that it is therefore the new leader. This is an issue for the lower-level protocols; the high-level algorithms act according to the best information available from the lower levels.

A ring-based election algorithm

An alternative is to use a RING algorithm in which processes are ordered cyclically, the order being known to all processes. A failed process can therefore be bypassed. The algorithm requires messages to be acknowledged so that any process that fails during its execution can be bypassed. All processes behave as follows, see Figure 22.2:

- P notices the coordinator is not functioning.
- P sends an **elect** message containing its own ID to the next process in the ring.
- on receipt of an **elect** message:
  (a)   without the receiver's ID – add this ID and pass on the message;
  (b)   with the receiver's ID (the message has been round the ring) – send a message (**coordinator**, highest ID in the message) around the ring.

The process with the highest ID then functions as coordinator; all the processes have found out this ID as the message traversed the ring.

   The algorithm involves fewer messages than the BULLY algorithm. Communication delay may again interfere with the algorithm, in that heavy loading of a process's node or the communication path to it may cause it to be bypassed. In both cases the algorithms are specified at a higher level than this.

22.3 Consistency of data replicas

Data that is needed to support the smooth operation of a system is often **replicated**. An example is the naming data held by name servers that was discussed in Section 15.11. Replication of data ensures that if a single computer that holds such data fails, another copy exists. Replication may also be used to ensure that there is a copy reasonably near to all points of the system, which is particularly relevant to large-scale systems. Data is therefore replicated for reasons of availability and performance. Applications and services in general may maintain data replicas for these reasons. Communications delay and distributed updates mean that replicas can get out of step. We may have sacrificed consistency to achieve availability.

When data replicas exist in a system there must be a policy about how changes to such data are handled. Alternative policies are as follows:

- **Weak consistency**: A change made to one of the replicas is visible immediately. The system will propagate the change to the other replicas in due course but in the meantime the system has become inconsistent.
- **Strong consistency**: Another approach is to attempt to make the change to all the copies before allowing the data to become visible again. The problem here is that even if all the computers holding the replicas are available, the process is much slower than updating one nearby copy.

Here we have a simpler model than in the transactional systems of Chapter 21. We have replicas of a single object which may be read and written by distributed processes. Another term which captures the requirement for strong consistency is **single copy serializability (SR1)**.

If any replica is on a system which is not available we have either to forbid the update or handle the inconsistency when the system becomes available again. It has been said that distributed computing means that the fact that a computer you have never heard of has crashed means that you can't get on with your work! We see how this problem can be alleviated in the next section.

Another scenario is that all the replicas may be on systems that are running but the network has become partitioned. There is the possibility of inconsistent updates being made within the separate partitions.

A special case of replication is that systems of moderate scale may maintain a **hot standby**. In this case a duplicate is maintained in step with the primary copy so that if the primary fails a switch can be made to the duplicate without loss of state. We shall not consider this option further but will focus on the more general case of multiple distributed replicas.

22.3.1 Quorum assembly for strong consistency

An approach to alleviating the problem of contacting every replica is to allow an update to take place when a **majority** of the replicas can be assembled to take part in the process. This is called a **write quorum**. A **read quorum** is also defined and its value is chosen to ensure that at least one of its member replicas contains the most recent update. If there are n replicas a write quorum WQ and read quorum RQ are typically defined to be:

$WQ > n/2$
$RQ + WQ > n$

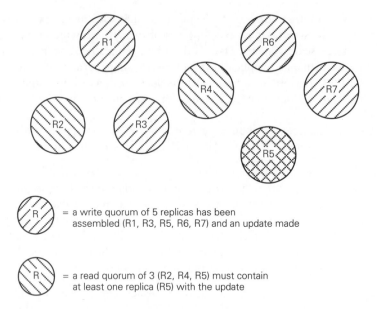

= a write quorum of 5 replicas has been
assembled (R1, R3, R5, R6, R7) and an update made

Figure 22.3
Quorum assembly.

= a read quorum of 3 (R2, R4, R5) must contain
at least one replica (R5) with the update

For example, if $n = 7$, you may have to assemble and write to 5 replicas and assemble 3 for reading. On reading you check the time of last update of all three and use the most recent. The system software is likely to attempt to bring all the replicas up to date behind the scenes. Figure 22.3 illustrates.

Note that the replicas are maintained by a group of processes of size n. Quorum assembly is tolerant of failure of the nodes. An atomic commitment protocol must then be used to commit (or fail to commit) the update for all (or no) members of the quorum; see Section 21.7. Quorum assembly is not tolerant of the group size being increased concurrently with assembly of a quorum and this must be taken into account in the protocol which implements join.

22.3.2 Large-scale systems

Quorum assembly alleviates the problem of having to contact every replica to make an update in a system where strong consistency is required. In large-scale systems the quorum size might still be large and the process of assembly very slow. Figure 22.4 illustrates how strong and weak consistency might both be used in a large-scale system. A hierarchy of replicas is created. Recall that a similar approach was used for NTP (network time protocol) to synchronize the clocks of computers on the internet; see Section 6.6.4.

Figure 22.4 shows a number of primary servers at the top level of the hierarchy. They are responsible for maintaining strongly consistent replicas. The system specification may be that all updates must be made by contacting some primary server. That server is then responsible for assembling a quorum among the primary servers then using an atomic commitment protocol to commit the update securely. The primary servers then propagate the update down their respective hierarchies.

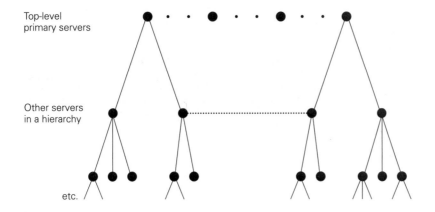

Top-level
primary servers

Other servers
in a hierarchy

etc.

Figure 22.4
Large-scale systems
of replicas.

A process which requires a **read** to be guaranteed to be up-to-date must contact a primary server. If a quick response is required any local server may be contacted. There is a small risk that an update to the data item required is still on its way to that server.

Ma (1992) used a hierarchical scheme of this kind for name servers. Adly *et al.* (1993; 1995) give a design which allows a variety of application semantics to be provided within a hierarchically structured system. The protocols are tolerant of changes in group membership. Adly *et al.* (1995) give an overview of replication algorithms for large-scale systems as well as describing this work in detail.

22.4 Ordering message delivery

We have seen that a group of processes may be set up and may execute distributed algorithms. Each member may be maintaining a data replica and we have seen how a single update may be committed by all members of the group or by none of them, using quorum assembly followed by an atomic commitment protocol. Concurrent update requests are serialized by the fact that only one quorum assembly can succeed. Strong consistency has been achieved, we have single copy serializability and have imposed a **total order** of updates system-wide (within the group).

In the above we did not take into account the order in which the update requests originated. We could specify an additional requirement: that updates are committed at the replicas in time-stamp order. In an application domain where this is appropriate it could well be beneficial to separate the application making updates from the message delivery system, as shown in Figure 22.5.

In some applications this strong consistency is not needed. If we remove the requirement for consistency we can allow messages to be delivered to the application in **any order**. We can ensure that every update reaches every replica eventually but the order in which the updates are made is not controlled.

Between these extremes we may require **causal ordering** of message delivery. Here we assert that a message received by a process can potentially affect any

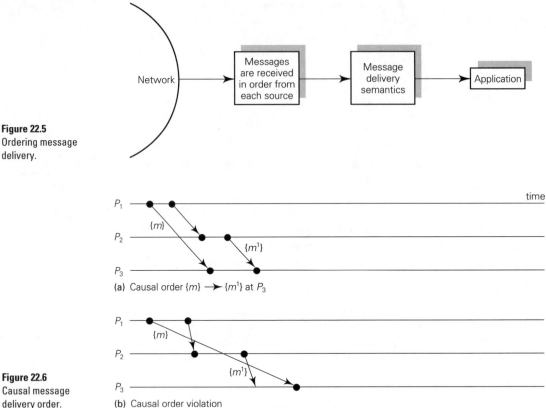

Figure 22.5
Ordering message
delivery.

(a) Causal order $\{m\} \longrightarrow \{m^1\}$ at P_3

Figure 22.6
Causal message
delivery order.

(b) Causal order violation

subsequent message sent by that process. Those messages should be received in that order at all processes. Unrelated messages may be delivered in any order. Figure 22.6 illustrates.

The causal ordering condition may be stated more formally as follows:

$$\text{send}_i(m) \rightarrow \text{send}_j(n) \text{ implies } \text{deliver}_k(m) \rightarrow \text{deliver}_k(n)$$

22.4.1 Vector clocks

We assume that every message is to be delivered eventually to every process. The message delivery system must be able to deliver messages to the application in causal order if required. This implies that some messages which are received 'early' must be held by the message delivery system before being delivered. A data structure must be maintained on which such decisions can be based. One approach is to use so-called 'vector clocks' (see the chapter by Babaoglu and Marzullo in Mullender (1993) and Figure 22.7).

We assume a fixed number n of processes, each with a corresponding entry in a vector. The entry for a process indicates the eventcount at that process; the idea is that described for logical time and event ordering in Section 6.6.3. Each

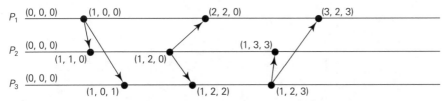

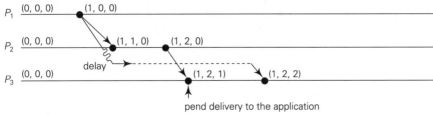

(a) Each message is multicast to the group and the vectors are maintained by each process

(b) Potential violation of causal order is detected

Figure 22.7
Example showing
vector clocks.

time a process sends or receives a message it increments its own eventcount (its entry in the vector).

SEND(vector, message)

When a process sends a message it tags the message with its value of the vector. This indicates the belief of that process about the state (eventcounts) of all other processes.

RECEIVE(vector, message)

When a process receives a message it updates its vector entries for other processes from the values in the vector when these are greater then the values in its locally maintained vector.

Each process, implementing the message service for an application, therefore maintains its best knowledge of the state of the system. Based on the values in the vector it can decide whether or not to pass a given message up to the application. Figure 22.7 illustrates.

Note that we have assumed that the number of processes is fixed. Each process has a name which indicates its slot in the vector. This notation has been used historically but a set notation would be more general. It would allow the group size to vary as processes join and leave and would avoid the problem of a gap in the vector caused by a leaving process.

22.5 Distributed, *N*-process mutual exclusion

Consider *n* processes executing on *n* processors with no shared memory. A problem discussed in the literature is to devise an algorithm to implement a critical region within each process. As discussed in Chapters 6 and 15 any such

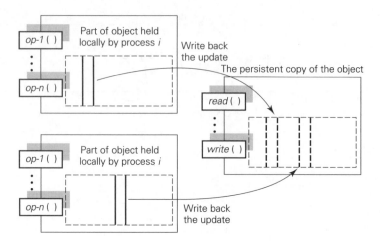

Figure 22.8
Centralized object, distributed operation invocation.

algorithm must take into account the possibility of independent failures of the components of distributed systems, the absence of global time and the delay involved in communications between components.

In order to explore the characteristics of applications for which a distributed mutual exclusion protocol may be appropriate we shall start from an example of a **centralized data object** with **distributed processing**.

Assume that n processes are cooperating to process data in a shared file and that the processes must use a conventional file server which sees a file as an unstructured byte sequence. Processes read the data in fixed size records, of size k bytes, process it, write it back to its original place in the file, read another record, and so on (see Figure 22.8). The processes may run at different speeds and the processing of the records may involve variable amounts of computing. The problem is to ensure that no record of the file is processed by more than one process and that all records are processed by some process.

If a process requests to read 'the next k bytes' (relative to some system-maintained pointer) the file server delivers a unique portion of the file to each process. Unfortunately, the process is unable to write back the record because it does not know the position of the record in the file; other processes may change the position of the pointer. If, instead, each process asks for a specific range of bytes, it is possible that more than one process will read a given range (or that some records will be missed) unless they coordinate their activities.

The file service interface does not provide the functionality required by the cooperating processes. We may adopt two approaches to solving this problem:

- *A centralized approach*: provide an 'access coordination server' (or coordinator) which tells the processes which record they may process.

  Note that we must avoid introducing extra data transfers into the distributed system. We must not put the coordinator on the data transfer path between the file server and the processes. Instead, each free process should ask the coordinator for a byte range in the file which it may process.

  Note that we are not implementing the coordinator as a server which functions as an object manager. It does not perform operation invocations

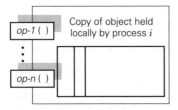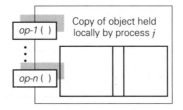

Figure 22.9
A replicated or
distributed object.

on the object: we wish to have these done in parallel by the processes.
Our coordinator is part of the process of assessing the object, similar to an
object location server which is transparent to client (object invoker) and
server (object manager).

- *A distributed approach*: the processes execute a protocol to ensure that no
record of the file is processed by more than one process and that all records
are processed by some process. Before going into the details of such protocols
we first consider some more general examples.

Replicated or distributed data objects

In the example above there is a single copy of the data object, and we arranged
carefully that no part of it would be acquired by more than one process. We
now consider the possibility that multiple copies of objects or parts of objects
might exist in a distributed system.

For example, suppose that a system supports object mapping. Suppose
that several processes have mapped a given object in their address spaces (see
Figure 22.9). When process *i* wishes to invoke an operation on its local copy of
the object it must first coordinate with the other processes to ensure that it has
exclusive access to the object or some specified part of it.

Another example is a distributed game with *n* players. Suppose each player
has a copy of the game's data and that only one player at once may make a
change to the data. The change is propagated to all the other players.

Another example is a multimedia, on-line conferencing system. Each delegate
sees some replicated objects and some private objects. A participant may only
make a change to a replicated object after executing a distributed mutual exclusion
protocol. A similar situation arises when a participant wishes to speak. It is agreed
that only one person may speak at once and obtaining permission to speak
requires a mutual exclusion protocol.

22.5.1 Algorithms

Three approaches to implementing *n*-process distributed mutual exclusion
are now outlined. The exercises which follow guide the reader in exploring
the trade-offs and potential problems. Raynal (1986) contains these and other
algorithms. The fully distributed approach was discussed in Lamport (1978)
and the algorithm presented below was devised by Ricart and Agrawala (1981).

Centralized algorithm

This approach is similar to that described above for a centralized access coordination server or coordinator. The idea is that one of the n processes is elected as coordinator. Each process sends a request to the coordinator before entering its critical region (CR). The coordinator checks whether any process is in the CR and, if so, accumulates a queue of requests. When the CR becomes free the coordinator sends a reply to a process, selected according to some specified scheduling policy, and this process receives the message and proceeds into its CR. On exit from its CR it sends a release message to the coordinator.

Token passing in a virtual ring of processes

The processes are ordered into a virtual ring and a 'token' is devised. The token comprises a message which all processes recognize as permission to enter the CR. The token is passed from process to process in the order specified. When a process receives the token it may, if it wishes, enter its CR. In this case it keeps the token and passes it on to the next process on exit from the CR. Otherwise it passes on the token immediately. Notice the similarity of the scheduling policy to that of the Eisenberg–McGuire algorithm for shared-memory systems (Section 9.3.3).

A distributed algorithm

The aim is to implement a first come first served scheduling policy. Recall the discussion of Section 6.6 on the ordering of events in distributed systems. When a process wishes to enter its CR it sends a request message to all processes, including itself, and includes a time-stamp with the message. The system has a policy for global ordering of time-stamps: for example, if any time-stamps are equal, the associated process IDs are used to achieve a unique global ordering of the request messages. On receiving a request message a process may reply immediately or may defer sending a reply as follows:

- If a process is in its CR it defers sending a reply.
- If a process does not want to enter its CR it sends a reply immediately.
- If a process wants to enter its CR but has not yet done so then it compares the time-stamp on its own request with the time-stamp of the incoming request. If its own time-stamp is greater than that of the incoming request it sends a reply immediately (the other process asked first). Otherwise it defers its reply.

A process that has received a reply from all the other processes may enter its CR. On exit from the CR the process replies to any requests that it has deferred. Notice the similarity of the scheduling policy to that of the bakery algorithm (Section 9.3.4).

The algorithms may be criticized as follows.

The centralized algorithm is fair: it implements first-come first-served priority. It is also economical in the number of messages required. However, it has a single point of failure and the coordinator will become a bottleneck for large-scale systems. The conditions of failure of the coordinator and denial of access to the CR cannot be distinguished. This can be solved by using an acknowledgement of the request. The requestor is then trusted to wait for the CR.

The token ring algorithm is reasonably efficient, although the token continues to circulate when no one wishes to enter the CR. It is not fair in that the ring ordering does not honour the order of requesting the CR. The algorithm is susceptible to loss of the token. Acknowledgement messages are needed to detect failure of components which must then be bypassed.

The distributed algorithm replaces a single point of failure with n separate points of failure and n bottlenecks. Although it is fair it is expensive in the number of messages required. As above, acknowledgement messages should be used to distinguish between failure and denial of the CR.

22.6 Summary of Part III

The model of an object with abstract operations is used throughout the book. Part II is concerned with implementing a single abstract operation correctly in the presence of concurrency and crashes. Part III is concerned with implementing a number of related operations comprising a single higher-level abstract operation.

The problems arising from uncontrolled concurrent execution of composite operations are incorrect results arising from certain interleavings of suboperations, and deadlock arising from some approaches to controlling this. Deadlock is discussed in Chapter 17. The concept of atomic transaction is developed in Chapter 18 and the ACID properties of transactions (atomicity, consistency, isolation and durability) are discussed. Concurrency control procedures must ensure consistency and isolation; storage management policies and crash recovery procedures must ensure atomicity and durability.

For concurrency control purposes we assume that information is stored at each object, including the time at which each invocation was made and by which transaction. The object also specifies which of its pairs of operations are conflicting (non-commutative).

On this basis the implementation of transactions in the presence of concurrent transactions and failures can be studied. Chapter 19 focuses on concurrency control; two-phase locking (2PL), time-stamp ordering (TSO) and optimistic methods (OCC) are discussed in general terms.

In Chapter 20 we are concerned with crash recovery. If a crash occurs it must be possible to recover any desired system state and therefore any desired state for any object. We have already set up the recording of a history of invocations at each object for concurrency control purposes. In theory, object state may be regarded as the result of a sequence of invocations starting from *create*. In theory, any state can be recovered by starting again from *create* and making any required sequence of invocations. In practice, our recovery procedures have to be efficient and have to allow for a crash at any time. We took a simple, state-based model for recovery in which object state was assumed to be recorded before and after an invocation. This allows any operation to be undone and redone, and these UNDO and REDO operations must be idempotent to allow for crashes during recovery.

Concurrency control and recovery are closely related because the mechanisms that must be in place for crash resilience in a transaction system can be used by a concurrency control method to achieve *abort*.

The object model used throughout Part III is not restricted to a centralized implementation. Most of the discussion in Chapters 16 to 20 is relevant to both centralized and distributed systems. Chapter 21 focuses on the issues specific to distributed systems; their special properties are discussed and the various methods for achieving concurrency control are reconsidered. Time-stamp ordering and optimistic concurrency control are shown to be immediately applicable to distributed systems; two-phase locking involves a good deal of extra work to distribute the deadlock detection procedure. In practice, if distributed two-phase locking was used for concurrency control, a timeout mechanism would be used. Any transaction which fails to achieve a lock in a given time is aborted.

In pessimistic methods commitment must be implemented atomically over all objects invoked by a transaction. In a centralized system the whole TPS is assumed to fail together. The recovery procedures must ensure the consistency of persistent memory on restart after a failure. In a distributed system we are concerned with the atomic commitment of distributed objects in the presence of partial failures of (components of) a system. We studied a two-phase commit protocol and outlined the recovery procedures of nodes that fail during the protocol.

In optimistic methods, we strive for high concurrency, that is, high availability of objects. If objects are involved in the atomic commitment of one transaction they are unavailable to others. We studied a two-phase validation protocol for distributed OCC during which shadow objects may still be taken by new transactions.

Finally we stepped back from transactions involving persistent data and examined some multicomponent distributed computations. The algorithms covered were suitable for use as building blocks within various categories of application. For each algorithm we considered the implications of the fundamental properties of distributed systems.

Exercises

22.1 How is the distributed deadlock detection algorithm of Section 17.10 affected by failure of the nodes involved?

22.2 Suppose a file server supports file caching at clients. Discuss how cache coherency might be maintained. Include possible interactions among the clients after server failure. What restart procedures would you expect at the server and at clients?

22.3 Discuss object coherency and failure semantics for a distributed object mapping system as described in Section 5.13.2.

22.4 Discuss how the nodes executing an atomic commitment protocol after write-quorum assembly should handle an incoming join or leave message from a process which is not in the write quorum.

22.5 For the BULLY and RING election algorithms:
   (a) How many messages are involved in electing a new coordinator?
   (b) What should happen when a failed coordinator restarts?

22.6 Give examples of applications which you would you expect to require strong consistency of data and of those which you would expect to prefer or tolerate weak consistency.

22.7 For the *n*-process mutual exclusion algorithms:
   (a) Is each algorithm correct and free from deadlock?
   (b) How many messages are required for the entry and exit protocols, with and without failure detection?
   (c) How many processes does each process need to communicate with?
   (d) How easy is it for the group of processes to be reconfigured by join and leave?

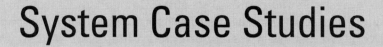

Part IV

System Case Studies

In Part IV we look at the design choices that were made in some real systems. Many papers, web pages, standards documents, and sometimes books, have been written on the systems we consider. A short case study cannot do full justice to any system and, for greater insight, the papers written by those involved in the design and everyday use of the systems are referenced.

The World Wide Web is a large-scale, widely distributed system, originally designed for document delivery. We look at how the standard distributed system architectural components introduced in Chapter 6, namely communication, naming, location, security, concurrency control and scalability have been addressed in the design of web browsers and web servers. We note that the fact that web documents are read-only over quite long periods of time helps to simplify the design. Because the web is ubiquitous it is coming to be used as the standard interface for many distributed systems and we discuss this trend and outline the standards designed for this purpose.

Chapter 24 discusses the design of middleware: a software layer or platform that may run above heterogeneous operating systems to create a common interface through which distributed applications can interoperate together with system services that run above the platform. We set up a framework for considering middleware paradigms then discuss current middleware in this context.

OMG's CORBA is discussed in detail because its design is object based and it is a widely accepted *de facto* standard. Java was originally designed with web servers and web browsers in mind but JavaSoft now offers the full range of services that might be expected in a general middleware platform. We describe Microsoft's Distributed Component Object Model (DCOM) and their recent middleware to support a web-server approach, .Net (dotNet). We discuss message-oriented middleware (MOM) and give two widely used examples: IBM's MQseries and TIBCO's TIB/Rendezvous. It should be noted that both CORBA and Java have been extended to include message passing services.

Chapter 25 first discusses how transaction processing systems might be implemented in terms of processes and IPC. We then outline some TP systems in the area of electronic funds transfer (EFT). The international Automatic Teller Machine network is then described in some detail. Security issues and some approaches to their solution are outlined.

The World Wide Web

The internet has existed in one form or another for decades, based on research in packet switching in the 1960s. Donald Davies of the National Physical Laboratory, UK, conceived the idea in 1965, coined the term 'packet switching' in 1966 and led a team that built a packet-switched network. The internet, as we know it today, has grown gradually since that time. The World Wide Web (henceforth 'the web') came into use in the early 1990s and has grown into the most popular and widely used distributed system. Non-specialists often confuse the internet and the web since the web is their only experience of network-based systems. The approach originated from the CERN research institute in Switzerland as a network-based hypertext system for nuclear physicists. The requirement was to share documents of various types across networked computers and the innovation was to combine hypertext and networking, using a simple protocol HTTP (Hypertext Transfer Protocol) above TCP. The development of the Mosaic browser for the web in 1993 led to the web's popular acceptance and extraordinary rate of growth. Mosaic was developed by Marc Andreesen, a student at the University of Illinois at Urbana-Champaign, while working for the NCSA (National Center for Supercomputing Applications). Andreesen left NCSA in 1994 and formed a company with Jim Clark which later became known as Netscape Communications Corporation.

In this chapter we first outline the system components involved in a simple interaction between a web client and a web server. As for all distributed systems, naming, location and the communications protocol must be defined. We then go on to describe how the web has evolved to provide more sophisticated facilities.

Web developments are initiated and controlled by the World Wide Web Consortium (W3C), a collaboration between CERN and MIT. Its home page is http://www.w3.org/. A recent trend in system design has been to use the web paradigm for the user interface to distributed systems in general. A remarkably general acceptance of this approach is emerging and we mention some of the W3C standards on which this approach is based.

To find more information about any of the topics in this chapter try using a web search engine, such as Google, to find an introductory tutorial or a standard document. There is a wealth of material about the web on the web.

23.1 A simple web-client, web-server interaction

The simplest way for a web service to operate is to deliver web pages on demand from clients. Figure 23.1 gives the overall architecture. This section gives an overview of the required naming, location and communication to make this happen together with an introduction to web server organization, document markup and display.

Web pages are **documents** which may take a variety of forms. They may be simple ASCII text, pdf or postscript but more usually are marked up according to a document standard. Document markup standards were of interest many years before the web was developed. The SGML (Standard Generalized Markup Language) ISO standard (8879) of the mid-1980s is widely used in electronic publishing. Web browsers have to display documents; that is, their format

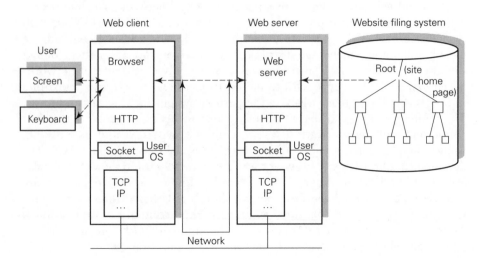

Figure 23.1
Architecture of a client–server interaction.

and style of display must be specified for the browser to implement. **HTML** (**HyperText Markup Language**) avoided the complexity of SGML and started off as a simple markup language focusing on format and display as well as document structure. More advanced features have been added over the years.

As well as defining a document's structure and how it should be displayed, HTML supports active links to other documents, so-called **hyperlinks**. Clicking on such a link initiates another interaction to get another document; in the case of the web, another web page from a web server. Later, W3C defined **XML** (**Extensible Markup Language**) which is a subset of SGML and is concerned not with display but with general document structure. Web documents are discussed further in Section 23.4; in particular we need to consider how users can interact with web pages.

A web server delivers web pages to clients on demand. A web page is a document that is stored as a file. The file system maintained by the web server contains the whole **website**. The web server and associated file system are available publicly, even though they may be located behind a firewall. As we saw in Chapter 7, this is achieved by using a well-known address and port, port 80 at the server's IP address, on which the server listens. Packets destined for this address are allowed through the firewall.

Like any shared file service, a web server holds pages that are owned by individuals and pages that belong to groups or projects. Let us first assume that each web page has a single owner or manager who is the only principal with write-access to the page. The page is published by making it available as a file in the web server's filing system. All the world may then read the page by requesting it to be fetched from the web server and displayed in the client's browser. It is possible to restrict access to web pages and this will be covered in Section 23.6. In order to access a page a client must know, or be able to find out, its name and location. A protocol must be followed for requesting and transmitting a page. The communication protocol for this purpose **HTTP** (**HyperText Transfer Protocol**) is described in Section 23.3.

The most common form of a web page name is a **URL** (**Uniform Resource Locator**). A URL is a concatenation of the web server's DNS address, the pathname of the file containing the required web page in the web server's filing system, and the access protocol to be used to request and transfer it. Notice that both naming and location are embodied in a URL, that is, it is a location-dependent name. For example, the University of Cambridge Computer Laboratory maintains a web server and the top-level or **home page** is accessed via the URL http://www.cl.cam.ac.uk. The DNS address is cl.cam.ac.uk. Following the Research path through the filing system we find http://www.cl.cam.ac.uk/Research/SRG. We discuss naming for the web more fully in Section 23.2.

Directory services are the standard approach for finding out about the existence of objects in distributed systems. Directory services exist for the web at dedicated websites, for example, a national directory of universities, but the most common approach is to use a **search engine** such as Google or Alta Vista. Here again we are seeing the expertise of a different community (information retrieval) incorporated into a world-wide distributed system. Web users commonly **bookmark** the URLs of sites of interest, thus creating their personal name cache. When a web page arrives at a browser it must detect the document type and display the page.

The browser may need to use a program such as acroread or ghostview to display pdf or postscript respectively. The browser usually causes a new window to pop up with such displays. Simple ASCII text is displayed directly in the browser's window. HTML documents are displayed in the browser's window by following the HTML instructions. Some document components may not be embedded in the marked up document but may be in a separate file, for example, images, audio and video. These have to be fetched in separate interactions with the web server. Active hypertext links have to be specially indicated.

We now give more detail of items introduced in the above overview. We then go on to show how more sophisticated web interactions, involving the execution of programs at the server and at the client, are supported and discuss the issues raised, such as protection of the client's host systems from such programs.

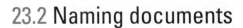 ## 23.2 Naming documents

The web is a very large-scale distributed system comprising many millions of documents stored at a large number of servers. The entities in a distributed system must be named uniquely and, as we saw in Chapter 6, there are well-known methods of designing a namespace and achieving unique names. The web uses a naming scheme which covers all kinds of documents, including books as well as web pages, called **Uniform Resource Identifiers (URIs)**. One form of URI is a hierarchical, location-dependent name called a **Uniform Resource Locator (URL)**. The other form of URI is a **Uniform Resource Name (URN)**. A URL is built around the DNS name of the server which holds the document. An example is:

> http://www.cl.cam.ac.uk/Research/SRG/opera/publications

As we have seen, cl.cam.ac.uk is the DNS name of the University of Cambridge Computer Laboratory and effectively indicates the root of the website. Research/SRG/opera/publications is one path through the website. The URL starts by selecting the protocol to be used, in this case HTTP. URLs have the general structure: **Scheme :// host name:port / pathname at host**. The scheme indicates how to access a document, for example via the HTTP protocol, via ftp or as a local file which may or may not not be stored at a public website. The host name may take the form of a DNS address or an IP address. If the port is omitted a default is used; port 80 is the usual convention. Other uses of URLs are possible such as for setting up telnet (a remote login protocol) or modem connections.

The other form of URI, a **URN**, is again globally unique but this time is a location-independent and persistent name for a document. A URN may be used for documents such as books and standards which are defined independently of website document hierarchies. The structure of a URN is:

> URN: name-space-identifier: document identifier within namespace

For example, for a book we might have: URN: ISBN: 0-201-17767-6.

As we saw in Chapter 6, directory services are needed to resolve names and bind them to locations. This is easy for a URL in that the already existing DNS directory structure, see Section 6.7.3, is used to locate the web server and a pathname within the server to locate the document. There is as yet no supporting directory structure for locating documents named only by a URN. Notice that a URN has a flat, rather than a hierarchical, namespace.

We also saw in Chapter 6 that using a hierarchical name makes it difficult to move an object. This is certainly true for web documents. When the owner renames a document, perhaps by reorganizing a directory structure, thus changing its pathname, the old pathname may lead to nothing, causing an 'error 404' message to be displayed, or the owner may replace it with a page indicating its new location and perhaps including a hyperlink to it. Web services have no responsibility for such dangling references: the problem is left for solution by the user. There may be many bookmarked copies of a URL and many hyperlinks embedding it in web pages and a judgement has to be made on how long to maintain a forward pointer at its old location to its new one.

23.3 Communication using HTTP

Communication between web browsers and web servers is via HTTP (Hypertext Transfer Protocol). The first version of HTTP, defined in 1990 at CERN, was a simple client–server protocol: a synchronous invocation, to the server, in which a client sends a request message to the server and awaits a response message. This version was for the transfer of raw data, while the next version HTTP 1.0 allowed MIME (Multipurpose Internet Mail Extensions) types to be specified and transferred; see Section 23.4. The most recent version at the time of writing is HTTP 1.1, decribed in the WC3's request for comment document, RFC2616.

HTTP is an application-level protocol built above TCP which is connection-oriented and reliable; see Section 3.9 and Figures 3.22 and 3.23. Figure 23.1 shows the overall architecture of a web client–server interaction. The early versions of HTTP were extremely inefficient, setting up a new TCP connection for every client request, server response interaction. A document typically contains embedded documents held as separate files at the server. For example, a web page containing text and several images would require an HTTP connection to fetch the HTML page and a further connection when the browser, on processing the page for display, found each image specification. This approach made transfers very slow. More recent versions allow a TCP connection to persist between a web client and server: the way TCP is supposed to be used. Also, instead of waiting for the response to a message before issuing another request message, a client may now issue a number of successive request messages. It is therefore now much faster to display a document implemented as several files. HTTP is, however, stateless at the application level and does not expect a server to maintain information on clients with open TCP connections.

The most commonly used HTTP request messages are:

HEAD   Request to return the header of a document
GET   Request to return a document to the client
PUT   Request to store a document under some filename
POST   Request to add a document to a collection such as a newsgroup
DELETE   Request to delete a document

All communication takes the form of request messages from client to server and response messages from server to client. The detailed format of these messages can be found in tutorials, standards and web development texts.

 # 23.4 Document representation

An HTML document is a tree of elements, including a head and body which includes headings, paragraphs, lists, etc. Embedded in the document specification is formatting detail such as text justification, the use of bold and italic text, background colour, etc. The coarse structure is:

<HEAD> ... the header of the document including its title
<TITLE> Example of HTML </TITLE>
</HEAD>
<BODY> ... the document including formatting instructions ... </BODY>

The body of the document may include, for example:

Paragraphs: <P> ... paragraph text ... </P>
Headings: <H1> first-level heading </H1>
              <H2> second-level heading </H2>
Images: <IMG src = "picture.jpeg" width = "200" height = "150">
Hyperlinks: <A HREF = "http://www.w3.org/" > W3C </A>
              where the text between <A ... > and </A>, in this case W3C, is
              usually displayed highlighted, in blue. If the hyperlink were to
              be displayed explicitly we would have:
              <A HREF = "http://www.w3.org/" > http://www.w3.org </A>

Lists may be bulleted, numbered or itemized, with nested lists as required.

HTML documents may also include **scripts** which are executed by the client browser during the process of preparing the page for display. This takes us further than the scenario represented in Figure 23.1 since it requires the client browser to interpret and execute the embedded script. We are seeing not only a document with instructions on how to display it but also the transmission of a program as part of the web page. When JavaScript is the scripting language we have:

<SCRIPT type = "text/javascript"> ... the script ... </SCRIPT>

Web pages may also include **forms** of various kinds, allowing users to interact with the web service. In a form, a user may be asked to type a response corresponding to a question; a single line might be:

Surname: <input name = surname >

A user might be presented with a list of alternatives and asked to select only one by clicking on that item. Alternatively, each element in a list may have an associated boolean response so that the user may select all items that apply by checking the associated boxes. A form may be presented to the user before a requested page is transferred, requesting authentication in the form of user name and password, thus controlling access to a web page. When a form is complete the user clicks on **submit**, the form is parsed and checked locally and, if correct, is transmitted to the web server in the form of an HTTP request to get a new page. The server must process the form data and carry out the required action such as sending a new page to the user and perhaps sending an email message confirming a completed transaction. The new page may be processed by the server to include the data in the form submitted by the user. We expand on the system architecture implied by these interactions in Figure 23.2.

Forms are used widely in e-commerce, for example for selecting and purchasing airline tickets, insurance policies, goods and services in general. The information in forms may be confidential and sometimes includes financial data such as credit card details. In Section 7.6.5 we introduced the **Secure Socket Layer** (**SSL**) protocol which is widely used for protecting such transfers.

As we have seen, HTML mixes the marked up document with how it should be displayed. W3C went on to define **XML** (**Extensible Markup Language**) which is concerned only with expressing the document structure and not with how it is to be displayed. XML is compatible with, but less complex than, SGML. XML allows the document author to define arbitrarily named structures.

Document types

Web services may store and present to users many types of document, for example pdf, postscript, images, audio or video. Such document types were already defined for email attachments when the web was designed and **MIME types** (**Multipurpose Internet Mail Extensions**) are also used for web documents. MIME defines types and subtypes. Some examples are:

Type	Subtype
Text	Plain
	HTML
	XML
Application	Octet-stream
	Postscript
	PDF
Image	GIF
	JPEG

23.5 Executing programs at server and client

We saw above that a web page may contain a script which is executed by the client's browser:

<SCRIPT type = "text/javascript"> ... the script ... </SCRIPT>

It is also possible for an HTML page to contain a script to be executed at the server side:

<SERVER type = "text/javascript"> ... the script ... </SERVER>

The result of executing the script, but not the script itself, is sent to the client along with the rest of the document. This facility might be used to personalize a page by inserting a 'welcome back' string before returning a page to a registered client. Figure 23.2 shows server-side and client-side script execution.

We also saw in Section 23.4 that forms may be sent for users to fill in either embedded in web pages or separately, perhaps for authentication before a requested page is returned. We now explore the software architecture that supports these activities and show extensions that allow programs (applets and servlets) as well as scripts to be executed.

Figure 23.3 shows one of the first enhancements of the basic client–server interaction shown in Figure 23.1. The non-intuitively-named **Common Gateway Interface (CGI)** is a protocol which defines how a web server should take user data as input, usually supplied by means of an HTML form, process it and generate HTML as output. A CGI script may be written in any language such as C or Perl. The client-side processing of the form causes the CGI program name and its input parameters to be sent to the server in the form of an HTTP GET request for a new page. The contents of the form are passed as a string of attribute value pairs. An attribute is what was output as part of the form, the

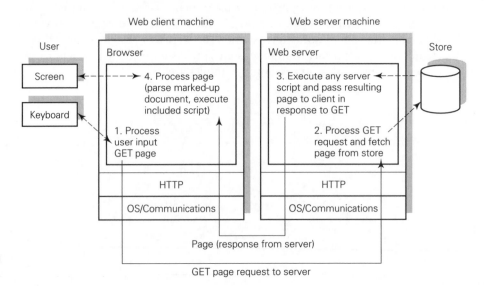

Figure 23.2
Client-server
interaction including
script processing.

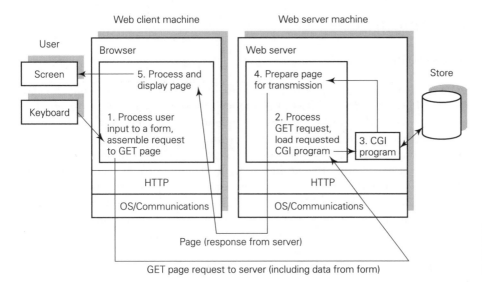

Web client machine   Web server machine

User

Screen   Browser   Web server
                5. Process and   4. Prepare page
                display page   for transmission

Keyboard   1. Process user   2. Process
                input to a form,   GET request,   3. CGI
                assemble request   load requested   program
                to GET page   CGI program

                HTTP   HTTP

                OS/Communications   OS/Communications

Store

Page (response from server)

GET page request to server (including data from form)

Figure 23.3
Client–server
interaction with forms
and CGI programs.

corresponding value is what the user typed in response or selected from a menu, for example:

http://host-dnsname/path-to-cgi-program/script.cgi/
   name1=value1&name2=value2

This basic scheme is routinely used to download files and images as well as to invoke CGI scripts. An example of the use of a CGI program is to send the form data to an email address as well as to generate the next HTML page to send to the user.

The web server causes the CGI program to be executed with these parameter values and in return expects a web page for sending on to the client. The CGI program may simply fetch the required page from storage, adding the data as appropriate, or may carry out more sophisticated page generation. Either way, the web server has delegated the task to the CGI program and a web page is returned to it; any page generation by the CGI program is not visible to the server. CGI programs may be passed to the web server and stored in the server's file system along with HTML documents. There are obvious security concerns as the server is being asked to execute an imported program; see Section 23.6.

As well as client-side and server-side scripts it is possible to include pre-compiled programs in HTML pages. Programs to be executed at the client side are **applets** and those to be executed at the server side are **servlets**. Current practice is that applets and servlets are written in Java and embedded in the form of Java bytecode. Many applets are available with Java, for example one applet might be designed to play a game with the user, such as noughts and crosses, another might show an animation as part of a web page. Applets are executed by the client browser; servlets are executed by the web server; the flow of control is therefore similar to that when scripts are interpreted as shown in Figure 23.2. Notice that a CGI program is executed by a separate process in a separate address space from the web server.

23.6 Security

Access control

We have seen above that a user might have to fill in a form before being allowed to see a document. The owner of the document associates a password and a list of user names with it and typically tells collaborators by telephone or by email what their names and passwords are. They must then fill in the form with this information before seeing the document. The approach is suitable as part of the management of collaborative authoring by distributed groups. Synchronization of access is currently left to the collaborators. This control is typically carried out through a combination of Readme files, email and telephone. The W3C is currently turning its attention to support for collaborative authoring.

An example where the web provides an ideal publishing forum yet where access control is important is in a conference management website, where authors submit papers for inclusion in the conference. A programme committee is responsible for reviewing the submissions and selecting the best papers for the conference. The papers and reviews are confidential documents. A selection of the papers will eventually appear in the published conference proceedings. Before the web existed, submitted papers were typically distributed as hard copy or by email. The submissions are now made available as part of a conference website but access to them must be strictly controlled.

Secure communication of confidential data

When buying goods and services via the web an option may be to pay on-line by supplying one's credit card details. This is information that must not be transmitted 'in clear'; the client must be assured that the data is securely encrypted before transmission. Many other forms of data may be deemed confidential, indeed those designing questionnaires using the HTML forms facility should be aware of the need to transmit user data securely. Users are informed that a secure communication is about to take place by a notification form in which they can click to proceed or cancel. The method in common use for implementing secure communication is the Secure Socket Layer (SSL) protocol described in Section 7.6.5.

Mobile code

We have seen examples of code originating at a web server being executed by a client browser. The code might take the form of scripts or applets, both specified in the document. There is reason for concern that an erroneous or malicious script or applet might be a trojan horse and, as well as carrying out its intended function, might damage the client's environment. For this reason, browsers run in virtual machines with controlled access to the environment in which they run.

The commonly used language for writing applets is Java and applets arrive at the client browser in the form of Java bytecode which is interpreted rather than executed directly. The interpreter functions as a controller, as part of a **Java Virtual Machine** in which the applet runs. Protection of the client's environment is through controlling the objects that can be created and monitoring every I/O request. The former results from the use of a trusted class loader and forbidding an imported program from using or generating its own class loader. I/O requests to local files are almost invariably disallowed and the only network connection that may be established is to the originating server. An applet is allowed access to the graphics library and to mouse and keyboard input which are necessary for user–browser interaction.

23.7 Concurrency control

Although there are many millions of web documents they are effectively read-only over a coarse time grain. Also, web documents tend to be read by human users at browsers rather than by other software. For these reasons, web software provides very little support for concurrency control. Any problems are left for the users to solve, as discussed in Section 23.2 for name changes leaving dangling references, and in Section 23.6 for synchronization for collaborative authoring.

The single writer, multiple readers paradigm applies to web documents, but strong consistency is not enforced. An owner may make changes to a page and replace an old version with a new one at any time. Many readers may be displaying the old version of the page while the change is being made. Once the page is replaced, any subsequent requests to the web server holding it will yield the new page. But, as we shall see below, there may be many cached copies of the old version and the new version will take time to propagate, depending on how the caches are managed.

More generally, a subtree of pages could be updated with related changes. Again, there is no support for transactional update and inconsistencies could be seen by readers. Because human users are involved, they can perceive and resolve such problems by forcing a reload of a page from its original source.

Servers must cope with a high volume of requests and each server instance must deploy multi-threading. At a website with high demand there may be many server machines. Again, concurrency control is made relatively simple by the read-only nature of web pages. Because the update rate is very low, the website data can be freely shared between threads and server machines without the need for complex locking or consistency maintenance.

23.8 Scalability issues

Web servers can come under extremely heavy load, for example when a news event breaks millions of people may turn to the web for immediate information and images. In general, because of the scale of the web, any website that provides a useful service may have very large numbers of client requests arriving effectively simultaneously. Designers therefore need to consider how **server architectures** can scale to handle large numbers of simultaneously ongoing client requests. One approach is to use **server clusters,** deploying a number of machines to provide the service. Another is to use **mirror sites** where a whole website is replicated. Users are not aware of server clusters but they are aware of the different server address components in mirrored URLs.

Because web documents are read-only over reasonably long timeframes, **caching** is potentially effective and is widely used; that is, copies of a document are stored local to clients who have accessed it recently. A cache may be for an individual, stored in the web browser's cache, or for a domain such as a university department. Such a domain runs a **web proxy** through which all requests for web pages pass. The web proxy passes a request for an uncached document to the external server and, when it is returned, stores the page in its own cache. The next time any client within the domain requests this page, the request is satisfied from the cache. Caches are of finite size and are managed according to a replacement algorithm such as 'least recently used'. There may be caches serving larger domains, such as universities or geographical regions, forming a hierarchical caching scheme.

Web pages may change. Users may request a reload from source, using the browser reload function, but users may often be in no position to know when this is appropriate. Cache management might include measures for consistency maintenance. A simple scheme is always to ask the originating server whether the page has changed since the time-stamp of the version held in the cache. Recall that one HTTP message option was GET HEADER which is used for this purpose. Although the amount of data transferred is greatly reduced by this procedure the number of interactions with the server is not. Alternative schemes are to use expiry times or to request servers to tell proxies when pages are changed. In practice cache hit rates have not been found to be very high, even for large caches, and cooperative caching is sometimes used. Here proxies are aware of each other and attempt to find a local copy of a page before going to the page-holding server.

23.9 Web-based middleware: XML and SOAP

XML generalized the simple, display-focused document markup of HTML to give a markup language with power and flexibility: a subset of SGML. XML documents are made up of storage cells called entities which contain either parsed or unparsed data. Parsed data is made up of characters, some of which form the markup and the rest character data. Markup encodes the document's logical structure. Users can define arbitrarily named headings and subheadings, nesting to any depth, for example:

```
<bank-account>  some-ID
              <name> <surname>owner's-surname</surname>
                        <forename>owner's-forename </forename> </name>
                        etc. – other account details
</bank-account>
```

In contrast, in HTML the only facility is to indicate the importance of the heading, selecting from a small number of levels, and the size and boldness of the type to be used for each heading. The user is in fact creating a document type when defining an XML document. A document begins in a root or 'document' entity and a well-formed document, with correct nesting, conforms to a grammar.

Each XML document has an associated **document type declaration** which indicates the defined markup names (the elements) and the types of their values, thus defining the document's grammar or **document type definition** (DTD). The DTD may be contained in the document itself, may be in a separate document or may have both components.

We appear to have discarded the ability to indicate how a document should be displayed compared with HTML. In fact, display requirements are specified in yet another associated document written in **XSL** (**Extensible Style Language**).

For example, a DTD might contain (where #PCDATA indicates a string of characters):

```
<!ELEMENT student (surname, forename, course, age-at-enrolment)>
<!ELEMENT surname (#PCDATA) >
<!ELEMENT forename (#PCDATA) >
<!ELEMENT course (#PCDATA) >
<!ELEMENT age-at-enrolment (#PCDATA) >
etc ...
```

An XML document with this DTD might contain many student records including:

```
<student>
        <surname>Smith</surname>
        <forename>John</forename>
        <course> Data Structures </course>
        <age-at-enrolment)>19 </age-at-enrolment)>
</student>
```

The web is an existing large-scale distributed system with an inbuilt scheme for naming and location based on DNS. Users are familiar with browsers which are therefore becoming almost essential interfaces to any distributed system. Browsers can transmit and receive messages in XML and this is leading to the widespread use of XML for a variety of purposes in addition to the definition and transmission of documents.

XML is suitable for marking up documents and giving them a type. Its use in general middleware, for specifying message contents and transmitting data in messages, has its pros and cons. XML is programming language independent yet can be generated from programming languages, therefore supporting the interworking of heterogeneous components. However, XML tends to express the transmitted data in external form as strings of characters. This is not ideal for transmission and is inappropriate if generalized to include storage of data in databases.

A W3C standard has been defined for the invocation of services using XML messages: the **Simple Object Access Protocol** (**SOAP**); see http://www.w3.org/TR/SOAP. SOAP is described by W3C as a lightweight mechanism for exchanging structured and typed information between peers in a decentralized distributed environment using XML. SOAP allows any service to be wrapped so to appear as a web server to its clients.

 ## 23.10 Summary

The internet-based World Wide Web is an example of a large-scale, widely distributed system. We studied its overall architecture and the mechanisms used for naming, location, communication, security and scalability. We saw that the commonly used names are location dependent, built above DNS. The web mechanisms do not address the avoidance of dangling references when the owner moves a page thus changing its name. The communications protocol HTTP is built above TCP. Its original design deficiencies, requiring a new TCP connection for every transfer involved in a composite document, were corrected in later versions thus improving on the original bad performance. The original document markup language HTML combined the specification of a document's structure with instructions for displaying it. XML is a generalization of HTML and a subset of SGML, the document standard ISO 8879 (ISO/IEC, 1986).

Web documents, unlike SGML-specified documents, need dynamic change and interaction with users. We saw how forms can be used for this purpose, how scripts can be executed at server or browser and how applets, servlets and CGI programs are located architecturally.

The fact that the web is concerned with delivering documents which are read-only over long periods simplifies concurrency control and makes it possible to exploit replication and caching successfully. The fact that a single owner or manager may write to a document, and this occurs infrequently, simplifies concurrency control. The web mechanisms do not address related changes to a number of different pages being made under transaction semantics. Consistency problems are left for the application level, the human users, to handle. The web is larger in scale than any other distributed system and scalability mechanisms are essential. Server clusters, hierarchical caching and mirror sites are widely deployed.

Recent developments are the use of web browsers as universal interfaces to distributed systems. This has led to the use of XML being extended from document markup to message definition and transfer and even data storage. This approach may or may not come to dominate future system usage. The W3C are active in defining standards. The recently defined SOAP allows any service to be wrapped so to appear as a web server to its clients.

Exercises

23.1 What is a document markup language? What is the fundamental difference between HTML and XML?

23.2 How is the information on how to display an XML document conveyed to a browser?

23.3 How is a website managed by a server inside a firewall made available for public access?

23.4 Discuss naming with respect to the Web:
  (a) How are unique names created for documents?
  (b) What happens when a web page is moved from one directory to another?
  (c) Give examples of where caching might usefully be used.

23.5 Criticize the original design of the HTTP protocol. How has it been improved over the years?

23.6 How is user interaction added to the basic functionality of displaying a document? How is such an interaction made secure, for example, for transmitting credit card details?

23.7 How are animations made part of documents and how are they executed when the document is displayed?

23.8 Web pages typically have a multiple reader, single writer pattern of access. To what extent is concurrency control enforced in the web environment?

23.9 How is potentially heavy load on web servers managed throughout the web architecture?

23.10 Outline the purpose of the SOAP protocol.

24

Middleware

Middleware was defined briefly in Section 2.8 as a layer of software that presents a uniform environment to the components of a distributed system. The middleware hides, or abstracts, any hetereogeneity in the underlying operating systems and communications services, as shown in Figure 2.19. As we saw in Chapter 6, all distributed systems need a naming scheme for their components, and services which map names to locations so that components can interwork, by making use of communications services. Chapter 15 started from same-machine inter-process communication and discussed how IPC might be integrated with communications services. There, we discussed message passing, remote procedure call and the socket interface to communications services. In this chapter we first give the historical development of the various styles of middleware, relating the paradigms that evolved to what we have studied already. We then describe the software that is available commercially or for free download.

24.1 Middleware paradigms

The widespread introduction of high bandwidth local area networks into the workplace during the 1980s led to distributed systems and the need to support the interworking of distributed software components. One approach was to build on communications services where untyped byte-streams or packets of bytes were transmitted. The ISO 7-layer model was defined by the communications community and included not only traditional communication in levels 1 through 4 but also its extension to support distributed applications in levels 5 (session), 6 (presentation) and 7 (application), see Section 3.8. Middleware can be seen as occupying layers 5 through 7 and **message-oriented middleware** (**MOM**) is a natural extension of the packet paradigm of communications. Note that message passing is an *asynchronous* style of communication. The sender does not block waiting for the recipient to participate in the exchange and, if there is a reply, it will also arrive asynchronously in due course. If the message service offers persistence and reliability then the receiver need not be up and running when the message is sent. Once a message is sent the system accepts responsibility for it and will buffer it if necessary until the receiver is ready. Again, this behaviour is following a communications paradigm, that of 'store and forward'. Later in this chapter we examine some examples of MOM.

Another approach to supporting distributed software development and deployment came from the computer science community and focused on programming. This led to remote procedure call (RPC) systems then remote object invocation, both of which offer typed communication between components of a distributed program; see Chapter 15. **Object-oriented middleware** is based on this style of communication together with related services to support the naming and location of objects system-wide so they can be invoked correctly. These services have various names such as Interface Trader, Yellow Pages, White Pages, Object Directory, Interface Repository, etc. Note that object invocation is a *synchronous* style of communication. The invoker blocks awaiting the return and the invoked object must be loaded and running to take the invocation.

The focus of the database community continued for some time to be of a centralized database with distributed clients making queries and receiving responses. Here, the role for middleware is limited to query and data shipping rather than closely-coupled, strongly-typed interaction between distributed components of a program. There is little need for strong typing in the communication, and message-oriented middleware was used. An example is IBM's CICS (Customer Information Control System), a transaction processing system supported by MQSeries reliable message passing; see Section 24.7.1.

In Chapter 23 we examined how document storage and delivery is distributed throughout the World Wide Web. In this case too, the communications protocol HTTP is based on message passing, simply being concerned with document transfer. The application (web browser or web server) interprets the marked-up document that is transferred but the communications service has no need to be aware of the document structure. As we discussed in Section 23.9, the web is larger in scale, and more widely used, than any other distributed system and web browsers are becoming the universal interfaces to distributed systems in general. A recent development that is becoming widely accepted is to use XML document markup as a type system for communication. Message passing is combined with XML data typing in the SOAP (simple object access protocol) standard of W3C, the World Wide Web Consortium. One use of SOAP is to wrap a service to make it appear as a web server to its clients. The web was covered in

Chapter 23. In this chapter we discuss the broad range of middleware, including object-oriented and message-oriented middleware.

24.1.1 Evolution of object-oriented middleware

Early work on **remote procedure call**, see Chapter 15, with associated services for naming and location, led to standard platforms such as ISO's ODP (ISO, 1992) and OSF's DCE (OSF, 1992). These early platforms were based on the **client–server model** but over the years a higher-level **object model** evolved along with object-oriented programming languages such as C++, Modula 3 and Java. Both approaches may use object concepts, in that the server in an RPC system may be an object manager. Both use client- and server-side stubs for marshalling and unmarshalling call and return parameters. In distributed object systems the client-side stub is usually called the **proxy** of the remote object. One conceptual difference has not been implemented in practice: in the more general object model an object with its methods is an independent entity that might migrate to the caller on invocation. In practice we have seen only implementations where servers are object managers, as in RPC systems. Exceptions are in research projects such as Comandos (Balter *et al.*, 1993) and Globe (van Steen *et al.*, 1999). An important difference is in naming. In RPC systems an interface specification in an interface definition language (IDL) is the basis for naming, location and invocation. As we saw in Figure 15.28 and Section 15.11.3, a server exports its interface to a name server, a client imports the interface from the name server in the form of an interface reference and invokes one of its procedures. Interface references are temporary handles for invoking operational services. In using procedures and arguments we are dealing with programming language entities which translate naturally into a language-neutral IDL.

Distributed object systems define system-wide unique object references. An object may, in some systems, be defined as persistent in which case it continues to exist if its managing server ceases execution. As in RPC systems, an object that is to be invoked remotely must be made known within the system and allocated a reference. In current systems, such as Java middleware and CORBA, the global name for an object is location dependent, containing the address of the managing server, the communication endpoint, the protocol to use for communication with it and the server's local identifier for the object. Potential users of the object must be able to obtain object references; this can be done via a name service as in RPC systems. Finally, when a client binds to an object, the language-independent, global name for an object which is returned to the client's system must be translated into an object reference within a local programming environment so that the client can invoke the object consistently with other objects. The use of global references for objects simplifies many of the issues we discussed for parameter passing in RPC systems. Object references may be passed as first-class values; that is, they are fully general, typed parameters which are meaningful system-wide.

The above discussion has assumed that interface specifications are known at compile time. It is quite possible that in some applications this is not always the

Client of object OID

Object OID's server

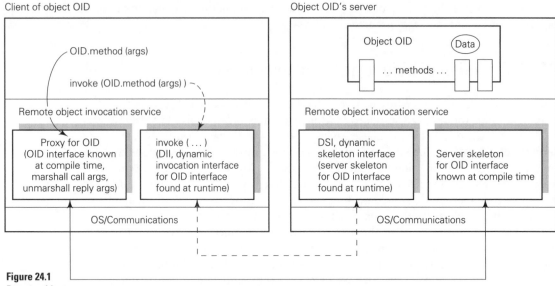

Figure 24.1
Remote object
invocation.

case. A client may look up an object specification at runtime and may then wish to invoke it. Most object-oriented middleware supports a dynamic invocation interface as well as providing a client proxy object at compile time. Figure 24.1 illustrates both modes of remote object invocation from a single client.

In the following sections we examine some examples of object-oriented middleware systems. We have used Java as a programming language throughout this book and Java-based middleware is our first case study. Note that Java middleware is **homogeneous** and **proprietary**. It is homogeneous in that a single programming language running a single environment, the Java Virtual Machine, is assumed throughout the system. Although this software is freely available, proprietary software can always be changed at the whim of the developing company. Our second case study is **OMG-CORBA**, the **Object Management Group's Common Object Request Broker Architecture**. OMG is concerned with the specification of **open standards** to create middleware for **heterogeneous** distributed systems; that is, components may be written in different languages and may run on different operating systems. One of these languages is Java, allowing it to be used as a programming language for CORBA systems. As our third case study we briefly outline Microsoft's Component Object Model COM which includes distributed objects, sometimes referred to as **DCOM** and also **.NET** for web-style programming. Microsoft were latecomers to the use of networks and distributed systems yet instead of participating in the open standards that had emerged, they developed **proprietary** middleware for their Windows operating systems which, unlike that of Sun Microsystems, is not freely available. Components can be written in different programming languages and this is achieved by forcing each language to use a uniform binary-level interface, in the form of a table of pointers, for COM objects.

Object-oriented middleware is based on the synchronous communication paradigm since the invoker of a remote object blocks, waiting for the call to return. This single paradigm has been found to be inadequate for meeting the needs of applications. The traditional way to program around blocking calls is to use multi-threading at the caller but there are still interaction needs that are not met by request–response synchronous invocation. Suppose, for example, that a server needs to send the same information to a large number of clients and does not need a response from each. The synchronous paradigm forces the server to send to each client in turn and wait for a null reply from each one before the next client can be contacted; a single slow or failed client delays all subsequent ones. Creating a thread to make a blocking call to each client is a complex solution and imposes a great deal of thread management overhead for large numbers of clients. We shall see that all the object-oriented middleware systems have grown to include asynchronous services.

24.2 Java middleware

From its outset Java was integrated with distributed programming by means of the web. Web programming was covered in detail in Chapter 23 and here we review the history and aspects that are relevant to this style of middleware.

24.2.1 Java for web programming

In 1990 Sun Microsystems set up a team of six, led by Patrick Naughton, to think afresh about support for distributed software development over heterogeneous systems. The team recognized the importance of a 'fun', easy to use interface and a language that allowed new media and devices to be programmed, and defined a minimal object-oriented language called Oak. Sun turned the team into a company called First Person which was in place, in 1993, ready to work with the World Wide Web and its browsers. Early in 1994 First Person decided to focus on a software system for online media with Oak as a 'language-based operating system'. A browser was built and the first applet, the Duke icon waving over the internet, was run. Oak was renamed Java by Sun and made available free on the internet. The browser was named HotJava. The company JavaSoft became responsible for all Java and internet development. Java is a language but its surrounding support system has evolved into a computing platform, a base on which software developers can build distributed applications. Novel aspects compared with traditional platforms are as follows:

- **Java programs are mobile,** that is, they can be migrated across a network. Data and the code to process it are transmitted together. A typical scenario is that Java programs (**applets**) are held on centralized servers and are downloaded on request. Note, however, that Java applications are mobile only once: their compiled images are loaded into Java interpreters and cannot move after they start executing. This is in contrast with some mobile programming languages, for example Scheme with state-saving continuations, where a program can be halted at any point and migrated to another node.

- **Heterogeneity is masked through interpretation**. Programs are transferred as intermediate code (bytecode). Object code can be produced on-the-fly for heterogeneous systems provided they have a Java interpreter. It is therefore unnecessary for an application to be ported to many different architectures. Java compilers also exist, of course; just-in-time compilers such as Kaffe (Wilkinson, 1997) translate a program's bytecode into native code after validating it. This allows long-running Java programs to be executed faster than under an interpreter, while at the same time ensuring that they do not access unauthorized areas of memory.
- **A browser interface** is often used; for example, the Netscape browser contains an embedded Java platform (is Java-compatible). The term applet was coined for a mini application that runs inside a web browser. A **Java application** is self-standing whereas an applet is not; see Section 23.5.
- **Security**. Although importing code into a system appears dangerous (we fear mobile viruses) the fact that it is interpreted by the client's interpreter and runs on a well-defined platform can be used to define its scope and confine its access. For example, an applet that is loaded over the network can't normally read or write files in the context of its executor; it can't make network connections except to the host that it came from. It can, however, invoke the public methods of other applets on the same page. Although Java interpreters attempt to execute their programs in this secure environment, some security breaches have been found (McGraw and Felten, 1996). A source of problems is that some programs that are rejected by a Java compiler may be accepted by a Java interpreter.

As we saw in Chapter 23, a popular use of Java is to develop applets for web pages. A Java applet is transferred, runs at the client site and may communicate externally only with its server. For a distributed application we need components to be loaded at several locations and then to interwork. When this is supported, serious, large-scale applications can be written in Java. We now look at the progress that has been made towards this end.

24.2.2 Java remote method invocation (RMI)

We have used Java for illustrative examples throughout this book. In Chapter 15 examples were given of, first, stream and socket programming, then Java RMI. The challenge of producing middleware for Java is much as we saw in Chapter 15 for the development of early RPC systems in the 1980s, in that a single programming language and a single environment, the Java Virtual Machine, are to be used. The difference is that Java is fully object-oriented and distributed objects have been integrated into the language. The approach taken for RMI is very much as outlined in Section 24.1.1, shown in Figure 24.1, and illustrated by example in Section 15.5. A remote object resides at one server and has a unique global reference which indicates this server. Its interface is made available to remote clients and the usual client proxy and server skeleton mechanisms are deployed. We mentioned the difficulty in general of translating global object references to and from the different local references required by different programming languages within a local programming environment. In homogeneous systems such as Java-based middleware this is much easier; a remote object's proxy appears as a local object in the client's address space.

We therefore appear to have distribution transparency since local and remote objects appear the same to the programmer. As discussed in Section 15.8, full distribution transparency is difficult to achieve, and possibly undesirable since certain local entities such as file descriptors and socket descriptors make no sense outside the local environment and the partial failures inherent in distributed systems must be dealt with. In an RMI, any primitive type and serializable object can be passed as a parameter. Local objects are passed by value which involves copying the object, however large. Remotely invocable objects are passed by passing their stubs which contain the object's managing server address and communication endpoint, the protocol to be used and the server's local identifier for the object.

Any Java object is an instance of a class and a class includes one or more interface implementations. A remote object has two components, one at the managing server and one for any client proxy. The server-side component is an instance of a class from which is generated the conventional object implementation and the server-side stub interface. The client-side component is an instance of a class which generates the client interface or proxy. The client proxy uses the server's address in the object reference to set up a connection to the server, create a message from the call arguments then await, receive, unmarshal and return the reply.

Because a proxy contains all the information necessary for invoking the remote object, proxies are self-standing and can function as global object references. Proxies can be marshalled in Java since a proxy can be treated in the same way as any other local object for the purposes of marshalling. On receipt the remote object can be invoked through the transmitted proxy since it contains the object reference and the invocation code. Note that this is only possible because we are operating in a homogeneous environment; the transmitted code will work when it arrives at another JVM. More detail, including optimizations of this process can be found in Waldo (1998).

Concurrency control on local objects is achieved by **synchronized** methods; see Section 11.2.1. Concurrency control on remote objects requires a distributed mutual exclusion protocol, see Section 22.5, since the crash of one client potentially affects others sharing the object. In general the use of remote objects can involve delay due to system failures or overload and this is best made explicit to systems programmers.

Note that unfortunate terminology was chosen for marshalling which is called **serialization** in Java, the intuition being 'flattening' for transmission. As we have seen in Part III, the concept of serializability had long been in use in the database community for a fundamental requirement on the concurrent execution of transactions.

24.2.3 Jini, including JavaSpaces

Jini's home page is http://www.sun.com/jini; the most useful descriptions are to be found in http://www.sun.com/jini/specs. Jini is intended for use within a Java environment where all computers run a JVM and where Java RMI is used for remote communication. Jini adds a service framework to a distributed Java system allowing service specifications to be published and discovered, a general middleware requirement we have seen in Chapter 15 and Section 24.1. Because of the homogeneity of distributed Java systems it is possible for both code and data to be freely transmitted; unusually, transmitted code will execute anywhere because of the universal use of the JVM, with its bytecode interpreter or just-in-time compiler, above all operating systems on all machine architectures.

JavaSpaces is an important and integral part of Jini. JavaSpaces provides facilities for storing into and retrieving from collections of (possibly) persistent objects in shared data spaces, for transactions and for event services. Both Jini services, and any services required by applications using Jini, can therefore be built as JavaSpaces in order to store and retrieve objects, manipulate them correctly under transactions and notify their clients of any changes in which they have registered interest. Jini supports more general communication patterns than synchronous method invocation; we shall see similar extensions in other object-oriented middleware systems.

JavaSpaces uses a tuple-space paradigm, first proposed for the Linda programming language, see Section 13.8.2, but, unlike Linda, JavaSpaces is object-oriented. A JavaSpace is a shared data space that stores tuples of Java objects. A system may have a number of named JavaSpaces but each JavaSpace has a single centralized implementation. Tuples are read using associative matching via a **template** which specifies for each field of the tuple either the value required or a wildcard. The primitives for using a JavaSpace are, as for Linda but renamed:

write write the given tuple into this JavaSpaces service;
read return either an entry that matches the template or 'no match';
take is like read except that the entry is removed from the space.

If a given JavaSpace is managed by a single server these operations can easily be made atomic by the server; that is, when, for example, a take operation returns, the matched tuple has been removed and cannot be read or taken by another client. Note, however, that two or more tuples in the space can have exactly the same value. If a distributed implementation was envisaged, the designers would have to worry about how to make the operations atomic to avoid race conditions between concurrent requests to write, read and take.

A JavaSpace service can also operate as an event notification service. A client can ask to be notified whenever a tuple is written which matches a template:

notify register a template for notification whenever a matching tuple is written.

The mechanism used is that the client supplies, with the notify request, a reference to an object which may be in its own or some other process's address space. This object is responsible for listening for notifications from the server so is called a listener object. The server's notification is calling back to the client so the object reference is known as a callback reference. The JavaSpaces service notifies this object using RMI; we are seeing asynchronous notification implemented using synchronous invocation. The notification is not reliable but a sequence number is associated with each notification so that the client is able to detect any missing deliveries.

JavaSpaces also offers a simple **transaction** service, allowing multiple operations and/or multispace updates to complete atomically. The normal ACID properties are guaranteed, see Section 18.4, and a two-phase commit protocol is used, see Section 21.8, for distributed, atomic commitment. When a primitive operation is used in isolation it is deemed to comprise a single-operation transaction. Finally, a tuple is written into a JavaSpace with a limited lifetime or **lease** to avoid the indefinite build-up of garbage resulting from client crashes. A lease is also associated with a template registered for event notification.

Jini was not designed as a replacement for relational or object-oriented databases. It provides small-scale storage, which may be persistent, for implementing more general communication patterns than RMI. When the storage is persistent the communicating partners can operate asynchronously; that is, they do not need to engage in communication at precisely the same time. Because communication can be indirect, via a JavaSpace, the parties need not know the naming and location necessary for RMI. An example is as follows:

- An academic wants to buy 20 copies of an out-of-print book for a specialist class. She writes a request into a public JavaSpace designed for this purpose.
- Specialist booksellers have registered for notification of requests for books. They are notified of this particular request if it matches their template and, if they have the book for sale, enter an offer of some number of copies into the JavaSpace specified in the request.
- At the time specified in the request, the buyer takes the offers out of the space and selects the 20 best ones.

Note that the buyer is communicating with previously unknown sellers, that is, making service discoveries. The fields of the tuples entered by the buyer and the templates of the sellers allow filtering of unwanted topics. The corresponding service in most other middleware styles would be a yellow pages service (YPS) where services, objects and attributes are specified for browsing by clients. But after discovering services via a YPS the client would then have to engage in one-to-one communication with each service whereas one-to-many and many-to-one communication is supported by a JavaSpace.

The detailed mechanisms of JavaSpaces are somewhat cumbersome. The fields of tuples are typed Java objects which are stored in marshalled form as type and value and may therefore be large. If two fields happen to hold the same object, two marshalled copies are stored there. The fields of templates are likewise typed, marshalled objects. The fields of tuples therefore always contain object values rather than object references.

Jini supports the development and deployment of system and application services and a number of system services are offered. An example is **JNDI**, the **Java Naming and Directory Interface**, which provides the standard middleware function of service interface publication and location. In addition, because of the notify facility of the underlying JavaSpaces, a JNDI client can ask to be notified of changes to JNDI. These could include addition of new objects or changes to existing objects and is useful in a dynamic environment. The naming service of JNDI provides a lookup function which returns objects matching a simple search request for a service name. The directory service is more powerful than the naming service, allowing applications to discover objects with common attributes by specifying the attributes for the search and returning a set of matching objects.

Jini was not designed for widely distributed implementations. It uses a multicast protocol and the underlying tuple-space paradigm makes it likely that services will be built with centralized implementations. The more recently defined Java Messaging Service (JMS) is potentially more scalable. We first introduce the Java component model then JMS.

24.2.4 The Java component model, JavaBeans

Applications of reasonable size are constructed from components – some bespoke (written specifically) and some reused. JavaBeans is a software component model that allows independently developed Java components (beans) to be combined and interwork.

Reusable software components can be the push buttons, text fields, list boxes, scrollbars or dialogues, typically sold by third parties as component sets, toolkits, or widget libraries. They might be as complex as calendars, spreadsheets, barcharts, graphical diagram editors or word processors. Components can be nested and arbitrarily complex.

In language terms a bean is a Java class which adheres to certain property and event interface conventions; that is, the interfaces and behaviour of independently developed components must be well defined: this is the purpose of the JavaBeans model. What differentiates beans from typical Java classes is introspection. Tools that recognize predefined patterns in method signatures and class definitions can 'look inside' a bean to determine its properties and behaviour. A bean's state can be manipulated at the time it is being assembled as a part within a larger application.

Tools have been developed to support the design and testing of beans: in Java terminology, the beans development kit is a Java application which depends only on the Java Development Kit (JDK). There is also a tool (a BeanBox) for testing beans which have a visual element and with which the user can interact. That is, the user can cause events by clicking on buttons (or words made into hypertext links) which cause methods to be invoked on the image.

Not all software modules need be beans. Beans are best suited to software components intended to be manipulated visually within builder tools. Some functionality, however, is still best provided through a textual interface, rather than a visual manipulation interface. For example, an SQL API would probably be better suited to packaging through a class library, rather than a bean.

Beans are intended for domain experts (financial analysts, scientists, linguists, factory process control experts), rather than systems programmers. The idea is to make applications easy for them to build.

In summary, JavaBeans have the following properties:

- Support for **introspection** allowing a builder tool to analyse how a bean works.
- Support for **customization** allowing a user to alter the appearance and behaviour of a bean.
- Support for **events** allowing beans to fire events, and informing builder tools about both the events they can fire and the events they can handle.
- Support for **properties** allowing beans to be manipulated by program, as well as to support the customization mentioned above.
- Support for **persistence** allowing beans that have been customized in an application builder to have their state saved and restored.

Enterprise Java Beans (EJB) is the JavaBean component architecture targeted for the business community and aiming to support the development of robust services within a multi-tier architecture. The most recent Java platform, engineered for the enterprise market is J2EE, the Java2 Platform Enterprise Edition. The current standard platform is J2SE, the Java2 Platform Standard Edition.

24.2.5 Java Messaging Service (JMS)

JMS specifies an API for applications to use message-oriented middleware. JMS supports both asynchronous reliable message passing via queues, comparable with IBM's MQSeries, and publish/subscribe comparable with the TIBCO Rendezvous. In both styles, an object is created as the destination through which messages are sent/received or published/subscribed-to by the clients. JMS does not support direct, source-to-sink communication. See Section 24.7 for details of MQSeries and TIBCO Rendezvous.

24.2.6 JXTA

JXTA, http:/www.jxta.org/, is associated with the Java2 Platform Micro Edition (J2ME), which is designed to support a wide range of consumer products including pagers, cellular phones, screenphones, digital set-top boxes and car navigation systems. JXTA technology is described as a set of open, generalized **peer-to-peer (p2p) protocols** that allow any connected device on the network to communicate and collaborate in a peer-to-peer manner. With the explosion of content on the network, and the existence of millions of connected devices, new styles of software and communications support are needed. For example, such devices may have relatively small amounts of memory and require a small software footprint. JXTA technology aims to enable new and innovative network applications to be created, giving access to content on this myriad of small, networked devices.

JXTA therefore aims to support networked, interoperable, p2p applications that can easily:

- find other peers on the network with dynamic discovery across firewalls;
- share files with anyone across the network;
- find up to the minute content at websites;
- create a group of peers that can easily find each other, across firewalls, on any device;
- monitor peer activities remotely;
- securely communicate with other peers on the network.

This is clearly a new application area, based on an evolution of communications services and devices, requiring new styles of middleware to be developed. It is not sufficient to develop new application-specific services, the approach often used by middleware producers to meet the needs of application domains such as finance or medicine. It brings with it the need to support mobile clients, services and applications.

Other ongoing developments for all middleware designers are associated with the need for interworking between different middlewares.

 ## 24.3 OMG and OMA

Our second case study is of an **open standard** for **heterogeneous**, object-oriented middleware. The **Object Management Group (OMG)** was formed to promote an object-oriented approach to distributed software design. More specifically, its aim was to develop, adopt and promote standards for the development and deployment of applications in distributed heterogeneous environments. In 1989 OMG issued a call for proposals for a new architecture **OMA (Object Management Architecture)** based on object invocation instead of client–server interaction: **OMG CORBA (Common Object Request Broker Architecture)** was defined. Since then the CORBA approach has gained industrial and commercial acceptance; the architecture has been refined and various implementations are available, at the time of writing 2.4 is widely used and 3.0 is coming into use. We examine CORBA in some detail below.

The OMG has grown to some 800 members who contribute technology and ideas in response to RFPs (requests for proposals) issued by the OMG. Based on these responses the OMG adopts and issues specifications after some iterations via RFCs (requests for comments). Its members include those who make products which implement the standards and those who build software which uses the standards. The vision is stated:

> The members of OMG have a shared goal of developing and using integrated software systems. These systems should be built using a methodology that supports modular production of software; encourages reuse of code; allows for useful integration along lines of developers, operating systems, and hardware; and enhances long-range maintenance of that code. Members of

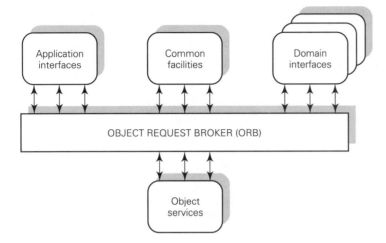

Figure 24.2
The OMA Reference
Model: Interface
categories.

OMG believe that the object-oriented approach to software construction best supports their goals. The OMG staff exists to support the vision of its membership and to promote object technology and its benefits.

The OMG home web page is at http://www.omg.org/ where the specifications may be obtained. An overview is given in Vinoski (1997) and further detail may be found in Pope (1998).

After CORBA became established the OMG reorganized itself in 1996, splitting the Technical Committee (TC) into two parts: the Domain TC and the Platform TC. The former includes task forces in the areas of medicine (master-patient indexing), telecommunications (management of quality of service for audio and video data) and business (a framework to support common business processes). The latter includes task forces in the areas of ORB object services and common facilities such as systems management.

24.3.1 OMA Reference Model component definitions

Figure 24.2 shows the main component types of the Object Management Architecture (OMA) Reference Model.

Object Request Broker (ORB)

At the heart of the OMA is an Object Request Broker Architecture, known commercially as CORBA. This provides the mechanisms by which objects transparently make requests and receive responses. It provides an infrastructure allowing objects to converse, independent of the specific platforms and techniques used to implement the objects. Compliance with the Object Request Broker standard guarantees portability and interoperability of objects over a network of heterogeneous systems.

Object services

These are general services (with specified interfaces) that are independent of any specific application domain. The CORBA services listed on the OMG website at the time of writing are:

Collection Service	Persistent Object Service
Concurrency Service	Property Service
Enhanced View of Time	Query Service
Event Service	Relationship Service
Externalization Service	Security Service
Licensing Service	Time Service
Life Cycle Service	Trading Object Service
Naming Service	Transaction Service
Notification Service	

We have already seen the need for some of these services and they are present in most CORBA systems. **Naming** allows a name to be associated with an object's identifier. **Trading** allows objects to publish their interfaces and clients to discover them. The **property** service allows clients to describe the properties of objects in the form of *attribute-value* pairs to provide information for potential clients to make a selection.

Other services may be used as required by the application. A **collection** service supports the grouping of objects into lists, sets, bags, etc., with corresponding access mechanisms so that elements can be inserted, selected and inspected. The **concurrency** service allows objects to be locked to support sharing by distributed clients. The **event** and **notification** services are an attempt to support asynchronous notification in addition to synchronous invocation.

Externalization is marshalling an object into a byte-stream for persistent storage or external transmission. The **licensing** service allows licensing conditions to be attached to an object. The **persistence** service allows objects to exist independently of the execution of their creator and managing server. Clients do not have to concern themselves with marshalling and unmarshalling objects for transfer to and from disk; this is the responsibility of the service. The **relationship** service allows connections between objects to be specified. The **transaction** service supports flat and nested transactions on method calls over multiple objects. Use of persistence, collections, relationships, and transactions should support at least some aspects of object and relational databases. The **security** service provides facilities for authentication, access control, auditing and secure communication. The **time** service provides the current time within a specified tolerance.

Common facilities

Common facilities provide a set of generic application functions that can be configured to the specific requirements of a particular configuration. These are facilities that sit closer to the user, such as printing, document management, database, system management and electronic mail facilities. Standardization leads to uniformity in generic operations and to better options for end-users for configuring their working environments.

Domain interfaces

Domain interfaces provide functionality of direct interest to end-users in particular application domains such as medical, financial and manufacturing. Domain interfaces are similar in function to common facilities and object services, but are designed to perform particular tasks for users within a certain market or industry. Figure 24.2 shows many different application domains.

Application interfaces

Application interfaces are developed specifically for a given application. OMG does not develop applications, only specifications, so these interfaces are not standardized. An application is typically built from a large number of basic objects: some specific to the application, some domain specific, some from object services and some built from a set of common facilities. These applications benefit greatly from unified object systems development. Better abstraction of the problem space and solution, reusability of components and simpler evolution contribute to good object application development. The application interfaces represent component-based applications performing particular tasks for a user and are important for a comprehensive system architecture.

24.3.2 The OMG Object Model

The OMG Object Model defines common object semantics for specifying the externally visible characteristics of objects in a standard and implementation-independent way. The common semantics characterize objects that exist in an OMG-conformant system. The OMG Object Model is based on a small number of basic concepts: **objects**, **operations**, **types** and **subtyping**.

An object can model any kind of entity such as a person, a car, a document and so on. Operations are applied to objects and allow one to conclude specific things about an object such as determining a person's date of birth. Operations associated with an object collectively characterize an object's behaviour.

Objects are created as instances of types. One can view a type as a template for object creation. An instance of type car could be a red car, 5 m long, with a seating capacity of five. A type characterizes the behaviour of its instances by describing the operations that can be applied to those objects. There can exist a relationship between types. For example, a racing car could be related to a generic form of car. The relationships between types are known as supertypes/subtypes.

The OMG Object Model defines a core set of requirements, based on the basic concepts, that must be supported in any system that complies with the Object Model standard. While the Core Model serves as the common ground, the OMG

Object Model also allows for extensions to the Core to enable greater commonality within different technology domains. The concepts, known as Components and Profiles, are supported by the OMA and are discussed in the OMA Guide.

24.4 CORBA

CORBA (Common Object Request Broker Architecture) is an application framework that provides interoperability between objects, built-in (possibly) different languages, running on (possibly) different machines in heterogeneous distributed environments.

CORBA 1.1 was introduced in 1991 and defined the **Interface Definition Language (IDL)** and the **Application Programming Interfaces (APIs)** that enable client–server object interaction within a specific implementation of an Object Request Broker (ORB); see Figure 24.3. CORBA 2.0, adopted in December 1994, tackled interoperability by specifying how ORBs from different vendors can interoperate.

An ORB is the middleware that establishes the client–server relationships between objects. Using an ORB, a client can transparently invoke a method on a server object, which can be on the same machine or across a network. The ORB intercepts the call and is responsible for finding an object that can implement the request, pass it the parameters, invoke its method, and return the results. The client does not have to be aware of where the object is located, its programming language, its operating system, or any other system aspects that are not part of an object's interface. In so doing, the ORB provides interoperability between applications on different machines in heterogeneous distributed environments.

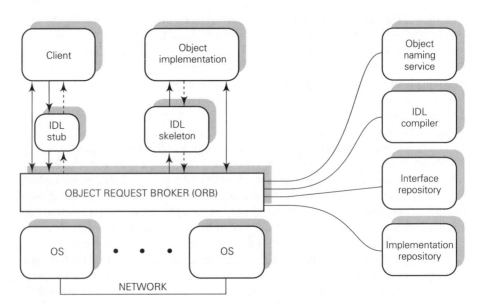

Figure 24.3
CORBA architecture.

The main features of CORBA 2.0 are:

- ORB core
- OMG Interface Definition Language (IDL)
- interface repository
- language mappings
- stubs and skeletons
- dynamic invocation and dispatch
- object adapters
- inter-ORB protocols.

The function of each is outlined below; further information may be obtained from the references. Some of the concepts were introduced in Chapter 15 in the context of RPC systems; other issues are language-level concerns.

24.4.1 The ORB core

The function of the ORB core is to support object invocation by clients on target objects. We therefore need a **naming scheme** for CORBA objects (see Section 6.7). When a CORBA object is created it is given an **object reference**, a unique identifier which is never reused. Object references can have standardized formats or proprietary formats.

Section 6.7

Objects are created by invoking a **create** operation on the appropriate **factory object**; an object reference is returned to the creator. An object reference may also be acquired through a directory lookup. For example, the CORBA Naming Service will supply the object reference for a named object; the Trading Service will supply the object reference for an object with specified properties. Object references may be stored persistently in files or databases for subsequent retrieval and use.

A client with an object reference may invoke any interface operation (service) supported by that object. The ORB is responsible for making this happen and achieves the following transparencies:

- **Location transparency.** The ORB must be able to locate the object from its reference.
- **Implementation transparency.** The client need not know how the target object is implemented, in what programming language it was written nor the operating system or hardware on which it is running.
- **Object execution state.** The ORB activates the object if necessary before delivering the request to it.
- **Communications mechanism.** The underlying protocol used by the ORB is transparent to the client.

24.4.2 OMG's Interface Definition Language (IDL)

As in all other object models we have seen, an object's interface is a specification of the operations and types that the object supports. Interfaces are defined in the OMG Interface Definition Language. As for other platforms, the idea is that an

IDL is programming language independent; interfaces are defined separately from object implementations. Objects may be written in different programming languages and still be able to communicate.

The OMG IDL **built-in types** are:

- long (signed and unsigned): 32-bit arithmetic types;
- long long (signed and unsigned): 64-bit arithmetic types;
- short (signed and unsigned): 16-bit arithmetic types;
- float, double and long double: IEEE 754(1985) floating point types;
- char and wchar: character and wide character types;
- boolean: boolean type;
- octet: 8-bit value;
- enum: enumerated type;
- any: a tagged type that can hold a value of any OMG IDL type, both built-in and user-defined.

The sizes of all types are specified in the standard to ensure interoperability across heterogeneous hardware implementations of CORBA.

The **constructed types** are:

- struct: a data aggregation construct, similar to C/C++;
- discriminated union: a type composed of a type discriminator and a value of one of several possible OMG IDL types that are specified in the union definition.

OMG IDL also supports **object reference types** and **template types** whose exact characteristics are defined at declaration time (for example, strings and sequences). Interfaces can inherit from one or more other interfaces; technically this is restricted multiple inheritance without overloading of operation names. The importance of inheritance is that an interface is open for extension but closed against modification (Meyer, 1988).

24.4.3 Other CORBA features

Interface repository

When a program containing a CORBA object invocation is type-checked at compile time, the interface specification of the object is needed. This may be a remote object written in another programming language but in all cases it must be specified in IDL. An interface repository (IR) holds these specifications. An alternative method of obtaining an interface specification is by invoking the **get-interface** operation which every object inherits. An IR may be interrogated dynamically at runtime as well as statically at compile time, see below.

Language mappings

OMG has standardized language mappings for Ada, C, C++, COBOL, CORBA scripting language, Lisp, Smalltalk, Java, Pl/1, Python and Smalltalk. Mappings for Perl, Eiffel and Modula3 exist but have not been submitted to OMG for acceptance as standards.

For each language it is necessary to be able to:

- invoke CORBA objects from a program written in the language;
- create an IDL interface specification for objects implemented in the language.

For each language a mapping of the language types to OMG IDL types is needed. In addition to the built-in types and constructors, types that are specific to IDLs must be mapped into the languages. An IDL interface is typically mapped to a class, as for C++, or an abstract data type, for C; an object reference may map to a pointer or an object instance. A CORBA object invocation is usually implemented as a function call in the language.

Stubs (proxies for remote objects) and skeletons

OMG IDL compilers generate client-side stubs and server- (target-)side skeletons. This automatic code generation from the IDL specification is an important component of IDL technology. The client-side stub creates and issues the request on behalf of the client; the skeleton delivers the request to the CORBA object implementation.

The programming languages that have mappings for CORBA may implement a CORBA object-operation invocation as a function call in the language or a local object invocation. In both cases the stub is invoked which functions as a proxy for the (possibly) remote target object. The stub, with the assistance of the ORB, marshalls the arguments that are to be transmitted. See Figure 24.1 and Section 24.1.1 for a general discussion.

Dynamic invocation and dispatch

CORBA supports two interfaces for dynamic invocation, roughly equivalent to the stub and the skeleton. These are the Dynamic Invocation Interface (DII) and the Dynamic Skeleton Interface (DSI). They can be seen as generic stubs and skeletons which are provided directly by the ORB and are independent of the IDL interfaces of the objects being invoked. By this means it is possible for an object to be invoked without compile-time knowledge of its interface. This is useful for external objects such as gateways and browsers which may evolve independently of the CORBA platform and for which interface information may be obtained by interface repository lookup or by interaction with a human user. See Figure 24.1 and Section 24.1.1 for a general discussion.

Object adapters

An object adapter is an object that adapts the interface of an object to that expected by its caller; it functions as a wrapper for external or legacy objects. There are language-level semantic issues in this area: the problem cannot be assumed to be solvable in general.

Inter-ORB protocols

Any one middleware platform abstracts above heterogeneous hardware and software. Alas, several different middleware platforms have been developed and standardized; we therefore have heterogeneous middleware. Distributed software running above different platforms may need to interoperate so the interworking of platforms has to be considered. Even different implementation of CORBA may need such services. CORBA 2.0 began to address interoperability.

The ORB interoperability architecture is based on the **General Inter-ORB Protocol (GIOP)** which specifies transfer syntax and a standard set of message formats for ORB interoperation over any connection-oriented transport. The **Internet Inter-ORB Protocol (IIOP)** specifies how GIOP is built over TCP/IP. The architecture also provides for other environment-specific inter-ORB protocols (**ESIOPs**). The first of these was for OSFs Distributed Computing Environment, the DCE Common Inter-ORB Protocol (**DCE-CIOP**). It can be used in environments where DCE is already installed and allows for integration of CORBA and DCE applications.

Object references must be understandable across interoperating platforms. CORBA specifies a standard object reference format: the **Interoperable Object Reference (IOR)**. An IOR contains information needed to locate and communicate with an object over one or more protocols.

CORBA 3 has three main new categories of specification: Java and Internet integration, quality of service control and the **CORBA component architecture (CCA)**. Allied with CCA, mappings have been specified to two scripting languages: Python and the specially defined **CORBA-specific scripting language**.

24.4.4 CORBA support for asynchronous communication

As discussed in Section 24.1, the synchronous communication paradigm does not meet all the interaction needs of applications. To some extent, multi-threading can be used to program around the blocking behaviour enforced by synchronous communication but this can add to software complexity. We saw a number of extensions for Java middleware to support more general communication patterns than one-to-one, directly-named, client–server interactions. A number of extensions have also been provided for CORBA to meet these needs.

CORBA one-ways were added to the request–response paradigm for calls that do not require a response. The semantics of one-ways was not clearly defined and some ORBs implemented them as synchronous calls: although no response is expected, the caller must block waiting for the called object to process the call. Another attempt to provide communication akin to message passing was **objects passable by value**, first included in 1999 in CORBA 2.3. Without this facility, programmers who require to transmit the data associated with an occurrence, typed using IDL, such as *observed (bus49, sensor123, threadneedle-street)* have to pass a fully-fledged object.

The **event service** of 1993 and the event **notification service** of 1998 were added to CORBA for applications that require asynchronous, best-effort notification of event occurrences. These services do not buffer events but operate either on a 'push' or a 'pull model'. The push model means that an event occurring at a source is notified first to the event service and then to any client registered with the event service. The pull model means that a client polls the event service which then polls event sources. The event service was soon found to be inadequate as no filtering of events is supported: a separate event service (event channel) would have to be used for each event type to avoid clients being flooded with events which they then have to filter. The notification service supports filtering and also deregistration at sources to avoid propagation of events for which there are no clients.

Asynchronous Message Invocation (AMI) was added to CORBA in late 2000 as part of release 2.4. Here, messages are typed using the IDL type system, unlike events in the event and notification services. AMI is still described in terms of invocation, where the result of the invocation may be notified to the caller by callback or the caller may pick the result up by polling. At least, a busy server with many notifications to make can send them all off without waiting for each reply. The general asynchronous paradigm, where all that is needed is an unreliable multicast, is still not envisaged.

24.5 ODMG

The Object Data Management Group (ODMG) is a consortium of object-oriented database management system (ODBMS) vendors and interested parties working on standards to allow portability of customer software across ODBMS products. The ODMG home page is http://www.odmg.org/.

By supporting the same interface, members expect to accelerate significantly progress towards effective adoption of the standard. The objectives of the ODMG are:

- To develop a standard set of specifications that may be freely incorporated in database and applications programs in order to permit applications to access information stored in object database management systems in a uniform manner.
- To make the definitions developed available to others for general industry use, and to submit them through appropriate channels for consideration by other standards-setting organizations, such as the International Standards Organization (ISO), the American National Standards Institute (ANSI) and the Object Management Group (OMG).

Although not part of the OMG, the consortium's work is therefore closely related to that of the OMG. The first standard to be published was ODMG-93 and the second edition is Cattell (1996) which should be consulted in preference; the first edition was quite heavily criticized and the problems are addressed in the second edition. As we saw in Section 24.3.1 there is some overlap with CORBA services which were developed in parallel. ODMG provides integrated object database support which is easier to comprehend than a combination of facilities provided by collection, persistence, relationship and transaction CORBA services.

For further information, see http://www.odmg.org/. Details can be found there on the ODMG object model, object definition language (ODL), object query language (OQL) and Java language binding for the second edition.

 ## 24.6 COM, DCOM and .NET

Microsoft's component object model COM, dating from 1993, was designed to make it easier for their software developers to create new releases of Windows operating systems that are compatible with previous versions and to encapsulate applications. It was necessary to be able to evolve and reuse existing components. To allow Windows operating systems to function as parts of distributed systems, COM was integrated with OSF's DCE, an RPC protocol, in NT 4.0. Product names such as Active/X, Network-OLE and DCOM were used but the term COM has come to subsume these and imply a distributed component object model.

Unlike other object-oriented middleware COM therefore supports **binary encapsulation** of server objects and **binary compatibility**. That is, the machine code deriving from components originally written in different programming languages, such as C++, Visual Basic or Visual J++, possibly by third parties, can be used without recompilation and invoked by clients in new environments. This is achieved by strict separation of interface and implementation. Like CORBA (and unlike Java RMI) COM allows components to be written in heterogeneous programming languages and an interface definition language is therefore needed, Microsoft's IDL, or MIDL to avoid confusion with OMG's IDL.

COM's object model

COM defines interfaces, implementations and classes.

A COM **interface** has a globally unique name: a 128-bit identifier into which is incorporated the physical network interface ID of the server computer and a time-stamp.

A COM **implementation** is a class of whatever programming language is used to program the component. An implementation may implement several interfaces and different views may be created for different client roles. COM (like CORBA) defines programming language bindings and these bindings determine how the languages are used to implement MIDL interfaces. An instance of a COM implementation is called a **COM object**. A COM object is identified by a pointer to a main memory location, called an **interface pointer**. If the client and the invoked object share an address space, the interface pointer points to the object itself. If the invoked object is remote, the interface pointer points to the invoked object's proxy. Note that although the COM object proxy is equivalent in functionality to CORBA's client stub, COM's interface pointer (main memory pointer) is a lower-level concept than CORBA's object reference or Java's proxy object reference. In general, binary compatibility is achieved by requiring every programming

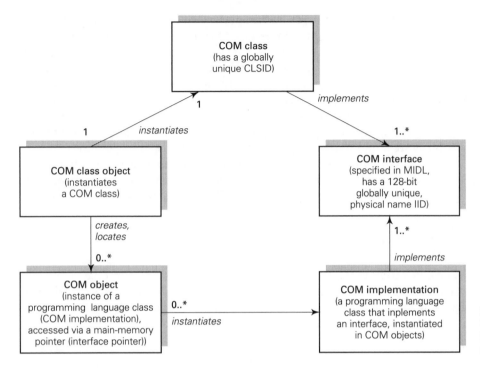

Figure 24.4
COM interfaces,
implementations
and classes.

language to treat the interface to an object as an array of pointers to the object's methods. The alternative is that the IDL compiler translates interfaces specified in IDL into programming language source code which is then compiled into code to invoke the object appropriate to that programming language.

COM defines **COM classes** to manage and locate COM objects. COM classes should not be confused with the programming language classes mentioned above which implement interfaces (see Figure 24.4). COM classes are instantiated in class objects and each COM class needs to have at least one class object. COM classes are the means by which COM objects are created and located. A COM class may make available one or more interfaces. COM classes have globally unique identifiers, **CLSIDs**, which take the same form as those for interfaces.

Types, interface specifications and invocations

COM supports base types which include **boolean, byte, small, short, long, float, double, char** and **enum,** and a limited number of type constructors; **records** and **arrays.** COM's object model is statically typed. Although interface pointers have a dynamic type they can only be used to request operations that are exported by that specific type and this is checked statically by the compilers used to build clients.

COM operations are specified with **in, out** and **inout** parameters. Multiple interfaces in COM can be used to provide client-role-specific views, although within a given interface all operations are visible to all clients who can see it.

COM supports single interface inheritance: every COM interface must inherit from another interface and the inheritance hierarchy forms a tree with a single root called **IUnknown**. IUnknown has three operations which every COM object must support: QueryInterface, AddRef and Release. The latter two are used to count the references to an object for garbage collection purposes; an object without a reference is deactivated.

Unlike CORBA, COM does not support the specification of attributes in interfaces: exposing instance variables would break binary encapsulation. Instead, attributes are unified with operations in the form of property operations.

Like CORBA, COM supports both static and dynamic invocation interfaces. The standard client proxy and server stub mechanisms are used when invocations are available at compile time. Idispatch is COM's dynamic invocation interface.

.NET (dotNET)

Microsoft's website for .NET is http://www.microsoft.com/net. Like all middleware providers Microsoft is seeing the importance of supporting web programming and access to services from, and on, a myriad small devices. .NET is middleware which supports an XML web services platform consisting of:

- a software platform for running web servers, databases, etc., and for XML message-based communication for invoking them;
- a programming model and tools to build and integrate XML web services;
- a set of programmable XML web services;
- a way to enable users to interact with a broad range of smart devices via the web, while ensuring that the user, rather than the application, controls the interaction;
- a way to provide users with applications, services and devices that are personalized, simple, consistent and secure.

It is envisaged that existing sevices and products, such as the Exchange messaging system and the Mobile Informations Server, will be integrated with .NET and form part of a naming and location infrastructure. Web services provide the services and information that users will require and expect and because these web services are programmable, they allow a user to use any device to access this information and to share it with other sites and services.

24.7 Message-oriented middleware (MOM)

Message-oriented middleware evolved alongside that based on object invocation, as we discussed in Section 24.1. MOM has a larger share of the middleware market than object-oriented middleware, being associated with database access within large business applications. In Chapters 12 and 13 we discussed message passing as a general IPC mechanism, applicable to same-machine, cross-address-space message passing. Section 15.3.1 showed how the distribution of message passing can be approached for network-based systems. Recall that in Chapter 13 we also discussed synchronous message passing, where processes have to make a handshake or rendezvous in order to communicate; that is, one party must block until the other is ready to communicate. Synchronous message passing was developed for multicomputer interconnects and message passing in network-based, distributed systems is almost invariably asynchronous. This, as always, implies that messages are buffered/queued by the message transport system. The characteristics of message passing as the basic communication service in MOM may be summarized as follows. We assume that every potential participant has a message queue for both outgoing and incoming messages:

- Message passing is **asynchronous**. The sender may send off a message and proceed immediately without blocking. The sender and receiver need not be parties to the communication at the same time, in a handshake or rendezvous. Indeed, they need not necessarily be running at the same time. The communicating parties are **loosely coupled**.
- Message passing may be reliable or best effort. A **reliable** service, after acknowledging acceptance of a message, guarantees to deliver it to the recipient's message queue exactly once. This implies that the message transport service must store messages in persistent storage to prevent their loss on system crashes.
- The recipient is responsible for retrieving the message from its queue and the message transport system makes no guarantee about when or whether a message is read.

A difference between single-machine message passing and MOM is that if a message is tagged as persistent (a reliable service is requested) the participants' output and input queues must be persistent and may be available independently of whether the participant is running. Also, a message may be routed through a number of queues, again using persistent storage for a reliable service, before eventual delivery into the recipient's queue. In practice, direct delivery from sender-queue to receiver-queue is often used.

MOM evolved to support the interaction of many clients with a few large services, for example financial databases. Unlike object-oriented middleware, MOM did not grow a large number of system services, even for service discovery and location. Instead, static routing was originally used for message transmission between queues. As the scope and size of MOM increased, static routing became difficult to organize and instead a number of routers, which know the whole message queuing topology, are used. Routers can also be used to achieve efficient multicast within a backbone structure, leaving the fan-out of multicast messages to be done close to their destinations instead of close to the source.

Communications services up to and including the transport level are not concerned with interpreting or preserving the internal structure of messages. We have seen that object-oriented middleware, through stubs, skeletons and proxies, ensures that the type checking within the distributed components of a program is preserved during communication. MOM is in general not concerned with the internal structure of messages and leaves this interpretation for the application. An exception is when MOM is used to integrate legacy systems. In this case a function of some components of the MOM is to translate message formats between the legacy format and that required by the existing services. Note that the contents of such messages are visible to the system performing the translation which must therefore be associated with known applications and trusted by them and their clients.

So far we have assumed that messages are addressed to their recipients, although the sender and recipient are loosely coupled and need not synchronize in order to communicate. In wide-area, large-scale systems it may be advantageous to decouple sources and sinks with respect to naming. We have already seen this in Jini/JavaSpaces where the tuple-space abstraction allows senders to insert tuples into a JavaSpace and receivers to receive tuples by supplying a template to a JavaSpace; fields of the template must be matched exactly by value or may be wildcards. By this means senders and receivers may be mutually anonymous.

Message passing systems have also been designed to decouple the naming of sources and sinks in so-called **publish-subscribe** systems. In these systems the message transport service must have knowledge of the message contents. Some publish-subscribe systems are **topic-based** (or **subject-based**): each message is given a topic and the internals of the message are not interpreted by the system. Others are **attribute-based**. Here, the message is structured as *attribute-value* pairs and the receiver may ask for filtering of the messages by requesting values of attributes or wildcards for each pair within a message.

We first consider an example of a reliable MOM service, then a topic-based, publish-subscribe system.

24.7.1 IBM's MQSeries

MQSeries (Gilman and Schreiber, 1996) was developed to serve CICS (Customer Information Control System), a transaction processing system running on IBM mainframes. Its architecture is very much as described above, is shown in Figure 24.5, and has the following components:

- **Queue manager**. Queue manager software resides on a message router. A queue manager is responsible for a number of input queues and a number of output queues. It holds routing tables which it uses to transfer each message from an input queue to the appropriate output queue, according to the routing table.
- **Message channel**. A message channel is a unidirectional reliable connection between a sending and receiving queue manager. It is associated with exactly one output and one input queue. In an internet-based system a message channel is implemented as a TCP connection.
- **Message-channel agent (MCA)**. An MCA is a component of a queue manager. A sending MCA is responsible for checking output queues for messages and sending them via the underlying transport service. A receiving MCA is responsible for listening for an incoming packet and storing the message therein in the appropriate queue.

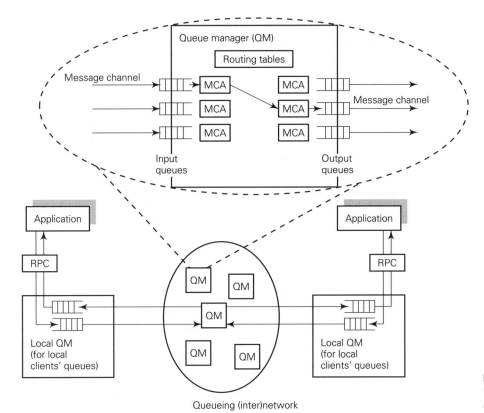

Figure 24.5
MQSeries
architecture.

Figure 24.5 shows these components in the blown-up view of a queue manager. It also shows the general architecture, with a queue manager for a domain, holding the input and output queues of the clients in the domain, together with an internetwork of queue managers acting as message routers. It is optional whether the input and output queues of a process are co-located on the same machine or are on a different, shared machine. This is transparent to the process as the same interface is used in either case:

MQopen   open a queue which may be local or remote, transparently to the application
MQclose close a queue
MQput   put a message into an open queue
MQget   get a message from a local queue

Messages may be defined as persistent (requesting a reliable service with transactional acceptance, transmission and delivery) or non-persistent. Messages are returned to the receiver on a priority basis and messages of equal priority are removed in first-in, first-out order. It is also possible to request notification that a message has arrived to avoid frequent polling of queues.

As there are no naming and directory services, and instead routing tables are used, there is a problem associated with propagating the knowledge of global names to all participants and handling name and location changes. This problem is solved by allowing clients to use aliases which are translated to and from global names by the MQSeries software.

24.7.2 TIB/Rendezvous

The basic TIB/Rendezvous is a subject-based, publish-subscribe system. Processes do not address each other directly but instead a source sends or publishes messages on a given subject and a sink receives messages on subjects to which it has subscribed. Note that all messages on a given subject are sent to subscribers since there is no attribute-based filtering. The architecture is shown in Figure 24.6.

Within a local networked domain each participating host runs a rendezvous daemon to handle subscriptions and publications. The rendezvous daemon keeps

Figure 24.6
TIB/Rendezvous
architecture.

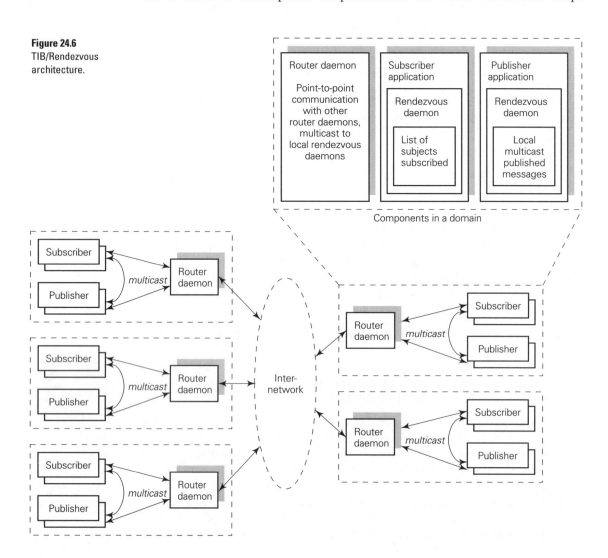

a record of the subjects subscribed to, listens for incoming multicast messages and delivers those tagged with a subject for which there are local subscriptions. The rendezvous daemon is also the first port-of-call for published messages which it multicasts to hosts within the local domain. It is possible to optimize and use direct communication instead of multicast when local subscribing hosts are known. For wide-area implementation, each domain runs a router daemon which communicates with other router daemons using standard communications addressing and routing. Unlike MQSeries, message acceptance, transport and delivery are not transactional and stored persistently en route. It is assumed that the underlying communication service is reliable; messages are held by the publishing host's rendezvous daemon for 60 seconds so that retransmissions can be requested; messages are given a sequence number by the publishing host's rendezvous daemon so that missing messages can be detected and retransmission requested.

On sending, a message is tagged with a subject name which is a sequence of character strings separated by dots. Subscribers can specify components of the sequence to be matched and wildcards for 'don't care' components. For example, a subject naming hierarchy might be created for stock values at stock exchanges, world wide. One generic name might be of the form **stocks.stock-exchange-name.stock-type.stock-subtype**. A subscription might take the form: **stocks.*.utilities.*** and would be matched by messages with any stock exchange in the second field and any utility in the fourth field, such as **stocks.New-York.utilities.water** and **stocks.Tokyo.utilities.electricity**. Subjects are assumed to be known statically, outside the transport system.

Messages consist of a number of named fields, each field comprises typed attributes and a typed data value as follows:

Name	string	the name of the field, possibly null and not necessarily message-unique
ID	integer	a two-byte integer that must be unique within the message
Size	integer	the size of the field in bytes
Count	integer	the number of elements if the data is an array
Type	constant	the type of the data in the field
Data	any type	the data in the field

This is a brief overview of a robust product and more details can be found at the TIBCO TIB-Rendezvous home page http://www.rv.tibco.com/.

24.8 Summary

The growth in acceptance of object-oriented design concepts embodied by CORBA and Java middleware has been steady, if relatively slow. This style of platform was designed primarily for workplace, industrial and commercial distributed systems and was evolving through the late 1980s and 1990s to exploit local area networks. This style of middleware primarily supports the interoperation of the distributed components of programs. They are assumed to be tightly coupled and continuously available for synchronous communication in the form of object invocation. Large-scale, wide-area, many-to-many communication among mutually anonymous parties was not envisaged.

Web browsers became available in 1993 and the explosive growth of popular interest in the internet and the web followed. Java took advantage of this popularly accepted style of interface and has become increasingly widely used, rather than just another object-oriented language. JavaSoft is looking to the ubiquitous computing market via web programming as well as working towards support for traditional distributed computing applications through the development of more traditional middleware products such as Jini, JavaSpaces and JMS with their related services. JXTA is an attempt to prepare for a world of myriad, small intercommunicating devices, as is CORBA version 3.0 and Microsoft's .NET.

Object concepts have stood the test of time in programming languages, operating systems and middleware platforms. Objects in themselves do not provide completely general interworking; there are many different object models and object-based middleware platforms, and middleware developers are increasingly concerned with interworking with different middleware.

Message-oriented middleware was an abstraction of communication services and is used by the database and transaction processing market. Here, clients and servers are assumed to be loosely coupled and asynchronous communication is essential. Reliable, store-and-forward communication is also provided. Initially, MOM had very little support for message structuring. More recently, XML has come to be used for message formatting.

We saw that object-oriented middlware came with a large number of services: some essential for the basic operations of naming and location, others optional but generic and others application-specific. MOM started with less of a service infrastructure and first used static routing then message routers.

It soon became apparent that synchronous object invocation alone was insufficient to meet the needs of all distributed applications and the asynchronous paradigm was added to object-oriented middleware in a variety of forms: Java RMI was augmented by Jini and JMS. CORBA was augmented by the event and notification services and by AMI. In all cases it is unclear to what extent truly asynchronous operation has been achieved since the asynchronous communication is often built above lower-level synchronous request–response.

As we saw with the use of Java for web programming, processors have become fast enough to make on-the-fly interpretation of code a feasible means of running applications. We had previously seen static clients and servers with data passed between them in some standard external form. It became possible to create programs which run above heterogeneous hardware and operating systems by interpreting intermediate code within the Java Virtual Machine. A simple form of mobility and heterogeneity is achieved relatively easily by this means. There is currently a great deal of interest in more general support for mobility which is beyond the scope of this book. There is also a great deal of interest in extending the web paradigm into general middleware, using browser interfaces and making all services look like web services.

Exercises

24.1 Contrast message-oriented middleware (MOM) with the message passing we defined in Chapters 13 and 15. (Hint: consider the reliability of the transmission.)

24.2 Contrast MOM with object-oriented middleware (OOM). List as many differences as you can.

24.3 What is meant by **open** interoperability? Contrast the approach taken by OMG CORBA with that of Sun's Java, and Microsoft's DCOM.

24.4 What interaction paradigm does a tuple space aim to support? What operations do the Linda programming language and JavaSpaces support? What problems would arise if a tuple space was to be distributed?

24.5 How is service naming and location supported in OMG CORBA and Java middleware?

24.6 What are the Java platforms J2SE, J2EE and J2ME designed to support?

24.7 What is the purpose of an Interface Definition Language (IDL)?

24.8 How have the OOM platforms been extended with asynchronous communication? Are these services equivalent to MOM services? To what extent has MOM moved towards the approach taken in OOM?

24.9 Contrast the approach taken in IBM's MQSeries MOM with that in the TIB/Rendezvous MOM. Contrast the design of names in the two systems.

24.10 How has the widespread acceptance of the web affected the design of middleware? Give examples of how recent middleware is adopting the web paradigm. What are the pros and cons of this?

25

Transaction processing monitors and systems

We first discuss systems aspects of transaction processing (TP) monitors. TP applications impose requirements on the underlying system in the following areas:

- the operating systems in the various computers involved, in particular, their support for processes, with or without multi-threading and inter-process communication (IPC);
- the communications support for the messages which flow to effect transactions;
- the higher-level transaction support to ensure correctness of stored data in the presence of failures in systems and communications;
- the requirements for transaction throughput, particularly in large-scale systems. Average, peak and emergency load should be considered.

We then look at some examples of transaction processing systems which are taken from the general area of electronic funds transfer (EFT). This application area is usually described from the viewpoint of security, since EFT systems are an obvious focus for criminals who want to steal money. Here, we are more concerned with general systems aspects and will leave a detailed study of encryption techniques for more specialized texts, for example Davies and Price (1984) and Meyer and Matyas (1982).

Terminology

In this chapter ATM stands for automatic teller machine and an ATM network allows you to obtain banking services internationally. In Chapter 3 an ATM network was one employing the asynchronous transfer mode of communication. We are suffering from a coincidence of TLAs (three-letter acronyms). Perhaps the term 'cashpoint machine' would be better.

25.1 Transaction processing monitors

Transaction processing applications were introduced in Chapter 1 and the theory underlying the correct execution of transactions was the core topic of Part III. A TP monitor coordinates the flow of information between users at terminals who issue transaction requests and TP applications that process the requests. Much of the integration of the software components (operating systems, communications and database management systems (DBMSs)) that are used by TP applications is done by the TP monitor. Figure 25.1 gives a model for a TP monitor, which follows Bernstein (1990). It is assumed that each transaction selects a pre-specified application service program. This is in contrast with a database transaction, which is composed in response to a query.

The figure shows the functions of the components of the TP monitor in the execution of a single transaction. In a typical TP system there are many instances of each of the components. Bernstein (1990) discusses the functions of each component in detail, together with standard message formats, etc. We shall focus on operating systems aspects.

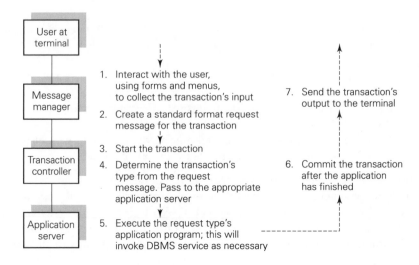

Figure 25.1
Components of a TP monitor.

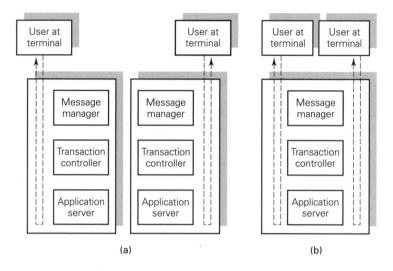

Figure 25.2
TP modules in a
single address space.
(a) Single-threading.
(b) Multi-threading.

25.1.1 Use of processes and IPC

A TP monitor is responsible for creating and managing the processes which execute the components shown in Figure 25.1. Design issues include the following:

- Should the components execute together in a single address space or separately in different address spaces?
- Is each process single-threaded or multi-threaded? (Multi-threaded processes were discussed in Section 4.11, throughout Chapters 4 and 8, and in Section 13.9.)

It is necessary to know the process model of the operating system and the IPC it provides when making these design decisions. We now consider the various options.

Single address space, single-threaded processes

The components are linked together into a single load module and are executed by a single process; see Figure 25.2(a). The control flow between the components is effected by a simple procedure call within the process. A simple strategy is to create such a process for each terminal. This model is used in small TP systems, but it does not scale well. A TP system may have a large number of active terminals. Even if the operating system is, in theory, able to support a large number of processes it may perform badly when a large number exist. This is because of the overhead of handling a large number of process descriptors for scheduling purposes, context switching overhead and memory overhead per process leading to the possibility of paging, etc. If the TP system is distributed there may be a process per terminal on each computer involved in a given transaction (see Chapter 21).

It is not clear how times of high activity, and therefore high load on the system, could be managed. An approach that is used in practice is to lower the priority of some request types. An example from a stock control system is that new orders would be given priority over requests from a management information system for the current stock level. We can assume the existence of a process dedicated to monitoring the load on the system. We can assume that each process, on decoding a request, could determine the current level of the load. We should then need a process to be able to request that its priority is lowered if the load is high and its request type is deemed unimportant. It may not be possible to do this and the crude approach of rejecting or aborting terminal transactions, whatever their type, might have to be used.

Single address space, multi-threaded processes

The components are linked together into a single load module and are executed by a multi-threaded process; see Figure 25.2(b). Each terminal is assigned a thread and each thread has a private data area for its local variables. We assume that a strongly typed language would offer protection of the private data.

The threads may be managed by the operating system or by a threads package in the TP monitor (see Chapter 4). In the latter case, the operating system must offer asynchronous system calls for this scheme to work effectively. Recall that a synchronous system call which results in blocking will block the whole process if the operating system is not aware of the separate threads of the process.

If the system is to run on a shared-memory multiprocessor, multi-threading implemented by the operating system allows the threads to run concurrently.

As we noted above, scheduling parameters may need to be adjusted at times of high load. The area of scheduling multi-threaded processes is still under active research and this is a requirement that should be taken into account.

TP monitors that use a single address space in practice use multi-threading. An example is IBM's CICS (Customer Information Control System) (see Yelavitch, 1985) but note that IBM has a proprietary network architecture to provide communications support for this product: System Network Architecture (SNA). Digital had a similar product (DECintact) and network support (DECNET).

Multiple address spaces, single-threaded processes

It is desirable to implement the components of the TP monitor as separate processes in the following circumstances:

- The system may comprise a large, geographically dispersed network of terminals. It is convenient to locate a message manager in a machine which is close to a group of terminals.
- The users submit transactions at workstations. The message manager component is best located in the workstation.
- The system may be partitioned so that some application servers execute specific request types. This may be because different parts of a business are concerned with different types of transaction and the business may most conveniently be served by such an arrangement.

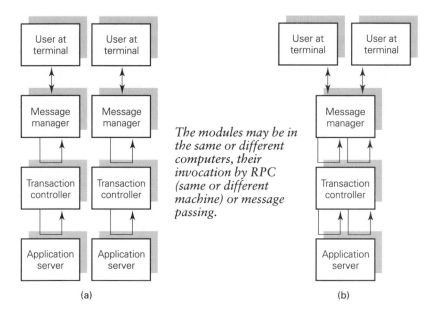

The modules may be in the same or different computers, their invocation by RPC (same or different machine) or message passing.

Figure 25.3
TP modules in separate address spaces.
(a) Single-threading.
(b) Multi-threading.

We now require IPC between the components of the TP monitor which is executing a given transaction. This may take the form of message passing or remote procedure call (RPC). Figure 25.3 shows the approach in general terms.

The modules shown there may be located in separate address spaces in the same computer or in separate computers. The IPC may be between different address spaces on the same machine or inter-machine. A wide-area network may separate some of the components.

Connection-oriented message passing is used in some systems (see Section 3.8.2). A process establishes a session, or virtual circuit, with another process after which they can exchange messages. In IBM's CICS, for example, a permanent half-duplex connection is set up and there is explicit transfer of control between the processes at the connection endpoints to form a conversation. Conversations are intended to be long-lived and to span many transactions. With this model a single transaction comprises a chain of processes. When each component process in the chain has finished its processing the transaction may be committed. Only then can the chain of connected processes start work on the next transaction.

When message passing is used between some components of the TP monitor and procedure call is used to invoke other components, the system configuration is made explicit in the programs. For example, the message manager might be in a dedicated machine, but the other components might run in a single address space. This could not be changed without reprogramming. The argument against using a separate address space for every component, even when they run on the same machine, is that the IPC would then be less efficient than procedure call.

We have seen that an RPC mechanism implements a client–server style of interaction. Each component of the TP monitor could be implemented as a separate process and RPC could be used for invocation. Some components are invoked as a server, then become a client of the next component in the line. The components could be invoked by same-machine RPC or cross-network RPC transparently to the application. This would make programming easy and reconfiguration possible without reprogramming. Digital's ACMS and Tandem's Pathway TP monitors used the client–server model.

Increasing the efficiency of general message passing and RPC is an active research area. If cross-address-space IPC can be made efficient it is preferable for the components of TP systems to be implemented as separate processes running in separate address spaces for the reasons mentioned above. However, if each of these processes is only single-threaded a large number of processes is needed when a large number of transactions must be handled. As we discussed for single address space implementations, this imposes a high overhead on the operating system and leads to a large amount of context switching overhead.

Multiple address spaces, multi-threaded processes

Here we again have the TP monitor's components in separate address spaces but this time they are executed by multi-threaded processes; see Figure 25.3(b). The context switching overhead between threads is much lower than between processes. Problems may arise (as discussed for single address space, multi-threaded processes) if the operating system does not support threads and has synchronous system calls.

Digital's ACMS and Tandem's Pathway TP monitors supported an 'application service class' abstraction to avoid this problem. The application service modules (which make potentially blocking system calls) are single-threaded and run as separate OS processes. A new transaction which requires an application service can make a request to the class and not to a specific instance of the application service. Any free application service process of this class can service the request. Similar mechanisms were discussed in Section 13.5.

25.1.2 Buffered transaction requests

The implication in the above discussion has been that a transaction is executed while the user waits. This may be the case in some applications. In others it may be convenient for the system to accumulate a batch of requests before carrying out processing. For example, a shop may record the items that have been sold during the day as a batch of transactions and may update the stock database overnight. Orders for new stock are then made on a daily basis. The shop may record the cheque or credit card purchases made by its customers as a batch of transactions to be sent to its bank for settlement.

A batch mode of working is natural for many systems. In others it may be that a transaction that would normally be executed on-line, such as an order to dispatch an item to a customer, might not be able to complete for some reason. A network connection or remote database system might be unavailable. In this case, it might be possible to enter the transaction into the system and have it guaranteed to execute but after some delay. The crucial requirement is that once the transaction is accepted it is not lost.

The TP monitor may therefore provide for messages to be stored securely and executed later. This allows batch working as described above and also allows the system to be used if there has been a network or server failure.

25.1.3 Monitoring system load and performance

TP systems are large and complex. Human managers or automated management systems need information on the throughput in transactions per second and the response times that are being achieved. This information allows the system to be expanded when it becomes necessary. It also allows parameters to be tuned dynamically to improve system performance.

A typical system will grade its transaction request types in priority, for example, into those which must, if possible, be carried out immediately and those which may be batched or delayed for a short time. When load becomes high, low-priority request types might be rejected or queued to ensure good response to high-priority types. A general requirement is that the operating system should allow the application to specify the relative priorities of its threads and should be able to change these priorities dynamically to respond to changing load levels.

25.2 Introduction to some electronic funds transfer (EFT) applications

An outline of some of the transaction processing which is carried out within EFT systems is now given.

25.2.1 Paying by cheque

Figure 25.4 outlines what is involved when goods are paid for by cheque.

I have bought a television and have paid the shop by cheque. My handwritten signature on the cheque is used to authenticate me, but only in the event of a dispute at a later stage.

1 The shop presents my cheque (and many others) to its bank.
2 The shop's bank transmits a file containing a batch of transactions to a central clearing house. A central clearing house service is used to avoid the necessity of every bank interacting with every other bank. One of these transactions corresponds to my cheque. The transactions are called **debit transfers** because they are requests to debit various accounts. The clearing house will need to interact with many different banks to establish whether the transactions can be carried out. These interactions are likely to be batched per bank rather than on-line.

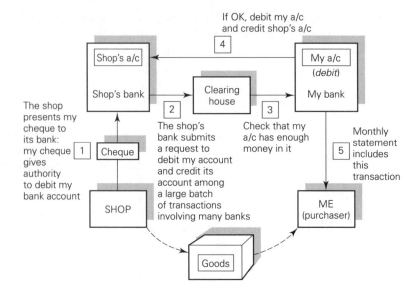

If OK, debit my a/c
and credit shop's a/c

| 4 |

Shop's a/c

Shop's bank

Clearing
house

| 2 |

My a/c
(*debit*)

My bank

| 3 |

The shop
presents my
cheque to
its bank:
my cheque | 1 |
gives
authority
to debit my
bank account

| Cheque |

The shop's
bank submits
a request to
debit my account
and credit its
account among
a large batch
of transactions
involving many banks

Check that my
a/c has enough
money in it

Monthly
statement
| 5 | includes
this
transaction

SHOP

ME
(purchaser)

| Goods |

Figure 25.4
Payment by cheque.

3 For each transaction, the clearing house asks the bank concerned whether the cheque can be honoured: whether there is enough money in the account. This process will involve a batch of transactions for each bank. The figure may imply something more interactive and immediate. The bank sends back bounced cheques after a day or two. Let us assume that I can pay for the television.

4 My account is debited and the shop's account is credited with the amount specified in the cheque. The mechanism for achieving this is again likely to involve a batch of accumulated transactions from my bank. This time, the transactions are credit transfers: they are a list of authorized credits.

5. I get a monthly bank statement which includes a record of this transaction.

Note that while the cheque is being cleared I cannot safely use the money represented by the cheque, nor can the shop that I have paid with it. The mechanism takes of the order of days because very large numbers of cheques are involved and the batch mode of working is used. This system therefore favours the banks since they can make use of the money in transit. Customer pressure and competition between banks will provide the motivation for developing more interactive systems.

We avoided discussing cheques that bounce. In practice, in Britain and some other countries, the shop would have insisted that I cover my cheque with a bank card which guarantees that the cheque will be honoured. It is then my bank's problem if the cheque bounces (to recover the money from me), and not the shop's. In this case, interaction 3 would merely pass the requirement to make the debit to my bank, whether my account could cover the cheque or not. Banks will not cover very large sums of money in this way, without a fee being paid, and other payment mechanisms are needed. For example, the goods might be held until the cheque is cleared, as described in 1 to 5 above.

The following points are relevant to an implementation of such a system:

- That the long time taken to clear a cheque by this means is tolerable to users of the system.
- A file transfer protocol is used to transfer the files of transactions. Copies of the various transaction files are kept so that any problems can be resolved. Early systems used magnetic tape to transfer batches of transactions.
- Encryption is used for security (see below).
- When transactions are being carried out at my bank, a transaction log records the debit to my account. If the system crashes during transaction processing, the log has a record of the old and new value of the account (see Chapter 20).
- When transactions are being carried out at the shop's bank, a transaction log records the credit corresponding to my cheque. This prevents the credit being made more than once, or not at all.

It must be ensured that each transaction is carried out exactly once, even when the systems or the networks connecting them fail. The use of a log for recovery was described in Chapter 20.

25.2.2 Paying by credit card

Figure 25.5 outlines what is involved when goods are paid for by credit card. This time, the shop is guaranteed payment by the credit card company (CCC). My credit card is issued by a member of the CCC which we shall call the credit card issuer (CCI). The CCI may be associated with a bank, for example.

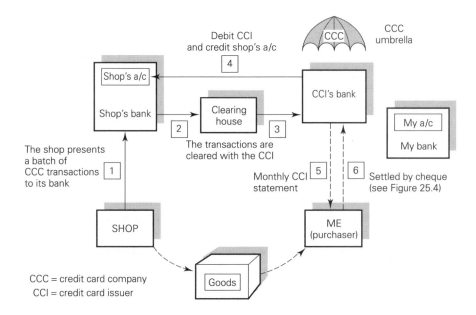

Figure 25.5
Payment by credit card.

My CCI notifies me of a batch of transactions in my monthly statement and I then pay the CCI for all of them (or pay to borrow money from the CCI). The CCC acts as a large, secure, high-level guarantor for the money involved in the transactions, shown as an umbrella in Figure 25.5. It is less likely to go broke than any one of its member CCIs and a card with its endorsement is more likely to be trusted by vendors of goods and services.

25.2.3 Paying by debit card: Point of sale transactions

A debit card is also likely to be guaranteed by an umbrella organization as described above for credit cards. If a debit card is used together with a hand-written signature on a payment slip, the procedure is similar to that described above for cheques. The debit card also acts as a guarantee that the issuer will cover the payment. At present there is no on-line interaction between the point of sale and the card issuer: the card merely functions as a cheque that is easy to clear. The card is put through the point of sale machine to check against a list of stolen card numbers (see below).

Most point of sale systems have traditionally used handwritten signatures for authentication but are gradually moving towards more secure methods.

Note that so far, a batch mode of working has been used to avoid the complexity of myriad interactive transactions between the many banks of purchasers, vendors and card issuers. The requirements on the operating system and communications support are less demanding for this batch mode of working than for on-line TP (OLTP). Interactive working implies that all parties wait in real time for accounts to be checked and authority to be given. When a batch mode is used, a system or communications line can go down for a short time without affecting the financial operations. If we move to interactive working, systems must be fault-tolerant. It would be intolerable for purchases, etc., to be held up when failures occur.

25.2.4 Some security issues

Cheque-books and cards can be stolen and forged. One of the critical issues for the financial card industry is the rate of loss due to fraud and forgery. In the USA, for example, this amounts to over 1.5% of the turnover of signature-based credit card transactions. For many issuing institutions this is over half of the profit made on credit card business. Much of the effort in designing EFT systems is therefore directed towards preventing and detecting both crime external to the EFT system (by its users), and internally (by those operating it).

After you have reported that your card is stolen, the credit card company is responsible for covering subsequent use of the card. It is in the company's interest to propagate information on stolen cards, so-called 'hot card numbers', as widely and rapidly as possible.

When a file of transactions is recorded it must be ensured that all these transactions are genuine and have not been augmented by transactions in favour of bank employees, nor have any transactions been changed to achieve this end. It must be guaranteed that only the intended transactions are processed when the file reaches its destination. Also, transactions must not be changed during transmission. In general, the requirement is that attacks on the transaction data must be prevented. An attack seeks to change data for the benefit of the attacker.

Security policies and mechanisms to achieve these aims are described in Davies and Price (1984) and Meyer and Matyas (1982).

25.3 International inter-bank payments: SWIFT

The discussion in the previous section has given some indication of the immense volume of EFT traffic. The implicit assumption was that the banks concerned were located in a single country, but many transactions involve the transfer of funds between countries. If you can find a garage when on holiday in the high Pyrenees it will almost certainly allow you to pay for your petrol by credit card. The supermarket in the provincial French town where you buy your holiday provisions will give you a choice of using a debit or a credit card.

The previous section described methods that are used for transactions involving a small amount of money. The methods described above would not be used for large sums. In the past, telephone or telex would have been used to arrange such transfers, but these methods are subject to misunderstandings and fraud. Increasingly, telecommunications are being used for this purpose, a major example being the Society for Worldwide Inter-bank Financial Telecommunications (SWIFT). SWIFT was formed in 1973 as a bank-owned, non-profit cooperative society, directed by about 1000 shareholding member banks which are located in about 50 countries worldwide. It has been operational since 1977. The costs of its message transfer service are paid for by members using a tariff based on the numbers of connections, their addresses and the volume of traffic.

Chapter 10 of Davies and Price (1984) covers the operation of SWIFT in detail and its interaction with the clearing houses of its member nations.

25.4 Authentication by PIN

In Section 25.2 we considered payment by cheque, credit card and debit card. In all of these cases a handwritten signature was the basis for authenticating the purchaser. In the next section we consider automatic teller machines (ATMs) which are EFT terminals which give cash dispensing and other banking services. For these machines a handwritten signature is not used. Before going on to the design of an ATM system we first consider authentication by personal identification numbers (PINs), a method suitable for banking and other applications. As well as being an authentication mechanism that is easier to automate than handwritten signatures, the PIN method has also been found to be very much less subject to fraud.

A PIN is a secret number assigned to, or selected by, the holder of a credit card or debit card. It authenticates the cardholder to the EFT system. The PIN is memorized by the cardholder and must not be recorded in any way that could be recognized by another person. At the time when the cardholder initiates an EFT transaction, the PIN is entered into the EFT terminal using a keyboard provided for this purpose. Unless the PIN, as entered, is recognized by the EFT system as correct for this particular account number (which is also recorded on the card) the EFT system refuses to accept the transaction.

This approach ensures that if someone steals a card or finds a lost card, he or she is unable to use it because the PIN is not known to them. Also, if a counterfeit copy of a card is made, it is useless without the corresponding PIN.

Chapter 10 of Meyer and Matyas (1982) discusses PINs in detail. The issues discussed there are summarized briefly below.

PIN secrecy

It is important that the users of the EFT system have confidence in its security. For example, if an applicant for a card were to be asked to specify a PIN on an application form it would be obvious that many employees of the card issuer would have access to the PIN. For this reason, we are issued with PINs instead of specifying our own.

Certain policies should hold, such as:

- A PIN should not be transmitted across a network connection 'in clear', that is, without first being encrypted.
- A clear PIN should never reside in a mainframe computer or database, even momentarily when in transit.
- A clear PIN should not be seen by an employee of the company at any time, including when it is being issued.
- Employees should not have access to the encryption keys used in the system.

PIN length

We are exhorted to use non-alphanumeric characters in our login passwords, whereas PINs are restricted to numeric characters to keep the EFT terminal's keyboard simple. As with computer passwords, the longer the PIN, the more difficult the system is to crack: the more unlikely it is that a guessed PIN will be correct. However, the method of guessing at random is thought to be infeasible for a would-be thief. It would be necessary to stand at an EFT terminal for many hours and this would not go without detection; see also 'allowable entry attempts' below.

Cardholders are required to memorize their PINs. The longer the PINs, the more likely we are to forget them. Four digits allow 10 000 different PINs, five digits give 100 000 and six digits 1 000 000. Four-digit PINs are often used, in order to be easy to remember, but this means that a lot of people will share a

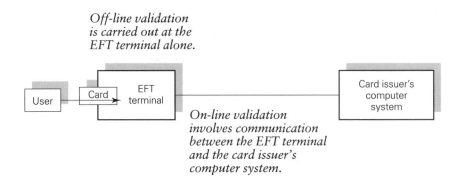

Off-line validation is carried out at the EFT terminal alone.

On-line validation involves communication between the EFT terminal and the card issuer's computer system.

Figure 25.6
PIN validation.

given PIN (each with a different account number of course), and occasionally they are found to live in the same house. In general, short PINs can be used because we do not tell them to each other.

Allowable PIN entry attempts

Notice a significant difference in the way passwords at login and PINs are used. When the card is inserted and a PIN is typed, the EFT system can monitor the process and can count the number of attempts which are made to type the correct PIN. The system typically refuses to allow more than a small number of attempts. A login procedure could do the same, but this would not prevent other methods of attempting to break a computer system's security. These often involve off-line computation; for example, a password file could be copied and many artificially constructed passwords could be put through the known encryption function and compared with the encrypted passwords in the file. The stored, encrypted PINs are not available to users of the EFT system. Off-line attacks on the master PIN key (see below) are still feasible, however.

The PIN validation mechanism

Suppose that the EFT terminal is owned by the card issuer. The two approaches to PIN validation are outlined in Figure 25.6. Either the PIN is validated off-line in the EFT terminal alone or it is validated on-line by an interaction between the EFT terminal and the card issuer's computer system.

Figure 25.7 gives a simplified view of one method of off-line validation. When the card and PIN are issued, the account number and a secret random number (the master PIN key) are put through an encryption function, giving the PIN as result. The PIN is not stored anywhere in the system and no bank employee sees it: it emerges in a sealed, addressed envelope.

When the card is used at an EFT terminal, the terminal must have the computing power and the information necessary to carry out the same encryption process. This information resides in the tamper-proof secure unit shown in the figure. The account number from the card's magnetic stripe and the stored secret

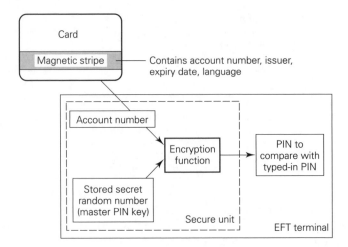

Figure 25.7
Off-line PIN validation
at the EFT terminal.

random number (the master PIN key) are put through the encryption function and the result is compared with the typed-in PIN. The reader is referred to Meyer and Matyas (1982) for details of this and other methods.

If an off-line validation method is used, some of the EFT services, such as cash dispensing, can still be offered when the EFT terminal is disconnected from the rest of the network. The EFT terminal must have stable storage to record the transactions. Other services, such as determining the balance of the account, may not be available.

Changing a PIN interactively

Some machines allow you to change your PIN. How can this be possible if PINs are not stored in the system? The method used is to store the difference between the original PIN and the new one the user has chosen. This stored information must be available to any EFT terminal. On-line validation is more appropriate for systems which offer a 'change PIN' service.

25.5 The international automatic teller machine (ATM) network service

Early ATMs were essentially cash dispensers. Their single function was to deliver cash in the form of banknotes and debit the corresponding bank account. Further facilities have now been added to these automatic tellers. You can enquire about the status of your bank accounts. You can move money between your own accounts and sometimes may be allowed to credit another person's account. It may be possible for travellers' cheques to be dispensed (in countries where these are needed). There may also be a simple deposit facility.

We have become used to the convenience of being able to put a card into an ATM anywhere in the world in order to draw cash from a bank account. You can now set off on holiday or on business with very little concern about how much cash to take with you.

This has happened recently and the design of the systems that support the service tends not to be discussed in the standard systems literature. When the systems are described, the emphasis is on the security aspects of their design. We give a short case study here which does not involve a deep discussion of security issues. An introduction to PINs and their validation was given in the previous section.

25.5.1 How bank accounts are held

A bank's account database is likely to be held on a relatively small number of large computer systems. Any given account is held at a primary site and a backup site, the 'hot standby' shown in Figure 25.8. As transactions involving the accounts are carried out at the primary site a log is kept as described in Chapter 20. If this computer should fail the bank accounts it holds should not become unavailable. This is the reason for the hot standby.

One approach to maintaining the hot standby would be to carry out each transaction on both machines but this would slow down the rate at which transactions could be processed. The log of transactions on the primary site is not lost on a crash, however, and it is therefore not necessary to keep the accounts exactly in step. The hot standby tends to be updated at a granularity of about ten minutes and the log can be used after a crash to bring the standby right up to date. With this approach, during normal working, a batch of transactions can be sent from the primary to the standby machine, thus optimizing both use of communication services and transaction processing at the standby.

25.5.2 Local control of ATMs

Figure 25.8 shows a number of ATM machines in a local area. The machines must be physically secure because they contain money. A secure authentication mechanism will not protect the machine from a brute force attack by heavy lifting gear. They therefore tend to be built into the foundations of the buildings where they are located. Each ATM has a keyboard through which the customer requests services and a screen to display information. Authentication of the customer is of primary importance and different approaches to achieving this were outlined in Section 25.4. Once the customer is authenticated, the transactions are carried out.

An ATM is typically owned and managed by a single bank, but the banks cooperate to allow transactions from each other's ATMs (not illustrated). Figure 25.8 shows a small computer which controls a number of local ATMs in

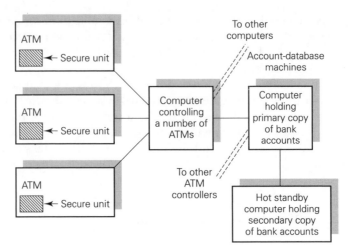

Figure 25.8
Local control of
ATMs.

addition to the main computers at which bank accounts are held. The rationale for the local computer is that while at work, for example, I regularly use the same few ATM outlets of my bank. The local computer can manage a large proportion of ATM traffic without interacting with the large account database storage systems. The functions of the ATM controller include the following:

- To keep a copy of information on selected local bank accounts. Hopefully, most transactions can be satisfied from this information. The less frequent cases are when a stranger uses this machine and when a local person goes elsewhere and uses a remote machine (see Section 25.5.3).

  The values of the various copies of a bank account (on the account-database machines and on the local ATM controller) are guaranteed to be synchronized on a 24-hour basis. In practice, transactions are carried out at a finer time grain and synchronization is more likely to be achieved after ten minutes or so. The information at the local controller can become out of date if the account is accessed remotely.

  The most recent value of each local account is remembered so if only local transactions are carried out, this value is up to date.

  All transactions are recorded in stable storage and a batch is sent to the account-database machine periodically, for example, every ten minutes.

- To keep a list of 'hot cards': those which have been notified as missing, presumed stolen. This is updated at least on a daily basis.
- To keep information on cards which have been used recently. This allows any attempt to use a stolen card repeatedly to be detected. It also allows a policy to limit the number of transactions per day or the amount of cash that can be withdrawn per day to be enforced.
- To cache information that may be useful in satisfying future requests.
- To communicate with other computers when requests cannot be satisfied from information held locally.

From the above it is clear that a local request is satisfied on the basis of the information held in the local controller.

25.5.3 Remote use

The following issues arise when an ATM is used by someone whose account information is not held by the ATM's controller.

The user belongs to the same bank or card issuer (CI) as the ATM's owner

- The ATM's stored encryption keys, the encryption function it uses and the encoding of the card are uniform for the CI. The PIN typed by the user at the ATM can therefore be validated.
- After PIN validation the ATM can carry out some services, such as dispensing cash. The transaction is recorded and in due course is passed to the account-holding database machine and the account is debited.
    If that user makes use of his or her local ATM on the way home, the value stored there for the balance of the account will not, in general, reflect this transaction.
- Certain services, such as giving the value of the account, may not be available. To provide such a service, it would be necessary to support interactive querying of the account database from this ATM's local controller. It might be that the account database is queried to ascertain and enforce the user's credit limit and the balance might or might not be divulged depending on the bank's policy for remote use.

Interactive TP is likely to become available increasingly in the future.

The user belongs to a different bank or card issuer (CI) from the ATM's owner

It is necessary for the user's CI and the ATM owner to have an agreement that their cards can be used in each other's machines. They may agree to use the same method of PIN validation (see Section 25.4), but the 'secret random number' (key) that is input to the encryption function when the card is issued, and when the PIN is validated, will be different for the two CIs. It must be possible for these secret numbers to be inserted into the tamper-proof secure unit in the ATM without being disclosed to the cooperating CIs. The program in the ATM which reads the card can detect the bank number and select the appropriate secret on that basis. An alternative method is to encrypt the information and transmit it for remote validation by the CI.

The service offered may differ slightly from that given to a customer of the owner's bank. It might be necessary that the account database is interrogated to enforce a 'no overdraft' policy, but the value is unlikely to be disclosed.

 ## 25.6 Load and traffic in TP systems

The above descriptions were presented in general terms. In order to understand the likely load on TP systems and the volume of traffic involved in this application area, knowledge of typical transaction sizes and the rates at which they are invoked is needed. If one is to design a TP system it is essential to know these values for the application areas it is intended to serve.

An example from ATM systems of the rate at which transactions can be executed is that a recent reimplementation of a widely used system has increased the potential transaction rate from 50 per second to 400 per second. The transaction rate could be limited by the line speed used for the connection between the ATM controller and the customer's host system, but is most often software-limited.

Another factor to bear in mind is peak load both in normal and exceptional circumstances. For example, ATM machines are used most heavily on Fridays and Saturdays around midday. The international stock exchanges' systems were unable to cope with the load generated on 'Black Monday' in October 1987. A TP system should have management procedures to cope with predicted high loads and projected emergency loads.

The size of a transaction depends on the number of instructions executed (the 'pathlength') and the number of input and output instructions it performs. Studies of real workloads have shown that pathlength provides a reasonable basis for comparison. Sharman (1991) classifies typical workloads as simple, medium and complex:

  simple: pathlength < 100 000 instructions
  medium: 100 000 < pathlength < 1 000 000
  complex: pathlength > 1 000 000 instructions

A typical mixed workload comprises simple and medium transactions. Complex transactions typically occur in applications which involve complex query analysis on a database, expert systems inference applications or very large components databases (such as the components involved in manufacturing various parts of an aircraft).

It is difficult to compare systems with widely varying transaction mixes. Figures indicating the number of transactions per second are quoted, but the transaction sizes must be known for these rates to mean anything. The non-profit Transaction Processing Performance Council (TPPC) was set up for this purpose in 1989. Its aim is to define standard benchmarks upon which both the industry and its customers can rely (see Gray, 1991). TPPC will define benchmarks based on typical applications and will specify the configurations which are needed to run them.

One benchmark, TPC-A, is based on a simplified banking transaction known as debit/credit which has a pathlength of 100 000 instructions. Typical prices of systems that can achieve one TPC-A transaction per second are in the range $20 000 to $40 000 (Sharman, 1991).

A customer may wish to purchase a TP system that will scale, for example, to handle from 0.1 to 1000 transactions per second. Different departments of the company may require different mixes and different rates, and any given part of a company will wish to be able to allow for growth of the system.

In addition to supporting some specified transaction rate a TP system (comprising the hardware and software of the attached computers and the network connections) is required to be highly available, to operate continuously and to be secure.

25.7 Summary and trends

This brief study of transaction processing systems has shown the relevance to them of the topics that we studied in the earlier parts of the book. We saw that it is necessary to know the process model and IPC facilities of the operating system over which a TP system is implemented. Ideally, the OS should support multi-threaded processes. The TP system can then be programmed naturally and without artificial restrictions. If only single-threaded processes are supported, and system calls are synchronous, the TP system implementor has to go to a great deal of trouble to program around the potential problems. We saw that multiple address spaces containing multi-threaded processes using RPC for communication could be used to provide a general and flexible implementation.

Examples of TP systems in the area of electronic funds transfer were given. They can be divided into those which use handwritten signatures for authentication and those which use personal identification numbers. The latter are more convenient to automate and more secure. The trend is therefore towards the use of PINs, and PIN validation is likely to come into use at point of sale terminals. IBM, however, go for signature verification.

We saw that file transfer and batched transaction processing are often used. This method uses processing power and communications efficiently, but is subject to delay. The trend is towards increasingly widespread use of on-line transaction processing, associated with the more conveniently automated PIN-based authentication.

Large distributed systems of this kind require management: configuration management and evolution in response to failures and bottlenecks and parameter tuning in response to varying load. At present, monitoring processes may report to human managers but the trend is towards increased automation of management processes. An example is that the transactions issued by one company to order goods from another may be input directly to the control mechanisms of the manufacturing processes of the supplying company.

Exercises

25.1 What problems arise from using one operating system process per user terminal?

25.2 How do the problems which arise when single-threaded processes are used for building multi-threaded servers apply to TP system implementations? How have these problems been addressed in practice?

25.3 Why is connection-oriented communication between the components of a TP system less elegant than an RPC system? Why might it be more efficient?

25.4 Why is the use of a separate process for each component of a TP system more flexible than a shared address space solution?

25.5 Indicate where buffered transaction processing is used when goods are paid for by cheque, credit card and debit card. How could on-line TP be brought into point of sale applications?

25.6 (a)   What are the factors affecting the design of PIN-based authentication?
     (b)   What would be the problems arising from a 12-digit PIN?
     (c)   Why shouldn't I choose a PIN and tell my card issuer by writing it on a form that includes my unencrypted name and address?

25.7 What would be involved in keeping the bank accounts in the bank account database computers and the ATM controllers completely up to date?

25.8 Why are TP benchmarks needed?

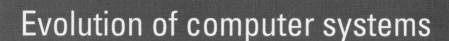

Appendix

Evolution of computer systems

A.1 Introduction, technological and commercial context

Since system design is technology-driven an outline of technological developments is given below. The development of hardware, computer systems and networks is included. Technology must be exploited, first in research projects and, when feasibility is demonstrated, in commercial products. The formation of selected major companies and software products is therefore included. The data below is based on the timeline created by the IEEE Computer Society for their 50th anniversary in 1996. See IEEE (1996) and http://www.computer.org/history/ for further reading.

We then go on to the evolution of software systems. The integrated approach taken throughout is relevant to operating systems, distributed operating systems, middleware, distributed services and database. A brief discussion of the major milestones in the evolution of these systems is given. The concepts can be followed up in the relevant section of the book.

Evolution and exploitation of technology

1801
A linked sequence of punched cards controls the weaving of patterns in Jacquard's loom.

1822–49
Charles Babbage works on his Difference Engine and Analytical Engine.

1844
Samuel Morse demonstrates the Morse code.

1854
George Boole develops Boolean algebra.

1858
First Atlantic telegraph cable.

1876
Alexander Graham Bell invents the telephone.

1882
William S. Burroughs embarks on inventing an adding machine.

1889
Herman Hollerith's Electronic Tabulating System is selected for use in the 1890 census. He establishes a company in 1896.

1895
Guglielmo Marconi transmits a radio signal.

1901
The keypunch appears.

1924
T. J. Watson renames the former CTR (originating from Hollerith) IBM.

1927
Television is demonstrated.

1936
Konrad Zuse files a patent application for the automatic execution of calculations including a combination memory.

1937
Howard Aiken proposes a digital calculating machine to IBM.
Claude Shannon publishes the principles for an electronic adder.
George Stibitz develops a binary circuit based on Boolean algebra.

Alan Turing publishes 'On Computable Numbers' giving the concepts of the Turing machine.
John Vincent Atanasoff devises the principles of the electronic digital computer.

1938
Hewlett Packard formed.
Zuse completes the electromechanical Z1.

1939
Atanasoff builds a prototype electronic digital computer based on binary arithmetic.

1940
Zuse completes the Z2, based on telephone relays.

1941
Zuse completes the Z3, the first fully functional, program-controlled electromechanical digital computer.

1943
The construction of ENIAC begins at the Moore School of Electrical Engineering in Philadelphia.
Colossus, the first all-electronic calculating device, is developed at Bletchley Park, UK by Turing and others.

1944
Harvard Mark 1 produced by Aiken.

1945
Eckert and Mauchley contract to build EDVAC.
ENIAC operational.
John von Neumann introduces the concept of a stored program in a draft report on the EDVAC design.

1946
ENIAC unveiled at the University of Pennsylvania.
Turing publishes a report on his design for ACE (Automatic

Computing Engine) to be built at the National Physical Laboratory (NPL), UK.

1947
Harvard Mark II is completed.
The magnetic drum is introduced as a data storage device.
Design for the first transistor at Bell Labs.

1948
Shannon publishes 'A Mathematical Theory of Communication'.
Manchester Mark I operational at Manchester University, UK.
EDSAC operational at Cambridge, UK.
The Hamming code is devised.

1949
Whirlwind goes into service at MIT.

1950
The Pilot ACE is completed at the NPL, UK.

1951
The first Univac I is delivered to the US Census Bureau.
David Wheeler, Maurice Wilkes and Stanley Gill introduce subprograms incorporating the 'Wheeler jump' mechanism.
Maurice Wilkes originates microprogramming.
Grace Murray Hopper develops the first compiler.

1952
EDVAC runs its first production program.
Illiac I is built at the University of Illinois.
von Neumann's bit-parallel machine is completed at Princeton.
Thomas J. Watson Jr becomes president of IBM.
Univac I predicts the outcome of the presidential election on TV.

1953
English Electric's LEO, a commercial version of EDSAC, goes into service for Lyons cafeterias.
The IBM 650 (Magnetic Drum Calculator) becomes the first mass-produced computer.
A Postgraduate Diploma in Computer Science is offered by the University of Cambridge, UK.

1957
Control Data incorporated.
John Backus and colleagues at IBM deliver the first Fortran compiler.

1958
Digital Equipment Corporation (DEC) is founded.

1959
The Codasyl committee is formed to create COBOL.
John McCarthy develops Lisp.

1960
Paul Baran at RAND develops the packet switching principle.
Algol 60 standards established by US and Europeans.
DEC introduces PDP-1, with a monitor and keyboard input.

1961
Fernando Corbato at MIT implements timesharing/multiaccess in CTSS.
IBM's Stretch (7030) completed.

1962
Atlas in the UK has paged virtual memory and pipelined operations.
Telstar satellite launched.
First video game.
Stanford and Purdue Universities establish departments of Computer Science.
Design and storage of synthesized music at Bell Labs.

1963

The ASCII 7-bit code becomes a standard.

1964

Seymour Cray's CDC 6600 achieves 9 megaflops – the first commercially successful supercomputer.
Doug Engelbart invents the mouse.
IBM announces (third generation) System/360.
IBM develops a CAD system.
IBM completes the Sabre airline reservation system.
BASIC is developed at Dartmouth by Kemeny and Kurtz.

1965

DEC introduces the PDP-8.
Project MAC embarks on the Multics operating system.
Maurice Wilkes proposes the use of a cache memory.

1967

Simula is developed.

1968

Burroughs introduces B2500 and B3500, the first computers to use integrated circuits.
Intel established by Noyce, Grove and Moore.
Seymour Cray's CDC 7600 achieves 40 megaflops.
The six-digit date format is established as a standard, ensuring a problem over year 2000.
Dijkstra invents semaphores for the THE operating system.

1969

The US Department of Defense commissions Arpanet for research networking. The first four nodes are UCLA, UC Santa Barbara, SRI and the University of Utah.

1970

UNIX developed at Bell Labs by Ritchie and Thomson (after withdrawing from the project MAC's Multics project in 1969).
Xerox PARC established for computer research.
Ted Codd defines the relational model.

1971

Niklaus Wirth develops Pascal.
First network email.
David Parnas defines the principle of information hiding.
Intel 4004 developed.

1972

DEC's PDP 11/45 is introduced.
Intel's 8008 and 8080 introduced, 8-bit microprocessors.
Prolog developed at the University of Marseilles.
Smalltalk developed at Xerox PARC.
C developed at Bell Labs.

1973

Robert Metcalfe describes the Ethernet as a modified Alohanet.
The Alto is developed at Xerox PARC.
Work begins on TCP.

1974

At Xerox PARC Charles Simonyi writes the first WYSIWYG (what you see is what you get) application.

1975

The first PC is available as a kit – the Altair 8800.
Fred Brookes writes *The Mythical Man-Month*.

1976

The Cray-1 vector/supercomputer is announced.
CP/M developed for 8-bit PCs.
OnTyme – the first commercial email service finds too few potential users.

Apple-I built by Steve Jobs and Steve Wozniak.

1977
Apple is formed and the Apple II establishes a personal computing environment.

Bill Gates and Paul Allen set up Microsoft, in Albuquerque, New Mexico.

1978
DEC introduces the VAX 11/780, a 32-bit computer.

Intel announces the 8086, its first 16-bit processor.

Wordstar becomes widely used on CP/M and later on DOS systems.

Rivest, Shamir and Adelman propose the RSA cipher as a public key cryptosystem for enciphering digital transmissions.

1979
Visicalc is unveiled – the first electronic spreadsheet.

Motorola introduces the MC68000, later to be used in the Macintosh.

1980
IBM selects PC-DOS from Microsoft as the operating system for its new PC.

David Patterson coins the term 'reduced instruction set computer' (RISC) in his work at Berkeley and develops the concept with John Hennessy of Stanford.

The Ada language emerges from the US Department of Defense. It is intended for process control and embedded applications.

DBase II is developed for the IBM PC.

1981
The open architecture IBM PC is launched.

Xerox introduces the Xerox Star. The Star then Viewpoint GUIs are developed.

1982
IBM PC clones are developed.

Autodesk is founded and AutoCAD is available.

John Warnock develops Postscript and with Charles Geschke founds Adobe Systems.

Japan launches its Fifth Generation project focusing on artificial intelligence.

Commercial email begins.

1983
The global internet is made by completion of the switchover to TCP/IP.

IBM PC-XT is available.

Lotus 1-2-3 is available for the IBM PC.

Apple's Lisa is launched.

1984
The Apple Macintosh is launched. MacPaint is available.

MIDI (Musical Instrument Digital Interface) standards are developed for interfacing computers and digital music synthesizers.

CD-ROM introduced by Sony and Philips.

1985
Microsoft Windows 1.0 is available for DOS-compatible computers.

The Inmos transputer is introduced.

Cray 2 and Thinking Machines' parallel processor Connection Machine is announced.

Intel introduces the 80 386 chip with 32-bit processing and on-board memory management.

PageMaker becomes the first desktop publishing program, first for the Macintosh and later for IBM compatibles.

1986
The term CASE (Computer Assisted Software Engineering) is popularized by a *Wall Street Journal* article.

1988
Motorola's 32-bit 88000 series of RISC processors is announced.
The internet worm program of graduate student Robert Morris Jr shows the need for better network security.

1989
Intel's 80486 chip is announced.

1990
Microsoft introduces Windows 3.0.
HP and IBM each announce RISC-based computers.
Intel's i486 and iPSC/860 become available.
Tim Berners-Lee writes the initial prototype for the World Wide Web.

1991
Cray Research unveils the Cray Y-MP C90 with 16 processors and a speed of 16 Gflops.
IBM, Motorola and Apple announce their PowerPC alliance.

1992
The first M-bone audio multicast is transmitted on the internet.
DEC introduces its first Alpha chip: a 64-bit RISC architecture.

1993
Apple releases the Newton, a personal digital assistant with a stylus pen.
Intel's Pentium is introduced.
The Mosaic browser is developed by NCSA (University of Illinois' National Center for Supercomputing).

1994
Jim Clark and Marc Andreesen found Netscape Communications.
Netscape's first browser becomes available.

1995
SUN Microsystems launches the Java programming language.
Microsoft Windows 95 is launched.

1996
The Intel Pentium Pro is announced.

A.2 Operating systems and distributed operating systems

The earliest computer systems had no operating systems. Programmers would book time on the computer or queue to use it. They would then read in their decks of cards or paper tapes and perhaps single-shot through the part of the program being debugged while watching the effect on the console display. The potential of computers for the business world was soon realized and the need for streamlining program execution became apparent.

One-at-a-time batch

During the 1960s computers were expensive and were located in air-conditioned machine rooms. The first operating systems were designed to run one program at once and the human was removed from the input process. The term SPOOL (simultaneous peripheral operation on line) was coined by IBM for a system in which a batch of jobs to be run was assembled on magnetic tape. The jobs were read into memory one at a time from the input spool and results were delivered to the output spool. This was faster than using other peripherals; a slower, less expensive computer could be used to generate the final output.

A one-day turnaround during program development and testing was deemed acceptable and the payroll program would run for many hours weekly. Although memory protection hardware would have been useful for this mode of operation to protect the operating system from the running program, early systems typically had no memory protection or relocation hardware. The operating system was frequently corrupted and had to be reloaded.

A.2.1 Multiprogramming batch

As technology improved, memory size increased, processors became faster and magnetic disks became available it was possible to give the operating system greater functionality. We still had batch working but multiprogramming batch operation became possible; that is, a number of programs could be in main memory at the same time. Each would run until it blocked for I/O when another program could take over to make use of this otherwise idle time. The batch of jobs could be input to disk, accessed in any order (unlike magnetic tape) and selected to run in memory. An aim was to achieve a good 'job mix' of jobs with varying resource requirements to avoid competition and make best use of the system's resources. This selection process was called high-level scheduling, as opposed to low-level or processor scheduling.

Note that memory protection is now essential to protect the operating system from the running programs and the programs from each other. It is no longer feasible to reload a corrupted operating system between jobs: jobs are continually terminating and being replaced from disk by other similar jobs. All multiprogramming systems had protection hardware; many did not have dynamic relocation hardware.

IBM OS/360 1964

IBM's OS/360 had two versions **MFT** (**multiple fixed task**) and **MVT** (**multiple variable tasks**), both requiring memory to be partitioned. Each program was assigned to a partition of memory in which it would always run. The partitions were associated with resources, for example, jobs requiring a large amount of memory and using magnetic tape, jobs of smaller size requiring some other peripherals and so on.

OS/360 (1964) was designed to run on a range of IBM machines, was written in assembler (as were all operating systems at the time), and was notoriously large. It had an extremely complex **job control language** (**JCL**) to allow for all possible options, which took weeks to learn. Over the years, the System 360 architecture evolved to the 370 series which finally provided virtual memory with segmentation and paging hardware and an address space per user. The operating system **MVS** is still basically a batch system but with some interactive use as an option: **time sharing option (TSO)**.

Atlas 1960

The Atlas computer was designed at the University of Manchester, UK in the late 1950s and early 1960s and ran at Manchester and London Universities (where I programmed it) as well as some government research laboratories. It was a spooled multiprogramming batch system as described above but also employed a magnetic drum; see below. It had several novel features which have since become standard; trap instructions were used for system calls (so-called extracodes) and device drivers were incorporated in the operating system.

Atlas memory management was remarkable in introducing paging hardware, virtual memory and demand paging from the 98K drum. The main (core) memory size was typically 16K. The page size was 512×48-bit words. The whole main memory was mapped in hardware in an associative memory (32 associative registers for a 16K memory). On a page fault a page replacement algorithm ran which could rely on one memory page being kept free so that the required page could be transferred in without delay.

Burroughs 1961

The Burroughs approach is worthy of note, the philosophy being to support the high-level language programmer. The architectures incorporated stack hardware (to mirror expression evaluation in languages such as Algol 60), and segmented memory management was used from the early 1960s.

A.2.2 Centralized time-sharing (interactive) systems

Batch operation works well for programs which run for a long time and change rarely. It is frustrating during the program development and testing period, since a small syntactic bug can mean a day or more wasted. As technology advanced computers became able to support interaction with users.

One model is a centralized system with an adequate supply of memory, good memory management hardware, plenty of file space, etc. The fact that humans type relatively slowly helped to make this mode of operation feasible. As communications improved users could logon from remote locations via dial-up lines and modems. Some early LAN-based systems used the LAN to provide access from terminals to centralized computer systems. The major new requirement was that the scheduling algorithm had to attempt to keep all the interactive users happy; thus time-slicing was invented. Some key system designs are outlined below but many others were developed, including Tops10 and Tenex for the DEC System10 (PDP 10), VMS for DEC VAXs and the Titan supervisor for the Atlas 2 computer at Cambridge University, UK.

CTSS 1962

The Compatible Time-Sharing System (CTSS) was designed at MIT (Corbato *et al.*, 1962). It ran on an IBM 7090 and was able to support up to 32 interactive users. The scheduling algorithm employed multi-level queueing; the time quantum associated with a queue doubled for each drop in priority level. The aim was to give high priority to interactive users who would run only for a short time and to allow compute-bound users to run for a reasonable time when the interactive users were all blocked. Memory management relied on swapping memory images rather than using demand paging hardware.

XDS 940, 1965

This was an interactive system designed at the University of California at Berkeley for a Rank Xerox machine (Lichtenberger and Pirtle, 1965). Although it had paging hardware for a 2K word page size, this was in the form of a memory map or hardware page table rather than making use of demand paging. When a process was running its entire page table had to be present in the hardware memory map, thus allowing dynamic address relocation. The memory map could contain entries for several processes and pages could be shared. The system was innovative in allowing any process to create subprocesses dynamically and supporting shared memory IPC between them.

THE 1968

THE design was described in detail in Chapter 10. The innovative aspect was the formalization of IPC through the definition of semaphores. The layered structure was also an attempt to master the complexity of operating systems and prove their correctness. Strict layering has not proved possible and modularity, especially through object orientation, has come to dominate. The process structure was static, unlike the other systems in this subsection.

Multics 1968

Multics was designed at MIT (Corbato and Vyssotski, 1965; Organick, 1972) as a natural successor to CTSS. It was funded under project MAC as a collaboration between MIT, GE, BBN and Bell Laboratories. The vision was a large time-sharing system that would offer continuous service. The hardware base was the specially developed GE645 which provided a large, paged and segmented virtual address space comprising an 18-bit segment number, a 16-bit word–offset and a 1K word page size. The operating system was written in a high-level language, PL/1.

A novel aspect was the integration of virtual memory with the filing system. A file became a segment when referenced and acquired a segment number dynamically. The design aim was to support full generality of file/segment sharing between processes. Process scheduling was similar to CTSS, with a multi-level queue structure.

A great deal of attention was paid to protection. As well as a flexible access control list specification for files, the hardware supported nested protection domains or rings. Sixty-four rings were envisaged but the operational system had eight. The innermost levels were used for highly privileged kernel functions such as interrupt servicing and process dispatching; outer levels were used for less sensitive functions. The operating system ran in-process, was invoked procedurally and inward ring crossing was monitored through hardware traps. Several levels were available for applications so that, for example, an instructor could assign software to examine students to a number of rings. The software to record the score could be made inaccessible to the software to test the student except through standard entry points.

MU5 1969

Various research machines were built at Manchester University, UK, including the Mark 1 in the late 1940s, Atlas in 1960 and a Dataflow machine in the 1980s. Research Machine 5 (MU5) (Morris and Detlefsen, 1969; Morris and Ibett, 1979) was built to explore paged, segmented memory management and included an early example of what would now be called an inverted page table. The use of large numbers of segments per process and the ability to share them was explored. The design was based on segment numbers rather than names (as in Multics) and naming conventions were necessary if renumbering was to be avoided. MU5 also employed message passing for IPC. The MU5 design was influential on **ICL's 2900** and the **George III** operating system.

UNIX 1970

UNIX was designed initially as a personal computing environment but soon came to implement time-sharing. The original design decisions on IPC have been used throughout the book as examples and a short case study was given as Section 12.9. A full case study can be found as Chapter 23 in the second edition of this book (Bacon, 1998).

RC4000 1973

The aim here was to provide a nucleus on which any kind of operating system could be built (Brinch Hansen, 1970). The hardware platform was the Danish Regnecentralen RC4000. The nucleus supported processes and message-based IPC. In this early system messages were fixed length (8 words) and the same message was used for a reply as that for the original request. Input and output was unified as message passing between processes and device drivers. A process could create subprocesses dynamically and allocate its resources among them.

Capability architectures

The focus here is on capability-based addressing for a secure environment. The designs can be seen as a generalization of the Multics ring structure (nested protection domains). The aim was to design general, hardware-enforced, domain-structured systems with capability-controlled domain entry. Examples include the **Plessey PP250** (England, 1972), **CAP** at Cambridge University, UK (Needham and Walker, 1977), the **Intel iAPX 432, Hydra** for **C.mmp** and StarOS for **Cm*** at Carnegie Mellon University. In general, the slow performance was found to be too great a penalty to pay for the enhanced security. Also, the advent of distributed systems meant that capabilities had to be transferred across the network (protected by encryption) rather than protected by hardware within a single system and the design emphasis changed.

A.2.3 Workstations and personal computers

During the 1970s and 1980s we saw the centralized time-sharing system replaced as the normal mode of computing provision by personal workstations. The workplace environment came to comprise a computer on the desk with a network connection and services such as printing and filing provided across the network.

We must now consider more than a single computer. During the 1970s at Xerox Palo Alto Research Center (**Xerox PARC**) researchers were given an environment comprising an **Ethernet LAN, Alto** workstations running the **Pilot** operating system (Lampson and Sproull, 1979; Redell *et al.*, 1980) and various shared servers such as the **XDFS** (Xerox Distributed File System) (Mitchell and Dion, 1982). For the first time, users were not constantly aware of the OS interface since a window-based GUI was provided above it. The work on the user interface at Xerox PARC was used as a basis for that of the Apple Macintosh personal computer. Distributed systems such as the **Grapevine** message passing and registration service (Birrell *et al.*, 1982) were built above this base.

The designers of Pilot used the term 'open operating system' for the concept that evolved into the microkernel approach to operating system design. The OS should support efficiently not only users developing and running programs but also shared servers and communications gateways. A common core should be provided.

UNIX was designed as a personal environment, was extended for centralized time-sharing systems and is now used in many workstations. As technology has developed workstations have become able to support a single local user and remote users simultaneously. There are many versions of UNIX.

Operating systems for LAN-based distributed systems include:

CDCS (Cambridge Distributed Computing System) (Needham and Herbert, 1982);
Thoth at the University of Waterloo, Ontario (Gentleman, 1981);
V system at Stanford (Cheriton, 1984);
Apollo Domain (Leach *et al.*, 1983);
Newcastle Connection (Brownbridge *et al.*, 1982);
Mach from Carnegie Mellon University (Rashid, 1986);
CHORUS from INRIA (Rozier *et al.*, 1988);
Amoeba at the Vrije Universiteit Amsterdam (Tanenbaum *et al.*, 1990);
Plan9 from Bell (Pike *et al.*, 1990; 1991).

A great deal of research effort has been directed towards applying object-oriented design principles to the internals of operating systems. Most of this effort has been by research teams at academic institutions, for example:

Clouds at the Georgia Institute of Technology (Dasgupta *et al.*, 1991);
Emerald at the University of Washington (Black *et al.*, 1986; 1987);
Choices at the University of Illinois (Campbell *et al.*, 1992);
Lipto at the University of Arizona (Druschel *et al.*, 1992);
Tigger at Trinity College Dublin, Ireland (Cahill, 1996).

Others, at government research institutions include:

Peace, at GMD, Germany (Schroeder-Preikschat, 1994);
Soul at INRIA, France (Shapiro, 1991).

A team at SUN Microsystems designed **Spring** (Hamilton and Kougiouris, 1993).
Personal computers had to be as inexpensive as possible. The OS had to fit into a small amount of memory, and features such as protected address spaces were inappropriate for this environment. Typically the operating system and all user-level software would run without restriction in a single address space; the OS could be corrupted and the user would have to reboot. The filing system was based on the assumption of a single owner; protection was not an issue. Examples are **CP/M** for early, 8-bit microprocessors, **MacOS** for Apple computers and **MS-DOS**, then **Windows 95** for IBM-compatible PCs. IBM's **OS/2** (Cook and Rawson, 1988) has been overtaken in popularity by Microsoft's **Windows NT** (Solomon, 1998). NT has an object-oriented design, offers protected address spaces, supports a multi-user filing system and is capable of running a broad range of applications, thus extending the scope of PC software.

 A.3 Databases

The field of database is large and, in this integrated approach to software systems design, we have focused on object data modelling, transaction processing, concurrency control, recovery, distribution and the requirements a database system imposes on the underlying operating system. We have not studied earlier approaches to data modelling and query language design. A very brief historical development is given here but a specialist database text should be consulted for background reading (Date, 1995; Korth and Silberschatz, 1991). Bell and Grimson (1992) focus on distributed database systems. Collections of papers edited by leading database researchers are Mylopoulos and Brodie (1989), Zdonik and Maier (1990) and Stonebraker (1994). Database products for microcomputers include **dBaseIII**; a spreadsheet/database product is **Lotus 1-2-3**.

Before the 1970s database functionality was achieved by indexed access to files structured as fixed-length records with file and record locking used to achieve concurrency control. During the 1970s complete DBMSs became available, based on the hierarchical (**IBM's IMS**) and network data models; that is links were used to create hierarchical structures of records. Record-level access control was imposed and the theory of transactions, with concurrency control and recovery as described in Part III of this book, began to emerge. A database became a general, linked, multifile structure.

Codd's classic paper in 1970 (Codd, 1970) introduced the **relational data model** and by the 1980s commercial relational DBMSs were available together with transactions and high-level query languages, such as **SQL** (structured query language), defined by ANSI in 1984 and described in Date (1987). Examples of relational systems are **INGRES**, from the University of California at Berkeley (Stonebraker, 1976; 1980) and **System R** from IBM San José (Astrahan *et al.*, 1976). **System R*** extended the project to a distributed database (Williams *et al.*, 1982).

The functional data model and related query languages emerged during the 1980s (Shipman, 1981; Buneman *et al.*, 1982).

In 1989 'The object-oriented database system manifesto' was published (Atkinson *et al.*, 1989) and in 1990 the 'Third generation database system manifesto'. There was general agreement on the directions in which DBMSs needed to move. The **ODMG-93** standard was a swift response to the two manifestos. The authors worked within the general framework of the Object Management Group (OMG), although as an independent consortium, the Object Database Management Group. Other OMG initiatives such as the object management architecture and CORBA are described in Chapter 24. The first edition of the ODMG standard was quite heavily criticized and a second edition is now available (Cattell, 1996). Cattell (1991) gives an excellent overview of object-oriented database systems.

Object-oriented databases have been designed and implemented during the 1990s but commercial systems still tend to follow the relational model. Some object-oriented systems with references are as follows:

Camelot (Spector *et al.*, 1986);
Gemstone (Bretl *et al.*, 1988);
IRIS (Fishman *et al.*, 1987);
O₂ (Bancilhon *et al.*, 1988);
ObjectStore;
ONTOS;
POSTGRES (Stonebraker and Rowe, 1986);
Starburst (Schwarz *et al.*, 1986).

Bibliography

Abrossimov V., Rozier M. and Gien M. (1989a). Virtual memory management in CHORUS. In *Proc. Progress in Distributed Operating Systems and Distributed Systems Management*, Berlin 1989. *Lecture Notes in Computer Science* **433**, pp. 45–59. Berlin: Springer Verlag.

Abrossimov V., Rozier M. and Shapiro M. (1989b). Generic virtual memory management in operating systems kernels. In *Proc. 12th ACM Symposium on Operating Systems Principles*, Dec. 1989.

ACM (1996). ACM OOPS Messenger. Special issue on object-oriented, real-time systems. January 1996.

Adly N., Bacon J.M. and Nagy M. (1995). Performance evaluation of a hierarchical replication protocol: synchronous versus asynchronous. *Proc. IEEE SDNE Services in Distributed and Networked Environments*, pp. 102–9, Whistler, British Columbia.

Adly N., Nagy M. and Bacon J.M. (1993). A hierarchical, asynchronous replication protocol for large scale systems. *Proc. IEEE PADS*, Princeton, New Jersey.

Aho A.V., Hopcroft J.E. and Ullman J.D. (1983). *Data Structures and Algorithms*. Reading MA: Addison-Wesley.

Aho A.V., Sethi R. and Ullman J.D. (1986). *Compilers: Principles, Techniques and Tools*. Reading MA: Addison-Wesley.

Almasi G.S. and Gottlieb A. (1989). *Highly Parallel Computing*. Redwood City CA: Benjamin/Cummings.

Almes G.T. (1985). The Eden System, a technical overview. *IEEE Trans SE* **11**(1).

AMD (1985). Advanced Micro Devices, Local Area Network Controller (Lance) *Am7990*.

Anderson R. (2001). *Security Engineering, A guide to building dependable distributed systems*. New York: Wiley.

Anderson T.E., Bershad B.N., Lazowska E.D. and Levy H.M. (1992). Scheduler activations: effective kernel support for the user-level management of parallelism. *ACM Trans. on Computer Systems* **10**(1).

Andrews G.R. (1991). *Concurrent Programming, Principles and Practice*. Redwood City CA: Benjamin/Cummings.

Andrews G.R. and Schneider F.B. (1983). Concepts and notations for concurrent programming. *ACM Computing Surveys* **15**(1).

ANSA (1989). *The Advanced Networks Systems Architecture (ANSA) Reference Manual.* Castle Hill, Cambridge, UK: Architecture Projects Management.

Arnold K. and Gosling J. (1996). *The Java Programming Language.* Reading MA: Addison Wesley Longman.

Astrahan M. *et al.* (1976). System R: A relational approach to database management. *ACM TODS* **1**(2), 97–137.

Atkinson M., Chisholm K. and Cockshot P. (1982). PS-algol: An Algol with a persistent heap. *ACM SIGPLAN Notices* **17**(7), 24–31.

Atkinson M.P., Bancillon F., DeWitt D., Dittrich K. and Zdonik S.B. (1989). The object oriented database manifesto. *Proc. 1st International Conference on Deductive and Object Oriented Databases*, Kyoto.

Atkinson M.P. (1996). Draft Pjava design 1.2. University of Glasgow, Department of Computer Science.

Bach M.J. (1986). *The Design of the UNIX Operating System.* Englewood Cliffs NJ: Prentice-Hall.

Bacon J.M. (1998). *Concurrent Systems*, 2nd edn. Harlow: Addison-Wesley.

Bacon J.M. and Hamilton K.G. (1987). Distributed computing with RPC: the Cambridge approach. In *Proc. IFIPS Conference on Distributed Processing* (Barton M. *et al.*, eds.). Amsterdam: North-Holland.

Bacon J.M., Leslie I.M. and Needham R.M. (1989). Distributed computing with a processor bank. In *Proc. Progress in Distributed Operating Systems and Distributed Systems Management*, Berlin 1989. *Lecture Notes in Computer Science* **433**, pp. 147–61. Berlin: Springer Verlag.

Badrinath B.R. and Ramamritham K. (1992). Semantics based concurrency control: beyond commutativity. *ACM Trans. on Database Systems* **17**(1), 163–99.

Baker M., Asami S., Deprit E., Ousterhout J. and Seltzer M. (1992). Non-volatile memory for fast, reliable file systems. *ACM Fifth International Conference on Architectural Support for Programming Languages and Operating Systems*, ASPLOS 92, 10–22.

Ball J.E., Feldman J.A., Low J.R., Rashid R.F. and Rovner P.D. (1976). RIG, Rochester's Intelligent Gateway, System Overview. *IEEE Trans SE* **2**(4), 321–8.

Balter R., Cahill V., Harris N. and Rousset de Pina X. (eds.) (1993). *The Comandos Distributed Application Platform.* Berlin: Springer Verlag.

Bancilhon F. *et al.* (1988). The design and implementation of O_2, an object oriented DBMS. In K.R. Dittrich (ed.) *Advances in Object Oriented Database Systems, Second Workshop on OODBMS*, Bad Munster, Germany *Lecture Notes in Computer Science* **334**. Berlin: Springer-Verlag.

Barton Davies P., McNamee D., Vaswani R. and Lazowska E. (1993). Adding scheduler activations to Mach 3.0. *Proc. 3rd Mach Symposium*, pp. 119–36, USENIX Association.

Bayer R., Graham R.M. and Seegmuller G., eds. (1978). Operating Systems – An Advanced Course. *Lecture Notes in Computer Science* **60**. Berlin: Springer Verlag.

Bell (1978). *Bell Systems Technical Journal*, Special Issue on UNIX 57(6), part 2.

Bell D. and Grimson J. (1992). *Distributed Database Systems.* Wokingham: Addison-Wesley.

Ben Ari M. (1990). *Principles of Concurrent and Distributed Programming.* Englewood Cliffs NJ: Prentice-Hall.

Bensoussan A., Clingen C.T. and Daley R.C. (1972). The Multics virtual memory: concepts and design. *Comm*. ACM **15**(5), 308–18.

Bernstein P.A. (1990). Transaction processing monitors. *Comm*. ACM **33**(11).

Bernstein P.A., Hadzilacos V. and Goodman N. (1987). *Concurrency Control and Recovery in Database Systems*. Reading MA: Addison-Wesley.

Bershad B.N., Anderson T.E., Lazowska E.D. and Levy H.M. (1990). Lightweight remote procedure call. *ACM Trans. on Computer Systems* **8**(1).

Bertsekas D.P. and Tsitsiklis J.N. (1989). *Parallel and Distributed Computation, Numerical Methods*. Englewood Cliffs NJ: Prentice-Hall.

Birman K. (1985). Replication and fault tolerance in the ISIS system. In *ACM 10th Symposium on Operating Systems Principles*, Dec.

Birman K.P. (1993). The process group approach to reliable distributed computing. *Comm ACM* **36**(12), 36–53.

Birman K.P. and Joseph T.A. (1987). Reliable communication in the presence of failures. *ACM TOCS* **5**(1), 47–76.

Birman K.P., Schiper A. and Stephenson A. (1991). Lighweight causal and atomic group multicast. *ACM TOCS* **9**(3) 272–314.

Birrell A.D. (1991). An introduction to programming with threads. In Nelson G., ed., *Systems Programming with Modula-3*. Englewood Cliffs NJ: Prentice-Hall.

Birrell A.D. and Needham R.M. (1980). A universal file server. *IEEE Trans. SE* **SE-6**(5).

Birrell A.D. and Nelson B.J. (1986). Implementing remote procedure calls. *ACM Trans. on Computer Systems* **2**(1).

Birrell A.D., Levin R., Needham R.M. and Schroeder M.D. (1982). Grapevine: an exercise in distributed computing. *Comm. ACM* **25**(4), 260–74.

Black A., Hutchinson E.J., Levy H. and Carter L. (1986). Object structure in the Emerald system. In *Proc. Conference on Object Oriented Programming Systems*. October 1986 and *ACM SIGPLAN Notices* **21**(11).

Black A., Hutchinson N., Jul E., Levy H. and Carter L. (1987). Distribution and abstract types in Emerald. *IEEE Trans. SE* **SE-13**(1), 65–76.

Booch G., Rumbaugh I. and Jacobson J. (1999). *Unified Modelling Language User Guide*. Reading MA: Addison-Wesley.

Bretl R., Maier D., Otis A., Penney J., Schuchardt B., Stein J., Williams H. and Williams M. (1988). The Gemstone data management system. In W. Kim and F.H. Lochovsky (eds) *Object Oriented Concepts, Databases and Applications*. Reading MA: Addison-Wesley.

Brinch Hansen P. (1970). The nucleus of a multiprogramming system. *Comm. ACM* **13**(4).

Brinch Hansen P. (1973a). *Operating System Principles*. Englewood Cliffs NJ: Prentice-Hall.

Brinch Hansen P. (1973b). Concurrent programming concepts. *ACM Computing Surveys* **5**(4).

Brinch Hansen P. (1977). *The Architecture of Concurrent Programs*. Englewood Cliffs NJ: Prentice-Hall.

Brinch Hansen P. (1978). Distributed processes: A concurrent programming concept. *Comm. ACM* **21**(11).

Brownbridge D.R., Marshall L.F. and Randell B. (1982). The Newcastle connection, or UNIXs of the world unite! *Software, Practice and Experience* **12**, 1147–62.

Buneman P., Fraenkel R.E. and Nikhil R. (1982). Implementation techniques for database query languages. *ACM TODS* **7**(2), 164–86.

Burns A. (1988). *Programming in occam 2*. Wokingham: Addison-Wesley.

Burns A. and Davies G.L. (1993). *Concurrent Programming*. Wokingham: Addison-Wesley.

Burns A. and Wellings A. (1989). *Real-Time Systems and their Programming Languages*. Wokingham: Addison-Wesley.

Burr W.E. (1986). The FDDI optical data link. *IEEE Communication Magazine* **25**(5).

Bustard D., Elder J. and Welsh J. (1988). *Concurrent Program Structures*. Englewood Cliffs NJ: Prentice-Hall.

Bux W., Janson P.A., Kummerle K., Muller H.R. and Rothauser E.H. (1982). A local area communication network based on a reliable token ring system. In *Proc. IFIP TCG Symposium on LANs*, Florence (Ravasio P.C., Hopkins G. and Naffah H., eds.). Amsterdam: North-Holland.

Cahill V. (1996). An overview of the Tigger object-support operating system framework, in *SOFSEM 96: Theory and Practice of Informatics*, K.G. Jeffery, J. Kral and M. Bartovsek (eds.) LNCS 1175, pp. 34–55, Berlin/Heidelberg: Springer-Verlag.

Campbell R.H. and Haberman N.A. (1974). *The Specification of Process Synchronization by Path Expressions. Lecture Notes in Computer Science* **16**. Berlin: Springer Verlag.

Campbell R.H. and Kolstad R.B. (1980). An overview of Path Pascal's design and Path Pascal user manual. *ACM SIGPLAN notices* **15**(9).

Campbell R.H., Islaam N. and Madany P. (1992). Choices, frameworks and refinement. *Computing Systems* **5**(3), 217–57.

Campione M. and Walrath K. (1996). *The Java Tutorial: Object-Oriented Programming for the Internet*. Reading MA: Addison Wesley Longman.

Carriero N. and Gelernter D. (1989). Linda in context. *Comm. ACM* **32**(4).

Cattell R.G.G. (1991). *Object Data Management: Object-Oriented and Extended Relational Database Systems*. Reading MA: Addison-Wesley.

Cattell R.G.G. (1996). *The Object Database Standard: ODMG-93 (Release 1.2)*. San Mateo CA: Morgan-Kaufmann.

Cellary W., Gelenbe E. and Morzy T. (1988). *Concurrency Control in Distributed Database Systems*. Amsterdam: North Holland.

CCITT (1998a) Recommendation X.500: The Directory – Overview of concepts, models and service. International Telecommunications Union, Place des nations 1211, Geneva, Switzerland.

CCITT (1998b) Recommendation X.500: The Directory – Authentication framework. International Telecommunications Union, Place des nations 1211, Geneva, Switzerland.

Ceri S. and Pelagatti G. (1984). *Distributed Databases, Principles and Systems*. New York: McGraw-Hill.

Cheriton D.R. (1984). The V kernel, a software base for distributed systems. *IEEE Software* **1**(2).

Cheriton D.R. and Zwaenpoel W. (1985). Distributed process groups in the V kernel. *ACM Trans. on Computer Systems* **3**(2).

Chou W., ed. (1977). *Computer Communications Vol II: Systems and Applications.* Englewood Cliffs NJ: Prentice-Hall.

Ciminiera L. and Valenzano A. (1987). *Advanced Microprocessor Architectures.* Wokingham: Addison-Wesley.

Clamen S.M. (1991). Data persistence in programming languages, a survey. TR CMU-CS-91-155. Dept. Comp. Sci., Carnegie-Mellon University, May.

Cockshot P., Atkinson M., Chisholm K., Bailey P. and Morrison R. (1984). Persistent object management systems. *Software Practice and Experience* **14**, 49–71.

Codd E.F. (1970). A relational model for large shared data banks. *Comm. ACM* **13**(6).

Coffman E.G. Jr., Elphick M.J. and Shoshani A. (1971). System deadlocks. *ACM Computing Surveys* **3**(2).

Comer D.E. (1991). *Internetworking with TCP/IP: Principles, Protocols and Architecture*, Vol. 1, 2nd edn. Englewood Cliffs NJ: Prentice-Hall.

Cook R.L. and Rawson F.L. III (1988). The design of OS/2. *IBM Systems Journal* **27**(2), 90–104.

Cooper E.C. and Draves R.P. (1987). *C Threads.* Technical Report, Carnegie-Mellon University.

Corbato F.J. and Vyssotsky V.A. (1965). Introduction and overview of the Multics system. In *Proc. AFIPS FJCC.*

Corbato F.J., Merwin-Daggett M. and Daley R.C. (1962). An experimental time-sharing system. *Proc. AFIPS*, Fall JCC, pp. 335–44.

Coulouris G.F., Dollimore J. and Kindberg T. (2001). *Distributed Systems, Concepts and Design*, 3rd edn. Harlow: Addison-Wesley.

Cristian F. (1989a). A probabilistic approach to distributed clock synchronization. In *Proc. IEEE 9th International Conference on Distributed Computing Systems (ICDCS)*, June 1989.

Cristian F. (1989b). Probabilistic clock synchronization. *Distributed Computing* **3**(3), 146–58.

Custer H. (1993). *Inside Windows NT.* Microsoft Press.

Custer H. (1994). *Inside Windows NT File System.* Microsoft Press.

Dasgupta P., LeBlanc Jr. R.J., Ahmad M. and Ramachandran U. (1991). The Clounds distributed operating system. *IEEE Computer* **24**(11), 34–44.

Date C.J. (1983, 1995). *An Introduction to Database Systems*, Vol. 1, 6th edn. (1995), Vol. 2 (1983). Reading MA: Addison-Wesley.

Date C.J. (1987). *A Guide to the SQL Standard.* Reading MA: Addison-Wesley.

Davari S. and Sha L. (1992). Sources of unbounded priority inversion in real-time systems and a comparative study of possible solutions. *ACM Operating Systems Review* **26**(2).

Davies D.W. and Price W.L. (1984). *Security for Computer Networks.* Chichester: Wiley.

DEC (1986). *DEQNA Ethernet: User's Guide.* Digital Equipment Corporation.

Denning P.J., Comer D.E., Gries D., Mulder M., Tucker A., Turner A.J. and Young P.R. (1989). Computing as a discipline. *Comm. ACM* **32**(1).

Dietel H.M. and Dietel P.J. (2002). *Java: How to Program*. 4th edn. Prentice-Hall International.

Diffie W. and Helman M.E. (1976). New directions in cryptography. *IEEE Trans. on Information Theory* **IT-22**, pp. 644–54.

Dijkstra E.W. (1965). Solution of a problem in concurrent programming control. *Comm. ACM* **8**(9).

Dijkstra E.W. (1968). The structure of THE operating system. *Comm. ACM* **11**(5).

Dijkstra E.W. (1975). Guarded commands, nondeterminacy and the formal derivation of programs. *Comm. ACM* **18**(8).

Dion J. (1980). The Cambridge File Server. ACM *Operating Systems Review* **14**(4).

Dowsing R. (1988). *An Introduction to Concurrency using occam*. London: Van Nostrand Reinhold.

Druschel P., Peterson L.L. and Hutchinson N.C. (1992). Beyond microkernel design: Decoupling modularity and protection in Lipto. *Proc. IEEE ICDCS*, pp. 512–20.

Eisenberg M.A. and McGuire M.R. (1972). Further comments on Dijkstra's concurrent programming control problem. *Comm. ACM* **15**(11).

Ellison C., Frantz B., Lampson B., Rivest R., Thomas B. and Ylonen T. (1999). SPKI Certificate Theory. Internet RFC 2693, September 1999.

Emmerich W. (2000). *Engineering Distributed Objects*. Chichester: Wiley.

England D.M. (1972). Architectural features of the System 250. *Proc. International Switching Symposium*, pp. 1–10.

Farber D.J., Feldman J., Heinrich F.R., Hopwood M.D., Larsen K.C., Loomis D.C. and Rowe L.A. (1973). The distributed computing system. In *Proc. 7th IEEE Comp. Soc. Int. Conf. (COMPCON)*, February 1973.

Fishman D. *et al.* (1987). IRIS: An object oriented database management system. *ACM Trans. on Office Information Systems* **5**(1).

Fishwick P. (1995). *Simulation Model Design and Execution*. Englewood Cliffs NJ: Prentice-Hall.

Fitzgerald R. and Rashid R.F. (1987). The integration of virtual memory and IPC in Accent. In *Proc. 10th ACM Symposium on Operating Systems Principles*, Dec. 1987.

Gelernter D. (1985). Generative communication in Linda. *ACM Trans. Prog. Lang. and Sys.* **7**(1).

Gentleman W.M. (1981). Message passing between sequential processes, the reply primitive and the administrator concept. *Software Practice and Experience* **11**(5), 435–66.

Gibbs S. and Tsichritzis D. (1994). *Multimedia Programming*. Wokingham: ACM Press/Addison-Wesley.

Gilman L. and Schreiber R. (1996). *Distributed Computing with IBM MQSeries*. New York: Wiley.

Gingell R.A., Moran J.P. and Shannon W.A. (1987). Virtual memory architecture in SunOS. *Proc. USENIX Assoc.* 81–94.

Gleeson T.J. (1989). *Aspects of Abstraction in Computing*. PhD Thesis, University of Cambridge.

Gomaa H. (1993). *Software Design Methods for Concurrent and Real-time Systems*. Wokingham: Addison-Wesley.

Goodenough J.B. and Sha L. (1988). The priority ceiling protocol: a method for minimising the blocking of high priority Ada tasks. *Ada Letters, Special Issue: Proc. 2nd International Workshop on Real-Time Ada Issues VIII*, 7, Fall 1988.

Gray J., ed. (1991). *The Benchmark Handbook for Database and Transaction Processing Systems*. San Mateo CA: Morgan Kaufmann.

Gray J. and Reuter A. (1993). *Transaction Processing: Concepts and Techniques*. San Mateo CA: Morgan Kaufmann.

Greaves D.J., Lioupis D. and Hopper A. (1990). *The Cambridge Backbone Ring*. Olivetti Research Ltd. Cambridge, Technical Report 2. Feb.

Guerni M., Ferrie J. and Pons J-F. (1995). Concurrency and recovery for typed objects using a new commutativity relation. *Proc. 4th International Conference on Deductive and Object Oriented Databases*, Singapore.

Gusella R. and Zatti S. (1989). The accuracy of clock synchronization achieved by TEMPO in Berkeley UNIX 4.3BSD. *IEEE Trans. Software Engineering* 15(7), 847–53.

Habert S., Mosseri L. and Abrossimov V. (1990). COOL: kernel support for object-oriented environments. *Proc. ECOOP/OOPSLA*, Oct. 1990.

Halsall F. (1996). *Data Communications, Computer Networks and OSI*, 4th edn. Wokingham: Addison-Wesley.

Hamilton G. and Kougiouris P. (1993). The Spring Nucleus: A microkernel for objects. *Proc. 1993 Summer USENIX Conference*, USENIX Association.

Hayes I., ed. (1987). *Specification Case Studies*. Englewood Cliffs NJ: Prentice-Hall.

Hennessy J.L. and Patterson D.A. (1996). *Computer Architecture, A Quantitative Approach*, 2nd edn. San Mateo CA: Morgan Kaufmann.

Herlihy M. (1990). Apologizing versus asking permission: optimistic concurrency control for abstract data types. *ACM Transactions on Database Systems* 15(1).

Hoare C.A.R. (1974). Monitors: an operating system structuring concept. *Comm. ACM* 17(10).

Hoare C.A.R. (1978). Communicating sequential processes. *Comm. ACM* 21(8).

Hoare C.A.R. (1985). *Communicating Sequential Processes*. Englewood Cliffs NJ: Prentice-Hall.

Hopper A. (1990). Pandora – an experimental system for multimedia applications. *ACM Operating Systems Review* 24(2).

Hopper A. and Needham R.M. (1988). The Cambridge Fast Ring networking system. *IEEE Trans. Computers* 37(10).

Hopper A., Temple S. and Williamson R. (1986). *Local Area Network Design*. Wokingham: Addison-Wesley.

Horn C. and Krakowiak S. (1987). Object Oriented Architecture for Distributed Office Systems. In *Proc 1987 ESPRIT Conference*. Amsterdam: North-Holland.

Humphrey W. (1995). *A Discipline for Software Engineering*. Wokingham: Addison-Wesley.

IEEE (1988). *IEEE Standard Portable Operating System Interface for Computer Environments (POSIX)*. IEEE 1003.1.

IEEE (1996). *50 years of computing*. *IEEE Computer*, October 1996.

IEEE (2002). *Pervasive Computing* **1**(1), January–March 2002, IEEE Computer Society

Inmos (1984). *occam Programming Manual*. Englewood Cliffs NJ: Prentice-Hall.

ISO (1981). *ISO Open Systems Interconnection, Basic Reference Model*. ISO 7498.

ISO (1986). *OSI: Specification of Abstract Syntax Notation 1 (ASN.1)*. ISO 8824.2.

ISO (1992). *Basic Reference Model of Open Distributed Processing*. ISO 10746.

ISO/IEC (1986). *Standard Generalized Markup Language* (SGML).

ISO/IEC (1992) *Entity Authentication Mechanisms Using Symmetric Techniques*. ISO/IEC 9798.

ITU/ISO (1997). Recommendation X.500 (08/97): *Open Systems Interconnection – The Directory: Overview of concepts, models and services*. International Telecommunications Union.

Jacky J. (1990). Risks in medical electronics. *Comm. ACM* **33**(12).

Johnson S. (1994). Objecting to objects. Invited Talk, USENIX Technical Conference, San Francisco CA, January.

Joseph M. (1992). *Problems, Promises and Performance: Some Questions for Real-Time System Specification*. *Lecture Notes in Computer Science* **600**, p. 315. Berlin: Springer Verlag.

Joseph M., ed. (1996). *Real-time Systems, Specification, Verification and Analysis*. UK: Prentice-Hall.

Kane G. and Heinrich J. (1992). *MIPS RISC Architecture*. Englewood Cliffs NJ: Prentice-Hall.

Khanna S., Sebree M. and Zolnowskey J. (1992). Real-time scheduling on SunOS 5.0. *Proc. USENIX*. Winter 1992.

Khoshafian S. (1993). *Object-oriented Databases*. Chichester: Wiley.

Kilburn T., Edwards D.B.G., Lanigan M.J. and Sumner F.H. (1962). One level storage systems. *IRE Trans. Electronic Computers* **EC**(11), April 1962.

Knapp E. (1987). Deadlock detection in distributed databases. *ACM Computing Surveys*, **19**(4), 303–28.

Kogan M.S. and Rawson S.L. III (1990). The design of Operating System/2. *IBM Systems Journal* **27**(2), 90–104.

Kohl J. and Neuman C. (1993). The Kerberos Network Authentication Service (V5). Internet RFC 1510, September 1993.

Korth H.F. and Silberschatz A. (1991). *Database System Concepts*, 2nd edn. New York: McGraw-Hill.

Korth H.F., Kim W. and Bancilhon F. (1990). On long-duration CAD transactions. In *Readings on Object-Oriented Database Systems* (Zdonik S.B. and Maier D., eds.). San Mateo CA: Morgan Kaufmann.

Lai W.S. (1982). Protocol traps in computer networks. *IEEE Trans. Commun.* **30**(6).

Lai X. and Massey J. (1990). A proposal for a new Block Encryption Standard. In *Proceedings, Advances in Cryptology, Eurocrypt 1990*, pp. 389–404. Berlin: Springer Verlag.

Lamport L. (1974). A new solution of Dijkstra's concurrent programming problem. *Comm. ACM* **17**(8).

Lamport L. (1978). Time, clocks and the ordering of events in a distributed system. *Comm. ACM* **21**(7).

Lamport L. (1987). A fast mutual exclusion algorithm. *ACM Trans. on Computer Systems* **5**(1).

Lamport L. (1990). Concurrent reading and writing of clocks. *ACM Trans. on Computer Systems* **8**(4).

Lamport L., Shostak R. and Peace M. (1982). The Byzantine Generals Problem. ACM *Trans. on Prog. Lang. and Systems* **4**(3).

Lampson B. (1981). Atomic transactions. In *Distributed Systems: Architecture and Implementation. Lecture Notes in Computer Science* **105**, 246–65. Berlin: Springer Verlag.

Lampson B. (1986). Designing a global name service. In *Proc. 5th ACM Symposium on Principles of Distributed Computing*.

Lampson B. and Sproull R.F. (1979). An open operating system for a single user machine. In *ACM 7th Symposium on Operating System Principles*, Dec. 1979.

Lantz K.A., Gradischnig K.D., Feldman J.A. and Rashid R.F. (1982). Rochester's Intelligent Gateway. *Computer* **15**(10), 54–68.

Lauer H.C. and Needham R.M. (1978). On the duality of system structures. *ACM Operating Systems Review* **13**(2).

Lea D. (1999). *Concurrent Programming in Java*, 2nd edn. Reading MA: Addison Wesley Longman.

Leach P.J., Levine P.H., Douros B.P., Hamilton J.A., Nelson D.L. and Stumpf B.L. (1983). The architecture of an integrated local network. *IEEE Journal on Selected Areas in Communications* **SAC-1**(5), 842–56.

Leffler S.J., McKusick M.K., Karels M.J. and Quarterman J.S. (1989). *The Design and Implementation of the 4.3 BSD UNIX Operating System*. Reading MA: Addison-Wesley.

Leslie I.M., McAuley D., Black R., Roscoe T., Barham P., Evers D., Fairbairns R. and Hyden E. (1996). The design and implementation of an operating system to support distributed multimedia applications. *ACM Journal of Selected Areas in Communication* **SAC14**(7), 1280–97.

Leslie I.M., Needham R.M., Burren J.W. and Adams G.C. (1984). The architecture of the UNIVERSE network. *Proc. ACM SIGCOMM '84*, **14**(2).

Levi S-T. and Agrawala A. (1990). *Real-time System Design*. New York: McGraw-Hill.

Li G.X. (1993). *Supporting Distributed Realtime Computing*. PhD Thesis, University of Cambridge and TR 322.

Lichtenberger W.W. and Pirtle M.W. (1965). A facility for experimentation in man–machine interaction. *Proc. AFIPS FJCC*, pp. 589–98.

Littlewood B. and Strigini L. (1992). *Validation of Ultra-High Dependability for Software-based Systems*. City University, London, Technical Report.

Liskov B.H. (1972). The design of the VENUS operating system. *Comm. ACM* **15**(3).

Liskov B.H. (1988). Distributed programming in Argus. *Comm. ACM* **31**(3).

Liskov B.H., Moss E., Schaffert C., Scheifler R. and Snyder A. (1981). *CLU Reference Manual. Lecture Notes in Computer Science* **114**. Berlin: Springer Verlag.

Lo S.L. (1995). *A Modular and Extensible Storage Architecture*. Distinguished Dissertations in Computer Science, Cambridge: Cambridge University Press.

Lynch N. (1993). *Distributed Algorithms*. Reading MA: Addison-Wesley.

Lynch N., Merritt M., Weilh W. and Fekete A. (1994). *Atomic Transactions*. San Mateo CA: Morgan Kaufmann.

Ma C. (1992). *Designing a Universal Name Service*. PhD Thesis, University of Cambridge and TR 270.

Manber U. (1989). *Introduction to Algorithms, A Creative Approach*. Reading MA: Addison-Wesley.

McAuley D. (1989). *Protocol Design for High Speed Networks*. PhD Thesis, University of Cambridge and TR 186.

McGraw G. and Felten E. (1996). *Java Security: Hostile Applets, Holes and Antidotes*. New York: Wiley.

McJones P.R. and Swart G.F. (1987). *Evolving the UNIX System Interface to Support Multithreaded Programs*. DEC SRC Technical Report, Sept.

McKusick M.K. and Karels M.J. (1987). *A New Virtual Memory Implementation for Berkeley UNIX*. Berkeley Technical Report.

Merkle R.C. (1978). Secure communication over insecure channels. *Comm. ACM* **21**(4), 294–9.

Messmer H-P. (1995). *The Indispensable Pentium Book*. Wokingham: Addison-Wesley.

Metcalfe R.M. and Boggs D.R. (1976). Ethernet: distributed packet switching for local computer networks. *Comm. ACM* **19**(6).

Meyer B. (1988). *Object-oriented Software Construction*. Englewood Cliffs NJ: Prentice-Hall.

Meyer C.H. and Matyas M. (1982). *Cryptography: A New Dimension in Computer Data Security*. Wiley.

Milenkovic M. (1990). Microprocessor memory management units. *IEEE Micro*, April.

Mills D.L. (1991). Internet time synchronization: the Network Time Protocol. *IEEE Trans. on Communications* **39**(10), 1482–93.

Milner R. (1989). *Communication and Concurrency*. Englewood Cliffs NJ: Prentice-Hall.

Mitchell J. and Dion J. (1982). A comparison of two network-based file servers. *Comm. ACM* **25**(4), 233–45.

Mockapetris P.V. and Dunlap K.J. (1988). Development of the Domain Name System. In *Proc. ACM SIGCOMM '88*, August 1988.

Morris D. and Detlefsen G.D. (1969). A virtual processor for real-time operation. In *Software Engineering: COINS III, Vol. 1, Proc. 3rd Symposium on Computer and Information Sciences*, Miami Beach, Florida, Dec. 1969. New York: Academic Press.

Morris D. and Ibett R.N. (1979). *The MU5 Computer System*. Basingstoke: Macmillan.

Mullender S.J., ed. (1993). *Distributed Systems*, 2nd edn. Wokingham: ACM Press/Addison-Wesley.

Mullender S.J. and Tanenbaum A.S. (1986). The design of a capability based operating system. *Computer Journal* **29**(4).

Mylopoulos J. and Brodie M.A., eds. (1989). *Readings in Artificial Intelligence and Databases*. San Mateo CA: Morgan Kaufmann.

Nakajima J., Yazaki M. and Matsumoto H. (1991). Multimedia/real-time extensions for the Mach operating system. In *Proc USENIX Summer Conference*, June 1991.

Needham R.M. (1993). Names. In *Distributed Systems* (Mullender S.J., ed.). Wokingham: ACM Press/Addison-Wesley.

Needham R.M. and Herbert A.J. (1982). *The Cambridge Distributed Computing System*. Wokingham: Addison-Wesley.

Needham R.M. and Schroeder M.D. (1978). Using encryption for authentication in large networks of computers. *Comm. ACM* **21**(12), 993–9.

Needham R.M. and Walker R.D.H. (1977). The Cambridge CAP computer and its protection system. *ACM SOSP6*, pp. 1–10.

Needham R.M., Herbert A.J. and Mitchell L.J.G. (1986). How to connect stable storage to a computer. *ACM Operating Systems Review* **17**(1).

Nelson G., ed. (1991). *Systems Programming with Modula-3*. Englewood Cliffs NJ: Prentice-Hall.

Object Design (1990). *ObjectStore Reference Manual*. Burlington, Object Design Inc.

Object Management Group (OMG) (1995a). *The Common Object Request Broker Architecture and Specification*, 2nd edn, July 1995.

Object Management Group (OMG) (1995b). *CORBAServices: Common Object Services Specification*, Revised edn, March 1995.

Object Management Group (OMG) (1996). *Description of the New OMA Reference Model*, Draft 1, OMG Document ab/96-05-02 May 1996.

O'Hara R. and Gomberg D. (1988). *Modern Programming Using REXX*. Englewood Cliffs NJ: Prentice-Hall.

Ontologic (1989). *ONTOS Reference Manual*. Billerica MA: Ontologic Inc.

Oppen D.C. and Dalal Y.K. (1983). The Clearinghouse: a decentralized agent for locating named objects in a distributed environment. *ACM Trans. Office and Information Systems*. **1**(3).

Organick E.I. (1972). *The Multics System: An Examination of its Structure*. Cambridge MA: MIT Press.

OSF (1992). *Introduction to OSF Distributed Computing Environment*. Englewood Cliffs NJ: Prentice-Hall.

Ousterhout J. (1994). *Tcl and the Tk Toolkit*. Reading MA: Addison-Wesley.

Ousterhout J.K., Scelza D.A. and Sindum P.S. (1980). Medusa: an experiment in distributed operating system structure. *Comm. ACM* **23**(2).

Ousterhout J.K., Cherenson A.R., Douglis F., Nelson M.N. and Welch B.B. (1988). The Sprite network operating system. *IEEE Computer* **21**(2). February.

Peterson G.L. (1981). Myths about the mutual exclusion problem. *Information Processing Letters* **12**(3), June.

Pham T.Q. and Garg P.K. (1996). *Multithreaded Programming with Windows NT*. Englewood Cliffs NJ: Prentice-Hall.

Pike R., Presotto D., Thomson K. and Trickey H. (1990). Plan 9 from Bell Labs. *Proc. Summer 1990 UKUUG Conference*. London July 90, pp. 1–9.

Pike R., Presotto D., Thomson K. and Trickey H. (1991). Designing Plan 9. *Dr Dobbs Journal* **16**(1).

Pope A. (1998). *The CORBA Reference Guide: Understanding the Common Object Request Broker Architecture*. Englewood Cliffs NJ: Prentice-Hall.

Quarterman J.S. and Hoskins J.C. (1986). Notable computer networks. *Comm. ACM* **29**(10).

Quinn M.J. (1987). *Designing Efficient Algorithms for Parallel Computers*. McGraw-Hill.

Rashid R.F. (1986). From RIG to Accent to Mach: the evolution of a network operating system. In *Proc. ACM/IEEE Fall Joint Conference*, November 1986.

Raynal M. (1986). *Algorithms for Mutual Exclusion*. Cambridge MA: MIT Press.

Raynal M. (1988). *Distributed Algorithms and Protocols*. New York: Wiley.

Redell D.D., Dalal Y.K., Horsley T.R., Lauer H.C., Lynch W.C., McJones P.R., Murray H.G. and Purcell S.C. (1980). Pilot, an operating systems for a personal computer. *Comm. ACM* **23**(2).

Reed D.P. and Kanodia R.K. (1979). Synchronization with eventcounts and sequencers. *Comm. ACM* **23**(2).

Ricart G. and Agrawala A.K. (1981). An optimal algorithm for mutual exclusion in computer networks. *Comm. ACM* **24**(1).

Richards M., Aylward A.R., Bond P., Evans R.D. and Knight B.J. (1979). TRIPOS: A portable real-time operating system for minicomputers. *Software Practice and Experience* **9**, June.

Richardson J.E., Carey M.J. and Schuh D.T. (1993). The design of the E programming language. *ACM TOPLAS* **15**(3), 494–534.

Ritchie D.M. and Thompson K. (1974). The UNIX operating system. *Comm. ACM* **17**(7).

Rivest R.L., Shamir A. and Adelman L. (1978). A method of obtaining digital signatures and public key cryptosystems. *Comm ACM* **21**(2), 120–6.

Roscoe T. (1995). *The Structure of a Multi-service Operating System*. PhD Thesis, University of Cambridge and TR 376.

Ross F.E. (1986). FDDI – a tutorial. *IEEE Communication Magazine* **25**(5), 25 May.

Rozier M., Abrossimov V., Armand F., Bowle I., Giln M., Guillemont M., Herrman F., Kaiser C., Langlois S., Leonard P. and Neuhauser W. (1988). CHORUS distributed operating systems. *Computing Systems Journal* **1**(4). The USENIX Assoc.

Rumbaugh I., Jacobson J. and Booch G. (1999). *Unified Modelling Language Reference Manual*. Reading MA: Addison-Wesley.

Saltzer J.H. (1974). Protection and control of information sharing in Multics. *Comm. ACM* **17**(7).

Saltzer J.H. (1979). On the naming and binding of objects. In *Operating Systems: An Advanced Course. Lecture Notes in Computer Science*, **60**, 99–208. Berlin: Springer Verlag.

Saltzer J. (1982). On the naming and binding of network destinations. In *Proc. IFIP/TC6 International Symposium on Local Computer Networks*, Florence, Italy, 1982.

Sandberg R. (1987). The Sun network file system design, implementation and experience. Technical Report, Mountain View CA.

Sandberg R., Goldberg D., Kleinman S., Walsh D. and Lyon B. (1985). The design and implementation of the Sun network file system. *Proc. USENIX Conference*, Portland OR.

Sansom R.D., Julin D.P. and Rashid R.F. (1986). *Extending a Capability Based System into a Network Environment*. Technical Report CMU-CS 86 116, Carnegie-Mellon University.

Satyanarayanan M. (1993). Distributed file systems. In *Distributed Systems*, 2nd edn. (Mullender S.J., ed.). New York: ACM Press/Addison-Wesley.

Satyanarayanan M., Howard J., Nichols D., Sidebotham R., Spector A. and West M. (1985). The ITC distributed file system: principles and design. In *Proc. 10th ACM Symposium on Operating Systems Principles*, December 1985.

Satyanarayanan M., Kistler J.J., Kumar P., Okasaki M.F., Siegal E.H. and Steere D.C. (1990). Coda, a highly available filing system for a distributed workstation environment. *IEEE Trans. on Computers* **39**(4).

Schlichting R.D. and Schneider F.B. (1983). Fail-stop processors: an approach to designing fault tolerant computing systems. *ACM Trans. on Computer Systems* **1**(3).

Schneier B. (1996). *Applied Cryptography: Protocols, Algorithms, and Source in C*, 2nd edn. New York: Wiley.

Schroeder-Preikschat W. (1994). *The Logical Design of Parallel Operating Systems*. London: Prentice-Hall.

Schwarz P. *et al.* (1986). Extensibility in the Starburst Database System. *Proc. International Workshop on Object Oriented Database Systems*, Pacific Grove CA.

Selic B., Gullekson G. and Ward P. (1995). *Real-time Object-oriented Modelling*. New York: Wiley.

Sha L., Rajkumar R. and Lehoczky J.P. (1990). Priority inheritance protocol: an approach to real-time synchronization. *IEEE Trans. Computers* **38**(9).

Shapiro M. (1986). Structure and encapsulation in distributed systems: the proxy principle. In *Proc. 6th Int. Conf. on Dist. Comp. Sys.* Boston MA, May 1986.

Shapiro M. (1991). Soul, an object-oriented framework for object support. In A. Karshmer and J. Nehmer (eds.), *Operating Systems of the 90s and Beyond*, *Lecture Notes in Computer Science* **563**. Berlin: Springer Verlag.

Sharman G.C.H. (1991). The evolution of online transaction processing systems. In *Aspects of Databases* (Jackson M.S. and Robinson A.E., eds.). Guildford: Butterworth Heinemann.

Shipman D. (1981). The functional data model and the data language DAPLEX. *ACM Trans. on Database Systems* **6**(1).

Siewiorek D., Bell G.B. and Newell A., eds. (1982). *Computer Structures: Readings and Examples*, 2nd edn. McGraw-Hill.

Silberschatz A., Galvin P.B. and Gagne G. (2001). *Operating Systems Concepts*, 6th edn. Wiley.

Singh S. (1999). The Code Book. Fourth Estate.

Singhal M. (1989). Deadlock detection in distributed systems. *IEEE Computer* **22**(11) 37–48.

Singhal V., Kakkad S.V. and Wilson P. (1992). Texas: an efficient, portable persistent store. In *Persistent Object Systems, Workshops in Computing* (Albano A. and Morrison R., eds.), pp. 11–33. Berlin: Springer Verlag.

Sloman M. and Kramer J. (1987). *Distributed Systems and Computer Networks*. Englewood Cliffs NJ: Prentice-Hall.

Solomon D.A. (1998). *Inside Windows NT*, 2nd edn.

Sommerville I. (1996). *Software Engineering*, 5th edn. Harlow: Addison Wesley Longman.

Spector A.Z., Bloch J., Daniels D., Draves R., Duchamp D., Eppinger J., Menees S. and Thompson D. (1986). The Camelot Project. Technical Report, CMU-CS-86-166, Carnegie Mellon University.

Stankovic J.A. and Ramamritham K., eds. (1988). Tutorial – Hard real-time systems. *IEEE Computer Society* no. 819, cat. EHO276–6.

Steiner J., Neuman C. and Schiller J. (1988). Kerberos: an authentication service for open network systems. *Proceedings USENIX Winter Conference*, Berkeley, CA.

Stoll C. (1989). *The Cuckoo's Egg*. London: Bodley Head.

Stonebraker M. (1976). The design and implementation of INGRES. *ACM Trans. on Database Systems* 1(3), 189–222, Sept.

Stonebraker M. (1980). Retrospective on a database system. *ACM TODS* 5(2), 225–40.

Stonebraker M., ed. (1994). *Readings in Database Systems*, 2nd edn. San Mateo CA: Morgan Kaufmann.

Stonebraker M. and Rowe L.A. (1986). The design of POSTGRES. *Proc. SIGMOD conference*, Washington DC.

Stonebraker M. *et al.* (The Committee for Advanced DBMS Function) (1990). Third generation database system manifesto. *ACM SIGMOD Record* 19(3).

Sun Microsystems Inc. (1989). *NFS: Network File System Protocol Specification*. TR RFC 1094 file available for anonymous ftp from the Internet Network Information Center – host: nic.ddn.mil, directory: /usr/pub/RFC

Tanenbaum A.S. (1987). *Operating Systems, Design and Implementation*. Englewood Cliffs NJ: Prentice-Hall.

Tanenbaum A.S. (1988). *Computer Networks*, 2nd edn. Englewood Cliffs NJ: Prentice-Hall.

Tanenbaum A.S. (1992). *Modern Operating Systems*. Englewood Cliffs NJ: Prentice-Hall.

Tanenbaum A.S. and van Steen M. (2002). *Distributed Systems*. Englewood Cliffs NJ: Prentice-Hall.

Tanenbaum A.S. and van Renesse R. (1985). Distributed operating systems. *ACM Computing Surveys* 17(4).

Tanenbaum A.S., van Renesse R., van Staveren H., Sharp G.J., Mullender S.J., Jansen J. and van Rossum G. (1990). Experiences with the Amoeba operating system. *Comm. ACM* 33(12).

Thacker C., Stewart L. and Satterthwaite E. Jr. (1987). *Firefly: A Multiprocessor Workstation*. DEC Systems Research Centre Technical Report 23, Dec. 1987.

Thakaar S.S., ed. (1987). *Selected Reprints on Dataflow and Reduction Architectures.* IEEE Computer Society Press (order number 759).

Treese G.W. (1988). Berkeley UNIX on 1000 workstations, Athena changes to 4.3BSD. *Proc. USENIX*, Winter 1988.

Tucker A.B., ed. (1991). A summary of the ACM/IEEE-CS joint curriculum task force report computing curricula 1991. *Comm. ACM* **34**(6).

van Steen M., Homberg P. and Tanenbaum A.S. (1999) Globe: A wide-area distributed system. *IEEE Concurrency*, January–March 1999, pp. 70–80.

Vinoski S. (1997). CORBA: Integrating diverse applications within distributed heterogeneous environments. *IEEE Comm* **35**(2) 46–55.

Wahl M., Howes T. and Kille S. (1997). The Lightweight Directory Access Protocol (v3). Internet RFC 2251.

Waldo J. (1998). Remote procedure call and Java remote method invocation. *IEEE Concurrency* **6**(3), 5–7, July 98.

Wall L., Christiansen T. and Schwartz R. (1996). *Programming Perl*, 2nd edn. Sebastopol CA: O'Reilly and Associates.

Weihl W.E. (1984). *Specification and Implementation of Atomic Data Types.* Technical Report MIT/LCS/TR-314, MIT Lab for Computer Science, March 1984.

Weihl W.E. (1989). Local atomicity properties: modular concurrency control for abstract data types. *ACM Trans. Prog. Lang. and Sys.* **11**(2).

Weiser M. (1993) Some computer science issues in ubiquitous computing. *CACM* **36**(7), 74–84.

Weiser M., Demers A. and Hauser C. (1989). The portable common runtime approach to interoperability. *Proc. ACM 12th Symposium on Operating Systems Principles*, pp. 114–22.

Welsh J. and Lister A. (1981). A comparative study of task communication in Ada. *Software, Practice and Experience* **11**, 256–90.

Whiddett D. (1987). *Concurrent Programming for Software Engineers.* Chichester: Ellis Horwood.

Wilkes M.V. and Needham R.M. (1979). *The Cambridge CAP Computer and its Operating System.* Amsterdam: North-Holland.

Wilkes M.V. and Wheeler D.J. (1979). The Cambridge Digital Communication Ring. In *Local Area Networks Communications Symposium* (sponsors Mitre Corp. and NBS), Boston MA, May 1979.

Wilkinson T. (1997). *Kaffe – A virtual machine to run Java code.* http://www.tjwassoc.demon.co.uk /kaffe/kaffe.htm

Williams R. *et al.* (1982). R*, An overview of the architecture. In P. Scheuerman (ed.) *Improving Database Usablity and Responsiveness.* New York: Academic Press, pp. 1–27.

Wong M.H. and Agrawal D. (1993). Context based synchronization: an approach beyond semantics for concurrency control. *12th Symposium on Principles of Database Systems*, pp. 276–87.

Yahalom R. (1991). *Managing the Order of Transactions in Widely Distributed Data Systems.* PhD Thesis, University of Cambridge and TR 231.

Yelavitch B.M. (1985). Customer information control system: an evolving system facility. *IBM Systems Journal* **24**(3/4).

Zdonik S.B. and Maier D., eds. (1990). *Readings on Object-Oriented Database Systems*. San Mateo CA: Morgan Kaufmann.

Zimmerman H. (1980). OSI reference model – the ISO model of architecture for open systems interconnection. *IEEE Trans. Computers* **28**(4).

Zöbel D. (1983). The deadlock problem, a classifying bibliography. *ACM Operating Systems Review* **17**(4).

Glossary

ACID	Atomicity, Consistency, Isolation, Durability	CBR	Cambridge Backbone Ring
ACL	Access Control List	CCA	CORBA Component Architecture
ADT	Abstract Data Type	CCC	Credit Card Company
AIX	IBM's version of UNIX	CCI	Credit Card Issuer
ALU	Arithmetic Logic Unit	CCITT	Comitée Consultatif International Télégraphique et Téléphonique
AMI	Asynchronous Message Invocation		
ANSA	Advanced Networked Systems Architecture	CDCS	Cambridge Distributed Computing System
ANSI	American National Standards Institute	CFR	Cambridge Fast Ring
		CGI	Common Gateway Interface
API	Application Programming Interface	CI	Card Issuer
ARM	Acorn RISC Machine	CICS	Customer Information Control System
ASCII	American Standard Code for Information Interchange	CISC	Complex Instruction Set Computer
ASN.1	Abstract Syntax Notation one	client	A computer program for which a *server* performs some computation; compare *user*
ATM	1. Asynchronous Transfer Mode 2. Automatic Teller Machine		
		COM	Component Object Model
BSD	Berkeley Software Distribution (of UNIX, for example BSD 4.3)	CORBA	OMG's Common Object Request Broker Architecture
		COW	Copy-On-Write
CA	Certification Authority	CPU	Central Processing Unit
CAD	Computer Aided Design	CR	1. Cambridge Ring 2. Critical Region
capability	A name for an object which includes access rights to the object		
		CRL	Certificate Revocation List

CSMA/CD	Carrier Sense Multiple Access with Collision Detection
DAN	Desk Area Network
DAP	1. Distributed Array Processor 2. Directory Access Protocol
DARPA	Defense Advanced Research Projects Agency
DBMS	Database Management System
DCE	Distributed Computing Environment
DEQNA	An Ethernet network interface of Digital Equipment Corporation
DES	Data Encryption Standard
DII	Dynamic Invocation Interface (OMG-CORBA)
DMA	Direct Memory Access
DN	Distinguished Name
DNS	Internet Domain Name Service
DRAM	Dynamic Random Access Memory
DSA	Data Signature Algorithm
DSI	Dynamic Skeleton Interface (OMG-CORBA)
DTD	Document Type Definition
EBCDIC	Extended Binary Coded Decimal Interchange Code
EDF	Earliest Deadline First – a real-time scheduling algorithm
EFT	Electronic Funds Transfer
EJB	Enterprise Java Beans
EPC	Exception Program Counter
ESIO	Environment Specific Inter-ORB Protocol
FCFS	First Come First Served
FDDI	Fibre Distributed Data Interface
FID	File IDentifier
FIFO	First In First Out
FTP	File Transfer Protocol
garbage	Inaccessible object occupying storage resources
GCHQ	Government Communications Headquarters (UK)
GEOS	Geostationary Operational Environment Satellite
GIOP	General Inter-ORB Protocol (OMG-CORBA)
GNS	Global Name Service
GNU	GNU's Not UNIX, a recursive acronym. The name of a project to make freely available UNIX-compatible software
GPS	Global Positioning System
GUI	Graphical User Interface
HAL	Hardware Abstraction Layer
host	A computer attached to a network, in particular, an IP network
HP-UX	Hewlett-Packard's version of UNIX
HTML	Hypertext Markup Language
HTTP	Hypertext Transfer Protocol
ID	IDentifier
IDEA	International Data Encryption Algorithm
IDL	Interface Definition Language
IEEE	Institute of Electrical and Electronics Engineers
IIOP	Internet Inter-ORB Protocol (OMG-CORBA)
inode	In the UNIX file system a file's index node or inode stores the file's metadata
internet	A global network connecting many commercial, academic and government sites, especially institutions engaged in research. The internet is an aggregate of many independently managed networks. The unifying factor is the Internet Protocol

I/O	Input/Output
IOR	Interoperable Object Reference
IP	Internet Protocol
IPC	Inter-Process Communication
IR	Interface Repository
ISDN	Integrated Services Digital Network
ISO	International Standards Organization
JDK	Java Development Kit
JMS	Java Messaging Service
JNDI	Java Naming and Directory Interface
JTS	Java Transaction Service
JVM	Java Virtual Machine
KDC	Key Distribution Centre
LAN	Local Area Network
LANCE	Local Area Network Controller for Ethernet
LDAP	Lightweight Directory Access Protocol
LPC	Local Procedure Call
LRU	Least Recently Used
LSF	Least Slack First – a real-time scheduling algorithm
LWP	Lightweight Process
MAN	Metropolitan Area Network
MCA	Message-Channel Agent
MIDL	Microsoft's Interface Definition Language
MIMD	Multiple Instruction Multiple Data
MIME	Multipurpose Internet Mail Extensions
MIPS	1. Millions of Instructions Per Second – an indicator of processor speed 2. A RISC processor made by MIPS Computer Systems Inc.

MIT	Massachusetts Institute of Technology
MMU	Memory Management Unit
MOM	Message-oriented Middleware
MS-DOS	Microsoft Disk Operating System. A single-user OS for the Intel 8088 microprocessor and its successors
MSNA	Multi-Service Network Architecture (Cambridge)
MTBF	Mean Time Between Failures
multi-threaded process	Used in systems where a process is the unit of resource allocation and a thread is the unit of execution on a processor. The threads of the process share its resources
Name service	Maps names to locations (see also *YPS*)
NFS	SUN's Network File System
NIST	National Institute of Standards and Technology (US)
node	A component computer of a distributed system, like *host*
NNTP	Network News Transfer Protocol
NSA	National Security Agency (US)
NT	New Technology
NTP	Network Time Protocol
NVRAM	Non-Volatile Random Access Memory
Object-based OS	An operating system which is object structured internally as well as supporting object-structured software
Object-support OS	An operating system which is designed to support object-structured software
OCC	Optimistic Concurrency Control, a method of concurrency control for transactions
ODBMS	Object-oriented Database Management System

ODL	Object Definition Language
ODMG	Object Data Management Group
ODMG-93	Object-oriented database standard
OLTP	On-Line Transaction Processing
OMA	Object Management Architecture
OMG	Object Management Group
OO	Object-oriented
OOM	Object-Oriented Middleware
OQL	Object Query Language
ORB	Object Request Broker
OS	Operating System
OSF	Open Software Foundation: a consortium of vendors led by IBM, DEC and Hewlett-Packard
OSI	Open Systems Inter-connection
OTS	Object Transaction Service (OMG-CORBA)
PC	1. Personal Computer 2. Program Counter
PGP	Pretty Good Privacy
PIN	Personal Identification Number
PKI	Public Key Infrastructure
POSIX	IEEE Standard 1000.3, Portable Operating System Interface for Computer (UNIX) Environments
PSR	Processor Status Register
pthreads	POSIX threads
PTT	Post, Telephone and Telegraph: the bodies within a country that are licensed to provide public data transmission services
QoS	Quality of Service
RAM	Random Access Memory
RARA	Request–Acknowledge–Reply–Acknowledge

RFC	Request For Comment
RFE	Return From Exception
RFP	Request For Proposal
RISC	Reduced Instruction Set Computer
RM	Resource Manager
RMI	(Java's) Remote Method Invocation
RMS	Rate Monotonic Scheduling – for real-time systems
RPC	Remote Procedure Call
RRA	Request–Reply–Acknowledge
RSA	Rivest, Shamir and Adleman algorithm
SAP	Service Access Point
SAR	Segmentation And Reassembly
SASOS	Single Address Space Operation System
SCSI	Small Computer System Interface. A standard I/O bus.
server	A computer or program designed to perform computations on behalf of other programs, its *clients*
SFID	System File IDentifier
SGML	Standard Generalized Mark-up Language
SHA	Secure Hash Algorithm
SHS	Secure Hash Standard
SIMD	Single Instruction Multiple Data
SISD	Single Instruction Single Data
SITA	Société Internationale de Télécommunications Aéronautiques
site	1. A component computer of a distributed system, like *host* and *node* 2. A local internetwork at some geographical locality, such as the Cambridge site
SLA	Single Logical Action
SMT	Simultaneous Multi-Threading

SMTP	Simple Mail Transport Protocol		Unicode	A 16-bit character encoding scheme
SOAP	Simple Object Access Protocol		UPS	Uninterruptable Power Supply – used to maintain a supply of power to equipment when the mains has failed
socket	An abstraction for a communication end-point			
SPARC	Scalable Processor ARChitecture, a RISC architecture		URI	Uniform Resource Identifier
			URL	Universal Resource Locator
SPKI	Simple Public Key Infrastructure		URN	Uniform Resource Name
SQL	Structured Query Language		user	A human operator of a computer system; compare *client*
SR1	Single-copy Serializability			
SSL	Secure Socket Layer		UTC	Universal Coordinated Time
SWIFT	Society for Worldwide Inter-bank Financial Telecommunications		VAX	A CISC processor proprietary to the Digital Equipment Corporation
TAS	Test-And-Set		VC	Virtual Circuit
Tcl-Tk	Tool command language and the Tk X11 toolkit		VLSI	Very Large Scale Integration
			VM	1. Virtual Machine 2. Virtual Memory
TCP	Transmission Control Protocol			
thread	A name for a unit of execution on a processor; see *multi-threaded process*		VME	A backplane bus standard, IEEE standard 104
TLB	Translation Lookaside Buffer		WAN	Wide Area Network
TLS	Transport Layer Security		WORM	Write Once Read Multiple, an optical storage technology
TP	Transaction Processing			
TPPC	Transaction Processing Performance Council		WWW	World Wide Web
TPS	Transaction Processing System		XDR	External Data Representation. A standard for representing data types so that they can be exchanged between different types of computer
TS	Tuple Space			
TSO	Time-Stamp Ordering, a method of concurrency control for transactions			
			XML	eXtensible Markup Language
			XSL	eXtensible Style Language
UDP	User Datagram Protocol		YPS	Yellow Pages Service, maps names to attributes
UFID	User File IDentifier			
UI	UNIX International: a consortium of vendors led by AT&T		2PL	Two-Phase Locking: a method of concurrency control for transactions
UID	Unique Identifier			
ULTRIX	Digital Equipment Corporation's version of UNIX		2PC	Two-Phase Commit: an atomic commitment protocol
UML	Unified Modelling Language		3PC	Three-Phase Commit: an atomic commitment protocol

Author index

Subject index

I

J

T

U

V

V system 130, 680
validation
    in system structure 68
    in transactions 540, 542–5
values 38
VAX (DEC) 60, 82, 676
vector clocks in message delivery ordering 590–1
Venus operating system 60, 299
videoconferencing 5
videomail 5
videophones 5
virtual address space 165
virtual communication 95
virtual machine 56
    definition 53
virtual processors 111
virtual ring of processes in distributed computations 594
virus 214
visibility of suboperations in composite operations 478
volatile storage 417

W

WAIT queue scheduling 288–9
wakeup 376
wake-up waiting 116
weak consistency in distributed computations 587
web browsers 602–3, 622
web proxy 612
website 603
WG94 processor 269
wide area networks 12
    architecture for 27
Win32 system 378, 380
window-based interfaces
    inherently concurrent systems 14
    system calls 145
Windows 95 680
Windows 2000 232
Windows NT 130, 185, 680
    asynchronous I/O by system threads 382–3
    asynchronous I/O calls 382

COM in 638
executive components 378–9
IPC support in 377–83
login 379–80
models used in design 378
processes, threads, concurrency control 380–1
structure 378
thread synchronization 381–2
working directories 173–4
workstations 9, 679–80
    in distributed systems 193–4
World Wide Web Consortium (W3C) 602, 603, 605, 618
World Wide Web servers
    client/server interaction 602–4
        executing programs 608–9
    communications
        security of 610
        using HTTP 605–6
    concurrency control 611
    in distributed systems 194
    document representation 606–7
    document types 607
    inherently concurrent systems 14–15
    middleware 612–14
    naming documents 604–5
    scalability issues 611–12
    security 610–11
        access control 610
        communications 610
        mobile code 610–11
worm programs 214
write locks 389
write operations 176, 242
write quorum 587
write-ahead in logging 558
write-ahead log 418
write-through 164

X

X.500 207
X.509 certification 229–30, 234
XDS 940 system 677
Xerox Courier 441, 452
Xerox Distribution File System (XDFS) 679
Xerox PARC 194, 206–7, 231, 679